SQL Server 2025 Query Performance Tuning

Troubleshoot and Optimize Query Performance

Seventh Edition

Grant Fritchey

SQL Server 2025 Query Performance Tuning: Troubleshoot and Optimize Query Performance, Seventh Edition

Grant Fritchey
Sapulpa, OK, USA

ISBN-13 (pbk): 979-8-8688-1864-6   ISBN-13 (electronic): 979-8-8688-1865-3
https://doi.org/10.1007/979-8-8688-1865-3

Copyright © 2026 by Grant Fritchey

This work is subject to copyright. All rights are reserved by the Publisher, whether the whole or part of the material is concerned, specifically the rights of translation, reprinting, reuse of illustrations, recitation, broadcasting, reproduction on microfilms or in any other physical way, and transmission or information storage and retrieval, electronic adaptation, computer software, or by similar or dissimilar methodology now known or hereafter developed.

Trademarked names, logos, and images may appear in this book. Rather than use a trademark symbol with every occurrence of a trademarked name, logo, or image we use the names, logos, and images only in an editorial fashion and to the benefit of the trademark owner, with no intention of infringement of the trademark.

The use in this publication of trade names, trademarks, service marks, and similar terms, even if they are not identified as such, is not to be taken as an expression of opinion as to whether or not they are subject to proprietary rights.

While the advice and information in this book are believed to be true and accurate at the date of publication, neither the authors nor the editors nor the publisher can accept any legal responsibility for any errors or omissions that may be made. The publisher makes no warranty, express or implied, with respect to the material contained herein.

    Managing Director, Apress Media LLC: Welmoed Spahr
    Acquisitions Editor: Shaul Elson
    Development Editor: Laura Berendson
    Coordinating Editor: Gryffin Winkler

Cover image designed by wrenchk on Freepik (www.freepik.com)

Distributed to the book trade worldwide by Springer Science+Business Media New York, 1 New York Plaza, New York, NY 10004. Phone 1-800-SPRINGER, fax (201) 348-4505, e-mail orders-ny@springer-sbm.com, or visit www.springeronline.com. Apress Media, LLC is a Delaware LLC and the sole member (owner) is Springer Science + Business Media Finance Inc (SSBM Finance Inc). SSBM Finance Inc is a **Delaware** corporation.

For information on translations, please e-mail booktranslations@springernature.com; for reprint, paperback, or audio rights, please e-mail bookpermissions@springernature.com.

Apress titles may be purchased in bulk for academic, corporate, or promotional use. eBook versions and licenses are also available for most titles. For more information, reference our Print and eBook Bulk Sales web page at http://www.apress.com/bulk-sales.

Any source code or other supplementary material referenced by the author in this book is available to readers on GitHub. For more detailed information, please visit www.apress.com/gp/services/source-code.

If disposing of this product, please recycle the paper

*Mom, you received a copy of the first of these I wrote.
Now you're gone, but this one is for you as well.*

Table of Contents

About the Author xxi

About the Technical Reviewer xxiii

Acknowledgments xxv

Introduction xxvii

Chapter 1: Query Performance Tuning 1

    The Query Performance Tuning Process 4

        Performance Issues 4

        A Repetitive Process 7

    Understanding What Defines "Good Enough" 11

    Establishing Comparison Points 11

    Most Likely Performance Issues 13

    Common Performance Issues 14

        Insufficient or Poor Indexes 15

        Inaccurate or Missing Statistics 15

        Bad T-SQL 16

        Problematic Execution Plans 16

        Excessive Blocking 17

        Deadlocks 17

        Non–Set-Based Operations 18

        Incorrect Database Design 18

        Poor Execution Plan Reuse 19

        Frequent Recompilation of Queries 19

    Summary 20

TABLE OF CONTENTS

Chapter 2: Execution Plan Generation and the Query Optimizer 21

The Query Optimization Process 21

    Optimization Preparation 22

Optimization 27

    Simplification 28

    Trivial Plan Match 28

    Optimization Phases 28

Generating Parallel Execution Plans 33

Execution Plan Caching 37

    Aging of the Execution Plan 37

Summary 38

Chapter 3: Methods for Capturing Query Performance Metrics 39

Methods to Capture Query Performance Metrics 40

    Include Client Statistics 40

    Connection Properties 41

    SET STATISTICS TIME/IO 41

    QueryTimeStats in the Execution Plan 42

    Trace Events (Profiler) 42

Dynamic Management Views 43

    Actively Executing Queries 44

    Previously Executed Queries 45

Query Store 47

Extended Events 47

    Creating an Extended Events Session 48

    Adding and Configuring Events 51

    Defining Targets 62

    Working with Sessions 66

    Adding Causality Tracking 67

    Scripting Extended Events 68

Live Data Explorer Window	70
General Recommendations for Using Extended Events	80
Summary	82

Chapter 4: Analyzing Query Behavior Using Execution Plans 83

Estimated vs. Actual Execution Plans	84
Capturing Execution Plans	85
SQL Server Management Studio	85
Dynamic Management Views	88
Query Store	90
Extended Events	91
What Is Inside an Execution Plan	93
Reading an Execution Plan	100
What Do You Look for in an Execution Plan?	102
First Operator	103
Warnings	104
Most Costly Operations	107
Fat Pipes	108
Extra Operators	108
Scans	110
Estimate vs. Actual	110
After the Signposts	113
Tools That Assist You with Execution Plans	113
SQL Server Management Studio	114
Third Party	125
Summary	126

Chapter 5: Statistics, Data Distribution, and Cardinality 127

Statistics in the Query Optimization Process	128
Statistics on Rowstore Indexed Columns	128
Statistics on Nonindexed Columns	137
Analyzing Statistics	146

TABLE OF CONTENTS

    Header 147

    Density 148

    Histogram 149

    Cardinality 150

    Statistics on a Multicolumn Index 154

    Statistics on a Filtered Index 157

    Controlling the Cardinality Estimator 159

Statistics Maintenance 162

    Auto Create Statistics 163

    Auto Update Statistics 163

    Auto Update Statistics Asynchronously 163

    Manual Maintenance 164

    Manage Statistics Settings 165

    Create Statistics Manually 167

Analyzing the Effectiveness of Statistics for a Query 168

    Resolving a Missing Statistics Issue 169

    Resolving an Outdated Statistics Issue 174

Recommendations on Statistics 177

    Backward Compatibility of Statistics 177

    Auto Create Statistics 177

    Auto Update Statistics 177

    Auto Update Statistics Asynchronously 178

    Amount of Sampling to Collect Statistics 178

Summary 179

Chapter 6: Using the Query Store for Query Performance and Execution Plans ... 181

Query Store Function and Design 182

    Information Collected by the Query Store 184

    Query Runtime Data 188

Controlling the Query Store 190

    Capture Mode 192

Query Store Reporting 194

Plan Forcing	200
Forcing Query Hints	202
Optimized Plan Forcing	203
Query Store for Upgrades	204
Summary	206

Chapter 7: Execution Plan Cache Behavior 207

Querying the Plan Cache	207
Execution Plan Caching and Plan Reuse	209
Ad Hoc Workload	210
Prepared Workload	221
sp_executesql	226
Prepare/Execute Model	229
Query Hash and Query Plan Hash	230
Execution Plan Cache Recommendations	234
Explicitly Parameterize Values in Your Query	235
Use Stored Procedures Where You Can	235
Use sp_executesql As an Alternative to Stored Procedures	235
Take Advantage of the Prepare/Execute Model	236
Avoid Ad Hoc Queries	236
Enable Optimize for Ad Hoc	236
Summary	236

Chapter 8: Query Recompilation 239

Benefits and Drawbacks of Recompilation	239
Identifying the Statement Being Recompiled	244
Analyzing Causes of Recompilation	245
Deferred Object Resolution	248
Avoiding Recompiles	251
Avoid Interleaving DDL and DML Statements	251
Reduce Recompilation Caused by Statistics Changes	253
Use Table Variables	257

TABLE OF CONTENTS

Use Temporary Tables Across Multiple Scopes 259

Avoid Changing SET Options Within a Batch 260

Controlling Recompile Results 261

Plan Forcing 262

Query Hints 262

Plan Guides 265

Hint Forcing 269

Summary 269

Chapter 9: Index Architecture 271

What Is a Rowstore Index? 271

The Benefits of Indexes 275

Index Overhead 277

What Is a Columnstore Index? 280

Columnstore Index Storage 281

Index-Design Recommendations 282

Type of Query Processing Being Performed 283

Determine Filtering Criteria 283

Use Narrow Indexes 286

Consider Selectivity of the Data 289

Determine the Data Type 292

Consider Column Order 292

Determine Data Storage 296

Ask an AI 296

Rowstore Index Behavior 296

Clustered Indexes 296

Nonclustered Indexes 307

Columnstore Index Behavior 310

Columnstore Recommendations 317

Missing Indexes 317

Summary 320

Chapter 10: Index Behaviors 321

Covering Indexes 321
A Pseudoclustered Index 324
Recommendations 324
Index Intersection 324
Index Joins 328
Filtered Indexes 330
Indexed Views 334
Benefit 334
Overhead 335
Usage Scenarios 336
Index Compression 340
Index Characteristics 342
Different Column Sort Order 342
Index on Computed Columns 343
CREATE INDEX Statement Processed As a Query 343
Parallel Index Creation 344
Online Index Creation 344
Considering the Database Engine Tuning Advisor 344
OPTIMIZE_FOR_SEQUENTIAL_KEY 345
Resumable Indexes and Constraints 345
Special Index Types 346
Full-Text 347
Spatial 347
XML 348
Vector 348
Summary 349

Chapter 11: Key Lookups and Solutions 351

Purpose of Lookups 351

Performance Issues Caused by Lookups 353

Analysis of the Causes of Lookups 354

Techniques to Resolve Lookups 357

    Create a Clustered Index 357

    Use a Covering Index 357

    Take Advantage of Index Joins 361

Summary 363

Chapter 12: Dealing with Index Fragmentation 365

Causes of Rowstore Fragmentation 366

    How Fragmentation Occurs in Rowstore Indexes 366

    How Fragmentation Occurs in Columnstore Indexes 371

Fragmentation Overhead 373

    Rowstore Overhead 374

    Columnstore Overhead 377

Analyzing the Amount of Fragmentation 378

Analyzing the Fragmentation of a Small Table 382

Fragmentation Resolutions 383

    Drop and Recreate the Index 383

    Recreating the Index with the DROP_EXISTING Clause 384

    Execute the ALTER INDEX REBUILD Command 385

    Execute the ALTER INDEX REORGANIZE Command 386

    Defragmentation and Partitions 393

Significance of the Fill Factor 395

Automatic Maintenance 399

Summary 399

Chapter 13: Parameter-Sensitive Queries: Causes and Solutions 401

How Does Parameter Sniffing Work? 401

Identifying Queries That Are Sensitive to Parameter Values 407

Mechanisms for Addressing Plan-Sensitive Queries 412

    Disable Parameter Sniffing 412

    Local Variables 414

    Recompile 414

    OPTIMIZE FOR Query Hint 415

    Force Plan 418

    Multiplan 419

Summary 428

Chapter 14: Query Design Analysis 431

Query Design Recommendations 431

Keep Your Result Sets Small 432

    Limit the Columns in Your SELECT List 432

    Filter Your Data Through a WHERE Clause 434

Use Indexes Effectively 435

    Use Effective Search Conditions 435

    Avoid Operations on Columns 443

    Custom Scalar UDF 448

Minimize Optimizer Hints 453

    JOIN Hint 454

    INDEX Hints 459

Using Domain and Referential Integrity 460

    NOT NULL Constraint 460

    User-Defined Constraints 463

    Declarative Referential Integrity 465

Summary 470

Chapter 15: Reduce Query Resource Use 471

Avoiding Resource-Intensive Queries 471
- Use Appropriate Data Types 472
- Test EXISTS Over COUNT(*) to Verify Data Existence 475
- Favor UNION ALL Over UNION 478
- Ensure Indexes Are Used for Aggregate and Sort Operations 481
- Be Cautious with Local Variables in a Batch Query 482
- Stored Procedure Names Actually Matter 486

Reducing Network Overhead Where Possible 486
- Execute Multiple Queries in Sets 487
- Use SET NOCOUNT 487

Techniques to Reduce Transaction Cost of a Query 488
- Reduce Logging Overhead 488
- Reduce Lock Overhead 491

Summary 493

Chapter 16: Blocking and Blocked Processes 495

Blocking Fundamentals 495
- A Short Discussion of Terminology 496
- Introducing Blocking 497

Transactions and ACID Properties 498
- Atomicity 498
- Consistency 502
- Isolation 502
- Durability 503

Lock Types 503
- Row Locks 504
- Key Locks 506
- Page Locks 507
- Extent Locks 508
- Heap or B-Tree Locks 508
- Rowgroup Locks 508

Table Locks	508
Transaction Locks	509
Database Locks	509
Lock Operations and Modes	509
Lock Escalation	510
Lock Modes	511
Lock Compatibility	519
Isolation Levels	520
Read Uncommitted	520
Read Committed	522
Repeatable Read	524
Serializable	526
Snapshot	528
Optimized Locking	528
TransactionID Locking	529
Lock After Qualification	531
Effect of Indexes on Locking	533
Effect of a Nonclustered Index	533
Effects of a Clustered Index	535
Capturing Blocking Information	536
Capturing Blocking Information Using T-SQL	537
Extended Events and the blocked_process_report Event	539
Recommendations to Reduce Blocking	544
Summary	546

Chapter 17: Causes and Solutions for Deadlocks 547

Deadlock Fundamentals	547
Choosing the Deadlock Victim	549
Analyzing the Causes of Deadlocks	550
Capturing Deadlock Information	550
Analyzing the Deadlock Graph	554
Error Handling for Deadlocks	564

TABLE OF CONTENTS

Mechanisms to Prevent Deadlocks 565

    Access Resources in the Same Order 565

    Decrease the Amount of Resources Accessed 566

    Minimize Lock Contention 567

Summary 568

Chapter 18: Row-by-Row Processing from Cursors and Other Causes 571

Cursor Fundamentals 571

    Cursor Location 572

    Cursor Concurrency 573

    Cursor Types 575

Cursor Cost Comparison 581

    Cost Comparison Based on Location 581

    Cost Comparison Based on Concurrency 583

    Cost Comparison Based on Cursor Type 585

Default Result Set 589

    Benefits 590

    Multiple Active Result Sets 591

    Drawbacks 591

Cursor Overhead 594

Cursor Recommendations 597

Summary 599

Chapter 19: Memory-Optimized OLTP Tables and Procedures 601

In-Memory OLTP Fundamentals 601

    System Requirements 603

    Basic Setup 603

Creating Tables 605

    In-Memory Table Variables 610

    In-Memory Indexes 613

    Statistics Maintenance 618

Natively Compiled Stored Procedures 620

Recommendations 623
    Baselines 623
    Correct Workload 623
    Memory Optimization Advisor 624
    Native Compilation Advisor 629

Summary 631

Chapter 20: Graph Databases 633

Introduction to Graph Databases 633

Querying Graph Data 647
    Shortest Path 649

Performance Considerations of Graph Data 652

Summary 654

Chapter 21: Intelligent Query Processing 655

Adaptive Query Processing 656
    Interleaved Execution 656
    Query Processing Feedback 667

Approximate Query Processing 681
    APPROX_COUNT_DISTINCT 682
    APPROX_PERCENTILE_CONT and APPROX_PERCENTILE_DISC 682

Table Variable Deferred Compilation 684

Scalar User-Defined Function Inlining 687

Summary 692

Chapter 22: Automated Tuning in Azure and SQL Server 693

Automatic Plan Correction 693
    Tuning Recommendations 694
    Enabling Automatic Tuning 700
    Automatic Tuning in Action 704

Azure SQL Database Automatic Index Management 705

Summary 711

TABLE OF CONTENTS

Chapter 23: A Query Tuning Methodology 713

Database Design 713

Use Entity-Integrity Constraints.. 714

Maintain Domain and Referential Integrity Constraints... 717

Adopt Index-Design Best Practices 720

Avoid the Use of the "sp_" Prefix for Stored Procedure Names 722

Minimize the Use of Triggers 722

Put Tables into In-Memory Storage 722

Use Columnstore Indexes 723

Take Advantage of Graph Storage 723

Use Appropriate Data Types... 723

Configuration Settings 723

Memory Configuration Options... 724

Cost Threshold for Parallelism.. 724

Max Degree of Parallelism.. 725

Optimize for Ad Hoc Workloads 726

Blocked Process Threshold 726

Database Compression... 726

Database Administration.. 726

Keep Statistics Up to Date 727

Maintain a Minimum Amount of Index Fragmentation 727

Avoid Database Functions Such As AUTO_CLOSE or AUTO_SHRINK................. 728

Query Design... 728

Use the Command SET NOCOUNT ON... 729

Explicitly Define the Owner of an Object 729

Avoid Non-sargable Search Conditions 729

Avoid Large IN Clauses 731

Avoid a Large Number of OR Clauses 731

Avoid Arithmetic Expressions on Filter Clauses... 731

Avoid Optimizer Hints 733

Stay Away from Nesting Views 733

Ensure No Implicit Data Type Conversions 733
Minimize Logging Overhead 734
Adopt Best Practices for Reusing Execution Plans 734
Adopt Best Practices for Database Transactions 736
Eliminate or Reduce the Overhead of Database Cursors 736
Use Natively Compiled Stored Procedures 737
Take Advantage of Columnstore for Analytical Queries 737
Enable the Query Store 737
Summary 738

Index **739**

About the Author

Grant Fritchey is a Microsoft Data Platform MVP and AWS Community Builder. He has more than 30 years of experience in IT technical support, development, and database administration. He currently works as a Product Advocate at Redgate Software. Grant writes articles for publication at SQL Server Central and SimpleTalk. He has published books, including *Introduction to PostgreSQL for the Data Professional*, *SQL Server Execution Plans*, and *SQL Server 2022 Query Performance Tuning* (Apress). Grant presents live sessions, virtual sessions, and recorded content online and in person, around the world.

About the Technical Reviewer

John Deardurff has been a Microsoft Certified Trainer (MCT) since July 2000 and specializes in teaching Azure SQL and SQL Server workshops. He is currently a Senior Cloud Solutions Architect for Microsoft and a Microsoft MVP alumnus.

Acknowledgments

Let's start off by thanking John Deardurff. This wouldn't have happened without your assistance, John. I'm truly grateful for all the work you put into the book. Any mistakes, I own, not John. Poor guy had to clean up after me. The Augean Stables were probably less work.

I have to thank my family. Every single time I finish a book, I declare it to be my last. Then someone asks me to write another and I'm off. I can get cranky while working on these things. My family puts up with a lot. Especially when some test or example isn't working right. Thanks to you all.

I also have to thank my work, Redgate Software, and my boss, Kirsty Roper. I mostly work on these books at night, in my own time. But they know it's "mostly" and are still willing to put up with me.

Finally, the team at Microsoft. You all do great work. Further, you put up with a lot of nitpicky questions from someone you are in no way associated with. THANKS! Your understanding and support are truly appreciated.

Introduction

It's never easy to "introduce" you to six to nine months of work. The concept of an introduction is simple enough: what's the purpose of the book, who is the book written for, tips on how best to use the book. However, the introduction also has to set the stage for the rest of the book. As you'll see when you read it, I open and close the book with a simple concept: query tuning is hard. When I present live sessions on this topic, I'll tell people up front. The easy way to tune queries is to simply throw money at the problem. Buy bigger hardware. Move to a higher service tier on your cloud provider. You can always make things faster by spending more money. It's when the money runs out that you might just need to spend something else, time. Time learning how to identify poorly performing queries, understand how to investigate them to see where the problem may lie, and then apply a fix and validate that it worked. That's where this book comes in.

I truly don't care what your title is. More and more, I see titles changing, rapidly. Yet, there's going to be a person responsible for making queries run faster. You may not want the job, it may be called any number of things, but at the root, the problem remains, which queries are problematic and how to make them not be. This book is for that person. You wrote some code, found some generated by a tool, who knows what the source may be. However, that code is running slow, and you need to figure out how to make it run fast. This is your book. Your title doesn't even enter the question.

The very best way to use the book is as a straight-through read. Many of the chapters build on knowledge from preceding chapters. However, an alternate way that could work for lots of people would be to read Chapters 1–10. They lay the foundations for most query behaviors and how to monitor those queries. The rest of the chapters are problem, or behavior, specific, so if you're not hitting that problem, or using that feature, you can safely skip that chapter, for the moment. Then read Chapter 23. It's not strictly a checklist, although I tried to make it as much like a checklist as I could. Or bounce around. Many of the chapters are largely stand-alone. It's kind of like query tuning: if it works for you, that's great.

CHAPTER 1

Query Performance Tuning

Query tuning is not easy.

It's 2025, and we still don't have a magic "run faster" switch. The goal of this book is to give you as many tools and as much knowledge as possible to make query tuning easier. However, it still won't be easy. In fact, the one easy way to make things run faster is to simply spend more money. It's a lot easier to buy bigger hardware and more of it. It's much easier to move to a higher service tier with your cloud provider. These solutions are the easy way to get performance to increase. Eventually though, there's a limit to how much you're going to be able to spend in order to fix your performance problems. Also, you could just try sending a request to a Large Language Model (LLM) or AI and see what it has to say. While this can be a useful shortcut, you still need to understand what it's telling you and validate that what it suggested actually helps. This is where the query performance tuning work starts.

You may be working in an environment that is purely run traditionally on large servers maintained in your building. On the other hand, you could be running your databases as a service through Google Cloud SQL, Amazon RDS, or Azure SQL Database. It's also possible that you are running through a virtualized environment on containers managed by Kubernetes or on more traditional virtual machines (VMs). In any of these environments where the SQL Server engine is running, when it comes time to deal with poor performance, the information provided in this book is going to help. In fact, when it comes to making many of these environments run faster, your only hope may be to know how to pick the best indexes, write code that performs well, and generally understand the tools that are going to help you wring more performance out of a limited resource.

What everyone wants right here is a simple formula: if you see "A," do "Z." Sadly, I'm unable to give you a simple formula because none exists. Instead, we're going to focus on two primary things throughout this book: understanding of how things work within

CHAPTER 1   QUERY PERFORMANCE TUNING

the SQL Server engine and a methodology for identifying what exactly has gone wrong. Here are a few of the topics we are going to cover to help you get to that understanding and methodology:

- Use Extended Events to collect information about query behavior, above and beyond anything you've been able to see before.

- Learn mechanisms for identifying and dealing with blocking within your queries.

- Understand what an execution plan is and how to go about pulling information from it to help you tune queries.

- Learn how statistics work and how you can actually use them to assist performance.

- Use modern indexing techniques such as columnstore indexes to make queries fly.

- Understand the causes of recompilation and how to deal with it when it becomes a problem.

- Take advantage of the Query Store to both identify poorly performing queries and fix or improve those queries.

- Develop knowledge of how the optimizer can automatically help you with some query performance.

- Spot places where you may be able to get some AI assistance to improve query performance.

- Learn how to implement a query tuning methodology that helps you make your queries run faster.

While I would love to dive straight into any one of these topics, we're first going to talk about the fundamentals behind query performance tuning. While you can turn to any chapter in the book or search the index to look up a topic that you think may help immediately, trying to tune queries without core concepts on how to go through the process and where to focus your efforts, you may not find the book as useful. Instead, we're going to spend this chapter talking through a few key points to set the general tone for the rest of the chapters:

- The query performance tuning process
- Understanding what defines "good enough"
- Establishing comparison points
- What the most likely performance issues are

With the understanding of the generally accepted approach defined here in this chapter, we can then use that approach through all the rest of the chapters of the book as a framework around which we build both our understanding and our abilities in performance tuning.

This edition of the book is an update to the 2022 version, which was a complete rewrite, from scratch. There have been a number of updates to indexing, statistics, and blocking over the years both in the 2025 release of SQL Server and in Azure SQL. I'll be working those in as we go as well as calling them out. There were also incomplete or missing details in the 2022 version of the book, which I'll be addressing here. While this won't be a complete rewrite again, it will be a new book, up to date and enhanced. I'm also going to try to work in situations where you may see true aid from an AI or LLM, because, situationally, these can be extremely useful tools.

At this point in previous editions, I spent a little time talking about what we won't be covering. Instead, I just want to focus on what is included in the book. For topics other than query tuning, look to other books.

While there are multiple tools available to you for working with SQL Server, the principal tool is SQL Server Management Studio (SSMS). I'm using the latest version, 21, to write the book. This version of Management Studio has been rebuilt by Microsoft to run as a part of Visual Studio, the first major upgrade of the tool since 2005. However, the majority of examples and screenshots are likely to behave perfectly well in older versions of SSMS and look mostly the same. You can get a copy of SSMS here: `https://learn.microsoft.com/en-us/ssms/download-sql-server-management-studio-ssms`.

Some of the examples in this book will be written from scratch, using generated tables, provided with those examples. However, most of the examples will be using the AdventureWorks database. I know that database is actually quite old at this point in time. However, all the errors in data types and bad data distribution as well as generally poor choices in data design (which were intentional when it was built) make it an excellent resource for showing how to identify and fix poorly performing queries, which is why I use it throughout the book. A few examples will use Wide World Importers, a newer database that was built to show off a better database design methodology, as well as newer SQL Server behaviors. The only problem with Wide World Importers is that it's too good. It doesn't offer as many opportunities for improvements as you see in AdventureWorks. Still, we'll put it to work in some spots in the book. These databases change a little over time, so you can't guarantee that the behavior you see will perfectly match mine. Go here to get these databases: https://github.com/microsoft/sql-server-samples/tree/master/samples/databases.

Let's move on and discuss the query performance tuning process.

The Query Performance Tuning Process

To begin tuning queries, you first have to identify which particular query needs your attention. You could rely on people telling you that they're experiencing pain while using your database, but a better approach is to be proactive. This means you need to first have a method for monitoring query performance. From there, you can identify the queries that are causing the most problems. With the query identified, you'll have to troubleshoot the potential causes of the slow performance. You can apply various mechanisms to resolve these issues. Then you have to quantify the performance after your changes. That's the complete process. What you'll find is that you repeat this process over and over.

Since no one thing will always fix performance problems, you need to be ready to experiment with various changes and solutions, measure their effects, and then decide which of them is helping the most. You will, over time, identify common issues with your code and structures, making things easier to address. You are also going to run into completely unique problems.

That is query tuning in as few words as possible. We'll now start to dig into the details of exactly how you achieve all of this.

Performance Issues

Performance tuning is not just about queries and indexes. Your hardware, operating system, cloud provider, network, and other applications can all negatively impact your servers. We're going to be focusing on query tuning and the query tuning process throughout this book, but you do need to know about some of the other issues that could impact your performance. Possibilities could include things like the following:

- An inadequate performance tier on your cloud provider.

- Applications other than SQL Server consuming resources on your server.

- Configuration of the SQL Server service.

- The capacity of the hardware, or the virtual machine, on which your server is running.

- Network hardware or configuration issues.

- Application code or reports running against the server may themselves be misconfigured or not optimized.

- Incorrectly or badly implemented container management and resources.

- The database design itself may not be optimized.

- You may be facing a situation where the relational data structure is the wrong choice.

Any one of these issues can lead to poor performance that completely overrides any sort of enhancements you can make by tuning queries. While we're not going to be drilling down into these types of issues in the rest of the book, we can have a short discussion about possible mechanisms for dealing with these issues here.

While the cloud is an excellent place to host databases and performance can be simply excellent, you have to make choices when configuring your systems, and those choices can be wrong. In order to deal with this issue, you will have to take advantage of the tools offered by the cloud provider. Whether we're talking about AWS or Azure, there are tools for measuring performance that are unique to each provider. You'll need to identify these tools and use them to understand if you're simply running out of resources on the service tier on which your database is operating. Conversely, you'll also want to use those tools to ensure that you're not using too high a service tier. It's not only possible to hurt performance, but you can hurt your company's bottom line by paying too much and using too little. Take some to learn how your cloud service provider supplies mechanisms for monitoring performance so that you can achieve a "just right" solution.

In this age of virtualized operating systems and containers, you may be in a situation where the only thing running within your VM or container is SQL Server. However, you may find that there are other virtual machines or other containers using up the resources. You may also find that another application is installed on your server, virtual or not, and it's using up all the resources. When SQL Server is waiting on access to resources, so are all the queries running on your system. This is why identifying what else may be running with your SQL Server instance is so important.

We will talk about a few server settings that are very directly related to query performance throughout the book. However, there are a number of configurations you could mess up on the SQL Server instance that can indirectly hurt performance. For example, misconfiguring memory can easily starve queries of the resources that they need. Learn how to use the system stored procedure sp_configure to take direct control of the system configurations. You can also query the configuration settings through the system table sys.configurations in the master database. SQL Server Management Studio has mechanisms for controlling SQL Server configurations. For the most part, in the majority of situations, the default settings within SQL Server should be adequate for good performance of the system. I will make a few suggestions on changes you may want to introduce as we go through the book. Following Microsoft best practices on most settings is the right way to go (with a few exceptions that I'll call out).

Ensuring that your servers are not overwhelmed while managing your data is very important. While query tuning is an important aspect to performance tuning in general, you first need to understand how your servers are working. Whether we're talking about a traditional install of SQL Server, a virtual machine (VM), or a Docker container, you'll want to learn how to capture performance metrics on each of these. You'll also need to plan for capturing vendor-specific metrics. For example, while both VMware and Hyper-V are hypervisors letting you virtualize your SQL Server instances, the underlying metrics defining behavior for each are very different. The same thing goes with VMs in the cloud. Focus on collecting metrics on waits and queues, especially around disk I/O, memory, and CPU as these are the resources most likely to be stressed as your data loads grow.

In addition to managing your hardware and virtual machines, you'll need to worry about your network. This is not just about your Internet download or upload speeds. It's also about the health of the routers, cables, and Wi-Fi repeaters you may have in use in your organization.

After talking about hardware, we have to mention that software can also be a problem, specifically when custom-built applications are not optimized in how they deal with the database. You could experience almost any issue from incorrect drivers causing connection timeouts to code that doesn't properly commit transactions that it opens, holding resources on your servers and negatively impacting performance all over the place. In addition to understanding the queries running on your system, don't forget to develop an understanding of the applications that are calling those queries. Also, how those applications are developed matters. Object Relational Mapping (ORM) software can be a huge boon to the speed of development. However, improperly configured, an ORM tool can introduce nightmare queries to your system. Work with your development teams to ensure they follow best practices in coding the applications.

It's also not uncommon for databases to simply be built poorly for the needs of the data and the application. Improper or incomplete data normalization can cause poor performance. Again, ORM tools can build databases that look like objects, which perform quite poorly, even as they make development easier. Take the time to evaluate your data structures to ensure you're designing the databases well, that data types are correct, and that your structures support the workload you're placing on them.

Finally, while SQL Server is an absolutely wonderful tool, it's not applicable to every situation. You may find that you're collecting data through massive Internet of Things (IoT) systems where unstructured or semi-structured information is being collected faster than SQL Server can process it. Sometimes, the right choice isn't to attempt to tune a query, a database, or a server. Instead, it's to change to a more appropriate data storage mechanism. Understand the business and technical needs of the data you're attempting to build a system to manage. You may be better served with an ID/Value database, a search engine, or some other type of nonrelational data store.

If all this sounds like a lot of work, it is. The best place for this work to occur is as you design and build your applications and databases. It's much harder to make the structural and code modifications after the system is already in production. While that may be the ideal, you're regularly going to be dealing with existing systems and attempting to fix them. Just remember that the best thing you can do is understand how your systems are behaving in order to identify the true bottlenecks. With the bottleneck identified, you can begin the process of addressing it.

A Repetitive Process

Performance tuning is something that you will repeat on any given system. On some systems, you're likely to repeat the process quite a lot as the data changes, your workload grows, and new applications are introduced. The core of the process is simple enough:

- Identify the bottleneck.
- Fix it.
- Validate the fix.
- Measure the impact and current performance.
- Start again with the next bottleneck.

One of the best habits you can develop is to change only one thing at a time. Any change to structure or code can have an impact beyond the immediate code you're working with currently. If you can limit your changes to one at a time, your ability to measure and understand the impact of those changes is enhanced. Further, you'll know for certain which change resulted in an improvement and which either didn't help or even hurt performance.

You may decide that adding an index will radically improve performance on a query, but it could cause other queries to run slower. The slowdown of other queries could be because they're now using that index and it's just not as good for them or because they are data modification queries and now another index must be modified as data gets added, changed, or removed from the system. Chapters 9 and 10 will help you deal with indexes. These types of issues are why it's very important to have a test or development system on which you can perform your code changes without negatively affecting the production system.

This is also a place where you can ask an AI for assistance. A couple of things about that though. You are going to want to be cautious about posting private information to a public AI. If there is proprietary stuff in your queries, don't do it. Second, don't blindly trust what the AI suggests. Hallucinations, when an AI makes up an answer, are real and can cause problems. As with the information I provide throughout the book, you should test and validate that the AI information is appropriate to solving your performance issues.

Tuning a single query will seldom fix all the performance issues on a system. Initially, you're likely to identify common problems across a large set of your queries. Addressing all these issues will help to clear a large percentage of your performance problems. At which point, before proceeding with simply trying to tune every query, you should establish best practices for query performance. One system I worked on in the past had a requirement that every query had to meet a three-second minimum operation. Happily, most of the queries were well below this. A few exceptions were allowed above it. Having set the minimum allowed us to focus our work on the worst offenders. This example is not a rule you should necessarily follow. It's just meant to convey how you can establish a minimum that's easy enough to clear. Once every query is running this fast, your system may need more help, and a new minimum can be established.

CHAPTER 1 ■ QUERY PERFORMANCE TUNING

All of this is just meant to emphasize the repetitive nature of query tuning. As the number of people using your system grows, you may see new needs for performance tuning. When the data stored within the database expands, additional query degradation can occur. As the data simply changes over time, you can see similar changes to the behavior of the queries. All of this will lead you to need to do additional query performance tuning. Figure 1-1 shows the general nature of the process over time using decision points based on your performance metrics and the monitoring of your system.

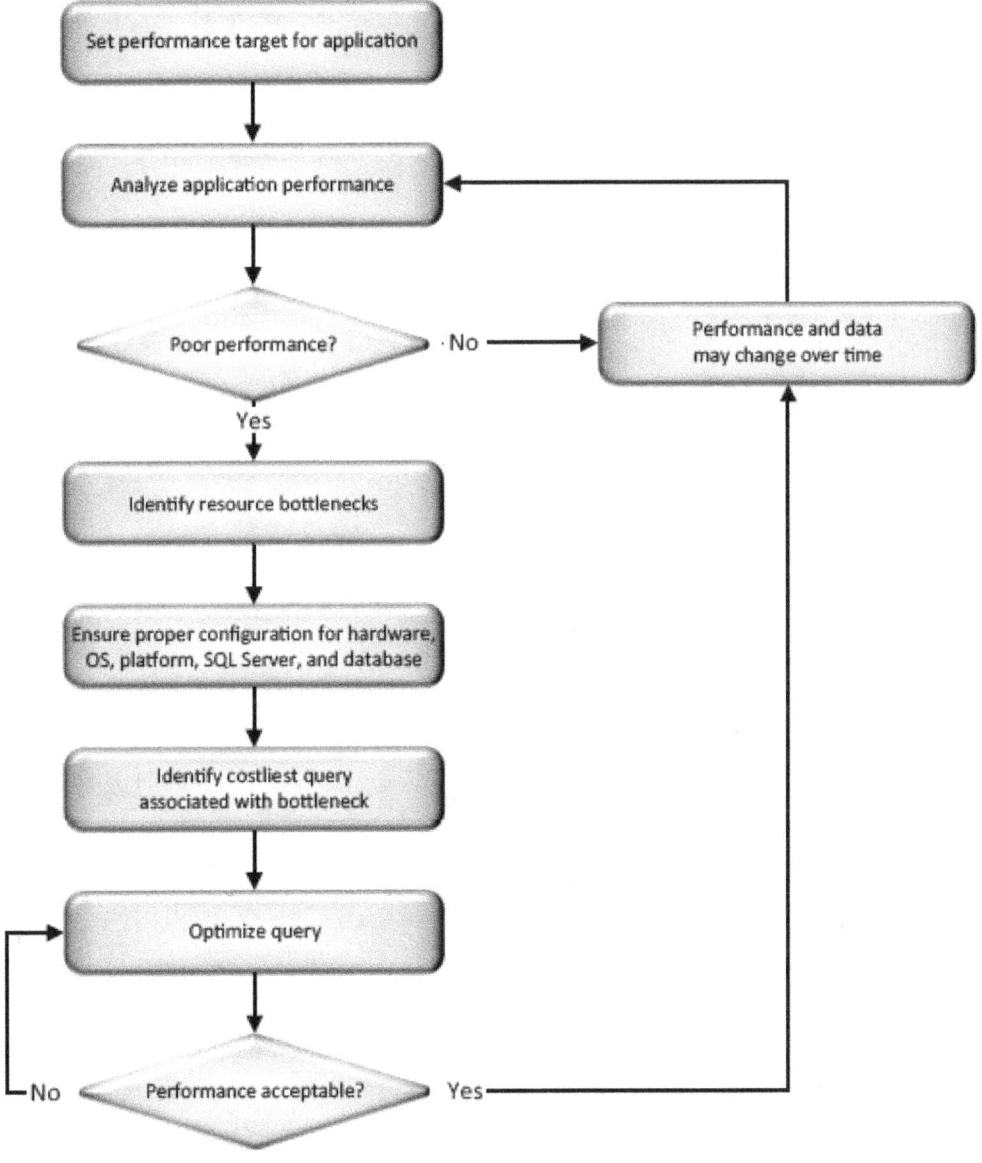

Figure 1-1. *The core performance tuning process*

9

CHAPTER 1 QUERY PERFORMANCE TUNING

The good news is for a lot of systems, all you really need to do is ensure you have a good system configuration and appropriate database settings. Then add some mechanism for capturing performance over time (covered in Chapter 3). Then, you'll need to go through the actual query tuning process as outlined in Figure 1-2.

Figure 1-2. *The core query tuning process*

While this process may seem complex, with practice, you'll find you can move through the steps and decision points rather quickly. The key is to take the time to understand the code, examine the execution plans if necessary, and then carefully assess your opportunities for improving performance. Testing the changes that they made to ensure actual improvements from your changes is also vital. Adopting a structured approach to your query tuning will ensure a higher degree of positive results instead of just poking at things.

Understanding What Defines "Good Enough"

The query optimizer uses a "good enough" method of optimization (we're going to cover the optimizer in Chapter 2). Instead of trying to get a perfect level of optimization for every query, it instead attempts to get enough optimization, without too much optimization. This is going to be the best approach for your query tuning. You simply won't be able to tune every query to the last possible microsecond of performance. There are simply too many databases with too many queries for any of us to do that. Instead, as I said in the last section, you're going to need to define what looks like "good enough" for your systems. There is no single right answer to this question. A query that runs in ten milliseconds is great, until that query gets called thousands of times in a minute. Then, shaving a millisecond or two from the query could be a lifesaver for your system. Yet another query runs in about 30 milliseconds, and it supports the system nicely. If it's only called a few times an hour, shaving a millisecond of performance off that query is absolutely not worth your time.

The key is time. Query tuning is a time-intensive undertaking. After you set up mechanisms for query monitoring (covered in Chapter 3 in detail, as well as several other chapters), you need to have some time to consume the data collected. Then, after you identify the query you intend to tune, you're going to spend quite a bit of time reading through the query in order to understand what it's doing, how, and why. Then, further time will be spent looking at the execution plan for the query (covered in Chapter 4) to understand if there are tuning opportunities. Finally, you're going to have to spend time testing solutions before you implement them on your production server.

Here is why you're not going to waste time getting an extra millisecond of performance out of every query. Only the ones that truly matter to your system are where you're going to spend time.

Establishing Comparison Points

In order to achieve the goals you set for your system and arrive at your "good enough" query tuning, you have to establish comparison points. Sometimes, people talk about establishing a baseline of behavior of your queries. However, you really don't have to have a perfect set of measures and metrics in order to identify poorly performing queries. All you need is the ability to compare before and after you tune your query, using any method you can.

The comparison points you need can include the following:

- A thorough measure of the queries on your system, possibly down to the individual statements on every database. You can then have detailed analysis to see if your query tuning has paid off.

- A measure of the performance of the application or reports that are calling your database. Their round-trip time frequently is all anyone cares about, so it's a good measure for query performance.

- An immediate look at the recent behavior of queries in the system using information stored in the plan cache, which is a memory space in your SQL Server instance. While not a detailed measure of performance, it does give you a comparison point.

- An immediate run of the query to see what performance looks like. Not recommended for systems under already-serious stress and certainly not for data modification queries, but if you can measure the query behavior, it gives you a comparison point.

- Running the query on a nonproduction system. While the full range of behaviors of a production environment may not be possible in other environments, a slow-running query is still a slow-running query.

Once you have a single point of measurement, your goal is then to perform the changes that you think will improve performance and then measure again so that you can compare the two behaviors. This comparison is the most important part of validation of your work. Without validation of the work you've done, you can't be sure you're making a real positive impact on your production systems.

Since you only need to really have two points for comparison purposes, this makes things much easier. You don't have to have a flawless data set to begin working on a query. The simplest initial measurement will enable you to understand the behavior of the system.

Also, when we talk about comparison points, I want to start emphasizing early on that you need to measure more than just the time a query takes to process. Certainly, the timing of the query is probably the most important aspect of query tuning. However, our systems can bottleneck on CPU use or disk I/O or memory. So we need to measure these metrics as well. When we're tuning, we are going to want to see if the CPU use was reduced as part of our tuning. Same goes for all the other metrics I just mentioned. In fact, in some cases, you will find if you're experiencing bottlenecks in a resource, making a query use less of that resource may be more important than making it run faster. You may even find letting a query run slower, but reducing the amount of I/O or memory it uses, can be a win on your systems. It all depends on where the problems are.

Throughout the book, I'll be showing more than one measurement and pointing out how any given tuning technique affects not just query time but CPU and all the rest.

Most Likely Performance Issues

As I said at the start of the chapter, there is not a simple query tuning formula. I truly wish there was and that I could be the one to give it to you. However, there are a number of very common problems. Most of those problems also have a well-defined set of solutions.

The good news here is there really are a few areas that are more important for you to spend time on. Figure 1-3 shows the results of a survey conducted several years ago by Paul Randal. It's still absolutely applicable today.

What were the root causes of the last few SQL Server performance problems you debugged?
(Vote multiple times if you want!)

Cause	Percentage	Count
CPU power saving	2%	6
Other hardware or OS issue	2%	7
Virtualization	2%	7
SQL Server/database configuration	3%	10
Out-of-date/missing statistics	9%	31
Database/table structure/schema design	10%	38
Application code	12%	43
I/O subsystem problem	16%	60
Poor indexing strategy	19%	68
T-SQL code	26%	94

Total: 364 responses

Figure 1-3. Root causes of poor performance

The top two most common problems are the T-SQL code itself and your indexing. Further, you can see that the design of the data structure and out-of-date statistics are also in the top six problems. That means that fully 64% of all performance problems are directly related to the topics discussed in this book.

As I also said at the beginning of this chapter, you can spend your way out of performance problems, buying bigger, faster, and more hardware or using a higher service tier. You'll still be dealing with the fact that 64% of your problems lie in your code, indexes, and statistics. In short, you can buy some of the wonderful hardware imaginable and still get bad performance if your code isn't good enough.

Common Performance Issues

After you've spent the money to try to improve performance, you're then going to turn to this list and focus your efforts on the most common performance problems. This is as close as we'll get to a simple formula for your query tuning efforts. The most common problems are as follows:

- Insufficient or poor indexes
- Inaccurate or missing statistics
- Bad T-SQL
- Problematic execution plans
- Excessive blocking
- Deadlocks
- Non–set-based operations
- Incorrect database design
- Poor execution plan reuse
- Frequent recompilation of queries

These are not the only problems you're likely to run into, they're just the most common. We'll address these in detail throughout the rest of the book, but let's run through them now to discuss how these problems come about and how to solve them.

Insufficient or Poor Indexes

While the joke goes that all you ever have to do is put an index on a table to fix performance problems, the fact is a missing index truly is one of the biggest problems for performance in SQL Server. You're also going to find that sometimes, while there is an index, it's not the right index, or it's an index with poor choices for keys. When there's no index on a given table, SQL Server has no choice but to read through the entire table any time it's attempting to filter information. This directly impacts disk performance and memory use. Further, you're going to see a lot of resource contention because of these scans leading to blocking. Chapters 9–11 are focused on indexes and index strategies.

Since indexes are vital for even the possibility of well-performing code, you need to work across teams to ensure appropriate indexes on your tables. You want the code to have indexes to use to make it run faster, and you want to ensure that the indexes you have will be used by the code. Because of this, you can't really divorce T-SQL coding from index creation. Instead, you need to ensure that the code and the indexes are created together.

While indexes are vital, you can actually create too many indexes. Every time you need to modify data through an INSERT, DELETE, or UPDATE operation, any index that has keys or INCLUDE columns from that data modification will also need to be updated. You can see massive performance hits on your data modification queries because they have to wait as indexes are updated. Also, SELECT queries will be blocked while the indexes get updated. While you do want to use and create indexes, you also must exercise restraint. This is where testing is going to come into play.

Inaccurate or Missing Statistics

The query optimizer within SQL Server does a lot of calculations on how exactly to satisfy a given query based on the number of rows that it expects to see affected by the query. Those row estimates come directly from the statistics that exist on indexes and columns in your database. If those statistics are missing or badly out of date, the choices the optimizer makes can be very bad indeed. You can see scans of entire tables where a seek against an index could have helped performance. Conversely, you may see seeks when a scan would be more efficient. Without good row estimates, the optimizer just can't make good choices.

Statistics are mostly created and maintained completely automatically by the system. This makes sense considering how important they are to the efficient operation of the system. However, depending on how the data in your system is changing, the statistics can quickly get out of date. There are also ways to disable the automatic creation and update of statistics, leading to the statistics being missing or incorrect. There are also potentially other issues that can crop up around statistics. We'll cover them in depth in Chapter 5.

Bad T-SQL

While indexes are going to help your queries run faster, and statistics will give the optimizer better row count estimates, you can completely negate all that with poor coding choices. Any number of problems can come from the code. You may be moving too much data, planning to filter it at the application. You may have written code in such a way that indexes can't be used, leading to scans and excessive I/O. You can also overcomplicate your code in such a way that the optimizer has a hard time picking it apart and providing a good execution plan. Finally, you can incorrectly use the different object types within SQL Server, resulting in very poor performance indeed. Common code smells, these regular poor coding practices we're talking about, are one area where AI can shine, so take advantage of it where possible. We'll discuss a bunch of these topics throughout the entire book and focus on mechanisms to ensure good coding practices in Chapter 23.

Problematic Execution Plans

There is no such thing as a bad, or incorrect, execution plan. Every execution plan generated by the optimizer will work. However, some execution plans are going to work better than others. While the optimizer is an amazing piece of software, it's not perfect. Execution plans that are not optimal for a given query can cause really bad performance. Most of the time, execution plans are fixed through changes in code, statistics updates, or adding an index. It is possible to feed an execution plan to an AI, and it can identify common issues exposed within it. Sometimes though, the execution plan is wrong for a given query due to a process known as parameter sniffing. Most of the time, parameter sniffing helps performance. However, parameter sniffing can go wrong. We'll spend the entire Chapter 13 addressing bad parameter sniffing.

> **Note** It is possible for the optimizer to have an error on plan generation, but this is extremely rare and usually caused by a bug within SQL Server itself.

Excessive Blocking

SQL Server guarantees that the data stored within it will be consistent and accurate through the application of the ACID mechanism: Atomicity, Consistency, Isolation, and Durability. In a nutshell, changes being made to the database won't be affected by other changes until they are complete. A query can only see data either before or after that modification is done. While there are ways to change this default behavior, they all still follow some basic rules.

This isolation of data modification allows multiple queries to access information in a shared fashion, without blocking. However, when more than one query attempts to access data that is being modified, or held for modification, you're going to see one of them waiting on the others. This is blocking in action. Blocking is exacerbated a little because SQL Server stores information on 8KB pages on the disk. Two processes that aren't even updating the same row can block each other.

Also, a lack of resources, not enough memory or CPU, or not fast enough disks can lead to additional blocking. As processes wait for the resources to be freed up, they're holding locks on rows or pages needed by other processes, all making blocking worse. We'll discuss blocking in Chapter 16.

Deadlocks

Deadlocks are related to blocking; in fact, they're caused by blocking. However, blocking and deadlocks are two, very different, topics and should be kept separate in your head. The core issue that causes a deadlock is when two processes each have an exclusive lock on a page that the other needs in order to complete a transaction. This is often referred to as a deadly embrace. One process must be given the go-ahead to complete. The other process is chosen as a deadlock victim, and its pending changes are rolled back.

The rollback is the real performance headache. Not only did a query not complete, but now SQL Server has to do work to remove the partially complete changes from the system. That can lead to more resource contention, more slowdowns, and additional blocking. In addition to this, you're pretty much guaranteed that the person experiencing the rollback will certainly resubmit their query, possibly multiple times. This exacerbates the performance problems caused by deadlocks.

At the root of the problem, deadlocks themselves are a performance-related problem. If all your queries complete fast enough, the chances of a deadlock are very slim. We'll discuss deadlocks in Chapter 17.

Non–Set-Based Operations

SQL in general and T-SQL in particular are designed to work with data in sets. Unlike many programming languages, you shouldn't be approaching your queries thinking about processing information a single row at a time. People use cursors and other types of loop operations to force a row-by-row–style processing on SQL Server. It frankly destroys performance. I address this in detail in Chapter 18.

Incorrect Database Design

SQL Server is a relational data storage engine. Of the many things this means, one of them is that SQL Server is designed to work with tables that use foreign key constraints as a mechanism to enforce the relationship between the tables. The methodology for creating these types of databases is called normalization. Ensuring that your database is properly normalized enhances performance. You reduce the number of columns by eliminating duplicate values. You reduce the number of rows by storing information in multiple tables. All this enhances performance when done correctly.

You can also use different modeling techniques with relational databases like SQL Server. An example might be a star schema for a data warehouse. These also suffer from incorrect design that can directly hurt performance.

A fundamental part of database design is also indexing. Clustered indexes and clustered columnstore indexes define data storage, which then controls data retrieval. The correct index and the right keys on that index (if it's a rowstore index) are as much a part of the database design as the table definitions.

Finally, storing data correctly, meaning a datetime goes into a datetime column and a string goes into a char, varchar, or nvarchar column, positively affects performance. Putting the wrong data types into the database can actually hurt performance since you'll have to work around the fact that since you don't have dates in your date column, but strings, you're giving up the possibility of date math functionality within SQL Server. This can also negatively impact index design and use.

We're going to discuss aspects of database design throughout the book, but this is a huge topic. I strongly recommend getting a copy of Louis Davidson's book: *Pro SQL Server Relational Database Design and Implementation: Best Practices for Scalability and Performance* (Apress, 2020).

Poor Execution Plan Reuse

The compilation of an execution plan by the query optimizer is an expensive operation. Because of this, SQL Server stores execution plans in a memory space referred to as the plan cache. The idea is simple. Many queries, maybe even most queries, are repetitious. Because of this, plans can be reused, tremendously reducing the overhead required to generate them. Parameterization of stored procedures and prepared statements makes plan reuse simpler. So does a process called simple parameterization where the optimizer adds parameters to simple queries. All of this is an attempt to reuse execution plans.

It is possible though that queries are structured such that they don't get to reuse plans, even though they are the same as queries run earlier. Generating dynamic T-SQL can lead to this problem. Badly configured ORM tools can generate inappropriate parameters, preventing plan reuse. All of that adds up to additional overhead on the system and slower performance. Chapter 7 covers this information.

Frequent Recompilation of Queries

Just as a lack of plan reuse causes excessive overhead on the system, a lot of recompilation of execution plans leads to a very similar problem. Generally speaking, recompiling of execution plans is a desirable process. The recompile is generally caused by changes in data, which leads to statistics getting updated. With new information, the optimizer might make better choices for your queries.

However, as with many other good things, too much is a problem. You may have highly volatile data sets that lead to a lot of recompiles. You can also get recompiles from poor coding practices. We'll discuss how to avoid recompiles in Chapter 8.

Summary

This chapter introduced us to the concepts that we'll be discussing throughout the rest of the book. The iterative nature of query tuning assumes that you'll be doing it quite a bit more than once over the lifetime of a given application and database. The core concepts though are always the same. First, measure performance on your system so you have something to compare against. Use those measurements to determine which queries could use help. Investigate and test possible solutions, validating any possible performance improvements against your metrics. Then, do the whole thing over again as the system changes and data changes.

The next chapter is going to cover how the query optimizer works. We'll also introduce execution plans, our window into the work done by the query optimizer. Since all of query performance is based on what the optimizer is doing, it makes a great place to get started understanding the mechanisms you can apply to make your systems run faster.

CHAPTER 2

Execution Plan Generation and the Query Optimizer

All performance within SQL Server starts, and frequently ends, with the query optimizer. Because the optimizer is so important to query performance, we're diving immediately into how the optimizer behaves in order to better understand why our queries perform the way they do. The optimization process results in an execution plan, a path for the query engine to follow as well as a mechanism for showing the choices the optimizer made. The optimization process is expensive in terms of resources, especially CPU, and can be somewhat time-consuming, affecting the execution time of your queries. We'll go over what the process is, how an execution plan is generated, and how that plan goes into memory in the plan cache in the hopes of reusing the plan.

In this chapter, we'll address the following topics:

- The query optimization process in general
- Execution plans and the plan cache
- Factors affecting parallel plan generation

The Query Optimization Process

The query optimizer in SQL Server uses a cost-based analysis mechanism to arrive at the necessary choices to satisfy the queries that you've submitted. In order to process a query, a large number of choices must be made. Which index to use to access a table, how to join two tables together, and whether or not the data has to be ordered, all these and many others are all given estimated costs by the optimizer. The optimizer is also aware of the structure of the database. From the data types in your columns to your primary key definitions, constraints, and foreign keys, these objects also affect the cost estimates that the optimizer uses to arrive at its decisions. Finally, your data is included in the cost through the use of statistics about the data (covered in more detail in Chapter 5).

As was mentioned in Chapter 1, the optimizer doesn't attempt to make a perfect execution plan. Instead, the optimizer uses mathematical models, based in part on the objects and statistics in your database, to arrive at a plan that is good enough. So the cost-based analysis tries to arrive at as optimal a plan as it can while using as few resources as it can and finishing up as quickly as it can.

Before optimization starts though, there are some initial, preparatory phases that must be accomplished.

Optimization Preparation

Because the optimizer needs so much metadata about your system, there are a number of steps before optimization takes place to put this information together. The order in which these steps are performed is as follows:

1. Parsing
2. Binding
3. Optimization

There is a complex set of inputs and outputs that don't really need to be explored in order to understand what's going on. However, just so we're clear, Figure 2-1 shows the process, the inputs, and the outputs.

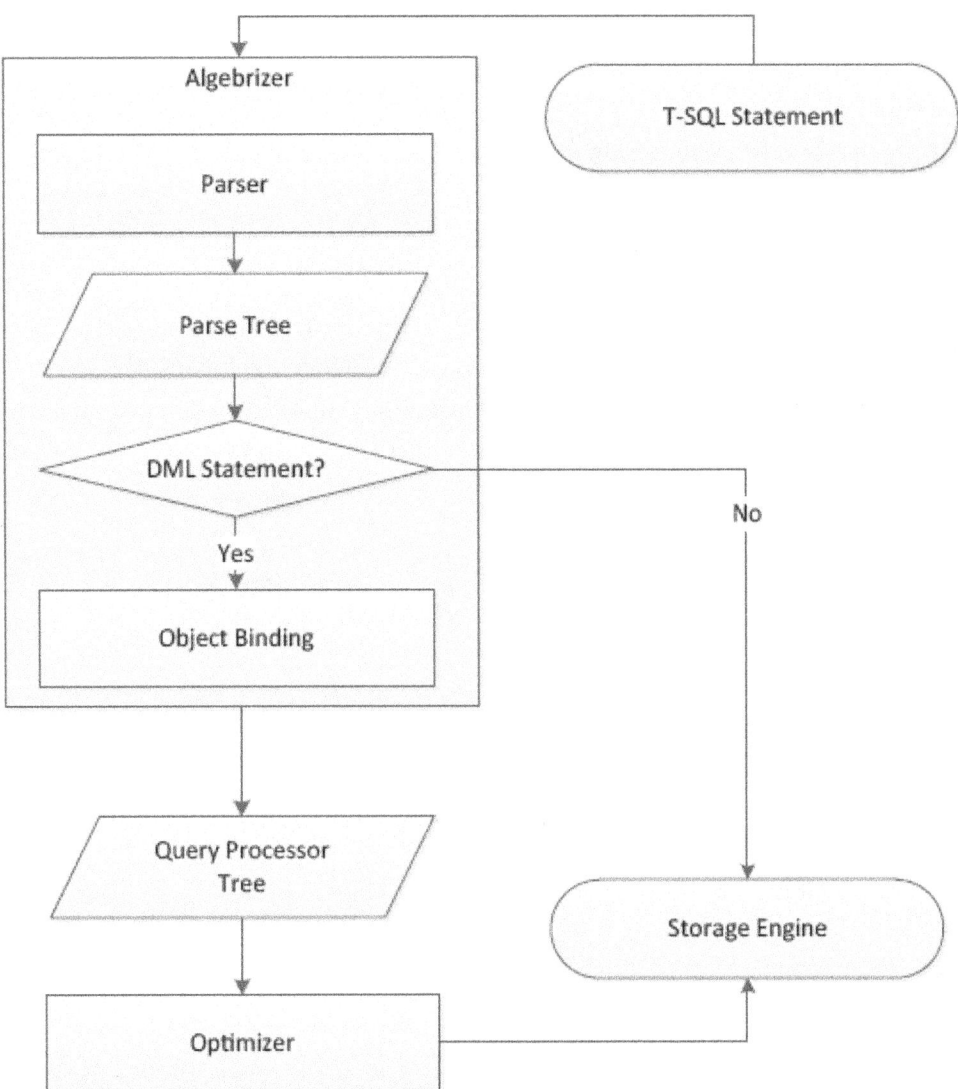

***Figure 2-1.** Steps leading up to the optimization process*

Let's take a look at the two steps that take place prior to the optimization process itself.

Parsing

A query first goes through the relational engine within SQL Server. This is the first part of two processes that deal with the query. The second is the storage engine that is responsible for data access, modification, and caching. The relational engine takes

CHAPTER 2 EXECUTION PLAN GENERATION AND THE QUERY OPTIMIZER

care of parsing the query through a process called the algebrizer. The relational engine executes a query per the execution plan generated and requests the data from the storage engine.

The algebrizer does several steps, but the first one is query parsing. The parsing process simply validates that you have correct syntax in your query. If there's an error in the syntax, the process is immediately terminated, and all optimization processes are circumvented. If multiple queries are submitted together as a single batch, then the batch is checked, and the batch is cancelled in the event of a syntax error anywhere within the batch. While you may have multiple syntax errors, the parser stops at the very first error and stops all other processing. The immediate interruption is just one aspect of how the optimizer attempts to reduce the overhead of the optimization process. Listing 2-1 shows a batch with an error.

Listing 2-1. A batch with a syntax error

```
CREATE TABLE dbo.Example
(
    Col1 INT
);
INSERT INTO dbo.Example
(
    Col1
)
VALUES
(1);
SELECT e.Col1
FORM dbo.Example AS e; -- Generates an error because of 'FORM'
```

Once the parsing process is passed, an internal-only structure called a parse tree gets created and passed on to the next step.

Binding

The parse tree is now used to identify all the objects that make up the query. This list of objects includes tables, columns, indexes, and more. This process is called binding. All the data types being processed are identified. Aggregations and other operations are also mapped out. All these objects and processes are put together into another internal structure called a query processor tree.

CHAPTER 2   EXECUTION PLAN GENERATION AND THE QUERY OPTIMIZER

The algebrizer will also handle implicit data conversions by adding steps to the processor tree. You may also see syntax optimizations occur where the code you passed to SQL Server actually gets changed. If you take the code from Listing 2-2 and capture an execution plan (covered in Chapter 4), you can actually see the changes in syntax.

Listing 2-2. The original code before binding

```
SELECT soh.AccountNumber,
       soh.OrderDate,
       soh.PurchaseOrderNumber,
       soh.SalesOrderNumber
FROM Sales.SalesOrderHeader AS soh
WHERE soh.SalesOrderID
BETWEEN 62500 AND 62550;
```

Figure 2-2 shows the change in syntax.

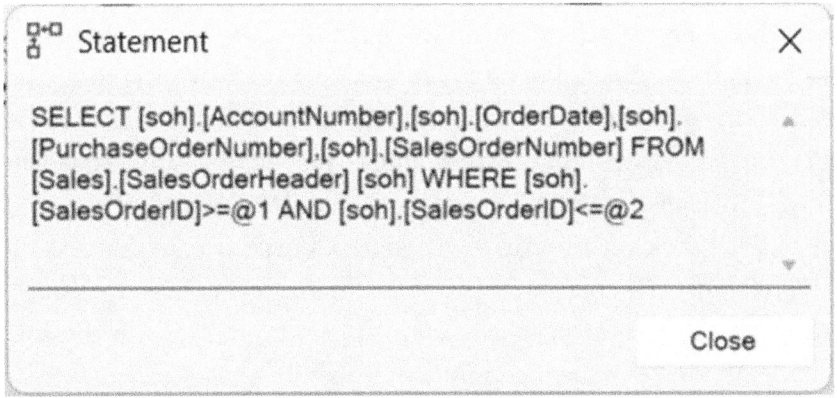

Figure 2-2. *Syntax-based optimization at work*

Two very distinct changes have been made. First, the BETWEEN statement has been replaced with ">=" and "<=". Second, a process called simple parameterization has been implemented through the @1 and @2 you see in the figure. We'll discuss more about parameterization later in this chapter. You can see further evidence of the binding process if we look at the execution plan generated in Figure 2-3.

CHAPTER 2   EXECUTION PLAN GENERATION AND THE QUERY OPTIMIZER

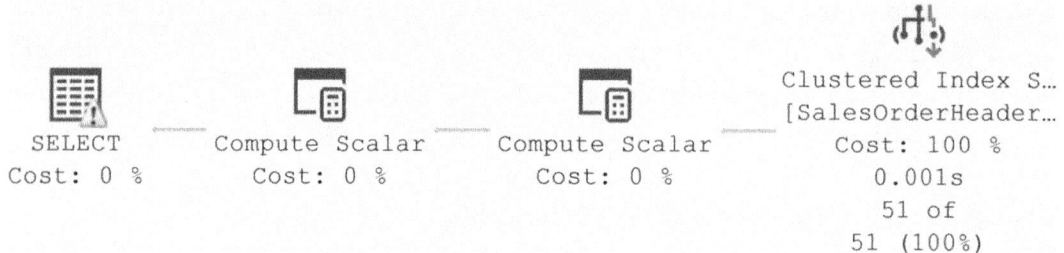

Figure 2-3. *A warning indicator on an execution plan*

The exclamation point visible on the very first operator on the left, labeled "SELECT," is an indication of a warning. Looking at the properties for that operator, you'll find that the SalesOrderID is actually going through a data type conversion:

Type conversion in expression (CONVERT(nvarchar(23),[soh].[SalesOrderID],0)) may affect "CardinalityEstimate" in query plan choice.

This example illustrates several points in addition to syntax-based optimization. First, warnings can sometimes be unclear. In this case, the warning is not actually from the SalesOrderID column as referenced in the WHERE clause of the query. Instead, it's from a calculated column, SalesOrderNumber. That calculation is converting the SalesOrderID, an integer, into a string and adding other information to it. In the way this calculation is being done, the optimizer recognizes that were this to be used as filtering criteria in a WHERE clause, or JOIN criteria, or even a HAVING clause, it would affect the ability to use statistics and indexes to get good performance. In this case though, the query doesn't reference the column in any of the filtering criteria, so we can safely ignore the warning. I like this example because it shows just how realistic AdventureWorks really is. A lot of this kind of issue creeps into real-world databases.

Unlike Data Manipulation Language (DML) queries that we've seen so far, Data Definition Language (DDL) queries, such as CREATE TABLE, do not get execution plans. There is only one way to run a CREATE VIEW query as an example. Therefore, most DDL doesn't go through the optimization process. The exception is CREATE INDEX DDL queries. The optimizer can take advantage of existing indexes to create another index more efficiently. So while you'll never see a CREATE PROCEDURE execution plan, you will see one when creating an index.

Once all the binding operations are complete, another internal structure is created, called the query processor tree. This is where optimization starts.

Optimization

The optimization process is a pretty amazing piece of software. Without a debugger, you can't really see it in action. However, we can see the results of the process in the execution plans that it creates. We can also use Dynamic Management Views (DMVs) and Extended Events to observe aspects of the optimization process. In this book, we'll see a lot of the evidence of optimization, but it's beyond the scope of the book to examine the code with a debugger. We'll stick to the tools immediately available to us. Let's start talking about the optimization process.

Figure 2-4 shows the processes that the optimizer uses to attempt to arrive at a "good enough" execution plan as quickly as possible.

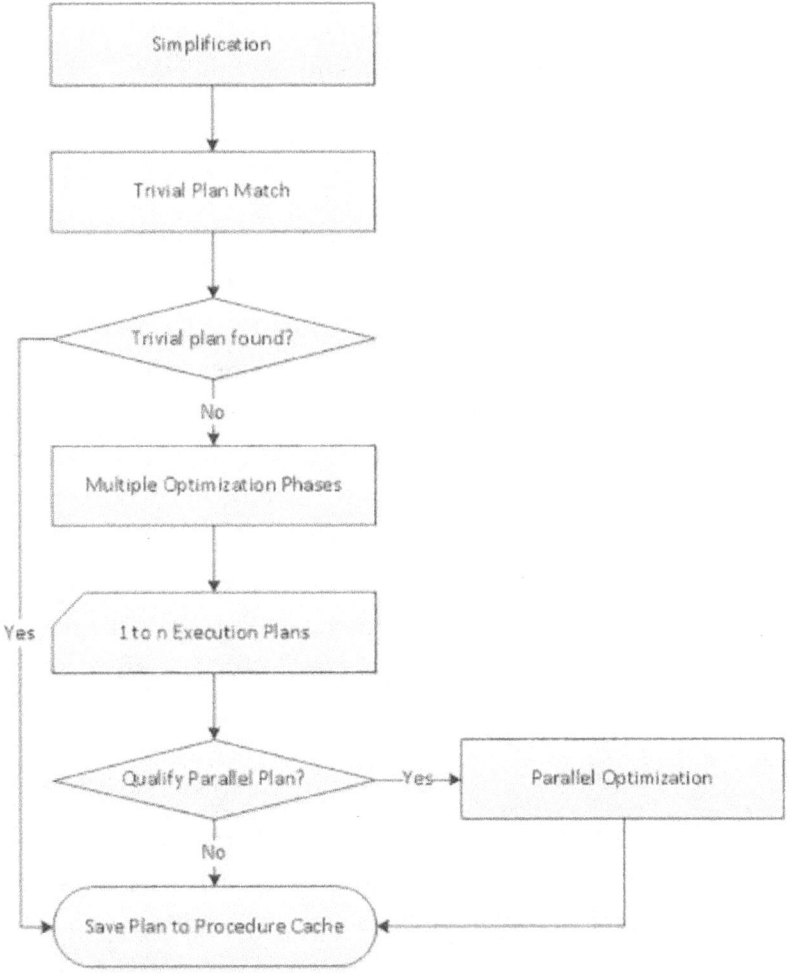

Figure 2-4. *The optimization process*

Let's discuss each step in order to understand how the optimizer arrives at an execution plan.

Simplification

The first step in optimization is a process called simplification. Here the optimizer ensures that all the objects that you reference in your query are actually in use. Statistics and row counts begin to be gathered and used. This step looks at the constraints such as foreign keys. When all this is taken together, you can see the optimizer actually change what is being processed. For example, you may write a query with a four-table join. However, only two tables are referenced in the SELECT list and the WHERE clause. Using the constraints, the optimizer can tell that it doesn't need the other two tables to satisfy the query and will therefore eliminate them from further processing, simplifying what is being queried–hence the name of this step.

Trivial Plan Match

When a query is extremely simplistic, it can match a pattern for which there are no options, but only one possible execution plan. That situation is referred to as a Trivial Plan. The simplest example is a table with no clustered index, referred to as a heap, and no other indexes. The only way this table can be accessed is through a table scan. Rather than even attempting to build an execution plan, the optimizer looks for the query pattern that matches existing Trivial Plans. When a pattern match is found, optimization, an expensive operation, is skipped entirely. Instead, the Trivial Plan is used to satisfy the query. As stated before, you'll only see Trivial Plans in extremely simple queries. You can see that a plan is marked Trivial in the properties of the execution plan (discussed in Chapter 4).

Optimization Phases

Once it's clear that a Trivial Plan won't be found, the optimizer will have to go through multiple optimization phases to attempt to arrive at a good enough execution plan. It breaks this process down into multiple steps, each one attempting to do as little work as possible. These are called

- Search 0 or Transaction: It's called Transaction since the types of queries that can be satisfied here are generally simple, Online Transaction Processing (OLTP)-style queries with few joins and no transformations needed, such as reordering joins.

- Search 1 or Quick Plan: This is where more complex operations occur such as reordering joins and other transformations to arrive at a good enough plan.

- Search 2 or Full Optimization: When queries are complex, they end up going through all three optimization steps to arrive at full optimization. This step includes more complex assessments such as composite index use and subquery unnesting (e.g., turning a correlated subquery into a JOIN).

The optimizer can short-circuit these searches, heading straight to Quick Plan or Full Optimization, skipping Transaction, depending on the query, its complexity, and the supporting objects such as indexes and constraints. These phases can each decide on how to perform a particular JOIN operation or access the data through scans or seeks.

The principal driver for most of the decisions within the optimizer are row counts. Row counts generally come from the statistics of the columns in the filtering criteria such as ON, HAVING, and WHERE predicates. With the statistics in hand, the optimizer begins to make choices and calculations based on how much estimated CPU, memory, and I/O are necessary to satisfy the query. These estimates are added up to a total cost for the execution of a query. That cost is not a measure based on your system. Rather it's an arbitrary calculation made by the optimizer and is purely a mathematical construct.

The optimizer will make a calculation on the number of iterations it needs to run through, attempting different plans, with different strategies. At the same time, it calculates what is likely to be the least cost plan. When it finds the plan that meets all the calculated requirements, it will stop optimization, even if a better plan could be found. This is known as Early Termination of Optimization. You'll also see the termination of optimization when the optimizer has gone through the calculated number of iterations. At that point, it will end optimization through what is referred to as a Timeout (more on that in Chapter 4).

If a query reaches Search 2, or Full Optimization, it may also be evaluated for conversion from a serial plan to a parallel plan (more on that later in the chapter).

CHAPTER 2 EXECUTION PLAN GENERATION AND THE QUERY OPTIMIZER

It's possible to see a lot of the work the optimizer is doing through the use of execution plans. Let's take the query in Listing 2-3 as an example.

Listing 2-3. A slightly complex query

```
SELECT soh.SalesOrderNumber,
       sod.OrderQty,
       sod.LineTotal,
       sod.UnitPrice,
       sod.UnitPriceDiscount,
       p.Name AS ProductName,
       p.ProductNumber,
       ps.Name AS ProductSubCategoryName,
       pc.Name AS ProductCategoryName
FROM Sales.SalesOrderHeader AS soh
    JOIN Sales.SalesOrderDetail AS sod
        ON soh.SalesOrderID = sod.SalesOrderID
    JOIN Production.Product AS p
        ON sod.ProductID = p.ProductID
    JOIN Production.ProductModel AS pm
        ON p.ProductModelID = pm.ProductModelID
    JOIN Production.ProductSubcategory AS ps
        ON p.ProductSubcategoryID = ps.ProductSubcategoryID
    JOIN Production.ProductCategory AS pc
        ON ps.ProductCategoryID = pc.ProductCategoryID
WHERE soh.CustomerID = 29658;
```

If we capture the execution plan for this query (again, covered in Chapter 4), we can see some of the behavior of the optimizer. This plan is hard to read within this context, but I don't want you to try to understand it all at this point. The plan is shown in Figure 2-5.

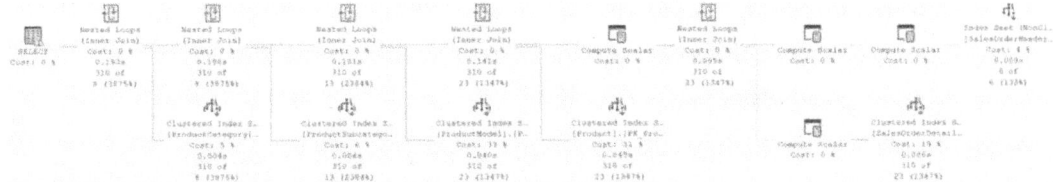

Figure 2-5. *Execution plan from the complex query*

Don't try to read that plan here in the book. It's much too small. Instead of reading the plan now, we're going to focus on one spot, the operator on the far-left side of the plan. In this case, since it's a SELECT query, the operator is labeled SELECT. The properties of this operator are all of the information about the execution plan itself. You can see the properties by right-clicking the operator and selecting "Properties" from the context menu. Again, we'll cover execution plans more in Chapter 4. These properties include information about the optimization process. We can see a subset of those properties in Figure 2-6.

Misc	
Cached plan size	72 KB
CardinalityEstimationModelVersion	140
CompileCPU	98
CompileMemory	1472
CompileTime	1197
Degree of Parallelism	1
Estimated Number of Rows for All Exe	0
Estimated Number of Rows Per Execut	7.78327
Estimated Operator Cost	0 (0%)
Estimated Subtree Cost	0.0832678

Figure 2-6. *Optimizer behaviors on display in the execution plan properties*

Some of the information immediately on display includes the following:

- CompileCPU: The amount of CPU time taken to compile this plan

- Estimated Number of Rows Per Execution: The row count that the optimizer arrived at for this query

- Estimated Subtree Cost: The combined estimates on CPU, I/O, and memory across all the operations in the plan arrived at through the optimization process

That's just a sample of the amount of information gathered here for how the optimizer works to arrive at an execution plan. We can also look to this data to see things like the Optimization Level and the Reason for Early Termination, the top and bottom properties shown in Figure 2-7.

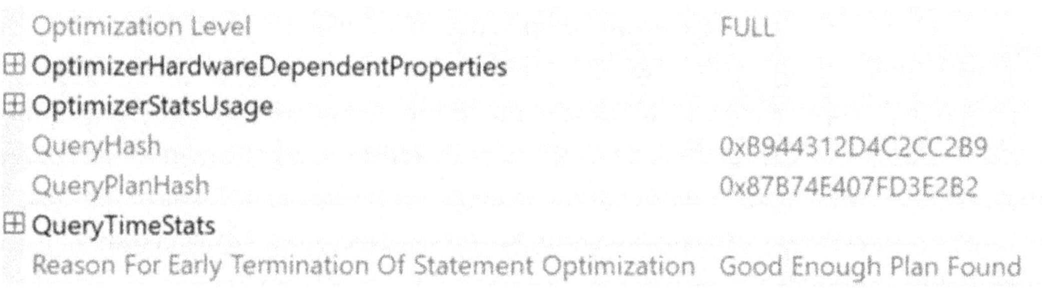

```
Optimization Level                                          FULL
⊞ OptimizerHardwareDependentProperties
⊞ OptimizerStatsUsage
QueryHash                                                   0xB944312D4C2CC2B9
QueryPlanHash                                               0x87B74E407FD3E2B2
⊞ QueryTimeStats
Reason For Early Termination Of Statement Optimization      Good Enough Plan Found
```

Figure 2-7. *Additional properties showing optimizer behaviors*

One point worth noting here, when we see the property *Optimization Level* and a value of "FULL," it doesn't necessarily mean that this plan went through *Search 2*. It only means that it's not a Trivial Plan.

Another way to observe some of the work by the optimizer is to use the Dynamic Management View (DMV) sys.dm_exec_query_optimizer_info. Named appropriately, this DMV shows aggregated data about the optimization process. An example of how to use this DMV is in Listing 2-4.

Listing 2-4. Querying the dm_exec_query_optimizer_info DMV

```
SELECT deqoi.counter,
       deqoi.occurrence,
       deqoi.value
FROM sys.dm_exec_query_optimizer_info AS deqoi;
```

A partial set of the results from the query are visible in Figure 2-8.

	counter	occurrence	value
1	optimizations	681	1
2	elapsed time	681	0.0456431718061674
3	final cost	681	0.0625588371393636
4	trivial plan	227	1
5	tasks	454	1307.15859030837
6	no plan	0	NULL
7	search 0	212	1
8	search 0 time	215	0.0403069767441861
9	search 0 tasks	215	2146.8976744186
10	search 1	242	1
11	search 1 time	242	0.00747107438016529
12	search 1 tasks	242	544.904958677686
13	search 2	0	NULL
14	search 2 time	0	NULL
15	search 2 tasks	0	NULL

Figure 2-8. *Aggregated information about the optimization processes*

You can see that the system I've run this on has done no complex optimizations so far. We can tell that because there have been no *Search 2* operations. You can see the other operations that have been done and the estimated time needed to accomplish them.

This information is only of limited use, but it's good to know where to go to get it in the event that you need to understand some of the processes that the optimizer is going through and the load it's placing on your systems.

You could also run this code before and after a query in order to see the types of optimizations that occurred on that query. However, you need to do this on an isolated system, or you're likely to see more than just the optimizations for the query you're investigating.

Generating Parallel Execution Plans

When plans become complex enough, they may benefit from parallel execution. Parallel execution is when more than one CPU is available to SQL Server, so multiple processors are put to work on a single query. However, parallel execution is an expensive operation, so you really want the query to benefit from parallelism before the query goes parallel. In fact, many queries executed in a parallel fashion can actually run slower because of the process. Further to this point, when queries that don't need parallelism are executed in parallel, you may see performance suffer as CPU resources are depleted. While there are benefits to parallel execution, due caution must be exercised in its use.

When the optimizer is deciding on whether or not a complex query will go parallel, it takes a number of factors into consideration:

- CPUs available to SQL Server, if more than one
- SQL Server edition
- Available memory
- Cost Threshold for Parallelism
- Query being executed
- Rows to be processed
- Active concurrent connections
- Max Degree of Parallelism

The three most important of these factors are the actual number of CPUs available to SQL Server, the *Max Degree of Parallelism*, and the *Cost Threshold for Parallelism*.

If there is only a single CPU or a single vCPU on a NUMA node available to SQL Server, then you won't see any query go parallel. You can also restrict parallelism and the number of CPUs used by it through the *Max Degree of Parallelism* setting. Setting that to a value of 1 will eliminate all parallel execution, but that's not recommended. One way to control the Max Degree of Parallelism, you have to use a server setting (Listing 2-5).

Listing 2-5. Changing the Max Degree of Parallelism

```
USE master;
EXEC sp_configure 'show advanced option', '1';
RECONFIGURE;
EXEC sp_configure 'max degree of parallelism', 2;
RECONFIGURE;
```

The changes defined by this query will take effect immediately. Determining the precise setting for this value is frequently of great debate. Your systems and your workloads should drive these decisions, not some arbitrary calculation based on the number of processors on your systems. Because of this, I'm not going to make a precise recommendation here, other than to emphasize again, parallel execution of some queries is very desirable, so you want to leave the possibility on your systems, meaning don't set the Max Degree of Parallelism to 1. However, for most systems, the default value of 0, meaning to use all CPUs available, is also not a desirable setting.

You can also control the degree of parallelism on a query-by-query basis through query hints. I'm going to say this multiple times in the book: query hints should be used extremely judiciously on your systems. Listing 2-6 shows how this works.

Listing 2-6. Controlling the degree of parallelism through a query hint

```
SELECT e.ID,
       e.SomeValue
FROM dbo.Example AS e
WHERE e.ID = 42
OPTION (MAXDOP 2);
```

If you want to more directly control which plans go parallel, the best way is controlling the process by changing the Cost Threshold for Parallelism (Listing 2-7). The default value of 5 is extremely low for the vast majority of systems. Microsoft generally doesn't agree, but I would immediately make that value higher on any system I was responsible for. Again, the precise value comes down to your system, queries, and load.

Listing 2-7. Changing the Cost Threshold for Parallelism

```
USE master;
EXEC sp_configure 'show advanced option', '1';
RECONFIGURE;
EXEC sp_configure 'cost threshold for parallelism', 35;
RECONFIGURE;
```

One way to determine a good value for the cost threshold would be to look at the estimated costs of the queries on your systems. Using any of the query metrics available, and the cost estimates from execution plans, you can see how your systems are behaving and make adjustments from there. There are a number of ways you could make a determination as to the appropriate value on your systems. The query in Listing 2-8, for example, will simply list all the estimated costs for all the execution plans in the plan cache in your system.

Listing 2-8. Retrieving every plan's estimated cost

```
WITH XMLNAMESPACES
(
    DEFAULT N'http://schemas.microsoft.com/sqlserver/2004/07/showplan'
)
, TextPlans
AS (SELECT CAST(detqp.query_plan AS XML) AS QueryPlan,
           detqp.dbid
    FROM sys.dm_exec_query_stats AS deqs
        CROSS APPLY sys.dm_exec_text_query_plan(
                                                deqs.plan_handle,
                                                deqs.statement_start_offset,
                                                deqs.statement_end_offset
                                              ) AS detqp ),
  QueryPlans
AS (SELECT RelOp.pln.value(N'@EstimatedTotalSubtreeCost', N'float')
AS EstimatedCost,
           RelOp.pln.value(N'@NodeId', N'integer') AS NodeId,
           tp.dbid,
           tp.QueryPlan
    FROM TextPlans AS tp
        CROSS APPLY tp.QueryPlan.nodes(N'//RelOp') RelOp(pln) )
SELECT qp.EstimatedCost
FROM QueryPlans AS qp
WHERE qp.NodeId = 0;
```

With the data returned, you could use it in calculations to arrive at an appropriate value for the cost threshold on your system.

Caution XML queries can be expensive to run and use quite a few resources. Be cautious running a query like this on your production systems.

As was stated earlier, parallel execution of queries is expensive. Parallel execution doesn't just take up more CPU but also considerably more memory. Because of this, SQL Server will take into account the amount of available memory, prior to executing a parallel plan. SQL Server will automatically reduce the amount of parallelism, or abandon it entirely, for a given query on a system under stress.

All DML queries are executed serially. However, the SELECT in an INSERT and the WHERE clauses of UPDATE or DELETE statements can be executed in parallel. All data changes are still applied in a serial fashion, never in parallel.

At execution time, SQL Server can change the behavior of parallel execution. It then sets the number of processing threads for a given query, and that number of threads is used throughout its execution. That value can be reexamined the next time the query executes and may change.

Execution Plan Caching

When the optimizer completes its processing, the result is an execution plan. The plan is saved in the memory of SQL Server in a place referred to as the plan cache. Saving the plan into cache is another optimization that SQL Server is performing in an attempt to make your queries faster. By saving the plan, it can be reused instead of going through the optimization process again. However, plans can be removed from cache through various processes. One of these processes is referred to as "aging."

Aging of the Execution Plan

The plan cache is part of SQL Server's buffer cache, which also holds data pages. As new execution plans are added to the plan cache, the size of the plan cache keeps growing, affecting the retention of useful data pages in memory. To avoid this, SQL Server dynamically controls the retention of the execution plans in the plan cache, retaining the frequently used execution plans and discarding plans that are not used for a certain period of time.

SQL Server keeps track of the frequency of an execution plan's reuse by associating an age field to it. When an execution plan is generated, the age field is populated with the cost of generating the plan. A complex query requiring extensive optimization will have an age field value higher than that for a simpler query.

At regular intervals, the current cost of all the execution plans in the plan cache is examined by SQL Server's lazy writer process (which manages most of the background processes in SQL Server). If an execution plan is not reused for a long time, then the current cost will eventually be reduced to 0. The cheaper the execution plan was to generate, the sooner its cost will be reduced to 0. Once an execution plan's cost reaches

0, the plan becomes a candidate for removal from memory. SQL Server removes all plans with a cost of 0 from the plan cache when memory pressure increases to such an extent that there is no longer enough free memory to serve new requests. However, if a system has enough memory and free memory pages are available to serve new requests, execution plans with a cost of 0 can remain in the plan cache for a long time so that they can be reused later, if required.

As well as changing the costs downward, execution plans can also find their costs increased to the max cost of generating the plan every time the plan is reused (or to the current cost of the plan for ad hoc plans). For example, suppose you have two execution plans with generation costs equal to 100 and 10. Their starting cost values will therefore be 100 and 10, respectively. If both execution plans are reused immediately, their age fields will be set back to that maximum cost. With these cost values, the lazy writer will bring down the cost of the second plan to 0 much earlier than that of the first one, unless the second plan is reused more often. Therefore, even if a costly plan is reused less frequently than a cheaper plan, because of the effect of the initial cost, the costly plan can remain at a nonzero cost value for a longer period of time.

Summary

While you don't need to understand every aspect of the query optimizer in order to make your queries run faster, having a degree of understanding will help. You've seen the basic process that the optimizer goes through from parsing and binding through to matching Trivial Plans and finally into the full optimization process. We've also discussed some of how parallel plans work and the ways in which execution plans end up in the plan cache.

The next chapter is going to discuss the best ways to capture query performance metrics.

CHAPTER 3

Methods for Capturing Query Performance Metrics

In order to understand which queries we should be focused on for query tuning, we need a method to accurately measure query performance. Also, as we make various attempts to improve query performance, we need to be able to capture the metrics that will enable us to understand how well our improvements are working or if they are working. Finally, we need to be able to measure the results of our improvements in order to both validate that they worked and also start the process over again, identifying the next poorly performing query.

While there are a large number of mechanisms for capturing query performance, we're going to focus our efforts around the three that I've found to be both the most accurate and the easiest to implement. While the other mechanisms work, I've found these three to work best. If you do choose to use another mechanism, just be consistent in what you measure because every metric gathering tool I've used seems to return different values from all the others.

In this chapter, we're going to learn about

- Using Dynamic Management Views
- Capturing detailed metrics using Extended Events
- Query performance metrics in the Query Store

Methods to Capture Query Performance Metrics

There are a large number of ways to capture query metrics. Most of them are equally accurate, but some are either easier to use, provide more complete information, or work better at scale on larger systems. Let me run through all the possibilities, and then we'll briefly discuss why I don't use some measures as much as others. The possible query performance measurement methods are as follows:

- Include Client Statistics
- Connection properties
- SET STATISTICS TIME/IO
- QueryTimeStats in the execution plan
- Query Store
- Dynamic Management Views (DMVs)
- Trace Events (Profiler)
- Extended Events

Since we're going to talk about the DMVs, Query Store, and Extended Events in the rest of the chapter, I want to talk about the others right here. Let's start with the one measure that is actually not accurate (unlike all the others), Include Client Statistics.

Include Client Statistics

You can get to this by right-clicking in a query window in SQL Server Management Studio (SSMS) and selecting "Include Client Statistics" from the context menu. It will capture the runtime and I/O from the client where you're running the query. This means that network times, local contention for resources, and everything else possible will negatively impact the performance measurement. The output of these values doesn't match in any way the output from other methods. Because of this, I simply never use it.

Connection Properties

This method is actually very handy, although I don't rely on it as my primary measure. Before, or even after, you run a query, right-click in the query window in SSMS and select "Properties" from the context menu. This will open the Properties window (which we're going to use a lot with execution plans throughout the book; I generally leave this window open, pinned, and available all the time while working). There you'll find the "Connection Details" information. The details include a "Connection elapsed time," which is actually an accurate measure of query performance. While you can see query performance at the bottom of the screen in SSMS, it only measures down to the second. The values here are accurate to milliseconds. The only problem is it doesn't give us a measure of I/O, so it's just not as useful as other measurements that give us both elapsed time and I/O and, in some cases, CPU use. However, if you forget to enable any other data collection mechanism, this one is always available to you, which, again, makes it very handy. Figure 3-1 shows the results of the last query I ran on the system.

Connection Details
Connection elapsed time   00:00:00.155

Figure 3-1. Connection properties showing elapsed time

SET STATISTICS TIME/IO

This is the classic mechanism for measuring performance when query tuning. Previous versions of the book made extensive use of these values. They are accurate, so if you choose to use them, you'll be fine. You can use them by going into the Options for SSMS, right-clicking and choosing them from the context menu, or using T-SQL to SET STATISTICS TIME ON.

Let me explain why I don't use them as much anymore. First, you only get a single measurement. I've found that I get more accurate results if I execute a query multiple times and then average the results. That's very hard using this method. You also don't get CPU use. Finally, if you capture both TIME and IO using this method, the IO capture can actually negatively impact the TIME capture, making it less accurate. You'll generally only see this on queries that are running in less than a second or even less than 100 milliseconds. However, when you most need accuracy is when you're down to tuning for those last few milliseconds. Having that accuracy upset detracts from the utility of this method. The one time I fall back on this measure though is when I need more granular IO measurement across the objects involved in a query. STATISTICS IO is always a simple way to get that measure.

QueryTimeStats in the Execution Plan

When you capture the runtime metrics with an execution plan, which is referred to as the "Actual Execution Plan" in SSMS, starting with 2016, you get query runtime metrics, including wait statistics. These are accurate measurements and are right there as a part of the execution plan. I will absolutely use these. However, again, they only show up for the one execution, making it very hard to get averages. Also, capturing execution plans negatively impacts the time measurement since capturing the runtime metrics along with the execution plan slows down the execution of the query. For this reason, when I want accurate performance metrics, I don't capture execution plans. That simple fact means I can't rely on this measure all the time.

Trace Events (Profiler)

This can be a sore subject. A lot of very experienced data professionals have been working with Trace Events and Profiler (the graphical user interface for creating and consuming Trace Event data) for a long time. They are comfortable using this tool, have developed excellent skills with Trace Events, and have no intention of stopping. I'm not going to stand in their way. However, for several reasons, I will not advocate for the use of Trace Events, and if you're just getting going with query performance tuning, I strongly suggest you don't use them either.

First, Trace Events are very expensive within the SQL Server operating system. Unlike Extended Events that, starting in SQL Server 2008, were incorporated directly into the internal behaviors of SQL Server, Trace Events were built and implemented separately. This causes them to have additional overhead in terms of memory and CPU, beyond that of Extended Events.

Because of the way Trace Events capture information, they can't be filtered at capture, like Extended Events. This means that all resources necessary to capture an event are consumed, but then filtering occurs and that event is removed from the results.

Another issue is the Profiler GUI. If you connect the Profiler GUI to a Trace Event on a live server, it instantiates an additional memory space on that server and uses that to help consume the events in real time, starving resources from your system.

Finally, the way you have to consume the data in Trace Events isn't as efficient as what you can do with the Live Data Explorer window in Extended Events.

Because of all these reasons, on any system that is SQL Server 2012 or greater, I won't use Trace Events to capture information. Prior to 2012, Trace Events are still the preferred mechanism.

I also would like to encourage the experienced data pro to, please, teach Extended Events instead of Trace to the up-and-coming data professionals.

That's all the other mechanisms for capturing query metrics. Now, let's move on and focus on the three that will serve you best over time.

Dynamic Management Views

There are a very large number of DMVs. Even if we limit ourselves to talking about the DMVs associated with query performance, there are still a very large number of DMVs. Because of this, I'm not going to attempt to document all of them or their uses here. Instead, we'll cover the core DMVs for query performance here, and we'll cover additional DMVs throughout the rest of the book (we introduced some in Chapter 2).

Note Some documentation, and older versions of this book, attempts to differentiate between Dynamic Management Views and Dynamic Management Functions. However, for the most part, people just use Dynamic Management Views, DMVs, as a catch-all, and so I'll do that here as well.

The DMVs are broken into two broad categories: the ones for currently executing queries and the ones for queries that have previously completed executing. The information gathered for previously executed queries is completely cache dependent. If for any reason the query has aged out of cache or been forcibly removed from cache, all query metrics go with it. Further, the information for previously executed queries is aggregate only. You have no way to differentiate between a query that ran at 2 AM and the same query executed at 3 AM, unless you use the DMVs to capture metrics at both times.

I use DMVs for query metrics frequently for several reasons. First, most of them are available in every single version of SQL Server from 2005 and up, including AWS RDS, Google Cloud SQL, and Azure SQL Database. That means I've always got a way of getting query performance metrics. Second, I won't always have other methods enabled on a server at all times. Some databases may have too heavy a load to run the Query Store. While Extended Events are extremely lightweight, they are not free, so I won't always have them running either. Yet I'll always be able to take a peek at query metrics through the DMVs.

Let's explore how you can capture actively executing queries first.

Actively Executing Queries

It's important to think about DMVs as building blocks or Legos. You can put them together all different ways. However, there are a few starting points you'll always fall back on. For queries that are actively executing, the starting point most of the time is sys.dm_exec_requests. This DMV captures a huge amount of information about actively running queries including things like the following:

- Starttime: When the query started to run
- Command Type: What kind of query is it
- Plan_handle: Used to get the execution plan from cache
- Sql_handle: Used to get the T-SQL text from cache
- Blocking_session_id: If the process is blocked, which session is blocking it
- Wait_type: If the process is waiting, what is it waiting on
- Total_elapsed_time: How long has the process been running so far
- Cpu_time: How much CPU has been consumed by the process
- Reads: How many reads have been done by this process
- Writes: How many writes have been done by this process

There's even more useful information that it collects, but you get the general idea. Each time you query sys.dm_exec_requests, it's a snapshot of a moment in time. You may not see the same queries on each call to the DMV. You also won't see those values changing unless you requery the DMV.

To really use the DMV to pull back interesting information, we'll need to combine it with a couple of other DMVs. The first is sys.dm_exec_query_plan(), which contains all the execution plans currently in the plan cache. The second is sys.dm_exec_sql_text(), which holds the T-SQL batch text for the executing query. Listing 3-1 shows one possible way of combining these DMVs to retrieve useful query metrics for currently executing queries.

Listing 3-1. Combining sys.dm_exec_requests with other DMVs

```
SELECT dest.text,
       deqp.query_plan,
       der.cpu_time,
       der.logical_reads,
       der.writes
FROM sys.dm_exec_requests AS der
    CROSS APPLY sys.dm_exec_query_plan(der.plan_handle) AS deqp
    CROSS APPLY sys.dm_exec_sql_text(der.plan_handle) AS dest;
```

You can get much more sophisticated with the queries against these DMVs so that you're returning individual statements rather than entire batches, filtering out the session_id for the query itself and more. However, this is enough to get you started.

Previously Executed Queries

To see queries that have been previously executed, we have a number of choices on where to start. The most common is to use sys.dm_exec_query_stats. This DMV has a lot of interesting information when it comes to query performance metrics:

- Sql_handle: Used to get the T-SQL for the batch
- Plan_handle: Used to get the execution plan for the query
- Last_execution_time: The last time this query was executed
- Execution_count: How many times has the query been executed
- Total_logical_reads: Accumulated logical reads
- Last_logical_reads: How many reads in the last run of the query
- Avg_logical_reads: The average reads across all the runs of the query

And as before, lots more. You can see the total, average, minimum, and maximum on a variety of measures including time, CPU, reads, and writes.

As before, you'll want to combine this with other DMVs to put together a more complete picture. Listing 3-2 shows one possible way to look at the data.

Listing 3-2. Combining sys.dm_exec_query_stats with other DMVs

```
SELECT dest.text,
       deqp.query_plan,
       deqs.execution_count,
       deqs.min_logical_writes,
       deqs.max_logical_reads,
       deqs.total_logical_reads,
       deqs.total_elapsed_time,
       deqs.last_elapsed_time
FROM sys.dm_exec_query_stats AS deqs
    CROSS APPLY sys.dm_exec_query_plan(deqs.plan_handle) AS deqp
    CROSS APPLY sys.dm_exec_sql_text(deqs.sql_handle) AS dest;
```

You can add a WHERE clause to search for particular text and so much more. There are also specific DMVs for particular object types:

- sys.dm_exec_procedure_stats: Operates similarly to sys.dm_exec_query_stats, but for stored procedures only

- sys.dm_exec_function_stats: Same idea but for user-defined functions (UDFs)

- sys.dm_exec_trigger_stats: Returns aggregated information about trigger performance

Between all these DMVs, you can get the information you need to show aggregated query performance for the queries currently in cache. I'll demonstrate a number of additional example queries using DMVs throughout the rest of the book.

Query Store

The Query Store was introduced in SQL Server 2016 and has gone through a number of updates in each release since then. The core behavior hasn't changed. The Query Store is enabled on a database-by-database basis. It will capture query metrics in an aggregated fashion and store them within the database where it is enabled. The aggregations are broken up by time; the default is 60 minutes, making it possible to compare performance over time, not simply relying on a single aggregation. We're going to cover the Query Store in detail in Chapter 6 because there is so much information. However, I wanted to bring it up here as one of the three principal methods of capturing query metrics.

Extended Events

Extended Events were first introduced in SQL Server 2008. However, at the time, they simply didn't provide an adequate level of functionality to make them useful for capturing query metrics. The upgrades to Extended Events introduced in SQL Server 2012, which included a GUI as well as several changes to their behavior and a whole slew of new events, made them not only viable for capturing query metrics, but the most efficient way to capture detailed query performance. Trace Events, and Profiler, still work within SQL Server, but not on Azure SQL Database. However, with the overhead they introduce to systems, and the lack of modern functionality, I won't use them in the book, and I do not recommend their use in any system running SQL Server 2012 or greater. Since that time, more and more events have been added to Extended Events, making them the primary instrument for understanding and monitoring all SQL Server behavior, not just for query metrics.

Extended Events consist of a number of different programmatic constructs; however, we're going to make our use of them as simple as we can. With that in mind, we'll be focusing on the following:

- Sessions: Which define which events will be captured; how they'll be stored, related to each other; and all other aspects of behavior of Extended Events.

- Events: The activities occurring within SQL Server, with one of our main focuses being on query performance, but also includes things like waits, recompiles, deadlocks, and more.

- Global Fields (Actions): These are additional pieces of information that can be added to a given event. They represent additional functional activity within SQL Server, so must be used judiciously.

- Event Fields: Each event consists of a combination of standard and optional information to be captured. This is the key data that makes Extended Events so very useful.

- Predicates: Quite simply, a WHERE clause that can be added to Extended Events to filter the information captured.

- Targets: This defines where the data that is captured will be stored. The default is the Ring Buffers, a memory space in Windows, but that should be avoided when possible in a production environment.

Extended Events can be created, edited, started, stopped, and removed through a GUI interface in SQL Server Management Studio or through T-SQL. We'll spend the majority of our time in this chapter looking through the GUI as it's the easiest way to get started with Extended Events. There is even a GUI introduced in SSMS called XEvent Profiler, which emulates the two most common templates from Profiler for capturing query information. It's a fast way to immediately see query metrics using Extended Events. However, we're not going to cover it in this book. We'll focus on showing you how to create your own custom Sessions. Finally, there is another GUI called the Live Data window that lets us explore the information captured by Extended Events.

Creating an Extended Events Session

There are actually two separate graphical interfaces in SSMS to create a custom Extended Events Session: the New Session Wizard and the New Session window. The wizard adds almost nothing to the process and can hide some functionality, so we're going to focus only on the New Session window. Also, the New Session window is just as easy to use as the wizard. You'll also use the New Session window when you want to edit a Session, so it's simply a good idea to get familiar with it right up front.

To access the New Session window, you'll need to navigate through the Object Explorer. Open the *Management* menu choice, then *Extended Events,* and, finally, *Sessions,* just like Figure 3-2.

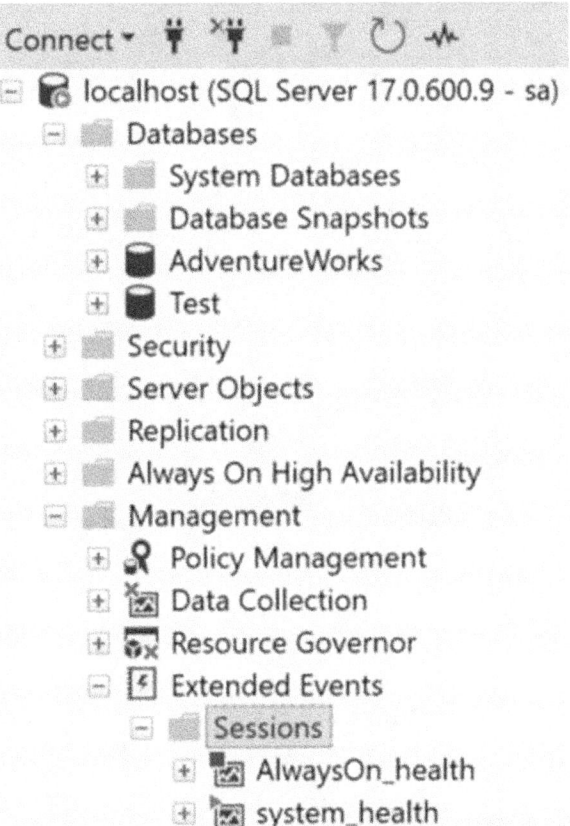

Figure 3-2. *The Object Explorer showing where Extended Events Sessions are located*

If you then right-click Sessions, you'll get a context menu. Select "New Session..." from that menu, and you'll get the New Session window as shown in Figure 3-3.

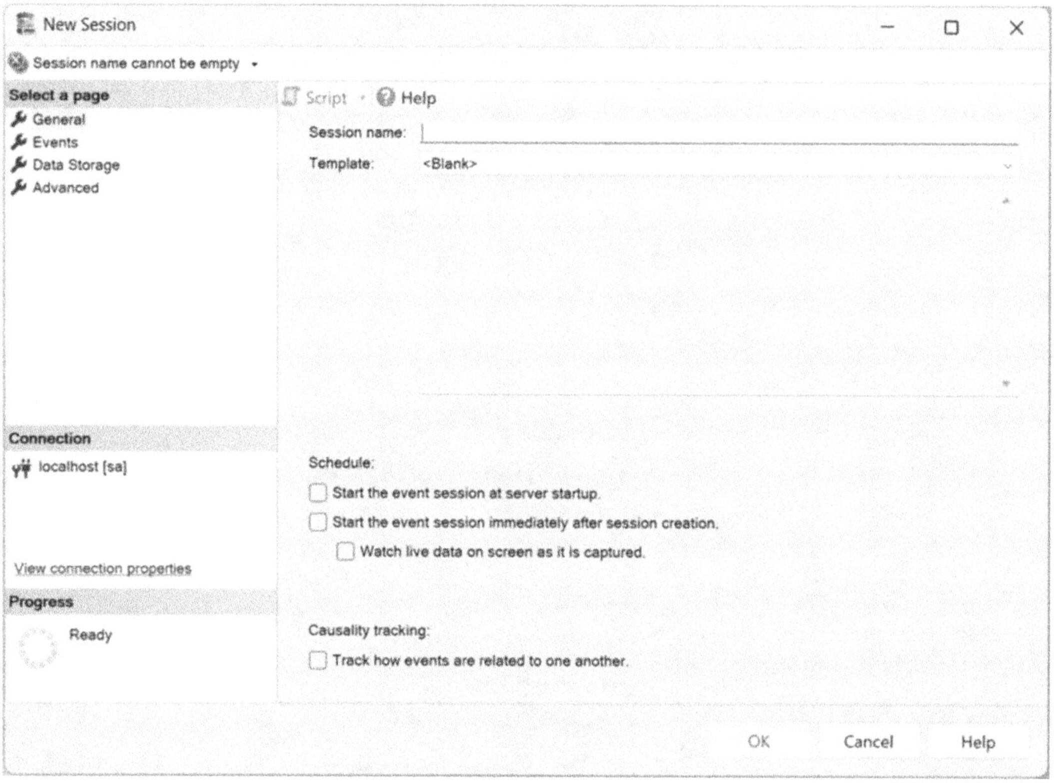

CHAPTER 3   METHODS FOR CAPTURING QUERY PERFORMANCE METRICS

Figure 3-3. The New Session window

The only thing you have to fill in here is the "*Session name.*" The rest of the settings here are optional. The name of the Session can have blanks. There is a maximum of 128 characters, and a given Session name must be unique on a server. I tend to try to use fairly descriptive names so it's clear what kind of monitoring the Session is performing. You can't create the Session yet though because each Session must have at least one Event.

You have the choice to go from here and add events in order to create a custom Session, or you can take advantage of the *Templates*. It's a drop-down menu with a large selection of different templates, most of them very oriented toward capturing performance metrics in different ways. You also get the option to load a session from a file. A few examples of the templates you can use include the following:

- Count Query Locks: A template that uses the histogram Target along with the query hash value to count locks per query.

CHAPTER 3   METHODS FOR CAPTURING QUERY PERFORMANCE METRICS

- TSQL: One of the "Profiler Equivalent" templates. It captures logins as well as batch and remote procedure call (RPC) completion.

- Query Batch Sampling: A template specific to Extended Events that uses a filter to only capture query metrics on 20% of all sessions running on the server.

- Query Detail Tracking: Captures all different sorts of statement, batch, and RPC completion while filtering out system queries and system databases.

- Query Wait Statistic: Another template only available to Extended Events whereby every query starting and completing as well as all the statements and the internal and external waits are captured across 20% of all sessions including *Causality Tracking* (explained in detail later in this chapter).

In other words, you have a lot to work from, or you can go on and customize your own Sessions with specific Events.

In the middle of the window visible in Figure 3-3, you can see some of the options available to your Session. You can enable or disable starting the Session when the server starts. You also have the ability to immediately start the Session after you're finished editing it. Along with this, you can immediately open the Live Data window to see the results of your Session. I use this feature quite a lot, especially when first setting up a Session. At the bottom of the screen is where you enable or disable Causality Tracking for the Session.

From there, you would click the left side of the screen where it says Events in order to start adding and configuring Events.

Adding and Configuring Events

Any given Session must have at least one Event added to it. Any given Session can have a large number of Events. However, I recommend caution when adding Events to a Session since you can seriously negatively impact a system by overloading it with Events.

When you first open the Events page, and you did not choose a template, it should be similar to Figure 3-4.

CHAPTER 3   METHODS FOR CAPTURING QUERY PERFORMANCE METRICS

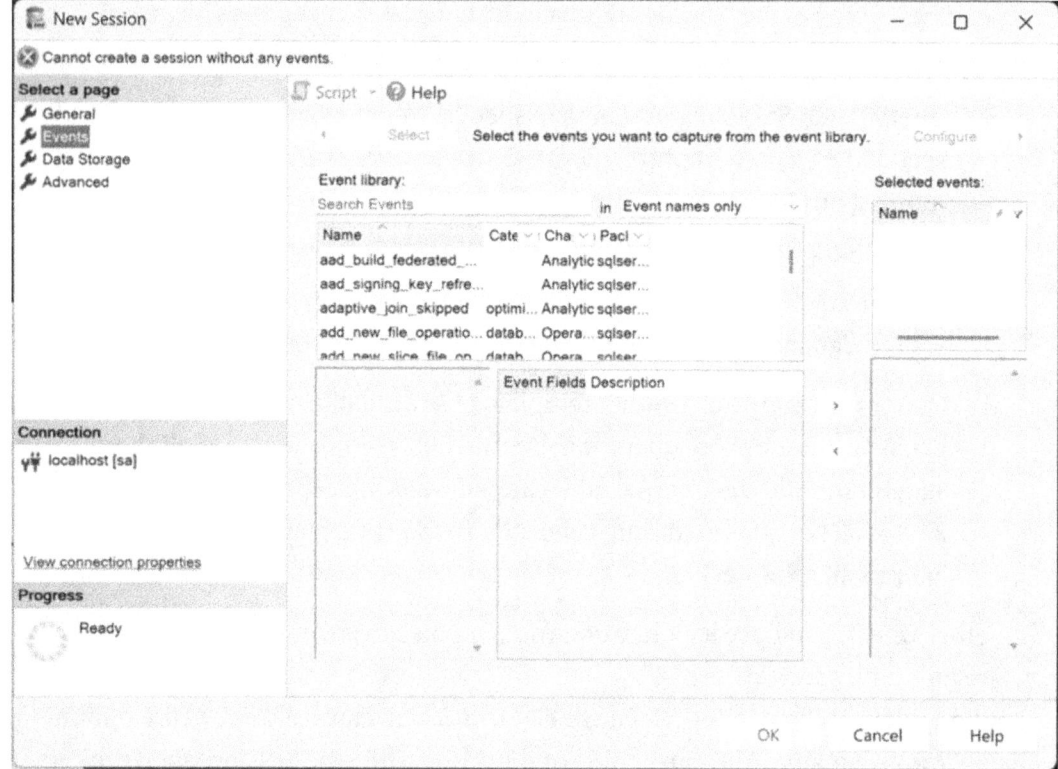

Figure 3-4. *Session selection for Extended Events*

This window can be maximized in order to make it possible to expand the columns, making it all a little easier to read. I'm going to leave it at the defaults, so you'll see roughly the same thing I see as you start.

The list of Events is right in the center. By default, all Events are listed; however, you have four different ways to filter the Events, right on the screen. At the top, there is a text box for inputting a search. It's automatically a wild card search. For example, if I was looking for the rpc_completed event, I could type "completed" into the window, and I'd end up with a fairly long list. I can scroll through that list to find what I want as shown in Figure 3-5.

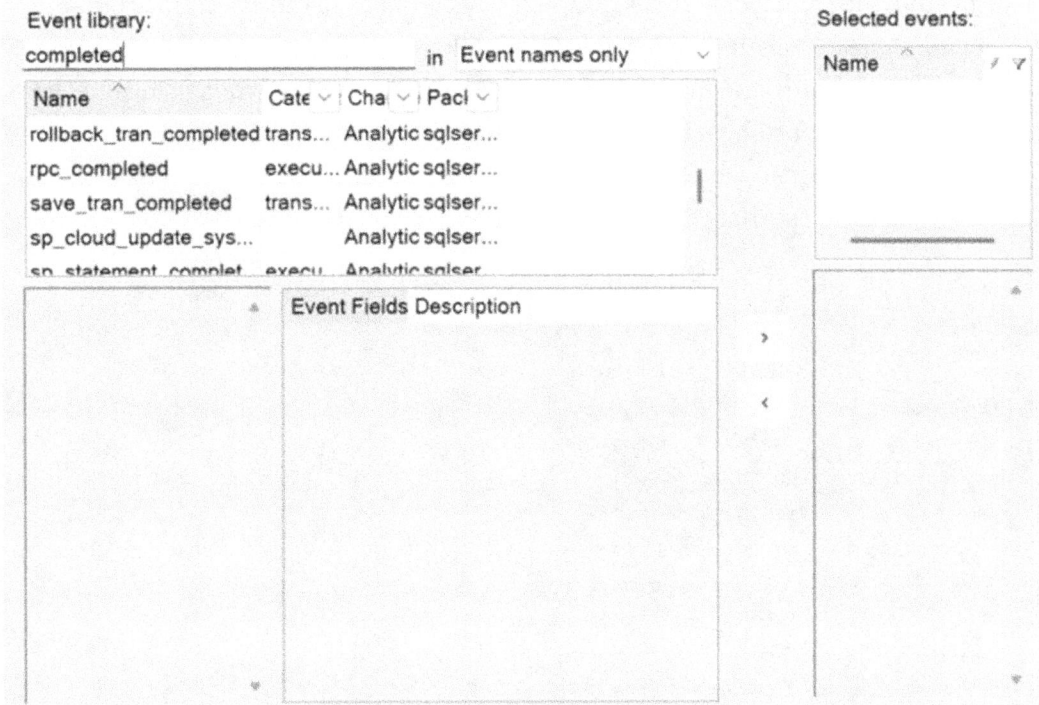

Figure 3-5. *Events filtered to only those that have the phrase "completed"*

You can also change the way the search works. By default, as shown in the drop-down immediately next to the text box, you'll only search in "Event names only." With the drop-down, you'll see other choices:

- Event names and descriptions
- Event fields only
- All

In addition to the search text box, you can also filter by Category, Channel, and Package. I generally leave these alone since I'm able to find what I need through the search box. The one exception is the Channel. There are only four channels:

- Admin
- Analytic
- Debug
- Operational

CHAPTER 3 METHODS FOR CAPTURING QUERY PERFORMANCE METRICS

By default, the Debug channel is disabled. This is because the Events in the Debug channel are subject to change by Microsoft without notice. Also, some of the Events in the Debug channel are dangerous. I recommend extreme caution when using the Debug channel Events. Better still, just leave that channel alone.

Once I've determined which Event I'm interested in, I can click that event, and then the window changes to what you see in Figure 3-6.

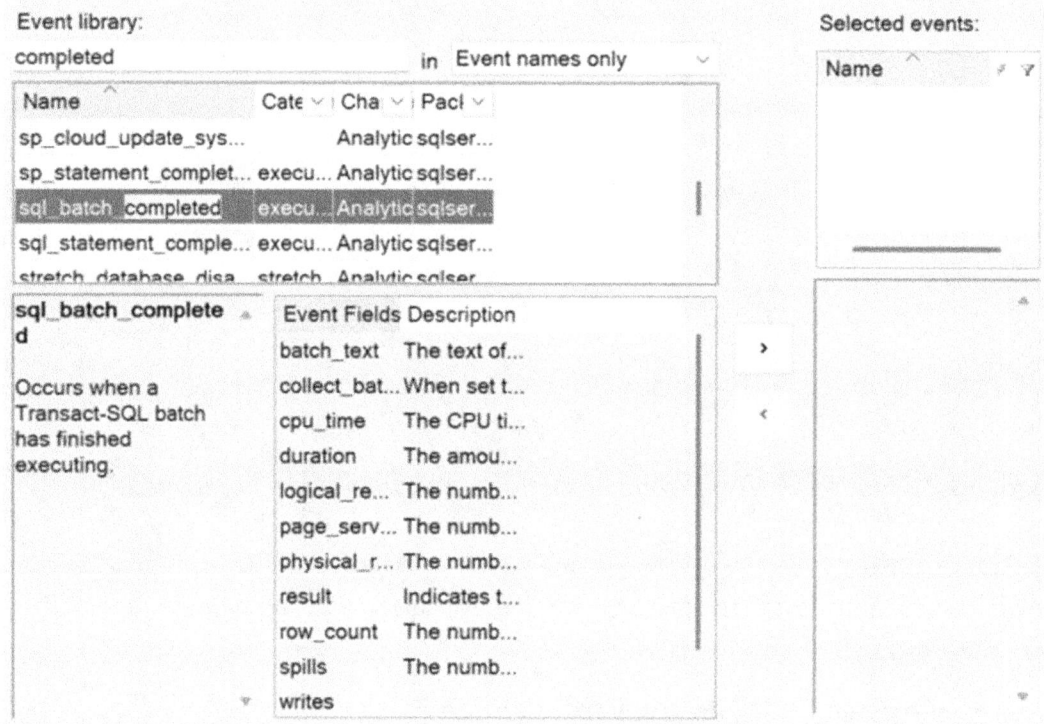

Figure 3-6. *Initially clicking an Event in Extended Events*

The two boxes below the Event list are now filled in. The first window is a description of the Event currently selected. The second window is a listing of the Fields associated with the event and a description of those fields including metric definitions. For example, the duration Field description informs you that the values are in microseconds. By default, those columns are narrow. However, you can resize them to make things easier to read.

CHAPTER 3 METHODS FOR CAPTURING QUERY PERFORMANCE METRICS

Once you've determined that a given Event is the one you wish to add to the Session, you click the arrow pointing to the right in the middle of the window. This will move the Event from the Event library on the left to the Selected events on the right. In Figure 3-7, I've selected two events, rpc_completed and sql_batch_completed, and added them to the Selected events list.

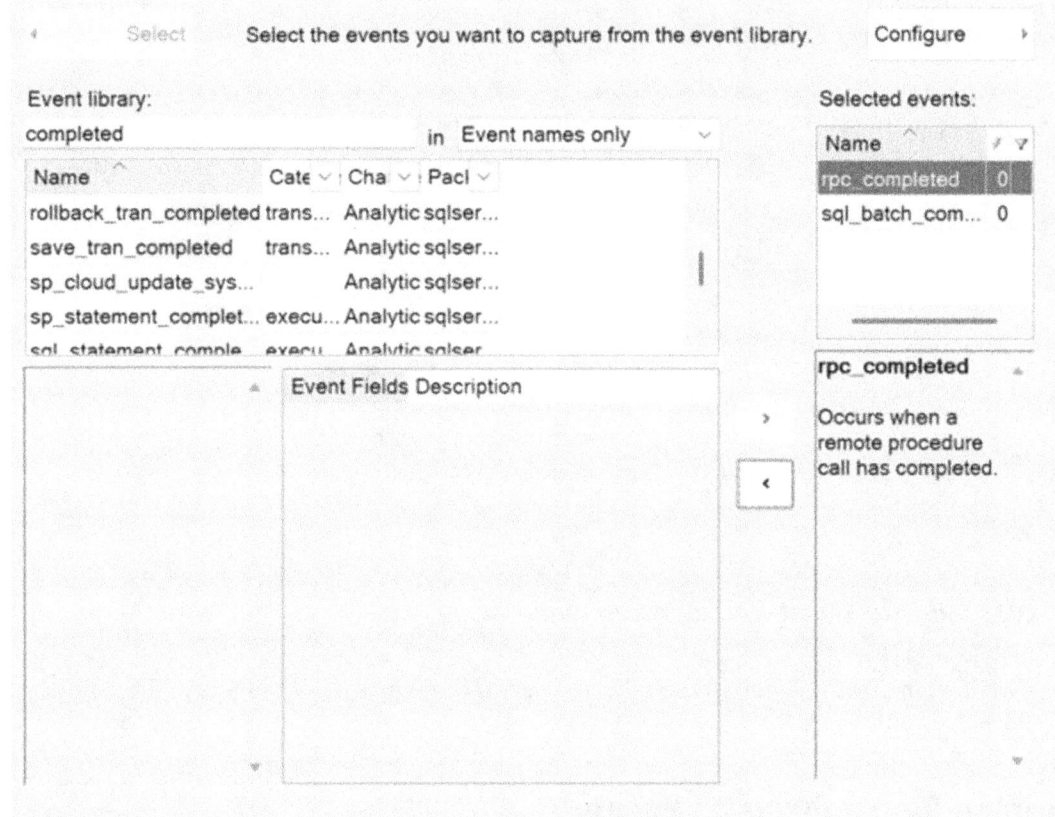

Figure 3-7. *Two Events added to the Selected events list*

From right here, we've done all we must do to create an Extended Events Session. We have provided the Session with a name, and we've added one or more Events. At this point, all the defaults will work, and we can create a Session. However, there's more to understand about how to configure the Events within a Session, so let's click the Configure button that is enabled after we add Events to the Session. This button is visible in the upper right of the dialog box as shown in Figure 3-7.

Clicking the button will shift us to another window, shown in Figure 3-8.

55

CHAPTER 3   METHODS FOR CAPTURING QUERY PERFORMANCE METRICS

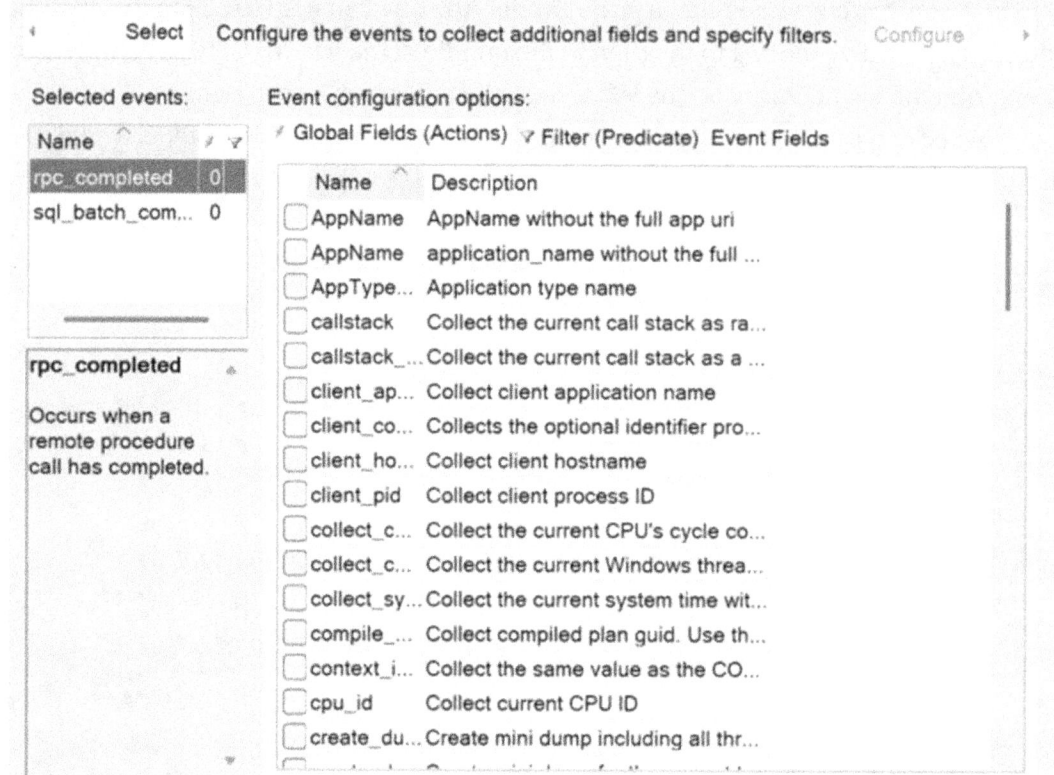

Figure 3-8. *The Event configuration window*

We'll walk through each of the tabs you see in the figure, Global Fields, Filter, and Event Fields.

Adding Global Fields to Events

The first tab open by default in the Event configuration window is Global Fields. These are also called Actions, which is more accurate. These are additional pieces of data that can be added to Events. As you can see, the columns are a little narrow by default. You can widen them to see better what kind of data is there. For each Action, you also get a description, telling you what will be created or collected through that Action.

You can highlight one or more Events on the left side of the screen. You can shift-click to select them or control-click to pick individual ones. A good example of an action that is worth adding for the kind of query metrics we're most interested in is the *query_hash* value and the *query_plan_hash* value. These are nicknamed the query fingerprints. We'll discuss the hash values more in later chapters. To add actions to the events we're collecting, I will select both events. Then, I'll scroll down to find the Actions and select them by clicking the box. My window now looks like Figure 3-9.

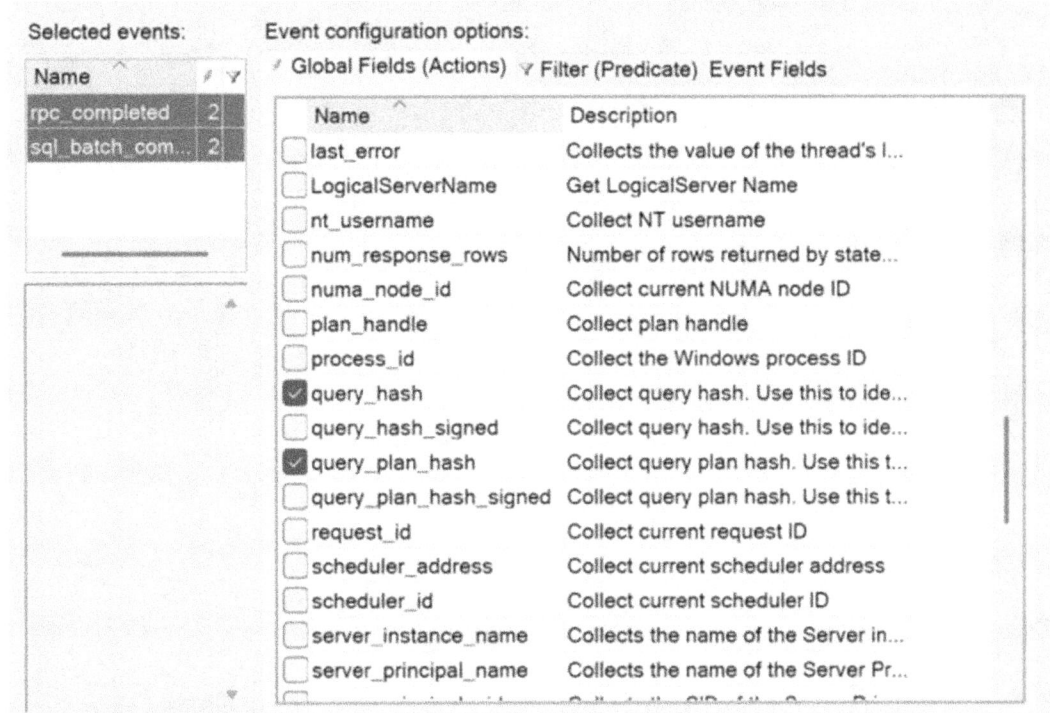

Figure 3-9. *Selecting Global Fields for multiple Events*

You can see in Figure 3-9 that I have both values selected. You can also see that the "Selected events" on the left has changed. Under the lightning bolt symbol, for each event, you can see the number two (2). This indicates that two Actions have been added. If you had different Actions selected for different events, those numbers may be different. If no Actions are selected, you'll see a value of zero (0), just as we had in Figure 3-8.

Using Predicates with Events

The next tab is where we define a Filter, or Predicate, for the Events. This Predicate functions just like a WHERE clause in a query. In fact, when we look at the T-SQL that defines a Session later in this chapter, you'll see that it is a WHERE clause, quite literally. When you first look at a customized Session as we're doing, the screen will be blank as you see in Figure 3-10.

CHAPTER 3   METHODS FOR CAPTURING QUERY PERFORMANCE METRICS

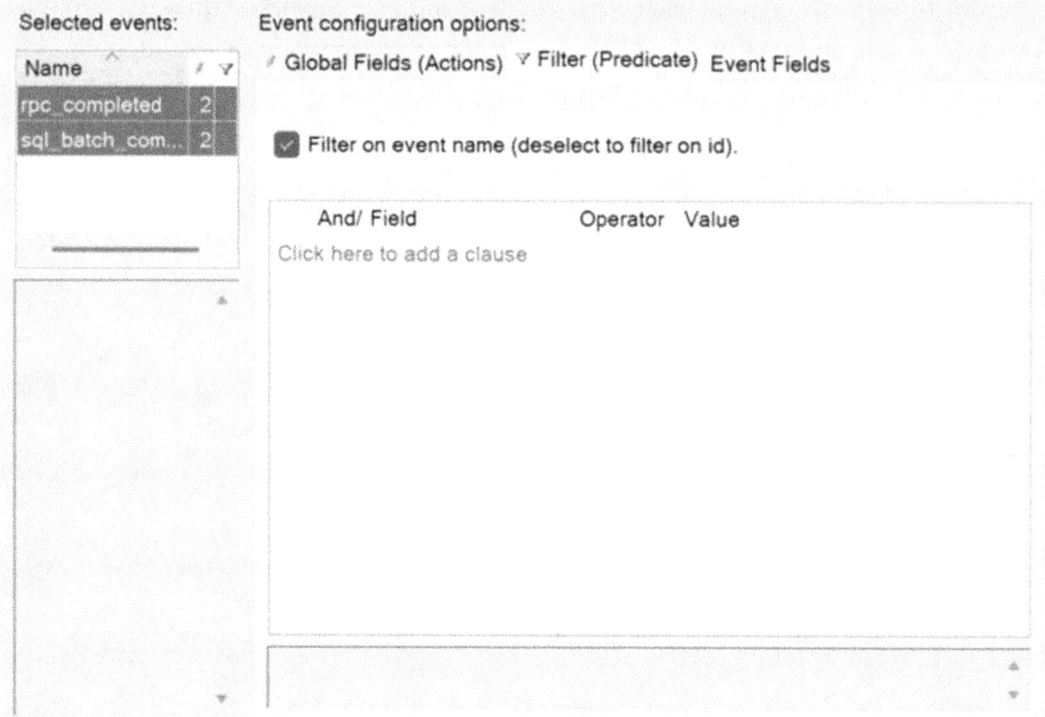

Figure 3-10. *The Filter or Predicate tab for configuring Events*

Just as with the Actions, you can individually select Events or group them together to define Predicates. The actual operation of the Predicates is straightforward. As you can see in Figure 3-10, you click where it says, "Click here to add a clause." You'll immediately get a new line as shown in Figure 3-11.

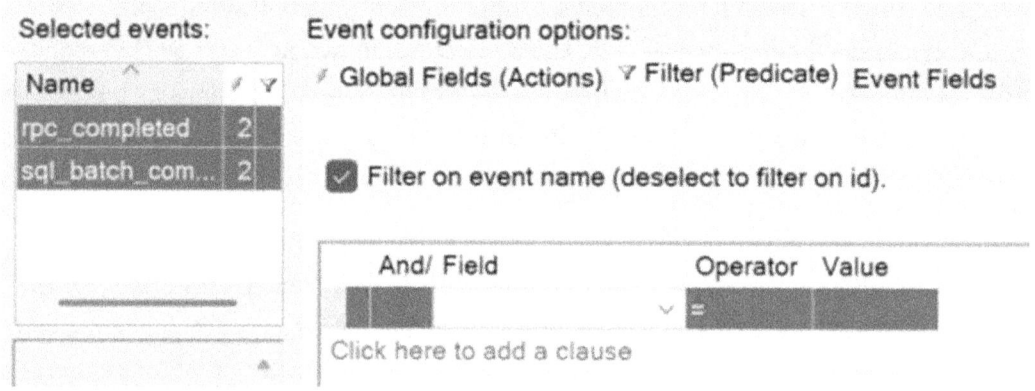

Figure 3-11. *Adding a Predicate to a set of Events*

Next, you click the drop-down box labeled "Field." This will open a customized list of values. It depends on what Event, or Events, you have selected on the left. If you have a single Event selected, you'll see all the Event Fields listing first, followed by a list of all Actions. You can filter by either. If you have more than one Event selected, as I do in my example, you'll get a list of common Event Fields first, followed by the Actions.

Extended Events filter the events based on the Predicate you provide at the capture of the Event. This means you want to be sure that you use the most stringent filtering criteria you can. Also, you want to ensure that the more stringent filter is applied first, to help reduce the overhead of capturing events.

For my example, I'm going to select the Action for the name of a database. This is displayed as sqlserver.database_name. This means that the Action itself is a part of the SQL Server system, as opposed to the SQL Server OS actions that are shown as sqlos.*.

After picking the field, I have to pick the operator. The default is an equals operation. So an exact match is necessary. Operators include, but are not limited to, the following:

- Equals: For an exact match
- Less Than: To determine values less than another
- Greater Than: To find values that are higher than another
- Like: To find pattern matches

There are a large number of other logical operators for filtering the Events. These are the most common.

Finally, you have to supply a value for the logical operator to compare. This can be string values, in the case of a database name, or numbers.

You can then add additional values for comparison. For my example here, I'm filtering to only capture queries for the database called AdventureWorks, and I'm only capturing queries that run longer than 1,000 microseconds. You can see the filter definition in Figure 3-12.

CHAPTER 3 METHODS FOR CAPTURING QUERY PERFORMANCE METRICS

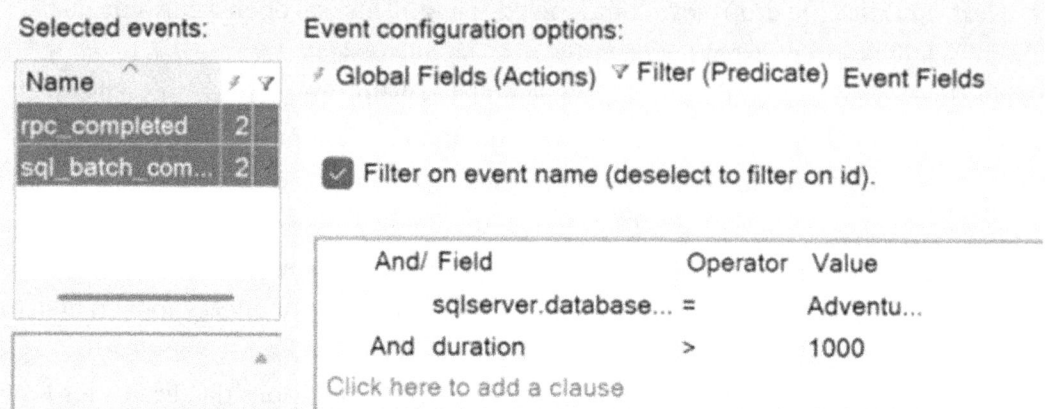

Figure 3-12. Multiple filter criteria for Events

As with the Actions, you can see a check mark has been added to indicate that there are filters on the Events at the left side of the screen in the "Selected events" box, under the funnel icon. You can also see the logical operation choice that I have between "And" and "Or" when defining more than one Predicate. In this case, I've chosen to use "And."

You can also see the description for the Field I'm filtering on at the bottom of the page, helping you through the whole process.

As before, maximizing this window will allow you to expand the size of columns, making them more readable. This is a good habit to get into when creating Extended Events Sessions.

Optional Event Fields

The final tab in the Event configuration window is the Event Fields tab. On this tab, you can only select a single Event at a time. Selecting more than one Event makes the tab go blank. In Figure 3-13, I have selected the rpc_completed event.

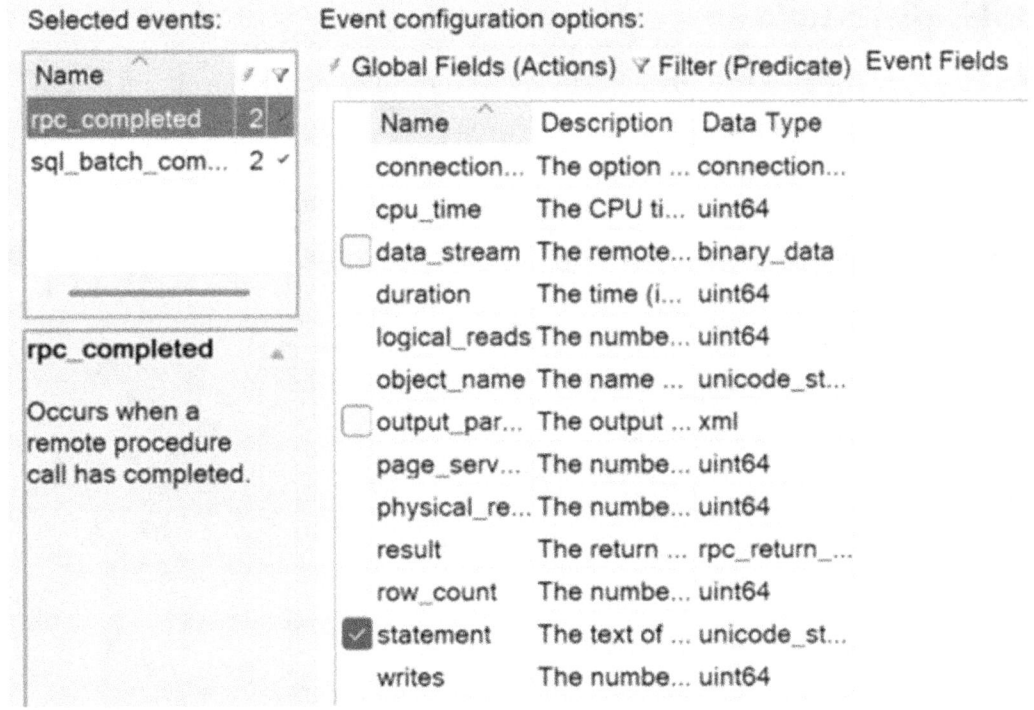

Figure 3-13. *Event Fields for the rpc_completed event*

The Fields that do not have a check box next to them are the ones that will always be returned by a given event. The ones with check boxes are optional Fields. By default, rpc_completed includes things like the duration, object_name, and row_count. However, statement is optional, although selected by default. You can turn this off to reduce the overhead of capturing this event, but you give up the ability to see the parameter values of the procedure call. You can optionally turn on output_parameters or data_stream as necessary, assuming you want to capture those values. Not all events have optional fields, but many do and so this is an area worth keeping an eye on when setting up your own events.

With all these values set, the next thing to do is define where the output from capturing the Events will go.

Defining Targets

By default, no Target has to be defined. When you create a Session, the output can go to a memory space called the Ring Buffers. However, this actually takes memory away from the operating system and SQL Server, so in production environments, or for certain tests in nonproduction environments, it's not a good idea at all to use the Ring Buffers. Instead, you get multiple options. The Data Storage, or Targets, page by default looks like Figure 3-14.

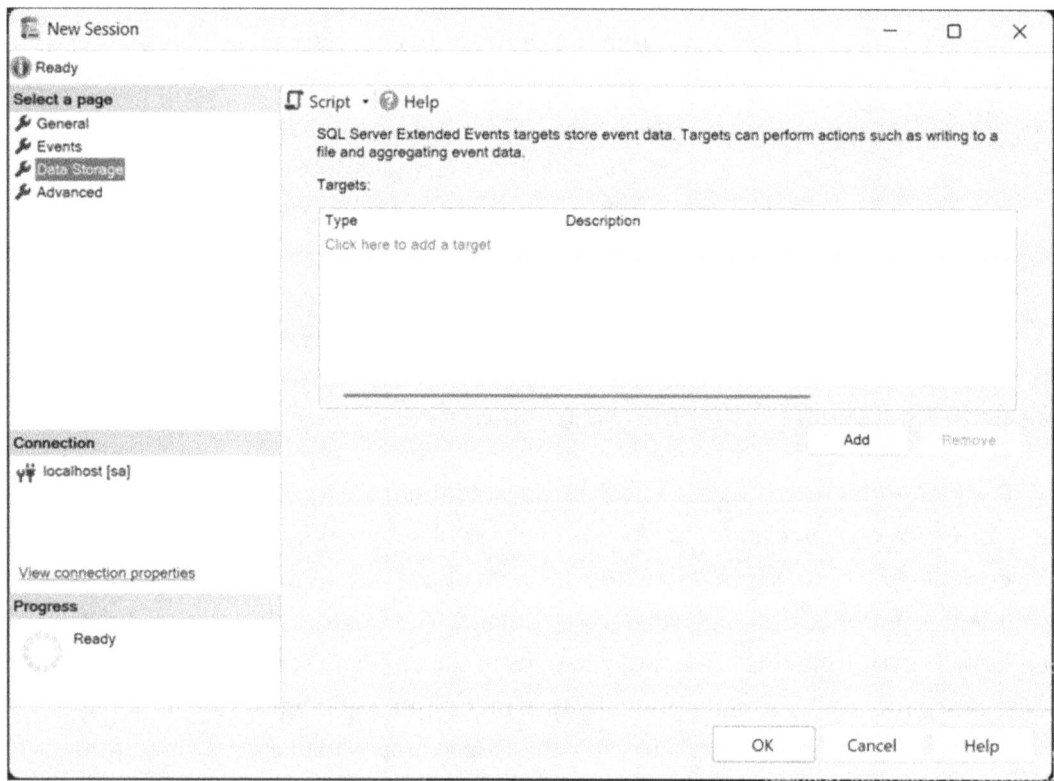

Figure 3-14. The Data Storage or Targets page

As the window says, "Click here to add a target" to get started. The options on Targets are as follows:

- etw_classic_sync_target: Event Tracing for Windows (ETW) output. This is rarely used, but available if you need it.

- event_counter: A count of the occurrences of the Event. A simple way to just track how often an Event happens on the system being monitored. It actually outputs to the OS events collection.

- event_file: Outputs all Events captured to a file. This is the most commonly used capture mechanism.

- Histogram: This Target allows you to identify an Event and then an Action or Field to group counts. This is extremely useful.

- pair_matching: You can define a mechanism to match pairs of events. This is somewhat difficult to use and not as handy as Causality Tracking.

- ring_buffer: The default memory space already explained. Again, this should be used quite judiciously in a production environment.

You can define one, or more, of these for any given Session. I'm going to explain how to use the event_file Target and the histogram Target. The other Targets, while useful in a given situation, are not applicable to standard query performance and query behavior monitoring.

Using the event_file Target

When you select the event_file Target, the Data Storage screen changes to what you see in Figure 3-15.

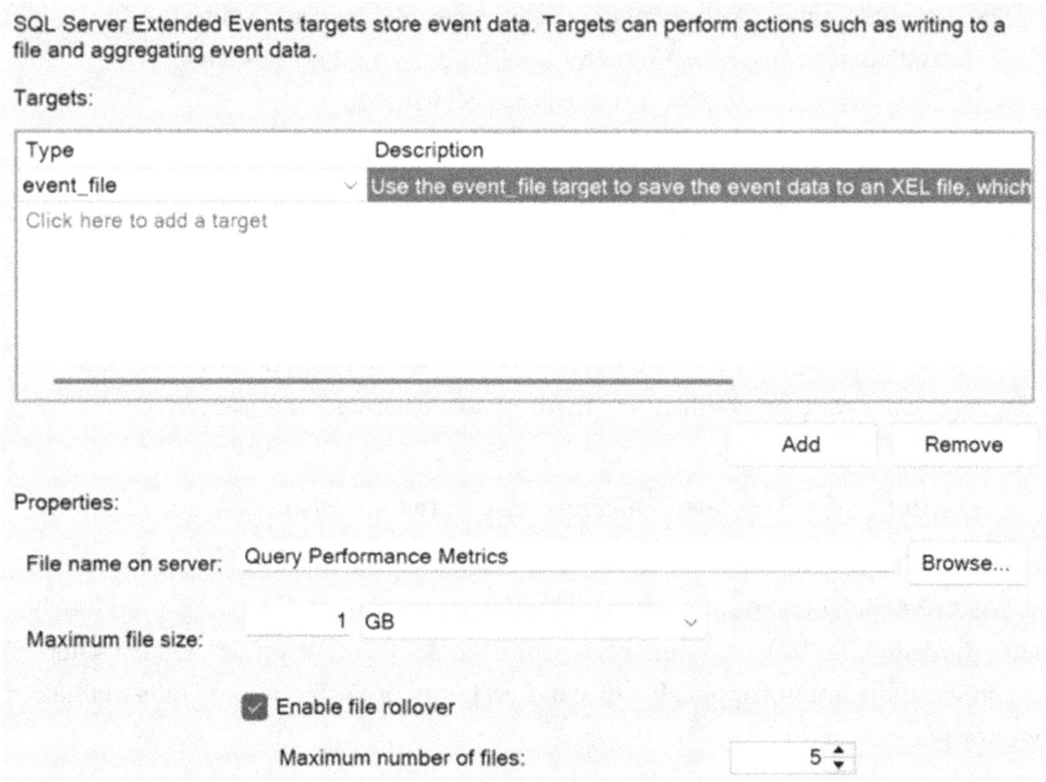

CHAPTER 3   METHODS FOR CAPTURING QUERY PERFORMANCE METRICS

Figure 3-15. Selecting the event_file Target

You must supply a file name and a path for the output of the Events. You can type it in or use the "Browse…" button to select a path. If you're running this on Azure SQL Database, the output must be Amazon storage, and you have to make sure that the security is set to allow output from your Azure SQL Database instances. In AWS RDS, you have a single location for the file: D:\rdsdbdata\log. With the file name and storage defined, you get to decide on the size of the file, either in gigabytes or megabytes. The default is 1GB, but that may be small for some systems. However, you don't want to go too large, or file management becomes more of an issue. Generally, somewhere between 5GB and 20GB works well for most systems. You can also define whether or not you're allowing file rollover. This is when you fill a file, another one is opened, and this continues until you hit the "Maximum number of files" that you define. Then, the Events will start writing to the first file again.

CHAPTER 3   METHODS FOR CAPTURING QUERY PERFORMANCE METRICS

Generally, this is the best approach for managing the data gathered by Extended Events. Output to a file puts the least load on the system. Having the files means you can save that data if needed and you can always open the files in the Live Data Explorer window (explained later in the chapter).

Using the histogram Target

The histogram Target is extremely useful. It's a handy way to simply count the number of times a given Event occurs, but with the information grouped by Fields or Actions. Figure 3-16 shows how the histogram Target could be configured to count the occurrences of different stored procedures being called.

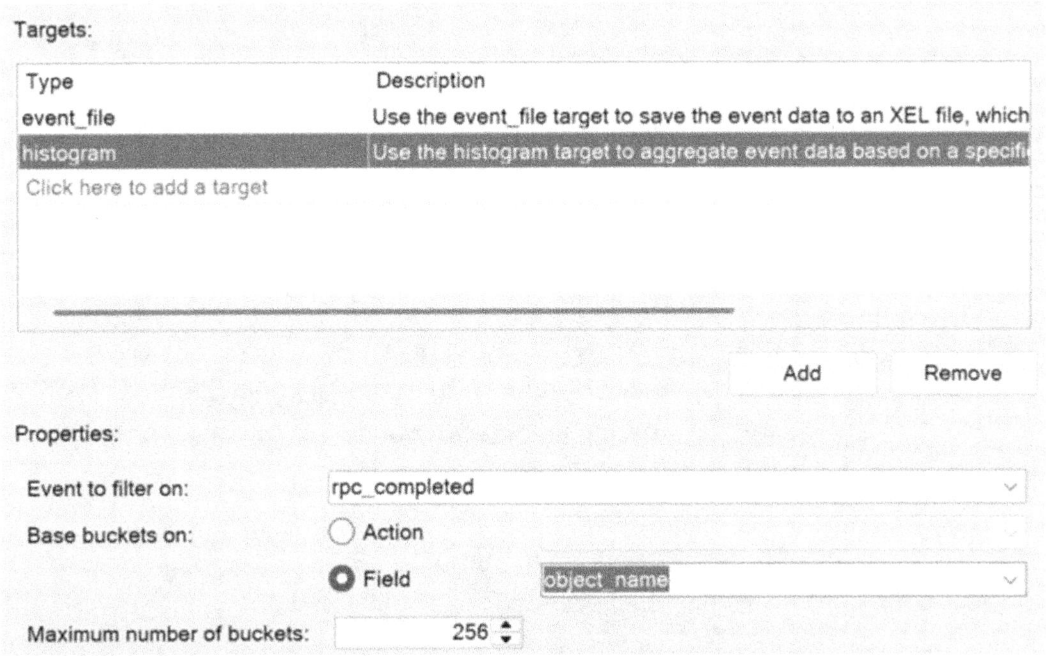

Figure 3-16. *Counting all occurrences of stored procedures using the histogram Target*

I've added this as a second Target, just to show how that would work. You can choose to only have one Target. It's all about what you hope to get out of a given Session.

Setting up the histogram Target involves first selecting which Event you wish to use from the drop-down. That will contain all the Events you defined on the Events page. Then, you have two radio buttons to choose either an Action or a Field from the event.

65

Chapter 3 Methods for Capturing Query Performance Metrics

I've picked the object_name from the rpc_completed event. That means each, distinct, stored procedure will get a count of the occurrences of that stored procedure being called. Finally, you set the number of buckets that define the histogram. The default value is 256, but you can adjust that up or down as needed. A larger number does put more of a load on the system, so be cautious when defining this value.

Working with Sessions

After you create a Session, it gets stored on the server you were connected to. You can see the sessions you have using the Object Explorer window in Management Studio or by querying system tables. Figure 3-17 shows Sessions currently on my machine.

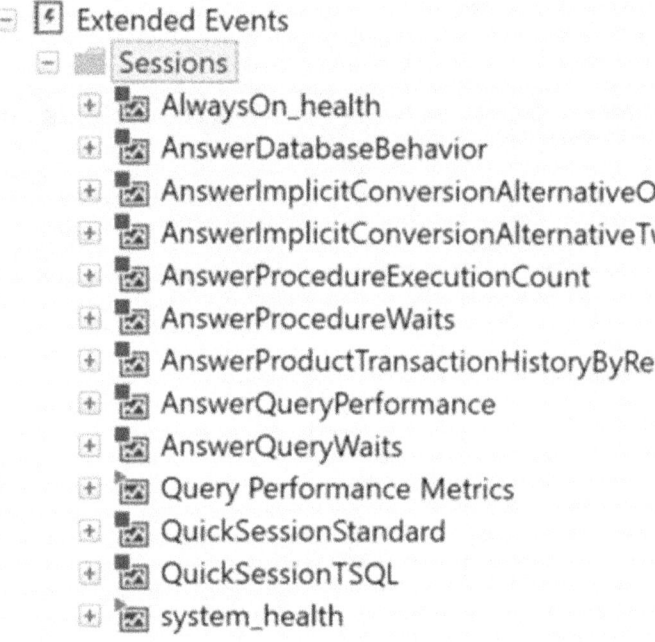

Figure 3-17. Extended Events Sessions in the Object Explorer window

You can tell which Sessions are running and which are stopped by looking at the green arrow or red square on the symbol next to the Session. From here, you can stop or start a Session, edit a stopped Session (except on AWS RDS—you can't edit a Session there), look at the properties of running Sessions, or remove Sessions. Simply right-click to get a menu choice.

You can also control sessions through T-SQL, covered later in this chapter.

Adding Causality Tracking

Causality Tracking is a powerful feature within Extended Events. It allows you to easily identify events that are related to one another. Further, it shows the precise sequence in which those events occur. That makes Causality Tracking extremely useful in situations like troubleshooting recompiles. You can capture the query metrics as well as recompile events and then directly relate them to each other.

You define Causality Tracking at the Session level. When you enable Causality Tracking, you are adding some additional overhead to the Extended Events capture. I use this frequently, but I also try to be cautious about just how much additional load I put on a system.

You'll see additional data added to the Events captured as shown in Figure 3-18.

Event:wait_completed (2025-05-07 19:32:31.3708722)
Details

Field	Value
attach_activity_id.guid	6D921247-1BBE-453B-BEE4-8...
attach_activity_id.seq	198

Figure 3-18. *Causality Tracking fields added to event results*

The Fields attach_activity_id.guid and attach_activity_id.seq are added to the Events. You can then group your data by the GUID and sort it by the seq, or sequence, to arrive at unique sets of data. We'll use this in various chapters throughout the book. You may also see a couple of additional columns like those in Figure 3-19.

Event:sql_batch_completed (2025-05-07 19:32:30.5640908)
Details

Field	Value
attach_activity_id.guid	5B8BC82E-1BB6-411C-A345-9...
attach_activity_id.seq	1
attach_activity_id_xfer.guid	C2AF07B7-0D13-4BD8-A6D6-...
attach_activity_id_xfer.seq	0

Figure 3-19. *Parent GUIDs in Causality Tracking*

These additional columns, attach_acity_d_xfer.guid and attach_activity_id_xfer.seq, are for the parent of the current set of events defined by the current attach_activity_id.guid. In cases such as parallelism, a second, or more, set of activity ID values will be generated to track those independently of the parent. Again, this permits you to group and sort activities by their related parent as well, adding to the capability of Extended Events.

Scripting Extended Events

While the GUI provides an easy way to set up and manipulate Extended Events sessions, you'll likely also use T-SQL. For example, T-SQL is a great way to move Sessions between servers. You can write the T-SQL directly or script out an existing Session from Management Studio. Listing 3-3 shows an example statement for creating a Session.

Listing 3-3. T-SQL to create an Extended Events Session

```
CREATE EVENT SESSION [Query Performance Metrics]
ON SERVER
    ADD EVENT sqlserver.rpc_completed
    (WHERE (
            [sqlserver].[database_name] = N'AdventureWorks'
            AND [duration] > (1000)
        )
    ),
    ADD EVENT sqlserver.sql_batch_completed
    (WHERE (
            [sqlserver].[database_name] = N'AdventureWorks'
            AND [duration] > (1000)
        )
    )
    ADD TARGET package0.event_file
    (SET filename = N'Query Performance Metrics');
```

The syntax is relatively straightforward. You do have to know which Events you want to add and any optional Fields they may have. Your Predicates are shown as WHERE clauses. You can define and control the Targets. In short, you can use T-SQL to do everything for setting up a Session.

CHAPTER 3   METHODS FOR CAPTURING QUERY PERFORMANCE METRICS

You can also start, stop, or drop a session with T-SQL. Listing 3-4 shows the scripts to start and stop the [Query Performance Metrics] session.

Listing 3-4. Stopping and starting a Session with T-SQL

```
ALTER EVENT SESSION [Query Performance Metrics]
ON SERVER
STATE = START;
ALTER EVENT SESSION [Query Performance Metrics]
ON SERVER
STATE = STOP;
```

Finally, you can read the output of Extended Events through T-SQL using a system function. Listing 3-5 shows an example demonstrating how this works.

Listing 3-5. Querying the Extended Event data directly

```
SELECT fx.object_name,
       fx.file_name,
       fx.event_data
FROM sys.fn_xe_file_target_read_file('.\Query Performance Metrics_*.xel',
                                      NULL,
                                      NULL,
                                      NULL) AS fx;
```

You can see the results of this query in Figure 3-20.

#	object_name	file_name	event_data
1	sql_batch_completed	C:\Program Files\Microsoft SQL Server\MSSQL17.MSS...	<event name="sql_batch_completed" package="sqlse...
2	sql_batch_completed	C:\Program Files\Microsoft SQL Server\MSSQL17.MSS...	<event name="sql_batch_completed" package="sqlse...
3	sql_batch_completed	C:\Program Files\Microsoft SQL Server\MSSQL17.MSS...	<event name="sql_batch_completed" package="sqlse...
4	sql_batch_completed	C:\Program Files\Microsoft SQL Server\MSSQL17.MSS...	<event name="sql_batch_completed" package="sqlse...
5	sql_batch_completed	C:\Program Files\Microsoft SQL Server\MSSQL17.MSS...	<event name="sql_batch_completed" package="sqlse...
6	sql_batch_completed	C:\Program Files\Microsoft SQL Server\MSSQL17.MSS...	<event name="sql_batch_completed" package="sqlse...
7	sql_batch_completed	C:\Program Files\Microsoft SQL Server\MSSQL17.MSS...	<event name="sql_batch_completed" package="sqlse...
8	rpc_completed	C:\Program Files\Microsoft SQL Server\MSSQL17.MSS...	<event name="rpc_completed" package="sqlserver" ti...
9	rpc_completed	C:\Program Files\Microsoft SQL Server\MSSQL17.MSS...	<event name="rpc_completed" package="sqlserver" ti...
10	rpc_completed	C:\Program Files\Microsoft SQL Server\MSSQL17.MSS...	<event name="rpc_completed" package="sqlserver" ti...
11	sql_batch_completed	C:\Program Files\Microsoft SQL Server\MSSQL17.MSS...	<event name="sql_batch_completed" package="sqlse...

Figure 3-20. *Output from querying Extended Event data directly*

You can see that this session is capturing both rpc_completed and sql_batch_completed events in the object_name column. You can see where the Session file is stored on the Linux container running SQL Server. Finally, the event_data is the XML containing all the information captured by each Event. We'll see examples on how to better use this functionality for troubleshooting in later chapters.

Additionally, the fantastic set of PowerShell tools called DBATools has a collection of scripts and mechanisms for dealing with the XML in Extended Events. If you're not already using this, it's well worth your time to explore: https://dbatools.io/.

Live Data Explorer Window

Because the output of Extended Events is XML, it can be difficult to read the information. While it is possible to write XQuery in T-SQL to deal with this, that's not easy either. Instead, as much as possible, I'll lean on the Live Data Explorer window in order to consume the output of Extended Events. Otherwise, I will go to DBATools to help with querying the XML.

You get to the Live Data Explorer window by either opening an Extended Events file or by right-clicking a running Session and choosing "Watch Live Data" from the context menu. Either way, the very first time you open the window and start capturing events, it will look similar to Figure 3-21.

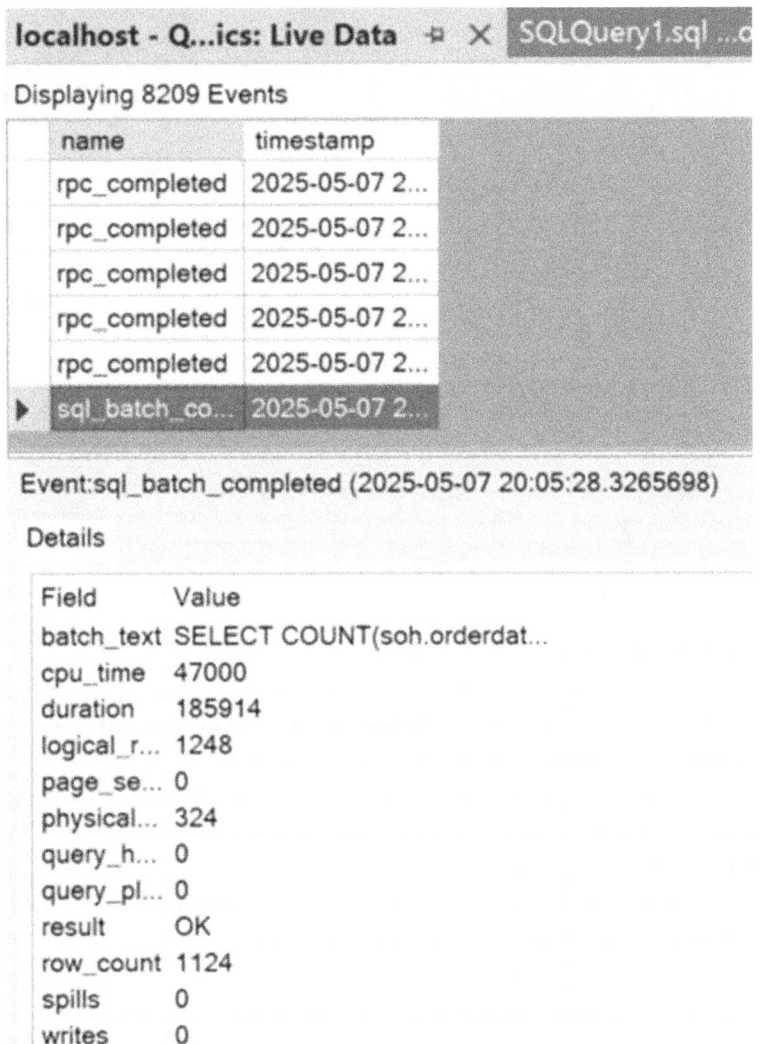

Figure 3-21. *Live Data window initial view*

The screen is split in two. The top is a list of the Events you have captured. The bottom is all the Fields for a given event. Selecting an event at the top will show the details in the bottom. While you can use the Live Data window this way, it's not efficient.

To really put the Live Data window to work, you need to change the behavior of the grid at the top of the screen. You can right-click a Field and select "Show column in table" from the context menu. I've done that and added duration to my grid in Figure 3-22.

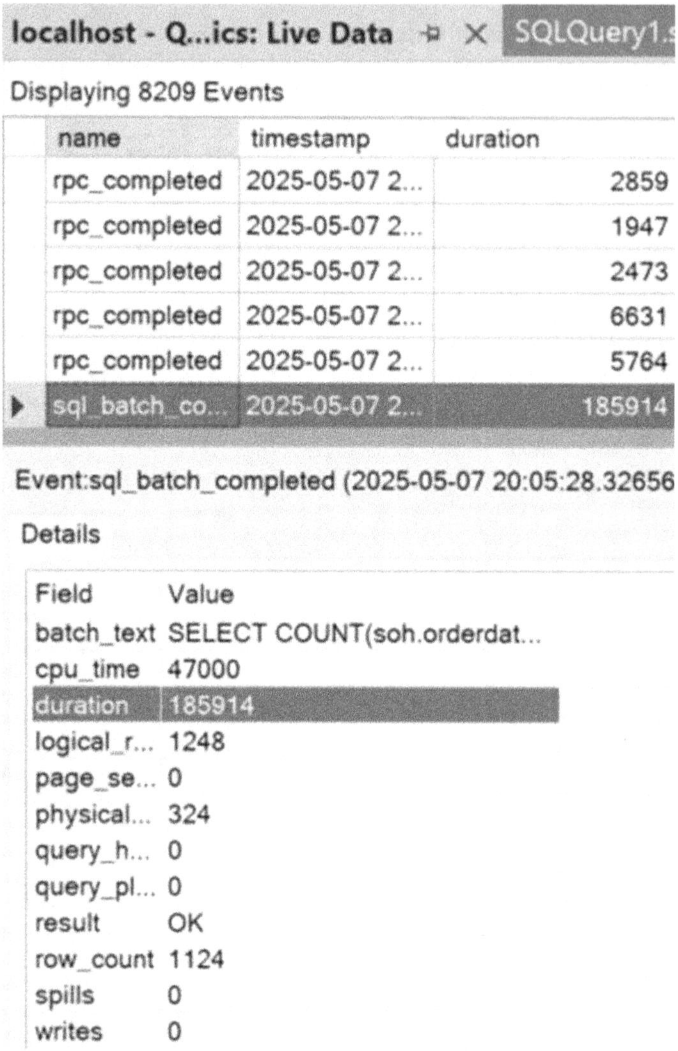

CHAPTER 3   METHODS FOR CAPTURING QUERY PERFORMANCE METRICS

Figure 3-22. Adding fields to the grid to make for easier viewing

You can now start to see how this can be a useful way to consume the information. Another way to control this is to take advantage of all the tools available within the Live Data Explorer. There should be a toolbar at the top of your screen similar to Figure 3-23 when you have the Live Data Explorer window selected.

Figure 3-23. The Live Data Explorer toolbar

Near the right side is a button labeled "Choose Columns…". Clicking this opens a new window to allow you to pick the columns you want as shown in Figure 3-24.

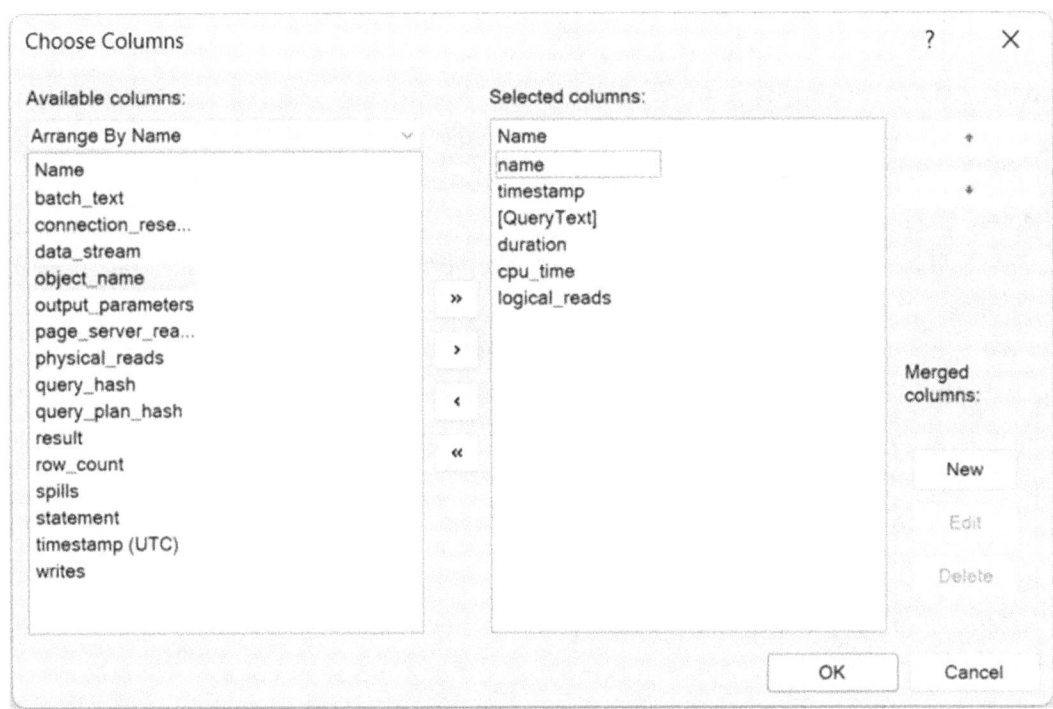

Figure 3-24. Choose Columns window in the Live Data Explorer

I've filled out the columns I want to see and ordered them using the controls on the screen. The left/right arrows allow you to add or remove Fields. The up/down arrows on the right are for controlling the order. Finally, I used the "Merged columns" function to create the column above labeled "[QueryText]" to combine the statement and batch_text Fields into a single column on the table. The results are shown in Figure 3-25.

name	timestamp	[QueryText]	duration	cpu_time	logical_reads
sql_batch_co...	2025-05-07 2...	SELECT * FROM Sales.SalesOrderHead...	902038	469000	2767
sql_batch_co...	2025-05-07 2...	SELECT COUNT(soh.orderdate), so...	86162707	313000	564
sql_batch_co...	2025-05-07 2...	SELECT e.BusinessEntityID, e.Org...	965214	391000	438
sql_batch_co...	2025-05-07 2...	SELECT ProductID FROM Production.Pr...	16578	0	431
rpc_completed	2025-05-07 2...	exec sp_executesql N'HumanResources....	237293	109000	1103
rpc_completed	2025-05-07 2...	exec sp_executesql N'dbo.uspGetWhere...	91025	63000	864

Figure 3-25. A new table with the columns selected on display

CHAPTER 3   METHODS FOR CAPTURING QUERY PERFORMANCE METRICS

You can now see a lot more information in the table, and it's much more useful for navigating and finding the information you're looking for. Now, I can take even more control over the information.

If you look again at the toolbar, as shown in Figure 3-23, on the left, you'll see a red box, or square. Pausing the mouse over this, you'll get a tooltip that says, "Stop the data feed." This is how you can pause the collection of data to the Live Data Explorer. It has no impact on the Extended Events Session. It's just the information on your screen that is affected. Clicking this enables a number of other buttons on the toolbar. If you're looking at a file that is not actively collecting data, your red box will be disabled, and the other buttons will already be enabled.

We're not going to go into detail for every single aspect of the Live Data Explorer, but we should hit a few highlights. First, with the data paused, you can add or remove bookmarks, making it easier to locate given Events. You can also sort the Events by clicking a column in the table. You can also search for events using the Find button, or CTRL-F, which will open a new window as shown in Figure 3-26.

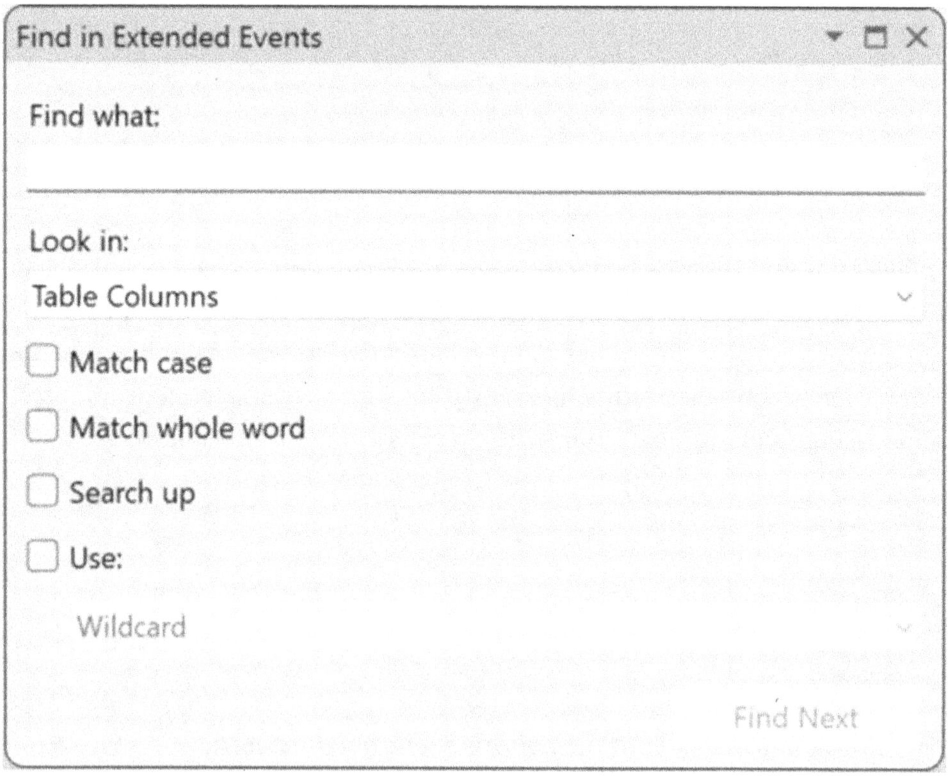

Figure 3-26. Using the search function within the Live Data Explorer

CHAPTER 3   METHODS FOR CAPTURING QUERY PERFORMANCE METRICS

You can also save the display settings to a file and share that with others on your team. You'll also find that after you've rearranged the columns on a session, your Management Studio instance will always open that same Session in the configuration in which you left it.

There are two additional functions that we're going to explore in more detail.

Filtering Live Data

The search function shown in Figure 3-26 lets you find information from within the Live Data Explorer. However, you can also directly filter the information so that only certain data is displayed. Clicking the "Filters..." button on the toolbar opens the Filters window. I've gone ahead and set a few options as you see in Figure 3-27.

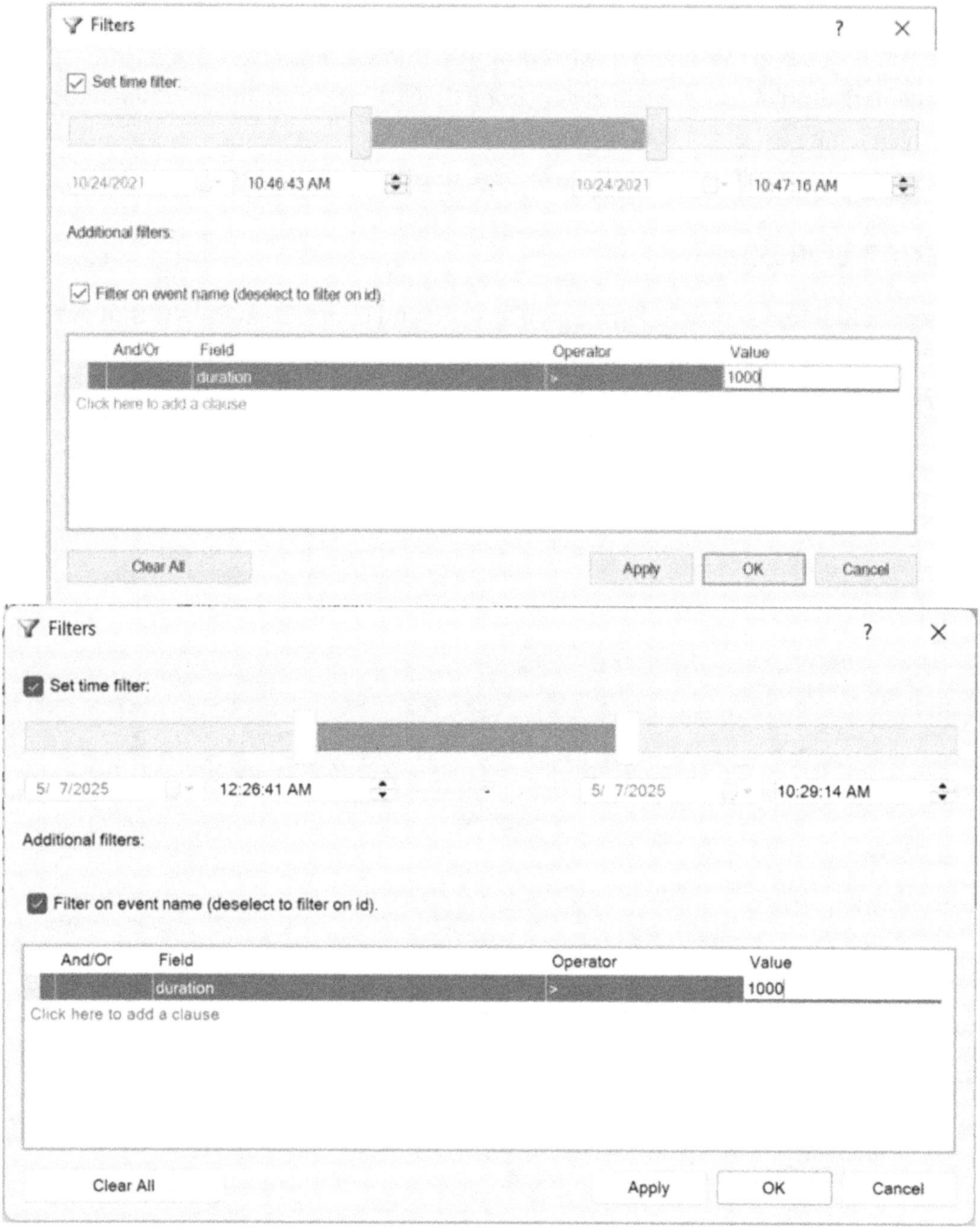

CHAPTER 3   METHODS FOR CAPTURING QUERY PERFORMANCE METRICS

Figure 3-27. Live Data Filters window set with various filters

The filter can use time as well as search criteria. In the example here in Figure 3-27, I've limited the time frame to about a ten-hour window. I've also added a filter on duration in order to only return values greater than 1,000 microseconds.

Once a filter is set, the data on view in the Live Data Explorer is limited to only that which meets the criteria set. You can also clear the filters as needed.

Aggregating Live Data

I use the ability of the Live Data Explorer to aggregate data all the time throughout the book. When you see the phrase "on average this query runs in X amount of time," it's because I've taken advantage of this mechanism. There are two different windows you have to use to put this to work. First is the Grouping button. Hitting that in the toolbar opens the window you see in Figure 3-28.

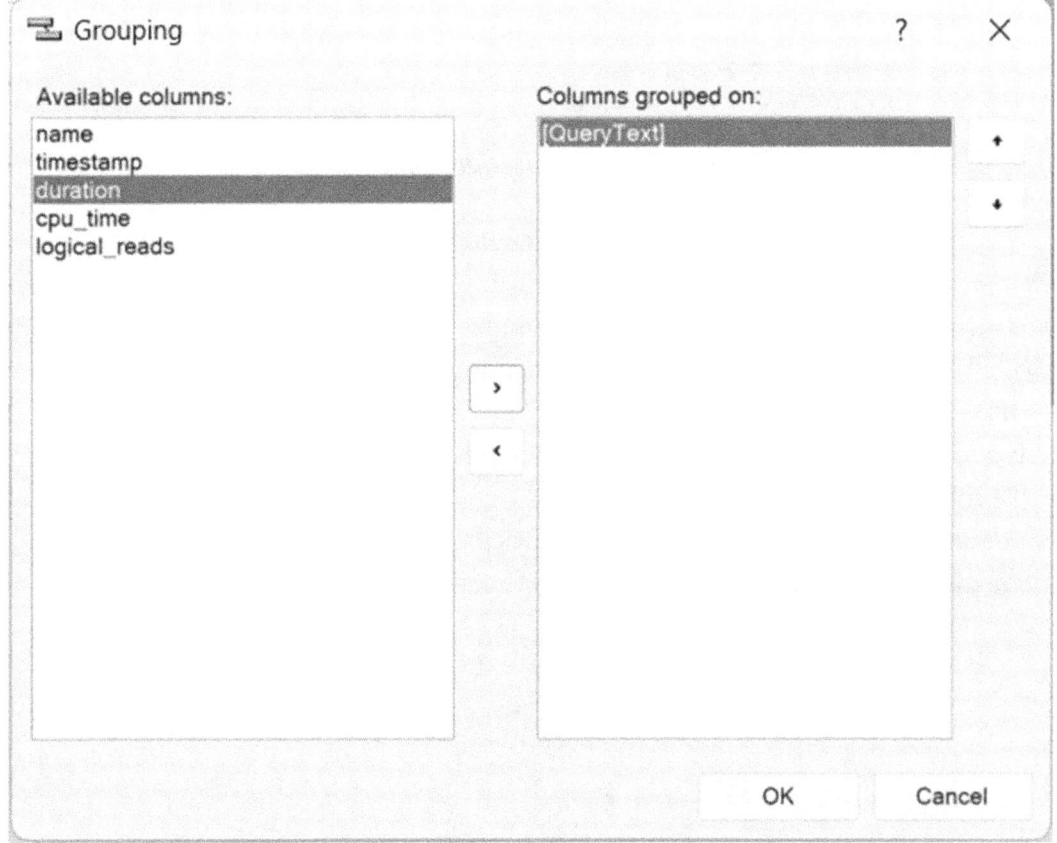

Figure 3-28. Live Data Explorer Grouping window

CHAPTER 3 METHODS FOR CAPTURING QUERY PERFORMANCE METRICS

I've selected one of the columns that I want to group on in this case, the artificial column, [QueryText]. The table in the Live Data Explorer window gets updated immediately. It groups based on the column, or columns, we select as shown in Figure 3-29.

Displaying 10895 Events

name	timestamp	[QueryText]	duration	cpu_time	logical_reads
⊞ [QueryText]: exec sp_executesql N'dbo.uspGetEmployeeManagers @BusinessEntityID =@EmpId',N'@EmpId int',@Empl...					(8)
⊞ [QueryText]: exec sp_executesql N'dbo.uspGetEmployeeManagers @BusinessEntityID =@EmpId',N'@EmpId int',@Empl...					(8)
⊞ [QueryText]: exec sp_executesql N'dbo.uspGetEmployeeManagers @BusinessEntityID =@EmpId',N'@EmpId int',@Empl...					(8)
⊞ [QueryText]: exec sp_executesql N'dbo.uspGetEmployeeManagers @BusinessEntityID =@EmpId',N'@EmpId int',@Empl...					(8)
⊞ [QueryText]: exec sp_executesql N'dbo.uspGetEmployeeManagers @BusinessEntityID =@EmpId',N'@EmpId int',@Empl...					(8)
⊞ [QueryText]: exec sp_executesql N'dbo.uspGetEmployeeManagers @BusinessEntityID =@EmpId',N'@EmpId int',@Empl...					(8)
⊟ [QueryText]: exec sp_executesql N'dbo.uspGetEmployeeManagers @BusinessEntityID =@EmpId',N'@EmpId int',@Empl...					(8)
rpc_completed	2025-05-07 2...	exec sp_executesql N'dbo.uspGetEmplo...	6123	0	125
rpc_completed	2025-05-07 2...	exec sp_executesql N'dbo.uspGetEmplo...	5515	15000	125
rpc_completed	2025-05-07 2...	exec sp_executesql N'dbo.uspGetEmplo...	11918	0	103
rpc_completed	2025-05-07 2...	exec sp_executesql N'dbo.uspGetEmplo...	14315	16000	103
rpc_completed	2025-05-07 2...	exec sp_executesql N'dbo.uspGetEmplo...	7725	16000	103
rpc_completed	2025-05-07 2...	exec sp_executesql N'dbo.uspGetEmplo...	10129	0	103
rpc_completed	2025-05-07 2...	exec sp_executesql N'dbo.uspGetEmplo...	9738	16000	125
rpc_completed	2025-05-07 2...	exec sp_executesql N'dbo.uspGetEmplo...	9339	0	125

Figure 3-29. *Table of the Live Data Explorer grouped by a column*

You can see that since we're using the statement for stored procedures, each different parameter value means a different string. Yet the one batch we have there are eight separate instances. I've shown that expanded so you can see that the columns you selected are still visible, maintaining the formatting.

If I wanted to group the stored procedures, I'd have to add the object_name to the table and then group by that instead of the [QueryText] as I did here. You can only group by the columns that are visible in the table.

After making that change, I'm going to click the Aggregation button. This opens another window. I've gone ahead and filled in some examples as you see in Figure 3-30.

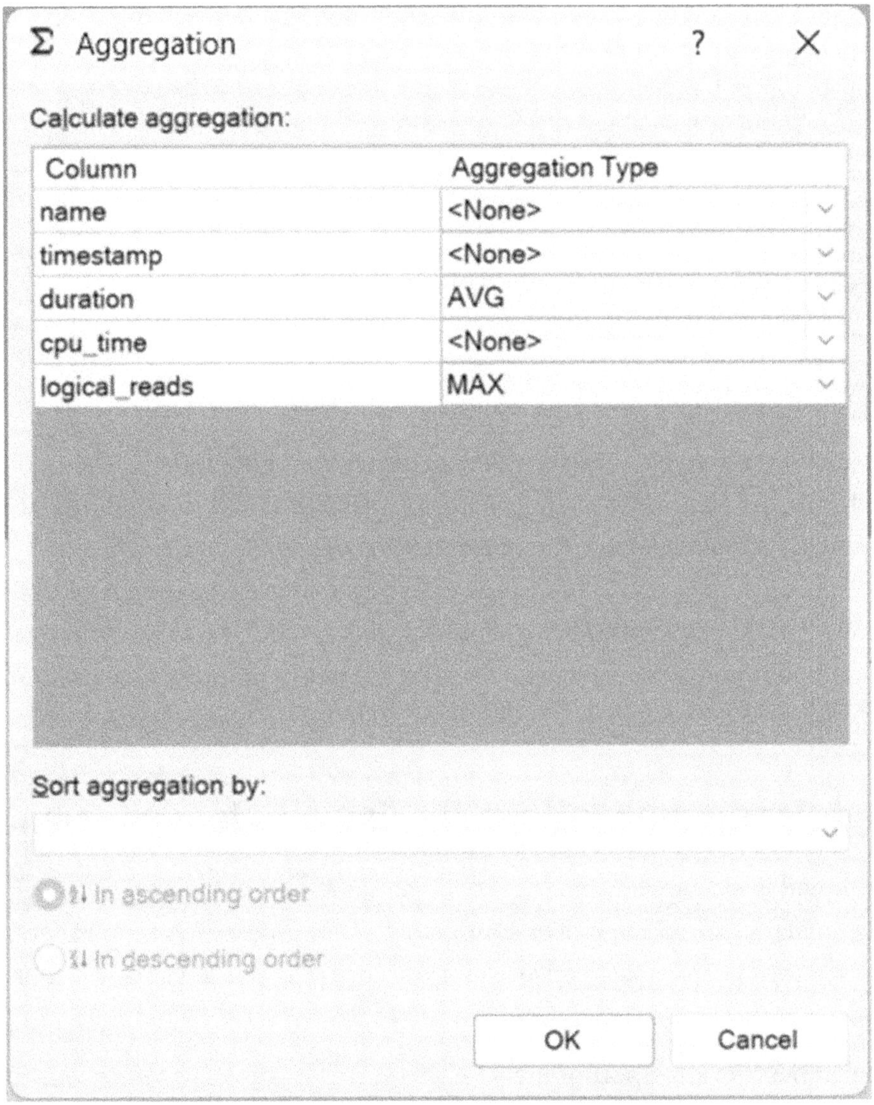

CHAPTER 3 METHODS FOR CAPTURING QUERY PERFORMANCE METRICS

Figure 3-30. Defining aggregation for the Live Data Explorer

You have a variety of aggregations to choose from:

- Minimum
- Maximum
- Average
- Summation
- Count

After I set the aggregations and click the OK button, my table changes again as you can see in Figure 3-31.

name	timestamp	object_name	duration	cpu_time	logical_reads
⊞ object_name: NULL (61)					
			AVG: 7842.475...		MAX: 640
⊞ object_name: sp_executesql (5362)					
			AVG: 2441.609...		MAX: 1696
⊞ object_name: ProductTransactionHistoryByReference (106)					
			AVG: 8181.811...		MAX: 1553

Figure 3-31. *Live Data Explorer table showing aggregated values*

I can now say, based on 106 executions of the stored procedure, ProductTransactionHistoryByReference, that on average, it executes in 8,181.811 microseconds. I can also see that the maximum logical_reads was 1,553.

You can see just how much utility is available here in the Live Data Explorer. This is an extremely handy way to quickly measure and understand query performance. You can of course combine these functions, filtering the data you want to look at and then applying aggregations to them or searching through them. Whatever it is you need to do.

General Recommendations for Using Extended Events

While Extended Events are a wonderful tool that has a minimal impact on your SQL Server instances, nothing is ever completely free from cost. There are a few recommendations I can make to ensure that your use of Extended Events is more successful:

- Set max file size appropriately.
- Avoid debug events.
- Avoid the use of No_Event_Loss.

I'll go over these in a little more detail in the following sections.

One quick side note that doesn't need much detail. In order to use lightweight statistics (covered in more detail in Chapter 4), if you're running SQL Server 2014, you'll need to create an Extended Events session with the query_thread_profile event.

Set Max File Size Appropriately

The default value for files is 1GB. That's actually very small when you consider the amount of information that can be gathered with Extended Events. It's a good idea to set this number much higher, somewhere in the 5–20GB range to ensure you have adequate space to capture information and you're not waiting on the file subsystem to create files for you while your buffer fills. This can lead to event loss. But it does depend on your system. If you have a good grasp of the level of output you can expect, set the file size more appropriate to your individual environment.

Avoid Debug Events

Not only do Extended Events provide you with a mechanism for observing the behavior of SQL Server and its internals in a way that far exceeds what was possible under Trace Events, but Microsoft uses the same functionality as part of troubleshooting SQL Server. A number of events are related to debugging SQL Server. These are not available by default through the wizard, but you do have access to them through the T-SQL command, and there's a way to enable them through the channel selection in the Session editor window.

Without direct guidance from Microsoft, do not use them. They are subject to change and are meant for Microsoft internal use only. If you do feel the need to experiment, you need to pay close attention to any of the events that include a break action. This means that should the event fire, it will stop SQL Server at the exact line of code that caused the event to fire. This means your server will be completely offline and in an unknown state. This could lead to a major outage if you were to do it in a production system. It could lead to loss of data and corruption of your database.

Avoid the Use of No_Event_Loss

Extended Events are set up such that some events will be lost. It's extremely likely, by design. But you can use a setting, No_Event_Loss, when configuring your session. If you do this on systems that are already under load, you may see a significant additional load placed on the system since you're effectively telling it to retain information in the buffer regardless of consequences. For small and focused sessions that are targeting a particular behavior, this approach may be acceptable.

Summary

In this chapter, you've seen two of the three best ways to capture query metrics. You can use aggregated data from cache through the DMVs. You can keep data with your databases in the Query Store (covered in detail in Chapter 6). You can get into extremely detailed behaviors through the use of Extended Events. You'll mix and match these as you go through the process of tracking your own query performance metrics.

In the next chapter, we'll get started on using execution plans as a way to understand how queries are behaving within SQL Server.

CHAPTER 4

Analyzing Query Behavior Using Execution Plans

Execution plans are the best window into understanding the choices made by the query optimizer as it attempts to make your query run quickly. Execution plans accurately describe the behaviors of your query, from the types of join operations to the indexes being used, as well as how they are used. Execution plans are absolutely not a measure of performance. That much must be made clear.

This chapter will outline what execution plans are, what they look like, and how you can read them. We'll do this by covering the following topics:

- How to capture execution plans
- The difference between actual and estimated plans
- What to look for in execution plans
- What some of the operators mean
- Tools available to you to help with execution plans

Execution plans are a huge topic. I'm going to cover some of the specifics around their use in this chapter, and then I'll be using them throughout the rest of the book as we learn how to tune queries through understanding the behavior shown through execution plans.

Execution plans themselves are common across all the SQL Server data platforms. A plan captured in Azure SQL Database, SQL Server 2025, AWS RDS, or Azure Managed Instance will be the same as any other. However, some newer behaviors show as new operators. For the most part, execution plans are a ubiquitous tool for understanding query behavior.

Estimated vs. Actual Execution Plans

Let's go ahead and start off with a hot topic and get it out of the way. I'm going to cover the methods used to capture execution plans in the next section. One of the ways is through SQL Server Management Studio (SSMS). SSMS shows us two different kinds of plans: estimated and actual. The problem is these are inaccurate names. There is only one kind of execution plan. However, it is possible to run a query and have SQL Server capture specific runtime metrics within the execution plan for that query. That, an execution plan with the addition of runtime metrics, is what is referred to when the term "actual execution plan" is used.

This goes against decades of documentation, including information I have written myself. However, it is absolutely true. As we're going to see in the next section, and throughout the book, we're going to get execution plans from all kinds of sources, from Dynamic Management Views (DMVs), Extended Events, and the Query Store. All those plans, for a given query, without a recompile, will be identical. However, if we execute a query and capture the runtime metrics, that plan will also be identical. It will just contain additional information.

The information added, the runtime metrics, is excellent data, and we're going to make use of it. That information includes, but isn't limited to, the following:

- Wait statistics for the query
- Duration of the query
- Actual row counts
- Actual number of executions of operators

However, this is just added data. The plan itself is always the same (except in the case of recompiles, which we'll cover in detail in Chapter 8). Most of the time, if you can, try to capture the execution plan with runtime metrics. The added information is frequently useful. However, since you sometimes can't run queries in a production environment, don't hesitate to use the execution plan that doesn't have the runtime metrics. It may be the one tool you have available. Further, when you retrieve a plan from the Query Store or you query the plan cache, that plan won't have runtime metrics. Yet, it's the plan used to run the query, so it's a valuable piece of information that you'll use to tune queries.

Capturing Execution Plans

There are a number of methods for capturing execution plans. The easiest is to use SSMS directly to get either an execution plan without query execution or an execution plan with runtime metrics after executing the query. You can also pull the queries directly from the plan cache in memory through the use of a DMV. If you have the Query Store enabled on a given database, that will also contain execution plans. Finally, you can put Extended Events to work to capture a variety of execution plans.

Before we get started on the details, a few notes about capturing execution plans. The act of capturing runtime metrics with an execution plan is an expensive operation, both because you're executing the query and because the engine is capturing metrics at a detailed level. Further, this process will directly, negatively, affect the query runtime and resource use. Because of this, you should get in the habit of either capturing an execution plan or capturing runtime metrics. Don't do both at the same time.

Behind the graphical execution plan, the one we'll use throughout the book is XML. That's how it's stored in memory, in the Query Store, and how most methods of getting the plan will have it. There is a method to capture what is known as a text plan, but they have a lot less information in them, so we won't be covering text plans here.

SQL Server Management Studio

Within SSMS, you can capture the execution plan, or you have the option of executing the query and getting both the execution plan and the runtime metrics. Let's take a simple query as our example, which we'll use throughout the chapter, so we won't have to post the graphical plan more than once. Listing 4-1 shows our example query.

Listing 4-1. Simple query to illustrate execution plans

```
SELECT soh.SalesOrderNumber,
       p.Name,
       sod.OrderQty
FROM Sales.SalesOrderHeader AS soh
    JOIN Sales.SalesOrderDetail AS sod
        ON sod.SalesOrderID = soh.SalesOrderID
    JOIN Production.Product AS p
        ON p.ProductID = sod.ProductID
WHERE soh.CustomerID = 30052;
```

CHAPTER 4   ANALYZING QUERY BEHAVIOR USING EXECUTION PLANS

To see the execution plan, we're going to click a button on the SQL Editor toolbar. However, before we do, we have to highlight the query from Listing 4-1. In a batch, every statement gets its own execution plan. So if we only want to see one execution plan, highlight that text. Otherwise, you'll get a plan for every statement in the batch.

The button we're going to click, after highlighting our query, is shown in the middle of Figure 4-1 with a white box around it. It also has a tooltip, "Display estimated execution plan."

Figure 4-1. *SQL Editor toolbar with the Display estimated execution plan button highlighted*

You can also use the keyboard to do the same action by pressing CTRL-L. As soon as you click the button, or press the keys, you'll immediately see an execution plan on a separate tab in your results pane within the SSMS query window just like Figure 4-2.

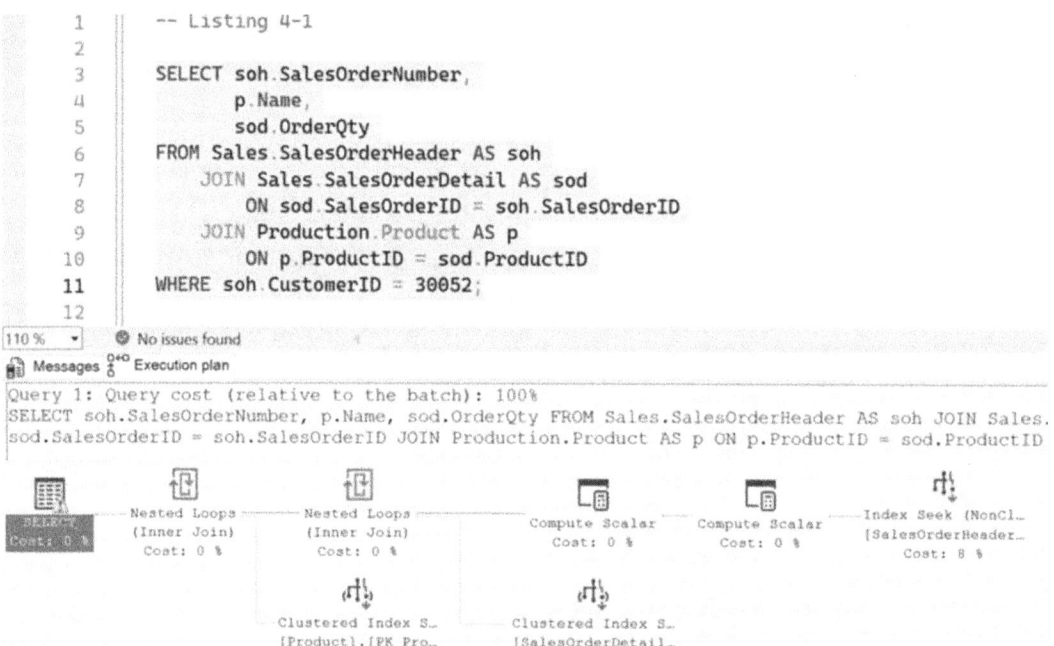

Figure 4-2. *Highlighted query and the execution plan*

CHAPTER 4   ANALYZING QUERY BEHAVIOR USING EXECUTION PLANS

We'll go over the objects, called operators, within the execution plan later in the chapter. For now, you've captured your first execution plan.

To add the runtime metrics to the plan, we'll have to execute the query, although we need to do one step first. We have to toggle the ability to capture the runtime metrics on through a different button on the SQL Editor toolbar. Mine is already enabled, so it's highlighted in the on position in Figure 4-3.

Figure 4-3. *SQL Editor toolbar with the Include actual execution plan button enabled*

The tooltip for the button reads "Include actual execution plan." You can also toggle it on or off from the keyboard, pressing CTRL-M. Unlike the first execution plan, nothing immediately happens other than the button showing as depressed. Again, to see the execution plan plus runtime metrics, a.k.a. the actual plan, you have to execute the query. After you execute the query, then, you'll get that same Execution plan tab in your results pane as shown in Figure 4-4. However, the results tab will be the one open by default, so you'll have to click the tab to see the execution plan.

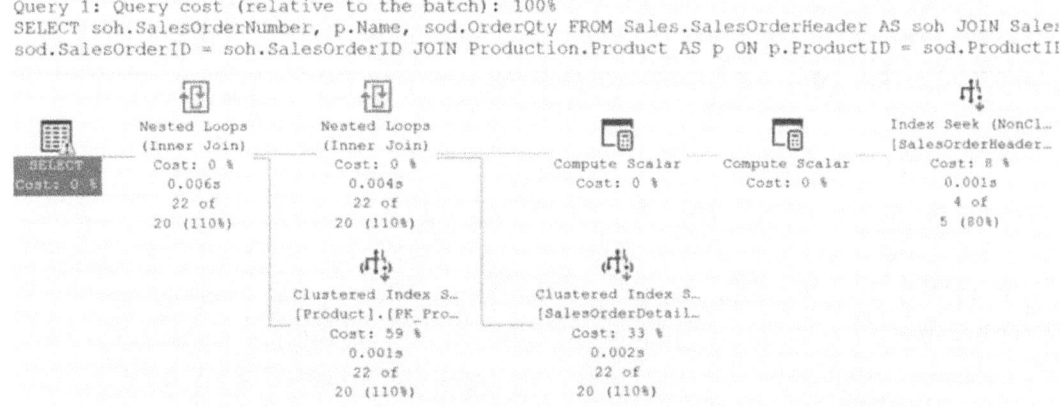

Figure 4-4. *An execution plan plus runtime metrics*

You can see that while the basic shape of the plan and the number of objects within it are the same, additional information is now visible on the plan. That additional information is the runtime metrics added to each operator in the plan.

87

Dynamic Management Views

We actually already covered capturing execution plans using DMVs in Chapter 3 with the examples there. Yet we should expand on it just a little. First, let's add a WHERE clause to our query from Chapter 3 so that we can locate just the query we're currently running. Listing 4-2 shows the WHERE clause.

Listing 4-2. Filtering for a particular query

```
SELECT dest.text,
       deqp.query_plan,
       deqs.execution_count,
       deqs.total_elapsed_time,
       deqs.last_elapsed_time
FROM sys.dm_exec_query_stats AS deqs
    CROSS APPLY sys.dm_exec_query_plan(deqs.plan_handle) AS deqp
    CROSS APPLY sys.dm_exec_sql_text(deqs.sql_handle) AS dest
WHERE dest.text LIKE 'SELECT soh.SalesOrderNumber,
       p.Name,%';
```

Using the LIKE operator saves a little room here in the book. To retrieve the data from your systems, you're probably better off using an equals clause and providing the whole query. The results are shown in Figure 4-5.

	text	query_plan	execution_count	total_elapsed_time	last_elapsed_time
1	SELECT soh.SalesOrderNumber, p.Nam...	<ShowPlanXML xmlns="http://schemas.microsoft.com...	1	11458	11458

Figure 4-5. *Results of querying the plan cache with a DMV*

Notice that the query_plan column is displaying XML data, but it's also underlined. That's because if you click it, it will recognize that it's an execution plan and will open it in another query window. Most plans can be queried and accessed in this fashion. When you open them though, you will only see the execution plan. You won't see runtime metrics as these are not stored in the plan cache.

Not all plans will work this way, though. Because the XML data type within SQL Server has a nesting limit, some execution plans for extremely large and complex queries could exceed it. Because of this, SQL Server also has a DMV called sys.dm_exec_text_query_plan. You query it the same way as sys.dm_exec_query_plan, providing a plan_ handle value. The results are in text, not XML. To convert that to a graphical execution plan, you have to save the text to a *.sqlplan file and then open that within SSMS.

One additional DMV is available to get the last actual plan for a query in cache, sys.dm_exec_query_plan_stats. However, to use this DMV, you must enable lightweight statistics profiling by either setting trace flag 2451 at the server level or using Listing 4-3 at the database.

Listing 4-3. Enabling last query plan stats

```
ALTER DATABASE SCOPED CONFIGURATION SET LAST_QUERY_PLAN_STATS = ON;
```

Once that's enabled, the DMV will hold the last execution plan with runtime metrics. I can now rewrite the query in Listing 4-2 to use this DMV as shown here in Listing 4-4.

Listing 4-4. Querying the sys.dm_exec_query_plan_stats DMV

```
SELECT dest.text,
       deqps.query_plan,
       deqs.execution_count,
       deqs.total_elapsed_time,
       deqs.last_elapsed_time
FROM sys.dm_exec_query_stats AS deqs
    CROSS APPLY sys.dm_exec_query_plan_stats(deqs.plan_handle) AS deqps
    CROSS APPLY sys.dm_exec_sql_text(deqs.sql_handle) AS dest
WHERE dest.text LIKE 'SELECT soh.SalesOrderNumber,
        p.Name,%';
```

If I click the plan in the results, it is an execution plan plus runtime metrics as shown in Figure 4-6.

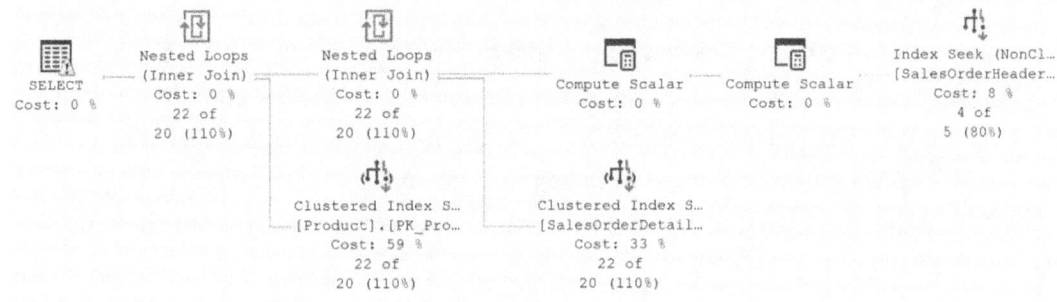

Figure 4-6. An execution plan with runtime metrics

You can see that there are actual row counts in there. You'll also find all the standard runtime metrics. You're not guaranteed to get a plan. First, the plan has to be in sys.dm_exec_cached_plans, or it won't be available at all. Next, if the query is extremely simple, you may only get the root node operator (SELECT in this case) instead of a full plan.

When the plan gets removed from cache, it's also removed from sys.dm_exec_query_plan_stats. Finally, if the plan can't be stored in cache, then it won't be available through the DMV either.

Query Store

We're going to cover the Query Store in depth in Chapter 6. However, we can take a quick look at how to retrieve an execution plan from the Query Store. The Query Store is enabled by default in SQL Server 2025 and must be enabled in order to get information from it. There are system tables that store the information for the Query Store. We can retrieve information from them in the same way we do any other as Listing 4-5 shows.

Listing 4-5. Retrieving a plan from the Query Store

```
SELECT qsq.query_id,
       qsq.query_hash,
       CAST(qsp.query_plan AS XML) AS QueryPlan
FROM sys.query_store_query AS qsq
    JOIN sys.query_store_plan AS qsp
        ON qsp.query_id = qsq.query_id
    JOIN sys.query_store_query_text AS qsqt
        ON qsqt.query_text_id = qsq.query_text_id
WHERE qsqt.query_sql_text LIKE 'SELECT soh.SalesOrderNumber,
       p.Name,%';
```

As with the DMV query, I've used LIKE just to save some space. It's not the best way to filter your queries against the Query Store. I've added the CAST to XML in order to get a plan that can be opened within SSMS. The Query Store keeps the XML data in a VARCHAR(MAX) column so it doesn't have to store it twice. You may still hit the XML nesting limit, but for most queries, this will work fine. The results are shown here in Figure 4-7.

CHAPTER 4　ANALYZING QUERY BEHAVIOR USING EXECUTION PLANS

	query_id	query_hash	QueryPlan
1	2	0x6BF6D3C13FB8FD7E	<ShowPlanXML xmlns="http://schemas.microsoft.com...

Figure 4-7. *Retrieving an execution plan from the Query Store*

Opening the plan, you would see something the exact same as Figure 4-2. The Query Store doesn't keep individual runtime metrics. As has already been said, to get those, you have to execute the query and capture the plan or use sys.dm_exec_query_plan_stats.

Extended Events

Another way to capture execution plans is through the use of Extended Events. There are several events that you can use to capture an execution plan:

- query_post_compilation_showplan: Takes place after a given query has gone through the compilation process

- query_pre_execution_showplan: Takes place after a query has gone through the optimization process, which is different from the compilation process and follows it in order of operations

- query_post_execution_plan_profile: Available in SQL Server 2017 and greater, uses the lightweight query profile process to capture the execution plan and runtime metrics

- query_post_execution_showplan: Takes place after the query finishes executing so that it captures both the execution plan and runtime metrics

---

Warning　Capturing execution plans with Extended Events can be a resource-intensive operation. Please exercise due diligence and filter your events carefully.

The most common use will either be to capture the execution plans after compilation or to use one of the post-execution methods to capture both the plan and the runtime metrics. Where possible, if you're capturing runtime metrics, use the lightweight query profile process in order to reduce the overhead of capturing plans.

The information captured from query_post_execution_plan_profile looks like Figure 4-8.

Event:query_post_execution_plan_profile (2025-05-12 10:42:41

Details Query Plan

Field	Value
cpu_time	224
database_name	
dop	1
duration	224
estimated_cost	0
estimated_rows	20
granted_memory_kb	0
ideal_memory_kb	0
nest_level	0
object_id	119976304
object_name	Dynamic SQL
object_type	ADHOC
requested_memory_kb	0
serial_ideal_memory_kb	0
showplan_xml	<ShowPlanXML xmlns="http://s..
source_database_id	5
used_memory_kb	0

Figure 4-8. *Extended Event fields after capturing an execution plan*

The plan itself is in the showplan_xml field. However, if you look at Figure 4-8, you can see that a tab has been added to the Extended Events results labeled Query Plan. If you click it, you'll see our familiar plan from earlier in the chapter as shown in Figure 4-9.

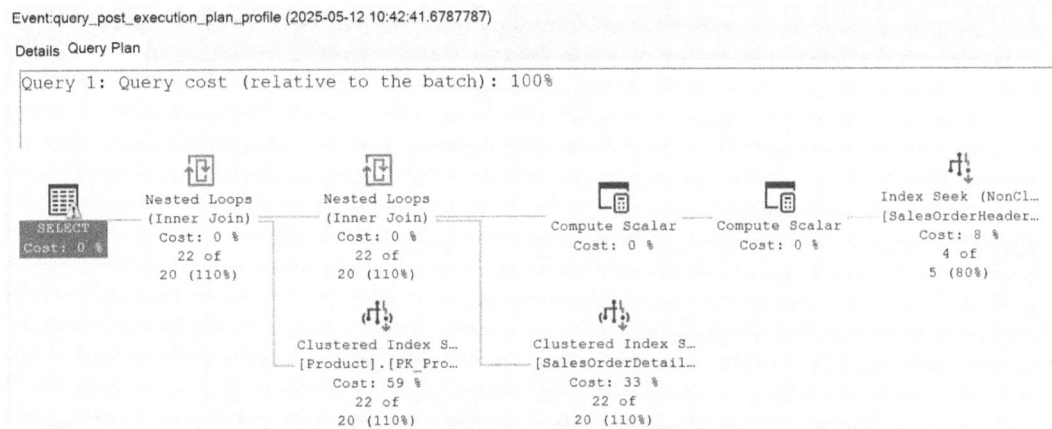

Figure 4-9. The execution plan inside of Extended Events

This is a fully functional graphical execution plan with all the properties and behaviors found in any other graphical plan within SSMS.

What Is Inside an Execution Plan

I've shown a couple of different execution plans in the book up to this point, but I haven't explained exactly what it is that you're seeing. Let's break that down now. When you look at a graphical plan, the first thing you're likely to notice is all the icons. These icons represent operators, also called iterators. Operators are the processes that are going to do something to the data in order to help satisfy your query. Figure 4-10 is an example of a Nested Loops operator.

Figure 4-10. The icon representing the Nested Loops operator

Below each operator are the logical name of the operator and the physical action that the operation represents like Figure 4-11.

Figure 4-11. *The icon plus the name of the operator and the action it represents*

Then, below each operator is the estimated cost of that operation. This cost is a calculation done within the optimizer and represents a figurative representation of a calculation of the amount of CPU, memory, and I/O needed to satisfy the query. It is always an estimated value and never an actual measure of any kind, even in plans that contain runtime metrics. You can see this in Figure 4-12.

Figure 4-12. *The estimated cost of the operator*

Finally, for execution plans that have added runtime metrics, two additional pieces of data are seen. These are the time involved with the given operation and the row count and estimated row counts plus their percentage as shown in Figure 4-13.

```
Nested Loops
(Inner Join)
Cost: 0 %
0.000s
22 of
20 (110%)
```

Figure 4-13. *The added values from the runtime metrics*

Between each of the operators are arrows, representing data flow. Because these arrows represent data flow, I generally refer to them as pipes, since pipes control and direct other types of flow. These pipes, or arrows, can vary in thickness with thin pipes showing small amounts of data movement and thicker pipes showing larger amounts of data movement. Two examples of these pipes from the same plan we've been exploring are visible in Figure 4-14.

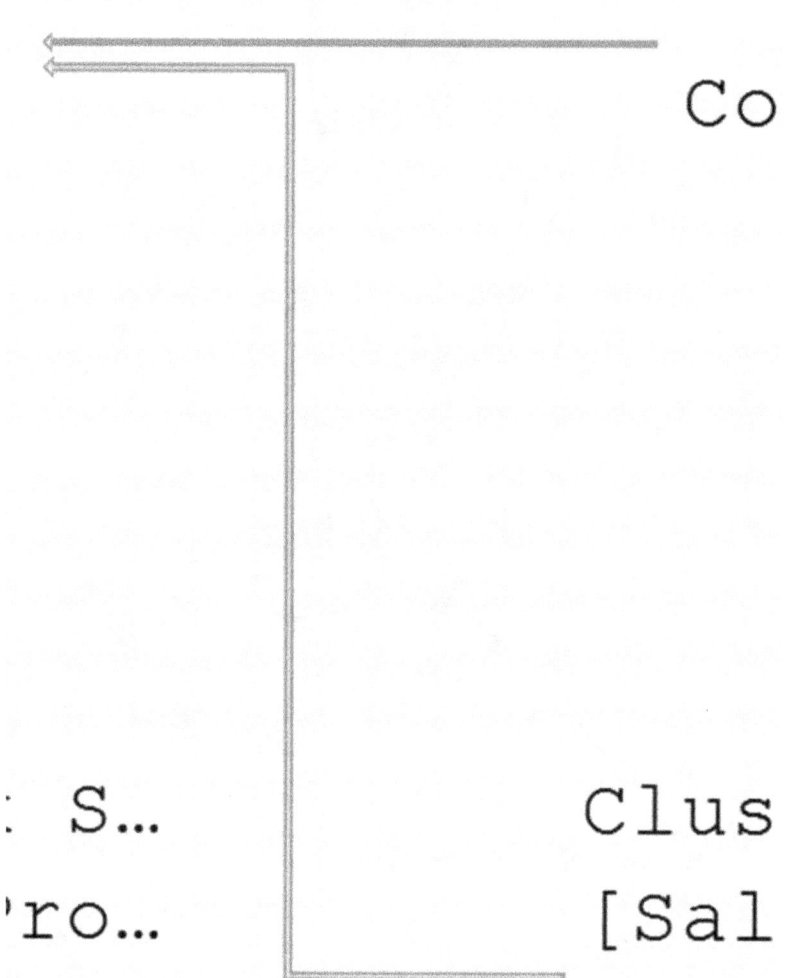

Figure 4-14. *Pipes representing data flow connect operators together*

As you can see, the pipe at the top of Figure 4-14 is a little thinner than the one below it, meaning less data is moving through it.

If you hover your mouse over any of the operators or pipes, you can get a tooltip to pop up, showing you additional information about that operator as shown in Figure 4-15.

Nested Loops

For each row in the top (outer) input, scan the bottom (inner) input, and output matching rows.

Physical Operation	Nested Loops
Logical Operation	Inner Join
Actual Execution Mode	Row
Estimated Execution Mode	Row
Actual Number of Rows for All Executions	22
Actual Number of Batches	0
Estimated Operator Cost	0.0000855 (0%)
Estimated I/O Cost	0
Estimated CPU Cost	0.0000855
Estimated Subtree Cost	0.0176668
Number of Executions	1
Estimated Number of Executions	1
Estimated Number of Rows for All Executions	20.4562
Estimated Number of Rows Per Execution	20.4562
Estimated Row Size	42 B
Actual Rebinds	0
Actual Rewinds	0
Node ID	1

Output List
[soh].SalesOrderNumber, [AdventureWorks].[Sales].[SalesOrderDetail].OrderQty, [AdventureWorks].[Sales].[SalesOrderDetail].ProductID

Outer References
[AdventureWorks].[Sales].[SalesOrderHeader].SalesOrderID

Figure 4-15. The tooltip for the Nested Loops operator

If you read through the information shown in the tooltip, you'll spot information that is likely to be quite useful, such as the estimated number of rows for this operator. However, all this information plus a whole lot more will be visible in the properties of the operator. Because there is so much more information in the properties, I almost never use the tooltips and find them to be a hindrance more than a help as they pop up and get in my way. However, one piece of information that is very useful from them is the description of the operator right at the top.

You can see the properties of an operator by right-clicking the operator and selecting "Properties" from the context menu. If you already have the Properties window open, you can refresh the information inside by clicking a given operator. The Properties window can be pinned inside SSMS. This is how I normally work with execution plans. It makes it much faster to get to more complete data sets from the operators. Figure 4-16 shows an example of the properties of an operator.

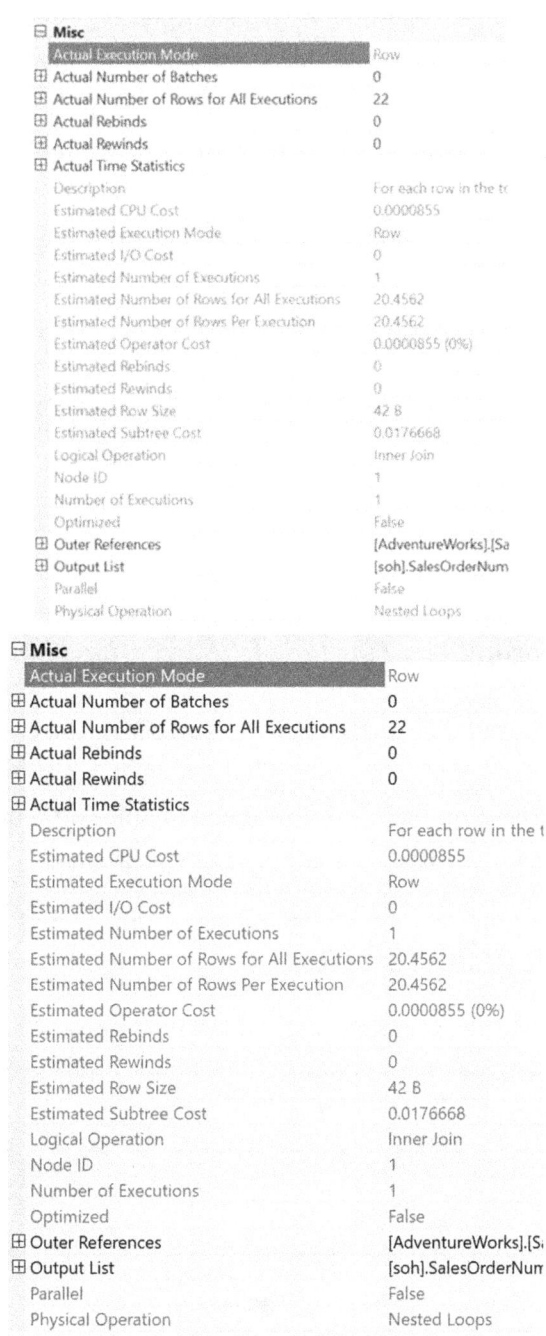

Figure 4-16. *Properties of the Nested Loops operator*

We'll be covering exactly what many of these represent as we work our way through the book. Some properties can be expanded to show additional values by clicking the plus sign. The values in the properties can be very long, so at the right edge of the value, there may be an ellipsis. Clicking that will open a window with the full value of the property selected.

At the top of a plan, you'll see varying pieces of information. First, you'll see a query count, if this is part of a batch of queries. Along with this there will be the estimated cost of this query in relation to the others. Second, you may see the query itself. There's an ellipsis there that lets you open it in another window. Finally, you may also see a Missing Index hint. We'll cover this later in the book. Figure 4-17 shows an example of the top of the execution plan.

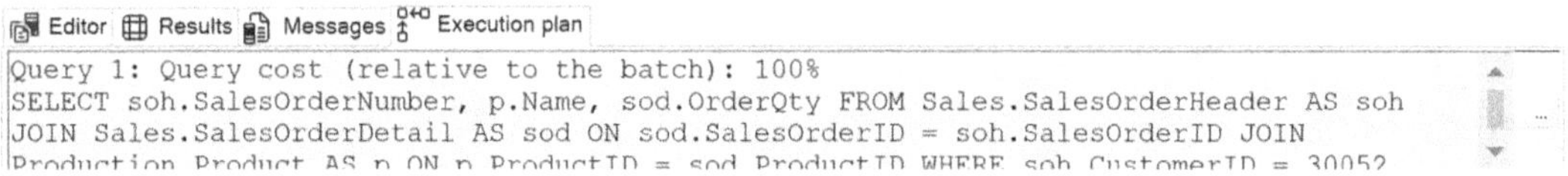

Figure 4-17. The information at the top of the execution plan

These are all the types of objects that make up an execution plan. Each of these objects can have a varying set of properties. All the objects represent different types of behaviors within the execution plan. Now, we need to talk a little bit about how to put these objects together in order to understand, or read, a plan.

Reading an Execution Plan

Let's take another look at the execution plan, without runtime metrics, generated from Listing 4-1 in Figure 4-18.

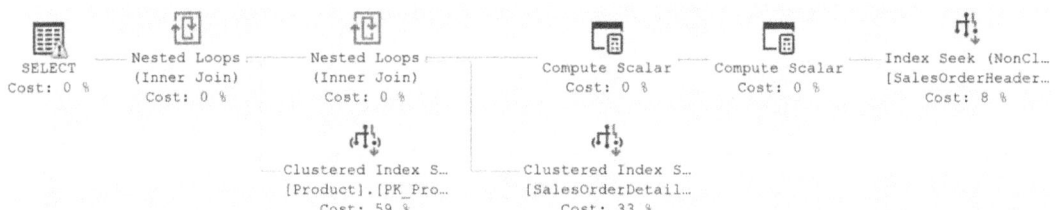

Figure 4-18. Execution plan from Listing 4-1

There are two ways to look at any execution plan. Logically, a plan is read like a book in English, from the left to the right. This means the first operator in the plan is the SELECT operator in the upper left. Next would be the first Nested Loops operator. Following that would be the second Nested Loops operator and so on down the line. You can also see this represented in the NodeID values for each operator. The leftmost operator, in this case, the SELECT, contains metadata about the plan itself, so it isn't given a NodeID. Purely technically, what I refer to throughout the book as the first operator, SELECT, INSERT, UPDATE, DELETE, is only metadata and not actually an operator. However, rather than give it another term and confuse things, let's just refer to it as an operator. The first numbered operator with a value for NodeID in this plan would go to the Nested Loops operator. It's given a value of zero (0), and then counting proceeds from there.

This logical reading of the plan follows how a plan is initialized within the query engine. Each operator requests data from those behind it in order until data is found and returned through the rest of the operators.

The second way to read a plan is by following the data flow. The data flow starts from the far-right side and at the top of the execution plan. In our example in Figure 4-18, it's the Index Seek operator against the IX_SalesOrderHeader_CustomerID index. The data then flows back to the left through the operators. Data flow through the operators depends on the processing mode. There are two: row and batch. We'll get into the details of this in later chapters, but suffice to say that row mode shows a single row being moved, while batch mode represents batches of rows being moved. These modes are why operators are sometimes called iterators. They iterate through data either a row at a time or in batches.

Next, you have to interpret what operators are doing. The description is a good place to start. For example, the description for the Nested Loops operator is as follows:

For each row in the top (outer) input, scan the bottom (inner) input, and output matching rows.

The Nested Loops operator is one of the JOIN operators (there are three others, and we'll introduce them throughout the book). A JOIN operation needs two sets of data, one from each data set that it's pulling information from. This why you can see that each of the two Nested Loops operators in Figure 4-18 has two inputs. The JOIN operation then outputs matching rows, represented by the single output from the Nested Loops operator.

One of the keys to reading a plan is not just understanding what each operator does, but also to track the input and output of each operator in order to understand what is happening to the data across the execution plan.

We'll be walking through a lot of examples of reading execution plans throughout the book.

What Do You Look for in an Execution Plan?

It's cumbersome, time-consuming, and probably impossible to attempt to read every single property of every single operator within an execution plan. So instead, we try to work from signposts. These are some shortcuts that can help make reading an execution plan easier. The first time I look at an execution plan, I look for these things:

- First Operator: The metadata about the plan in the operator on the far left of the plan.

- Warnings: Indications of potential issues with the plan are visually identifiable.

- Most Costly Operations: Operators with the highest estimated cost are likely to be the most expensive operations in reality.

- Fat Pipes: Large pipes represent data movement.

- Extra Operators: Any time you see an operator that you don't know what it is, or you don't know why it's there, it should draw your eye.

- Scans: Seeks are not naturally good and scans are not naturally bad, but scans do represent I/O, which is frequently an issue.

- Estimate vs. Actual Counts: When the actual values vary wildly from the estimated values, it can be a sign of issues with the query.

Let's take a moment and walk through these in a little more detail so it's clear why you use these as your signposts.

CHAPTER 4 ANALYZING QUERY BEHAVIOR USING EXECUTION PLANS

First Operator

The first operator, the one all the way on the left side of the plan, contains metadata about the plan itself. Not all plans will have this operator. Plans captured using Trace won't have it at all. Plans captured using older versions of Extended Events may not have it. Regardless, the data is still there, in the XML. It's just not within a readily identifiable graphical operator.

The reason we go there is obvious when we look at the properties in Figure 4-19.

Misc	
Cached plan size	40 KB
CardinalityEstimationModelVersion	140
CompileCPU	51
CompileMemory	928
CompileTime	60
Estimated Number of Rows for All Executions	0
Estimated Number of Rows Per Execution	20.4562
Estimated Operator Cost	0 (0%)
Estimated Subtree Cost	0.0429188
⊞ MemoryGrantInfo	
Optimization Level	FULL
⊞ OptimizerHardwareDependentProperties	
⊞ OptimizerStatsUsage	
QueryHash	0x6BF6D3C13FB8FD7E
QueryPlanHash	0x7AE51EDE67A98772
Reason For Early Termination Of Statement Optimization	Good Enough Plan Found
RetrievedFromCache	false
SecurityPolicyApplied	False
⊞ Set Options	ANSI_NULLS: True, ANSI_PA
Statement	SELECT soh.SalesOrderNun
⊞ TraceFlags	
⊞ Warnings	Type conversion in express

Figure 4-19. Properties of the first operator in an execution plan

We don't have the space to go through all of these in detail. Plus, we already covered some of the information gathered here in Chapter 2 talking about query optimization. However, let me point out a few places where you will look regularly. First, the

"Cached plan size" shows just how big this plan is in memory. The value for "QueryHash" is considered a given query's fingerprint and can be used to search for similar queries. The same goes for the "QueryPlanHash." These are simply hash values created from the T-SQL itself, in the case of the QueryHash, and the execution plan, in the case of the QueryPlanHash. As hash constructs, it's possible to see duplicate values, meaning neither of these is necessarily perfectly unique. However, they are a mechanism for searching for similar, or identical, queries or plans in your system. The "Set Options" are the ANSI connection settings, and differences here can result in different execution plans, so they're stored with the plan. You can also see a query's parameterization type and, when dealing with a parameterized query, the compile values and, if you have runtime information for the plan, the runtime values. You can also see the "MemoryGrantInfo" to see how much memory SQL Server thought needed to be allocated for the plan. If you have runtime metrics, you'll also get the actual memory use, which is a great comparison point, talked about in a later section. Finally, at the bottom of Figure 4-19, you can see the "Warnings" that are associated with this plan, all in one place.

All this information describing how the plan was compiled, its settings, and the rest is why I start here when looking at a plan for the first time.

Warnings

Warnings are indicators of the possibility of an issue that could affect query performance. They're not automatically a problem, but they are an indicator for the potential for problems. The plan we've been looking at throughout this chapter has a warning on it as shown in Figure 4-20.

CHAPTER 4   ANALYZING QUERY BEHAVIOR USING EXECUTION PLANS

Figure 4-20. *The SELECT operator with a warning indicator*

That visual indicator lets you know that there may be an issue. The tooltip of the operator will show the warning, and you can see it inside the properties as shown in Figure 4-21.

```
⊟ Warnings                              Type conversion in expression (CONVERT(nva
    ⊟ Type conversion in expression (({0})
        ConvertIssue                        CardinalityEstimate
        Expression                          CONVERT(nvarchar(23),[soh].[SalesOrderID],0)
```

Figure 4-21. *Details of a warning within the properties of the operator*

This warning is letting us know that a data conversion operation is being run against a column, SalesOrderID, that could affect row estimates, CardinalityEstimate, negatively impacting performance. You'll see a single indicator for a warning, but you can have multiple warnings. If there is more than one, you'll see it in the properties.

Note   This is not saying that an actual problem exists, just that it could.

In fact, in this case, the warning is a false positive, because the column in question isn't used in any filtering operations, so it can't affect the row estimates. We'll discuss these sorts of issues in later chapters.

There's another warning indicator that we should take a quick look at in Listing 4-6.

Listing 4-6. A query without JOIN criteria

```
SELECT pv.OnOrderQty,
       a.City
FROM Purchasing.ProductVendor AS pv,
     Person.Address AS a
WHERE a.City = 'Tulsa';
```

If we look at the execution plan for this query, it should look like Figure 4-22.

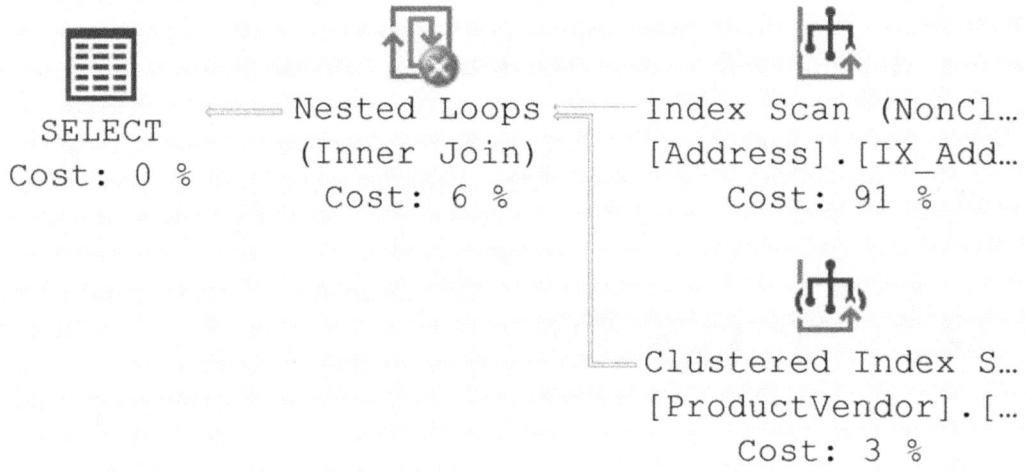

Figure 4-22. *An execution plan showing another kind of warning*

The operator with the warning is where we can see the details of the warning itself. Figure 4-23 shows the properties from the Nested Loops operator.

Figure 4-23. *Warning description from the Nested Loops operator*

This warning is very clear: we have no JOIN predicate. In this case, I wrote the query without one just so that we can see the error. You might have a query where you intentionally left off the criteria in order to get a Cartesian product result set (everything joined to everything). However, it's also a possibility that someone just messed up.

There are a number of other possible causes for warnings. They'll all show up as either the exclamation point or the red "X." Some warnings will only be visible in execution plans with runtime metrics. Others will show up in both, including the two examples we just discussed.

Most Costly Operations

Even though the values of the costs for the operators are all estimates, these are the absolute numbers that the optimizer uses to make its decisions. Therefore, they become a driving factor behind our interpretation of execution plans. If you look at the execution plan for the query (Listing 4-6) we used to generate the warning earlier, you can see that the Index Scan against the IX_Address_AddressLine1_AddressLine2_City_StateProvinceID_PostalCode index is the highest cost, by far, as shown in Figure 4-24.

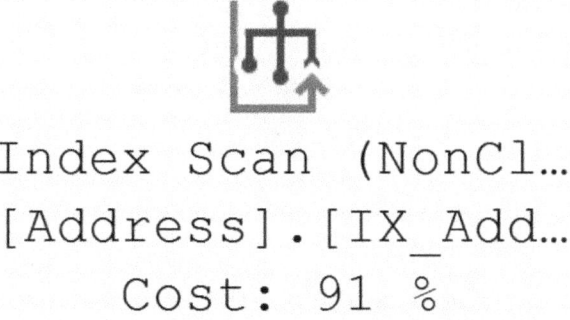

Figure 4-24. The highest cost operator in the execution plan

As we'll see throughout the book, processes that cause more I/O generally also cause queries to run slower. The estimated cost associated with this Index Scan is the most likely place to focus our efforts if we want this query to run faster.

Just remember, while an estimated cost may be high, it is still just an estimate. You may find that the real culprit for slow query performance lies elsewhere. In this case though, if we were to look at the actual number of rows vs. the estimated number of rows, both values are 19,614, showing that the estimated cost of this operation is accurate.

Fat Pipes

Since the pipes represent data movement, identifying large amounts of data movement can help us interpret an execution plan in order to identify the most likely cause of performance issues. Another thing we look for when looking at the pipes is transitions, either from fat pipes to thin ones or the reverse, thin pipes growing ever fatter.

In the first case, fat pipes becoming thinner, you're seeing late filtering of the data. It's possible that an index could help, or maybe some changes to the code.

In the second case, you're seeing data being multiplied as the execution of the query progresses. Again, this increase in data movement means more I/O and more memory resources being used. This may be a place where adjustments to code are necessary again.

Extra Operators

There is actually no such thing as an "extra operator." Every operator has a purpose, and they are put to use executing the query. However, I needed a shorthand way to describe the situation where you need to investigate a given operator because you have a lack of knowledge. If you don't know what an operator is, that should be one that draws your eye so that you can better understand how the query is being processed.

If you don't know why a given operator is being used in a particular situation, that can also be a signpost for further investigation. If we go back to the query from Listing 4-2 and look at its execution plan, we've lightly discussed what each of the operators is except for the two Compute Scalar operators, visible here in Figure 4-25.

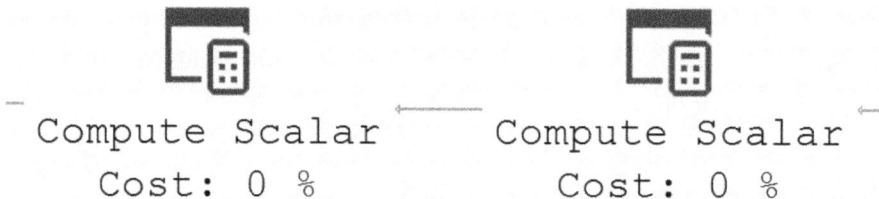

Figure 4-25. *Two Compute Scalar operators represent extra operators*

Since we don't yet know what a Compute Scalar operator is, this represents an extra operator in this case. If we look at the description of the operator, we get a definition of what it does:

Compute new values from existing values in a row.

But now, we're still faced with these being "extra operators" since we don't know why the operations are being done. Selecting the second Compute Scalar operator, we can look at the properties in Figure 4-26 within the execution plan to try to understand what this is doing.

Figure 4-26. *The details behind the Defined Values property of a Compute Scalar operator*

What all of that is defining for us is this bit of T-SQL code:

```
Scalar Operator(isnull(N'SO'+CONVERT(nvarchar(23),[AdventureWorks].[Sales].
[SalesOrderHeader].[SalesOrderID] as [soh].[SalesOrderID],0),
N'*** ERROR ***'))
```

If you look at the structure of the tables, you'll find that the SalesOrderHeader table contains a computed column, SalesOrderNumber, and that T-SQL is the calculation necessary to generate values for that column.

Now, not only have we answered most of the questions around this operator, we've also identified the source of the warning from earlier in the chapter. It's this CONVERT function causing the warning.

Scans

Scans are a signpost for us simply because they represent data movement. More data movement means more disk and memory access, and this is frequently the cause of performance problems. So looking for scans is one way to more quickly understand where problems may lie within execution plans.

However, if we look at a query like the one in Listing 4-7, the only way that query can be satisfied is through a scan.

Listing 4-7. A query that can only use a Scan operation

```
SELECT *
FROM Production.UnitMeasure AS um;
```

Without any kind of filtering criteria, the optimizer can only choose a scan. A seek in this case would actually run slower than the scan. We'll get to exactly why in Chapter 9. Just know that scans are not inherently bad and seeks are not inherently good. It's just that scans represent data movement, one of the more common causes of performance issues, which is why we use them as a signpost.

Estimate vs. Actual

When we execute the query and capture runtime metrics along with the execution plan, we can add one more signpost to our list, comparing the estimated values and the actual values of the operations. Figure 4-27 shows the costliest operation within the plan from Listing 4-1, the Clustered Index Seek against the PK_Product_ProductID index.

CHAPTER 4 ANALYZING QUERY BEHAVIOR USING EXECUTION PLANS

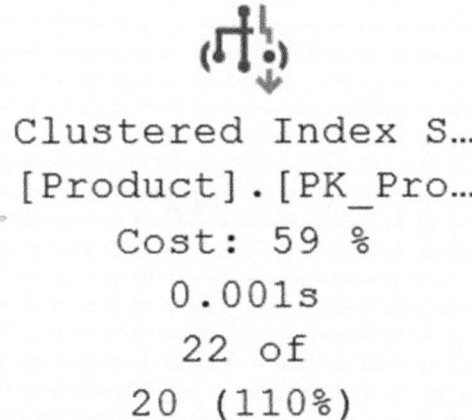

Figure 4-27. *Estimated values compared with actual values in an execution plan*

You can see immediately that the estimated number of rows to be processed by this operator was 20. The actual number of rows was 22, 110% of the total. In this case, that's not far enough off to give us concern. In fact, you wouldn't worry until you were seeing at least threefold or more increases, or, conversely, one-fifth or fewer decreases, in the comparison. Those aren't hard numbers, just general examples.

You can also get more detailed comparisons by looking to the properties, visible in Figure 4-28.

Misc

Actual Execution Mode	Row
⊞ Actual I/O Statistics	
⊞ Actual Number of Batches	0
⊞ Actual Number of Rows for All Executions	22
⊞ Actual Number of Rows Read	22
⊞ Actual Rebinds	0
⊞ Actual Rewinds	0
⊞ Actual Time Statistics	
⊞ Defined Values	[AdventureWorks].[Prc
Description	Scanning a particular
Estimated CPU Cost	0.0001581
Estimated Execution Mode	Row
Estimated I/O Cost	0.003125
Estimated Number of Executions	20.456203
Estimated Number of Rows for All Executions	20.456203
Estimated Number of Rows Per Execution	1
Estimated Number of Rows to be Read	1
Estimated Operator Cost	0.0251665 (59%)
Estimated Rebinds	19.3468
Estimated Rewinds	0.109403
Estimated Row Size	61 B
Estimated Subtree Cost	0.0251665

Figure 4-28. Comparing the estimated and actual values in the properties

You can see the row estimates again here, along with the actuals, but let's see something with more disparity. If you look at the *Estimated Rebinds*, at the bottom of Figure 4-28, and compare that with the *Actual Rebinds*, you'll see real disparity, 19.3468 compared with 0. We'll discuss exactly what a Rebind is later in the book, but you can see that in this case, what was estimated is not what happened. That disparity could be a strong indicator for all sorts of performance problems, which is why we will use these types of comparisons for one of our signposts.

After the Signposts

We can use the signposts to quickly identify potential issues within an execution plan. This is especially helpful the first time you look at a given execution plan. However, those only carry you so far in understanding what is going on within an execution plan. After you've exhausted the simple process of using the signposts, what's left is the hard work of understanding what's happening in a plan where the signposts don't give you enough information to go on.

First, get in the habit of tracking the *NodeID* value for the operators. Knowing what the NodeID is lets you know the order in which the operators were instantiated, helping you understand how the query is being processed. You'll also run into operators that refer back to other operators, so keeping an eye out for references to other NodeID values helps you understand the execution plan.

Next, get in the habit of tracking the output of each operator. Many operators change, or add, columns to the result set. Knowing where those columns came from can be helpful in understanding the plan.

Finally, get in the habit early of using the properties of the operators. Yes, in some cases, the information you need immediately is in the tooltip. However, frequently, it's not. Having that more complete picture at your fingertips will help you read and understand execution plans better.

Tools That Assist You with Execution Plans

The more you get into reading execution plans, the more you need to have a little help in navigating and understanding the plans. The first tool I want to recommend to you is another book I wrote, *SQL Server Execution Plans*, Third Edition (Redgate Press). It's a large book focused only on what execution plans are, how they work, and how to interpret them. The book goes into detail on plans but doesn't cover query tuning to any degree. That's what this book is for.

After that, there are some functions within SSMS and some third-party tools you might consider.

CHAPTER 4   ANALYZING QUERY BEHAVIOR USING EXECUTION PLANS

SQL Server Management Studio

A couple of points immediately about SQL Server Management Studio (SSMS). Since you're likely to be getting a lot of your plans through Extended Events, querying the DMVs, or through the Query Store, you're naturally going to do more work with plans in SSMS. Understanding how it can help you will make execution plans easier.

A few points here, and then we'll get into some of the details. First, you can simply drag a plan around on your screen by clicking with your mouse and then dragging. It will move the plan around. You can also zoom in and out on plans through either CTRL-scroll or by right-clicking and selecting from a context menu. Finally, for plans that are exceeding the size of the screen, there's a small plus sign that will appear in the lower right of the graphical part of the plan. Clicking it will open a small screen as you see here in Figure 4-29.

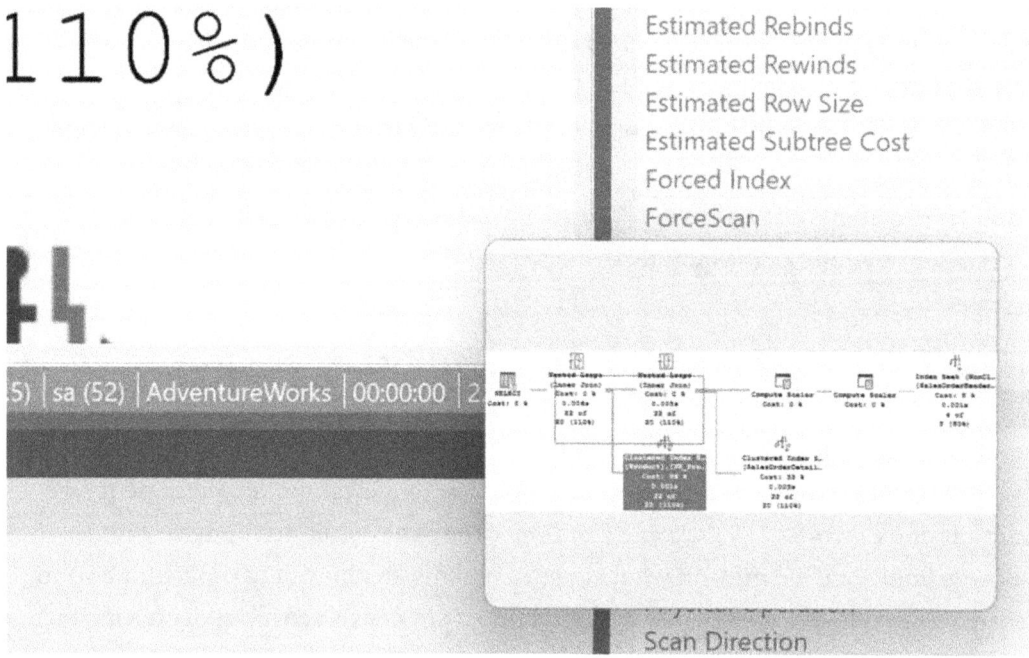

Figure 4-29. The screen for dragging around the view of an execution plan

While you can drag a plan around on your screen, this enables you to simply drag the view of the screen around the plan. It can be useful if you're not sure where to go on the plan, since it gives you a full view of the shape of the plan so you can decide where you'd like to move in order to look at things in the plan.

After that, we get into some more detailed functionality of execution plans within SSMS.

Find Node

When execution plans become large, tracking down particular operators can be much more difficult. You can use the Find Node functionality within a plan to search for a particular node. Right-click within a plan and select *Find Node* from the context menu, or hit CTRL-F in a plan. A small window is opened in the upper right of the execution plan window as shown in Figure 4-30.

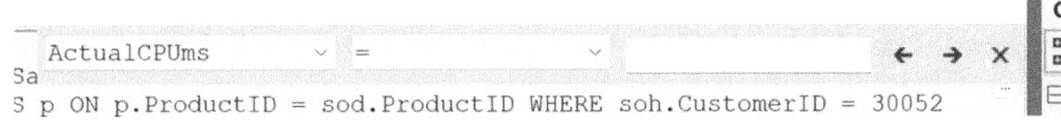

Figure 4-30. *The Find Node window open within an execution plan*

You can use the first drop-down to pick from a list of all possible properties within the current execution plan, a portion of which is shown in Figure 4-31.

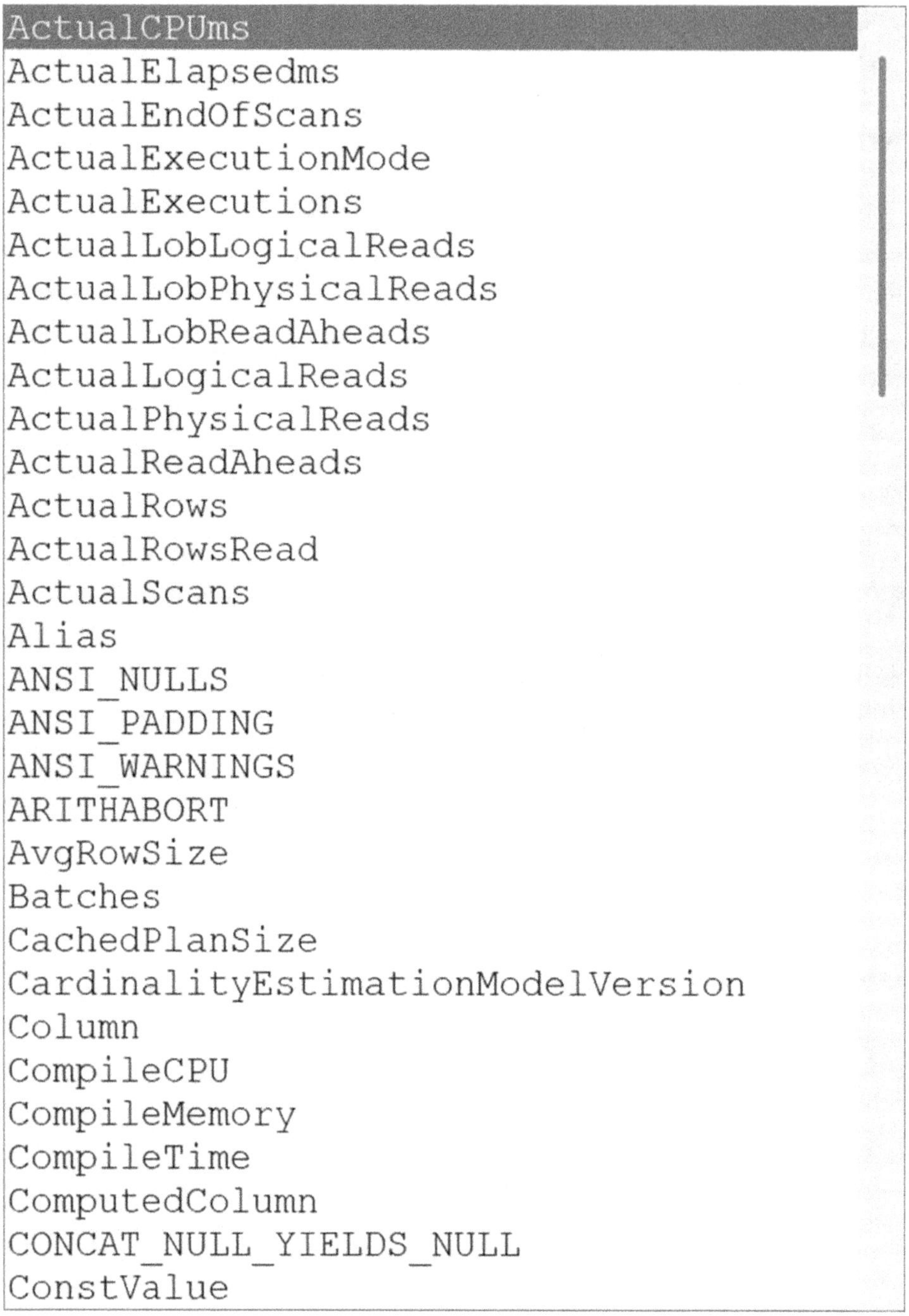

CHAPTER 4 ANALYZING QUERY BEHAVIOR USING EXECUTION PLANS

```
ActualCPUms
ActualElapsedms
ActualEndOfScans
ActualExecutionMode
ActualExecutions
ActualLobLogicalReads
ActualLobPhysicalReads
ActualLobReadAheads
ActualLogicalReads
ActualPhysicalReads
ActualReadAheads
ActualRows
ActualRowsRead
ActualScans
Alias
ANSI_NULLS
ANSI_PADDING
ANSI_WARNINGS
ARITHABORT
AvgRowSize
Batches
CachedPlanSize
CardinalityEstimationModelVersion
Column
CompileCPU
CompileMemory
CompileTime
ComputedColumn
CONCAT_NULL_YIELDS_NULL
ConstValue
```

Figure 4-31. Part of the list of properties in the Find Node drop-down menu

Selecting one of the properties means you'll be searching for values within that property. You can only search for one property at a time.

CHAPTER 4 ANALYZING QUERY BEHAVIOR USING EXECUTION PLANS

The next drop-down gives you two choices:

- Equals
- Contains

Or, in other words, you can search for a specified value or do a loose match, no wild card replacements necessary. Then the two arrows, pointed left and right, will move you through the plan to the operators that match, highlighting those operators, as shown in Figure 4-32.

***Figure 4-32.** Results of searching for operators using Find Node*

CHAPTER 4　ANALYZING QUERY BEHAVIOR USING EXECUTION PLANS

I did a search for any operator where the ActualRows equaled the value of "4." The Index Seek operator returned four rows.

Compare Plans

You can compare two execution plans and find all their differences and similarities using SSMS. One of the plans must be saved as a file. You save a plan to a *.sqlplan file by right-clicking the plan itself and choosing *Save Execution Plan As* from the context menu.

From the plan that is not a file, right-click the plan and select *Compare Showplan* from the context menu. You'll be given the window for selecting a file. Pick the *.sqlplan file, and then your screen will change to something like what you see in Figure 4-33.

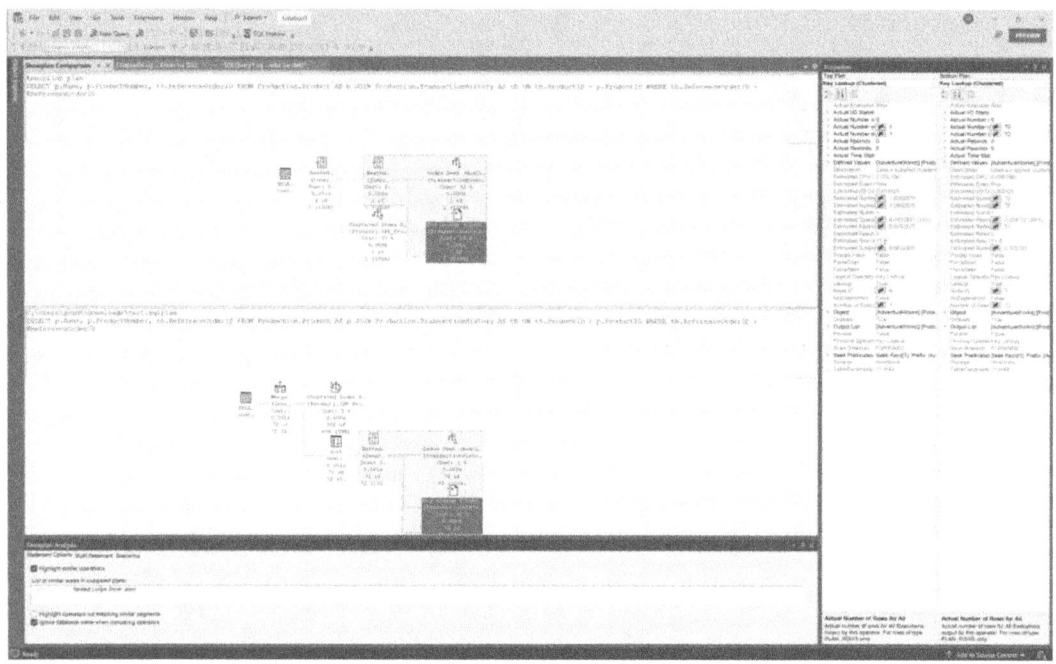

Figure 4-33. *Comparing two execution plans within SSMS*

That's hard to see, so let's break down the view into the three areas of functionality within the Showplan Comparison window.

First, in the upper left, you have the two plans you're comparing. In my case, I'm comparing the execution plan from two different executions of a stored procedure we'll be using later in the book. Similarities between the plans are highlighted as you can see in Figure 4-34.

118

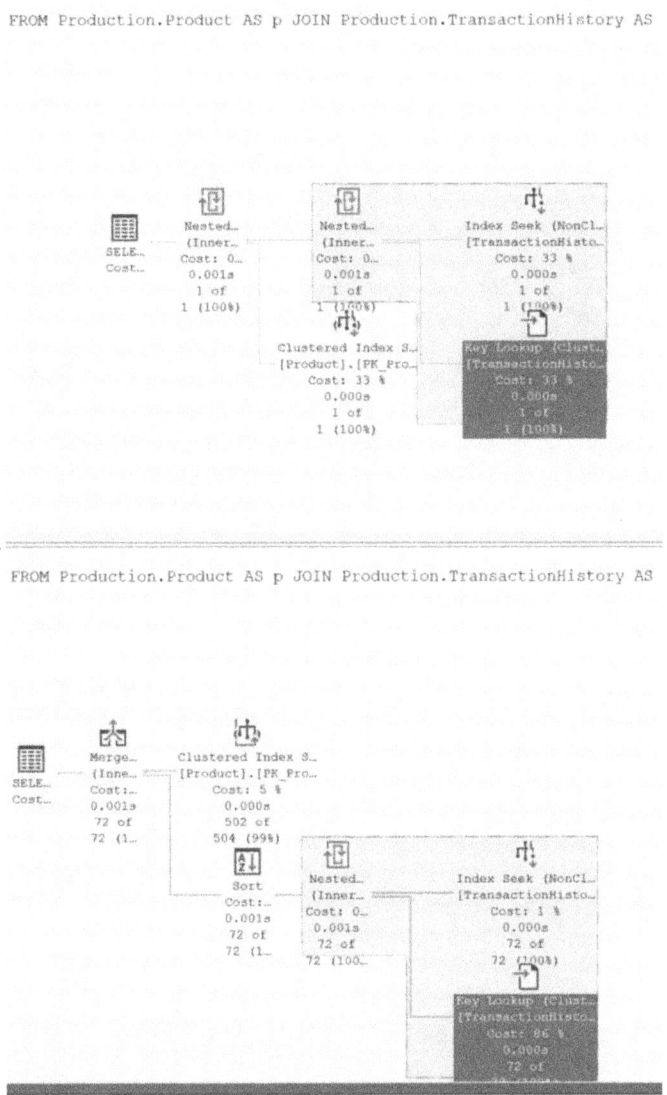

Figure 4-34. *Compared plans showing common characteristics*

In the example, the similarities are where both plans have a Nested Loops join, an Index Seek, and a Key Lookup. We'll cover these types of patterns in later chapters. For now, you can see that the difference is the top plan, the plan I'm comparing, has another Nested Loops join, whereas the bottom plan, the plan from the file, has a Merge Join. There are other differences as well. Plans in the Showplan Comparison window otherwise behave the same as plans anywhere else within SSMS.

Next, you get the ability to compare the properties of each operator on the right side of the screen, as shown in Figure 4-35.

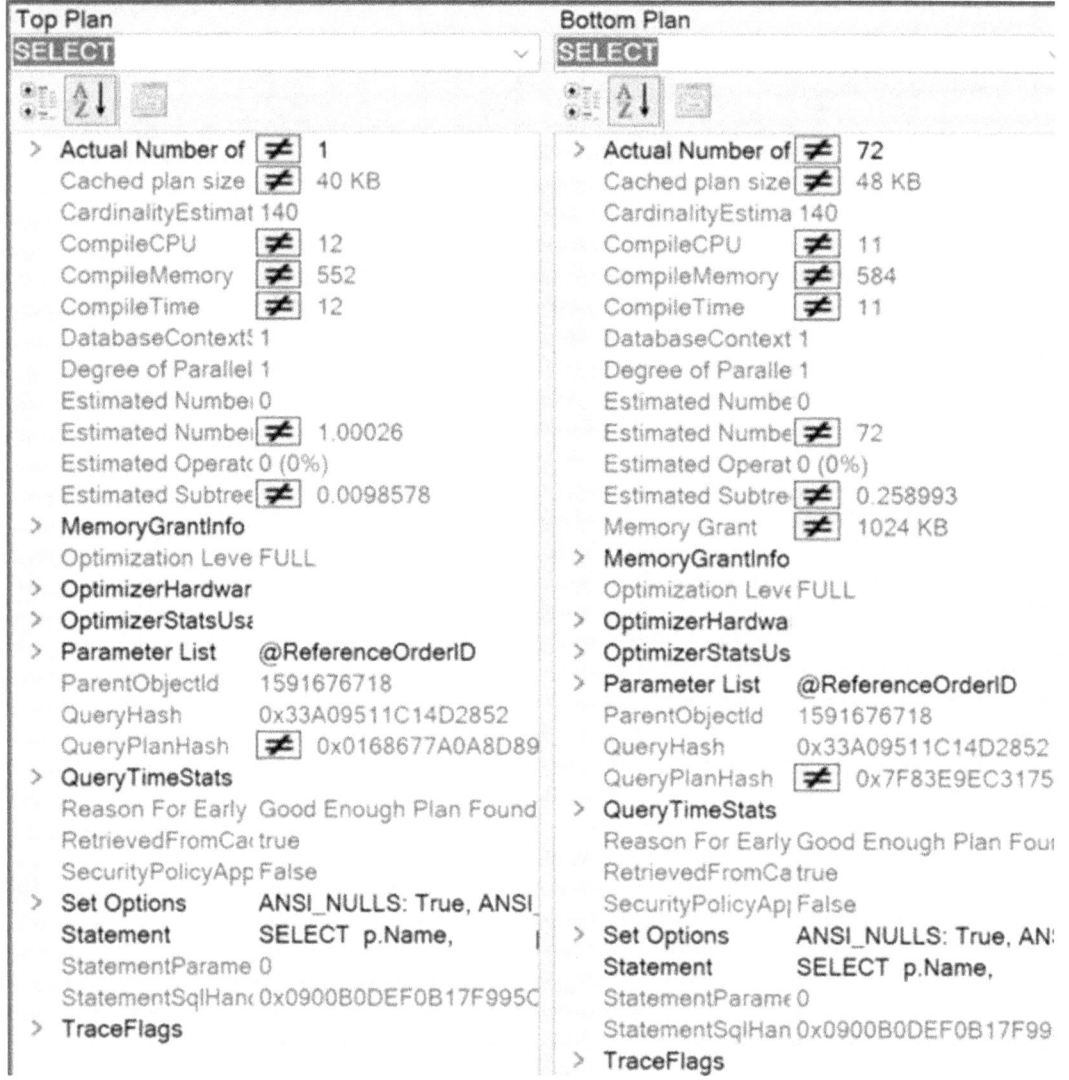

Figure 4-35. Comparing the values of properties between two plans

You can see the property values that match and those that don't match. If a given operator exists in a plan, but not the other, you won't see a comparison here.

Finally, at the bottom of the screen, on the first tab, you have some options you can set to control the behavior of the plan comparison as shown in Figure 4-36.

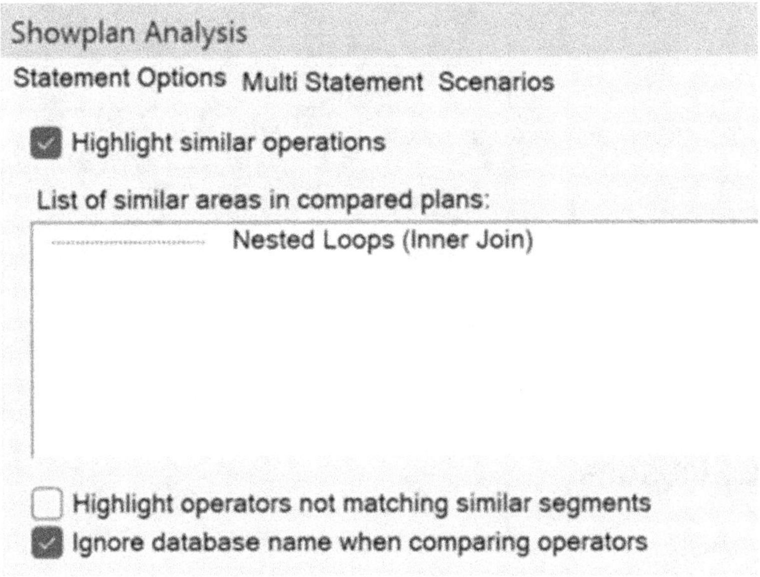

CHAPTER 4   ANALYZING QUERY BEHAVIOR USING EXECUTION PLANS

Figure 4-36. *Options for comparing execution plans*

You enable or disable the highlight of similar parts of the plan. You can also choose to highlight the parts of the plan that do not match. Finally, you can choose to ignore the database name when making comparisons, which is very handy when testing disparate systems.

The second tab is for when you have multiple statements. You can pick and choose which statement to compare. In this case, both are single-statement plans, so there's nothing to change as you see in Figure 4-37.

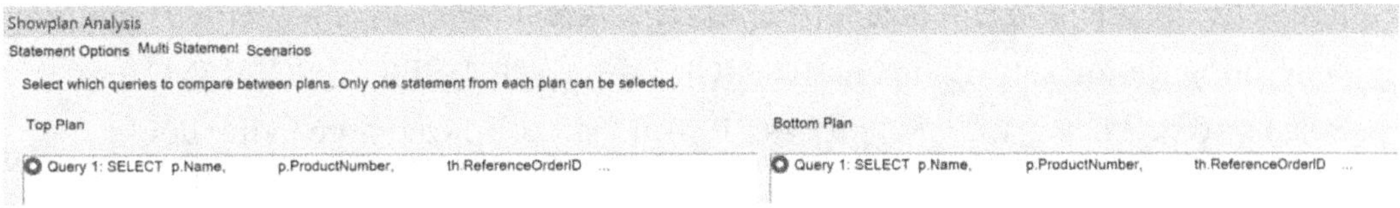

Figure 4-37. *Multi-statement selection in a plan comparison*

The final tab is a guidance tool provided by Microsoft called Showplan Analysis. It currently only supports a single scenario, Inaccurate Cardinality Estimation when looking at a single plan or Different Estimated Rows when comparing two plans. While this is helpful, since only one scenario is supported, the utility is somewhat limited. You can see the highlighted differences between our two plans in Figure 4-38.

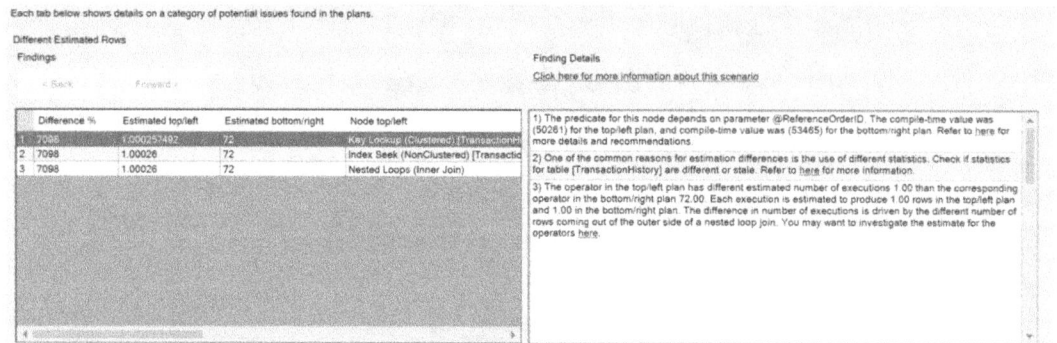

Figure 4-38. Three operators with different estimated rows

Live Query Statistics

One additional tool is available within SSMS, Live Query Statistics. This functionality enables you to see the rows moving through an execution plan in real time. It's only really useful for queries that run a very long time. Also, in order to use it, you have to meet some additional criteria.

In SQL Server 2014, you must be running an Extended Events session using the query_thread_profile event. That will enable the live plan.

With SQL Server 2016 and 2017, you can use the Extended Events session as well. However, there's a trace flag, 7412, that you can set for the server. This enables what is called lightweight profiling. You can also use the query hint, QUERY_PLAN_PROFILE, to enable it at the query level.

For SQL Server 2019 and greater, as well as Azure SQL Database, lightweight profiling is enabled by default. You can disable it at the database level using one of the Database Scoped Configuration settings to change LIGHTWEIGHT_QUERY_PROFILING = OFF.

Because this is a live, moving, process, it won't show up well here in the book. However, I'll walk through a query and show how you can view it yourself. Listing 4-8 shows a query that runs for approximately 10–15 seconds on a laptop.

Listing 4-8. A long-running query

```
SELECT o.*,
       o2.*
FROM sys.objects AS o,
     sys.objects AS o2;
```

CHAPTER 4 ANALYZING QUERY BEHAVIOR USING EXECUTION PLANS

To see the live execution plan, you can click the switch in the center in Figure 4-39.

Figure 4-39. *Include Live Query Statistics*

This is a toggle like the "Actual Execution" toggle right next to it. You turn it on and then execute the query. The output of query execution is shown here in Figure 4-40.

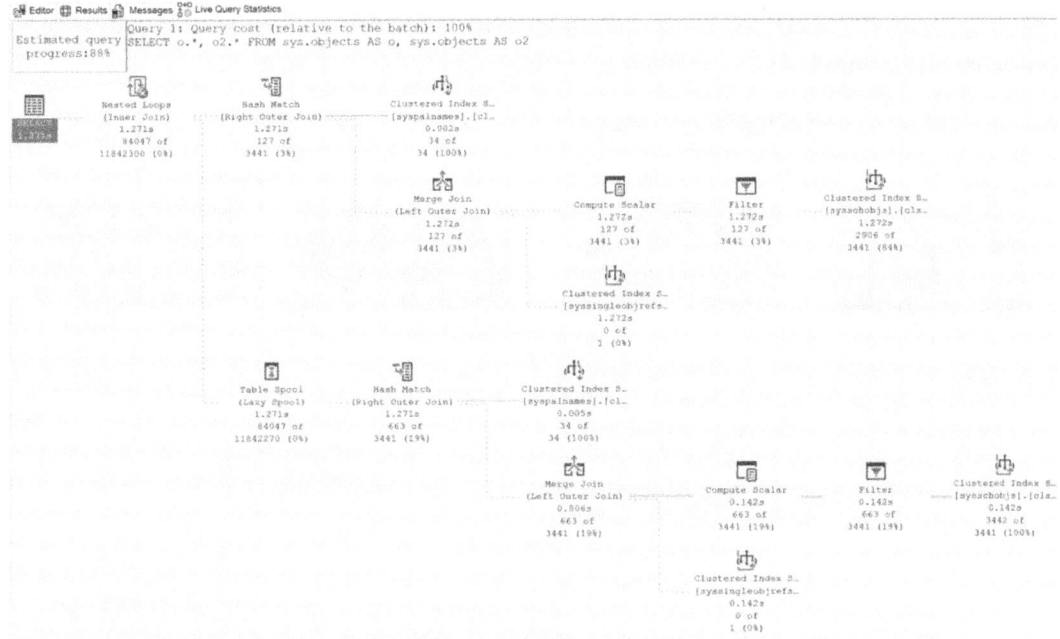

Figure 4-40. *A live execution plan in action*

Notice how some of the pipes are solid and some are dashed lines. The solid pipes represent completed activity. The dashed lines actually move and show data movement in action. The row counts below the operators get updated in real time, showing which ones are complete and the completion status of those still active. At the top left is even a percentage complete readout. I know this is small, but it's at 88% at the moment I took the readings.

CHAPTER 4   ANALYZING QUERY BEHAVIOR USING EXECUTION PLANS

Other than being live, this is an execution plan like any other; you can get tooltips and properties and see all the expected detail there as outlined in the rest of this chapter.

All of this is driven by a DMV, sys.dm_exec_query_profiles. You can retrieve information from that DMV as queries are running, and you'll see the active row counts, same as before.

Finally, you can also simply look at live execution plans of long-running queries without having to execute them yourselves. Right-clicking a server in the Object Explorer window, you'll get a menu choice for "Activity Monitor." Selecting that will open a new window. In that window, you'll see a series of overviews of performance as well as Processes, Resource Waits, Data File I/O, Recent Expensive Queries, and Active Expensive Queries. Open either Processes or Active Expensive Queries, and you'll see a query list like Figure 4-41.

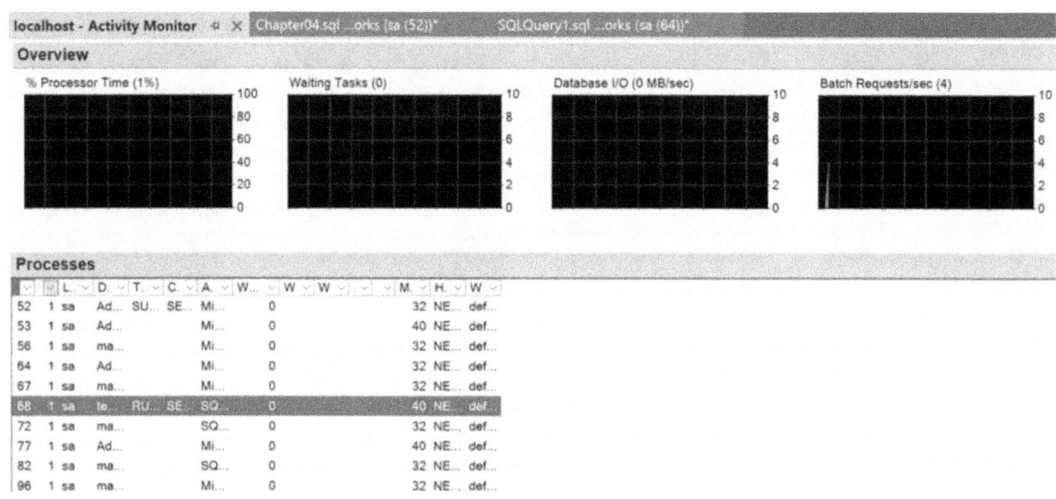

Figure 4-41. *The Activity Monitor window in SSMS*

Right-clicking a query that is currently in a state of RUNNING, you'll get a context menu like Figure 4-42.

- Details
- Show Live Execution Plan
- Kill Process
- Trace Process in SQL Server Profiler

Figure 4-42. *Context menu that lets you select Show Live Execution Plan*

Clicking "Show Live Execution Plan" will also open up the window shown in Figure 4-40 with the plan for the running query.

This is a somewhat expensive process and can place noticeable load on the servers, so only use it when you need to. Live execution plans are very useful for extreme long-running queries like data loads to get a sense of their completion. Always remember that the row counts are based on estimates, so if there's disparity between the estimated and actual rows, the percentage complete of any given operator for the entire query won't be accurate.

Third Party

We're not going to document how to use these tools. I'm merely going to point out how these tools can help you understand and read execution plans.

SolarWinds Plan Explorer

Plan Explorer is an incredibly powerful tool. Not only will it display your execution plans in a variety of different formats, but a whole slew of analysis tools are available to help you better read and understand the execution plan. Some of the analysis can even point you right to where the performance problem exists as illustrated by the execution plan. One big option is the ability to make a plan anonymous, removing all index names, column names, and values in the query. This makes it easier to share plans with others.

While Plan Explorer integrates with SSMS, you can't actually replace your SSMS plan behavior with it. This tool hasn't received as many updates as in the past, but it still has value.

Plan Explorer is free to download and available at http://solarwinds.com.

Supratimas

Supratimas is a web-based plan analysis tool. It's not as extensive as Plan Explorer. However, it does give you some help in looking at execution plans. You paste your XML into its web page, and you can then see the highest cost operations, ordered. You also get a list of operators that are causing I/O, again ordered from highest to lowest. Clicking the list takes you to the operator in question. This can absolutely make it easier to understand what's happening within your plans.

Supratimas is available at http://supratimas.com.

Paste The Plan

Paste The Plan is the simplest of the third-party tools. This is just a way to share execution plans easily with others. You paste the XML of your plan into the web page, similar to Supratimas. You can then get a URL to share with others so that they can see your plan in the graphical explorer provided or download it to their machines.

The graphical plan is limited and doesn't show all properties. Also, you may want to use Plan Explorer to anonymize your plan prior to posting it on a completely public website.

Paste The Plan is available from Brent Ozar at `https://brentozar.com/pastetheplan`.

AI

It is entirely possible to take the XML of an execution plan and paste it into one of the Large Language Models (LLMs). Since reading an execution plan is all about pattern recognition, the AI can do basic interpretation. However, as the complexity of the plan goes up, the likelihood of hallucination, made-up answers, becomes higher. Using these tools can act as a bit of a shortcut to speed up your understanding of the behavior of a given query through its execution plan. You must not assume that everything the LLM tells you is accurate. Your watch words must be "Trust but verify." Also, remember, don't put private information into public AIs.

Summary

In this chapter, you learned what execution plans are and the beginnings of how to read them. The differences between execution plans and execution plans with runtime metrics were established. You also went through a set of signposts that help in understanding execution plans. We finished with some tools that can make working with execution plans easier.

In the next chapter, we're going to be discussing statistics and how they're used to understand the distribution of data, cardinality, and the row counts that drive the decisions of the query optimizer.

CHAPTER 5

Statistics, Data Distribution, and Cardinality

In Chapter 2, we talked about the query optimization process and how it uses the indexes, constraints, and other objects within your database in order to figure out how best to satisfy the query. All those objects in combination are how the optimizer arrives at its estimated values. However, one of the single biggest driving factors in what leads the optimizer to choose one method of query behavior over another is row counts. Since SQL Server can't realistically count all the rows ahead of time, it maintains information about the distribution of data within a column. That information is called statistics. Statistics are used to establish estimates on row counts for the optimizer so that it can make better choices.

In this chapter, we'll discuss the importance of statistics in query optimization. Specifically, I will cover the following topics:

- Statistics in query optimization
- The behavior of statistics on columns with indexes
- Statistics on nonindexed columns when used in join and filter criteria
- Analysis of single-column and multicolumn statistics, including the computation of selectivity of a column for indexing
- Statistics maintenance
- Effective evaluation of statistics used in query execution

Statistics in the Query Optimization Process

As you know from Chapter 2, the optimizer uses a cost-based optimization process. The optimizer picks the appropriate data access and join mechanisms by determining the selectivity of the data, meaning how unique is it. Columns in the SELECT clause don't need statistics. It's the columns used in the filtering mechanisms—WHERE, HAVING, and JOIN—that have to have statistics. When an index is created (we'll be discussing indexes in detail starting in Chapter 9), statistics are automatically created based on the data contained within the column or columns that define the index key. Statistics will also be automatically created, by default, on columns that are not a part of an index if those columns are used in filtering criteria.

Having the statistics about the data and the distribution of the data in the columns referenced in predicates is a major driving factor in how the optimizer determines the best strategies to satisfy your query. The statistics allow the optimizer to make a fast calculation as to how many rows are likely to be returned by a given value within a column. With the row counts available, the optimizer can make better choices to find the more efficient ways to retrieve and process your data. In general, the default settings for your system and database will provide adequate statistics so that the optimizer can do its job efficiently. Also, the default statistics maintenance will usually give the optimizer the most up-to-date values within the statistics. However, you may have to determine (through the information in the "Analyzing Statistics" section) if your statistics are being adequately created and maintained. In many cases, you may find that you need to manually take control of the creation and/or maintenance of statistics.

Statistics on Rowstore Indexed Columns

The degree to which a given index can help your queries run faster is largely driven by the statistics on the column, or columns, that define the key of the index. The optimizer uses the statistics from the index key columns to make row count estimates, which drive many of the other decisions. SQL Server has two ways of storing indexes: rowstore and columnstore (we'll be covering them both in Chapter 9). For rowstore indexes, statistics are created automatically along with the index. This behavior cannot be modified. You can add statistics to a columnstore index if you choose. Nonclustered indexes added to columnstore indexes do have statistics because they are still rowstore indexes.

Changes in data can affect index choice. If a table has only one row for a certain column value, then using the index could be a great choice. If the data changes over time and a large number of rows now match that value, it could be that the index becomes less useful. This is why you need to ensure that you have up-to-date statistics.

By default, SQL Server will update statistics on your indexes as the indexed column's data changes over time. You can disable this behavior if you choose. There is a setting called Auto Update Statistics that can be changed to control this behavior.

SQL Server uses two methods for updating statistics. The default method, for SQL Server 2016 and greater, works well for most data sets. The algorithm that drives the automatic update for statistics depends on if we're talking about a permanent table or a temporary table. The default behavior is shown in Table 5-1.

Table 5-1. Default automatic statistics maintenance

Table Type	Number of Rows in the Table	Update Threshold
Temporary	Less than 6	6 changes
Temporary	Between 6 and 500	500 changes
Permanent	Less than 500	500 changes
Both	Greater than 500	MIN(500+(0.2 * n), SQRT(1,000 * n))

Changes here could be INSERT, UPDATE, or DELETE. The total value is in combination, so, for example, in a permanent table with less than 500 rows, 200 rows inserted, 200 rows deleted, and 100 rows modified would trigger automated statistics update. In the calculation, "n" represents the number of rows in the table. You're basically getting the MIN, or minimum, of the two calculations. Let's assume a larger table with five million rows. The first calculation results in a value of 1,000,500. The second calculation results in a value of 70,710. This would then mean that data modifications to only 70,710 rows will result in a statistics update.

The older method, which can be enabled by changing the database compatibility mode, didn't work well for larger data sets. That behavior is outlined in Table 5-2.

Table 5-2. Old statistics maintenance thresholds

Table Type	Number of Rows in the Table	Update Threshold
Temporary	Less than 6	6 changes
Temporary	Between 6 and 500	500 changes
Permanent	Less than 500	500 changes
Both	Greater than 500	500 + (.2 * n)

With the older method, more than 1,000,500 rows would have to be inserted, updated, or deleted before the statistics would update automatically. As you can see, that would mean a lot fewer statistics updates and, therefore, more out-of-date statistics.

You can also make the choice to update statistics asynchronously. Normally, when statistics need to be updated, a query stops and waits until that update is complete. However, with asynchronous statistics updates, the query will complete, the statistics will update, and then any other queries using those statistics will get the updated values.

You can disable the automatic statistics maintenance using the ALTER DATABASE command. I strongly recommend that you keep this enabled on your systems. Exceedingly few systems suffer from the automatic statistics maintenance, and most systems benefit from it. You can decide to turn on the asynchronous statistics update if you're seeing timeouts and waits caused by the statistics update.

Note I'll explain ALTER DATABASE later in the chapter.

Benefits of Updated Statistics

Let's explore how statistics updates benefit query performance. In order to directly control the data in the tables, instead of using AdventureWorks tables for this example, Listing 5-1 will create a table for the test.

Listing 5-1. Creating a table and index

```
DROP TABLE IF EXISTS dbo.Test1;
GO
CREATE TABLE dbo.Test1
```

```
(
    C1 INT,
    C2 INT IDENTITY
);
SELECT TOP 1500
       IDENTITY(INT, 1, 1) AS n
INTO #Nums
FROM master.dbo.syscolumns AS sC1,
     master.dbo.syscolumns AS sC2;
INSERT INTO dbo.Test1
(
    C1
)
SELECT n
FROM #Nums;
DROP TABLE #Nums;
CREATE NONCLUSTERED INDEX i1 ON dbo.Test1 (C1);
```

We can now run a query against that table that will return one row and use the index as shown in Listing 5-2.

Listing 5-2. Retrieving a single row from the table

```
SELECT t.C1,
       t.C2
FROM dbo.Test1 AS t
WHERE t.C1 = 2;
```

We can see the execution plan for the query in Figure 5-1.

CHAPTER 5   STATISTICS, DATA DISTRIBUTION, AND CARDINALITY

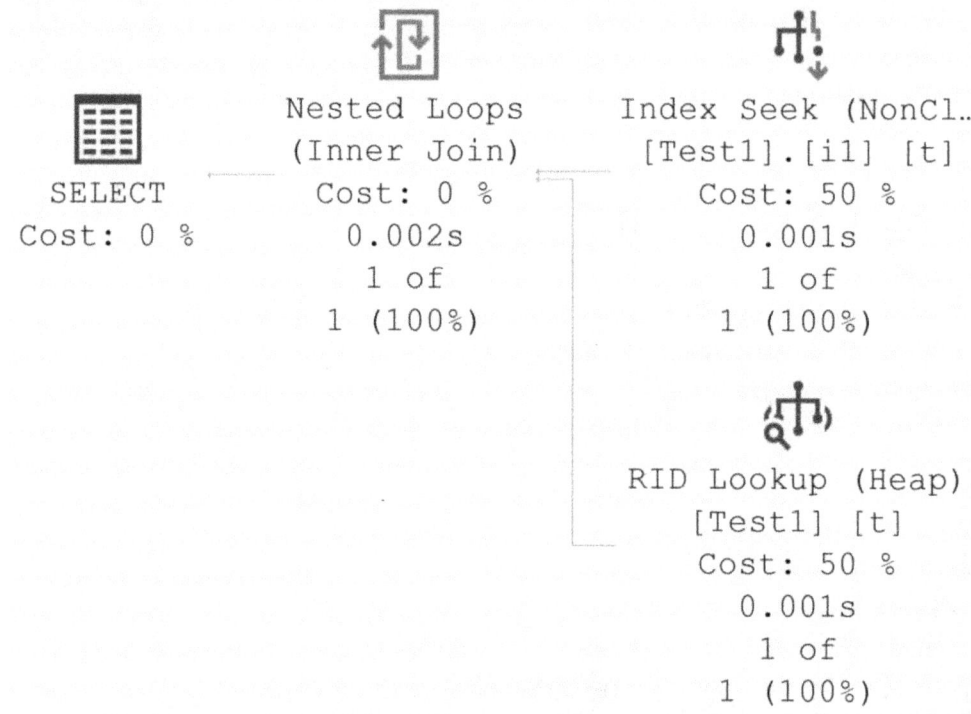

Figure 5-1. *An Index Seek is used to retrieve data*

We're going to use an Extended Events session to watch the behavior of the statistics update processes, as well as capture query performance. Listing 5-3 shows how to set up such a session, including filtering to the database I'm working in.

Listing 5-3. Creating and starting an Extended Events session

```
CREATE EVENT SESSION [Statistics]
ON SERVER
    ADD EVENT sqlserver.auto_stats
    (ACTION
     (
         sqlserver.sql_text
     )
     WHERE (sqlserver.database_name = N'AdventureWorks')
    ),
    ADD EVENT sqlserver.sql_batch_completed
    (WHERE (sqlserver.database_name = N'AdventureWorks'));
```

CHAPTER 5 STATISTICS, DATA DISTRIBUTION, AND CARDINALITY

```
GO
ALTER EVENT SESSION [Statistics] ON SERVER STATE = START;
```

We're going to add a row to the table (Listing 5-4).

Listing 5-4. Adding a single row to the Test1 table

```
INSERT INTO dbo.Test1
(
    C1
)
VALUES
(2 );
```

If we run the SELECT query from Listing 5-2 again, the execution plan is still the same as what we see in Figure 5-1. Figure 5-2 shows the output of the Extended Events session (I have here, and throughout the book, selected columns for display in Extended Events).

Figure 5-2. *Extended Events output showing no statistics updates*

We don't see any updates from the statistics because adding a single row won't cross the threshold for statistics updates. Even if it did, just one more row also wouldn't result in a new execution plan. To understand the effect of data modification on statistics, we'll add 1,500 rows to the table (Listing 5-5).

Listing 5-5. Adding 1,500 rows

```
SELECT TOP 1500
        IDENTITY(INT, 1, 1) AS n
INTO #Nums
FROM master.dbo.syscolumns AS sc1,
     master.dbo.syscolumns AS sC2;
INSERT INTO dbo.Test1
(
```

CHAPTER 5   STATISTICS, DATA DISTRIBUTION, AND CARDINALITY

```
    C1
)
SELECT 2
FROM #Nums;
DROP TABLE #Nums;
```

Now when we execute the SELECT query from Listing 5-2, we're going to be retrieving a very large data set, 1,502 rows out of only 30,001. Since a large result set is being requested, scanning the table directly will be preferable to going to the nonclustered index. This is especially true since the Nested Loops join will require us to access that index 1,501 times. You can see the execution plan resulting from the data changes in Figure 5-3.

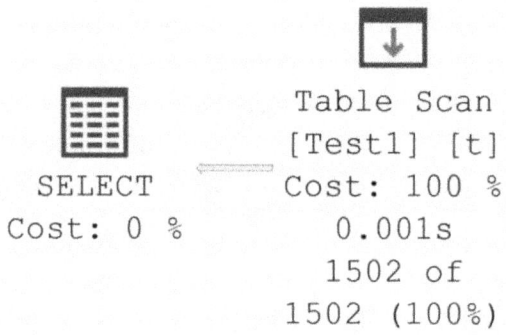

Figure 5-3. Execution plan showing a table scan

Figure 5-4 shows the resulting output from the Extended Events session.

name	timestamp	batch_text	duration	row_count	statistics_list	status
auto_stats	2025-05-23 2...	NULL	0	NULL	Loading and updating: dbo.Test1.i1	Loading and updating stats
auto_stats	2025-05-23 2...	NULL	24590	NULL	Updated: dbo.Test1.i1	Other
sql_batch_completed	2025-05-23 2...	SELECT t.C1, t.C2 FROM dbo.T...	184956	1503	NULL	NULL

Figure 5-4. Session output including the auto_stats event

Since we updated so many rows, we exceeded the threshold, so the statistics were updated. I captured the column showing the statistics_list and status from the auto_stats event. You can see that auto_stats was called twice: once to load and update the dbo.Test.i1 statistics and the second time showing that those statistics were successfully updated.

Then, the query ran. The statistics were updated, which resulted in a change to the execution plan. It now has a single table scan instead of 1,501 seek operations. This also illustrates why you want to test carefully if asynchronous statistics updates are desirable. This query could have run with the old execution plan.

Drawbacks of Outdated Statistics

In the previous section, the statistics within SQL Server were automatically updated. The updated statistics are then used to create a new, better, execution plan. That illustrates the advantages of up-to-date statistics. Statistics can become outdated. Then, the optimizer may make poor choices that don't accurately reflect the data within the system, which will lead to bad performance.

I'm now going to demonstrate what happens when statistics are out of date. To do this, follow these steps:

1. Run Listing 5-1 again to recreate the test table with 1,500 rows and the nonclustered index.

2. Disable automatic statistics updates using Listing 5-6.

Listing 5-6. Disabling automatic update of statistics

```
ALTER DATABASE AdventureWorks SET AUTO_UPDATE_STATISTICS OFF;
```

3. Add 1,500 rows to the table using Listing 5-5.

4. Run the query from Listing 5-2.

With that setup we'll see the execution plan plus runtime metrics shown in Figure 5-5.

CHAPTER 5 STATISTICS, DATA DISTRIBUTION, AND CARDINALITY

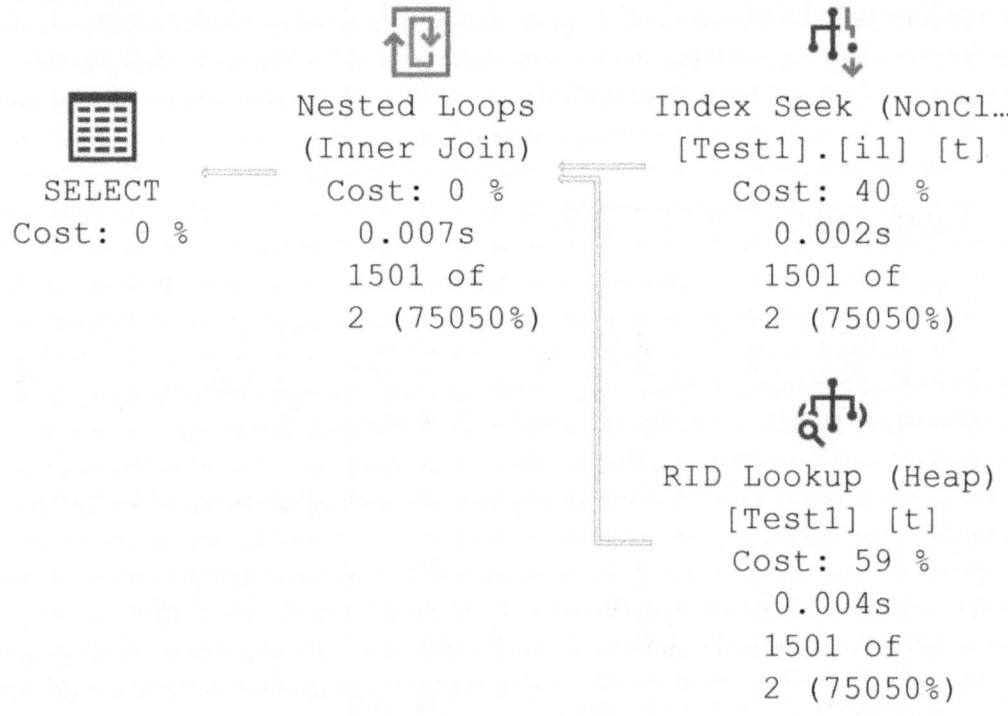

Figure 5-5. Inaccurate execution plan due to out-of-date statistics

Because the automatic statistics maintenance has been disabled, the optimizer chose an execution plan based on bad estimates of row counts. You readily see that in the execution plan in Figure 5-5, the estimated number of rows is 2 and the actual is 1,501, a 75,050% variance.

Let's also look at the differences in the performance metrics of the query. Table 5-3 shows the average duration and the reads of the query with up-to-date statistics and out-of-date statistics.

Table 5-3. Performance measurements of different statistics maintenance

Statistics Update Status	Execution Plan	Avg. Duration (ms)	Number of Reads
Up to date	Figure 5-3	44.2	11
Out of date	Figure 5-5	63.6	1,510

The number of logical reads and the duration are significantly higher with out-of-date statistics. That performance degradation and the difference in the number of reads are despite the fact that we are running the exact same query with the exact same result sets. The differences in how the optimizer satisfies a query, even with everything else being identical, result in serious performance changes. The benefits of keeping statistics up to date usually far outweigh the cost of performing the updates.

Before we finish this section, turn AUTO_UPDATE_STATISTICS back on (Listing 5-7).

Listing 5-7. Enabling automatic statistics update

```
ALTER DATABASE AdventureWorks SET AUTO_UPDATE_STATISTICS ON;
```

Statistics on Nonindexed Columns

It's very common to see columns that are not a part of the index key being used in filtering and join criteria. When this happens, the optimizer still needs to understand the cardinality and data distribution of the column, just like one that has an index on it, in order to make better choices for the execution of the query.

While a column not taking part in an index means that no index exists to help retrieve the data, the optimizer can still use the statistics to create a better plan. This is why, by default, SQL Server will automatically create indexes on columns used for filtering. One scenario where you may consider disabling the automatic creation of statistics is where you are executing a series of ad hoc T-SQL queries that will never be executed again. It's possible that creating statistics on columns in this scenario could cost more than it benefits you. However, even here, testing to validate how performance is positively or negatively impacted is necessary. For most systems, you should keep the automatic creation of statistics enabled unless you have very clear evidence that the creation of those statistics is actively causing your system pain.

Benefits of Statistics on a Nonindexed Column

To see the benefits of statistics on a column that is not a part of an index, Listing 5-8 will create two test tables with wildly varying data distributions. Both tables contain 10,001 rows. Table *Test1* contains only one row for the column *Test1_C2* equal to 1 with the remaining 10,000 rows showing that value as 2. Table *Test2* is exactly the opposite data distribution (Listing 5-8).

CHAPTER 5 STATISTICS, DATA DISTRIBUTION, AND CARDINALITY

Listing 5-8. Two test tables with varying data distributions

```
DROP TABLE IF EXISTS dbo.Test1;
GO
CREATE TABLE dbo.Test1
(
    Test1_C1 INT IDENTITY,
    Test1_C2 INT
);
INSERT INTO dbo.Test1
(
    Test1_C2
)
VALUES
(1  );
SELECT TOP 10000
        IDENTITY(INT, 1, 1) AS n
INTO #Nums
FROM master.dbo.syscolumns AS sc1,
     master.dbo.syscolumns AS sC2;
INSERT INTO dbo.Test1
(
    Test1_C2
)
SELECT 2
FROM #Nums;
GO
CREATE CLUSTERED INDEX i1 ON dbo.Test1 (Test1_C1);
--Create second table with 10001 rows, -- but opposite data distribution
IF
(
    SELECT OBJECT_ID('dbo.Test2')
) IS NOT NULL
    DROP TABLE dbo.Test2;
```

```
GO
CREATE TABLE dbo.Test2
(
    Test2_C1 INT IDENTITY,
    Test2_C2 INT
);
INSERT INTO dbo.Test2
(
    Test2_C2
)
VALUES
(2 );
INSERT INTO dbo.Test2
(
    Test2_C2
)
SELECT 1
FROM #Nums;
DROP TABLE #Nums;
GO
CREATE CLUSTERED INDEX il ON dbo.Test2 (Test2_C1);
```

We need to verify that SQL Server is still running with the default statistics creation behavior. We can do that using the DATABASEPROPERTYEX function shown in Listing 5-9.

Listing 5-9. Checking database properties using DATABASEPROPERTYEX

```
SELECT DATABASEPROPERTYEX('AdventureWorks', 'IsAutoCreateStatistics');
```

The resulting value should be 1. If it's 0, you've disabled the automatic creation of statistics at some point and need to reenable it (Listing 5-10).

Listing 5-10. Enabling the automatic creation of statistics

```
ALTER DATABASE AdventureWorks SET AUTO_CREATE_STATISTICS ON;
```

CHAPTER 5   STATISTICS, DATA DISTRIBUTION, AND CARDINALITY

With all that set, we can now test the behavior of statistics on columns that are not a part of an index key. Listing 5-11 shows a SELECT statement that joins our two tables together. A large set of data from Test1 will be returned and a small set of data from Test2 because of the data distribution we have created. Worth noting, the columns used in the join and filter operations have no index on either table.

Listing 5-11. Joining the two test tables

```
SELECT t1.Test1_C2,
       t2.Test2_C2
FROM dbo.Test1 AS t1
   JOIN dbo.Test2 AS t2
       ON t1.Test1_C2 = t2.Test2_C2
WHERE t1.Test1_C2 = 2;
```

Figure 5-6 shows the execution plan plus runtime metrics for Listing 5-11.

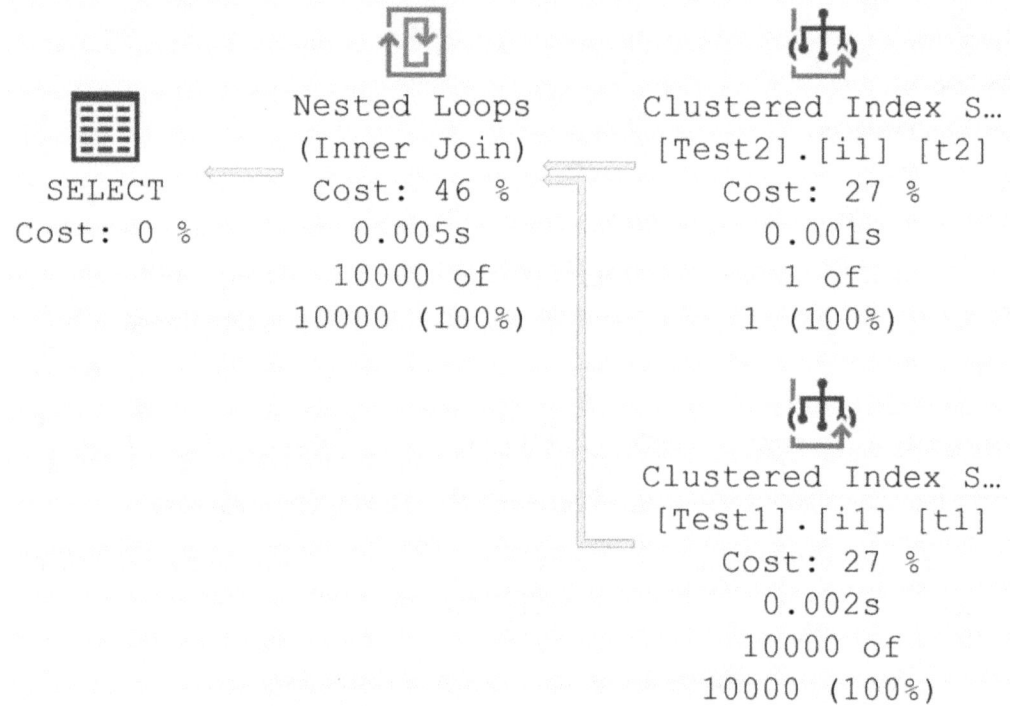

Figure 5-6. *Execution plan on two tables without indexes*

CHAPTER 5 STATISTICS, DATA DISTRIBUTION, AND CARDINALITY

You can see that the estimated and actual rows match what we expect based on the data we created in the tables. A single row returned from Test2 and 10,000 from Test1.

Our Extended Events session output shows four auto_stats events, creating the statistics on the columns used in the JOIN and WHERE clauses of the query from Listing 5-11. Figure 5-7 shows the output.

name	timestamp	batch_text	duration	row_count	statistics_list	status
auto_stats	2025-05-23 2...	NULL	11820	NULL	Created: Test1_C2	Other
auto_stats	2025-05-23 2...	NULL	0	NULL	Loading without updating: dbo.Test...	Loading stats without updat...
auto_stats	2025-05-23 2...	NULL	13421	NULL	Created: Test2_C2	Other
auto_stats	2025-05-23 2...	NULL	0	NULL	Loading without updating: dbo.Test...	Loading stats without updat...
sql_batch_completed	2025-05-23 2...	SELECT t1.Test1_C2, t2.Test2_...	244828	10002	NULL	NULL

Figure 5-7. *Extended Events session showing auto_stats events*

You can see in the *statistics_list* property how the statistics are created on a column and then those statistics loaded for use by the optimizer. To see the statistics created, we run a query against the *sys.stats* table from Listing 5-12.

Listing 5-12. Querying the sys.stats table to see table statistics

```
SELECT s.name,
       s.auto_created,
       s.user_created
FROM sys.stats AS s
WHERE object_id = OBJECT_ID('Test1');
```

You can see the results for the query in Figure 5-8.

name	auto_created	user_created
i1	0	0
_WA_Sys_00000002_76B698BF	1	0

Figure 5-8. *Automatic statistics created for table Test1*

The auto_created column lets you know that statistics were automatically created with a value of 1. However, you can also see the standard naming convention with "_WA_Sys*" for all automatically created statistics. Noteworthy mentioning here is that the statistics for the index, i1, were automatically created along with the index, but they don't actually count as being auto_created.

CHAPTER 5 STATISTICS, DATA DISTRIBUTION, AND CARDINALITY

The naming convention for automatically created statistics is as follows:

- "_WA": Signifying the state of Washington where Microsoft is headquartered. Yes, seriously
- "_Sys": Letting us know this is system generated
- "_00000002": The ordinal position of the column in the table on which statistics are being created
- "76B698BF": A unique value to identify the statistic created and differentiate it from other automatically created statistics

We can see the optimizer making different choices based on the statistics if we change the query from Listing 5-11 into the query in Listing 5-13 where we filter on the value 1 instead of 2.

Listing 5-13. Filtering on different criteria

```
SELECT t1.Test1_C2,
       t2.Test2_C2
FROM dbo.Test1 AS t1
    JOIN dbo.Test2 AS t2
        ON t1.Test1_C2 = t2.Test2_C2
WHERE t1.Test1_C2 = 1;
```

The resulting execution plan is just a little bit different as you can see in Figure 5-9. However, the difference might not be immediately apparent.

CHAPTER 5 STATISTICS, DATA DISTRIBUTION, AND CARDINALITY

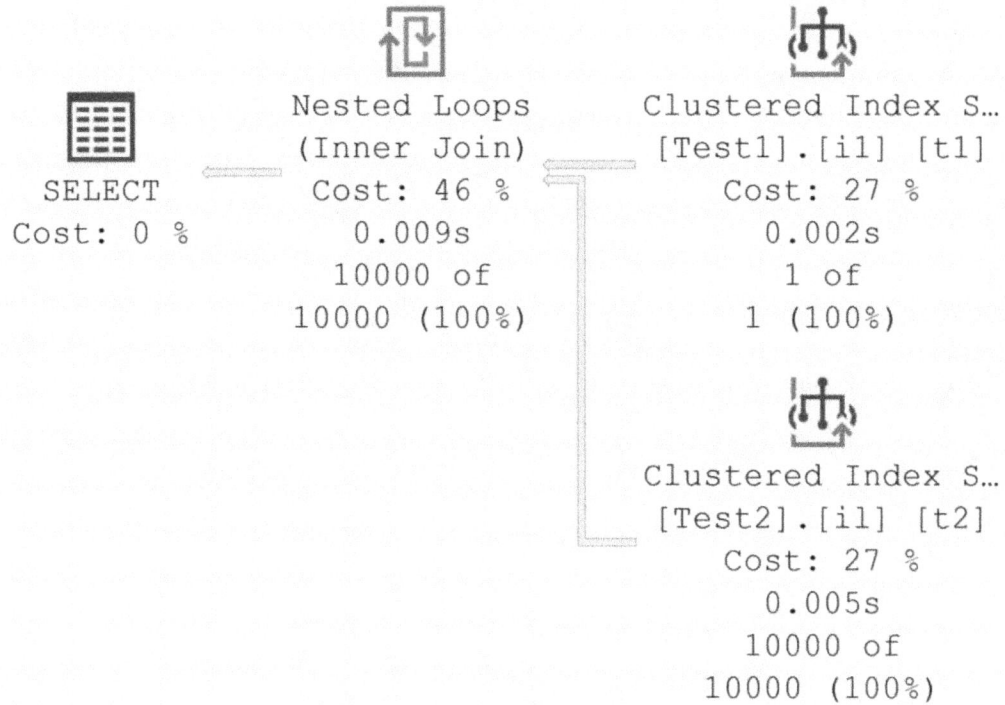

Figure 5-9. *Execution plan changes as the data returned changes*

When I executed the query, there were no auto_stats events since the statistics are already in place. What we do see is that by changing the query, the execution plan has changed. In Figure 5-6, Test2 was the inner table of the Nested Loops join operation. In Figure 5-9, we've swapped to Test1 being the inner table. The optimizer can justify this change based on the difference in the data as reflected in the statistics that were automatically created on the columns in question. The optimizer knows that with the change to the filter criteria in the WHERE clause of Listing 5-13, only a single row is going to be returned from table Test1.

Obviously, if we were concerned with improving performance, we'd likely need to add indexes to the columns in question. However, you can see that the optimizer can use statistics on nonindexed columns that will change plan behaviors.

CHAPTER 5 STATISTICS, DATA DISTRIBUTION, AND CARDINALITY

Comparing Performance with Missing Statistics

Just as we saw in the section earlier in the chapter, if the statistics are missing from columns, the optimizer will make less optimal choices. Run Listing 5-8 to recreate our tables without any automatically created statistics. Alternatively, you can identify the names of the automatic statistics and use the DROP STATISTICS command. Either way, we need to disable the automatic creation of statistics using Listing 5-14.

Listing 5-14. Disabling the automatic creation of statistics

```
ALTER DATABASE AdventureWorks SET AUTO_CREATE_STATISTICS OFF;
```

The SELECT query in Listing 5-11 will result in the execution plan you see in Figure 5-10.

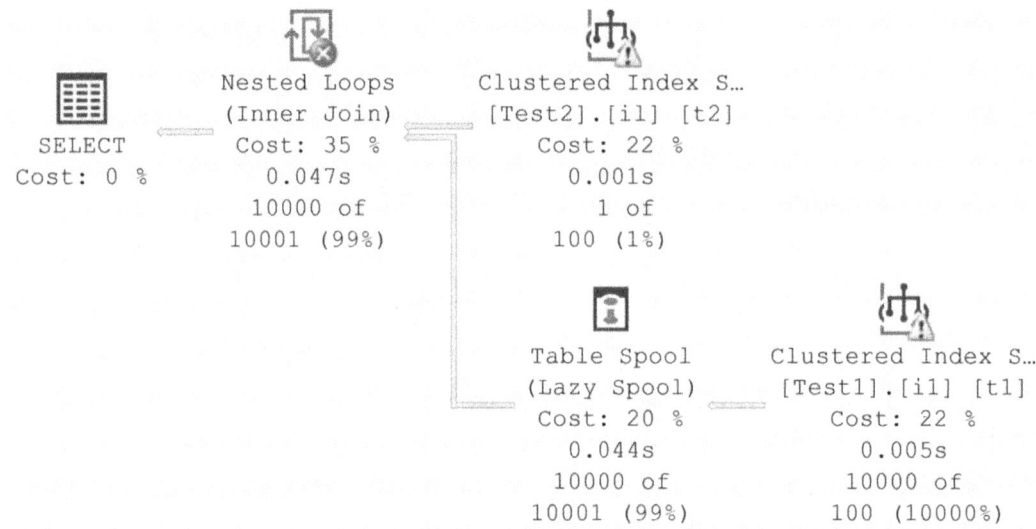

Figure 5-10. *Execution plan with a number of warnings*

Without statistics, the query optimizer made some very different choices in how it satisfied the query. You can immediately see the warnings on the Clustered Index Scan operations. Here is one of the warnings:

Columns With No Statistics: [AdventureWorks].[dbo].[Test2].Test2_C2

CHAPTER 5   STATISTICS, DATA DISTRIBUTION, AND CARDINALITY

This shouldn't be a surprise since we reset our table and disabled the ability of SQL Server to create statistics. So the optimizer recognizes that these columns are in use in filtering operations, but without statistics.

The Nested Loops join also has a warning:

No Join Predicate

In short, because there is no way for the optimizer to estimate row counts, it's effectively assuming that all values will have to be matched to all values. Because of this, it has chosen to add a Table Spool, a temporary storage mechanism within execution plans, as a way to store the data read from the Clustered Index Scan against table Test1. By doing this, it thinks it can reduce the number of times it has to scan the table. You can also see that the optimizer assumes a value of 100 rows when it has no statistics on a given column.

Table 5-4 shows the comparison of performance between the two execution plans for the identical query and result set.

Table 5-4. *Runtime metrics for two different execution plans*

Existence of Statistics	Execution Plan	Avg. Duration (ms)	Number of Reads
With statistics	Figure 5-6	57.9	48
Without statistics	Figure 5-10	72.5	20,248

The number of reads and the duration were much higher on the query without statistics. Because it didn't have statistics, the optimizer simply made guesses, using mathematical heuristic calculations of course, as to how the data might be distributed. These guesses are simply not as accurate as having actual data for decision-making.

If you do disable the automatic creation of statistics, it might be a very good idea to keep an eye on just how many queries have a need for statistics. Extended Events provide an event called missing_column_statistics.

Analyzing Statistics

Statistics are composed of three sets of data:

- Header: Information about the set of statistics you're looking at
- Density Graph: A mathematical construct of the selectivity of the column or columns that make up the statistic
- Histogram: A statistical construct that shows how data is distributed across actual values within the first column of the statistic

The most commonly used of these data sets is the histogram. The histogram will show a sample of the data, up to 200 rows worth, and a count of the occurrences of values within each step, one of the 200 rows. If the column allows NULL values, you may see 201 rows, with one added for the NULL value. The steps are generated from the data in question, from a random distribution across the data.

In order to see statistics in action, I'm going to create a new test table as shown in Listing 5-15.

Listing 5-15. Creating a testing table for statistics analysis

```
DROP TABLE IF EXISTS dbo.Test1;
GO
CREATE TABLE dbo.Test1
(
    C1 INT,
    C2 INT IDENTITY
);
INSERT INTO dbo.Test1
(
    C1
)
VALUES
(1  );
SELECT TOP 10000
        IDENTITY(INT, 1, 1) AS n
INTO #Nums
FROM master.dbo.syscolumns sc1,
```

CHAPTER 5 STATISTICS, DATA DISTRIBUTION, AND CARDINALITY

```
    master.dbo.syscolumns sc2;
INSERT INTO dbo.Test1
(
    C1
)
SELECT 2
FROM #Nums;
DROP TABLE #Nums;
CREATE NONCLUSTERED INDEX FirstIndex ON dbo.Test1 (C1);
```

The final command creates a nonclustered index on the table. When that happens, SQL Server automatically creates statistics based on the index key. We can retrieve the statistics for the nonclustered index, FirstIndex, by executing the DBCC SHOW_STATISTICS command in Listing 5-16.

Listing 5-16. Retrieving statistics using DBCC SHOW_STATISTICS

```
DBCC SHOW_STATISTICS(Test1, FirstIndex);
```

The results of the query in Listing 5-16 are visible here in Figure 5-11.

	Name	Updated	Rows	Rows Sampled	Steps	Density	Average key length	String Index	Filter Expression	Unfiltered Rows	Persisted Sample Percent
1	FirstIndex	May 24 2025 11:29PM	10001	10001	2	0	4	NO	NULL	10001	0

	All density	Average Length	Columns
1	0.5	4	C1

	RANGE_HI_KEY	RANGE_ROWS	EQ_ROWS	DISTINCT_RANGE_ROWS	AVG_RANGE_ROWS
1	1	0	1	0	1
2	2	0	10000	0	1

Figure 5-11. *Statistics on index FirstIndex*

You get three distinct result sets from the SHOW_STATISTICS command. I outlined what they are at the start of this section: header, density graph, and histogram. Let's step through these in a little detail and discuss what each means.

Header

The header contains information about the statistics. Some of the data is straightforward such as the Name and the Updated value. The rest is descriptive about the statistics. The *Rows* column represents the number of rows in the table at the time that the statistics were created or updated. The Rows Sampled column shows how many of the rows were sampled to create the statistics, in this case, 10,001. The header lists how many *Steps* are in the histogram, here, only 2. The *Density* is shown as the average key length for the index. The rest of the columns are just describing the state of the statistics in question and are dependent on other settings, which we'll cover later in the chapter.

Density

The next data set, visible in the middle of Figure 5-11, is the measure of the density. When creating an execution plan, the optimizer analyzes the statistics of columns used in JOIN, HAVING, and WHERE clauses. A filter with high selectivity limits the number of rows that will be retrieved from a table, which helps the optimizer keep the query cost low. A column with a unique index will have a very high selectivity since it limits the number of matching rows to one.

On the other hand, filters with low selectivity will return larger results from the table. A filter with low selectivity can make a nonclustered index ineffective. Navigating through a nonclustered index to the base table for a large result set is less efficient than simply scanning the clustered index (or the base table in the case of a heap).

Statistics track the selectivity of a column in the form of a density ratio. There are two calculations: one for a single column set of statistics like what we're dealing with here and a second for compound statistics consisting of more than one column. We'll cover the compound statistics in a later section. The basic calculation is as follows:

Density = 1/Number of distinct values for a column

Density will always come out as a number somewhere between 0 and 1. The lower the density, the more suitable it is for use as an index key. If you want to check the values yourself, you could run a T-SQL command as shown in Listing 5-17.

Listing 5-17. Calculating the density value

```
SELECT 1.0 / COUNT(DISTINCT C1)
FROM dbo.Test1;
```

The results will be the same as those shown in Figure 5-11, 0.5.

The density is used to estimate the number of rows when the histogram won't work. The calculation is simple: multiply the density value times the number of rows to get an estimate on the average number of rows for any given distinct value within the table.

Histogram

The most used piece of data in the statistics is the histogram. It's the third data set, so I covered it last, but it is the most important data set within statistics to understand. It consists of only five columns and up to 200 rows, or steps. The columns are as follows:

- RANGE_HI_KEY: The top value of each range. There may or may not be values within the range. This value will be an actual value from the data in the column. If it's a number column, like our INT in the example, it will be a number. If it's a string, as we'll show in later examples, it will have some value within the column shown as a string, for example, "London" from a City column.

- EQ_ROWS: The number of rows within the range at the point when the statistics were updated, or created, that match the RANGE_HI_KEY value.

- RANGE_ROWS: The number of rows between the previous top value and the current top value, not counting either of those two boundary points.

- DISTINCT_RANGE_ROWS: The number of distinct values within the range. If all values are unique, then the RANGE_ROWS and DISTINCT_RANGE_ROWS will be equal.

- AVG_RANGE_ROWS: The number of rows equal to any potential key value within the range. Basically, RANGE_ROWS/DISTINCT_RANGE_ROWS is the calculation to arrive at this value.

The optimizer will have a value; let's say 1 from our example. It will then look at the histogram to determine an estimated number of rows. Since the value 1 is the RANGE_HI_KEY for the first range, or step, it knows that the EQ_ROWS has a value of 1 and therefore doesn't have to do any other calculations. Since our example data set only has a pair of values, 1 and 2, we only have two steps to examine. Let's take a look at another set of statistics (Listing 5-18).

Listing 5-18. Retrieving statistics from the Sales.SalesOrderDetail table

```
DBCC SHOW_STATISTICS('Sales.SalesOrderDetail', 'IX_SalesOrderDetail_
ProductID');
```

Figure 5-12 shows a subset of the histogram from these statistics.

	RANGE_HI_KEY	RANGE_ROWS	EQ_ROWS	DISTINCT_RANGE_ROWS	AVG_RANGE_ROWS
76	809	0	507	0	1
77	811	216	98	1	216
78	813	0	270	0	1
79	815	226	232	1	226
80	819	218	195	2	109
81	820	0	206	0	1
82	822	0	356	0	1
83	824	148	265	1	148
84	825	0	258	0	1
85	826	0	305	0	1
86	831	110	198	3	36.66667
87	832	0	256	0	1
88	833	0	88	0	1
89	835	0	489	0	1

Figure 5-12. Histogram from the IX_SalesOrderDetail_ProductID statistics

So now, let's assume we have a value, 827. If we look at the RANGE_HI_KEY values, the closest one, above our value, is 831. If we then look over at the AVG_RANGE_ROWS, we get the value 36.66667. If the optimizer were creating an execution plan, it would estimate that there would be 36.66667 rows that matched the value, 827.

Cardinality

The statistics, consisting of the histogram and density, are used by the query optimizer to calculate how many rows are to be expected by each operation within the execution plan for the query. This calculation to determine the number of rows is called the cardinality estimate. Cardinality represents the number of rows in a set of data, which means it's directly related to the density measures in SQL Server. Most of the time, this information is pulled from the histogram as outlined previously. But when multiple columns are used

CHAPTER 5 STATISTICS, DATA DISTRIBUTION, AND CARDINALITY

for filtering, the cardinality calculation has to take into account the potential selectivity of each column. The calculation on any instance that is SQL Server 2014 or higher is as follows:

Selectivity1*Power(Selectivity2,1/2)*Power(Selectivity3,1/4)...

This estimate is predicated on the idea that columns of data are related to one another. By getting the power of 1/2 of the selectivity, then 1/4, 1/8, etc., depending on the number of columns involved, the data is treated as if the columns were interrelated, which they usually are.

If you're running an older version of SQL Server, or in an older compatibility mode, then the calculation is different:

Selectivity1*Selectivity2*Selectivity3...

Another calculation takes effect when dealing with monotonically increasing values, such as an IDENTITY column. With a fresh set of statistics, which have been created using a FULLSCAN (explained later in the "Statistics Maintenance" section), everything simply works as expected. However, if you have used a sampled method to create the statistics, or there have been additions to the table, then the cardinality estimation (CE) assumes an average number of rows from the statistics. Prior to SQL Server 2014, the assumption was that all data only returned one row, whether it did or not. The newer method ensures more accurate execution plans in most cases. However, if you have uneven distribution in your data, referred to as skewed data, it can lead to bad cardinality estimations that can result in badly performing execution plans.

You can use Extended Events to observe how cardinality estimations get made. It's only useful if you really don't understand where a particular estimate is coming from. Usually that information is easily correlated between the information in the execution plan and the statistics on the columns or indexes. The event in question is query_optimizer_estimate_cardinality.

Note The query_optimizer_estimate_cardinality event is part of the Debug channel within Extended Events. The Debug events should be used with extreme care, after careful testing on nonproduction systems. The events in the package are subject to change or removal without notice.

CHAPTER 5 STATISTICS, DATA DISTRIBUTION, AND CARDINALITY

Listing 5-19 shows an example Extended Events session you could use to monitor cardinality estimation in action.

Listing 5-19. Extended Events session for query_optimizer_estimate_cardinality

```
CREATE EVENT SESSION [CardinalityEstimation]
ON SERVER
    ADD EVENT sqlserver.auto_stats
    (WHERE ([sqlserver].[database_name] = N'AdventureWorks')),
    ADD EVENT sqlserver.query_optimizer_estimate_cardinality
    (WHERE ([sqlserver].[database_name] = N'AdventureWorks')),
    ADD EVENT sqlserver.sql_batch_completed
    (WHERE ([sqlserver].[database_name] = N'AdventureWorks')),
    ADD EVENT sqlserver.sql_batch_starting
    (WHERE ([sqlserver].[database_name] = N'AdventureWorks'))
    ADD TARGET package0.event_file
    (SET filename = N'cardinalityestimation')
WITH
(
    TRACK_CAUSALITY = ON
);
```

I have a query that is slightly complex in order to generate a larger execution plan with plenty of operators and therefore more cardinality estimation events in Listing 5-20.

Listing 5-20. SELECT query against several tables

```
SELECT so.Description,
       p.Name AS ProductName,
       p.ListPrice,
       p.Size,
       pv.AverageLeadTime,
       pv.MaxOrderQty,
       v.Name AS VendorName
FROM Sales.SpecialOffer AS so
    JOIN Sales.SpecialOfferProduct AS sop
        ON sop.SpecialOfferID = so.SpecialOfferID
```

```
    JOIN Production.Product AS p
        ON p.ProductID = sop.ProductID
    JOIN Purchasing.ProductVendor AS pv
        ON pv.ProductID = p.ProductID
    JOIN Purchasing.Vendor AS v
        ON v.BusinessEntityID = pv.BusinessEntityID
WHERE so.DiscountPct > .15;
```

The first time I run this query, I will generate a number of calls to get cardinality estimation from the optimization process. You can see the output of my Extended Events session in Figure 5-13.

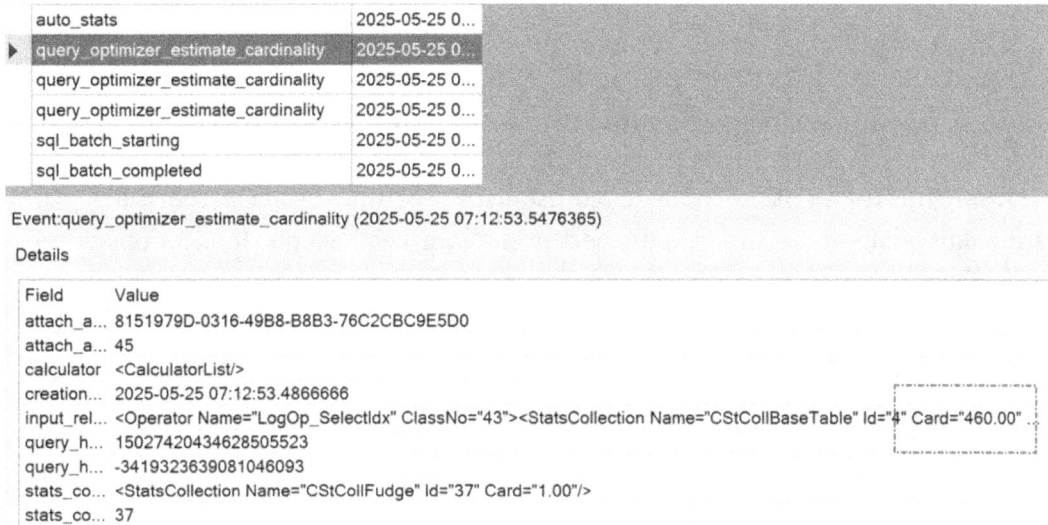

Figure 5-13. *Session showing output from the query_optimizer_estimate_ cardinality event*

You can see the auto_stats events firing as they did earlier. Then, highlighted, I have the first query_optimizer_estimate_cardinality event selected, so you can see all the properties of the event at the bottom of the screen. The two areas we have to focus on are the input_relation value and the stats_collected value. Both are XML. The interesting numbers are the Card values. The first is 460.00 (highlighted, at the right, with the dashed box around it), showing the overall cardinality of the table, the number of rows. The second value is 1.00, the estimated number of rows from the statistics in question.

Now, we can use this in correlation with the execution plan. Pull the plan from any source, with or without runtime metrics. Then, using the Find Node functionality (described in Chapter 4), we can look for the stats_collection_id value of 37, shown at the bottom of Figure 5-13. That will take us to Node 6 in the plan, the Clustered Index Seek operator against the ProductVendor table. You can see the values in Figure 5-14.

Scan Direction	FORWARD
⊞ Seek Predicates	Seek Keys[1]: Prefix: [/
StatsCollectionId	37
Storage	RowStore
TableCardinality	460

Figure 5-14. *StatsCollectionId matching the operator to the properties*

Again, this is only useful in rare circumstances because, as you can see, the cardinality values are included in the operators. Only if you need to look for obscure issues will this be useful.

Another piece of information returned by this event is the cardinality estimation engine version. This is useful when you're dealing with upgrades or issues caused by the Cardinality Estimator (we'll discuss this some more later in the chapter).

This event is not available on Azure SQL Database.

Statistics on a Multicolumn Index

When dealing with an index with a single key column, statistics are defined by the histogram and the density value for that column. When an index has a compound key, more than one column defining the key, then the information is a little different. The histogram stays the same. The first column in a compound key is always the one used to create a histogram. This makes choosing the order of your columns in a key important because only that first column will ever get a histogram, so you want to use the column that has the best data distribution, generally, the most selective column, the one with the lowest density. Then density values include the density for the first column and then for each additional column in the index key. Multiple density values ensure that the optimizer can get more accurate row estimates when multiple columns from the index

CHAPTER 5 STATISTICS, DATA DISTRIBUTION, AND CARDINALITY

are used in the predicates of a WHERE, HAVING, or JOIN clause. Here again, column order will matter in the density calculation as described in the earlier section.

You will only get multicolumn density graphs through the creation of an index with a compound key or the use of manually created statistics (discussed later in the chapter). You'll never see a multicolumn density graph created from the automatic statistics creation process. We can see that in action. Listing 5-21 shows a query with two columns used in the WHERE clause that could easily generate a compound statistic.

Listing 5-21. Query with two columns in the WHERE clause

```
SELECT p.Name,
       p.Class
FROM Production.Product AS p
WHERE p.Color = 'Red'
      AND p.DaysToManufacture > 15;
```

An index on the columns p.Color and p.DaysToManufacture would have a multicolumn density value. Before we run the query, let's look at a list of statistics on the table using Listing 5-22.

Listing 5-22. Querying the system tables to return a list of statistics

```
SELECT s.name,
       s.auto_created,
       s.user_created,
       s.filter_definition,
       sc.column_id,
       c.name AS ColumnName
FROM sys.stats AS s
   JOIN sys.stats_columns AS sc
      ON sc.stats_id = s.stats_id
         AND sc.object_id = s.object_id
   JOIN sys.columns AS c
      ON c.column_id = sc.column_id
         AND c.object_id = s.object_id
WHERE s.object_id = OBJECT_ID('Production.Product');
```

CHAPTER 5 STATISTICS, DATA DISTRIBUTION, AND CARDINALITY

If we run that query, you can see the results in Figure 5-15.

	name	auto_created	user_created	filter_definition	column_id	ColumnName
1	PK_Product_ProductID	0	0	NULL	1	ProductID
2	AK_Product_ProductNumber	0	0	NULL	3	ProductNumber
3	AK_Product_Name	0	0	NULL	2	Name
4	AK_Product_rowguid	0	0	NULL	24	rowguid
5	_WA_Sys_0000000C_1CBC4616	1	0	NULL	12	SizeUnitMeasureCode
6	_WA_Sys_0000000D_1CBC4616	1	0	NULL	13	WeightUnitMeasureCode
7	_WA_Sys_00000014_1CBC4616	1	0	NULL	20	ProductModelID
8	_WA_Sys_00000013_1CBC4616	1	0	NULL	19	ProductSubcategoryID

Figure 5-15. *List of statistics on the Product table*

None of the existing statistics has more than one column. I'm going to run the query from Listing 5-21 and then run the query from Listing 5-22 again. The results are visible in Figure 5-16.

	name	auto_created	user_created	filter_definition	column_id	ColumnName
1	PK_Product_ProductID	0	0	NULL	1	ProductID
2	AK_Product_ProductNumber	0	0	NULL	3	ProductNumber
3	AK_Product_Name	0	0	NULL	2	Name
4	AK_Product_rowguid	0	0	NULL	24	rowguid
5	_WA_Sys_0000000C_1CBC4616	1	0	NULL	12	SizeUnitMeasureCode
6	_WA_Sys_0000000D_1CBC4616	1	0	NULL	13	WeightUnitMeasureCode
7	_WA_Sys_00000014_1CBC4616	1	0	NULL	20	ProductModelID
8	_WA_Sys_00000013_1CBC4616	1	0	NULL	19	ProductSubcategoryID
9	_WA_Sys_0000000F_1CBC4616	1	0	NULL	15	DaysToManufacture
10	_WA_Sys_00000006_1CBC4616	1	0	NULL	6	Color

Figure 5-16. *Added statistics to the Product table*

As you can see, rather than creating a multicolumn set of statistics, one set of statistics for each of the columns in question has been added.

To see the density values in a multicolumn index, I'll modify the nonclustered index we created back in Listing 5-1 as shown in Listing 5-23.

Listing 5-23. Changing the index to have two keys

```
CREATE NONCLUSTERED INDEX FirstIndex
ON dbo.Test1 (
                C1,
                C2
            )
WITH (DROP_EXISTING = ON);
```

Figure 5-17 then shows the statistics that now exist on the index.

	Name	Updated	Rows	Rows Sampled	Steps	Density	Average key length	Strir
1	FirstIndex	May 26 2025 11:36AM	10001	10001	2	0	8	NO

	All density	Average Length	Columns
1	0.5	4	C1
2	9.999E-05	8	C1, C2

	RANGE_HI_KEY	RANGE_ROWS	EQ_ROWS	DISTINCT_RANGE_ROWS	AVG_RANGE_ROWS
1	1	0	1	0	1
2	2	0	10000	0	1

Figure 5-17. *Statistics with a multicolumn density graph*

You can now see that the density has changed to show just the density of the first column and then the density with the addition of the second column. Nothing has changed in the histogram because it's always, only, on the first column.

Statistics on a Filtered Index

Filtered indexes (discussed in Chapter 9) are meant to limit the data that makes up the index through the use of a WHERE clause. By its nature then, the density and histogram will consist of different data in support of that index. To see this in action, we'll create an index on the Sales.SalesOrderHeader table as shown in Listing 5-24.

Listing 5-24. Creating an index on the PurchaseOrderNumber column

```
CREATE INDEX IX_Test ON Sales.SalesOrderHeader (PurchaseOrderNumber);
```

The resulting output from DBCC SHOWSTATISTICS against this new index is shown in Figure 5-18.

CHAPTER 5 STATISTICS, DATA DISTRIBUTION, AND CARDINALITY

	Name	Updated	Rows	Rows Sampled	Steps	Density	Average key length	String Index	Filter Expression	Unfiltered Rows	Persisted Sample Percent
1	IX_Test	May 26 2025 11:41AM	31465	31465	152	1	7.01516	YES	NULL	31465	0

	All density	Average Length	Columns
1	0.000262674	3.01516	PurchaseOrderNumber
2	3.178134E-05	7.01516	PurchaseOrderNumber, SalesOrderID

	RANGE_HI_KEY	RANGE_ROWS	EQ_ROWS	DISTINCT_RANGE_ROWS	AVG_RANGE_ROWS
1	NULL	0	27659	0	1
2	PO10005144378	0	1	0	1
3	PO10092142501	14	1	14	1
4	PO10150121946	15	1	15	1
5	PO10179199539	17	1	17	1
...	...	...			
149	PO8352178578	63	1	63	1
150	PO8903194371	127	1	127	1
151	PO9280166971	63	1	63	1
152	PO9976195169	149	1	149	1

Figure 5-18. *Statistics on an unfiltered index*

If the same index is recreated to filter out NULL values to help make a more effective index, the code would look like Listing 5-25.

Listing 5-25. Altering the index to make it filtered

```
CREATE INDEX IX_Test
ON Sales.SalesOrderHeader (PurchaseOrderNumber)
WHERE PurchaseOrderNumber IS NOT NULL
WITH (DROP_EXISTING = ON);
```

The updated statistics are visible in Figure 5-19.

	Name	Updated	Rows	Rows Sampled	Steps	Density	Average key length	String Index	Filter Expression	Unfiltered Rows	Persisted Sample Percent
1	IX_Test	May 26 2025 11:48AM	3806	3806	151	1	28.92696	YES	([PurchaseOrderNumber] IS NOT NULL)	31465	0

	All density	Average Length	Columns
1	0.000262743	24.92696	PurchaseOrderNumber
2	0.000262743	28.92696	PurchaseOrderNumber, SalesOrderID

	RANGE_HI_KEY	RANGE_ROWS	EQ_ROWS	DISTINCT_RANGE_ROWS	AVG_RANGE_ROWS
1	PO10005144378	0	1	0	1
2	PO10092142501	14	1	14	1
3	PO10150121946	15	1	15	1
4	PO10179199539	17	1	17	1
5	PO10208129572	0	1	0	1
147	PO7917120732	63	1	63	1
148	PO8352178578	63	1	63	1
149	PO8903194371	127	1	127	1
150	PO9280166971	63	1	63	1
151	PO9976195169	149	1	149	1

Figure 5-19. *New statistics based on the filtered index*

The first thing to note between the information in Figures 5-18 and 5-19 is the number of rows, going from 31,465 to 3,806. You can also see that the key length has increased since we no longer have NULL values. You can also see a Filter Expression for the first time in this chapter in Figure 5-19.

The density measures are an interesting case. The density is close to the same for both values, but the filtered density is slightly lower, meaning fewer unique values. This is because the filtered data, while marginally less selective, is actually more accurate, eliminating all the empty values that won't contribute to filtering the data. The density of the second value, which is the clustered index pointer (discussed in Chapter 6), is identical with the value of the density previously because each represents the same amount of unique data. Finally, the histogram shows a NULL value in step 1 in Figure 5-18, but not in Figure 5-19 with a reduction in the size of the histogram from 152 rows, or steps, to 151.

You can create filtered statistics as well. Doing this lets you create finely tuned histograms. These are especially useful on partitioned tables. This is necessary because statistics are not automatically created on partitioned tables, and you can't create your own using CREATE STATISTICS. You can create filtered indexes by partition and get statistics or create filtered statistics specially by partition.

Before continuing, remove the index we created using Listing 5-26.

Listing 5-26. Removing the test index

```
DROP INDEX Sales.SalesOrderHeader.IX_Test;
```

Controlling the Cardinality Estimator

Running SQL Server 2014 or greater, you'll be automatically set to the latest cardinality estimation engine. The principal way this is controlled is through the database compatibility level. If it's set to 120 or greater, you're on the latest estimator. If you're on 110 or less, it's the old estimator. You can control which estimator is in use one of several ways, depending on the version of SQL Server you're on:

- Database compatibility level
- Trace flag 9481
- LEGACY_CARDINALITY_ESTIMATION database setting
- FORCE_LEGACY_CARDINALITY_ESTIMATION query hint
- Query Store hint for FORCE_LEGACY_CARDINALITY_ESTIMATION

Which of these you choose depends on how granular a manner you need to adjust how cardinality is estimated on your system and what version of SQL Server you're on. The least granular option is to set the database compatibility level; for SQL Server 2014 and up, this is controlled by altering the database as shown in Listing 5-27.

Listing 5-27. Changing the database compatibility level

```
ALTER DATABASE AdventureWorks SET COMPATIBILITY_LEVEL = 110;
```

That would make the database behave as if it were a SQL Server 2012 database. This means that much of the more modern behaviors of the database are also disabled. This is generally a poor choice.

The next setting in order is trace flag 9481, available in SQL Server 2014 and greater. However, controlling database behavior through trace flags is somewhat old-fashioned. Further, it makes it difficult to look at the settings on individual databases and servers since the trace flags will only ever return a set of numbers. Using the Database Scoped Configuration, we can see exactly the choices being made. A better approach is shown in Listing 5-28.

Listing 5-28. Controlling the legacy cardinality estimation engine

```
ALTER DATABASE SCOPED CONFIGURATION SET LEGACY_CARDINALITY_ESTIMATION = ON;
```

It's much easier to understand what you're doing and easier to query the behaviors you have set through DATABASE SCOPED CONFIGURATION, available in SQL Server 2016 and greater. Further, with the new SQL Server Management Studio 21, you can even look at the configuration settings for your database in Object Explorer. Right-click a given database, select "Properties" from the context menu, and then select the "Configurations" page. Figure 5-20 shows the full set of choices, including the fact that the legacy cardinality estimation is set to ON for this database.

CHAPTER 5   STATISTICS, DATA DISTRIBUTION, AND CARDINALITY

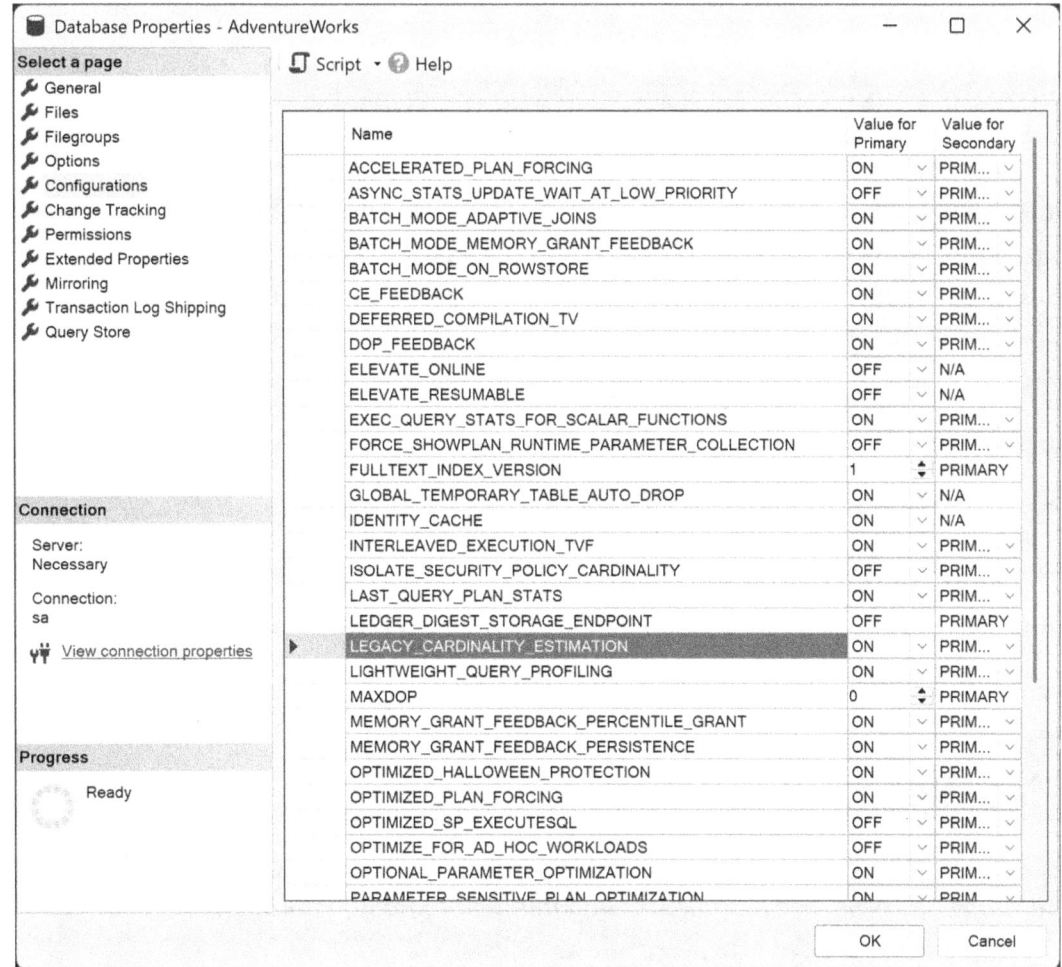

Figure 5-20. All Database Scoped Configuration settings

You can even use this interface to control the Database Scoped Configuration settings, even for Primary and Secondary replicas.

You can also choose to use LEGACY_CARDINALITY_ESTIMATION as a query hint on a query. An example of how this would work is shown in Listing 5-29.

Listing 5-29. Controlling cardinality through a query hint

```
SELECT p.Name,
       p.Class
FROM Production.Product AS p
```

161

```
WHERE p.Color = 'Red'
    AND p.DaysToManufacture > 15
OPTION (USE HINT ('FORCE_LEGACY_CARDINALITY_ESTIMATION'));
```

You can also apply trace flag 9481 through a query hint if you choose or you're on an older version of SQL Server. It will behave the same way. If you look at the execution plan for the query in Listing 5-29, you can validate which cardinality estimation engine is in use by looking at the properties of the first operator. Find the CardinalityEstimationModelVersion property as shown in Figure 5-21.

CardinalityEstimationModelVersion   70

Figure 5-21. Execution plan property showing the cardinality estimation engine

And finally, you can use the Query Store hint feature if you're on SQL Server 2022 and up or in Azure SQL Database and Azure Managed Instance. We'll cover the Query Store hint feature in Chapter 6.

Statistics Maintenance

SQL Server allows a user to manually override the maintenance of statistics in an individual database. The four main configurations controlling the automatic statistics maintenance behavior of SQL Server are as follows:

- Auto Create Statistics: New statistics on columns with no index
- Auto Update Statistics: Updating existing statistics automatically
- Sampling rate of statistics
- Auto Update Statistics Asynchronously: Updating statistics after query execution

You can control these settings across a database, or you can control them on individual indexes and statistics. The Auto Create Statistics is applicable to columns without an index only because SQL Server automatically creates statistics when an index gets created.

Auto Create Statistics

We've already discussed how statistics get created on columns without an index when those columns are used as filtering criteria in a JOIN, WHERE, or HAVING clause. This behavior is enabled by default and generally should be left in place.

Auto Update Statistics

We've already discussed how statistics get updated. As before, you should leave the defaults in place unless strong testing shows that disabling it on a given system is worth having out-of-date statistics. If you do disable the automatic update of statistics, ensure that you build your own statistics maintenance routines to ensure your statistics are up to date.

Auto Update Statistics Asynchronously

We've mentioned this several times in the chapter, but we haven't yet explained how it works in detail. When Auto Update Statistics Asynchronously is set to on, the basic behavior of statistics in SQL Server isn't changed radically. When a set of statistics is marked as out of date through the formula established, the statistics update process does not interrupt the execution of the query, like what normally happens. Instead, the query finishes execution using the older set of statistics. Once the query completes, the statistics are updated. This approach can be attractive because when statistics are updated, the current execution plan is removed from cache and a new execution plan is created. Depending on the query in question, creating a new execution plan could be a time-consuming process, delaying the execution of the query. Rather than making a query wait for both the update of the statistics and the generation of the new execution plan, the query completes its run. The next time the same query is called, it will have updated statistics waiting for it, and it will have to recompile only.

Although this functionality does make the steps needed to update statistics and recompile plans faster, it can also cause queries that could benefit immediately from updated statistics and a new execution plan to suffer with the old execution plan. Testing is required before enabling this functionality to ensure it doesn't cause more harm than good.

> **Note** If you are attempting to update statistics asynchronously, you must also have AUTO_UPDATE_STATISTICS set to ON.

Manual Maintenance

Even though SQL Server does a decent job of automatically maintaining statistics, you may still need to intervene directly in some circumstances:

- When Experimenting with Statistics: Please don't run the experiments outlined here on your production servers and databases.

- After Upgrading from a Previous Version to a New Version of SQL Server: Assuming you're moving to a SQL Server instance of 2016 or greater, you should take advantage of the Query Store as part of your upgrade process. This also means I wouldn't immediately start updating statistics on your databases. Rather, let them get updated as before. Then, when you change the compatibility mode through your Query Store upgrade process (outlined in Chapter 6), then you may want to also update all statistics.

- While Executing One-Time Ad Hoc SQL Activities: In such cases, you may have to decide between automatic statistics maintenance and a manual process where you control exactly when and how statistics get updated. This is usually only a concern for much larger than normal databases.

- Automatic Update of Statistics Is Not Firing Frequently Enough: This can be caused by a lot of reasons. You'll usually identify it when you have slow performance on a query and on looking at the execution plan you have a large disparity between the estimated and actual row counts. In these cases, you may need to manually intervene, either as a one-time activity or as a part of regular maintenance to assist with the automatic maintenance.

Manage Statistics Settings

You can control the Auto Create Statistics setting at a database level. To disable this setting, use the `ALTER DATABASE` command shown in Listing 5-30.

Listing 5-30. Turning Auto Create Statistics off

```
ALTER DATABASE AdventureWorks SET AUTO_CREATE_STATISTICS OFF;
```

You can control the Auto Update Statistics setting at different levels of a database, including all indexes and statistics on a table, or at the individual index or statistics level. To disable Auto Update Statistics at the database level, use the `ALTER DATABASE` command as shown in Listing 5-31.

Listing 5-31. Turning off Auto Update Statistics

```
ALTER DATABASE AdventureWorks SET AUTO_UPDATE_STATISTICS OFF;
```

Disabling this setting at the database level overrides individual settings at lower levels. Auto Update Statistics Asynchronously requires that the Auto Update Statistics be on first. Then you can enable the asynchronous update, visible in Listing 5-32.

Listing 5-32. Turning on asynchronous statistics update

```
ALTER DATABASE AdventureWorks SET AUTO_UPDATE_STATISTICS_ASYNC ON;
```

To configure Auto Update Statistics for all indexes and statistics on a table in the current database, use the `sp_autostats` system stored procedure as shown in Listing 5-33.

Listing 5-33. Turning off automatic update of statistics on a single table

```
USE AdventureWorks;
EXEC sp_autostats
    'HumanResources.Department',
    'OFF';
```

You can also use the same stored procedure to configure this setting for individual indexes or statistics. To disable this setting for the AK_Department_Name index on HumanResources.Department, execute the following statement in Listing 5-34.

Listing 5-34. Disabling automatic statistics on a single index

```
EXEC sp_autostats
    'HumanResources.Department',
    'OFF',
    AK_Department_Name;
```

You can also use the UPDATE STATISTICS command's WITH NORECOMPUTE option to disable this setting for all or individual indexes and statistics on a table in the current database. The sp_createstats stored procedure also has the NORECOMPUTE option. The NORECOMPUTE option will not disable automatic update of statistics for the database, but it will for a given set of statistics.

Avoid disabling the automatic statistics features, unless you have confirmed through testing that this brings a performance benefit. If the automatic statistics features are disabled, then you are responsible for manually identifying and creating missing statistics on the columns that are not indexed and then keeping the existing statistics up to date. In general, you're only going to want to disable the automatic statistics features for very large tables.

If you want to check the status of whether a table has its automatic statistics turned off, you can use this in Listing 5-35.

Listing 5-35. Determining the status of statistics on a table

```
EXEC sp_autostats 'HumanResources.Department';
```

Reset the automatic maintenance of the index so that it is on where it has been turned off from Listing 5-36.

Listing 5-36. Resetting statistics on tables and indexes

```
EXEC sp_autostats
    'HumanResources.Department',
    'ON';
EXEC sp_autostats
```

```
'HumanResources.Department',
'ON',
AK_Department_Name;
```

Create Statistics Manually

You can create statistics yourself in two ways:

- CREATE STATISTICS: You can use this command to create statistics on a single or multiple columns of a table or an indexed view. Unlike the CREATE INDEX command, CREATE STATISTICS uses sampling by default.

- sys.sp_createstats: This stored procedure creates single-column statistics for all eligible columns for all user tables in the current database. Ineligible columns are excluded: NTEXT, TEXT, GEOMETRY, GEOGRAPHY, IMAGE, and sparse columns, columns that already have statistics or are the first column of an index key. This is a backward compatibility function, and I do not recommend using it.

You will see a statistics object get created for a columnstore index, but the values inside that set of statistics are null. Individual columns on a columnstore index can have system-generated statistics. When dealing with a columnstore index, if you find you're still referencing individual columns in filtering queries, it's possible that creating a multicolumn statistic is useful.

With the execution of individual column statistics, and any you create, there is no need to worry about the automatically created index statistic on a columnstore index. The only exception to this rule is if you partition the columnstore index (partitioning is not a performance enhancement tool; it's a data management and storage tool). In this case, you'll need to change your statistics to be incremental using the command in Listing 5-37.

Listing 5-37. Making a statistic incremental to deal with partitioning

```
UPDATE STATISTICS dbo.bigProduct
WITH RESAMPLE,
    INCREMENTAL = ON;
```

To update statistics manually, use one of the following options:

- UPDATE STATISTICS: You can use this command to update the statistics of an individual index or all indexes and nonindexed columns of a table or an indexed view.

- sys.sp_updatestat: This system stored procedure is used to update statistics of all user tables in the current database. However, it can only sample statistics and can't use FULLSCAN. It will also update statistics when only a single action has been performed on a given statistic. In short, this is a rather blunt instrument for maintaining statistics.

You may find that allowing the automatic updating of statistics is not quite adequate in all circumstances. Scheduling UPDATE STATISTICS for the database during off-hours is a perfectly acceptable way to deal with this issue. UPDATE STATISTICS is the preferred mechanism because it offers a greater degree of flexibility and control. It's possible, because of the distribution of your data, that the sampling method for gathering statistics may not be accurate enough. The sampled method is the default because it's faster. However, if you are hitting a case where the statistics aren't accurately reflecting the data, you can force a FULLSCAN so that all the data is used to update the statistics. This is the same as when a statistic is initially created. FULLSCAN can be a costly operation, so it's best to be selective about which statistics receive this treatment.

When you create your own statistics, they are treated as a permanent object. As such, they can prevent changes to the table. Automatically created statistics are automatically dropped as needed when tables and indexes are modified. Starting in SQL Server 2022, you can modify the creation of your statistics to include the ability to automatically drop. Simply add WITH AUTO_DROP = ON to the end of the statistics creation. You can also modify statistics to automatically drop by adding the same WITH statement during an UPDATE of statistics.

Analyzing the Effectiveness of Statistics for a Query

In order to assist the optimizer in creating the best possible plans for your queries, you must maintain the statistics on your database objects. Issues with old or incorrect, missing, or inaccurate statistics are quite common. You need to keep your eyes open to the possibility of problems with statistics while analyzing the performance of a query. In fact, checking that the statistics are up to date at the beginning of a query tuning session eliminates an easily fixed problem. In this section, you'll see what you can do in the event you find statistics to be missing or out of date.

The focus here is going to be on the execution plan. You need to look for the following points:

- Indexes are available on the columns referred to in the filter and join criteria.

- In the case of a missing index, statistics should be available on the columns. It is generally preferable to have the index.

- Since outdated statistics are of no use and can even cause harm to your execution plans, it is important that the estimates used by the optimizer from the statistics are up to date.

Resolving a Missing Statistics Issue

In order to demonstrate what happens when statistics are missing, Listing 5-38 is going to show a series of steps. First, I'm going to disable automatic statistics creation and updates. Then I'll set up a test table, index, and data.

Listing 5-38. Setting up test for missing statistics

```
ALTER DATABASE AdventureWorks SET AUTO_CREATE_STATISTICS OFF;
ALTER DATABASE AdventureWorks SET AUTO_UPDATE_STATISTICS OFF;
GO
DROP TABLE IF EXISTS dbo.Test1;
GO
CREATE TABLE dbo.Test1
(
    C1 INT,
    C2 INT,
    C3 CHAR(50)
);
INSERT INTO dbo.Test1
(
    C1,
```

CHAPTER 5 STATISTICS, DATA DISTRIBUTION, AND CARDINALITY

```
    C2,
    C3
)
VALUES
(51, 1, 'C3'),
(52, 1, 'C3');
CREATE NONCLUSTERED INDEX iFirstIndex ON dbo.Test1 (C1, C2);
SELECT TOP 10000
        IDENTITY(INT, 1, 1) AS n
INTO #Nums
FROM master.dbo.syscolumns AS sc1,
     master.dbo.syscolumns AS sC2;
INSERT INTO dbo.Test1
(
    C1,
    C2,
    C3
)
SELECT n % 50,
       n,
       'C3'
FROM #Nums;
DROP TABLE #Nums;
```

Since the index is created on the columns C1 and C2, the statistics on the index contain a histogram for the first column, C1, and density values for the combination of columns (C1 and C1*C2). There are no histograms or density values alone for column C2.

When the optimizer gets the query in Listing 5-39, it won't be able to generate statistics for the column C2.

Listing 5-39. Query demonstrating missing statistics

```
SELECT t.C1,
       t.C2,
```

```
    t.C3
FROM dbo.Test1 AS t
WHERE t.C2 = 1;
```

Figure 5-22 shows the resulting execution plan with runtime metrics.

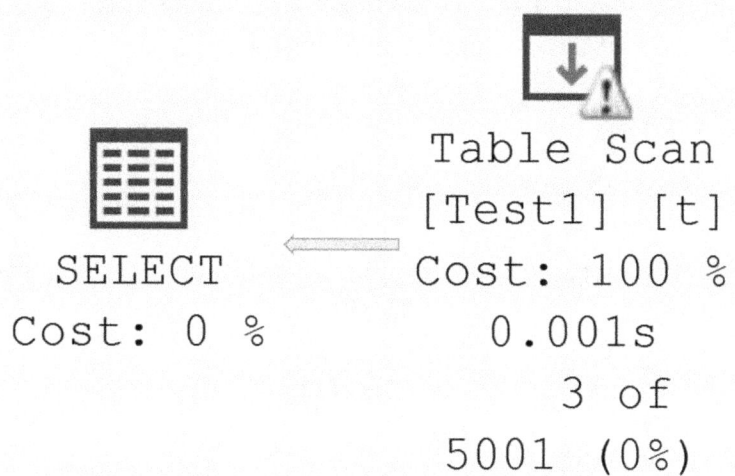

Figure 5-22. Index scan caused by missing statistics

The first two things to note on the execution plan are the warning and the fact that only three rows were returned, but 5,001 were expected. The warning is letting us know that there is a problem with the Table Scan operation. If we look at the Properties page, we'll find the warning shown in Figure 5-23.

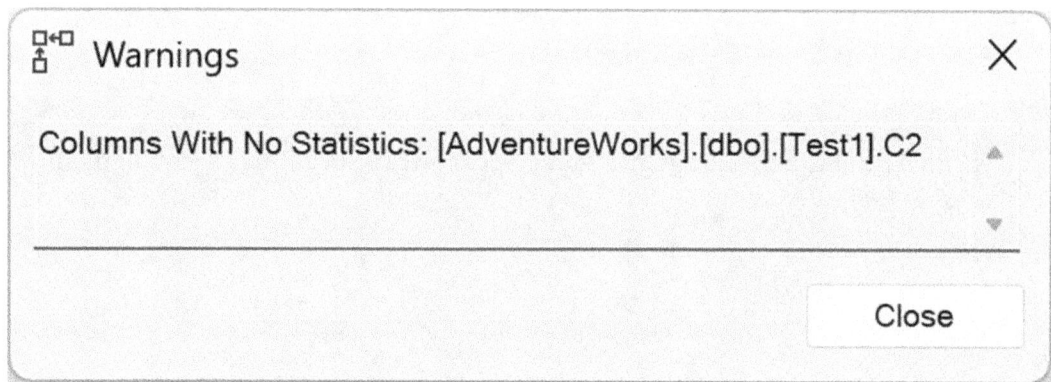

Figure 5-23. Property values from the warning in the Table Scan operator

CHAPTER 5 STATISTICS, DATA DISTRIBUTION, AND CARDINALITY

You get a warning when there are no statistics on a column used in a filtering operation because the optimizer knows that it's not going to be able to ensure accurate row estimates. Between this clear warning and the huge disparity between estimated and actual rows, you know that you're missing statistics. On average, this query ran in 2.1ms with 92 reads.

To resolve the missing statistics issue, I'm going to create statistics on the C2 column using the CREATE STATISTICS statement in Listing 5-40.

Listing 5-40. Using CREATE STATISTICS on a column

```
CREATE STATISTICS Stats1 ON Test1(C2);
```

Before we run the query again, we're going to use Listing 5-41 to remove it from cache.

Listing 5-41. Removing a query from the cache

```
DECLARE @Planhandle VARBINARY(64);
SELECT @Planhandle = deqs.plan_handle
FROM sys.dm_exec_query_stats AS deqs
    CROSS APPLY sys.dm_exec_sql_text(deqs.sql_handle) AS dest
WHERE dest.text = 'SELECT  *
FROM    dbo.Test1
WHERE   C2 = 1;';
IF @Planhandle IS NOT NULL
BEGIN
    DBCC FREEPROCCACHE(@Planhandle);
END;
```

If we then run Listing 5-39 again, Figure 5-24 shows the resulting execution plan.
Reads: 34
Duration: 8.3ms

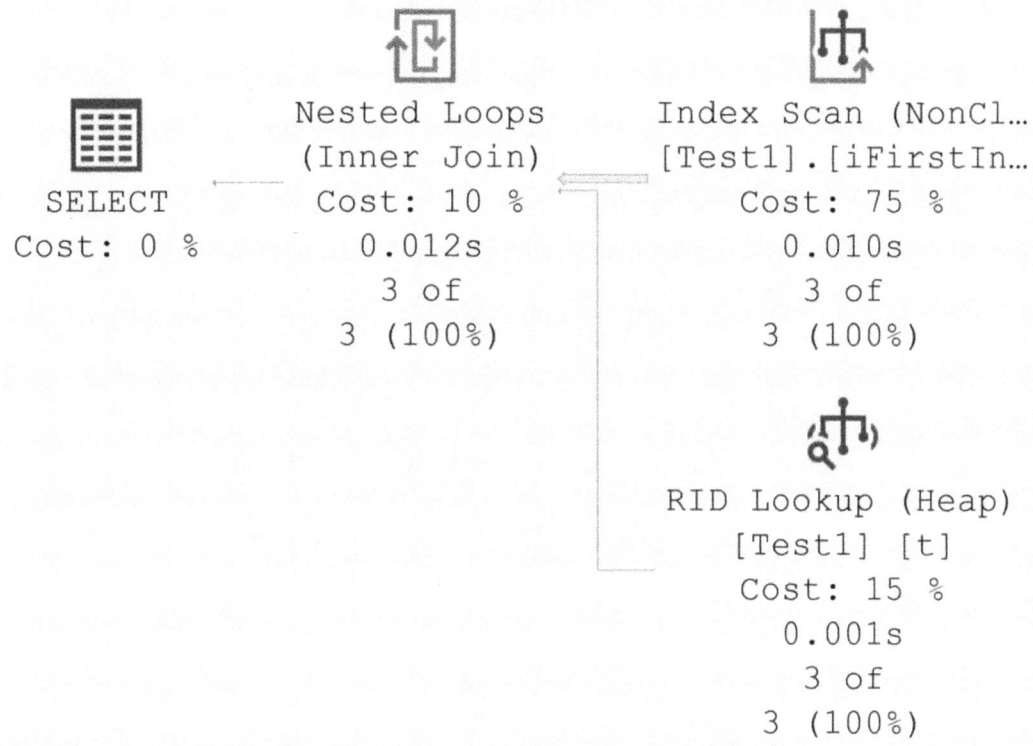

Figure 5-24. *A different execution plan, thanks to statistics*

Because it now has statistics to work with, the optimizer can accurately estimate that only three rows are going to be returned by the query. Because of this, the optimizer also decides that a better approach would be to use the index iFirstIndex to scan for the data. However, because the index only contains some of the data, we have to go to the table and perform a row lookup using the RID Lookup operation. The number of reads went from 88 to 34, a win. However, because of the extra processing needed for the Nested Loops join and the RID Lookup, the duration actually increased from 2.1ms to 8.4ms, a loss. A fix is possible here. Adding the C3 column as an INCLUDE on the index would result in improved performance. We'll be covering that sort of solution in later chapters in more detail.

CHAPTER 5   STATISTICS, DATA DISTRIBUTION, AND CARDINALITY

Resolving an Outdated Statistics Issue

Outdated or incorrect statistics are just as damaging as missing statistics. The choices the optimizer makes may be highly inappropriate for the current data distribution. Unfortunately, the execution plan won't show the same glaring warnings for outdated or incorrect statistics as it does for missing statistics. Instead, you're going to be looking primarily at the comparison of estimated rows to actual rows in the execution plan.

There is a Debug Extended Event that can show you some events when the statistics are wildly off. It's called inaccurate_cardinality_estimate. However, since it's a debug event, I'd urge a very cautious approach to its use and only when you have strong filtering in place and only for short periods of time.

Listing 5-42 will retrieve the statistics from our test index, iFirstIndex.

Listing 5-42. Using DBCC SHOW_STATISTICS on iFirstIndex

```
DBCC SHOW_STATISTICS (Test1, iFirstIndex);
```

The resulting information is shown in Figure 5-25.

	Name	Updated	Rows	Rows Sampled	Steps	Density	Average key length	String Index	Filter Expression	Unfiltered Rows	Persisted Sample Percent
1	iFirstIndex	May 26 2025 12:43PM	2	2	2	0	8	NO	NULL	2	0

	All density	Average Length	Columns
1	0.5	4	C1
2	0.5	8	C1, C2

	RANGE_HI_KEY	RANGE_ROWS	EQ_ROWS	DISTINCT_RANGE_ROWS	AVG_RANGE_ROWS
1	51	0	1	0	1
2	52	0	1	0	1

Figure 5-25. *Statistics for iFirstIndex*

We're going to run the query in Listing 5-43.

Listing 5-43. A SELECT query against the Test1 table

```
SELECT C1,
       C2,
       C3
FROM dbo.Test1
WHERE C1 = 51;
```

The resulting execution plan is shown in Figure 5-26.

Reads: 94

Duration: 2.5ms

CHAPTER 5   STATISTICS, DATA DISTRIBUTION, AND CARDINALITY

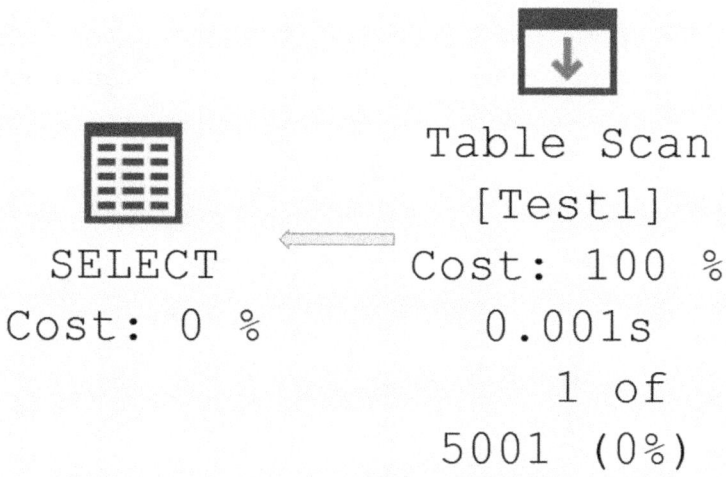

Figure 5-26. An execution plan with out-of-date statistics

Looking at the execution plan with runtime metrics, we can see that only one row was returned, but that 5,001 were estimated based on our out-of-date statistics. You can also see the estimated number of rows and the actual number of rows in the properties of the operator.

When you see a disparity between estimated and actual where it is several times off, in either direction, it's possible that the processing strategy chosen by the optimizer may not be cost-effective for the existing data distribution.

To help the optimizer make a more accurate estimation, the statistics need to be updated on the index in question, iFirstIndex. If I had left the automatic update of statistics enabled, it would have been done during the data load. However, instead, we'll be updating them ourselves using Listing 5-44.

Listing 5-44. Updating the statistics on iFirstIndex

```
UPDATE STATISTICS Test1 iFirstIndex
WITH FULLSCAN;
```

A FULLSCAN might not be necessary in this situation. The sampled method of creating and updating statistics is usually fairly accurate and is much faster, using less resources. However, on systems that aren't experiencing stress, or during off-hours, I tend to favor using FULLSCAN because of the improved accuracy. Either approach

CHAPTER 5 STATISTICS, DATA DISTRIBUTION, AND CARDINALITY

is valid as long as you're not negatively impacting the system and your statistics are good enough.

Running the query from Listing 5-43 results in a different execution plan shown in Figure 5-27.

Reads: 4

Duration: 419mcs

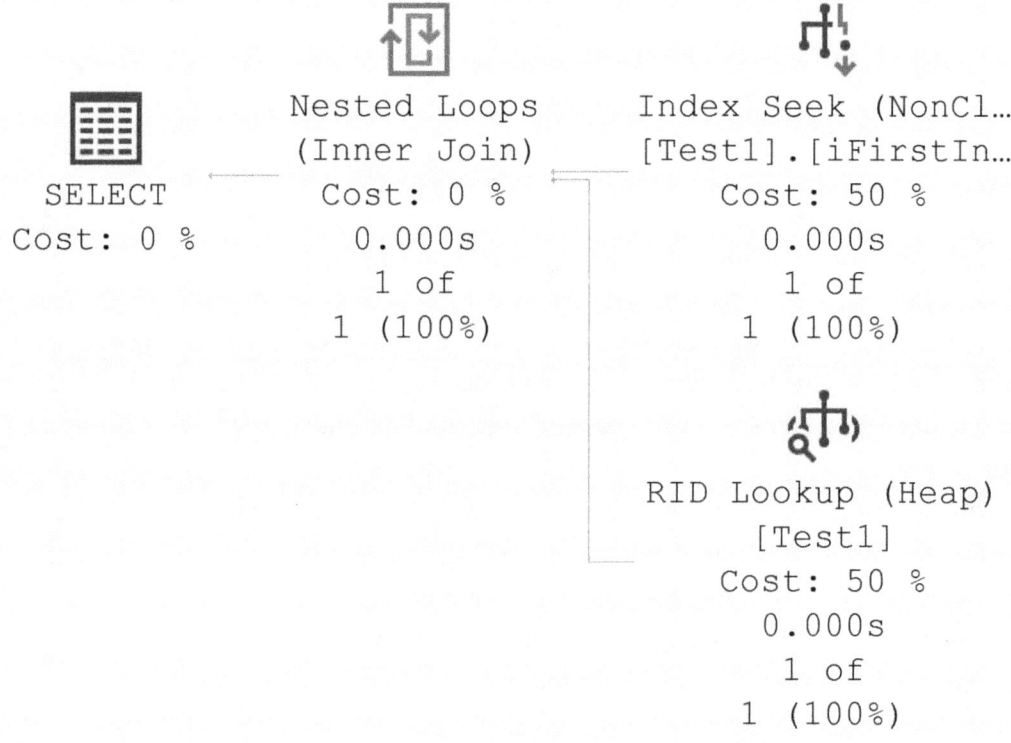

Figure 5-27. A different execution plan after the statistics are updated

With updated statistics, the optimizer came up with a completely different execution plan. Instead of 5,001 rows, it knows that it's only got one row to deal with, so retrieving the data from iFirstIndex with an Index Seek operation was chosen. It still had to go and retrieve the rest of the data from the heap.

However, the changes resulted in the reads going from 88 to 4 and the execution time reducing from 2.1ms to 419mcs, more than five times faster.

Before continuing, turn the statistics back on for the database (Listing 5-45).

Listing 5-45. Enabling automatic creation and update of statistics

```
ALTER DATABASE AdventureWorks SET AUTO_CREATE_STATISTICS ON;
ALTER DATABASE AdventureWorks SET AUTO_UPDATE_STATISTICS ON;
```

Recommendations on Statistics

Throughout the chapter, I've made a number of recommendations on how to maintain and manage your statistics. For easy reference, I've consolidated these recommendations here along with some extra details.

Backward Compatibility of Statistics

When upgrading your databases between different versions of SQL Server, using the Query Store as a mechanism during the upgrade (outlined in Chapter 6) is generally a good idea. Because of this, the statistics will update naturally over time as the data changes. I recommend letting this happen rather than attempting to update all the statistics after an upgrade. However, this assumes that you're using Query Store. If not, it's probably a good idea to update all the statistics after an upgrade to ensure that any changes to the behavior of statistics get incorporated right away.

Auto Create Statistics

This feature should be left on. SQL Server can then create statistics it needs on columns that do not have an index, which will result in better execution plans and usually better performance. You might find that creating compound statistics yourself is beneficial in some circumstances.

Auto Update Statistics

This feature should also be left on, allowing SQL Server to get more accurate execution plans as the data distribution changes over time. Usually, the performance benefit outweighs the overhead cost.

If you do come across issues with the Auto Update Statistics feature and decide to disable it, then you must ensure that you create an automated process to update the statistics on a regular basis. For performance reasons, where possible, run that process during off-peak hours.

You will likely need to supplement the automatic statistics maintenance. Whether you need to do it across your entire database or just for specific indexes or statistics will be driven by the behavior of your systems.

Auto Update Statistics Asynchronously

Waiting for statistics to be updated before plan generation will be fine in most cases. In cases where the statistics updates, or the recompiles of execution plans from those updates, are more expensive than the cost of working with out-of-date statistics, then enable this functionality. Just understand that it may mean that queries that would benefit from more up-to-date statistics will suffer until the next time they are run. Don't forget that you need automatic update of statistics enabled in order to enable asynchronous updates.

Amount of Sampling to Collect Statistics

It is generally recommended that you use the default sampling rate. This rate is decided by an efficient algorithm based on the data size and number of modifications. Although the default sampling rate turns out to be best in most cases, if for a particular query you find that the statistics are not very accurate, then you can manually update them with FULLSCAN. You also have the option of setting a specific sample percentage using the SAMPLE number. The number can be either a percentage or a set number of rows.

If this is required repeatedly, then you can add a SQL Server job to take care of it. For performance reasons, ensure that the SQL job is scheduled to run during off-peak hours. To identify cases in which the default sampling rate doesn't turn out to be the best, analyze the statistics effectiveness for costly queries while troubleshooting the database performance. Remember that FULLSCAN is expensive, so you should run it only on those tables or indexes that you've determined will really benefit from it.

Summary

SQL Server's cost-based optimization process requires accurate statistics on columns used in filtering criteria to determine an efficient processing strategy. Statistics on an index are always created during the creation of the index, and by default, SQL Server also keeps the statistics on indexed and nonindexed columns updated automatically as the data changes over time. This enables the optimizer to determine the best processing strategies based on the current data distribution.

Even though you can disable both the automatic creation and automatic update of statistics, it is recommended that you leave these features enabled. Their benefit to the optimizer is almost always more than their overhead cost. For a costly query, analyze the statistics to ensure that the automatic statistics maintenance lives up to its promise. You can supplement the automatic process with your manual processes as necessary.

Now that we have a firm foundation in how plans are generated from Chapter 4 and how statistics affect that generating from this chapter, we're going to look at how you can use the Query Store to further understand query and execution plan behavior inside SQL Server in the next chapter.

CHAPTER 6

Using the Query Store for Query Performance and Execution Plans

The Query Store adds a large amount of functionality to SQL Server and Azure SQL Database that helps you in tuning queries. First, the Query Store captures performance metrics on any database that has it enabled, allowing you to look at a historical set of measures. Next, it captures execution plans so that you can see how plans and behaviors change over time. Then, it gives you the ability to control execution plans through a mechanism called plan forcing and another through query hints. All these taken together make the Query Store a very powerful tool for tuning queries.

In this chapter, I cover the following topics:

- How the Query Store works and the information it collects
- Reports and mechanisms for the Query Store in Management Studio
- Plan forcing, a way to force SQL Server to use a particular plan
- Query hints through the Query Store, allowing you to put in hints without editing code
- An upgrade method that helps you protect your system's performance

CHAPTER 6   USING THE QUERY STORE FOR QUERY PERFORMANCE AND EXECUTION PLANS

Query Store Function and Design

The Query Store was first introduced in SQL Server 2016. Prior to that version, the Query Store simply didn't exist. The Query Store has a variety of functionality, but the chief thing it does is to collect aggregate information on the queries running within a given database, including both performance and wait metrics. In addition to this information collection, it also gathers the execution plans for those queries. The Query Store is enabled by default in Azure SQL Database. Starting with SQL Server 2022, the Query Store is also enabled by default. In SQL Server 2025, readable secondaries in an Availability Group will also be enabled by default. Any of these can be disabled individually. Prior to SQL Server 2022, the Query Store was disabled by default. Enabling, or disabling, the Query Store can be easily done through T-SQL and doesn't require a server restart. A small aside here worth noting, in an Availability Group, since secondaries are read-only, the information captured on the secondary for the Query Store is stored within the primary database and then written to the secondary as a part of the standard operation of Availability Groups. You can query it using any of the mechanisms outlined in this chapter or the rest of the book. Listing 6-1 enables the Query Store on my database.

Listing 6-1. Enabling the Query Store on AdventureWorks

```
ALTER DATABASE AdventureWorks SET QUERY_STORE = ON;
```

You can also use the database properties within SQL Server Management Studio to control the Query Store. I'll cover that in detail later in the chapter.

When the Query Store is enabled, the behavior is illustrated in Figure 6-1.

Chapter 6 Using the Query Store for Query Performance and Execution Plans

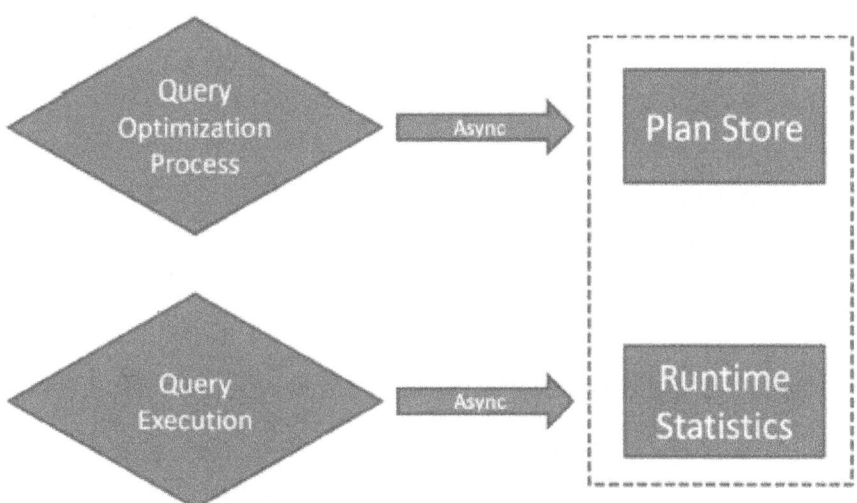

Figure 6-1. *Behavior of the Query Store when collecting data*

Query optimization is normally not affected directly by the Query Store. When a query is submitted to the system, an execution plan gets generated as outlined in Chapter 2. Normally, the plan then gets stored in the plan cache (which we'll cover in detail in Chapter 7), but plan forcing in the Query Store can change that behavior. I'll detail how plan forcing changes the standard behavior later in the chapter. Assuming there is no forced plan, after the plan gets stored in the plan cache, an asynchronous process copies the plan to a separate memory area for temporary storage. Then, another asynchronous process writes the plan to the Query Store within the database system tables. These asynchronous processes are meant to reduce the overhead from the Query Store as much as possible.

Query execution then proceeds as normal. When the query completes executing, the runtime metrics such as duration, reads, wait statistics, and more are written to a separate memory space through an asynchronous process. That data is aggregated as it's stored. Then another asynchronous process ensures that the information gets written to the system tables on your database. The default aggregation interval is 60 minutes, and you can adjust that up or down as appropriate for your system.

The information captured by the Query Store is written into the databases on which it is enabled. The query metrics and the execution plans are kept with the database. They get backed up with the database and will get restored with the database. These are system tables and will be stored on the main drive with all other system tables. If your system is to go offline for some reason, or when failing over, it is possible to lose the Query Store information that is in memory and not yet written to disk. The default interval for writing the information to disk is 15 minutes, and you can control that as well. Since this is aggregate information, the possibility of data loss in this case is not concerning.

When you query the information from the Query Store, you get both the in-memory data and the data that has been written to disk. This is automatic, and you don't have to do anything to make it happen.

Information Collected by the Query Store

The core piece of data that drives the Query Store is the individual query itself. Any given query may be part of a stored procedure or a collective batch of queries. That doesn't matter when it comes to the Query Store. It collects information based on the individual query statement. You can easily match it back to a stored procedure, the object_id is captured, but you can't connect it back to any given batch processes, except through the text of the T-SQL itself.

There are seven system tables that store the Query Store information:

- sys.query_store_query: The main table for information about the queries within the Query Store.

- sys.query_store_query_text: The T-SQL code for a given query.

- sys.query_store_plan: All the plans for a given query.

- sys.query_store_runtime_stats: The aggregated runtime metrics gathered by the Query Store.

- sys.query_store_wait_stats: Aggregated wait statistics for each query.

- sys.query_store_runtime_stats_interval: The start and stop times for each of the intervals within the Query Store.

- sys.database_query_store_options: This is a store showing the various settings within the Query Store on a given database.

There are a number of reports within Management Studio to enable you to look at Query Store information, but I also write a lot of queries to pull information I want quickly. For example, if you wanted to see information about a particular stored procedure, you could do something like Listing 6-2.

CHAPTER 6 USING THE QUERY STORE FOR QUERY PERFORMANCE AND EXECUTION PLANS

Listing 6-2. Querying the Query Store for a stored procedure query

```
SELECT qsq.query_id,
       qsq.object_id,
       qsqt.query_sql_text,
           qsp.plan_id,
       CAST(qsp.query_plan AS XML) AS QueryPlan
FROM sys.query_store_query AS qsq
   JOIN sys.query_store_query_text AS qsqt
       ON qsq.query_text_id = qsqt.query_text_id
   JOIN sys.query_store_plan AS qsp
       ON qsp.query_id = qsq.query_id
WHERE qsq.object_id = OBJECT_ID('dbo.
ProductTransactionHistoryByReference');
```

While each individual query statement is stored within the sys.query_store_query table, you also get the object_id value, so you can use functions like OBJECT_ID() as I did to identify my stored procedure by name. I also used the CAST command on the query_plan column. This is because the Query Store rightly stores this column as NVARCHAR(MAX), not XML. The XML data type has a nesting limit. You can see this in action in the DMVs where you have two places to get execution plans: sys.dm_exec_query_plan and sys.dm_exec_text_query_plan. The Query Store wisely eliminates the need for two kinds of storage, again, making it more efficient by design. So if you want to be able to click the results of the query, as shown in Figure 6-2, you'll need to use CAST as I did in Listing 6-2.

	query_id	object_id	query_sql_text	plan_id	QueryPlan
1	121	1591676718	(@ReferenceOrderID int)SELECT p.Nam...	9	<ShowPlanXML xmlns="http://schemas.microsoft.com...
2	121	1591676718	(@ReferenceOrderID int)SELECT p.Nam...	11	<ShowPlanXML xmlns="http://schemas.microsoft.com...
3	121	1591676718	(@ReferenceOrderID int)SELECT p.Nam...	55	<ShowPlanXML xmlns="http://schemas.microsoft.com...

Figure 6-2. *One query and multiple plans for a query within a stored procedure*

Here, you can see that I have a stored procedure with one statement, identified as query_id = 121. However, for that one query, there are three different execution plans in the plan_id: 9, 11, and 55.

CHAPTER 6 USING THE QUERY STORE FOR QUERY PERFORMANCE AND EXECUTION PLANS

Something important to take note of here is how the text of the query is stored in the Query Store. Since this statement is part of a stored procedure with parameters, the parameter definition is included with the T-SQL text. This is what the statement looks like within the Query Store (formatting left as is):

```
(@ReferenceOrderID int)SELECT   p.Name,                    p.
ProductNumber,              th.ReferenceOrderID      FROM     Production.
Product AS p      JOIN     Production.TransactionHistory AS
th            ON th.ProductID = p.ProductID       WHERE
th.ReferenceOrderID = @ReferenceOrderID
```

You can see the parameter definition at the start of the query. The actual stored procedure I'm using is in Listing 6-3.

Listing 6-3. Procedure definition for ProductTransactionHistoryByReference

```
CREATE OR ALTER PROC dbo.ProductTransactionHistoryByReference
(@ReferenceOrderID int)
AS
BEGIN
    SELECT p.Name,
           p.ProductNumber,
           th.ReferenceOrderID
    FROM Production.Product AS p
        JOIN Production.TransactionHistory AS th
            ON th.ProductID = p.ProductID
    WHERE th.ReferenceOrderID = @ReferenceOrderID;
END;
```

The statement stored in the Query Store is different than the statement in the stored procedure because of that parameter definition. This can lead to some minor issues when attempting to find a particular query within the Query Store. Listing 6-4 has another interesting example.

Listing 6-4. Batch process running a simple query

```
SELECT a.AddressID,
       a.AddressLine1
```

```
FROM Person.Address AS a
WHERE a.AddressID = 72;
```

While this is a batch and not a stored procedure, it can still be parameterized through simple parameterization. Luckily, the Query Store has a function for dealing with parameterization, sys.fn_stmt_sql_handle_from_sql_stmt. That function retrieves the SQL handle that can be used to identify the query as shown in Listing 6-5.

Listing 6-5. Putting sys.fn_stmt_sql_handle_from_sql_stmt to work

```
SELECT qsq.query_id,
       qsq.query_hash,
       qsqt.query_sql_text,
       qsq.query_parameterization_type
FROM sys.query_store_query_text AS qsqt
    JOIN sys.query_store_query AS qsq
        ON qsq.query_text_id = qsqt.query_text_id
    JOIN sys.fn_stmt_sql_handle_from_sql_stmt(
            'SELECT a.AddressID,
        a.AddressLine1
FROM Person.Address AS a
WHERE a.AddressID = 72;',
            2) AS fsshfss
        ON fsshfss.statement_sql_handle = qsqt.statement_sql_handle;
```

The formatting and white space all have to be the same in order for the function to succeed. The hard-coded value can be different, because it's going to get replaced anyway, but the other parts of the T-SQL have to be identical. The bad news is sys.fn_stmt_sql_handle_from_sql_stmt only works with automatic parameterization. It won't help you with prepared statements or stored procedures. To retrieve that information, you will be forced to use the LIKE command when searching for text. This is why I usually just use the object_id or query_hash values to track things down when I can. The output from Listing 6-5 is shown here in Figure 6-3.

	query_id	query_hash	query_sql_text	query_parameterization_type
1	303	0xDE0BD0B755E53296	(@1 tinyint)SELECT [a].[AddressID],[a].[AddressL...	2

Figure 6-3. *Getting the query_id for a parameterized query*

The columns should all make sense based on what we've discussed throughout the book and this chapter, but query_parameterization_type is new. It can return four different values:

- 0: Meaning no parameterization has occurred.
- 1: A user has parameterized the query.
- 2: Simple parameterization.
- 3: Forced parameterization.

We'll discuss more on parameterization elsewhere throughout the book.

Query Runtime Data

The query and the execution plan are great pieces of information to have. However, you also want to see runtime metrics. The runtime metrics are a little different than you would initially expect. First of all, the runtime metrics are matched to a given execution plan, not the query. Since each plan could, and probably will, behave differently, the runtime metrics are captured for the plan. Second, the runtime metrics are aggregated by the runtime interval. The default value for the interval is 60 minutes. This means that for each interval, you'll have a different set of runtime metrics if your query was run during that interval.

You can easily combine the runtime metrics with the information on the query itself. Because the information is aggregated into discrete intervals, it may be necessary to aggregate the aggregates, meaning sum up or average the accumulated values. While this may seem like a pain, the purpose for the aggregation intervals is extremely helpful. You have the aggregates broken up so that you have more than one point of reference. You can track how a query's behavior changes over time. Having comparison points is how you can tell if performance is degrading or improving. You get some of the granularity and detail of using Extended Events with the ease of simply querying cache, combined in the Query Store.

Listing 6-6 shows one example of how you can retrieve metrics for a specific moment in time.

CHAPTER 6 USING THE QUERY STORE FOR QUERY PERFORMANCE AND EXECUTION PLANS

Listing 6-6. Retrieving runtime information from the Query Store

```
DECLARE @CompareTime DATETIME = '2025-05-29 12:22';
SELECT CAST(qsp.query_plan AS XML),
       qsrs.count_executions,
       qsrs.avg_duration,
       qsrs.stdev_duration,
       qsws.wait_category_desc,
       qsws.avg_query_wait_time_ms,
       qsws.stdev_query_wait_time_ms
FROM sys.query_store_plan AS qsp
    JOIN sys.query_store_runtime_stats AS qsrs
        ON qsrs.plan_id = qsp.plan_id
    JOIN sys.query_store_runtime_stats_interval AS qsrsi
        ON qsrsi.runtime_stats_interval_id = qsrs.runtime_stats_interval_id
    LEFT JOIN sys.query_store_wait_stats AS qsws
        ON qsws.plan_id = qsrs.plan_id
           AND qsws.plan_id = qsrs.plan_id
           AND qsws.execution_type = qsrs.execution_type
           AND qsws.runtime_stats_interval_id = qsrs.runtime_stats_interval_id
WHERE qsp.plan_id = 11
    AND @CompareTime BETWEEN qsrsi.start_time
                     AND     qsrsi.end_time;
```

The query in Listing 6-6 pulls back both the average duration and the standard deviation for that average in order to better understand how accurate the average is. The results for my query are shown in Figure 6-4.

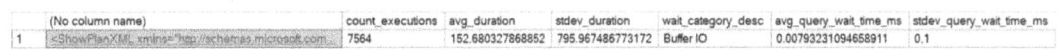

Figure 6-4. *Runtime metrics and wait statistics for a plan within one time interval*

In addition to associating the performance with a given plan, the execution context is also taken into account. A query from a batch and the same query in a stored procedure may have different behaviors.

You can combine all the metrics for a given query using Listing 6-7.

Listing 6-7. Taking an average of all Query Store runtime metrics for a query

```
WITH QSAggregate
AS (SELECT qsrs.plan_id,
            SUM(qsrs.count_executions) AS CountExecutions,
            AVG(qsrs.avg_duration) AS AvgDuration,
            AVG(qsrs.stdev_duration) AS StDevDuration,
            qsws.wait_category_desc,
            AVG(qsws.avg_query_wait_time_ms) AS AvgQueryWaitTime,
            AVG(qsws.stdev_query_wait_time_ms) AS StDevQueryWaitTime
    FROM sys.query_store_runtime_stats AS qsrs
        LEFT JOIN sys.query_store_wait_stats AS qsws
            ON qsws.plan_id = qsrs.plan_id
                AND qsws.runtime_stats_interval_id = qsrs.runtime_stats_interval_id
    GROUP BY qsrs.plan_id,
            qsws.wait_category_desc)
SELECT CAST(qsp.query_plan AS XML),
        qsa.*
FROM sys.query_store_plan AS qsp
    JOIN QSAggregate AS qsa
        ON qsa.plan_id = qsp.plan_id
WHERE qsp.plan_id = 11;
```

I use a LEFT JOIN here because you won't always have wait statistics since the Query Store only captures waits longer than 1ms. This will retrieve all performance for the plan_id specified, regardless of the interval.

Controlling the Query Store

At the start of the chapter, I showed how to enable the Query Store in Listing 6-1. There are a number of other commands you can use to take charge of how the Query Store behaves on your system. You can, of course, turn it off on a database the same way as you turned it on in Listing 6-1, just changing the value to *OFF*. Disabling the Query Store will not remove the information within it. If you wish to do that, you can run Listing 6-8.

Listing 6-8. Removing all information from the Query Store

```
ALTER DATABASE AdventureWorks SET QUERY_STORE CLEAR;
```

You can also get selective. Listing 6-9 shows how to remove either a query or a plan from the Query Store. The key is you have to know either the query or plan identifier within the Query Store.

Listing 6-9. Removing a query or a plan from the Query Store

```
EXEC sys.sp_query_store_remove_query @query_id = @QueryId;
EXEC sys.sp_query_store_remove_plan @plan_id = @PlanID;
```

The queries earlier in the chapter showed how to get both the plan_id and query_id values by searching for queries or objects using the information stored within the Query Store.

Since the Query Store uses an asynchronous process to write from memory to disk, it is possible to lose information that the Query Store has captured. If you're in a situation where you're going to perform a controlled shutdown or failover, you can ensure that you force the data out of memory and down to disk using the command shown in Listing 6-10.

Listing 6-10. Flushing the Query Store from memory to disk

```
EXEC sys.sp_query_store_flush_db;
```

Finally, you can change the default behaviors of the Query Store. There are a number of them, and we're not going to detail them all here. However, to see the current settings, you can query the information using the system view sys.database_query_store_options as shown in Listing 6-11.

Listing 6-11. Retrieving all current Query Store settings

```
SELECT *
FROM sys.database_query_store_options AS dqso;
```

Listing 6-11 is intentionally using SELECT * in order to retrieve every column. You would normally, of course, be more selective in the columns you want to retrieve. You can modify these values using T-SQL, shown in Listing 6-12, or using SQL Server Management Studio (SSMS). First is using T-SQL.

Listing 6-12. Changing the maximum storage size for the Query Store

```
ALTER DATABASE AdventureWorks SET QUERY_STORE (MAX_STORAGE_SIZE_MB = 200);
```

If you make changes to the settings within the Query Store, they take effect immediately. There are no reboots or resets of any kind required. The default values are adequate for many systems. However, there is one set of values you may want to adjust on your systems, and that's the Query Store Capture Mode.

Capture Mode

Prior to SQL Server 2019, you had only three options for how the Query Store captured queries. The default is *All*, meaning it will capture all queries. You also have the option of setting the Capture Mode to *None*. This means that the Query Store remains enabled, so you can do things like plan forcing (explained later in this chapter), but you stop capturing new data within the Query Store. Finally, you had Auto as an option. The old behavior here meant that the Query Store would only capture queries that had been executed three times or had run longer than one second. This helped reduce some of the overhead of the Query Store and helped it work well with "Optimize for Ad Hoc," a setting that helps with plan cache memory management (we'll discuss this in Chapter 7).

In Azure SQL Database and any version of SQL Server greater than 2019, you have a completely different way to control how the Query Store captures queries. Figure 6-5 shows the database properties for the Query Store within SSMS.

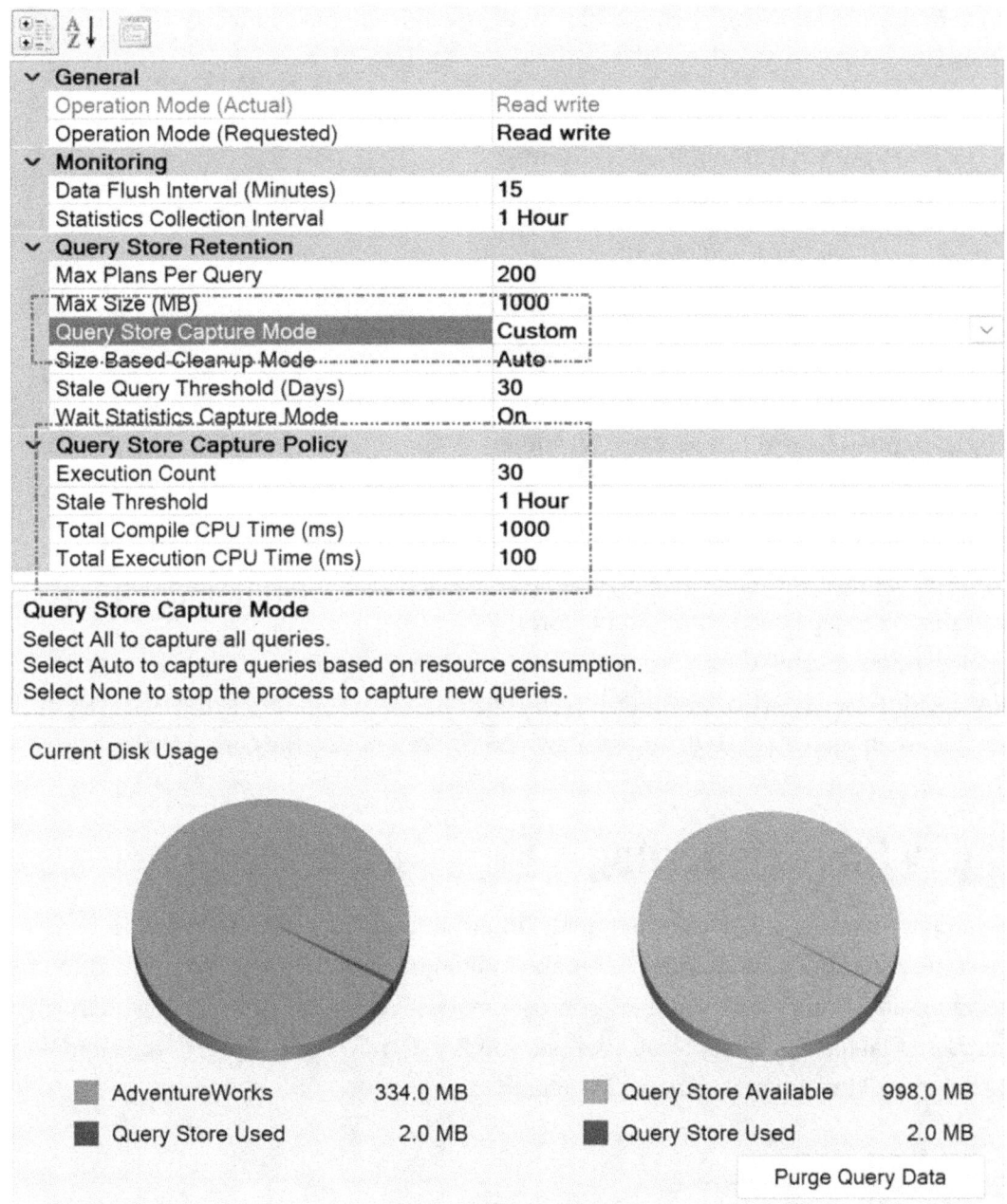

***Figure 6-5.** Changing the Capture Mode to Custom*

I've highlighted two areas in Figure 6-5. The first, on top, shows where you change the Query Store Capture Mode. It's set to Custom, the new mechanism for controlling the Query Store. When you select Custom from the drop-down menu, it enables the second

CHAPTER 6   USING THE QUERY STORE FOR QUERY PERFORMANCE AND EXECUTION PLANS

set of properties I have highlighted there in Figure 6-5. You have four settings you can control:

- Execution Count: The number of times a query must run before you capture it within the Query Store

- Stale Threshold: The time period in which the query must meet the other criteria you're setting

- Total Compile CPU Time (ms): The total amount of CPU used during the time period before it gets captured

- Total Execution CPU Time (ms): As with compile CPU time, but measuring the execution CPU time

Obviously, some information is captured on these queries in order for the Query Store to know when it must capture all the information it would normally capture. However, using these filters allows you to take very direct control over how much information is captured by the Query Store.

Just remember, all these settings for the Query Store are on a database level only. If you decide to set a particular value and you want it to be a standard across the system, you'll have to set it on each database on which you're running the Query Store.

Query Store Reporting

In addition to using T-SQL to consume the information captured by the Query Store, there are a number of customizable reports built into SSMS. These reports provide a very full set of functionality, making consuming these reports flexible and easy. On any database that has the Query Store enabled, you'll see a new folder, Query Store, and inside of it all the reports as shown in Figure 6-6.

CHAPTER 6 USING THE QUERY STORE FOR QUERY PERFORMANCE AND EXECUTION PLANS

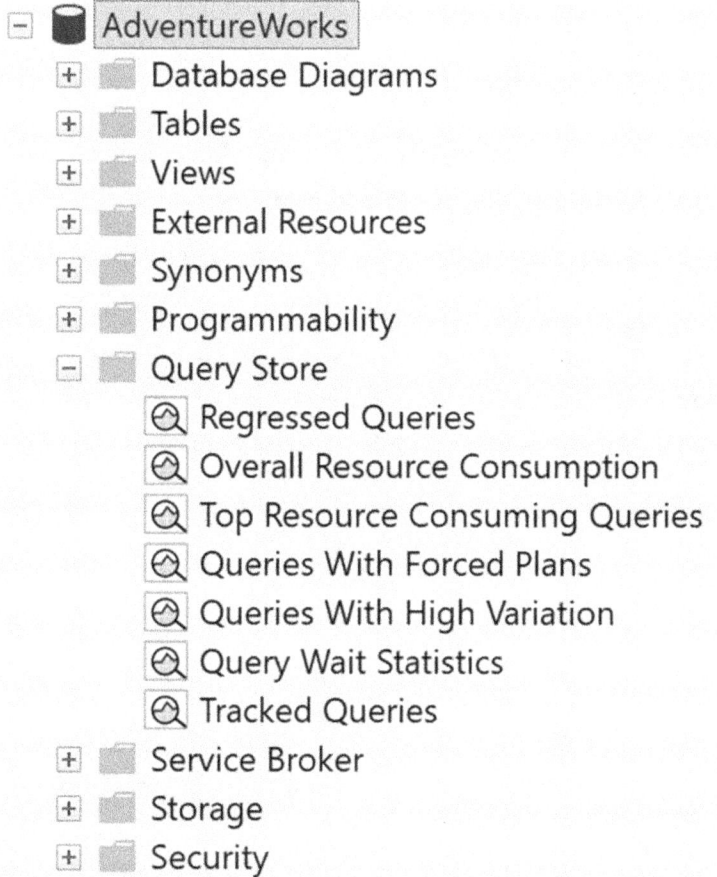

Figure 6-6. *Query Store reports within a database*

The reports are as follows:

- Regressed Queries: Queries that have suffered negative impacts from a change in execution plan.

- Overall Resource Consumption: This report shows the resource consumption over a given time period, by default, one month.

- Top Resource Consuming Queries: The queries that are using the most resources based on the information currently in the Query Store.

- Queries With Forced Plans: Any queries where you have enabled plan forcing.

195

CHAPTER 6   USING THE QUERY STORE FOR QUERY PERFORMANCE AND EXECUTION PLANS

- Queries With High Variation: A report that displays queries that have a high degree of variation in their runtime metrics, frequently with more than one execution plan.

- Query Wait Statistics: Focused on the waits taking place on your database, broken down by query and wait type.

- Tracked Queries: You can mark a query in the Query Store and then use this report to track the behavior of all marked queries.

We don't have the space to cover every report in detail. I'm going to focus on the report you're most likely to make use of, Top Resource Consuming Queries. Double-click the report to open it, and you'll see something similar to Figure 6-7.

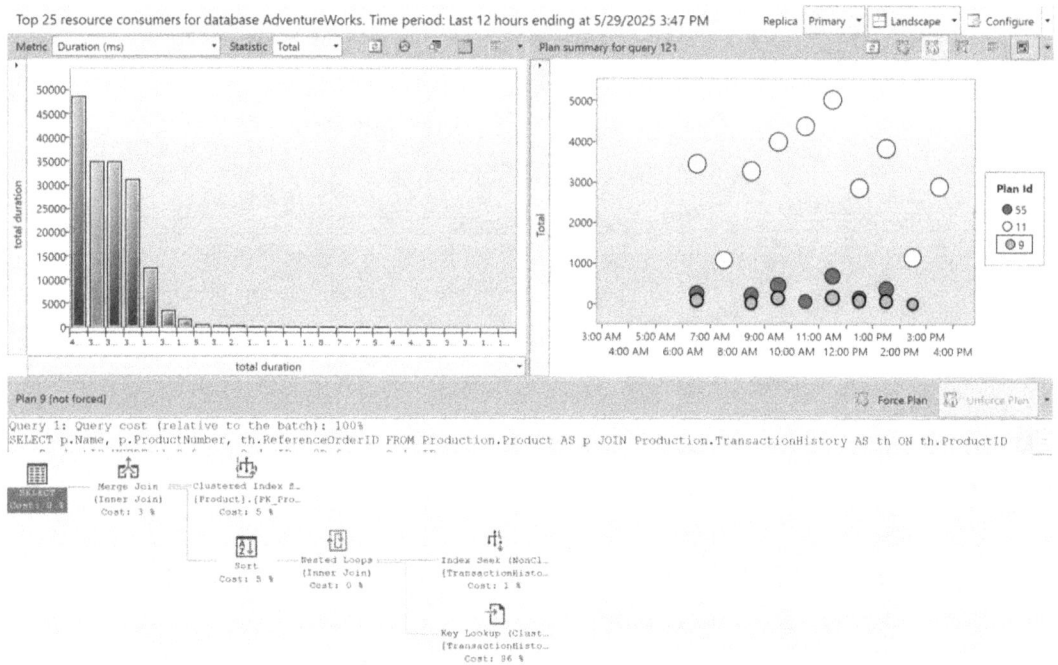

Figure 6-7. *Top 25 Resource Consumers report from the Query Store*

The report consists of three different pieces of data. On the top left is a listing of the most costly reports. On the top right are the execution plans for the query that is currently highlighted on the left. At the bottom is the execution plan.

Hover the mouse over the queries on the left, and you'll get information about the query in question as you can see in Figure 6-8.

CHAPTER 6 USING THE QUERY STORE FOR QUERY PERFORMANCE AND EXECUTION PLANS

Query Id   121

Object Id   1591676718

Object Name   ProductTransactionHistoryByReference

Total Duration (ms) 34898.4

Execution Count   166589

Plan Count   3

```
(@ReferenceOrderID int)SELECT  p.Name,
       p.ProductNumber,
       th.ReferenceOrderID
FROM   Production.Product AS p
JOIN   Production.TransactionHistory AS th
       ON th.ProductID = p.ProductID
WHERE  th.ReferenceOrderID = @ReferenceOrderID
```

Figure 6-8. *Properties about the query from the report*

You can see important pieces of information such as the execution count, the query itself, and the number of plans associated.

You can also hover over the plans on the right side of Figure 6-7, and you'll get information about that execution plan, something like Figure 6-9.

CHAPTER 6   USING THE QUERY STORE FOR QUERY PERFORMANCE AND EXECUTION PLANS

Plan Id	11
Execution Type	Completed
Plan Forced	No
Interval Start	2025-05-29 14:00:00.000 +02:00
Interval End	2025-05-29 15:00:00.000 +02:00
Execution Count	7564
Total Duration (ms)	1154.87
Avg Duration (ms)	0.15
Min Duration (ms)	0.04
Max Duration (ms)	66.85
Std Dev Duration (ms)	0.8
Variation Duration (ms)	5.21

Figure 6-9. Properties about a given execution plan

Each of those plans represents different moments in time between plan compiles and recompiles as well as plan changes. You can see the performance metrics for the plan in question including such things as the execution count for the plan, as opposed to the one for the query.

On the top right of the report is a button labeled Configure. Clicking that brings up the full configuration screen for the report as shown in Figure 6-10.

CHAPTER 6 USING THE QUERY STORE FOR QUERY PERFORMANCE AND EXECUTION PLANS

Figure 6-10. *Report configuration window*

You can pick any of those metrics to get a whole new report. You can also decide between various aggregations for those metrics. Below that, you can pick the time interval, including full customization. The number of queries can be controlled by setting the Return value. Finally, you can filter the data based on the number of execution plans per query.

The report has one last piece of functionality worth mentioning. On both the plan runtime metrics and the plan itself, there is a button that lets you force or unforce a given plan. Figure 6-11 shows the buttons from the execution plan.

Figure 6-11. *Forcing and unforcing plans from the reports*

We're going to cover plan forcing in detail in the next section.

Plan Forcing

The majority of the functionality in the Query Store is very much focused around capturing the plans, runtime metrics, and wait statistics of the queries on the database. There is, however, one additional piece of functionality, plan forcing. Plan forcing is simply the ability to mark an execution plan as the preferred plan. The optimization process occurs as per normal. Then, a check is made to see if there is a forced plan. If there is one, then that plan will be used, if it's a valid execution plan.

The main point of forcing plans is the ability to ensure consistent behavior from your queries. A recompile of a query could lead to changes in behavior that negatively impact the system. Forcing a plan makes that behavior go away by ensuring one plan is used instead of any other.

Most queries support plan forcing. If there are any that don't, you will get an error. Only two types of cursors support plan forcing: fast forward and static.

Plan forcing is very easy to implement. You have to supply the query_id and the plan_id. That's it. Listing 6-13 shows the T-SQL.

CHAPTER 6   USING THE QUERY STORE FOR QUERY PERFORMANCE AND EXECUTION PLANS

Listing 6-13. Forcing an execution plan

```
EXEC sys.sp_query_store_force_plan 121, 11;
```

After running this command, any time the query in question gets compiled or recompiled, the plan represented by the ID value, 11, will be used. However, there is a rare exception where the optimizer can use a different plan after recompiling. The plan will be almost exactly the same. The actual term used by Microsoft for this event is "a morally equivalent plan." Again, this is a rare event, but it does happen.

With a forced plan in place, we can take a look at the "Queries With Forced Plans" report, visible in Figure 6-12.

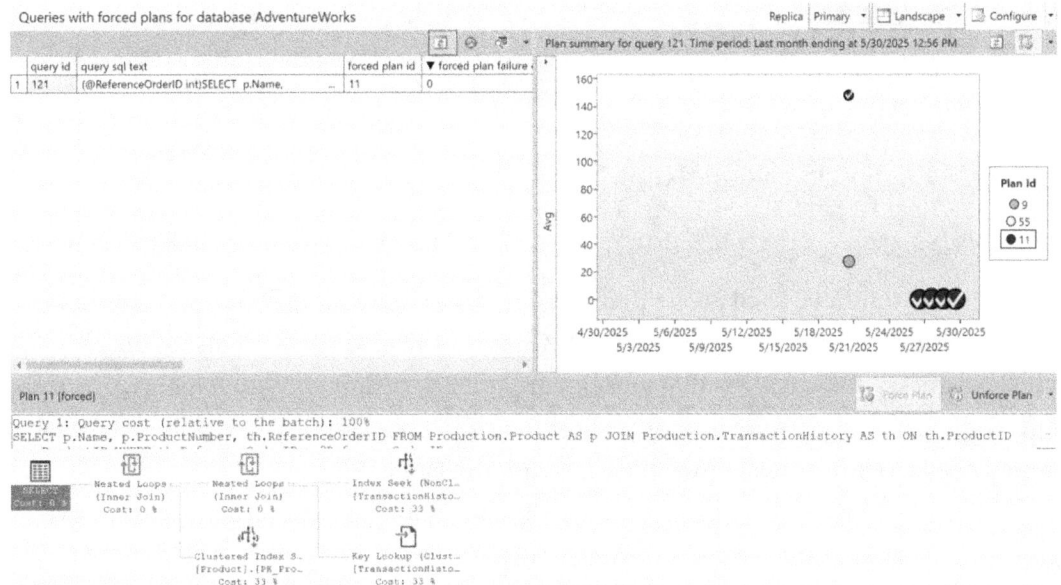

Figure 6-12.   *Queries With Forced Plans*

As you can see, the report looks similar to the Top 25 Resource Consumers shown in Figure 6-7. The behaviors are all largely the same as well. The key difference is that the upper left simply shows a list of all queries with forced plans. Another difference is visible in the list of plans where we can see that one plan has a check mark on it. This is showing the plan that is currently being forced.

I can unforce the plan by ensuring it's selected and then hitting the appropriate button from Figure 6-11.

Forcing Query Hints

Query hints are a badly named piece of functionality. Instead of suggestions, or hints, they are quite literally commandments. There are a large number of query hints, and several will be shown throughout the book.

> **Note** Query hints take away choices from the optimizer. Their use must be done extremely judiciously after thorough testing and as a last resort.

Using the Query Store to force a hint on a query is available in Azure SQL Database and SQL Server 2022 and greater. The concept is almost the same as plan forcing. Identify the query you wish to add a query hint to. Get its ID value from the Query Store. Then, use the code in Listing 6-14.

Listing 6-14. Forcing a query hint

```
EXEC sys.sp_query_store_set_hints 550, N'OPTION(OPTIMIZE FOR UNKOWN)';
```

The query hint I've used is one that is common when dealing with bad parameter sniffing issues (discussed at great length in Chapter 13). The beauty of using the sp_query_store_set_hints code is that you can apply a query hint without having to change your code in any way. There is another method called plan guides, that's similar, but it simply doesn't work as well as what we get with the Query Store.

Unlike plan forcing, hint forcing isn't visible in SSMS. You have to run queries to see which queries have hints applied (Listing 6-15).

Listing 6-15. Querying to see which queries have hints

```
SELECT qsqh.query_hint_id,
       qsqh.query_id,
       qsqh.query_hint_text,
       qsqh.source_desc
FROM sys.query_store_query_hints AS qsqh;
```

Finally, you can remove hints as shown in Listing 6-16.

Listing 6-16. Clearing hints from the Query Store

```
EXEC sp_query_store_clear_hints @query_id = 550;
```

Just like with plan forcing, forcing a hint is persisted in the event of a reboot or failover. Hints that are not valid will be ignored.

Optimized Plan Forcing

Intelligent Query Processing (covered in detail in Chapter 21) is a number of internal enhancements for query performance addressing common issues. One of those common issues is the query optimization process. Sometimes, generating the execution plan can be a very resource-intensive operation. As such, starting with SQL Server compatibility level 160 (which means SQL Server 2022 and Azure SQL Database), Microsoft has changed the way some plan generation occurs.

When a plan is generated and it crosses internal thresholds within the optimizer, a portion of the optimization will be stored in a hidden attribute within the XML in the Query Store. What's stored there is a replay script for the optimization process, making for faster optimization.

The trade-off is additional storage vs. savings in processing. The optimizer estimates how long optimization will take. If it's wrong on that estimate and the resources, counted by objects, number of joins, optimization tasks, and optimization time, exceed internal thresholds, the script is persisted.

In SQL Server 2022 or greater and Azure SQL Database, this behavior is enabled by default on new databases. You can disable it using Database Scoped Configuration like in Listing 6-17.

Listing 6-17. Disabling optimized plan forcing

```
ALTER DATABASE SCOPED CONFIGURATION SET OPTIMIZED_PLAN_FORCING = OFF;
```

You can also use a query hint to disable optimized plan forcing for a single query, DISABLE_OPTIMIZED_PLAN_FORCING.

Not all queries are eligible for optimized plan forcing. If the optimization process is anything other than FULL, the query can't get this benefit. Distributed queries are ineligible. Queries with the RECOMPILE hint are also not allowed.

Even though you can't see the replay script, you can see which queries and plans have one. Simply query the Query Store tables like in Listing 6-18.

Listing 6-18. Using the has_compile_replay_script column

```
SELECT qsqt.query_sql_text,
       TRY_CAST(qsp.query_plan AS XML) AS query_plan,
       qsp.is_forced_plan
FROM sys.query_store_plan AS qsp
    INNER JOIN sys.query_store_query AS qsq
        ON qsp.query_id = qsq.query_id
    INNER JOIN sys.query_store_query_text AS qsqt
        ON qsq.query_text_id = qsqt.query_text_id
WHERE qsp.has_compile_replay_script = 1;
```

Finally, you can disable optimized plan forcing by forcing a plan using the disable_optimized_plan_forcing parameter. You can query for these using the is_optimized_plan_forcing_disabled column.

Query Store for Upgrades

While general query performance monitoring and tuning may be the day-to-day common use for the Query Store, one of the most powerful purposes behind the tool is its use as a safety net for upgrading SQL Server.

Let's assume that you are planning to migrate from SQL Server 2016 to SQL Server 2025. Traditionally, you would upgrade your database on a test instance somewhere and then run a battery of tests to ensure that things are going to work well. If you catch and document all the issues, great. Unfortunately, it might require some code rewrites because of some of the changes to the optimizer or the cardinality estimation engine. That could cause delays to the upgrade, or the business might even decide to try to avoid it altogether (a frequent, if poor, choice). That assumes you catch the issues. It's entirely possible to miss that a particular query has suddenly started behaving poorly because of a change in estimated row counts or something else.

This is where the Query Store becomes your safety net for upgrades. First, you should do all the testing and attempt to address issues using standard methods. That shouldn't change. However, the Query Store adds additional functionality to the standard methods. Here are the steps to follow:

1. Restore your database to the new SQL Server instance or upgrade your instance. This assumes the production machine, but you can do this with a test machine as well.

2. Leave the database in the older compatibility mode. Do not change it to the new mode because you will enable both the new optimizer and the new cardinality estimation engine before we've captured data.

3. Enable the Query Store. It can run in compatibility mode.

4. Run your tests or run your system for a period of time that ensures that you have covered the majority of queries within the system. This time will vary depending on your needs.

5. Change the compatibility mode to the latest value.

6. Let your load run for a period of time. Run the report "Query With High Variation" or "Regressed Queries." One of these reports will find queries that have suddenly started running slower than they had previously.

7. Investigate those queries. If it's obvious that the query plan has changed and that is the cause of the change in performance, then pick a plan from prior to the change and use plan forcing to make that plan the one used by SQL Server.

8. Where necessary, take the time to rewrite the queries and/or restructure the system to ensure that the query can, on its own, compile a plan that performs well with the system.

This approach won't prevent all problems. You still must test your system. However, using the Query Store will provide you with mechanisms for dealing with internal changes within SQL Server that affect your query plans and subsequently your performance. You can also use similar processes to apply a Cumulative Update.

CHAPTER 6 USING THE QUERY STORE FOR QUERY PERFORMANCE AND EXECUTION PLANS

Summary

With the Query Store, you have one more tool in your toolbox to assist in identifying poorly performing queries. When you need detailed analysis, you'll still rely on Extended Events. However, when you want fast access to data with the ability to do comparisons between points in time, the Query Store has you covered. With the ability to capture multiple execution plans per query so you can see how that changes performance over time, you've got even more than you had before. Finally, you can force plans and force hints to get the behavior you want out of your queries.

In the last several chapters, we've discussed how execution plans get created, how to read them, and even how to force them through the Query Store. In the next chapter, we discuss how the query plan cache behaves in SQL Server and how it can impact the performance of your systems.

CHAPTER 7

Execution Plan Cache Behavior

The query optimization process is expensive. Because of this, SQL Server keeps the execution plans it has created in memory in order to reuse those plans. The space where these plans are stored is referred to as the *plan cache*. Understanding how plans get into, and out of, the plan cache is an important part of query tuning. In this chapter, I will walk you through the mechanisms you can use to monitor and observe the plan cache and plan reuse.

I will cover the following topics:

- Querying the plan cache
- Using the query plan hash and query hash as mechanisms for identifying problematic queries
- Mechanisms to improve plan reuse through the cache
- Interactions between the Query Store and plan cache

Querying the Plan Cache

The first place to go for information about the plan cache is the Dynamic Management Views. Listing 7-1 shows how to query the sys.dm_exec_cached_plans DMV.

Listing 7-1. Querying the plan cache for useful information

```
SELECT decp.refcounts,
       decp.usecounts,
       decp.size_in_bytes,
```

```
        decp.cacheobjtype,
        decp.objtype,
        decp.plan_handle
FROM sys.dm_exec_cached_plans AS decp;
```

Table 7-1 defines the information we're retrieving from sys.dm_exec_cached_plans with this query.

Table 7-1. *Useful information in sys.dm_exec_cached_plans*

Column Name	Description
refcounts	The number of objects in cache referencing this plan. It will always be at least 1.
usecounts	Number of times the plan has been looked up. That doesn't equal the number of times a query used the plan though.
size_in_bytes	The size of the plan in cache.
cacheobjecttype	One of several different types of plans available. It's driven by the query, the object type, and whether or not *Optimize for Ad Hoc* has been enabled (covered later in the chapter).
objtype	The exact object type this plan has been created for. Ad hoc queries get an ad hoc type here.
plan_handle	The plan_handle for the plan. This is used to join to other DMVs like sys.dm_exec_query_plan.

This DMV can be combined with other DMVs to get information like currently running metrics from sys.dm_exec_requests, aggregations from sys.dm_exec_query_stats, and, as was already mentioned, sys.dm_exec_query_plan to get the execution plan.

Plans don't remain in cache forever. Rebooting the server, shutting down SQL Server, failovers, detaching a database, any of these, and many more can remove all plans from cache. Also, plans age in cache and can be removed due to memory pressure. We'll cover a lot of this in detail in Chapter 8 when we discuss query recompiles. When a plan is removed from cache, for any reason, you also will no longer see it in this, or any other, DMV.

Execution Plan Caching and Plan Reuse

As soon as a query is submitted to SQL Server, after checking the syntax, SQL Server will look for a matching execution plan in the plan cache. If one is not found, then the optimization process occurs as outlined in Chapter 2. If there is a forced plan from the Query Store, its plan will be used instead of this newly compiled plan. If there is a plan that matches both the query and the execution context (ANSI settings and others; we'll go over it as we proceed), then that plan is reused instead of going through the compilation process again. This saves CPU and some memory.

Whether you're dealing with ad hoc queries, stored procedures, or something else, it's always a good idea to provide filter criteria to limit the result set. The mechanisms of filtering data absolutely affect plan reuse as we're going to outline. As a general practice, the old-school saying "only move the data you need and only when you need it" still very much applies in this modern age. So please, do use filtering criteria as much as possible on your queries. This will be a frequent topic throughout the book.

You can very broadly classify all queries within SQL Server into two categories that will drive how and when those plans get reused:

- Ad hoc

- Prepared

In the following sections, we'll define what kind of queries both of these represent and show how they may, or may not, get reused. As a part of this, we're going to be removing plans from cache manually throughout the chapter. There are two methods you can use:

- DBCC FREEPROCCACHE: Running this command will remove all plans from cache, across all databases, forcing new compilations of each of your plans. You can alter this command to remove only a single plan by passing the plan_handle value. You can also use the sql_handle or resource pool name with this command.

- ALTER DATABASE SCOPED CONFIGURATION CLEAR PROCEDURE_CACHE: This command will only remove the plans from the database you run the command in. Starting with SQL Server 2019, and in Azure SQL Database and Managed Instance, you can also supply a plan_handle to remove only one plan from cache.

As we work through the chapter, use any method that works for you. Earlier chapters showed how to get the plan_handle, and we'll include more examples later in this chapter.

Caution Running DBCC FREEPROCCACHE on a production environment without focusing through the plan_handle or sql_handle can lead to serious negative performance repercussions. Exercise caution when using this command.

Ad Hoc Workload

Queries can be submitted to SQL Server without defining parameters. These types of queries, whether they're using hard-coded values or variables, are referred to as ad hoc, either workloads or queries. Most of the examples in the book up to this chapter have been ad hoc queries. Listing 7-2 shows an example of an ad hoc query that we'll use to explore plan cache behavior.

Listing 7-2. An ad hoc query retrieving information from SQL Server

```
SELECT soh.SalesOrderNumber,
       soh.OrderDate,
       sod.OrderQty,
       sod.LineTotal
FROM Sales.SalesOrderHeader AS soh
    JOIN Sales.SalesOrderDetail AS sod
        ON soh.SalesOrderID = sod.SalesOrderID
WHERE soh.CustomerID = 29690
    AND sod.ProductID = 711;
```

The values in the WHERE clause here are hard-coded, meaning they can't change. As structured, this query will always have those same values. Even if we substitute local variables and add the values there, it's not the same thing as preparing a parameterized query. Because of this, any change in these values basically means you're getting a new execution plan because the query is fundamentally not the same. We'll cover how prepared queries differ in the next section.

CHAPTER 7 EXECUTION PLAN CACHE BEHAVIOR

When the query in Listing 7-2 gets submitted, an execution plan is created and stored in cache in anticipation of the exact same query getting submitted more than once. The hard-coded values define the plan and are stored with it. For a plan to get reused from cache, the T-SQL must match exactly. This includes all spaces and carriage returns plus any values supplied with the query. If any of these change, the plan cannot be reused.

If we execute the query in Listing 7-2, a plan is created and stored in cache. We can then query sys.dm_exec_cached_plans to see information about the query as you see in Listing 7-3.

Listing 7-3. Retrieving information about an ad hoc query

```
SELECT c.usecounts,
       c.cacheobjtype,
       c.objtype
FROM sys.dm_exec_cached_plans AS c
    CROSS APPLY sys.dm_exec_sql_text(c.plan_handle) AS t
WHERE t.text = 'SELECT soh.SalesOrderNumber,
       soh.OrderDate,
       sod.OrderQty,
       sod.LineTotal
FROM Sales.SalesOrderHeader AS soh
    JOIN Sales.SalesOrderDetail AS sod
        ON soh.SalesOrderID = sod.SalesOrderID
WHERE soh.CustomerID = 29690
    AND sod.ProductID = 711;';
```

A couple of quick points. I carefully executed the query, highlighting it so the text matches t.text in Listing 7-3. Also, I made sure that the formatting, including white space, in Listing 7-3 was exactly the same as Listing 7-2. Figure 7-1 shows the results.

	usecounts	cacheobjtype	objtype
1	1	Compiled Plan	Adhoc

Figure 7-1. Results of one execution of an ad hoc query

CHAPTER 7 ■ EXECUTION PLAN CACHE BEHAVIOR

Figure 7-1 outlines exactly what we should have expected from the earlier descriptions. A plan was compiled and added to cache. It was executed once, and it's marked as an Adhoc plan. If we execute the query in Listing 7-2 a second time and then query the plan cache, you can see the change in Figure 7-2.

	usecounts	cacheobjtype	objtype
1	2	Compiled Plan	Adhoc

Figure 7-2. *A second execution shown for the ad hoc query*

This is confirmation of plan reuse in effect. However, if we were to change something about the query in Listing 7-2 to look like Listing 7-4, where soh.CustomerID is now 29500, different behavior occurs.

Listing 7-4. Changing the ad hoc query

```
SELECT soh.SalesOrderNumber,
       soh.OrderDate,
       sod.OrderQty,
       sod.LineTotal
FROM Sales.SalesOrderHeader AS soh
    JOIN Sales.SalesOrderDetail AS sod
        ON soh.SalesOrderID = sod.SalesOrderID
WHERE soh.CustomerID = 29500
    AND sod.ProductID = 711;
```

If we were to rerun Listing 7-2 again, we wouldn't see a change. Instead, let's modify the query against sys.dm_exec_cached_plans to return information about both ad hoc queries as you see in Listing 7-5.

Listing 7-5. Showing the existence of a new execution plan in cache

```
SELECT c.usecounts,
       c.cacheobjtype,
       c.objtype,
       t.text,
       c.plan_handle
FROM sys.dm_exec_cached_plans AS c
```

```
        CROSS APPLY sys.dm_exec_sql_text(c.plan_handle) AS t
WHERE   t.text LIKE 'SELECT  soh.SalesOrderNumber,
            soh.OrderDate,
            sod.OrderQty,
            sod.LineTotal
FROM    Sales.SalesOrderHeader AS soh
JOIN    Sales.SalesOrderDetail AS sod
            ON soh.SalesOrderID = sod.SalesOrderID%';
```

The results from Listing 7-5 are shown in Figure 7-3.

	usecounts	cacheobjtype	objtype	text		plan_handle
1	2	Compiled Plan	Adhoc	SELECT soh.SalesOrderNumber,	soh.OrderDa...	0x06000500F53A601F0069101E1102000001000000000000...
2	1	Compiled Plan	Adhoc	SELECT soh.SalesOrderNumber,	soh.OrderDa...	0x060005006E4AFD27609577101102000001000000000000...

Figure 7-3. *The existing plan was not reused*

You can see that there are now two plans in cache: one that has been executed twice and a second with only one execution. You can validate that there are in fact two plans by looking at the plan_handle values. If we were to continue changing the values from Listing 7-2 and Listing 7-4, we would continue generating new execution plans. This behavior increases the load on the CPU and uses up a lot of memory. However, there are ways to change the behavior of some ad hoc queries.

Optimize for Ad Hoc Workloads

When you have a system with a lot of ad hoc queries, you can get some improvement through enabling a setting called *Optimize for Ad Hoc Workloads*. This setting is enabled at the server level, and it changes the way SQL Server deals with ad hoc queries. Instead of saving the plan in cache, after the compile is complete, a plan stub is stored. A stub doesn't actually store the execution plan, saving all that memory. Instead, the plan stub has just enough information to identify the query. When the same query is called a second time, then the plan is stored in cache.

Enabling Optimize for Ad Hoc on the server is straightforward as you see in Listing 7-6.

Listing 7-6. Enabling Optimize for Ad Hoc Workloads

```
EXEC sys.sp_configure 'show advanced option', '1';
GO
RECONFIGURE;
GO
EXEC sys.sp_configure 'optimize for ad hoc workloads', 1;
GO
RECONFIGURE;
```

After changing this option, I'm going to flush the cache using one of the mechanisms outlined earlier in the chapter. I'm going to execute our ad hoc query from Listing 7-2. Then, I'm going to modify Listing 7-3 so that it includes size_in_bytes_column. With that added to the query, the results are visible in Figure 7-4.

	usecounts	cacheobjtype	objtype	size_in_bytes
1	1	Compiled Plan Stub	Adhoc	456

Figure 7-4. *Results from sys.dm_exec_cached_plans showing size_in_bytes*

The current size in bytes for this query is 456. That is a plan stub. We know this primarily because cacheobjtype says so. However, we can validate it. If we execute the query from Listing 7-2 a second time and then query sys.dm_exec_cached_plans again, we'll see a change in Figure 7-5.

	usecounts	cacheobjtype	objtype	size_in_bytes
1	1	Compiled Plan	Adhoc	131072

Figure 7-5. *The plan stub has been replaced by a compiled plan*

The cacheobjtype has changed to Compiled Plan, and the size has increased from 456 to 131072. You can now see exactly the kind of memory savings available when using *Optimize for Ad Hoc Workloads*. Before proceeding, use Listing 7-7 to disable this setting.

Listing 7-7. Disabling Optimize for Ad Hoc Workloads

```
EXEC sp_configure 'optimize for ad hoc workloads', 0;
GO
RECONFIGURE;
GO
EXEC sp_configure 'show advanced option', '0';
GO
RECONFIGURE;
```

I recommend enabling this on most systems. As with any recommendation made by anyone, you should test this on your environment to be sure. There is a cost when a query runs a second time; you have to recompile that query. However, the savings in memory can be fairly radical, depending on your environment. In all the tests I've run, this is a beneficial setting with very little downside.

Simple Parameterization

Part of the optimization process has the optimizer examining your queries to see if it can identify places where a parameter can be substituted for hard-coded values. When it does identify such a situation, it will parameterize your execution plan through a process called *simple parameterization*.

During the process of simple parameterization, the optimizer ensures that if the ad hoc query is parameterized, the changes in parameter values won't wildly change the execution plan. If it determines that parameterization is safe, the actual structure of the query is changed, and an execution plan based on that restructured query is generated. Listing 7-8 shows a query that will go through the simple parameterization process.

Listing 7-8. A simple ad hoc query that is a candidate for parameterization

```
SELECT a.AddressLine1,
       a.City,
       a.StateProvinceID
FROM Person.Address AS a
WHERE a.AddressID = 42;
```

Executing this query and then looking at sys.dm_exec_cached_plans, Figure 7-6 shows the results.

CHAPTER 7 EXECUTION PLAN CACHE BEHAVIOR

usecounts	cacheobjtype	objtype	text
1	Compiled Plan	Adhoc	SELECT a.AddressLine1, a.City, a.StateProvinc...
1	Compiled Plan	Prepared	(@1 tinyint)SELECT [a].[AddressLine1],[a].[City],[a].[StateP...

Figure 7-6. *sys.dm_exec_cached_plans showing simple parameterization*

Highlighted in Figure 7-6 is the line showing the execution plan that has been compiled using simple parameterization. You can see the addition of a parameter definition at the front of the text column, *(@1 tinyint)*. Also, the objtype has been changed to *Prepared*.

While the original ad hoc query is not executed, you can see a plan has been added to cache for it, just above the one highlighted in Figure 7-6. Before creating the parameterized plan, it has to create the full query tree as part of the process. That's the plan you see.

Worth noting is the data type of the parameter, tinyint. This is because of the value being used in the query. If we were to change Listing 7-8 to Listing 7-9, we would see different results.

Listing 7-9. Same query with a higher hard-coded value

```
SELECT a.AddressLine1,
       a.City,
       a.StateProvinceID
FROM Person.Address AS a
WHERE a.AddressID = 32509;
```

Querying sys.dm_exec_cached_plans, a new plan has been added as you can see in Figure 7-7.

	usecounts	cacheobjtype	objtype	text
1	1	Compiled Plan	Adhoc	SELECT a.AddressLine1, a.City, a.StateProvince...
2	1	Compiled Plan	Prepared	(@1 smallint)SELECT [a].[AddressLine1],[a].[City],[a].[Stat...
3	2	Compiled Plan	Adhoc	SELECT c.usecounts, c.cacheobjtype, c.objtype, ...
4	1	Compiled Plan	Adhoc	SELECT a.AddressLine1, a.City, a.StateProvince...
5	1	Compiled Plan	Prepared	(@1 tinyint)SELECT [a].[AddressLine1],[a].[City],[a].[StateP...

Figure 7-7. *A change in the simple parameterization*

CHAPTER 7 ■ EXECUTION PLAN CACHE BEHAVIOR

You can see why a new plan has been generated. The plan from before used a parameter value of a tinyint. The new hard-coded value, 32509, will not fit inside a tinyint. So, instead, a new plan has been created using a smallint as a parameter. Yes, if you sent the query with an even higher value, you'd get a new plan using an int. While this adds some overhead to the amount of memory being used in the plan cache, it's not even remotely as much as what would be needed to store each ad hoc plan.

We'll change the query one more time as shown in Listing 7-10.

Listing 7-10. *Another query using a tinyint*

```
SELECT a.AddressLine1,
       a.City,
       a.StateProvinceID
FROM Person.Address AS a
WHERE a.AddressID = 56;
```

Once again, querying sys.dm_exec_cached_plans, we see Figure 7-8.

usecounts	cacheobjtype	objtype	text
1	Compiled Plan	Prepared	(@1 smallint)SELECT [a].[AddressLine1].[a].[City].[a].[Stat...
3	Compiled Plan	Adhoc	SELECT c.usecounts, c.cacheobjtype, c.objtype, ...
1	Compiled Plan	Adhoc	SELECT a.AddressLine1, a.City, a.StateProvince...
2	Compiled Plan	Prepared	(@1 tinyint)SELECT [a].[AddressLine1].[a].[City].[a].[StateP...

Figure 7-8. *The prepared plan has now been used twice*

You can see in Figure 7-8 the plan used by the query was the same one originally parameterized. The parameterization means that this is the plan that will be reused as long as the data types match. Also, no additional compiles are necessary through the optimizer, helping to reduce resource usage.

Another thing to note about the parameterized query shown in Figure 7-8 is that the text of the query has been modified beyond simply adding the parameter definition at the front. You also see brackets that have been added around all the object names. SQL Server creates this new code from a template, and it uses brackets to deal with the fact that you may have object names that require them. However, it also means that additional code changes can be made. Take Listing 7-11 for an example.

217

CHAPTER 7 ■ EXECUTION PLAN CACHE BEHAVIOR

Listing 7-11. A SELECT query using the BETWEEN operator

```
SELECT a.AddressLine1,
       a.PostalCode
FROM Person.Address AS a
WHERE a.AddressID
BETWEEN 40 AND 60;
```

Querying sys.dm_exec_cached_plans and sys.dm_exec_sql_text as before, we get the results in Figure 7-9.

usecounts	cacheobjtype	objtype	text
1	Compiled Plan	Adhoc	SELECT a.AddressLine1, a.PostalCode FROM Perso...
1	Compiled Plan	Prepared	(@1 tinyint,@2 tinyint)SELECT [a].[AddressLine1],[a].[Posta...

Figure 7-9. *Changes to the query result in changes in the cache*

You can pretty easily see that the simple parameterization has been done for the two hard-coded values used in the BETWEEN operation. However, there's more that may not be readily apparent. This is the unformatted code from sys.dm_exec_sql_text:

(@1 tinyint,@2 tinyint)SELECT [a].[AddressLine1],[a].[PostalCode] FROM [Person].[Address] [a] WHERE [a].[AddressID]>=@1 AND [a].[AddressID]<=@2

The key point to notice here is that the original query was a BETWEEN operator, but instead, the optimizer has chosen to change to >= and <= for compiling the plan. In fact, let's try running this query itself as an ad hoc query shown in Listing 7-12.

Listing 7-12. Changing the query to what the optimizer liked

```
SELECT a.AddressLine1,
       a.PostalCode
FROM Person.Address AS a
WHERE a.AddressID >= 40
      AND a.AddressID <= 60;
```

Now if we look at the output from sys.dm_exec_cached_plans, we'll see something interesting in Figure 7-10.

usecounts	cacheobjtype	objtype	text
1	Compiled Plan	Adhoc	SELECT a.AddressLine1, a.PostalCode FROM Perso...
2	Compiled Plan	Prepared	(@1 tinyint,@2 tinyint)SELECT [a].[AddressLine1],[a].[Posta...

Figure 7-10.* Reuse of the parameterized query*

We see here that the plan that was compiled for Listing 7-11 is now used for Listing 7-12, which matches what the optimizer wanted to do anyway. So not only will SQL Server modify the queries when it parameterizes them, but it can spot the template it used and will then automatically reuse that template.

Simple parameterization is used fairly sparingly. SQL Server takes a conservative approach to the application of parameterization because ad hoc queries frequently benefit from unique plans for unique hard-coded values. If any of our sample queries had a JOIN to one or more additional tables, it wouldn't be considered for simple parameterization. As your system scales, you'll seldom see simple parameterization.

Forced Parameterization

Parameterization not only affects plan reuse but can lead to superior performance (although there can also be issues, which we'll discuss when we get to parameter sniffing in Chapter 14). If you're looking at a lot of ad hoc queries, you may want to attempt to increase the number of queries that are automatically parameterized. There is a database setting that will attempt to put more queries through the automated parameterization process called Forced Automation. To test this out, we have to modify the database using Listing 7-13.

Listing 7-13.* Enabling forced parameterization*

```
ALTER DATABASE AdventureWorks SET PARAMETERIZATION FORCED;
```

This time, instead of a simple query, let's look at something a little more realistic. Listing 7-14 shows a somewhat more complicated query.

Listing 7-14.* SELECT statement from multiple tables*

```
SELECT ea.EmailAddress,
       e.BirthDate,
       a.City
FROM Person.Person AS p
```

```
        JOIN HumanResources.Employee AS e
            ON p.BusinessEntityID = e.BusinessEntityID
        JOIN Person.BusinessEntityAddress AS bea
            ON e.BusinessEntityID = bea.BusinessEntityID
        JOIN Person.Address AS a
            ON bea.AddressID = a.AddressID
        JOIN Person.StateProvince AS sp
            ON a.StateProvinceID = sp.StateProvinceID
        JOIN Person.EmailAddress AS ea
            ON p.BusinessEntityID = ea.BusinessEntityID
WHERE ea.EmailAddress LIKE 'david%'
        AND sp.StateProvinceCode = 'WA';
```

With parameterization set to FORCED, when we look at the plans in cache, we can see that this query is now a Prepared plan in Figure 7-11.

usecounts	cacheobjtype	objtype	text
1	Compiled Plan	Adhoc	SELECT ea.EmailAddress, e.BirthDate, a.City FR...
1	Compiled Plan	Prepared	(@0 varchar(8000))select ea . EmailAddress . e . BirthDate...

Figure 7-11. *A query has gone through forced parameterization*

Our WHERE clause had two hard-coded values, but in Figure 7-11, we can only see one. If we look at the unformatted query, it looks like this:

(@0 varchar(8000))select ea . EmailAddress , e . BirthDate , a . City from Person . Person as p join HumanResources . Employee as e on p . BusinessEntityID = e . BusinessEntityID join Person . BusinessEntityAddress as bea on e . BusinessEntityID = bea . BusinessEntityID join Person . Address as a on bea . AddressID = a . AddressID join Person . StateProvince as sp on a . StateProvinceID = sp . StateProvinceID join Person . EmailAddress as ea on p . BusinessEntityID = ea . BusinessEntityID where ea . EmailAddress like 'david%' and sp . StateProvinceCode = @0

There are a number of restrictions on how forced parameterization works, and we can see one of them at play here. The clause with LIKE 'david%' did not get parameterized. Also, pay attention to the parameter for 'WA'. While the string is only two characters long, the parameter is defined as 8000. While this value is different from what's in the database, it won't cause any issues with indexes or statistics.

Let's take a look at some of the restrictions on forced parameterization:

- INSERT ... EXECUTE queries
- Statements inside procedures, triggers, and user-defined functions since they are already prepared statements
- Client-side prepared statements (we'll discuss these more later in the chapter)
- Queries with the RECOMPILE query hint
- Pattern and escape clause arguments used in a LIKE statement (as we just saw previously)

For the complete list, please consult Microsoft documentation. However, with this list, you get some idea of the kinds of queries that won't benefit from forced parameterization.

Before continuing, use Listing 7-15 to disable forced parameterization.

Listing 7-15. Disabling forced parameterization

```
ALTER DATABASE AdventureWorks SET PARAMETERIZATION SIMPLE;
```

Prepared Workload

Queries that are defined as a prepared workload are using parameters as a fundamental part of the process. They can still be written using local variables or hard-coded values, but the entire idea behind prepared workloads, also called statements, is to take advantage of parameters as an easy way to change the results of a query without changing the code. There are three techniques for creating prepared workloads:

- Stored Procedures: A stored procedure allows you to create one or more T-SQL statements that can accept, and return, user-defined and supplied parameters.
- sp_executesql: This command within SQL Server executes a T-SQL statement that may contain parameters but isn't defined as a stored procedure. In fact, they can be run within stored procedures.

- Prepare/Execute Model: Allows a client application to request the generation of a query plan that can be reused in subsequent executions of the query using parameters, just like a stored procedure. This is a common practice for Object Relational Mapping (ORM) tools like Entity Framework.

Stored Procedure

Using stored procedures is, among other things, a very standard technique for improving the effectiveness of plan caching. Stored procedures get compiled when they are executed (this is different from native compiled procedures, which we'll discuss in Chapter 19). A plan gets generated for each SQL statement within the procedure. The execution plan is then reused as the procedure gets called with different parameter values.

In addition to using sys.dm_exec_cached_plans as we did in the previous section, you can also track plan caching using Extended Events. Table 7-2 shows the events used to track cache behavior.

Table 7-2. Events to analyze plan caching

Event	Description
sp_cache_hit	After a search a plan is found in cache.
sp_cache_miss	No plan was found when searching the cache.
sp_cache_insert	A new plan has been generated and added to cache.
sp_cache_remove	A plan has been removed from cache.

In order to test this through the rest of the chapter, Listing 7-16 shows a stored procedure.

Listing 7-16. Stored procedure definition for dbo.BasicSalesInfo

```
CREATE OR ALTER PROCEDURE dbo.BasicSalesInfo
    @ProductID INT,
    @CustomerID INT
AS
SELECT soh.SalesOrderNumber,
```

```
        soh.OrderDate,
        sod.OrderQty,
        sod.LineTotal
FROM Sales.SalesOrderHeader AS soh
    JOIN Sales.SalesOrderDetail AS sod
        ON soh.SalesOrderID = sod.SalesOrderID
WHERE soh.CustomerID = @CustomerID
    AND sod.ProductID = @ProductID;
```

In order to get a remote procedure call, we can execute the procedure using a simple PowerShell script, taking advantage of DBATools as shown in Listing 7-17.

Listing 7-17. Executing the dbo.BasicSalesInfo stored procedure

```
$credential = Get-Credential 'sa'
$instance = Connect-DbaInstance -SqlInstance "localhost" -SqlCredential
$credential

Invoke-DbaQuery -SqlInstance $instance -Query 'dbo.BasicSalesInfo'
-SqlParameter @{ CustomerId = 29690; ProductID = 711 }  -Database
'AdventureWorks' -CommandType StoredProcedure
```

If we look at the Extended Event information, we can see that the remote procedure call is started, the plan is added to cache, and then the execution of the procedure completes as illustrated in Figure 7-12.

name	timestamp	object_name
rpc_starting	2025-06-09 19:44:14.948...	BasicSalesInfo
sp_cache_insert	2025-06-09 19:44:14.973...	BasicSalesInfo
rpc_completed	2025-06-09 19:44:14.974...	BasicSalesInfo

Figure 7-12. *Adding a stored procedure to cache*

We could see the behavior also if we were to modify the code such that we execute for @ProductID = 777. Executing the procedure results in the Extended Events output you see in Figure 7-13.

name	timestamp	object_name
rpc_starting	2025-06-09 19:49:02.055...	BasicSalesInfo
sp_cache_hit	2025-06-09 19:49:02.055...	
rpc_completed	2025-06-09 19:49:02.063...	BasicSalesInfo

Figure 7-13. *The stored procedure was found in cache*

Now you can see the procedure beginning to execute, then it's found in cache, and it finishes executing. This means that the optimizer was not engaged in this second execution, even though the parameter value was changed. That sp_cache_hit event is a clear example of prepared statements in use.

Worth noting, I'm executing these procedures remotely using PowerShell. If you're running the procedure from a batch command within SSMS or ADS, you may see a sp_cache_miss before you see the sp_cache_hit. This is because the batch command isn't in cache, so you're getting a cache miss for the batch, followed by a cache hit for the procedure.

Stored procedures have a few distinct behaviors that are worth discussing in more detail:

- When stored procedures are compiled
- Mechanisms for stored procedures to enhance performance
- Nonperformance benefits of stored procedures

When Stored Procedures Are Compiled

Stored procedures only get compiled when they are executed for the first time. There is an old myth that stored procedures were compiled when they were created. This still lurks around on the Internet, but it has never been true. When you run a CREATE PROCEDURE statement, no optimization occurs. Instead, the CREATE statement itself, not the queries inside, gets parsed, and the stored procedure is added to the database. This means you can create stored procedures before you create the objects that the stored procedure uses. Listing 7-18 shows a stored procedure that will parse and store just fine.

Listing 7-18. A stored procedure that will save but can't execute

```
CREATE OR ALTER PROCEDURE dbo.MyNewProc
AS
SELECT MyID
FROM dbo.NotHere; --Table dbo.NotHere doesn't exist
```

If you attempt to execute this query without first creating the table dbo.NotHere, you'll get an error. This is how you can tell for certain that a stored procedure is only compiled when it gets executed.

Performance Benefits of Stored Procedures

There is nothing that automatically makes stored procedures superior from a performance standpoint. For SQL Server, a query is a query. You can see some benefits from plan reuse as I've explained throughout this chapter, although you can also get that with other types of prepared statements. You may also get a benefit from parameter sniffing, where the parameter value passed to the procedure at compile time is used with statistics to make a more specific execution plan (we'll discuss this in a lot more detail in Chapter 13).

You can also see some other performance enhancements from the use of stored procedures:

- Business Logic Near the Data: A common suggestion is that business logic doesn't belong in the database. However, some business logic is very data specific and absolutely should be performed where the data is stored, rather than moving larger amounts of data. So aggregations and other set-based operations that can be done at the point of data access reside nicely inside stored procedures.

- Network Traffic Can Be Reduced: By providing a means of filtering data at the point of querying and, more specifically, within the SQL Server engine, you move less data across the network. Further, since a stored procedure only requires the procedure name and parameters, if any, it also results in a reduction of network traffic as opposed to large T-SQL batches.

Nonperformance Benefits of Stored Procedures

While the focus of the book is absolutely on performance enhancements, a few behaviors that stored procedures offer should be quickly discussed:

- The Application Can Be Isolated from Data Structure Changes: Data access that is accomplished through stored procedures can make it possible to change data structures without necessarily changing application code. The stored procedure can deal with these structural changes instead of forcing them back on the application.

- There Can Be a Single Point of Administration: The business logic implemented in stored procedures is maintained as part of the database. This means that code, access, and behaviors can all be managed directly through the database. This isn't always ideal, any more than always having all data access managed through application logic.

- Security Can Be Enhanced: User privileges to the tables of a given database can be restricted, and access can be granted only to stored procedures (or views, or other similar objects). By doing this, you hide data structures from the users, helping to enhance security.

Stored procedures aren't magic. They do add some overhead to a system especially in terms of storage and maintenance. You may see situations where most queries get executed one time only or very few times. In those cases, trying to get a stored procedure together may be tough. This situation is where you may benefit from using sp_executesql.

sp_executesql

sp_executesql is a system procedure that gives you a mechanism to submit an ad hoc query as a prepared workload. You can create parameters for an ad hoc query and therefore get plan reuse in the same way as stored procedures. We can take the query from our example stored procedure, `dbo.BasicSalesInfo`, and execute it through sp_executesql as shown in Listing 7-19.

CHAPTER 7 ■ EXECUTION PLAN CACHE BEHAVIOR

Listing 7-19. Putting sp_executesql to work

```
DECLARE @query NVARCHAR(MAX),
        @paramlist NVARCHAR(MAX);
SET @query
    = N'SELECT soh.SalesOrderNumber,
        soh.OrderDate,
        sod.OrderQty,
        sod.LineTotal
FROM Sales.SalesOrderHeader AS soh
    JOIN Sales.SalesOrderDetail AS sod
        ON soh.SalesOrderID = sod.SalesOrderID
WHERE soh.CustomerID = @CustomerID
    AND sod.ProductID = @ProductID';
SET @paramlist = N'@CustomerID INT, @ProductID INT';
EXEC sys.sp_executesql @query,
                      @paramlist,
                      @CustomerID = 29690,
                      @ProductID = 711;
```

You have to use Unicode when working with sp_executesql. That's why I declared the variables as NVARCHAR and use the letter "N" in front of the string definition. Listing 7-20 lets us query the cache to see how sp_executesql was put together.

Listing 7-20. Querying the cache to observe sp_executesql queries

```
SELECT c.usecounts,
       c.cacheobjtype,
       c.objtype,
       t.text
FROM sys.dm_exec_cached_plans AS c
    CROSS APPLY sys.dm_exec_sql_text(c.plan_handle) AS t
WHERE text LIKE '(@CustomerID%';
```

Figure 7-14 displays the results.

usecounts	cacheobjtype	objtype	text
1	1	Compiled Plan	Prepared	(@CustomerID INT, @ProductID INT)SELECT soh.Sales...

Figure 7-14. A prepared statement built by sp_executesql

Even though this is a batch statement, the use of sp_executesql has resulted in a prepared statement. We can modify the batch to change the parameter value of @ProductID to 777 and then execute the query again. If we then look at the cache, you'll see something like Figure 7-15.

usecounts	cacheobjtype	objtype	text
1	2	Compiled Plan	Prepared	(@CustomerID INT, @ProductID INT)SELECT soh.Sales...

Figure 7-15. Second use of the prepared plan from sp_executesql

Even though we've changed the batch commands, because we're using sp_executesql to run the query, you can see that it is acting as a prepared statement and the usecounts has increased to 2.

The trick here, if you're going to use this type of query throughout your code, is to ensure that the text of the T-SQL is identical in every way, or you won't see plan reuse. For example, something as simple as changing the definition of the parameter @CustomerID to @customerid will result in a new prepared plan as you see in Figure 7-16.

	usecounts	cacheobjtype	objtype	text
1	1	Compiled Plan	Prepared	(@CustomerID INT, @ProductID INT)SELECT soh.Sales...
2	2	Compiled Plan	Prepared	(@CustomerID INT, @ProductID INT)SELECT soh.Sales...

Figure 7-16. A new prepared plan is created

As you see in Figure 7-16, a new prepared plan was created. You can even see where the changes to the parameter are visible in the text. While every other aspect of the query is identical, these case changes are enough to cause the optimizer to think a new plan is necessary. This is one of the many reasons why it pays to be extremely consistent when it comes to coding T-SQL.

The goal of using sp_executesql is twofold. First, and most importantly, you can ensure a degree of plan reuse, even with a batch query as we have in Listing 7-19. Second, by using parameter values, we can ensure that they are strongly typed in order to help avoid SQL Injection attacks in our batch processes.

You can also issue prepared statements through ODBC and OLEDB commands using SQLExecDirect and ICommandWithParameters, respectively. This is how most Object Relational Mapping (ORM) tools, such as Entity Framework, execute their queries, through prepared statements (we'll look at an example in the next section).

Prior to SQL Server 2025, there was one distinct weakness associated with sp_executesql. The compile process for sp_executesql was not serialized like it is for stored procedures. This means that you could get what was termed a "compile storm" if a number of different processes all tried to execute the same query. Introduced in SQL Server 2025, and available in Azure SQL Database, you can now enable the Database Scoped Configuration setting OPTIMIZE_SP_EXECUTESQL.

When this setting is optimized, the compile becomes serialized, just like a stored procedure. Making this change will eliminate the potential for cache bloat and thrashing due to multiple statements compiling at once. This setting is off by default. However, turning it on is as easy as Listing 7-21.

Listing 7-21. Enabling the Database Scoped Configuration setting OPTIMIZE_SP_EXECUTESQL

```
ALTER DATABASE SCOPED CONFIGURATION
SET OPTIMIZED_SP_EXECUTESQL = ON;
```

One caveat is associated with enabling this. Microsoft suggests that you enable asynchronous statistics updates as we discussed in Chapter 4. In addition, they recommend enabling the Database Scoped Configuration setting ASYNC_STATS_UPDATES_WAIT_AT_LOW_PRIORITY. Enabling both can make it so you see fewer waits in the event of a long compile time when using sp_executesql.

Prepare/Execute Model

ODBC and OLEDB provide a prepare/execute model to submit queries as a prepared workload. Similar to how sp_executesql works, this model allows you to parameterize queries. The prepare phase allows SQL Server to generate the execution plan for the query and return a handle to the application code for that execution plan. You can then use the plan handle to execute the query while passing it parameter values. This reduces network overhead, not requiring you to pass the full string of T-SQL every time you want to execute a query. You can't use this mechanism within T-SQL itself, only external code.

Note: For a detailed description on how to use the prepare/execute model in an application, please refer to this Microsoft document: "SqlCommand.Prepare Method" (https://bit.ly/2DBzN4b).

Query Hash and Query Plan Hash

SQL Server creates a hash value for the query and for the query plan. These hash values become very useful for searching for queries and plans that may have similarities. It's really common for people to create patterns in their code. These patterns can lead to common queries, or common query plans. When you identify that the pattern you're following is working well, being able to quickly identify multiple queries or plans to make changes wherever the pattern exists is a great utility.

The query hash and the query plan hash are stored in DMVs like sys.dm_exec_query_stats or sys.dm_exec_requests. The hash values are also stored in the Query Store. You can even retrieve them as part of some Extended Events or by adding them as an Action. In short, there are a lot of ways to get at these hash values. Like any hash value, the possibility exists for queries or plans that are not actually similar to have the same value. So the hash values, while useful, are not unique identifiers for queries or plans.

To see the hash values in action, we're going to run two queries, in two steps, as a single batch each, as shown in Listing 7-22.

Listing 7-22. Similar queries for testing hash values

```
SELECT p.Name AS ProductName,
       ps.Name AS SubCategory,
       pc.Name AS Category
FROM Production.Product AS p
    JOIN Production.ProductSubcategory AS ps
        ON p.ProductSubcategoryID = ps.ProductSubcategoryID
    JOIN Production.ProductCategory AS pc
        ON ps.ProductCategoryID = pc.ProductCategoryID
WHERE pc.Name = 'Bikes'
      AND ps.Name = 'Touring Bikes';
SELECT p.Name AS ProductName,
       ps.Name AS SubCategory,
       pc.Name AS Category
```

```
FROM Production.Product AS p
    JOIN Production.ProductSubcategory AS ps
        ON p.ProductSubcategoryID = ps.ProductSubcategoryID
    JOIN Production.ProductCategory AS pc
        ON ps.ProductCategoryID = pc.ProductCategoryID
where pc.Name = 'Bikes'
    and ps.Name = 'Road Bikes';
```

The only significant difference between the two queries is the hard-coded values used in the WHERE clause on ProductSubcategory.Name. However, you'll also note that there is a lowercase "where" and an "and" in the second statement. I'm going to execute each query shown previously, separately. Then, I'm going to pull the hash values from sys.dm_exec_query_stats using the query in Listing 7-23.

Listing 7-23. Retrieving the hash values from the cache

```
SELECT deqs.execution_count,
       deqs.query_hash,
       deqs.query_plan_hash,
       dest.text
FROM sys.dm_exec_query_stats AS deqs
    CROSS APPLY sys.dm_exec_sql_text(deqs.plan_handle) AS dest
WHERE dest.text LIKE 'SELECT p.Name AS ProductName%';
```

The results are here in Figure 7-17.

execution_count	query_hash	query_plan_hash	text	
1	0xFAD418608AA1941F	0xB473BE5020ABF67D	SELECT p.Name AS ProductName,	ps.Name AS ...
1	0xFAD418608AA1941F	0xB473BE5020ABF67D	SELECT p.Name AS ProductName,	ps.Name AS ...

Figure 7-17. *Retrieving the hash values from cache*

The queries are complex enough that simple parameterization didn't occur. Also, forced parameterization is off. Because of this, with two different WHERE clauses, we now have two different execution plans. However, you can see that the query_plan_hash values match. This means the plans are likely to be identical. You can also see that both query_hash values match. Despite the minor changes to the text of the query, it wasn't enough to get a new hash value.

If I edit the SELECT criteria so that our code now looks like Listing 7-24, then things change.

Listing 7-24. Removing two columns from the SELECT list

```
SELECT p.Name AS ProductName
FROM Production.Product AS p
    JOIN Production.ProductSubcategory AS ps
        ON p.ProductSubcategoryID = ps.ProductSubcategoryID
    JOIN Production.ProductCategory AS pc
        ON ps.ProductCategoryID = pc.ProductCategoryID
WHERE pc.Name = 'Bikes'
    AND ps.Name = 'Touring Bikes';
```

The results from cache are in Figure 7-18.

execution_count	query_hash	query_plan_hash	text
1	0xFAD418608AA1941F	0xB473BE5020ABF67D	SELECT p.Name AS ProductName, ps.Name AS Sub...
1	0x34FA892A8C0244DF	0xB473BE5020ABF67D	SELECT p.Name AS ProductName FROM Production.Pr...
1	0xFAD418608AA1941F	0xB473BE5020ABF67D	SELECT p.Name AS ProductName, ps.Name AS Sub...

Figure 7-18. *A new query_hash value*

The structure of the query without the two additional columns changes, so you see a new query_hash value on the second line. However, the query structure is effectively the same, so an identical query plan was created, hence the matching query_plan_hash value.

You can now see the utility of using the hash values to search for queries. If these queries were performing poorly and you identified a fix, you could quickly search for matching query_plan_hash values to find all the places where you need to apply that fix.

You can get the reverse too, identical query_hash values, but different query_plan_hash values. To explore this, we need two more queries from Listing 7-25.

Listing 7-25. Nearly identical queries that produce two execution plans

```
SELECT p.Name,
        tha.TransactionDate,
        tha.TransactionType,
        tha.Quantity,
```

CHAPTER 7 EXECUTION PLAN CACHE BEHAVIOR

```
        tha.ActualCost
FROM Production.TransactionHistoryArchive AS tha
    JOIN Production.Product AS p
        ON tha.ProductID = p.ProductID
WHERE p.ProductID = 461;
SELECT p.Name,
       tha.TransactionDate,
       tha.TransactionType,
       tha.Quantity,
       tha.ActualCost
FROM Production.TransactionHistoryArchive AS tha
    JOIN Production.Product AS p
        ON tha.ProductID = p.ProductID
WHERE p.ProductID = 712;
```

Figure 7-19 shows the hash values retrieved from the cache.

execution_count	query_hash	query_plan_hash	text
1	0xD4FA47AE35195F89	0xA366B147B0F12C2F	SELECT p.Name, tha.TransactionDat...
1	0xD4FA47AE35195F89	0x2567346B1381B053	SELECT p.Name, tha.TransactionDat...

Figure 7-19. *Changes to the query_plan_hash value*

Once again, the small differences in the text are not enough to change the query_hash values. However, the different values passed through each WHERE clause result in radically different execution plans, on display in Figure 7-20.

233

CHAPTER 7 EXECUTION PLAN CACHE BEHAVIOR

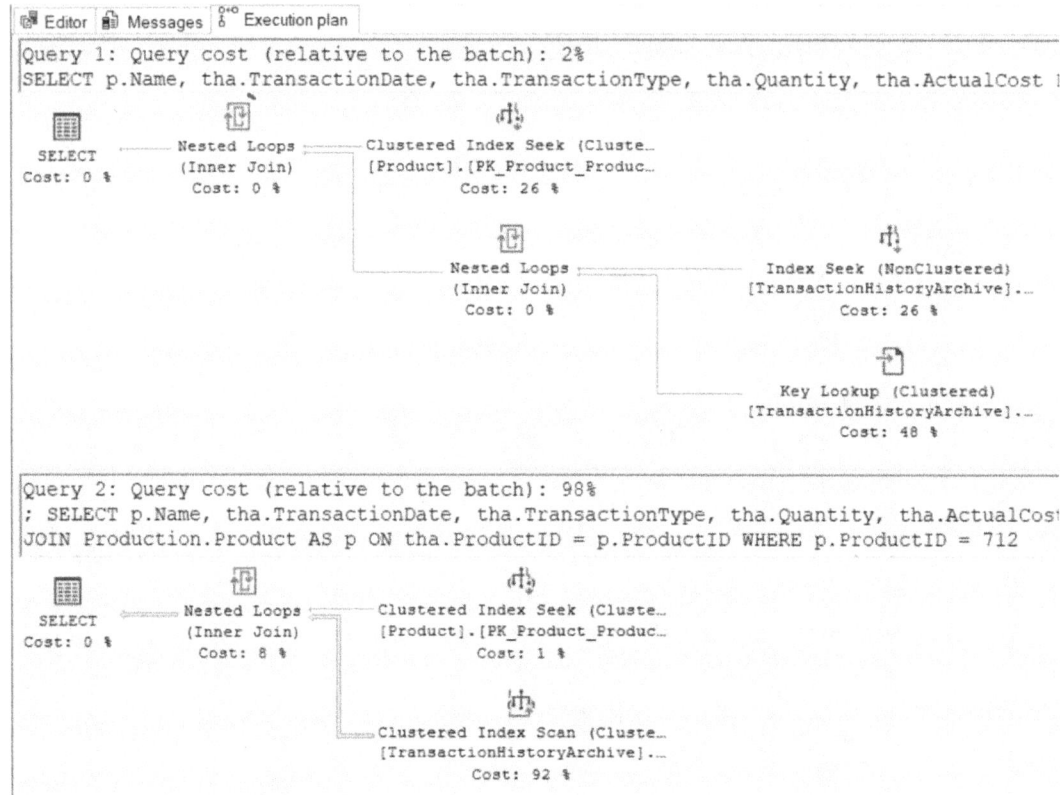

Figure 7-20. Radically different execution plans

The hash values are a handy tool for looking for either nearly identical code or identical plans. However, as you've seen, the code doesn't have to be a perfect match to get the same hash values.

Execution Plan Cache Recommendations

The core principle for the plan cache is to reuse execution plans in order to reduce the overhead caused by compiling execution plans. In order to take advantage of this behavior, your queries need to be written in such a way that they can be reused. Where possible, avoid ad hoc queries and instead rely on prepared statements. Here are some recommendations to help ensure good plan cache management:

- Explicitly parameterize values in your query.
- Use stored procedures where you can.

- Use sp_executesql as an alternative to stored procedures.
- Take advantage of the prepare/execute model.
- Avoid ad hoc queries.
- Enable *Optimize for Ad Hoc*.
- Use sp_executesql over EXECUTE for dynamic queries.

Let's take a moment to briefly discuss each of these recommendations.

Explicitly Parameterize Values in Your Query

It's extremely common for a given query to be executed repeatedly, but with different values in the WHERE clause. You can get more plan reuse by parameterizing your queries so that the static and variable parts of the query are separated. You can take advantage of simple and forced parameterization, but they do have their limits. Explicitly parameterizing your workloads will help with plan reuse and reduce the amount of plans in cache. Just be aware that some plans are sensitive to the values passed in parameters, and this can lead to difficulties (which we'll cover in Chapter 13).

Use Stored Procedures Where You Can

Parameterizing queries within stored procedures is a great way to assist with cache management. Since only the parameters need to be sent in addition to the stored procedure name, network traffic will be less than with ad hoc queries. Since stored procedures are reused from cache, in many cases, they will run faster than ad hoc queries, which require a compile every single time they run.

Like anything else, it is possible to have too much of a good thing. There are business processes that are best placed within the database, but there are also business processes that should never be placed within the database.

Use sp_executesql As an Alternative to Stored Procedures

You may find situations where a procedure doesn't make sense. If you take advantage of sp_executesql, you can still have code that is made into a prepared workload. The full query must be passed to sp_executesql. This sometimes becomes very difficult when the queries are complex and large. The use of sp_executesql through parameters also helps to reduce the possibility of SQL Injection attacks.

While you can use EXECUTE with an ad hoc string, I would strongly caution you against this practice. First, you won't be able to parameterize the code. Second, you are very likely to open up a vector for SQL Injection. If you must build and execute strings within your code, do it with sp_executesql.

Take Advantage of the Prepare/Execute Model

If you are building strings in the application that you're then going to send over the network using sp_executesql, you might want to consider using prepare/execute instead. Using this method, you will only have to send the full string of the query across the network once. Further, since you only need the plan handle, more than one user connection can take advantage of prepared plans.

Avoid Ad Hoc Queries

A certain amount of ad hoc queries seem almost inevitable in most systems. However, do what you can to minimize them. Since ad hoc queries almost never get plan reuse, they add the overhead of additional compile time. They also lead to cache bloat, filling the cache with useless plans.

Enable Optimize for Ad Hoc

Since ad hoc queries do seem somewhat unavoidable, keep them out of your cache as much as possible. You can do this by enabling Optimize for Ad Hoc on your database. Then, a plan only goes into the cache in the event that query is executed more than once.

Summary

Query optimization is an expensive process. The plan cache is designed with this issue in mind. By storing plans in the cache, these plans can be reused in order to avoid optimization. The best way to ensure plan reuse is to take advantage of one of the methods of parameterizing queries. Stored procedures are generally considered to be the best technique for ensuring plan reuse. However, sp_executesql provides another mechanism. Finally, the prepare/execute model gives you yet one more method to ensure plan reusability.

The next chapter is also about query optimization and the plan cache. We're going to be discussing how queries age out of the cache and, in other ways, get recompiled.

CHAPTER 8

Query Recompilation

In order to minimize the overhead from compiling execution plans, the plans are stored in a memory space called the plan cache. When prepared statements, whether as stored procedures or the other mechanisms for creating parameterized queries, are used, the process takes advantage of the plans being in cache. However, a number of things can cause plans to be removed from cache. Sometimes, this is a good thing. Either data has changed, statistics have been updated, or something has happened so a different execution plan may enhance performance. Sometimes, this is a bad thing, and you get a lot of recompiles, placing excessive load on the processor and interfering with the general good behavior of queries on the system. This chapter covers the following topics:

- The benefits and drawbacks of recompilation
- How to identify the statements being recompiled
- Analyzing the causes of recompilation
- Methods to avoid recompilation

Benefits and Drawbacks of Recompilation

Compiling and recompiling execution plans is an expensive operation. However, as data changes over time, statistics will also change. The optimizer can find better execution and processing strategies as the data distribution and statistics get updated. The addition of new indexes and constraints on a given table may also benefit from a new execution plan.

Since the recompiles are always done at the statement level instead of at the procedure, two things happen. First, you're likely to see a higher overall recompile count than if entire procedures were recompiled. However, this is offset by the second thing, which is reduced time, processing and blocking by only recompiling the individual statement that needs it.

The standard recompile process is modified when plan forcing is enabled from the Query Store. The recompile process will still occur, but the recompiled plan will not be used. Instead, the forced plan will be substituted. In addition, if the Query Store is forcing a query hint, then that hint will be applied when the recompile process occurs. However, if the forced plan has been marked as invalid, due to structural changes or something else, then the recompiled plan will be used. For more on the Query Store, refer back to Chapter 6.

To understand how recompilation can be beneficial, I'm going to create this procedure in Listing 8-1.

Listing 8-1. Creating the dbo.WorkOrder procedure

```
CREATE OR ALTER PROCEDURE dbo.WorkOrder
AS
SELECT wo.WorkOrderID,
       wo.ProductID,
       wo.StockedQty
FROM Production.WorkOrder AS wo
WHERE wo.StockedQty
BETWEEN 500 AND 700;
```

If I execute the procedure, it results in the execution plan visible in Figure 8-1.

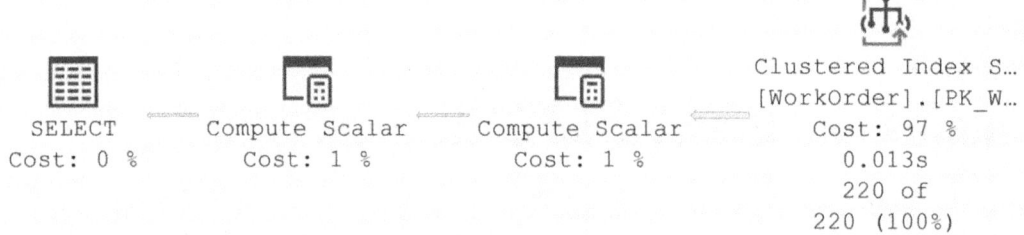

Figure 8-1. *Execution plan with runtime metrics for the dbo.WorkOrder procedure*

We'll be talking more about indexes in Chapters 9 and 10, but suffice to say, an index scan in this scenario is less than ideal. The optimizer is even suggesting an index through a Missing Index hint on the plan (covered in Chapter 9), although not the same index as I'm proposing. We could improve performance by adding an index to the WorkOrder table similar to Listing 8-2.

Listing 8-2. Creating a new index on the WorkOrder table

```
CREATE INDEX IX_Test ON Production.WorkOrder (StockedQty, ProductID);
```

When the index gets created, SQL Server will automatically mark plans that reference the Production.WorkOrder table for recompile. This means the optimizer can now consider using our new index. After creating the index and rerunning the procedure, Figure 8-2 displays the resulting execution plan with runtime metrics.

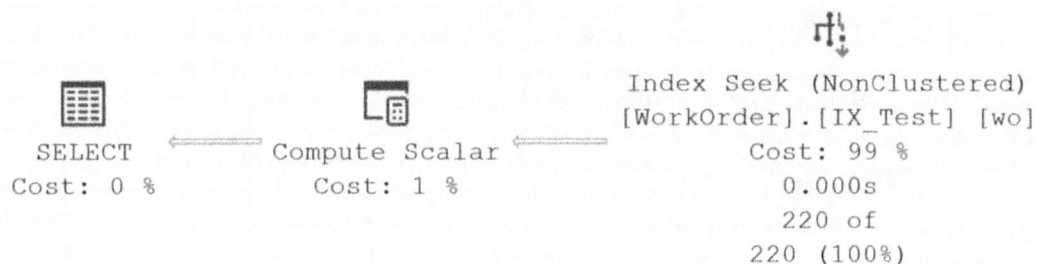

Figure 8-2. *New execution plan for dbo.WorkOrder*

The principal reason for a recompile comes after statistics get updated. SQL Server will then automatically mark queries that used those statistics as needing to be recompiled. Any time a statement gets marked, it will get recompiled at its next execution, and the application calling the query will wait until the recompile is complete.

Listing 8-3 cleans up the test index created in Listing 8-2.

Listing 8-3. Removing the new index on the WorkOrder table

```
DROP INDEX Production.WorkOrder.IX_Test;
```

You may not always generate a better plan after a recompile. Listing 8-4 shows a problematic query within a procedure, using SELECT * with no filtering criteria.

Listing 8-4. Creating the procedure dbo.WorkOrderAll

```
CREATE OR ALTER PROCEDURE dbo.WorkOrderAll
AS
--intentionally using SELECT * as an example
SELECT *
FROM Production.WorkOrder AS wo;
```

CHAPTER 8 QUERY RECOMPILATION

I'm going to create the procedure, but I don't want to execute it just yet. When I do execute it, because it's returning all rows and all columns, the best way to satisfy the query will always be a Clustered Index Scan of Production.WorkOrder (we'll talk about why in Chapter 9). Even if I am to try adding a nonclustered index, it's not going to help the query, and it's going to lead to a recompile.

Before we execute the query, I'm going to set up an Extended Events session to capture recompile events as shown in Listing 8-5.

Listing 8-5. CREATE statement for the QueryAndRecompile session

```
CREATE EVENT SESSION [QueryAndRecompile]
ON SERVER
    ADD EVENT sqlserver.rpc_completed
    (WHERE ([sqlserver].[database_name] = N'AdventureWorks')),
    ADD EVENT sqlserver.rpc_starting
    (WHERE ([sqlserver].[database_name] = N'AdventureWorks')),
    ADD EVENT sqlserver.sp_statement_completed
    (WHERE ([sqlserver].[database_name] = N'AdventureWorks')),
    ADD EVENT sqlserver.sp_statement_starting
    (WHERE ([sqlserver].[database_name] = N'AdventureWorks')),
    ADD EVENT sqlserver.sql_batch_completed
    (WHERE ([sqlserver].[database_name] = N'AdventureWorks')),
    ADD EVENT sqlserver.sql_batch_starting
    (WHERE ([sqlserver].[database_name] = N'AdventureWorks')),
    ADD EVENT sqlserver.sql_statement_completed
    (WHERE ([sqlserver].[database_name] = N'AdventureWorks')),
    ADD EVENT sqlserver.sql_statement_recompile
    (WHERE ([sqlserver].[database_name] = N'AdventureWorks')),
    ADD EVENT sqlserver.sql_statement_starting
    (WHERE ([sqlserver].[database_name] = N'AdventureWorks'))
    ADD TARGET package0.event_file
    (SET filename = N'QueryAndRecompile')
WITH
(
    TRACK_CAUSALITY = ON
);
```

```
GO
ALTER EVENT SESSION QueryAndRecompile ON SERVER STATE = START;
```

With this Extended Events session up and running, Listing 8-6 illustrates how we're going to execute `dbo.WorkOrderAll`.

Listing 8-6. Executing the procedure and creating an index

```
EXEC dbo.WorkOrderAll;
GO
CREATE INDEX IX_Test ON Production.WorkOrder(StockedQty,ProductID);
GO
EXEC dbo.WorkOrderAll; --After creation of index IX_Test
```

I will change the columns in the grid in the Live Data window as explained in Chapter 3. After executing, we can see that despite the fact that no recompile is going to help this query, a recompile occurred anyway, as shown in Figure 8-3.

name	timestamp	recompile_cause	batch_text	statement
sql_batch_st...	2025-06-13 1...	NULL	EXEC dbo.WorkOrderAll; --A...	NULL
sql_statemen...	2025-06-13 1...	NULL	NULL	EXEC dbo.WorkOrderAll
sp_statement...	2025-06-13 1...	NULL	NULL	SELECT * FROM Production....
sql_statemen...	2025-06-13 1...	Schema changed	NULL	
sp_statement...	2025-06-13 1...	NULL	NULL	SELECT * FROM Production....
sp_statement...	2025-06-13 1...	NULL	NULL	SELECT * FROM Production....
sql_statemen...	2025-06-13 1...	NULL	NULL	EXEC dbo.WorkOrderAll
sql_batch_co...	2025-06-13 1...	NULL	EXEC dbo.WorkOrderAll; --A...	NULL

Figure 8-3. *A useless statement recompile*

I've highlighted the recompile event so we can see why it happened. The recompile_cause column informs us that the reason was "Schema changed." That was me creating the nonclustered index before executing the procedure again.

In this case, the recompile served no useful purpose. The execution plan is exactly the same. Because the conditions were met for a recompile, a recompiled occurred. This means extra processing was done to remove the plan from cache, create a new plan, and then add that plan to cache, all before executing the query. This is why excessive or unnecessary recompiles can be a major performance issue. Before we proceed, run Listing 8-3 again to remove the test index.

Identifying the Statement Being Recompiled

Within a large, stored procedure, consisting of a number of individual statements, knowing exactly which statements are being recompiled could be a challenge. This is why I created the Extended Events session in Listing 8-5.

The code there is taking advantage of the various events related to batch and procedure execution, individual statements in both batches and procedures, and the recompile event and tying it all together through Causality Tracking.

Let's look again at the output in Figure 8-3. Since I ran my stored procedure call as a batch from SSMS, the first event we see is sql_batch_starting, and you can see the batch_text shows "EXEC dbo.WorkloadAll". Let's walk through the rest of the events in order:

1. sql_batch_starting: The start of the batch process.

2. sql_statement_starting: The batch in this case consists only of the execution of the procedure, so that's what we see here in the statement column.

3. sp_statement_starting: The procedure consists of just one statement, and now it is starting to execute. However, the plan used by that statement has been marked for recompile due to the change in the schema.

4. sql_statement_recompile: The recompile event occurs as described.

5. sp_statement_starting: Now our stored procedure statement starts again because it was interrupted by the recompile event.

6. sp_statement_completed: The stored procedure statement finishes.

7. sql_statement_completed: Now the statement in the batch, started up at #2 in this list, is completed.

8. sql_batch_completed: The batch itself can now complete.

You don't have to do all of this in order to capture recompile events. You can simply capture just the event itself. In most cases, you'll see the individual statement as part of the recompile event. However, this case illustrates an example where that's not true. So setting up a system where we can observe the start and stop of each step allows us to better understand which individual statement is causing the recompile.

CHAPTER 8   QUERY RECOMPILATION

Because my system isn't under load, the order of the timestamp values is enough to see the sequence I outlined. However, on a busy system, I would take advantage of the Causality Tracking to group and order events. Figure 8-4 shows how the output would look using the activity ID and sequence to order the events.

name	timestamp	recompile_cause	batch_text	statement	attach_activity_i...	attach_activity_i...
⊞ attach_activity_id.guid: E2CA02AC-4775-4580-B979-DE3A93E3E99F (6)						
⊞ attach_activity_id.guid: 08E369E1-151B-48E4-9719-5C1AB97F9267 (6)						
⊟ attach_activity_id.guid: 544D98B2-A2DC-4810-8D1D-9443BE5B21D8 (8)						
sql_batch_st...	2025-06-13 1...	NULL	EXEC dbo.WorkOrderAll; --A...	NULL	544D98B2-A2DC...	1
sql_statemen...	2025-06-13 1...	NULL	NULL	EXEC dbo.WorkOrderAll	544D98B2-A2DC...	2
sp_statement...	2025-06-13 1...	NULL	NULL	SELECT * FROM Production....	544D98B2-A2DC...	3
sql_statemen...	2025-06-13 1...	Schema changed	NULL		544D98B2-A2DC...	4
sp_statement...	2025-06-13 1...	NULL	NULL	SELECT * FROM Production....	544D98B2-A2DC...	5
sp_statement...	2025-06-13 1...	NULL	NULL	SELECT * FROM Production....	544D98B2-A2DC...	6

Figure 8-4. *Using the attach_activity_id_guid to group the data and sequence to order it*

All this lets me identify exactly which statement was recompiled and when.

Analyzing Causes of Recompilation

While a recompile can help performance by creating a more appropriate execution plan, it's entirely possible for recompiles to become excessive and seriously negatively impact performance. Every single compile of an execution plan uses up valuable CPU time. In addition, you're moving plans in and out of memory as a part of the process, thereby using up those resources too. When a query is recompiling, any processes that need that execution plan will be blocked until the compile process completes. This means even if you have prepared plans, a high-volume system with frequent calls to a given query can see poor performance. For all these reasons, you should know the conditions that result in recompilation. Knowing when recompiles occur can help you avoid them when they become excessive. Some of the causes for statement-level recompiles are as follows:

- Schema Changes: If a table, temporary table, or view referred to by a statement changes, including structure, metadata, and indexes, a recompile is necessary.

- Binding Changes: When a binding, like a default, of a column in a table or temporary table changes.

- Statistics Updates: Whether automatic or manual, when statistics used by a query get updated.

- Deferred Object Resolution: If an object necessary for a query gets created as part of the execution of a batch, a recompile is necessary. A query can compile without an object, but then, when that object gets created, a recompile for the referencing statement(s) is required.

- SET Options: If the SET options of a given query change.

- Sp_recompile: An explicit call to the system procedure sp_recompile will result in a recompile.

- RECOMPILE Hint: The use of the RECOMPILE query hint does what's in the name.

- Parameter-Sensitive Plans (PSPs): When a multi-plan query has one of the plans recompile or when the dispatcher plan changes.

- Optional Parameter Optimization (OPO): If one of the plans made is recompiled or the dispatcher plan changes, same as PSPs.

We'll cover PSPs and OPO more in Chapter 13. Suffice to say that they have no impact on the fundamental causes of any given plan being recompiled. Nor do they interfere with the standard recompile process, beyond their normal processing, again, discussed in detail in Chapter 13.

Listing 8-7 shows how to get the complete list of causes from the Extended Events system tables.

Listing 8-7. Querying sys.dm_xe_map_values

```
SELECT dxmv.map_value
FROM sys.dm_xe_map_values AS dxmv
WHERE dxmv.name = 'statement_recompile_cause';
```

The results are shown in Figure 8-5.

	map_value
1	Schema changed
2	Statistics changed
3	Deferred compile
4	Set option change
5	Temp table changed
6	Remote rowset changed
7	For browse permissions changed
8	Query notification environment changed
9	PartitionView changed
10	Cursor options changed
11	Option (recompile) requested
12	Parameterized plan flushed
13	Test plan linearization
14	Plan affecting database version changed
15	Query Store plan forcing policy changed
16	Query Store plan forcing failed
17	Query Store missing the plan
18	Interleaved execution required recompilation
19	Not a recompile
20	Query Store hints changed
21	Query Store hints application failed
22	Query Store recompiling to capture cursor query
23	Recompiling to clean up the multiplan dispatcher ...
24	Recompiling due to NCCI in broadcast mode error
25	Recompiling to clean up the multiplan opo dispat...

Figure 8-5. All the reasons for a plan recompile

This list grows regularly as new functionality is added to SQL Server over time. We simply don't have room to discuss every possible cause for a recompile event. Most of them are relatively self-explanatory. However, we can walk through a few examples so that you can see how to use the Extended Events session to understand recompile causes.

Deferred Object Resolution

It's very common to have a batch that dynamically creates database objects and then uses them in subsequent statements. When such a batch is executed for the first time, the initial plan won't contain the information about the objects being created. The processing strategy is deferred until the runtime of the query. When a DML statement referring to the objects being created is executed, the query recompiles in order to generate a new plan.

Both tables and local temporary tables can be created within a batch in order to hold intermediate result sets. The recompilation of the statement because of deferred object resolution behaves differently for a table when compared with a local temporary table.

Recompilation on a Table

To see the deferred compilation in action, we'll start with Listing 8-8.

Listing 8-8. Stored procedure that creates a table

```
CREATE OR ALTER PROC dbo.RecompileTable
AS
CREATE TABLE dbo.ProcTest1
(
    C1 INT
);
SELECT *
FROM dbo.ProcTest1;
DROP TABLE dbo.ProcTest1;
```

When the stored procedure is executed for the first time, an execution plan is generated before the actual execution of the queries. Since the table doesn't exist in Listing 8-8, the plan that gets created won't include the processing strategy for the SELECT statement. Therefore, a recompile is necessary, as shown in Figure 8-6.

CHAPTER 8 QUERY RECOMPILATION

name	timestamp	recompile_cause	batch_text	statement
sql_batch_st...	2025-06-13 1...	NULL	exec dbo.RecompileTable;	NULL
sql_statemen...	2025-06-13 1...	NULL	NULL	exec dbo.RecompileTable
sp_statement...	2025-06-13 1...	NULL	NULL	CREATE TABLE dbo.ProcTest...
sp_statement...	2025-06-13 1...	NULL	NULL	CREATE TABLE dbo.ProcTest...
sp_statement...	2025-06-13 1...	NULL	NULL	SELECT * FROM dbo.ProcTe...
sql_statemen...	2025-06-13 1...	Deferred compile	NULL	
sp_statement...	2025-06-13 1...	NULL	NULL	SELECT * FROM dbo.ProcTe...
sp_statement...	2025-06-13 1...	NULL	NULL	SELECT * FROM dbo.ProcTe...
sp_statement...	2025-06-13 1...	NULL	NULL	DROP TABLE dbo.ProcTest1
sp_statement...	2025-06-13 1...	NULL	NULL	DROP TABLE dbo.ProcTest1
sql_statemen...	2025-06-13 1...	NULL	NULL	exec dbo.RecompileTable
sql_batch_co...	2025-06-13 1...	NULL	exec dbo.RecompileTable;	NULL
sql_batch_st...	2025-06-13 1...	NULL	exec dbo.RecompileTable;	NULL
sql_statemen...	2025-06-13 1...	NULL	NULL	exec dbo.RecompileTable
sp_statement...	2025-06-13 1...	NULL	NULL	CREATE TABLE dbo.ProcTest...
sp_statement...	2025-06-13 1...	NULL	NULL	CREATE TABLE dbo.ProcTest...
sp_statement...	2025-06-13 1...	NULL	NULL	SELECT * FROM dbo.ProcTe...
sql_statemen...	2025-06-13 1...	Schema changed	NULL	
sp_statement...	2025-06-13 1...	NULL	NULL	SELECT * FROM dbo.ProcTe...
sp_statement...	2025-06-13 1...	NULL	NULL	SELECT * FROM dbo.ProcTe...
sp_statement...	2025-06-13 1...	NULL	NULL	DROP TABLE dbo.ProcTest1
sp_statement...	2025-06-13 1...	NULL	NULL	DROP TABLE dbo.ProcTest1
sql_statemen...	2025-06-13 1...	NULL	NULL	exec dbo.RecompileTable
sql_batch_co...	2025-06-13 1...	NULL	exec dbo.RecompileTable;	NULL

Figure 8-6. *Multiple recompile events from two executions of the procedure*

I've highlighted the first recompile event with the recompile_cause listed as Deferred compile. When the procedure is executed the second time, another recompile occurs. When we drop the table at the end of the batch within the stored procedure, the execution plan that was recompiled for that table doesn't get dropped. It's still there and can be referenced the next time the query executes. However, because the table gets recreated, SQL Server considers that a change to the schema. All of that is neatly laid out for us by the Extended Events.

Recompilation on a Temporary Table

It's more common to create temporary tables within your batches. Listing 8-9 shows a simple query to illustrate deferred object resolution in a temporary table.

CHAPTER 8 QUERY RECOMPILATION

Listing 8-9. Stored procedure that creates a temporary table

```
CREATE OR ALTER PROC dbo.RecompileProc
AS
CREATE TABLE #TempTable (C1 INT);
INSERT INTO #TempTable (C1)
VALUES (42);
```

If I create and then execute this stored procedure, twice, the Extended Events output is shown in Figure 8-7.

name	timestamp	recompile_cause	batch_text	statement
sql_batch_st...	2025-06-13 1...	NULL	exec dbo.RecompileProc;	NULL
sql_statemen...	2025-06-13 1...	NULL	NULL	exec dbo.RecompileProc
sp_statement...	2025-06-13 1...	NULL	NULL	CREATE TABLE #TempTable ...
sp_statement...	2025-06-13 1...	NULL	NULL	CREATE TABLE #TempTable ...
sp_statement...	2025-06-13 1...	NULL	NULL	INSERT INTO #TempTable (C...
sql_statemen...	2025-06-13 1...	Deferred compile	NULL	
sp_statement...	2025-06-13 1...	NULL	NULL	INSERT INTO #TempTable (C...
sp_statement...	2025-06-13 1...	NULL	NULL	INSERT INTO #TempTable (C...
sql_statemen...	2025-06-13 1...	NULL	NULL	exec dbo.RecompileProc
sql_batch_co...	2025-06-13 1...	NULL	exec dbo.RecompileProc;	NULL
sql_batch_st...	2025-06-13 1...	NULL	exec dbo.RecompileProc;	NULL
sql_statemen...	2025-06-13 1...	NULL	NULL	exec dbo.RecompileProc
sp_statement...	2025-06-13 1...	NULL	NULL	CREATE TABLE #TempTable ...
sp_statement...	2025-06-13 1...	NULL	NULL	CREATE TABLE #TempTable ...
sp_statement...	2025-06-13 1...	NULL	NULL	INSERT INTO #TempTable (C...
sp_statement...	2025-06-13 1...	NULL	NULL	INSERT INTO #TempTable (C...
sql_statemen...	2025-06-13 1...	NULL	NULL	exec dbo.RecompileProc
sql_batch_co...	2025-06-13 1...	NULL	exec dbo.RecompileProc;	NULL

Figure 8-7. *Statement-level recompile caused by deferred compilation*

You can see the deferred compile explanation in the recompile_cause column. The first statement in the procedure creates a temporary table, and then the second inserts data into it. That second statement had to be deferred until the object was actually created. However, unlike the table in the example in the previous section, the temporary table being created isn't considered a change to the schema. Therefore, no second recompile is necessary, and the execution plan is reused.

Avoiding Recompiles

I can't emphasize enough that a recompile can be extremely beneficial for a given query. If the data has changed sufficiently, the optimizer can make better choices for a given plan. However, there are coding practices that can cause unnecessary recompiles to occur. You can also see excessive recompiles due to code changes and other events, as outlined previously. So there are practices we can follow that will help us reduce the frequency of recompiles. The following practices can help reduce the number of recompiles:

- Avoid interleaving DDL and DML statements.
- Reduce recompilation caused by statistics changes.
- Use the KEEPFIXED PLAN hint.
- Disable automatic statistics maintenance on a table.
- Use table variables.
- Use temporary tables across multiple scopes.
- Avoid changing SET options within a batch.

Avoid Interleaving DDL and DML Statements

It's a common practice to use local temporary tables with a batch or procedure. Frequently, you'll see people modify the schema or add indexes as part of the practice. Making these changes will affect the validity of the execution plan, therefore causing a recompilation for the statements that reference those temporary tables, mostly from *deferred compilation*. Listing 8-10 shows a procedure that can lead to recompilations.

Listing 8-10. Procedure with interleaved DDL and DML

```
CREATE OR ALTER PROC dbo.TempTable
AS
--All statements are compiled initially
CREATE TABLE #MyTempTable
(
    ID INT,
```

```sql
    Dsc NVARCHAR(50)
);
--This statement must be recompiled
INSERT INTO #MyTempTable
(
    ID,
    Dsc
)
SELECT pm.ProductModelID,
       pm.Name
FROM Production.ProductModel AS pm;
--This statement must be recompiled
SELECT mtt.ID,
       mtt.Dsc
FROM #MyTempTable AS mtt;
CREATE CLUSTERED INDEX iTest ON #MyTempTable (ID);
--Creating index causes a recompile
SELECT mtt.ID,
       mtt.Dsc
FROM #MyTempTable AS mtt;
CREATE TABLE #t2
(
    c1 INT
);
--Recompile from a new table
SELECT c1
FROM #t2;
```

Because of all the interleaved structural changes, more recompiles are needed than would be necessary if we changed the code around a little. Figure 8-8 shows the Extended Events output.

name	timestamp	recompile_cause	batch_text	statement
sql_batch_st...	2025-06-13 1...	NULL	EXEC dbo.TempTable;	NULL
sql_statemen...	2025-06-13 1...	NULL	NULL	EXEC dbo.TempTable
sp_statement...	2025-06-13 1...	NULL	NULL	CREATE TABLE #MyTempTa...
sp_statement...	2025-06-13 1...	NULL	NULL	CREATE TABLE #MyTempTa...
sp_statement...	2025-06-13 1...	NULL	NULL	INSERT INTO #MyTempTable ...
sql_statemen...	2025-06-13 1...	Deferred compile	NULL	
sp_statement...	2025-06-13 1...	NULL	NULL	INSERT INTO #MyTempTable ...
sp_statement...	2025-06-13 1...	NULL	NULL	INSERT INTO #MyTempTable ...
sp_statement...	2025-06-13 1...	NULL	NULL	SELECT mtt.ID, mtt.Dsc ...
sql_statemen...	2025-06-13 1...	Deferred compile	NULL	
sp_statement...	2025-06-13 1...	NULL	NULL	SELECT mtt.ID, mtt.Dsc ...
sp_statement...	2025-06-13 1...	NULL	NULL	SELECT mtt.ID, mtt.Dsc ...
sp_statement...	2025-06-13 1...	NULL	NULL	CREATE CLUSTERED INDEX...
sp_statement...	2025-06-13 1...	NULL	NULL	CREATE CLUSTERED INDEX...
sp_statement...	2025-06-13 1...	NULL	NULL	SELECT mtt.ID, mtt.Dsc ...
sql_statemen...	2025-06-13 1...	Deferred compile	NULL	
sp_statement...	2025-06-13 1...	NULL	NULL	SELECT mtt.ID, mtt.Dsc ...
sp_statement...	2025-06-13 1...	NULL	NULL	SELECT mtt.ID, mtt.Dsc ...
sp_statement...	2025-06-13 1...	NULL	NULL	CREATE TABLE #t2 (c1 I...
sp_statement...	2025-06-13 1...	NULL	NULL	CREATE TABLE #t2 (c1 I...
sp_statement...	2025-06-13 1...	NULL	NULL	SELECT c1 FROM #t2
sql_statemen...	2025-06-13 1...	Deferred compile	NULL	
sp_statement...	2025-06-13 1...	NULL	NULL	SELECT c1 FROM #t2
sp_statement...	2025-06-13 1...	NULL	NULL	SELECT c1 FROM #t2
sql_statemen...	2025-06-13 1...	NULL	NULL	EXEC dbo.TempTable
sql_batch_co...	2025-06-13 1...	NULL	EXEC dbo.TempTable;	NULL

Figure 8-8. *Multiple recompiles from interleaved DDL and DML*

It's good to remember every statement in a procedure gets a plan initially. However, because objects are referenced that don't exist, additional work is necessary at every execution of this procedure.

Reduce Recompilation Caused by Statistics Changes

In most cases, the changes in data over time that result in statistics updates need a new execution plan. This means the cost associated with the recompile can be beneficial overall to the system. However, in some cases, the plans may be identical because the data distribution is the same, even after a statistics update. If this were to happen frequently, the recompiles could be very painful. In the rare instance where this is the case, you have a couple of options to deal with recompiles from statistics updates:

CHAPTER 8 QUERY RECOMPILATION

- Use the KEEPFIXED PLAN hint.
- Disable the automatic statistics maintenance on a table.

Use the KEEPFIXED PLAN Hint

In the event you'd like to avoid recompiles as much as possible, you can apply a query hint, KEEPFIXED PLAN. We haven't discussed query hints yet. In a nutshell, they're slightly misnamed. Instead of a hint, a suggestion, a query hint is a commandment to the optimizer, or, in the instance of this particular hint, the SQL engine. Instead of removing this plan from cache to recompile it, the same plan will remain in place. Listing 8-11 contains the necessary code to test this hint.

Listing 8-11. Script to create a table and procedure for a query hint

```
IF
(
    SELECT OBJECT_ID('dbo.Test1')
) IS NOT NULL
    DROP TABLE dbo.Test1;
GO
CREATE TABLE dbo.Test1
(
    C1 INT,
    C2 CHAR(50)
);
INSERT INTO dbo.Test1
VALUES
(1, '2');
CREATE NONCLUSTERED INDEX IndexOne ON dbo.Test1 (C1);
GO
--Create a stored procedure referencing the previous table
CREATE OR ALTER PROC dbo.TestProc
AS
SELECT t.C1,
```

```
        t.C2
FROM dbo.Test1 AS t
WHERE t.C1 = 1
OPTION (KEEPFIXED PLAN);
GO
--First execution of stored procedure with 1 row in the table
EXEC dbo.TestProc; --First execution
--Add many rows to the table to cause statistics change
WITH Nums
AS (SELECT 1 AS n
    UNION ALL
    SELECT Nums.n + 1
    FROM Nums
    WHERE Nums.n < 1000)
INSERT INTO dbo.Test1
(
    C1,
    C2
)
SELECT 1,
       Nums.n
FROM Nums
OPTION (MAXRECURSION 1000);
GO
--Reexecute the stored procedure with a change in statistics
EXEC dbo.TestProc;
```

The results of the Extended Events are visible in Figure 8-9.

sql_batch_starting	2025-06-13 1...	NULL	--First execution of stored pr...	NULL
sql_statement_starting	2025-06-13 1...	NULL	NULL	EXEC dbo.TestProc
sp_statement_starting	2025-06-13 1...	NULL	NULL	SELECT t.C1, t.C2 FROM dbo.Test1 AS t ...
sp_statement_completed	2025-06-13 1...	NULL	NULL	SELECT t.C1, t.C2 FROM dbo.Test1 AS t ...
sql_statement_complet...	2025-06-13 1...	NULL	NULL	EXEC dbo.TestProc
sql_statement_starting	2025-06-13 1...	NULL	NULL	WITH Nums AS (SELECT 1 AS n UNION ALL...
sql_statement_complet...	2025-06-13 1...	NULL	NULL	WITH Nums AS (SELECT 1 AS n UNION ALL...
sql_batch_completed	2025-06-13 1...	NULL	--First execution of stored pr...	NULL
sql_batch_starting	2025-06-13 1...	NULL	--Reexecute the stored proc...	NULL
sql_statement_starting	2025-06-13 1...	NULL	NULL	EXEC dbo.TestProc
sp_statement_starting	2025-06-13 1...	NULL	NULL	SELECT t.C1, t.C2 FROM dbo.Test1 AS t ...
sp_statement_completed	2025-06-13 1...	NULL	NULL	SELECT t.C1, t.C2 FROM dbo.Test1 AS t ...
sql_statement_complet...	2025-06-13 1...	NULL	NULL	EXEC dbo.TestProc
sql_batch_completed	2025-06-13 1...	NULL	--Reexecute the stored proc...	NULL

Figure 8-9. Results of the KEEPFIXED PLAN query hint

You can see that the procedure executed the first time and didn't have a recompile. Then, the script in Listing 8-11 modified the data sufficiently that a recompile would absolutely be necessary under normal circumstances. However, you can see that we didn't get a recompile on the second execution of the procedure, despite the change in data and statistics. This is due to the KEEPFIXED PLAN hint.

> **Caution** Using any query hint should only come after extensive testing has proven that it is the best solution. KEEPFIXED PLAN could result in a poor execution plan being kept on the system when a better one would result in superior performance.

Another query hint that might be useful here is KEEP PLAN. This hint is specific to temporary tables. It will keep the plan in place until the 500-row threshold is met for statistics updates. It can help reduce the amount of recompiles you see when using temporary tables. It does come with the same caveats though.

Disable Automatic Statistics Maintenance on a Table

You have the option of disabling statistics updates, either for the database entirely or for individual tables. Listing 8-12 shows how to turn off a table's statistics maintenance.

Listing 8-12. Disabling automatic statistics maintenance on one table

```
EXEC sys.sp_autostats 'dbo.Test1', 'OFF';
```

Now, regardless of data changes, statistics are not updated on this table. That means that no queries will be marked for recompile because of changes in data.

Once again, we are in a situation where this could prove extremely problematic. Extensive testing to validate that this won't hurt other queries should be undertaken before implementing this. Also, if you do choose to disable the automatic statistics updates, you should plan to have a manual process to update those statistics and then deal with the recompile in a more controlled manner.

Use Table Variables

Temporary tables and table variables are almost identical in every regard. However, table variables have one singular distinction: they do not have statistics. Because table variables do not have statistics, they don't suffer from some recompiles that do occur on temporary tables. If we look at Listing 8-13, we can see an example with a temporary table.

Listing 8-13. Updating a temporary table

```
DECLARE @count INT;
CREATE TABLE #TempTable
(
    C1 INT PRIMARY KEY
);
SET @count = 1;
WHILE @count < 8
BEGIN
    INSERT INTO #TempTable
    (
        C1
    )
    VALUES
    (@count);
    SELECT tt.C1
    FROM #TempTable AS tt
        JOIN Production.ProductModel AS pm
            ON pm.ProductModelID = tt.C1
```

CHAPTER 8   QUERY RECOMPILATION

```
        WHERE tt.C1 < @count;
        SET @count += 1;
END;
DROP TABLE #TempTable;
```

Figure 8-10 has part of the output from the execution of Listing 8-13.

name	timestamp	recompile_cause	batch_text	statement
sql_statement_complet...	2025-06-13 1...	NULL	NULL	WHILE @count < 8
sql_statement_starting	2025-06-13 1...	NULL	NULL	INSERT INTO #TempTable (C1) ...
sql_statement_complet...	2025-06-13 1...	NULL	NULL	INSERT INTO #TempTable (C1) ...
sql_statement_starting	2025-06-13 1...	NULL	NULL	SELECT tt.C1 FROM #TempTable AS tt ...
sql_statement_recompile	2025-06-13 1...	Statistics changed	NULL	
sql_statement_starting	2025-06-13 1...	NULL	NULL	SELECT tt.C1 FROM #TempTable AS tt ...
sql_statement_complet...	2025-06-13 1...	NULL	NULL	SELECT tt.C1 FROM #TempTable AS tt ...
sql_statement_starting	2025-06-13 1...	NULL	NULL	SET @count += 1;
sql_statement_complet...	2025-06-13 1...	NULL	NULL	SET @count += 1;
sql_statement_starting	2025-06-13 1...	NULL	NULL	WHILE @count < 8

Figure 8-10. *A recompile caused by a statistics change*

Since the threshold of six rows has been exceeded on the temporary table, a recompile has occurred. We can change this code to what we see in Listing 8-14.

Listing 8-14. Updating a table variable

```
DECLARE @TempTable TABLE
(
    C1 INT PRIMARY KEY
);
DECLARE @Count TINYINT = 1;
WHILE @Count < 8
BEGIN
    INSERT INTO @TempTable
    (
        C1
    )
    VALUES
    (@Count );
    SELECT tt.C1
    FROM @TempTable AS tt
        JOIN Production.ProductModel AS pm
```

```
      ON pm.ProductModelID = tt.C1
      WHERE tt.C1 < @Count;
   SET @Count += 1;
END;
```

In this case, there is no statistics update. I'm not going to display the Extended Events output here because there is nothing new or different to see. No recompile occurs in this instance.

For very small data sets like this one, table variables are preferable because the lack of statistics avoids recompiles. As the data set grows, however, statistics become helpful to the optimizer, and temporary tables will perform better, usually despite the recompile.

Use Temporary Tables Across Multiple Scopes

You can declare a temporary table in one procedure and then use that same temporary table in a second procedure, called by the first procedure. Prior to SQL Server 2019, and outside of Azure SQL Database, this resulted in a recompile, every single time the query was called. However, new changes to the engine mean you won't see those recompiles.

Listing 8-15 shows an example of this in action.

Listing 8-15. Nested procedures to avoid recompiles

```
CREATE OR ALTER PROC dbo.OuterProc
AS
CREATE TABLE #Scope
(ID INT PRIMARY KEY,
ScopeName VARCHAR(50));
EXEC dbo.InnerProc
GO
CREATE OR ALTER PROC dbo.InnerProc
AS
INSERT INTO #Scope
(
    ID,
    ScopeName
)
```

```
VALUES
(   1,      -- ID - int
    'InnerProc' -- ScopeName - varchar(50)
    );
SELECT s.ScopeName
FROM #Scope AS s;
GO
```

Creating a procedure like dbo.OuterProc, you will receive a message that it has a dependency on dbo.InnerProc. However, both procedures can be created, and then, when the outer procedure gets executed, you won't see recompiles from the inner procedure.

Avoid Changing SET Options Within a Batch

Changing the environment settings while executing a procedure will lead directly to recompiles. For ANSI compatibility, it's generally recommended that you keep the following SET options ON:

- ARITHABORT
- CONCAT_NULL_YIELDS_NULL
- QUOTED_IDENTIFIER
- ANSI_NULLS
- ANSI_PADDING
- ANSI_WARNINGS
- NUMERIC_ROUNDABORT should be set to OFF

Listing 8-16 shows code that doesn't follow these guidelines.

Listing 8-16. Changing environment settings within a procedure

```
CREATE OR ALTER PROC dbo.TestProc
AS
SELECT 'a' + NULL + 'b'; --1st
SET CONCAT_NULL_YIELDS_NULL OFF;
SELECT 'a' + NULL + 'b'; --2nd
```

CHAPTER 8   QUERY RECOMPILATION

```
SET ANSI_NULLS OFF;
SELECT 'a' + NULL + 'b';--3rd
GO
EXEC dbo.TestProc; --First execution
EXEC dbo.TestProc; --Second execution
```

Some of the results from the Extended Events are visible in Figure 8-11.

name	timestamp	recompile_cause	batch_text	statement
sp_statement_starting	2025-06-13 1...	NULL	NULL	SELECT 'a' + NULL + 'b'
sql_statement_recompile	2025-06-13 1...	Set option change	NULL	
sp_statement_starting	2025-06-13 1...	NULL	NULL	SELECT 'a' + NULL + 'b'
sp_statement_completed	2025-06-13 1...	NULL	NULL	SELECT 'a' + NULL + 'b'
sp_statement_starting	2025-06-13 1...	NULL	NULL	SELECT 'a' + NULL + 'b'
sql_statement_recompile	2025-06-13 1...	Set option change	NULL	
sp_statement_starting	2025-06-13 1...	NULL	NULL	SELECT 'a' + NULL + 'b'

Figure 8-11. *Recompiles caused by SET option changes*

The first execution of the queries results in recompiles for the statements after the SET option changes. However, you'll note that the second execution doesn't show any recompile. That's because the SET options are now a part of the execution plan, so no further recompiles are necessary. However, for identical queries, there are now three plans in cache.

Worth noting, changing the SET NOCOUNT environment setting doesn't cause recompiles.

Controlling Recompile Results

In the previous section, we went over several ways you can attempt to reduce the number of recompiles. However, sometimes, the recompile is unavoidable. In that case, you need to have some mechanisms to control the output of the recompile. You have four options:

- Plan forcing
- Plan guides
- Query hints
- Hint forcing

Plan Forcing

We already talked a little about plan forcing in Chapter 6 when we talked about the Query Store. We'll cover it some more in Chapter 13 when we talk about dealing with parameter-sensitive execution plans. However, it's worth a little detail right here in this chapter too.

Plan forcing will not prevent a recompile from occurring. Should any of the listed criteria be met, the plan will recompile. However, plan forcing allows you to control the outcome of the recompile. Instead of an all-new plan, you'll get the plan chosen for forcing. This does assume that the plan was not rendered invalid due to code or structure changes. Otherwise, this is one way to control the results of a recompile.

Query Hints

I introduced the concept of query hints earlier in the chapter when we used KEEPFIXED PLAN to eliminate recompiles and KEEP PLAN to reduce the occurrence of recompiles for temporary tables. Many of the query hints available are directly related to forcing choices on the optimizer. We'll address a number of different hints throughout the book. However, there's one in particular I'd like to bring up here: OPTIMIZE FOR.

The OPTIMIZE FOR hint allows you to control the values of parameters used during the compile process. You can use OPTIMIZE FOR with a specified value for a parameter to get a precise plan. You can also use OPTIMIZE FOR UNKNOWN to get a more generic plan. We'll cover these hints further in Chapter 13, but let's look at an example right now in Listing 8-17.

Listing 8-17. A parameter-sensitive stored procedure with a query hint

```
CREATE OR ALTER PROCEDURE dbo.CustomerList @CustomerID INT
AS
SELECT soh.SalesOrderNumber,
       soh.OrderDate,
       sod.OrderQty,
       sod.LineTotal
FROM Sales.SalesOrderHeader AS soh
    JOIN Sales.SalesOrderDetail AS sod
        ON soh.SalesOrderID = sod.SalesOrderID
```

```
WHERE soh.CustomerID >= @CustomerID
OPTION (OPTIMIZE FOR (@CustomerID = 1));
```

Using a query hint like I do in Listing 8-17 does require that the code gets modified. There are possible ways around that, discussed in the next two sections. However, regardless of the recompile process, the query in this procedure will always get one plan, based on the value provided to @CustomerID within the OPTIMIZE FOR hint.

We can see it in action if we run the queries in Listing 8-18.

Listing 8-18. Executing the CustomerList procedure with different values

```
EXEC dbo.CustomerList @CustomerID = 7920 WITH RECOMPILE;
EXEC dbo.CustomerList @CustomerID = 30118 WITH RECOMPILE;
```

Executing the procedure while specifying WITH RECOMPILE will ensure that the optimizer is forced to recompile the entire procedure. The execution plans from each of these values are here in Figure 8-12.

CHAPTER 8 QUERY RECOMPILATION

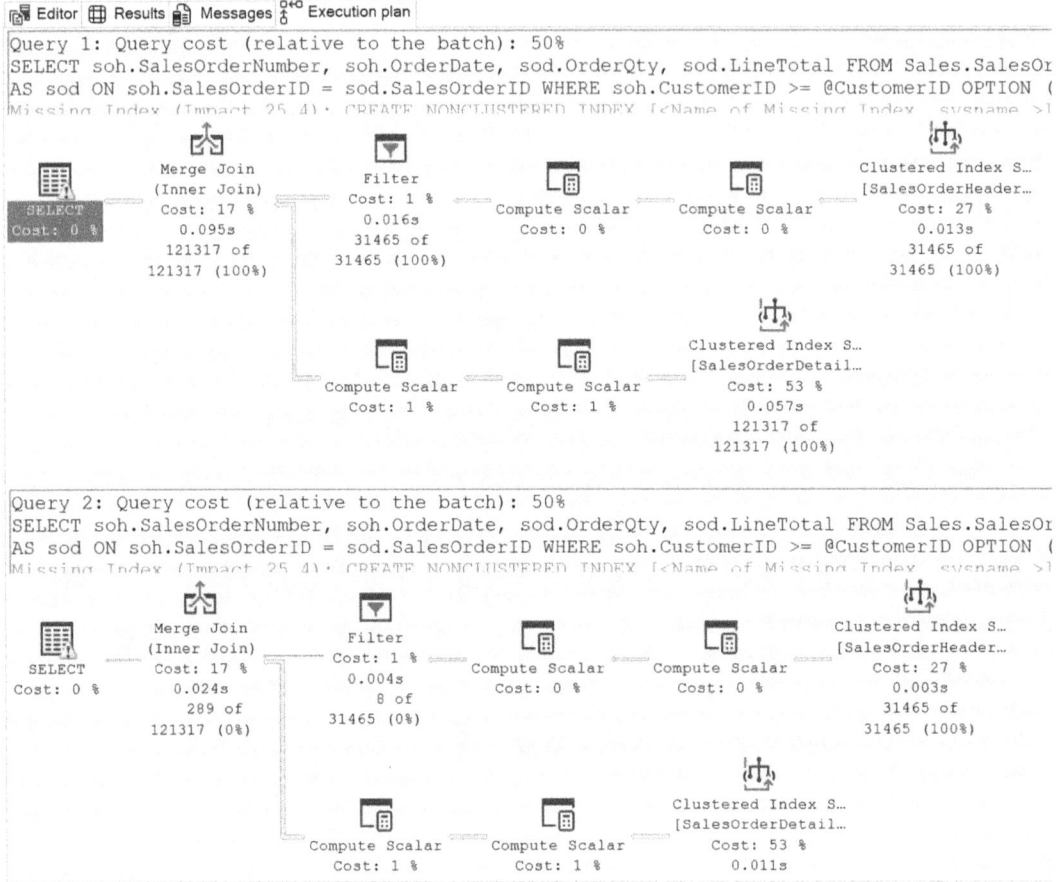

Figure 8-12. *Two identical execution plans*

You can see that both execution plans are the same. However, since I have runtime metrics, you can see substantial differences that would have, under other circumstances, resulted in different execution plans. The first query shows that it's returning 121,317 rows out of 121,317 rows expected. In short, that plan is correct for the parameter passed in. However, the second plan is returning only 289 rows. That suggests pretty strongly a different execution plan could have been used for the second parameter value.

We can see evidence of the work done by the query hint within the execution plan. If you look at the properties of the first operator, in the second execution plan, you'll see the Parameter Compiled Value in Figure 8-13.

CHAPTER 8   QUERY RECOMPILATION

Parameter List	@CustomerID
Column	@CustomerID
Parameter Compiled Value	(1)
Parameter Data Type	int
Parameter Runtime Value	(30118)

Figure 8-13. *Parameter list from the first operator*

So while the query was executed with the value of 30118, the compile value was 1. This, despite the fact that the query was recompiled as it was executed.

Plan Guides

In the previous section, we used a stored procedure with a query hint added to it. What if you wanted to try to use a query hint, but you really didn't want to modify the code? Plan guides can sometimes do that job for us. Listing 8-19 shows the procedure and query without the query hint.

Listing 8-19. The CustomerList procedure without the query hint

```
CREATE OR ALTER PROCEDURE dbo.CustomerList @CustomerID INT
AS
SELECT soh.SalesOrderNumber,
       soh.OrderDate,
       sod.OrderQty,
       sod.LineTotal
FROM Sales.SalesOrderHeader AS soh
    JOIN Sales.SalesOrderDetail AS sod
        ON soh.SalesOrderID = sod.SalesOrderID
WHERE soh.CustomerID >= @CustomerID;
```

If I decided that I need to add a query hint, but for whatever reason, I can't modify the code, I'm going to create a plan guide as you see in Listing 8-20.

Listing 8-20. Creating a plan guide

```
sp_create_plan_guide @name = N'MyGuide',
                     @stmt = N'SELECT soh.SalesOrderNumber,
       soh.OrderDate,
       sod.OrderQty,
       sod.LineTotal
FROM Sales.SalesOrderHeader AS soh
    JOIN Sales.SalesOrderDetail AS sod
        ON soh.SalesOrderID = sod.SalesOrderID
WHERE soh.CustomerID >= @CustomerID;',
                     @type = N'OBJECT',
                     @module_or_batch = N'dbo.CustomerList',
                     @params = NULL,
                     @hints = N'OPTION (OPTIMIZE FOR (@CustomerID = 1))';
```

You'll notice that I copied the formatting, as well as the text, of the query. That's because in order to get plan guides to work, you have to match the white space exactly. However, with that plan guide in place, if I were to execute the procedure again, as I did in Listing 8-18, the execution plans would be identical again. We can see whether or not the guide was used in a couple of ways. There is an event in Extended Events. You can also look directly at the execution plan properties in Figure 8-14.

Parameter List	@CustomerID
PlanGuideDB	AdventureWorks
PlanGuideName	MyGuide
QueryHash	0x3A3D3A1BB29006AE
QueryPlanHash	0xE049A058F67475F7

Figure 8-14. *The PlanGuideName property in an execution plan*

The property PlanGuideName is added to an execution plan, in the properties of the first operator, only when a plan guide is used. You can see this one right there, by name, MyGuide.

Listing 8-20 represents an object plan guide. This means the plan guide itself is associated only with the defined module, CustomerList. You can also create a plan guide just for queries, like ad hoc batches. This is known as a SQL plan guide. Just like with the object plan guide, you have to get the white space and everything just right.

Listing 8-21 shows an ad hoc query version of the same code we've been using.

Listing 8-21. An ad hoc query in need of a query hint

```
SELECT soh.SalesOrderNumber,
       soh.OrderDate,
       sod.OrderQty,
       sod.LineTotal
FROM Sales.SalesOrderHeader AS soh
    JOIN Sales.SalesOrderDetail AS sod
        ON soh.SalesOrderID = sod.SalesOrderID
WHERE soh.CustomerID >= 1;
```

If we wanted to take control of the recompile to force a particular behavior, we could create a SQL plan guide like Listing 8-22.

Listing 8-22. Forcing an index seek through a plan guide

```
EXECUTE sp_create_plan_guide @name = N'MyGoodSQLGuide',
                             @stmt = N'SELECT soh.SalesOrderNumber,
       soh.OrderDate,
       sod.OrderQty,
       sod.LineTotal
FROM Sales.SalesOrderHeader AS soh
    JOIN Sales.SalesOrderDetail AS sod
        ON soh.SalesOrderID = sod.SalesOrderID
WHERE soh.CustomerID >= 1;',
                             @type = N'SQL',
                             @module_or_batch = NULL,
                             @params = NULL,
                             @hints = N'OPTION (TABLE HINT(soh, FORCESEEK))';
```

Executing the query from Listing 8-21 results in the execution plan shown in Figure 8-15 (broken in two, top to bottom, for visibility).

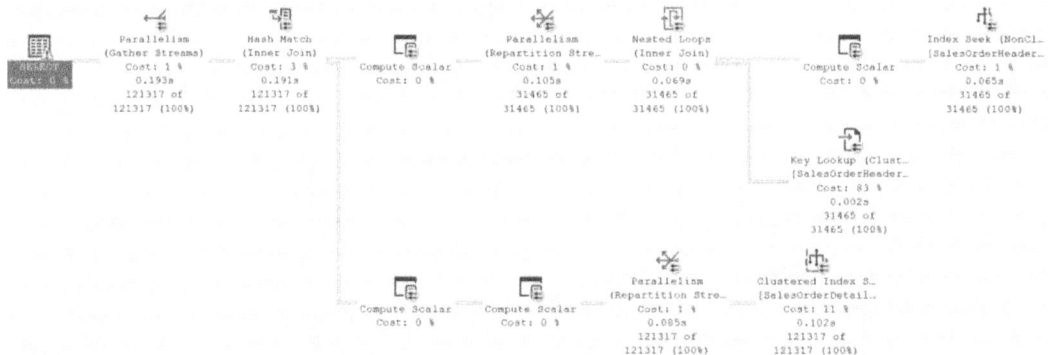

Figure 8-15. *The execution plan after applying a hint through a plan guide*

That's a radically different execution plan, despite compiling from a value that should result in the plan in Figure 8-12.

One other method for controlling the results of a recompile is possible. To see this in action, I'm first going to clear the cache to ensure there are no plans at all. Second, I'm going to remove the plan guides we have created using Listing 8-23.

Listing 8-23. Removing plan guides

```
EXECUTE sp_control_plan_guide @operation = 'Drop', @name = N'MyGoodSQLGuide';
EXECUTE sp_control_plan_guide @operation = 'Drop', @name = N'MyGuide';
```

With that done, I'm going to go back and execute the query in Listing 8-21. That will mean that the original plan is now in cache. I can now take advantage of one more plan guide mechanism, creating a plan guide from an execution plan. Listing 8-24 shows how to get this done.

Listing 8-24. Using sp_create_plan_guide_from_handle

```
DECLARE @plan_handle VARBINARY(64),
        @start_offset INT;
SELECT @plan_handle = deqs.plan_handle,
       @start_offset = deqs.statement_start_offset
FROM sys.dm_exec_query_stats AS deqs
```

```
    CROSS APPLY sys.dm_exec_sql_text(sql_handle)
    CROSS APPLY sys.dm_exec_text_query_plan(deqs.plan_handle, deqs.
    statement_start_offset, deqs.statement_end_offset) AS qp
WHERE text LIKE N'SELECT soh.SalesOrderNumber%';
EXECUTE sp_create_plan_guide_from_handle
@name = N'ForcedPlanGuide',
    @plan_handle = @plan_handle,
    @statement_start_offset = @start_offset;
```

This is very similar to plan forcing but clearly involves quite a few more steps. However, it is a way to control the output of a recompile.

I want to emphasize that using plan guides can be a dangerous approach to fixing problems. As data changes over time, the plans that were working well for you may no longer be. If you do choose to implement plan guides, ensure you have a regularly scheduled reassessment of whether or not they are appropriate.

Hint Forcing

In Azure SQL Database and SQL Server 2022 and greater, you have one final option for controlling the output of a recompile: hint forcing. We covered how this works in Chapter 6.

Summary

Most of the time, recompiles are helping us. Data, structures, or code has changed, and a fresh execution plan will help enhance performance. However, as we discussed throughout the chapter, this isn't always the case. Extended Events are a great way to understand why a given statement is being recompiled. You now have several methods to reduce the volume of recompiles you experience on your system. Finally, we walked through several ways to control the results of the recompile. With your ability to understand why recompiles are occurring, it will make it possible to avoid unnecessary recompiles.

The last several chapters were all about the internals of how SQL Server generates and manages execution plans. The next several chapters are going to talk about specific database structures that can hurt, or help, your performance. We're going to start with the most important: indexes.

CHAPTER 9

Index Architecture

Choosing the correct index can be one of the single most effective mechanisms for enhancing performance within SQL Server. Because of this simple fact, it's vital that you understand how indexes work in order to help you select the correct one for the job. Back in SQL Server 2016, the clustered columnstore index was introduced. Today, we actually get to pick our best storage mechanism for the data, whether a clustered rowstore or a clustered columnstore index, for the most common data access. Then we can add additional indexes to each to assist other query paths to the data.

In this chapter, I will cover the following topics:

- What is an index
- Recommendations for choosing an index
- Clustered and nonclustered rowstore index behavior
- Clustered and nonclustered columnstore index behavior
- Recommendations on index use

What Is a Rowstore Index?

The existence of an index on a table can be the difference between looking at every single row on the table, in what's called a scan, and simply going right to the row of information you need. To say that this helps performance, especially I/O, would be a gross understatement. A good analogy for an index in a database is the index in this book. For example, if you were interested in the term *deadlock*, without an index in the book, you'd have to look at every single page. With the index, you can go directly to the page you need. In the same way, an index in the database takes you right to the information you need.

CHAPTER 9 INDEX ARCHITECTURE

To see this in action, let's look at some data from a table in AdventureWorks. Let's say we wanted to see all the Products in the Production.Product table and we wanted to see them ordered by Name of the product. The query would look something like Listing 9-1 (for illustration purposes, I'll just retrieve ten rows).

Listing 9-1. Retrieving all Products ordered by Name

```
SELECT TOP 10
       p.ProductID,
       p.[Name],
       p.StandardCost,
       p.[Weight],
       ROW_NUMBER() OVER (ORDER BY p.NAME DESC) AS RowNumber
FROM Production.Product p
ORDER BY p.NAME DESC;
```

The output is in Figure 9-1.

	ProductID	Name	StandardCost	Weight	RowNumber
1	852	Women's Tights, S	30.9334	NULL	1
2	853	Women's Tights, M	30.9334	NULL	2
3	854	Women's Tights, L	30.9334	NULL	3
4	867	Women's Mountain Shorts, S	26.1763	NULL	4
5	868	Women's Mountain Shorts, M	26.1763	NULL	5
6	869	Women's Mountain Shorts, L	26.1763	NULL	6
7	870	Water Bottle - 30 oz.	1.8663	NULL	7
8	842	Touring-Panniers, Large	51.5625	NULL	8
9	965	Touring-3000 Yellow, 62	461.4448	30.00	9
10	964	Touring-3000 Yellow, 58	461.4448	29.79	10

Figure 9-1. *Data ordered and numbered by Product.Name*

You can think about this result set as if it were an index. The data is sorted and stored by Name. You can look up the data by the RowNumber value. In the database, the query shown previously scanned all the data in the table because there is no WHERE clause.

If we were interested in filtering our data and the business requirement was to return only those values where the StandardCost is greater than 200, we'd have to scan the entire table, comparing the values, to determine if a given row exceeded that value. We can take a couple of approaches to create an "index" on this data.

CHAPTER 9 INDEX ARCHITECTURE

The first way would be to store it more like a dictionary. The data will be ordered but will have duplicate values. If we modified the query in Listing 9-1 to sort by StandardCost DESC, we'd get results similar to Figure 9-2.

	ProductID	Name	StandardCost	Weight	RowNumber
1	749	Road-150 Red, 62	2171.2942	15.00	125
2	753	Road-150 Red, 56	2171.2942	14.68	126
3	752	Road-150 Red, 52	2171.2942	14.42	127
4	751	Road-150 Red, 48	2171.2942	14.13	128
5	750	Road-150 Red, 44	2171.2942	13.77	129
6	774	Mountain-100 Silver, 48	1912.1544	21.42	170
7	773	Mountain-100 Silver, 44	1912.1544	21.13	171
8	772	Mountain-100 Silver, 42	1912.1544	20.77	172
9	771	Mountain-100 Silver, 38	1912.1544	20.35	173
10	778	Mountain-100 Black, 48	1898.0944	21.42	174

Figure 9-2. *Data reordered by StandardCost*

Note, I left the ROW_NUMBER function still sorting by Name, so you see the original values there.

Finding the values that are greater than 200 would be a simple matter of going to the first value that's above that and then returning the rest. An index that both sorts the data and stores it in that sorted fashion is a clustered index. Because SQL Server is oriented around the storage of clustered indexes, this is the single most important index to define on your tables. I'll explain even more later in the chapter.

Another way to create an index is, again, like a book's index. There we create a second, sorted set of values, but we're not changing the storage of the data, the book itself. Instead, we keep all the values and a page number to refer back to where the data is stored. If we wanted to use RowNumber as this pointer, the data in the index would look like Table 9-1.

273

Table 9-1. An "index" on the StandardCost column

StandardCost	RowNumber
2171.2942	125
2171.2942	126
2171.2942	127
2171.2942	128
2171.2942	129
1912.1544	170

A structure like this is similar to a nonclustered index. We have a pointer back to the data, in the form of the RowNumber, which would be the primary key on a clustered index, or a row identifier (RID) in a heap (more about heaps a little later). Again, the value for StandardCost acts as a guide to the value we're interested in, and then the data is stored with the clustered index.

I've already talked about the common types of indexes, either rowstore or columnstore and clustered or nonclustered. There are also several other index types that we'll deal with in other parts of the book. These include the following:

- Hash: Part of the memory-optimized table structure, covered in Chapter 19

- Memory-Optimized Nonclustered: Another part of the memory-optimized table structure, also covered in Chapter 19

- Spatial: Indexes that work with geometry or geography data in order to optimize search and retrieval of spatial objects, covered in Chapter 10

- XML: Indexes for the XML data type, covered in Chapter 10

- Full-Text: Indexes built and maintained by the full-text engine within SQL Server, also covered in Chapter 10

- Vector Index: Indexes to help speed up operations with the Vector data type used in AI operations, covered in Chapter 10

The Benefits of Indexes

In order for SQL Server to actually be useful, you need to be able to retrieve the data stored in it. When you have no clustered index defined on a table, the storage engine will be left with no choice but to read through the entire table to find information. A table that has no clustered index is called a heap. A heap is just an unordered stack of data with a row identifier as a pointer to the storage location. The only way to search through the data in a heap is going row by row in a process called a scan. When creating a clustered index, the data itself is reordered and stored by the key you define for that index. The key becomes the pointer to the data, as well as the ordering mechanism. A nonclustered index, as described previously, will have a pointer back to the data, either consisting of the RID to a heap or the key to the clustered index. So the first benefit of indexes is the fact that the data is ordered, making it easier to search.

Data within SQL Server is stored on an 8KB page. A page is the minimum amount of information that moves from the disk into memory. How much data you can store on a given page becomes very important for this reason. Generally speaking, a nonclustered index is going to be small, consisting of the key column, or columns, and any INCLUDE columns that you add. Because of this, retrieving data from a nonclustered index means more rows on a page. This makes for better performance because you have to move fewer pages off disk and into memory, depending on the query of course.

Another benefit of a nonclustered index is that it is stored separately from the table. You can even put it onto a different disk entirely, helping make searches faster.

All rowstore indexes, and parts of the columnstore index, store their data in a balanced tree, referred to as a B-Tree. The B-Tree is used in order to minimize the number of reads required to find a given row. To illustrate this, I want to go through a thought experiment. Imagine a table with one column and 27 rows in a random order. For our thought experiment, only three rows can be stored on a given page. The layout of the data would look like Figure 9-3.

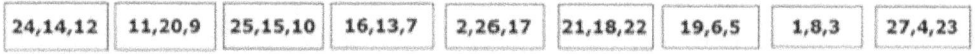

Figure 9-3. *Twenty-seven rows in a random order stored in pages*

To search for the value of 5, SQL Server will have to scan all the rows on all the pages. Even though you find the value of 5, the scan continues because the last page could also contain the value of 5. The number of reads depends on the number of pages accessed;

nine read operations (retrieving the pages from disk and storing them in memory) will be performed on the table since there is no index.

If we were to create an index on the column, the data would be reordered as shown in Figure 9-4.

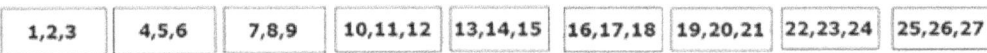

Figure 9-4. *Twenty-seven rows stored in sorted order on the pages*

If SQL Server were to look for the value of 5, just from this ordered list, only two reads would be required, because the second page has the value. Further, because it's the key value in an index, SQL Server knows that the data is sorted, so when it hits the value 6, it knows it can stop reading pages. If we were to search for the value of 25, though, we're back to nine reads again. This is where the B-Tree structure comes into play. The data in our index is actually stored as shown in Figure 9-5.

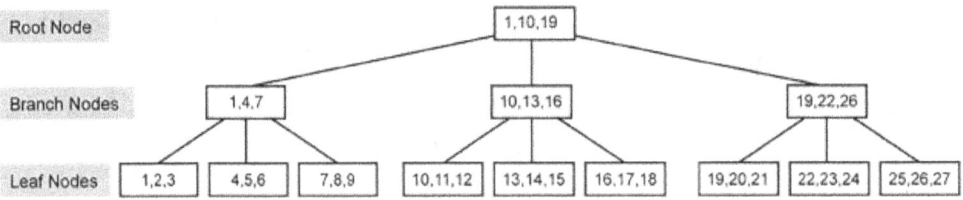

Figure 9-5. *Twenty-seven rows stored in a B-Tree*

A B-Tree consists of a starting node (or page) called a root node. It has a number of branch nodes (again, or pages) that are below it. Finally, below them are the leaf nodes (pages, also called interior nodes). The root node stores pointers to the branch nodes. The branch nodes store pointers to the leaf nodes. All values are stored in the leaf nodes. The key values that define our index are kept sorted at all times. The balanced nature of the B-Tree is that each of these nodes will be distributed evenly as shown in Figure 9-5. Each of the leaf nodes is in what is referred to as a doubly linked list, meaning each page points to the page that follows it and the page that precedes it. The doubly linked list means that when scanning the values, you won't have to go back up the chain of nodes to find the next page.

The B-Tree algorithm minimizes the number of pages accessed, speeding up data retrieval. For the value of 5, you would start at the root node. It's going to point to the first branch node, because its starting value is 1, which is less than 5, while the next page starts at 10, so it can be ignored. The branch node page is read, and here, we find a page that starts at the value of 4, greater than the value of 1 and less than the value of 7. It then goes down and reads the leaf node page, reading through all the rows on the page, to return the value of 5. So it took three reads to find 5. While that sounds like more than two, remember, it will also only take three reads to find the value of 25.

So indexes put the data into ordered storage to help speed processing. They reduce the number of pages to be accessed, again, increasing performance, and, through the B-Tree, further reduce the number of pages to be accessed, again, increasing performance.

There are a number of other benefits from indexes that we'll explore throughout the book, from enforcing unique values (which can also help performance) to compressed storage and more. Further, we'll discuss the benefits of the columnstore index in a section later in the chapter.

Index Overhead

Nothing comes for free. While we get a performance benefit from indexes, there is also a cost. A table with an index requires more storage and memory space than an equivalent heap table. Data manipulation queries (INSERT, UPDATE, and DELETE statements) can take longer. More processing time is required to maintain the indexes. This is because, unlike a SELECT statement, data manipulation queries modify the content of a table. If an INSERT statement adds a row to the table, then it also has to add a row in the index structure. Since the data is stored in order, it could mean rearranging data within the pages to get it stored in the correct position. Similar issues arise from UPDATE and DELETE.

There are going to be two things to think about when deciding whether or not to add an index. First, will that index help performance? Next, how much will that index negatively impact performance? You will absolutely want to measure the performance improvements that come with an index. However, you should have the capabilities to also measure its impact. I'll cover that in some detail in Chapter 23. Your best tool here is Extended Events. However, you'll also want to use the DMVs that show how indexes behave: sys.dm_db_operational_stats and sys.dm_db_index_usage_stats. The operational stats show the behaviors of the indexes including locks and I/O. The usage stats give you statistics counts of index operations over time. I'll cover these in more detail in Chapter 16.

CHAPTER 9 INDEX ARCHITECTURE

> **Note** Most of the measurements I show throughout the book are done using Extended Events as outlined in Chapter 3. However, for some detailed situations, I will use STATISTICS IO and STATISTICS TIME. However, using both of these together in some situations can cause problems. The time it takes to retrieve and transmit the IO data gets added to the time data, making it less accurate. This is why unless I need the object-level measurement of IO, I stick to Extended Events.

To understand how indexes can cause some negative impact on systems, we can start with a simple example. First, we'll use Listing 9-2 to build a table.

Listing 9-2. Building a table with 10,000 rows

```
IF
(
    SELECT OBJECT_ID('IndexTest')
) IS NOT NULL
    DROP TABLE dbo.IndexTest;
GO
CREATE TABLE dbo.IndexTest
(
    C1 INT,
    C2 INT,
    C3 VARCHAR(50)
);
WITH Nums
AS (SELECT TOP (10000)
        ROW_NUMBER() OVER (ORDER BY (SELECT 1)) AS n
    FROM MASTER.sys.all_columns ac1
        CROSS JOIN MASTER.sys.all_columns ac2)
INSERT INTO dbo.IndexTest
(
    C1,
    C2,
    C3
)
```

```
SELECT n,
       n,
       'C3'
FROM Nums;
```

With the table created, I'll run Listing 9-3, but with STATISTICS IO (detailed in Chapter 3) enabled.

Listing 9-3. Updating the IndexTest table

```
UPDATE dbo.IndexTest
SET C1 = 1,
    C2 = 1
WHERE C2 = 1;
```

The output from STATISTICS IO is then

```
Table 'Test1'. Scan count 1, logical reads 29
```

With that baseline established, let's change the table from a heap to a clustered index in Listing 9-4.

Listing 9-4. Creating a clustered index on IndexTest

```
CREATE CLUSTERED INDEX iTest
ON dbo.IndexTest(C1);
```

If I then run the UPDATE statement from Listing 9-3 again, the IO becomes

```
Table 'Test1'. Scan count 1, logical reads 42
Table 'Worktable'. Scan count 1, logical reads 5
```

The reads go up because the data has to be reordered in the index. That's more work than just making the change to the row within the heap table.

Note A worktable is a temporary table used internally by SQL Server to process the immediate results of a query. Worktables are created in tempdb and are dropped automatically after execution. In this case, the worktable was for sorting the data.

While there is overhead associated with maintaining indexes as data changes, it's important to remember that SQL Server must find the row in order to update or delete it. This means even while a given data manipulation query may experience overhead due to the index being there, it also gets the benefits of the index in locating the correct row. Frequently, the performance benefit here outweighs the cost.

I can show the benefits of an index on data modification queries by adding another index to our test table from Listing 9-5.

Listing 9-5. Creating a new index on IndexTest

```
CREATE INDEX iTest2
ON dbo.IndexTest(C2);
```

Now, running Listing 9-3 again results in the following IO:

```
Table 'IndexTest'. Scan count 1, logical reads 15
Table 'Worktable'. Scan count 1, logical reads 5
```

We've taken the reads from 42 down to 20. That's even fewer reads than the original heap table, at 29. All because the index helped us more quickly identify which row to modify from our query. While there is certainly overhead to indexes, there are, with equal certainty, benefits to indexes.

What Is a Columnstore Index?

Simply put, a columnstore index stores data by columns instead of by rows. By pivoting the storage of the information, the columnstore index becomes extremely useful when working with analytical-style queries. These are queries with a lot of aggregations and counts. Because the data is stored at the column, instead of the row, aggregations are extremely fast because you don't have to access a large number of rows. You also see benefits because you're only retrieving data from the columns you want, instead of rows full of columns, some of which you don't want. You'll also see performance benefits from columnstore indexes because the data is stored there in a compressed manner by default (you can add compression to rowstore indexes, and I'll discuss that in Chapter 10).

Columnstore indexes come in two types: clustered and nonclustered. Like the clustered rowstore index, a clustered columnstore index determines the storage for the data of the table. A nonclustered columnstore index is one that gets added to heaps or rowstore clustered indexes. Like the rowstore nonclustered index, you'll generally see a subset of columns in the nonclustered columnstore index. There are a few restrictions on columnstore indexes:

- Some data types cannot be used such as binary, test, varchar(MAX), clr, or XML.

- You can't create a columnstore index on a sparse column.

- A table with a clustered columnstore index cannot have constraints, including primary and foreign keys.

- Prior to SQL Server 2016, nonclustered indexes cannot be updated.

Columnstore indexes are designed to work best with larger data sets, above 100,000 rows. You can see some benefits on smaller data sets, but not always.

Because AdventureWorks doesn't have large-scale tables, I'm going to use Adam Machanic's script, make_big_adventure.sql, to create large tables: dbo.bigTransactionHistory and dbo.bigProduct. The script is available for download from here: http://dataeducation.com/thinking-big-adventure/.

Columnstore Index Storage

I've already said it in this chapter, but it bears repeating. Because we now have both rowstore and columnstore clustered indexes, we get to choose data storage that is optimal for the majority of our queries.

Columnstore is not stored in a B-Tree as described earlier. Instead, the data is pivoted and aggregated on each column within the table. Further, the data is broken up into rowgroups. Each rowgroup consists of approximately 102,400 rows (although it's easier to just think of them as being grouped in sets of 100,000). As data is loaded into a columnstore, it automatically gets broken up into rowgroups.

As data is updated in columnstore indexes, changes are stored in what is called the deltastore. The deltastore is a B-Tree index managed by the SQL Server engine. Added and modified rows are accumulated in the deltastore until there are 102,400 of them. At which point, they will be pivoted, compressed, and stored as a rowgroup.

Deletes from columnstore indexes are not actually immediately removed. Instead, another B-Tree index, again, controlled internally and not visible to the user, tracks a list of identifiers for the rows removed. When the index goes through a rebuild or reorganization, the data is then physically removed.

If you only ever perform batch loads to the columnstore, you really won't have to worry about the deltastore. However, if you're doing small batch loads, or a lot of updates, you will be dealing with the deltastore. This is very likely when you have a nonclustered columnstore on a rowstore table. By and large, the deltastore manages itself just fine. However, it's not a bad idea to rebuild the columnstore index in order to clear out the logically deleted rows and get compressed rowgroups. We'll cover rebuilds and reorgs in Chapter 11.

The pivoted, grouped, and compressed storage in the columnstore index leads to excellent performance with analytical-style queries. However, it's much slower when performing single-row or limited-range lookups needed for OLTP-style queries.

The overall behavior of a clustered or nonclustered columnstore index is the same. The difference is that the clustered columnstore, like the clustered rowstore, is literally defining data storage for the table. The nonclustered columnstore must have the data stored and managed elsewhere, through either a clustered index or a heap. One more thing is common between the clustered and nonclustered columnstore indexes in SQL Server 2025. Nonclustered columnstore indexes are now sorted, just like the clustered columnstore index, helping to improve their performance even more.

Index-Design Recommendations

When deciding on how to build an index, you have several options you need to consider:

- Type of query processing being performed.
- Determine filtering criteria.
- Use narrow indexes.
- Consider the uniqueness of the data.
- Determine the data type.
- Consider column order.
- Determine data storage.
- Ask an AI.

I'll discuss each of these in detail in order to help explain what I mean.

Type of Query Processing Being Performed

You first have to determine if your queries are primarily the kind of point lookup and limited-range scans commonly associated with an Online Transaction Processing (OLTP) system or if you are looking at more large-scale data analytic queries involving aggregations. If you are supporting a primarily OLTP system, then you should be looking at rowstore indexes. More specifically, you should be looking at rowstore clustered indexes for data storage. On the other hand, if you are doing a lot of large analytical queries, then you should be focused on columnstore indexes.

Because you can combine each approach using nonclustered rowstore indexes on your clustered columnstore or using nonclustered columnstore indexes on your clustered rowstore, you should first decide what style the majority of your queries are. After that, you can adjust by adding nonclustered indexes as needed.

Determine Filtering Criteria

The query optimizer goes through a series of checks directly affected by the filtering criteria:

- Each column used in a WHERE, JOIN, or HAVING clause is identified.

- Indexes on these columns are identified.

- The usefulness of the index is determined by looking at the selectivity of the index (i.e., the number of rows that would be returned) based on statistics on the index.

- If no indexes exist for a column used in filtering, statistics are gathered or created for evaluation.

- Constraints such as foreign keys or check constraints are assessed and used by the optimizer.

- Finally, the optimizer goes through all this and creates cost estimates for the least costly method of retrieving the matching rows.

To see the effects of a WHERE clause in action, let's start with Listing 9-6, which doesn't yet have a WHERE clause.

CHAPTER 9 INDEX ARCHITECTURE

Listing 9-6. Retrieving all data from a table

```
SELECT p.ProductID,
       p.NAME,
       p.StandardCost,
       p.Weight
FROM Production.Product p;
```

When I execute this query, a Clustered Index Scan is performed. You get a Clustered Index Scan and not a table scan, because the data is stored with the clustered index, not as a heap. Figure 9-6 shows the resulting execution plan plus runtime metrics.

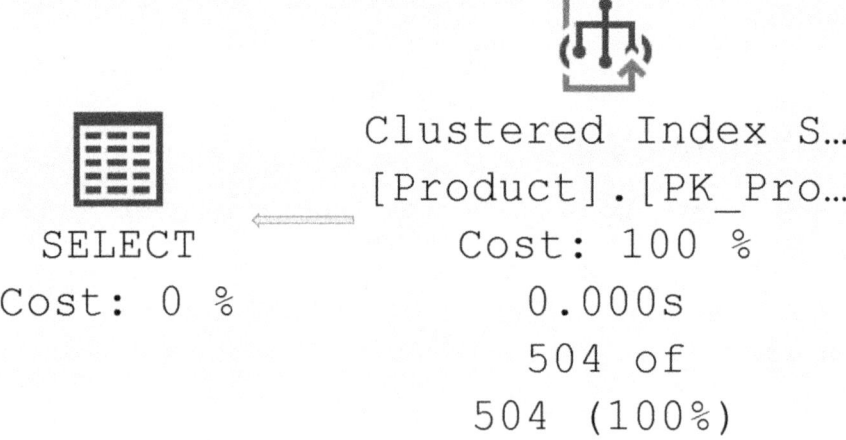

Figure 9-6. *A Clustered Index Scan to retrieve all data*

The number of reads is as follows:

```
Table 'Product'. Scan count 1, logical reads 15
```

Now, let's see what happens when we put a WHERE clause in place in Listing 9-7.

Listing 9-7. Introducing the WHERE clause

```
SELECT p.ProductID,
       p.NAME,
       p.StandardCost,
```

```
    p.Weight
FROM Production.Product AS p
WHERE p.ProductID = 738;
```

Before, the optimizer had no choice in how to satisfy the query. Now, decisions can be made. The ProductID column has an index, PK_Product_ProductID. Not only an index, but a unique index, which means extremely high selectivity. The optimizer rightly decides to satisfy this query in a different manner than earlier (Figure 9-7).

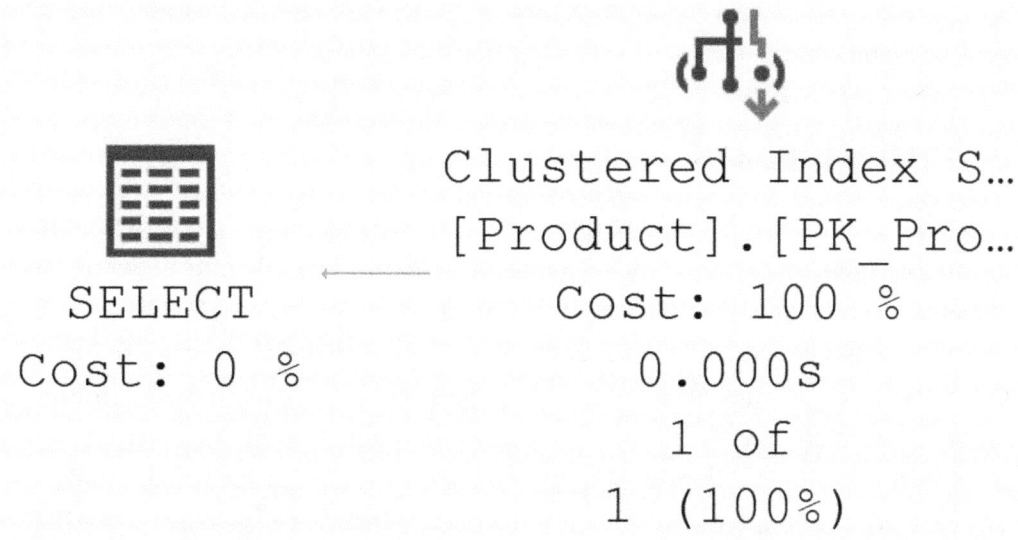

Figure 9-7. A Clustered Index Seek because of the WHERE clause

The number of reads goes to

```
Table 'Product'. Scan count 0, logical reads 2
```

Also, the execution time for the query went from 534mcs on average to 132mcs.

Note Don't forget when measuring execution time, you shouldn't also capture STATISTICS IO or execution plans. Both negatively impact the recorded execution time, skewing your results.

You can see visibly how introducing a WHERE clause gives the optimizer information to work with in making better choices for retrieving data. This is also applicable if you have a JOIN between two tables or a HAVING clause as part of an aggregation. The optimizer could simply scan all tables to retrieve the data. That will work. However, it's not efficient. The combination of a good index and filtering criteria gets us more efficient data retrieval.

When the amount of data inside a table is so small that it fits on a single page (8KB), you may only ever see a scan. In this case, with such a small amount of data, a scan is every bit as efficient as a seek. In short, you won't always see a SEEK operation, even if there is a good index in place.

Use Narrow Indexes

To help enhance performance, where possible, use as narrow a data type as is practical. Narrow in this context means as small a data type as you can use. A column defined as an integer (INT) is smaller than a column defined as a variable string, VARCHAR(50). That said, if you need to index on a wider column because that's how the queries are going to be written, you may have to skip this suggestion. However, another common practice is to sacrifice a bit of disk space and add a surrogate key column to avoid indexing a wider column. Experimentation and testing are always the order of the day.

The reason you should at least consider the possibility is because a narrower key column can fit more rows on your 8KB page, which reduces I/O. You'll also see improved data caching because fewer pages have to be read into memory.

To see the effect of a narrow index, let's use Listing 9-8 to set up a test table.

Listing 9-8. Creating a test table and index

```
IF
(
    SELECT OBJECT_ID('Test1')
) IS NOT NULL
    DROP TABLE dbo.Test1;
GO
CREATE TABLE dbo.Test1
(
    C1 INT,
```

```
    C2 INT
);
WITH Nums
AS (SELECT 1 AS n
    UNION ALL
    SELECT n + 1
    FROM Nums
    WHERE n < 20)
INSERT INTO dbo.Test1
(
    C1,
    C2
)
SELECT n,
       2
FROM Nums;
CREATE INDEX iTest ON dbo.Test1 (C1);
```

This is a narrow index, and all the rows can fit on a single 8KB page. To validate this, we'll query the DMV sys.dm_db_index_physical_stats as shown in Listing 9-9.

Listing 9-9. Getting the size of the index

```
SELECT i.NAME,
       i.type_desc,
       ddips.page_count,
       ddips.record_count,
       ddips.index_level
FROM sys.indexes i
    JOIN sys.dm_db_index_physical_stats(DB_ID(N'AdventureWorks'), OBJECT_
    ID(N'dbo.Test1'), NULL, NULL, 'DETAILED') AS ddips
        ON i.index_id = ddips.index_id
WHERE i.OBJECT_ID = OBJECT_ID(N'dbo.Test1');
```

The results are in Figure 9-8.

CHAPTER 9 INDEX ARCHITECTURE

	name	type_desc	page_count	record_count	index_level
1	NULL	HEAP	1	20	0
2	iTest	NONCLUSTERED	1	20	0

Figure 9-8. *Number of pages for a narrow index*

I've combined a couple of system objects here. First, sys.indexes is a system table, unique to each database, showing all the indexes in that database. I combined it with the DMV to get detailed information about how the index is being stored (I'll spend more time on how to use the DMV in Chapter 12).

To see how a wider data type affects the index, I'm going to modify the table using Listing 9-10.

Listing 9-10. Changing the data type on the existing table

```
DROP INDEX dbo.Test1.iTest;
ALTER TABLE dbo.Test1 ALTER COLUMN C1 CHAR(500);
CREATE INDEX iTest ON dbo.Test1 (C1);
```

The INT data type has a width of 4 bytes. The CHAR(500) data type has a length of 500 bytes. All the data no longer fits on a single page. We can validate this by running the query from Listing 9-9 again. The results are shown in Figure 9-9.

	name	type_desc	page_count	record_count	index_level
1	NULL	HEAP	2	25	0
2	iTest	NONCLUSTERED	2	20	0
3	iTest	NONCLUSTERED	1	2	1

Figure 9-9. *Number of pages for a wider index*

A larger number of pages means more memory use, more I/O, and generally slower performance. You won't always be able to choose which column to index, but when you can, go for the narrower column.

Consider Selectivity of the Data

Marking an index as unique can enhance performance in multiple ways. The optimizer will know that only a single row can match any given value, or set of values for a compound key; this will change the choices it makes when retrieving the data, but also when performing a join operation as well as other behaviors.

Just because an index is unique doesn't necessarily make it superior. Consider a column like MaritalStatus on the HumanResources.Employee table. It only contains the values 'M' or 'S'. You couldn't make a unique index on the column unless you only had two rows in the table. A limited set of rows like that won't lend themselves to indexes. Listing 9-11 shows how you can look at a column to determine its selectivity for an index.

Listing 9-11. Determining a column's selectivity

```
SELECT COUNT(DISTINCT E.MaritalStatus) AS DistinctColValues,
       COUNT(E.MaritalStatus) AS NumberOfRows,
       (CAST(COUNT(DISTINCT E.MaritalStatus) AS DECIMAL) / CAST(COUNT(E.
       MaritalStatus) AS DECIMAL)) AS Selectivity,
       (1.0 / (COUNT(DISTINCT E.MaritalStatus))) AS Density
FROM HumanResources.Employee AS E;
```

Just change the column and table to run that anywhere.

While MaritalStatus by itself is not selective, in combination with another column or columns, it could be. Listing 9-12 shows a simple query filtering on both MaritalStatus and BirthDate.

Listing 9-12. Retrieving information from the Employee table

```
SELECT e.BusinessEntityID,
       e.MaritalStatus,
       e.BirthDate
FROM HumanResources.Employee AS e
WHERE e.MaritalStatus = 'M'
      AND e.BirthDate = '1982-02-11';
```

No indexes exist on the Employee table that will support this query, so any execution of it will result in a scan of the clustered index. We'll need to build an index if we want to make the query run faster. We could start with the index in Listing 9-13.

Listing 9-13. Adding an index to the Employee table

```
CREATE INDEX IX_Employee_Test ON HumanResources.Employee (MaritalStatus);
```

If we run the SELECT query from Listing 9-12, we're still going to get a Clustered Index Scan, and the performance will be 336mcs with nine reads. We could try to force the index use as shown in Listing 9-14.

Listing 9-14. Forcing the index use through a query hint

```
SELECT e.BusinessEntityID,
       e.MaritalStatus,
       e.BirthDate
FROM HumanResources.Employee AS e WITH (INDEX(IX_Employee_Test))
WHERE e.MaritalStatus = 'M'
      AND e.BirthDate = '1982-02-11';
```

I now won't see an index scan in the execution plan. You can see the plan in Figure 9-10.

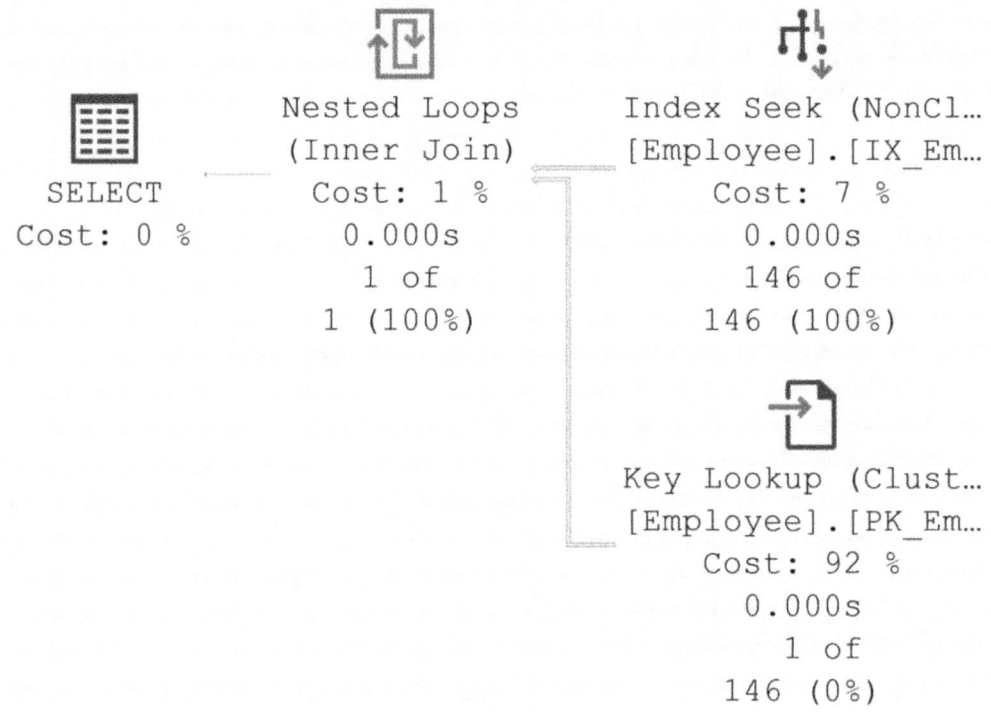

Figure 9-10. *Forcing an index seek*

Performance went down to 466mcs and 294 reads. This is not a healthy choice for performance optimization. We did get the index seek we wanted, but it read 146 rows in order to return 1 and it had to perform a Key Lookup operation to get the rest of the data. All this together took the reads from 9 to 294 and performance degraded. Instead, let's modify the index like Listing 9-15.

Listing 9-15. Changing the IX_Employee_Test index

```
CREATE INDEX IX_Employee_Test
ON HumanResources.Employee (
                    BirthDate,
                    MaritalStatus
                )
WITH DROP_EXISTING;
```

With the new index in place, performance goes to 211mcs and two reads with the execution plan you see in Figure 9-11.

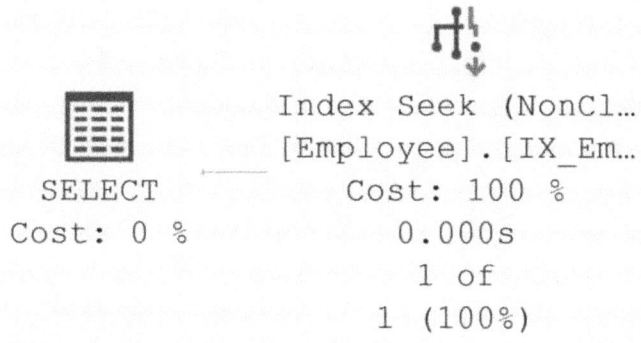

Figure 9-11. *Index is now covering the query*

Without the need for a query hint (and the modification of the code that requires, unless we forced a hint through the Query Store or a plan guide), modifying the index results in a radically faster query and much fewer reads.

As you can see, a more selective index can lead to serious performance improvements.

Before moving on, I'm removing the test index (Listing 9-16).

CHAPTER 9 INDEX ARCHITECTURE

Listing 9-16. Removing the test index

```
DROP INDEX IF EXISTS IX_Employee_Test ON HumanResources.Employee;
```

Determine the Data Type

The data type of an index matters. For example, an index search on integer keys is fast because of the small size and easy arithmetic manipulation of the INTEGER (or INT) data type. You can also use other variations of integer data types (BIGINT, SMALLINT, and TINYINT) for index columns, whereas string data types (CHAR, VARCHAR, NCHAR, and NVARCHAR) require a string match operation, which is usually costlier than an integer match operation.

Suppose you want to create an index on one column and you have two candidate columns—one with an INTEGER data type and the other with a CHAR(4) data type. Even though the size of both data types is 4 bytes in SQL Server 2017 and Azure SQL Database, you should still prefer the INTEGER data type index. Look at arithmetic operations as an example. The value 1 in the CHAR(4) data type is actually stored as 1 followed by three spaces, a combination of the following four bytes: 0x35, 0x20, 0x20, and 0x20. The CPU doesn't understand how to perform arithmetic operations on this data, and therefore, it converts to an integer data type before the arithmetic operations, whereas the value 1 in an integer data type is saved as 0x00000001. The CPU can easily perform arithmetic operations on this data.

Further, use the correct data type on columns. While you can store numbers in text columns, they're going to be much bigger than the same number column. An integer stores up to 2,147,483,647 in a 4-byte column. For a VARCHAR to store the same thing, it will have to be 10 bytes in size. That will make for a poor index.

Of course, most of the time, you won't have the simple choice between identically sized data types, allowing you to choose the more optimal type. Keep this information in mind when designing and building your indexes.

Consider Column Order

In the case of a compound key (more than one column) on an index, the data is sorted on the first column of the key and then sub-sorted on each additional column in the key. The first column in a compound index is frequently referred to as the leading edge of the index. An example unsorted table would look like Table 9-2.

CHAPTER 9 ■ INDEX ARCHITECTURE

Table 9-2. *An unsorted table*

Column1	Column2
1	1
3	1
2	1
3	2
1	2
2	2

If I was to create an index on my sample table on the columns (Column1, Column2), then the subsequent index would look like Table 9-3.

Table 9-3. *A sorted index*

Column1	Column2
1	1
1	2
2	1
2	2
3	1
3	2

The data is sorted first on Column1, as the leading edge of the index, and then on Column2.

To see how the column order affects queries, I'm going to create an index on the Person.Address table as shown in Listing 9-17.

Listing 9-17. *Creating a new index on the Address table*

```
CREATE INDEX IX_Address_Test ON Person.ADDRESS (City, PostalCode);
```

With the index in place, I'm going to run the query in Listing 9-18.

CHAPTER 9　INDEX ARCHITECTURE

Listing 9-18. Querying the Address table

```
SELECT A.AddressID,
       A.City,
       A.PostalCode
FROM Person.ADDRESS AS A
WHERE A.City = 'Dresden';
```

Executing the query, I get the following performance and the execution plan you see in Figure 9-12:

156mcs

2 reads

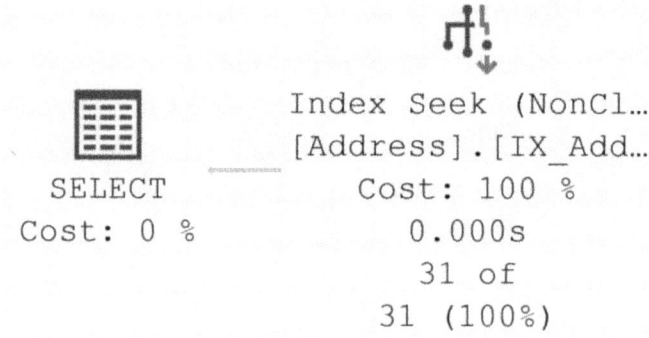

Figure 9-12. *Execution plan that can use the index created*

The index provides exactly what the query needs in order to perform quickly. The histogram supplies an accurate row count for the number of rows that are going to be equal to the value of "Dresden."

Now, if we try to run the query in Listing 9-19, the behavior changes.

Listing 9-19. A different query for the Address table

```
SELECT A.AddressID,
       A.City,
       A.PostalCode
FROM Person.ADDRESS AS A
WHERE A.PostalCode = '01071';
```

CHAPTER 9 INDEX ARCHITECTURE

It's worth noting that the PostalCode value being passed is the one for Dresden. In theory, it could use the same index to find the data since we know that they're stored together. However, when I run the query in Listing 9-19, I get the following performance and execution plan in Figure 9-13:

2.7 sec
106 reads

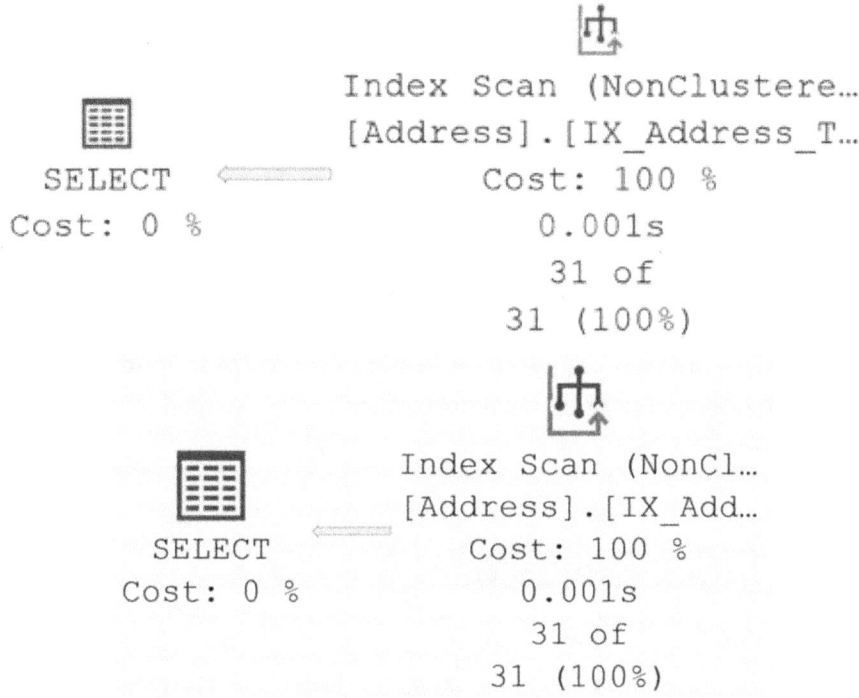

Figure 9-13. *The index could not be fully used*

We went from 2 reads to 108. It is still using the same test index that we created, but because it's not looking at the leading edge of the index, it must be scanned to find the matching rows. This also illustrates the power of the covering index, which we'll cover in Chapter 10.

I'm removing the test index (Listing 9-20).

Listing 9-20. Dropping the test index

```
DROP INDEX IF EXISTS IX_Address_Test ON Person.ADDRESS;
```

CHAPTER 9 INDEX ARCHITECTURE

Determine Data Storage

You have to determine how your data is best stored. The storage is driven by the predominant types of queries run against the data. Online Transaction Processing (OLTP) largely consists of smaller sets of data, even single rows. This style of query is best served by rowstore indexes. Analytical queries that aggregate large data sets are best served by columnstore indexes. So first determining how to store your data helps you pick your first index on a given table.

There are additional index types, but we'll address them in Chapter 10.

Ask an AI

Designing indexes can very much be an art form. There are aspects to choosing exactly which kind of index, settings on the index, all the things we just discussed, that prevent this from being a simple formula. However, there are very common patterns associated with choosing an index. Any time you see a pattern, well, that's a place where an AI may be able to assist. You can pass both your table definitions and the code you're looking to tune to an AI. Their results can be informative. As always, you need to validate that the answers are accurate.

Rowstore Index Behavior

The more traditional type of index in SQL Server is the rowstore index. Because of this, I don't refer to those indexes as "rowstore clustered index" or "rowstore nonclustered index" but instead simply as either a clustered or nonclustered index. However, we do need to take into account that there is more than one way to store and retrieve data, so we'll approach each in turn, starting with the rowstore indexes.

Clustered Indexes

The data is stored at the leaf level of clustered indexes with the key to the index supplying the order for data storage. Because of this, you get one clustered index per table.

> **Tip** When you create a primary key constraint, by default, it will be a unique clustered index, that is, if a clustered index doesn't already exist on the table and you don't specify that this constraint should be nonclustered. While having the primary key be a clustered index is a default behavior, it's not in any way required. You can choose to make the clustered index on columns other than the primary key.

Heap Tables

A table without a clustered index is referred to as a heap table. The data in a heap is not stored in any kind of order. It's this unorganized structure that gave it the name heap. As data in a heap grows, more and more overhead is necessary to deal with the unstructured nature of the storage. Except in cases where extensive testing suggests otherwise, it's best to have a clustered index of some kind on every table in your database.

Relationships with Nonclustered Indexes

A nonclustered index only stores the key values and any INCLUDE values. In order to get at the underlying data, a pointer is stored with the nonclustered index. In the case of a heap table, this is the row identifier (RID). In the case of a clustered index, this is the key to the clustered index. The pointer is called a row locator.

We've seen this in action with a couple of queries already in this chapter. However, let's look at another example. The table dbo.DatabaseLog doesn't have a clustered index. Instead, it has a nonclustered primary key. Listing 9-21 shows a query against this table.

Listing 9-21. Querying the heap table DatabaseLog

```
SELECT dl.DatabaseLogID,
       dl.PostTime
FROM dbo.DatabaseLog AS dl
WHERE dl.DatabaseLogID = 115;
```

Running this query results in the execution plan shown in Figure 9-14.

CHAPTER 9 INDEX ARCHITECTURE

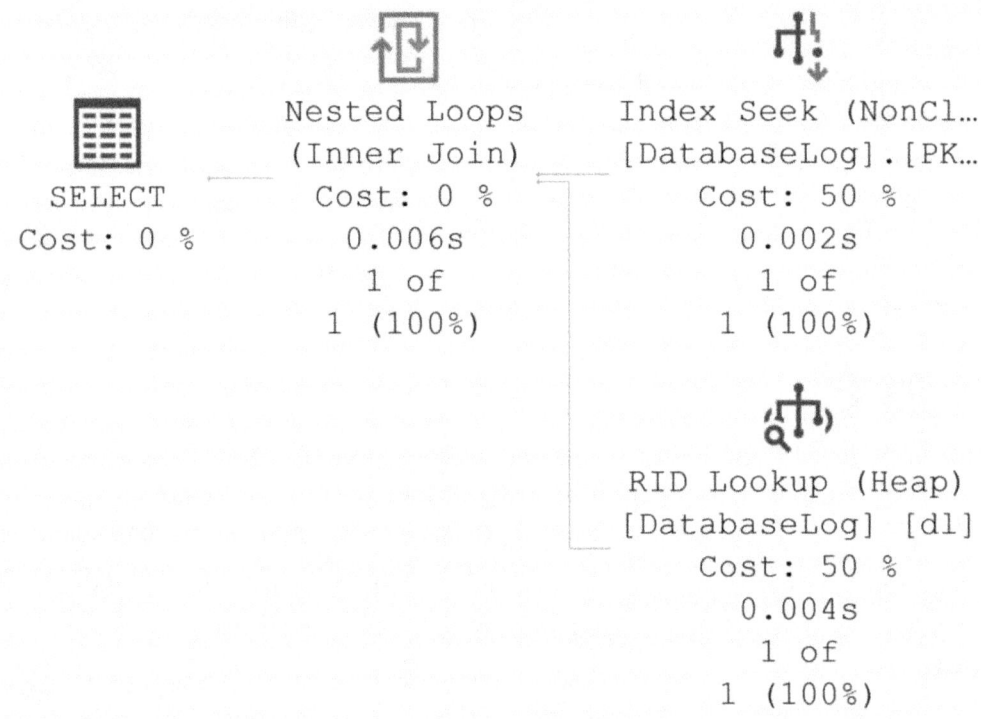

Figure 9-14. An RID lookup is needed to satisfy the query

The nonclustered index, the primary key, was helpful to the query as you can see with the Index Seek operation. However, because the data is stored separately, two additional operations are necessary: RID Lookup and Nested Loops. The Nested Loops operator is only there to bring the data together from the other two operations. The RID Lookup is the optimizer going to the heap to retrieve additional data. We'll go into more on this later in the chapter.

A query run against a table with a clustered index would look something like Listing 9-22 with the execution plan in Figure 9-15.

Listing 9-22. Querying a table stored on a clustered index

```
SELECT d.DepartmentID,
       d.ModifiedDate
FROM HumanResources.Department AS d
WHERE d.DepartmentID = 10;
```

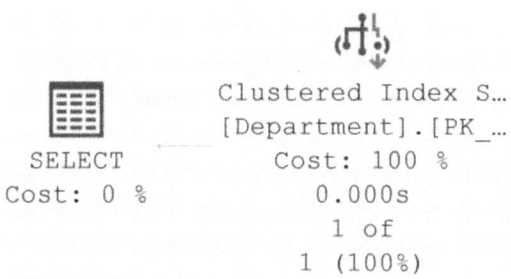

Figure 9-15. *No lookup required on this query*

The query in Listing 9-21 against the heap used the primary key to find the correct row but then had to look up the remaining data. The query in Listing 9-22 used the primary key to find the correct row; then, because the data is stored with the key, no additional operations were needed to satisfy the query.

To navigate from a nonclustered index row to a data row, this relationship between the two index types requires an additional indirection for navigating the B-Tree structure of the clustered index. Without the clustered index, the row locator of the nonclustered index would be able to navigate directly from the nonclustered index row to the data row in the base heap table. The presence of the clustered index causes the navigation from the nonclustered index row to the data row to go through the B-Tree structure of the clustered index, since the new row locator values point to the clustered index key.

On the other hand, consider inserting an intermediate row in the clustered index key order or expanding the content of an intermediate row. For example, imagine a clustered index table containing four rows per page, with clustered index column values of 1, 2, 4, and 5. Adding a new row in the table with the clustered index value 3 will require space in the page between values 2 and 4. If enough space is not available in that position, a page split will occur on the data page (or clustered index leaf page). Even though the data page split will cause relocation of the data rows, the nonclustered index row locator values need not be updated. These row locators continue to point to the same logical key values of the clustered index key, even though the data rows have physically moved to a different location. In the case of a data page split, the row locators of the nonclustered indexes need not be updated. This is an important point since tables often have a large number of nonclustered indexes.

Things don't work the same way for heap tables. While page splits in a heap are not a common occurrence, and when heaps do split, they don't rearrange locations in the same way as clustered indexes; you can have rows move in a heap, usually due to updates causing the heap to not fit on its current page. Anything that causes the location of rows to be moved in a heap will result in a forwarding record being placed into the original location pointing to that new location, necessitating even more I/O activity.

Clustered Index Recommendations

The general behavior of the clustered index and its relationship to nonclustered indexes means you should take a few things into consideration when working with clustered indexes.

Create the Clustered Index First

Since all nonclustered indexes contain the clustered index key within their rows, the order of creation for nonclustered and clustered indexes is important from a performance standpoint. For example, if the nonclustered indexes are built on a table before the clustered index, all the row locators are going to be the RID of the heap table. Creating the clustered index will then entail recreating all the nonclustered indexes because they need to have the key values replace the RID as row locator.

I recommend you create the clustered index before you create nonclustered indexes. This won't affect most operations, but it will require additional work, adding to the overhead on the system during the creation process.

As part of creating the clustered index, I also suggest you design the tables in your OLTP database around that index. It should be the first index created because you should be storing your data as a clustered index by default.

I'll address data warehouse and analytical-style queries in the columnstore section later in this chapter.

Keep Clustered Indexes Narrow

Because all nonclustered indexes must carry the clustered index key values, for best performance, keep the size of the clustered index key as small as possible. If you create a wide clustered index, for example, CHAR(500), in addition to having fewer rows per page in the cluster, you will have fewer rows per page in every nonclustered index as 500 bytes gets added to them.

CHAPTER 9 INDEX ARCHITECTURE

Keep the number, data type, and size of the clustered index keys in mind when designing them. This doesn't mean if the correct key is wider than other possible columns, you should not use that key. No, please, do use the appropriate key. Simply look for opportunities to use a better key structure where possible.

We can see how data is stored with a narrow key if we look at the structure in Listing 9-23.

Listing 9-23. Queries to create clustered and nonclustered indexes

```
IF
(
    SELECT OBJECT_ID('Test1')
) IS NOT NULL
    DROP TABLE dbo.Test1;
GO
CREATE TABLE dbo.Test1
(
    C1 INT,
    C2 INT
);
WITH Nums
AS (SELECT TOP (20)
           ROW_NUMBER() OVER (ORDER BY (SELECT 1)) AS n
    FROM MASTER.sys.all_columns ac1
        CROSS JOIN MASTER.sys.all_columns ac2)
INSERT INTO dbo.Test1
(
    C1,
    C2
)
SELECT n,
       n + 1
FROM Nums;
CREATE CLUSTERED INDEX iClustered ON dbo.Test1 (C2);
CREATE NONCLUSTERED INDEX iNonClustered ON dbo.Test1 (C1);
```

We can then run a query to get the size of the index using the query in Listing 9-24.

Listing 9-24. Getting the size of the indexes on the test table

```
SELECT i.NAME,
       i.type_desc,
       s.page_count,
       s.record_count,
       s.index_level
FROM sys.indexes i
   JOIN sys.dm_db_index_physical_stats(DB_ID(N'AdventureWorks'), OBJECT_
ID(N'dbo.Test1'), NULL, NULL, 'DETAILED') AS s
       ON i.index_id = s.index_id
WHERE i.OBJECT_ID = OBJECT_ID(N'dbo.Test1');
```

The results are visible in Figure 9-16.

	name	type_desc	page_count	record_count	index_level
1	iClustered	CLUSTERED	1	20	0
2	iNonClustered	NONCLUSTERED	1	20	0

Figure 9-16. *The size of indexes with a narrow key*

We can now make the index wider using the code in Listing 9-25.

Listing 9-25. Adjusting the size of the column

```
DROP INDEX dbo.Test1.iClustered;
ALTER TABLE dbo.Test1 ALTER COLUMN C2 CHAR(500);
CREATE CLUSTERED INDEX iClustered ON dbo.Test1 (C2);
```

Running the query from Listing 9-24 to get the size of the indexes results in Figure 9-17.

	name	type_desc	page_count	record_count	index_level
1	iClustered	CLUSTERED	2	20	0
2	iClustered	CLUSTERED	1	2	1
3	iNonClustered	NONCLUSTERED	2	20	0
4	iNonClustered	NONCLUSTERED	1	2	1

Figure 9-17. *Wider indexes mean more pages*

Just those small changes, with small data sets, result in significantly more pages being used. Therefore, a wide clustered key has ramifications beyond its own storage.

Rebuild the Clustered Index in a Single Step

Because of the dependency of nonclustered indexes on the clustered index, rebuilding the clustered index has two statements, DROP INDEX and CREATE INDEX, which causes all nonclustered indexes to get rebuilt two times. To avoid this, use WITH DROP_EXISTING as part of the CREATE INDEX statement. That results in a single atomic step and impacts the nonclustered indexes only once.

Where Possible, Make the Clustered Index Unique

Because the clustered index defines data storage, each distinct row has to be identified separately. When the clustered index is a unique value, each row is then identified through that value. However, when the clustered index is not unique, SQL Server must add a value to the index key in order to make it unique. This is called the uniquifier. The uniquifier consists of what is, to all intents and purposes, an IDENTITY column added to your index key. It adds a little overhead to storage and processing for that index, 4 bytes per row to be exact. It's also possible to run out of uniquifier values (although this is relatively rare). For these reasons, where possible, define the clustered index as unique.

When to Use a Clustered Index

Clustered indexes are best used in a couple of scenarios. However, remember, one of the driving factors for a clustered index is that it's not just a retrieval mechanism. The clustered index also defines storage of the data.

Accessing the Data Directly

Since all columns for the table are stored at the leaf level of the clustered index, this should be the most common path to the data. When the data is directly retrieved from the clustered index without intervening steps, performance is generally enhanced. When you get into performing lookup operations to get data after the rows have been identified, you are adding overhead to the system.

It bears repeating, frequently, the most common access path to the data is through the primary key of the table, hence why so many are clustered. There may be other columns in the table that would make for a better access path.

The clustered index works well when you're retrieving data from the table. If you're retrieving only a small subset of that data, only a few columns, a nonclustered index can become more useful.

If the majority of your queries are analytical in nature, you may be better off using the clustered columnstore index.

Retrieving Pre-sorted Data

Clustered indexes are useful when the data retrieval needs to be sorted (a covering nonclustered index is also good for this). If the clustered index exists on the columns that you need to sort by, then the rows will be physically stored in that order, eliminating the overhead of sorting the data after it is retrieved.

To see this in action, we'll create a table without any indexes from the code in Listing 9-26.

Listing 9-26. Building the od table from the PurchaseOrderDetail table

```
IF
(
    SELECT OBJECT_ID('od')
) IS NOT NULL
    DROP TABLE dbo.od;
GO
SELECT pod.PurchaseOrderID,
       pod.PurchaseOrderDetailID,
       pod.DueDate,
       pod.OrderQty,
       pod.ProductID,
       pod.UnitPrice,
       pod.LineTotal,
       pod.ReceivedQty,
       pod.RejectedQty,
       pod.StockedQty,
```

```
        pod.ModifiedDate
INTO dbo.od
FROM Purchasing.PurchaseOrderDetail AS pod;
```

I'm then going to execute the query in Listing 9-27.

Listing 9-27. Retrieving a large range of rows

```
SELECT od.PurchaseOrderID,
       od.PurchaseOrderDetailID,
       od.DueDate,
       od.OrderQty,
       od.ProductID,
       od.UnitPrice,
       od.LineTotal,
       od.ReceivedQty,
       od.RejectedQty,
       od.StockedQty,
       od.ModifiedDate
FROM dbo.od
WHERE od.ProductID
BETWEEN 500 AND 510
ORDER BY od.ProductID;
```

The performance of the query is

```
3.4ms
82 reads
```

We can try improving performance with a nonclustered index. However, unless we INCLUDE all columns, the behavior and performance are going to be the same as the existing results. Let's try a clustered index (Listing 9-28).

Listing 9-28. Creating a clustered index on the table

```
CREATE CLUSTERED INDEX i1 ON od (ProductID);
```

With that, we can run the query from Listing 9-27 again. The performance is

```
988mcs
8 reads
```

We've cut the execution time by a third and reduced the reads from 82 to 8. Having the data stored in order makes the query faster.

Poor Design Practices for a Clustered Index

Clustered indexes are extremely important within SQL Server. However, there are situations where you can negatively impact performance on clustered indexes.

Frequently Updated Columns

If the columns that define the key of the clustered index are frequently updated, this has a direct performance impact. Since the key columns act as the row identifier for nonclustered indexes, each of these nonclustered indexes has to be updated along with the clustered index. That adds quite a bit of additional resource use and will cause blocking as other queries will wait until the data update is complete.

We can see this in action. The Sales.SpecialOfferProduct table has a composite clustered index on the primary key, which is also a foreign key from two other tables. This represents a classic many-to-many mapping within the database. In Listing 9-29, I'm going to update one of the columns in the key. I use a transaction with a rollback in order to keep the data intact for additional testing. Also, unlike earlier metrics, I'm going to use STATISTICS IO here so I can see the details on the objects involved, not just the total count.

Listing 9-29. Updating the key on the Sales.SpecialOfferProduct table

```
BEGIN TRAN;
SET STATISTICS IO ON;
UPDATE Sales.SpecialOfferProduct
SET ProductID = 720
WHERE SpecialOfferID = 1
    AND ProductID = 721;
SET STATISTICS IO OFF;
ROLLBACK TRAN;
```

The STATISTICS IO output shows the reads performed during the execution:

```
Table 'Product'. Scan count 0, logical reads 2
Table 'SalesOrderDetail'. Scan count 1, logical reads 1248
```

CHAPTER 9 INDEX ARCHITECTURE

```
Table 'SpecialOfferProduct'. Scan count 0, logical reads 10
```

I can add a nonclustered index to the column as in Listing 9-30.

Listing 9-30. Adding a nonclustered index to the SpecialOfferProduct table

```
CREATE NONCLUSTERED INDEX ixTest
ON Sales.SpecialOfferProduct (ModifiedDate);
```

If I rerun the query from Listing 9-29, here are the reads:

```
Table 'Product'. Scan count 0, logical reads 2
Table 'SalesOrderDetail'. Scan count 1, logical reads 1248
Table 'SpecialOfferProduct'. Scan count 0, logical reads 19
```

You can see that we went from 10 reads to 19, just because additional work has to be done on the nonclustered index.

Drop the test index before proceeding (Listing 9-31).

Listing 9-31. Dropping the ixTest index

```
DROP INDEX ixTest ON Sales.SpecialOfferProduct;
```

Wide Keys

I've already talked about this earlier in the chapter. A wider clustered key means fewer rows per page in the nonclustered index. Where possible, keep the size on your key columns down.

Nonclustered Indexes

The core concept with a nonclustered index is a mechanism to add more ways to sort the data, making more possibilities for retrieving the data. A nonclustered index doesn't affect the order of the data in the table pages because it's storing its information separately from the rest of the table. A pointer (row locator) is required to navigate from a nonclustered index to the actual data row, whether on a heap or a clustered index. For a heap, the row locator is the RID for the data row. With a clustered index, the key columns from the clustered index act as the row locator. When you have a nonclustered index on a clustered columnstore index, an 8-byte value consisting of the columnstore's row_group_id and an offset value make up the row locator.

Nonclustered Index Maintenance

In a table that is a heap, where there is no clustered index, to optimize this maintenance cost, SQL Server adds a pointer to the old data page to point to the new data page after a page split, instead of updating the row locator of all the relevant nonclustered indexes. Although this reduces the maintenance cost of the nonclustered indexes, it increases the navigation cost from the nonclustered index row to the data row within the heap, since an extra link is added between the old data page and the new data page. Therefore, having a clustered index as the row locator decreases this overhead associated with the nonclustered index.

When a table is a clustered columnstore index, the storage values of exactly what information is stored where, change as the index is rebuilt and data moves from the deltastore into compressed storage. This would lead to all sorts of issues except a new bit of functionality within the clustered columnstore index allows for a mapping between where the nonclustered index thought the value was and where it actually is. Funny enough, this is called the Mapping Index. Values are added to it as locations of data change within the clustered columnstore. It can slightly slow nonclustered index usage when the table data is contained in a clustered columnstore.

Defining the Lookup Operation

When a query requests columns that are not part of the nonclustered index chosen by the optimizer, a lookup is required. This may be a key lookup when going against a clustered index, columnstore or not, or an RID lookup when performed against a heap. The lookup fetches the corresponding data row from the table by following the row locator value from the index row, requiring a logical read on the data page besides the logical read on the index page and a join operation to put the data together in a common output. However, if all the columns required by the query are available in the index itself, then access to the data page is not required. This is known as a *covering index*.

These lookups are the reason that large result sets are better served with a clustered index. A clustered index doesn't require a lookup since the leaf pages and data pages for a clustered index are the same. I'll go over lookups in a lot more detail in Chapter 11.

Nonclustered Index Recommendations

Nonclustered indexes are meant to offer flexibility for your data retrieval. While you only get one clustered index, you can have multiple nonclustered indexes, although it's a good idea to keep these as minimal as possible since they do come with maintenance overhead.

When to Use a Nonclustered Index

A nonclustered index is most useful when all you want to do is retrieve a small number of rows and columns from a large table. As the number of columns to be retrieved increases, the ability to have a covering index decreases. Then, if you're also retrieving a large number of rows, the overhead cost of any lookup rises proportionately. To retrieve a small number of rows from a table, the indexed column should have a high selectivity.

Furthermore, there will be indexing requirements that won't be suitable for a clustered index, as explained in the "Clustered Indexes" section:

- Frequently updatable columns
- Wide keys

In these cases, you can use a nonclustered index since, unlike a clustered index, it doesn't affect other indexes in the table. A nonclustered index on a frequently updatable column isn't as costly as having a clustered index on that column. That isn't to say there is no cost, but that there is a reduced cost. The UPDATE operation on a nonclustered index is limited to the base table and the nonclustered index. It doesn't affect any other nonclustered indexes on the table. Similarly, a nonclustered index on a wide column (or set of columns) doesn't increase the size of any other index, unlike that with a clustered index. However, remain cautious, even while creating a nonclustered index on a highly updatable column or a wide column (or set of columns), since this can increase the cost of action queries, as explained earlier in the chapter.

When Not to Use a Nonclustered Index

Nonclustered indexes are not suitable for queries that retrieve a large number of rows, as a percentage of the size of the table. Such queries are better served with a clustered index, which doesn't require a separate lookup to retrieve a data row. Since a lookup requires additional logical reads to get to the data page besides the logical read on the nonclustered index page, the cost of a query using a nonclustered index increases significantly for a large number of rows, such as when in a loop join that requires one lookup after another. The SQL Server query optimizer takes this cost into effect and accordingly can discard the nonclustered index when retrieving a large result set. Nonclustered indexes are also not as useful as columnstore indexes for analytics-style queries with more aggregates.

CHAPTER 9 INDEX ARCHITECTURE

If your requirement is to retrieve a large result set from a table, then having a nonclustered index on the filter criterion (or the join criterion) column will probably not be useful unless you use a special type of nonclustered index called a *covering index*. I describe this index type in detail in Chapter 10.

Columnstore Index Behavior

I wrote earlier about how the columnstore indexes are stored, but we didn't look at them in action. We'll start with a query against the BigAdventure tables created earlier. Listing 9-32 shows an analytical-style query.

Listing 9-32. Aggregate query against BigAdventure tables

```
SELECT bp.Name AS ProductName,
       COUNT(bth.ProductID),
       SUM(bth.Quantity),
       AVG(bth.ActualCost)
FROM dbo.bigProduct AS bp
    JOIN dbo.bigTransactionHistory AS bth
        ON bth.ProductID = bp.ProductID
GROUP BY bp.Name;
```

I don't yet have any columnstore indexes on my BigAdventure tables, so the execution plan with runtime metrics looks like Figure 9-18.

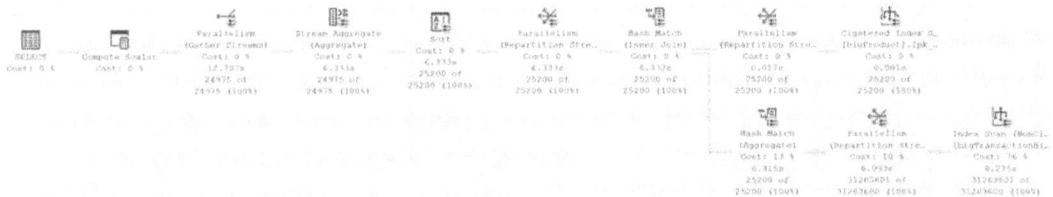

Figure 9-18. *Execution plan for an aggregate query without columnstore indexes*

Because there are no filtering criteria in Listing 9-32, we're scanning the tables to retrieve the data. Several other operations, including two different Stream Aggregate operations, are necessary to pull the data together for the SUM, COUNT, and AVG (average). Also, you may notice the little yellow icons on most of the operators. This plan went parallel (discussed in more detail in Chapter 2).

The detailed reads from STATISTICS IO show how much information we're dealing with:

```
Table 'bigTransactionHistory'. Scan count 1, logical reads 132815
Table 'bigProduct'. Scan count 1, logical reads 629
Table 'Worktable'. Scan count 0, logical reads 0
Table 'Worktable'. Scan count 0, logical reads 0
```

The execution time on average was 4.8 seconds. In short, this is a very expensive query. We could migrate one of the tables to a clustered columnstore, but the overall behavior is very similar, so I'm just going to use Listing 9-33 to create a nonclustered columnstore on the bigTransactionHistory table.

Listing 9-33. Creating the first columnstore index

```
CREATE NONCLUSTERED COLUMNSTORE INDEX ix_csTest
ON dbo.bigTransactionHistory (
                        ProductID,
                        Quantity,
                        ActualCost
                );
```

Once the index is created, we can immediately run Listing 9-32 again. No code changes are necessary to take advantage of the columnstore index. The optimizer immediately recognizes what it has and creates a very different execution plan as you see in Figure 9-19.

CHAPTER 9 INDEX ARCHITECTURE

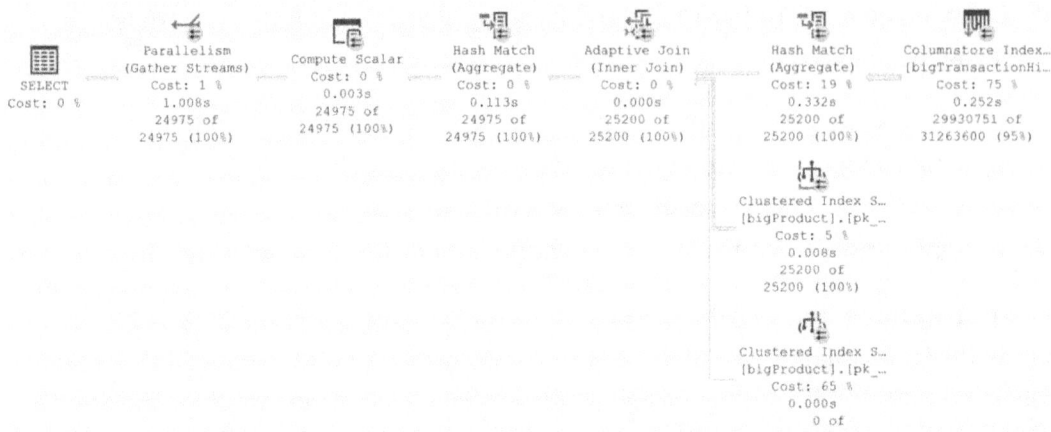

Figure 9-19. *Columnstore indexes in an execution plan*

There's a whole bunch of new behavior introduced here. Before we break it down, let's take a look at the STATISTICS IO output and execution time:

Table 'bigTransactionHistory'. Scan count 40, logical reads 0
Table 'bigTransactionHistory'. Segment reads 49
Table 'bigProduct'. Scan count 21, logical reads 629
Table 'Worktable'. Scan count 0, logical reads 0
Table 'Worktable'. Scan count 0, logical reads 0

The execution time was 409ms on average.

Just to emphasize this, we've gone from 4.8 seconds on the Linux container running SQL Server 2025 on my laptop to return 24,975 rows to 409 milliseconds. Ignoring the change in the reads, that's about 12 times faster.

Now that we're all suitably impressed, let's explore the execution plan in order to understand what's happening. We'll start with the physical data access, a Columnstore Index Scan, shown in Figure 9-20.

```
Columnstore Index...
[bigTransactionHi...
    Cost: 75 %
      0.166s
   29930751 of
  31263600 (95%)
```

Figure 9-20. Columnstore Index Scan of bigTransactionHistory

This is a new operator introduced just for columnstore indexes. It reveals a number of functions internally. You can see that this plan went parallel as well. You can tell that a plan is parallel by the addition of those two yellow circles with arrows indicating that a given operation is being done through parallel processing. Parallel processing takes advantage of the fact that you have more than one CPU on a system in order to split up the work done between processors.

As with most execution plan operators, the really interesting stuff is in the properties of the operator. At the top of the property sheet are several concepts we need to talk about. First, among them is batch-mode processing. Figure 9-21 shows the Execution Mode for this operator.

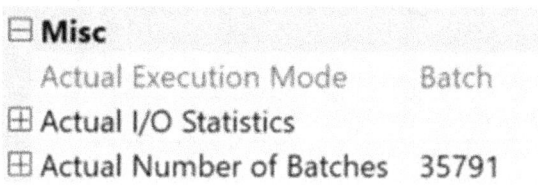

Figure 9-21. Batch-mode processing and the number of batches

Batch-mode processing was introduced along with columnstore indexes. It's a much faster way to process the data than with row-mode processing. Row-mode processing worked through execution plans, a row at a time, passing the rows between operators. Batch-mode processing operates on approximately 1,000 rows at a time. In fact, you can see in Figure 9-21 that the Columnstore Index Scan operated as batch mode and that there were 35,791 batches. There were 29,930,751 rows processed. Doing the math, that comes out to about 836 rows per batch.

Prior to SQL Server 2019, batch-mode processing was only available to columnstore indexes. Starting in SQL Server 2019, rowstore indexes can also benefit from batch-mode processing. We'll see that in Chapter 10.

Another piece of functionality within columnstore indexes is the pushdown aggregate. Because of how the data is stored in a columnstore index, it's possible for some aggregations to occur at the point of data retrieval. If we look at the properties in the Columnstore Index Scan operator, you can see this value, visible in Figure 9-22.

⊞ Actual Number of Locally Aggregated Rows	1332850
⊞ Actual Number of Rows for All Executions	29930751

Figure 9-22. *Showing the Locally Aggregated Rows*

The property *Actual Number of Locally Aggregated Rows* shows that 1,332,850 rows were aggregated as the data was retrieved. This behavior is yet another enhancement on performance in the columnstore index in support of analytical queries.

It's generally a good practice to put any column that you're likely to query against into the columnstore index. It's not like creating a key in a rowstore index.

Another behavior introduced by columnstore indexes is the Adaptive Join, now available in rowstore as well. Figure 9-23 shows that part of the execution plan.

CHAPTER 9   INDEX ARCHITECTURE

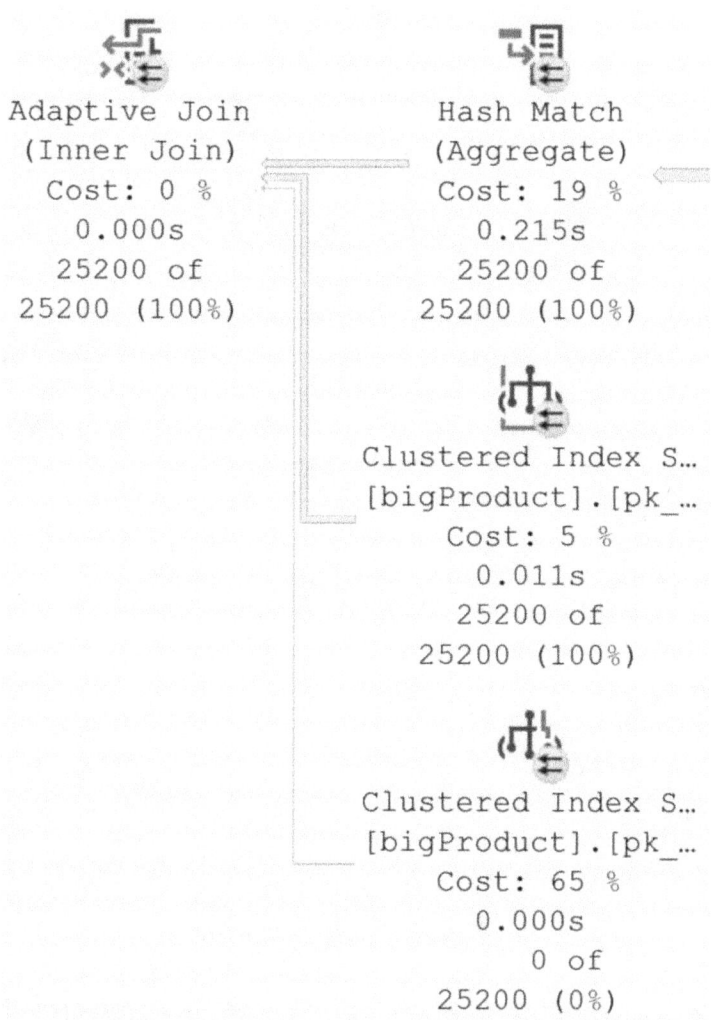

Figure 9-23. The Adaptive Join operator

We'll be talking about join types throughout the book, as we have already. The Adaptive Join is part of the automated tuning mechanisms that we'll cover in detail in Chapter 21. For larger data sets, the Nested Loops join can perform poorly. For smaller data sets, a Hash Join can also perform poorly. The Adaptive Join establishes a data threshold based on the statistics available from the objects involved in the query. Below that threshold, a Nested Loops join will be used. Above that threshold, a Hash Join will be used.

In Figure 9-23, you see the Adaptive Join operator in the upper left of the image. Immediately to its right is a Hash Match operator. That is performing some of the aggregation necessary for the query. Below that are the two possible branches for the Adaptive Join. The top branch always represents the Hash Match join. The bottom branch always represents the Nested Loops join. In this case, we can see that there were 0 rows processed from the Clustered Index Seek and 25,200 rows processed from the Clustered Index Scan. This tells us, thanks to the runtime metrics captured with the execution plan, that in this case, a Hash Match join was used. We can look at the properties of the Adaptive Join operator to see the row threshold visible in Figure 9-24.

Actual Number of Rows for All Executions	25200
Actual Rebinds	0
Actual Rewinds	0
Actual Time Statistics	
Adaptive Threshold Rows	1955.09
Defined Values	[[Adventure
Description	Chooses dy
Estimated CPU Cost	0.0000504
Estimated Execution Mode	Batch
Estimated I/O Cost	0
Estimated Join Type	HashMatch

Figure 9-24. *Properties of the Adaptive Join operator*

I'd like to point out several properties here. First, and most importantly, I have highlighted the *Adaptive Threshold Rows* property. The value is 1,955.09. That means as soon as 1,956 rows are passed to the Adaptive Join operator, it will choose the Hash Join branch. Since 25,200 rows were processed, as we see on the Actual Number of Rows for All Executions property, we have exceeded that value. You can also see at the bottom of Figure 9-24 the *Estimated Join Type* has a value of *HashMatch*. That shows the optimizer assumed the number of rows processed was likely to exceed the threshold. You can also see the *Actual Join Type,* which also has a value of *HashMatch*. This means you can reliably know which branch was chosen by the Adaptive Join without just looking at row counts. Finally, as a side note, at the top of Figure 9-24, you can see that this operator was also performing in batch mode.

One other point from this query and the resulting execution plan, you can mix and match columnstore and rowstore indexes and tables in a single query. The optimizer will make appropriate choices for each.

Columnstore Recommendations

It bears repeating, columnstore indexes are best for large-scale, analytical-style queries. If you have a more OLTP set of queries, rowstore indexes will serve you well.

Because you can add nonclustered rowstore indexes to a clustered columnstore and you can add nonclustered columnstore indexes to a clustered rowstore, you can deal with exceptional situations in either direction. While you will gain the most benefit from columnstore indexes when you exceed the 102,400-row rowgroup threshold, smaller tables may still get some benefit, depending on the style of queries. Test your system to know for sure.

There are a few points to bear in mind when working with columnstore indexes:

- Load the data into the columnstore in either a single transaction or in batches that are greater than 102,400 in order to take advantage of compressed rowgroups.

- Where possible, minimize small-scale updates within columnstore in order to avoid the overhead of dealing with the deltastore.

- Plan to have an index rebuild for both clustered and nonclustered columnstore indexes in order to eliminate deletion of data completely from the rowgroups and move modified data from the deltastore into the rowgroups.

- Maintain the statistics on your columnstore indexes similar to how you do the same on your rowstore indexes. While they are not visible in the same way as rowstore indexes, they still must be maintained.

Missing Indexes

This may have already been visible in some of the execution plans in the book, but let's take Listing 9-34.

CHAPTER 9 INDEX ARCHITECTURE

Listing 9-34. A query in need of an index

```
SELECT a.AddressID,
       a.AddressLine1,
       a.AddressLine2,
       a.City,
       sp.Name AS StateProvinceName,
       a.PostalCode
FROM Person.Address AS a
    JOIN Person.StateProvince AS sp
        ON a.StateProvinceID = sp.StateProvinceID
WHERE a.City = 'London';
```

Looking at the execution plan, it should look similar to Figure 9-25.

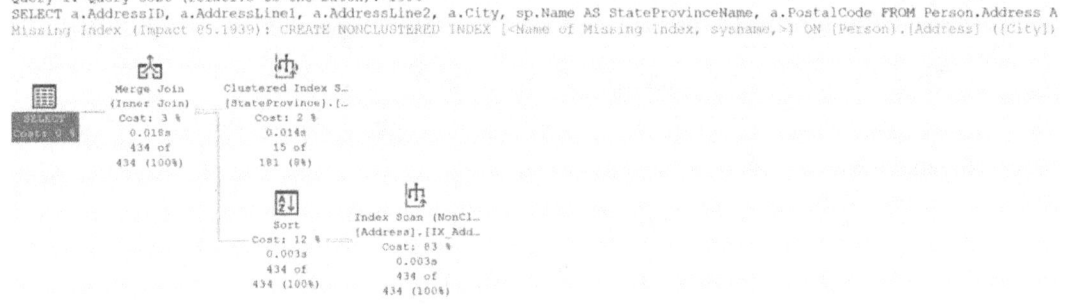

Figure 9-25. *An execution plan with a Missing Index suggestion*

Immediately below the query itself at the top of the execution plan, you can see the following text:

Missing Index (Impact 85.1939): CREATE NONCLUSTERED INDEX [<Name of Missing Index, sysname,>] ON [Person].[Address] ([City])

This is a Missing Index suggestion from the query optimizer. Depending on the query in question, the optimizer may make multiple suggestions for improving performance. First, it suggests a possible impact to the performance if this index was created, 85.1939. Then, it defines the suggested index with a name to be defined later.

If there is more than one suggestion, you can see them in the properties of the first operator, in this case, the SELECT operator on the far left of the execution plan. Figure 9-26 shows that for this query, there is only the one suggestion.

Figure 9-26. *The Missing Index properties in an execution plan*

There are several points I need to make about these Missing Index suggestions from the optimizer. First, and most importantly, they are suggestions. These are not commandments. They're not requirements. I do use the Missing Index information as a starting point at times for tuning queries, but I will not simply create an index each time one is suggested.

Next, you have to know that the optimizer won't always make the best index choices. It won't ever suggest a unique index, even though that can be a massive performance enhancement, because a unique index has further implications. The optimizer doesn't take into account existing indexes either. Also, the optimizer won't suggest columnstore indexes.

If you do decide that you at least wish to test this index, please, rename the index. The number of times I've found databases with indexes named [<Name of Missing Index, sysname>] is far too much. Further, you'll see [<Name of Missing Index, sysname>1], [<Name of Missing Index, sysname>2], etc., as people try to deal with creating indexes with the same names over and over.

Finally, there are Missing Index DMVs that you can query as well. In the strongest possible words, I'm going to suggest that you ignore their existence. Yes, if you query the DMV, you'll find the suggestion that we have from Figure 9-25. However, what you won't find is any correlation between the suggested Missing Index and an actual query. The DMVs do not track which query they are from. So a given missing index in the DMVs may be from a query called hundreds of times in a second and could absolutely benefit from a new index, but you won't be able to tell. Conversely, the Missing Index suggestion could be for a query that was run one time and will never be run again. Creating that Missing Index has negative impact as an extra, unused, and unneeded index.

The Missing Index information is nothing more than a suggestion by the optimizer. Treat it as such.

Summary

In this chapter, I introduced the two major types of indexes: rowstore and columnstore. I also walked you through the importance of understanding how your data is being queried in order to help you choose the correct storage mechanism for the data. We explored the strengths and weaknesses of each of the different index types and how they work together to support you storing and retrieving your data in an efficient manner. Finally, we explored how these different index types affect query performance, both positively and negatively.

In the next chapter, we're going to continue to explore indexes. We'll look at several modifications you can make to index behavior and some of the special types of indexes available.

CHAPTER 10

Index Behaviors

In the previous chapter, I introduced the core indexes within SQL Server, both rowstore and columnstore, clustered and nonclustered. This chapter takes that information and describes additional functionality related to indexes. I'll also introduce some new indexes in this chapter. There are a number of index settings that affect their behavior, which we'll discuss.

In this chapter, I'll cover the following topics:

- Covering indexes
- Index intersection
- Index joins
- Filtered indexes
- Indexed views
- Index characteristics
- Special index types

Covering Indexes

A covering index is a nonclustered index that contains all the columns required to satisfy a query without going to the heap or the clustered index for a lookup. We've already had several covering indexes in examples throughout the book.

If we take the query in Listing 10-1, the existing structure of the Person.Address table does not have a covering index for it.

CHAPTER 10   INDEX BEHAVIORS

Listing 10-1. A query that does not have a covering index

```
SELECT A.PostalCode
FROM Person.ADDRESS AS A
WHERE A.StateProvinceID = 42;
```

If we were to execute this query, we'd get the following performance metrics (using an average of multiple executions captured using Extended Events) and the plan in Figure 10-1:

316mcs
19 reads

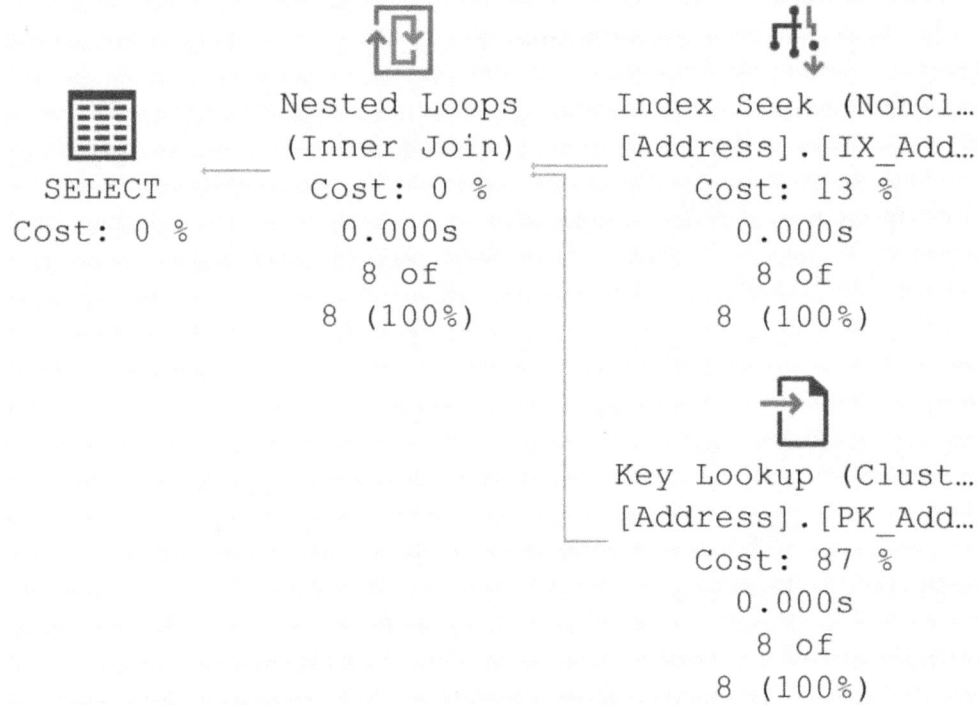

Figure 10-1. *Execution plan for a query without a covering index*

This is a classic lookup query with the Key Lookup operator pulling the PostalCode data from the clustered index and joining it with the Index Seek operator against the IX_Address_StateProvinceID index. In order for this index to be covering, it needs to include the PostalCode column, either in the key or stored at the leaf level as part of the INCLUDE operation. If you add the column to the key, it changes the fundamental structure of the index. Adding it to the leaf through INCLUDE just adds some size to the index. Listing 10-2 shows how I'm going to modify the index in this case.

Listing 10-2. Recreating the IX_Address_StateProvinceID index

```
CREATE NONCLUSTERED INDEX IX_Address_StateProvinceID
ON Person.ADDRESS (StateProvinceID ASC)
INCLUDE (PostalCode)
WITH (DROP_EXISTING = ON);
```

Now when I run the query from Listing 10-1, I see the following performance and execution plan in Figure 10-2:

167mcs

2 reads

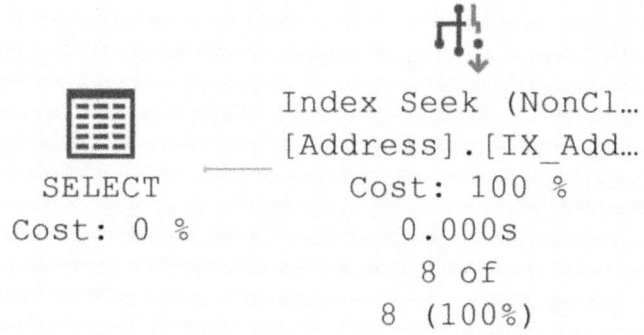

Figure 10-2. *Execution plan for the query with a covering index*

Performance was cut in half, and the reads went from 19 to 2. You can see the results in the execution plan where only our nonclustered index was referenced. Clearly, a covering index can be a useful mechanism for increasing query performance. Modifying the key of the index would have done the same thing, but then the index would be structurally different. Using the INCLUDE operator worked because we didn't need that column to be used in a WHERE, JOIN, or HAVING clause. If that was the case, you'd then be better off modifying the key.

Before continuing, I'm going to reset the table back to its original index from Listing 10-3.

Listing 10-3. *Reverting the index to its previous shape*

```
CREATE NONCLUSTERED INDEX IX_Address_StateProvinceID
ON Person.ADDRESS (StateProvinceID ASC)
WITH (DROP_EXISTING = ON);
```

A Pseudoclustered Index

A covering index physically organizes the data in the key columns in a sequential order, in the order of the keys. Any data included at the leaf level is then ordered by the key column(s) in the same way. That means, for a query this index satisfies as covering, it becomes effectively the same as a clustered index. In some cases, you'll see superior performance from a covering index, even when the data is being ordered, over a clustered index because the covering, nonclustered, index is generally smaller, with only a subset of the columns of the clustered index.

Conversely, you can make a nonclustering index effectively a full clustered index by adding all the columns through INCLUDE. However, this adds the possibility of considerable overhead since any change to any column now results in updates to the clustered index and the nonclustered index.

Recommendations

A common, and old, admonition when it comes to writing queries is to only move the data you need. This is why people will frequently advocate against using SELECT *. The same is true of trying to make an index into a covering index. Be judicious in the columns that you add, either to the key or through the INCLUDE operation. If you do add columns to the key of the index, you are making that index wider, allowing for fewer rows per page, which could also hurt performance. All of this is absolutely a balancing act and why it's so important to set up testing for your systems to ensure you know how these changes are going to affect other queries.

Index Intersection

When there are multiple indexes on a table, SQL Server can use more than one index to satisfy a query. It will use a set of data from each index and then combine them for a result.

CHAPTER 10 ■ INDEX BEHAVIORS

This combination of indexes is called index intersection. While it sounds like a great thing, it's actually pretty rare to see it in action. You can't count on it as a regular occurrence.

Let's start with a query that's performing badly in Listing 10-4.

Listing 10-4. A query performing a Clustered Index Scan

```
SELECT soh.SalesPersonID,
       soh.OrderDate
FROM Sales.SalesOrderHeader AS soh
WHERE soh.SalesPersonID = 276
      AND soh.OrderDate
      BETWEEN '4/1/2013' AND '7/1/2013';
```

I'll capture the performance metrics and the execution plan in Figure 10-3:

2.7ms
686 reads

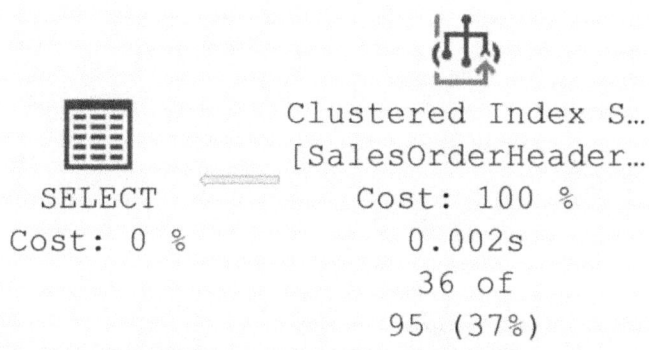

Figure 10-3. *No indexes help the query, so a scan ensues*

There is an index on the PersonID column of the SalesOrderHeader table, but it doesn't help since I'm also filtering on the OrderDate. The optimizer just chose to do a scan of the clustered index. This can frequently be the default behavior. However, let's try to modify it by adding an index in Listing 10-5.

Listing 10-5. Adding an index in the hopes of index intersection

```
CREATE NONCLUSTERED INDEX IX_Test
ON Sales.SalesOrderHeader (OrderDate ASC);
```

Executing Listing 10-4 again results in a change in both the performance metrics and the execution plan, visible in Figure 10-4:

1.8ms
10 reads

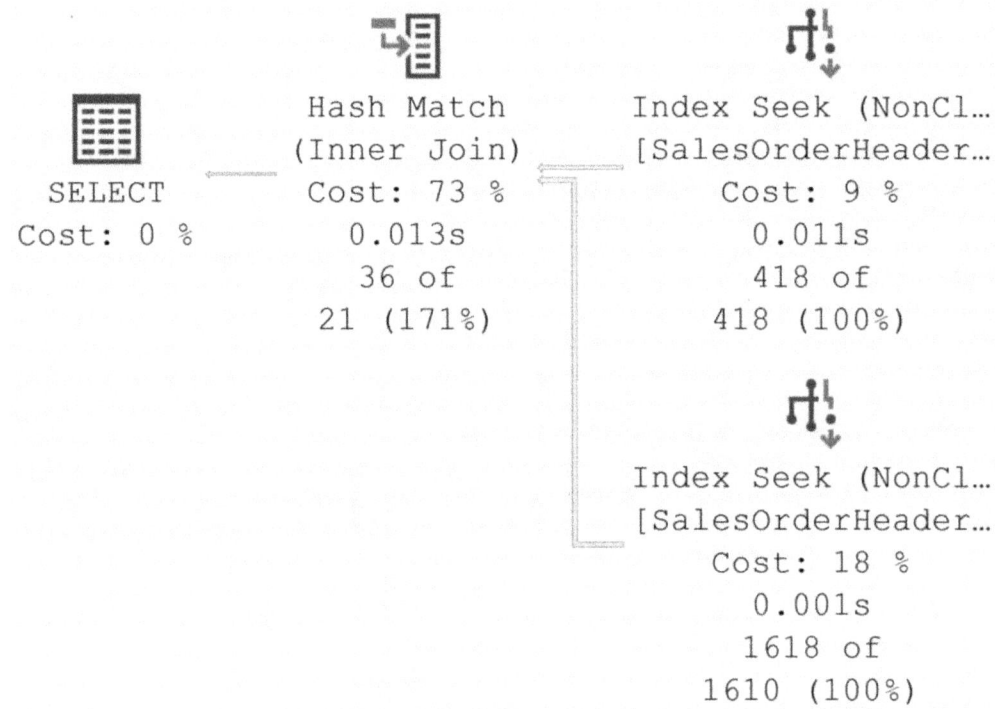

Figure 10-4. *An index intersection*

We've successfully arrived at an index intersection. The key point here is the Hash Match join. If we saw either a Nested Loops or Merge, that would be an index join (covered in the next section), which is extremely similar to index intersection, but not exactly the same.

In an index intersection, the optimizer has assumed it can put together a match, but it doesn't have a guaranteed mechanism to ensure the match. If it did, you'd see the other join types. The optimizer has chosen to build a temporary table (the hash table), and the probe against that has to find the combined data. So it seeks 418 rows from one index and 1,618 from the other and then combines them into 36 matching rows (per the values in the execution plan with runtime metrics).

CHAPTER 10 INDEX BEHAVIORS

The performance went from 2.7ms to 1.8ms, which isn't huge. However, the reads went from 689 to 10. That's the difference between index seeks and an index scan, even if you have to then process a join to get to the result set.

I'd like to repeat that this is a fairly rare occurrence, as are index joins. More often than not, a compound index can actually improve performance even more. Let's modify the index as shown in Listing 10-6.

Listing 10-6. Creating a compound key on the test index

```
CREATE NONCLUSTERED INDEX IX_Test
ON Sales.SalesOrderHeader (
                        SalesPersonID,
                        OrderDate ASC
                    )
WITH DROP_EXISTING;
```

Now execute Listing 10-4 again, and we'll see the following performance metrics and the execution plan in Figure 10-5:

165mcs
2 reads

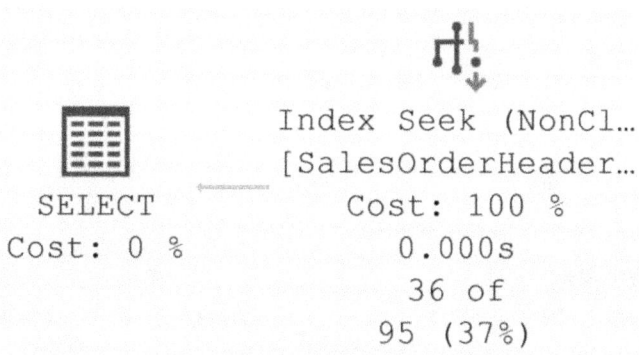

Figure 10-5. *Replacing the index intersection*

Now we see a radical improvement in performance, going from 1.8ms to 165mcs and from ten reads to two. Creating a compound key, while it did change the index structure and make the index wider, resulted in an even more serious performance improvement.

327

CHAPTER 10　INDEX BEHAVIORS

You may be in a situation where creating a separate nonclustered index is a superior choice:

- Reordering the columns in one of the existing indexes would have a negative impact on other queries.
- Some of the columns required to make a covering index are not a part of the existing indexes.

If you are limited in the changes you can make to an index, sometimes, just adding another nonclustered index might be a good solution if it results in index intersection, or, as we'll see in a second, an index join.

Before we go on, we should remove the test index as shown in Listing 10-7.

Listing 10-7. Removing the test index

```
DROP INDEX IX_Test ON Sales.SalesOrderHeader;
```

Index Joins

The index joins are, to a very large degree, just a variation on index intersection. Only, instead of having to build a temporary table in order to hash the values together, joins are used. Let's just see one in action from Listing 10-8.

Listing 10-8. A query that will perform an index join

```
SELECT poh.PurchaseOrderID,
       poh.RevisionNumber
FROM Purchasing.PurchaseOrderHeader AS poh
WHERE poh.EmployeeID = 261
    AND poh.VendorID = 1500;
```

The execution plan returned is visible in Figure 10-6.

CHAPTER 10 INDEX BEHAVIORS

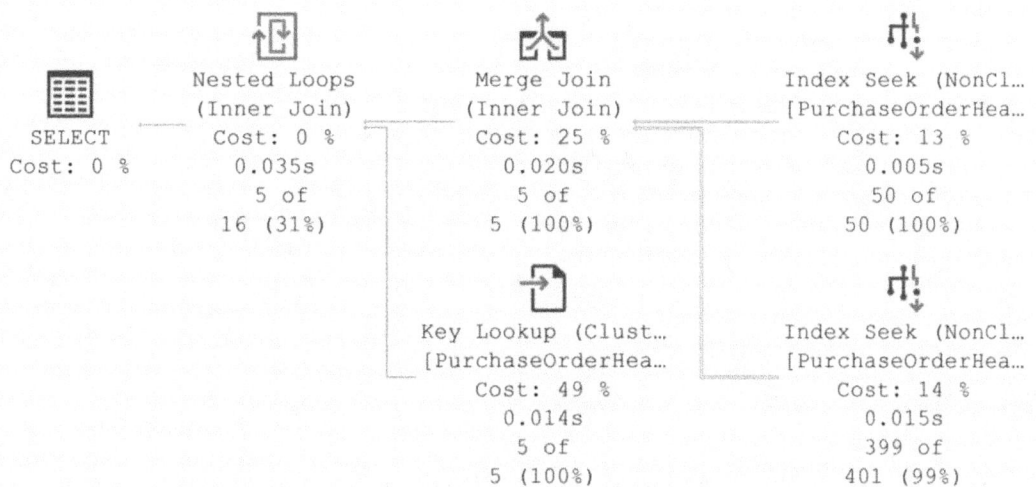

Figure 10-6. *An index join*

There are a couple of points to make here. First, you see the two indexes being used to seek for the appropriate data in the filter criteria. One is from the index on EmployeeID, and one is from the index on VendorID. They are then using a Merge Join to combine the two data sets.

Second, note the Key Lookup operation. Because I included the RevisionNumber column, the join between the two indexes was not covering. That means it had to go to the clustered index to retrieve the rest of the data. In most circumstances, you won't see this with an index intersection. The combined indexes have to be covering. However, with an index join, you can see lookups.

You can even see what is being used to perform the join in the properties of the Merge Join operator. Figure 10-7 shows the *Where (join columns)* property.

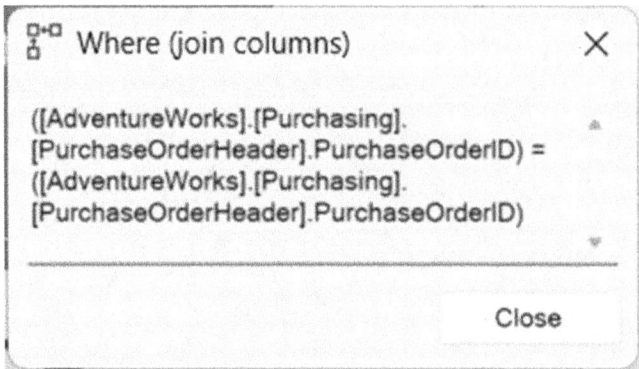

Figure 10-7. *Join criteria in the Where (join columns) property*

As was shown in the previous section, sometimes, wider indexes perform better. Sometimes, you may find that index intersection and index join allow you to use narrower indexes. Testing and validation are always going to be necessary to know what's going to work best for a given query, within a given system.

Filtered Indexes

A filtered index is a nonclustered rowstore index that uses a filter, simply a WHERE clause, to create a more selective index. For example, a column with a large number of NULL values may be stored as a sparse column to reduce the overhead of those NULL values. Adding an index that eliminates NULLs could be useful.

Let's look at an example. The SalesOrderHeader table contains 30,000 rows. Of those, 27,000+ have a NULL value in the PurchaseOrderNumber column and the SalesPersonID column. If you wanted to get a list of purchase order numbers where there is a sales person, you might run the query in Listing 10-9.

Listing 10-9. A query to retrieve purchase order numbers

```
SELECT soh.PurchaseOrderNumber,
       soh.OrderDate,
       soh.ShipDate,
       soh.SalesPersonID
FROM Sales.SalesOrderHeader AS soh
WHERE PurchaseOrderNumber LIKE 'PO5%'
      AND soh.SalesPersonID IS NOT NULL;
```

Running the query, you'll get a Clustered Index Scan since there are no good indexes. You'll also see these performance metrics:

6.5ms
686 reads

To eliminate the scan, we can create an index like you see in Listing 10-10.

Listing 10-10. An index to improve query performance

```
CREATE NONCLUSTERED INDEX IX_Test
ON Sales.SalesOrderHeader (
                        PurchaseOrderNumber,
                        SalesPersonID
                    )
INCLUDE (
        OrderDate,
        ShipDate
    );
```

Executing this query gets us to the following performance metrics and the execution plan in Figure 10-8:

533mcs
5 reads

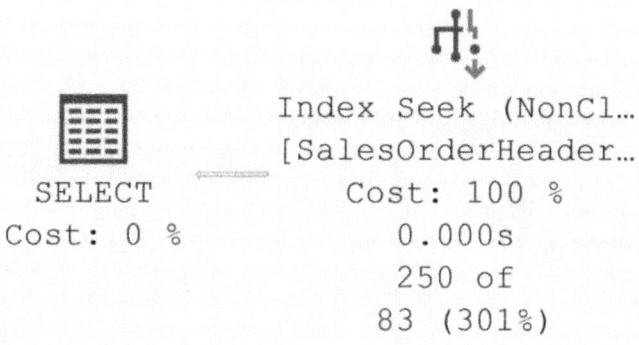

Figure 10-8. *The scan is gone, and an index seek is operating*

By ensuring that we had a covering index, we took the reads from 686 down to 5, and performance went from 6.5ms to 533mcs. On many systems, that would be good enough, and you could walk away a winner. However, on some systems, squeezing the last drop of performance may be required. To improve this query, we can eliminate the NULL values from the index. We just have to modify it using Listing 10-11.

Listing 10-11. Eliminating the NULL values from the index

```
CREATE NONCLUSTERED INDEX IX_Test
ON Sales.SalesOrderHeader (
                    PurchaseOrderNumber,
                    SalesPersonID
                )
INCLUDE (
        OrderDate,
        ShipDate
    )
WHERE PurchaseOrderNumber IS NOT NULL
    AND SalesPersonID IS NOT NULL
WITH (DROP_EXISTING = ON);
```

Notice at the end of the index definition that a WHERE clause has been added. We're removing any row from the index where either PurchaseOrderNumber or SalesPersonID has NULL values. Executing the query again, we get the following metrics:

```
317mcs
4 reads
```

I recognize that's not a major performance enhancement. However, it is an enhancement. Imagine this query is called thousands of times a minute. Reducing its time and resource use constitutes a win.

We can't look at the execution plan because it's actually identical to what you see in Figure 10-8. However, there is one small change. So we're going to use the plan comparison facility within SQL Server Management Studio to compare the two execution plans, with results in Figure 10-9.

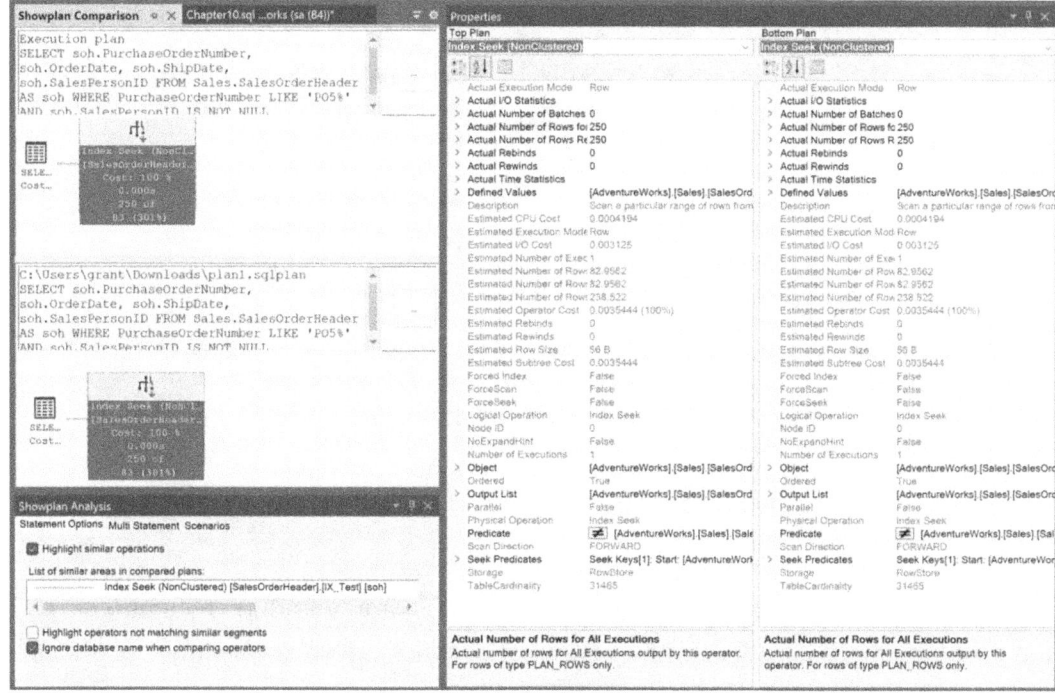

***Figure 10-9.** Comparison between two nearly identical execution plans*

You'll notice that almost every single property in both Index Seek operators is identical. However, the one difference is highlighted. It's the Predicate. The simplification process within the query optimizer removed the IS NOT NULL from the query since the index eliminates NULL values.

While filtered indexes can improve performance, they are not without cost. You might see issues where parameterized queries don't perfectly match the WHERE clause in the index, therefore preventing its use. Statistics are not updated on the filtering criteria, but rather on the entire table, just like a regular index. Testing on your own system to see where, and when, this helps performance is a must.

The most frequent purpose for using a filtered index is the example we just saw, the elimination of NULL values. You can also isolate frequently accessed sets of data with a filtered index so that queries against that data perform faster. You can use the WHERE clause to filter data in ways that are similar to creating indexed views (covered in the next section) without the extensive data maintenance headaches associated with indexed views. Following the example shown previously and making the nonclustered, filtered, index into a covering index further enhance performance.

You must have specific ANSI settings when using filtered indexes:

- On: ANSI_NULLS, ANSI_PADDING, ANSI_WARNINGS, ARITHABORT, CONCAT_NULL_YIELDS_NULL, and QUOTED_IDENTIFIER
- Off: NUMERIC_ROUNDABORT

Before moving on, remove the index using Listing 10-12.

Listing 10-12. Removing the test index

```
DROP INDEX IX_Test ON Sales.SalesOrderHeader;
```

Indexed Views

A view in SQL Server does not store any data. A view is simply a SELECT statement, stored within an object called a view. That view does act as if it were a table, but it's just a query. You define a view using the CREATE VIEW command. Once created, it can be used like a table. However, just to reiterate, it's still only a SELECT statement.

You can also take a view and perform an action called materialization. You're basically creating a new clustered index, based on the query that defines the view. This is called an indexed view or a materialized view. When you create a materialized view, the data is actually persisted to disk and stored within the database, at which point, it is, to all intents and purposes, effectively the same as a table. You can even create nonclustered indexes on the indexed view.

Benefit

You can use an indexed view to increase the performance of a query in the following ways:

- Aggregations can be precomputed and stored in the indexed view to minimize expensive computations during query execution.
- Tables can be pre-joined, and the resulting data set is materialized.
- Combinations of joins or aggregations can also be materialized.

Overhead

Nothing comes without a cost. Materialized views can produce major overhead on a database. Some of the overhead from indexed views is as follows:

- Any change in the base tables has to be reflected in the indexed view by executing the view's SELECT statement.

- Any changes to a base table on which an indexed view is defined may initiate one or more changes in the nonclustered indexes on the indexed view. The clustered index will also have to be changed if the clustering key is updated.

- The indexed view adds to the ongoing maintenance overhead of the database, along with the statistics that also must be maintained.

- Additional storage is required.

There are a number of restrictions on exactly how an index view can be created:

- Whatever keys define the indexed view, it must be a unique index.

- Nonclustered indexes on an indexed view can be created only after the unique clustered index is created.

- The view definition must be deterministic—that is, it is able to return only one possible result for a given query (a list of deterministic and nondeterministic functions is available in the SQL Server documentation).

- The indexed view must reference only base tables in the same database, not other views.

- The indexed view must be schema bound to the tables referred to in the view to prevent modifications of the table (frequently a major problem).

- There are several restrictions on the syntax of the view definition (a complete list is provided in the SQL Server documentation).

- The list of SET options that must be set is as follows:

  - On: ARITHABORT, CONCAT_NULL_YIELDS_NULL, QUOTED_IDENTIFIER, ANSI_NULLS, ANSI_PADDING, and ANSI_WARNING

  - Off: NUMERIC_ROUNDABORT

Usage Scenarios

Dedicated reporting and analysis systems generally benefit the most from indexed views. OLTP systems with frequent writes may not be able to take advantage of indexed views because of the increased maintenance overhead associated with updating both the underlying tables and the view itself, all within a single transaction. The net performance improvement provided by an indexed view is the difference between the total query execution savings and the cost of storing and maintaining the view. Careful testing here is a must. Just remember, for analytical systems, chances are high that columnstore indexes will do even more for the system than materialized views. Materialized views are, however, one more tool in the toolbox.

If you are using the Enterprise edition of SQL Server (or the Developer edition), an indexed view need not be referenced in the query for the query optimizer to use it during query execution. This allows existing applications to benefit from the newly created indexed views without changing those applications. Otherwise, you would need to directly reference the view within your T-SQL code. The query optimizer considers indexed views only for queries with nontrivial cost.

To see indexed views in action, let's start with the queries in Listing 10-13.

Listing 10-13. Analysis-style queries

```
SELECT p.[Name] AS ProductName,
       SUM(pod.OrderQty) AS OrderOty,
       SUM(pod.ReceivedQty) AS ReceivedOty,
       SUM(pod.RejectedQty) AS RejectedOty
FROM Purchasing.PurchaseOrderDetail AS pod
    JOIN Production.Product AS p
        ON p.ProductID = pod.ProductID
GROUP BY p.[Name];
```

```sql
SELECT p.[Name] AS ProductName,
       SUM(pod.OrderQty) AS OrderQty,
       SUM(pod.ReceivedQty) AS ReceivedQty,
       SUM(pod.RejectedQty) AS RejectedQty
FROM Purchasing.PurchaseOrderDetail AS pod
    JOIN Production.Product AS p
        ON p.ProductID = pod.ProductID
GROUP BY p.[Name]
HAVING (SUM(pod.RejectedQty) / SUM(pod.ReceivedQty)) > .08;

SELECT p.[Name] AS ProductName,
       SUM(pod.OrderQty) AS OrderQty,
       SUM(pod.ReceivedQty) AS ReceivedQty,
       SUM(pod.RejectedQty) AS RejectedQty
FROM Purchasing.PurchaseOrderDetail AS pod
    JOIN Production.Product AS p
        ON p.ProductID = pod.ProductID
WHERE p.[Name] LIKE 'Chain%'
GROUP BY p.[Name];
```

All three queries are aggregating data from the PurchaseOrderDetail table. An indexed view that precomputes the aggregations could reduce the cost of these queries. I'm going to use STATISTICS IO to show the detailed reads involved with these queries and, as usual, Extended Events to capture the performance time:

```
Table 'Workfile'. Scan count 0, logical reads 0
Table 'Worktable'. Scan count 0, logical reads 0
Table 'Product'. Scan count 1, logical reads 6
Table 'PurchaseOrderDetail'. Scan count 1, logical reads 66
Table 'Workfile'. Scan count 0, logical reads 0
Table 'Worktable'. Scan count 0, logical reads 0
Table 'Product'. Scan count 1, logical reads 6
Table 'PurchaseOrderDetail'. Scan count 1, logical reads 66
Table 'PurchaseOrderDetail'. Scan count 5, logical reads 894
Table 'Product'. Scan count 1, logical reads 2
```

5.6ms

4.6ms

1.5ms

Listing 10-14 contains the indexed view definition.

Listing 10-14. Creating an indexed view

```
CREATE OR ALTER VIEW Purchasing.IndexedView
WITH SCHEMABINDING
AS
SELECT pod.ProductID,
       SUM(pod.OrderQty) AS OrderQty,
       SUM(pod.ReceivedQty) AS ReceivedQty,
       SUM(pod.RejectedQty) AS RejectedQty,
       COUNT_BIG(*) AS COUNT
FROM Purchasing.PurchaseOrderDetail AS pod
GROUP BY pod.ProductID;
GO
CREATE UNIQUE CLUSTERED INDEX iv ON Purchasing.IndexedView (ProductID);
```

As I mentioned earlier, some functions, such as AVG, are disallowed since it's nondeterministic (again, the complete list is in the SQL Server documentation). If aggregates are included in the view, you must include COUNT_BIG by default.

Creating the clustered index writes all the aggregations to the disk. Now, calculations will only be made as the data changes in the root tables. Queries will be able to access the calculations on the fly. Without modifying the existing queries from Listing 10-13, I can rerun them now, and I get the following IO and execution times:

```
Table 'Product'. Scan count 1, logical reads 13
Table 'IndexedView'. Scan count 1, logical reads 4
Table 'Product'. Scan count 1, logical reads 13
Table 'IndexedView'. Scan count 1, logical reads 4
Table 'IndexedView'. Scan count 0, logical reads 10
Table 'Product'. Scan count 1, logical reads 2
```

968mcs

639mcs

290mcs

Without touching the code, we've radically reduced reads and increased performance speeds on all the queries. You can also see how we've eliminated worktables (temporary tables for performing aggregations) from the process in the reads. One of the execution plans is shown in Figure 10-10.

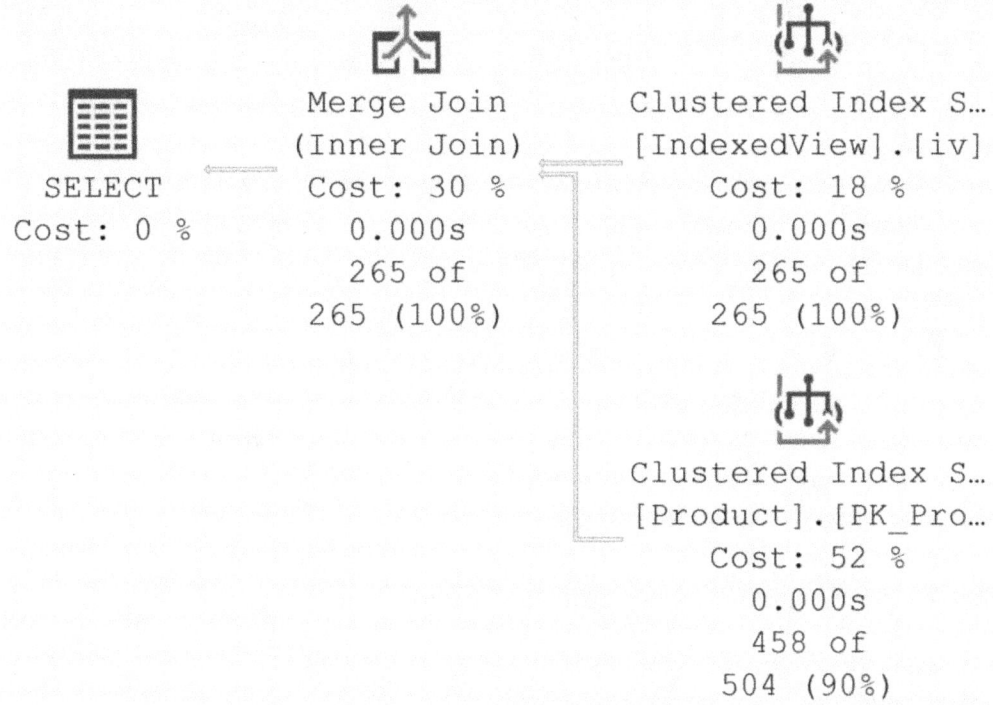

Figure 10-10. *The use of an indexed view in a query*

The optimizer can tell that the indexed view can satisfy the needs of the query, so it just uses that instead of the tables.

Before we proceed, I'm going to remove the indexed view from the database in Listing 10-15.

Listing 10-15. Removing the indexed view

```
DROP VIEW Purchasing.IndexedView;
```

CHAPTER 10 INDEX BEHAVIORS

Index Compression

Using compression on an index means using algorithms to reduce the amount of space taken up by data, thereby putting more data on a given page. More data on a page means fewer pages need to be read from disk. Fewer reads mean better performance. You also get the compressed pages in memory, so you're reducing memory use as well. You will see added overhead on the CPU since compression and decompression will be going through calculations. This overhead means that this won't be a viable solution for all indexes.

By default, indexes are not compressed. You have to call for compression on your indexes. There are two different kinds of index compression: row- and page-level compression. Row-level compression identifies the columns that can be compressed (for details, see the SQL Server documentation) and then compresses the data in those columns. It does this on a row-by-row basis. Page-level compression actually does row-level compression and then additional compression on top to reduce storage size for the non-row elements stored on a page. Non-leaf pages in an index receive no compression under the page type.

Let's take an example index from Listing 10-16.

Listing 10-16. Creating a noncompressed index

```
CREATE NONCLUSTERED INDEX IX_Test
ON Person.ADDRESS (
            City ASC,
            PostalCode ASC
        );
```

You may recognize that index from an earlier chapter. For the sake of comparison, I'm going to create two more indexes using the same key columns, but we'll compress those indexes using row and page compression (Listing 10-17).

Listing 10-17. Creating compressed indexes

```
CREATE NONCLUSTERED INDEX IX_CompRow_Test
ON Person.ADDRESS (
            City,
            PostalCode
```

CHAPTER 10 INDEX BEHAVIORS

```
                )
WITH (DATA_COMPRESSION = ROW);
CREATE NONCLUSTERED INDEX IX_CompPage_Test
ON Person.ADDRESS (
                City,
                PostalCode
                )
WITH (DATA_COMPRESSION = PAGE);
```

> **Note** Just so we're very clear, these three indexes are for example purposes only. Three indexes with identical keys just add overhead to the system and may cause confusion in the optimizer.

With the indexes all created, let's take a look at the physical characteristics of these indexes using sys.dm_db_index_physical_stats in Listing 10-18.

Listing 10-18. Getting a count of pages and compressed pages

```
SELECT i.NAME,
       i.type_desc,
       s.page_count,
       s.record_count,
       s.index_level,
       s.compressed_page_count
FROM sys.indexes AS i
   JOIN sys.dm_db_index_physical_stats(DB_ID(N'AdventureWorks'), OBJECT_
   ID(N'Person.Address'), NULL, NULL, 'DETAILED') AS s
        ON i.index_id = s.index_id
WHERE i.OBJECT_ID = OBJECT_ID(N'Person.Address');
```

The results of this query are visible in Figure 10-11.

	NAME	type_desc	page_count	record_count	index_level	compressed_page_count
1	PK_Address_AddressID	CLUSTERED	344	19614	0	0
2	PK_Address_AddressID	CLUSTERED	1	344	1	0
3	PK_Address_AddressID	CLUSTERED	1	0	0	NULL
4	PK_Address_AddressID	CLUSTERED	1	0	0	NULL
5	AK_Address_rowguid	NONCLUSTERED	64	19614	0	0
6	AK_Address_rowguid	NONCLUSTERED	1	64	1	0
7	IX_Address_AddressLine1_AddressLine2_City_StateP...	NONCLUSTERED	211	19614	0	0
8	IX_Address_AddressLine1_AddressLine2_City_StateP...	NONCLUSTERED	3	211	1	0
9	IX_Address_AddressLine1_AddressLine2_City_StateP...	NONCLUSTERED	1	3	2	0
10	IX_Address_StateProvinceID	NONCLUSTERED	34	19614	0	0
11	IX_Address_StateProvinceID	NONCLUSTERED	1	34	1	0
12	IX_Test	NONCLUSTERED	106	19614	0	0
13	IX_Test	NONCLUSTERED	1	106	1	0
14	IX_CompRow_Test	NONCLUSTERED	63	19614	0	0
15	IX_CompRow_Test	NONCLUSTERED	1	63	1	0
16	IX_CompPage_Test	NONCLUSTERED	25	19614	0	25
17	IX_CompPage_Test	NONCLUSTERED	1	25	1	0

Figure 10-11. Pages being used by indexes on the Address table

The original index, IX_Test, uses 107 pages. The row compression takes it down to 64, and the page compression goes down to 26 pages in total, with 25 of them being compressed. Performance will improve on queries that use these indexes since they will have to move fewer pages to arrive at identical data sets.

Before we proceed, I'll remove these indexes (Listing 10-19).

Listing 10-19. Removing the test indexes

```
DROP INDEX IX_Test ON Person.ADDRESS;
DROP INDEX IX_CompRow_Test ON Person.ADDRESS;
DROP INDEX IX_CompPage_Test ON Person.ADDRESS;
```

Index Characteristics

There are a number of other properties and settings available on indexes that can help you improve performance in some situations. Let's walk through them in detail.

Different Column Sort Order

The default sort order for indexes is ascending. You can control that sort order when you create the index. Further, you can control each column in the key individually so that the data is stored in a sorted fashion best suited to the query. If you were to create an index in this manner, it would look something like Listing 10-20.

CHAPTER 10 ■ INDEX BEHAVIORS

Listing 10-20. Changing the sort order of an index

```
CREATE NONCLUSTERED INDEX IX_Test
ON Person.ADDRESS (
                City ASC,
                PostalCode DESC
            );
```

Index on Computed Columns

SQL Server allows you to create indexes on computed columns. However, the result of the computation has to be deterministic and can only reference columns on the same table.

CREATE INDEX Statement Processed As a Query

Creating indexes is a costly process. As such, SQL Server will put the creation process through the optimizer in an attempt to find ways to create the index more efficiently by the use of other indexes.

For example, Listing 10-21 shows the creation of an index on the City column of the Address table, but with a rollback, so we can see the execution plan but not really create the index.

Listing 10-21. Creating a new index

```
BEGIN TRAN
CREATE NONCLUSTERED INDEX IX_Test
ON Person.Address(City);
ROLLBACK TRAN
```

If I capture the execution plan for this query, it looks like Figure 10-12.

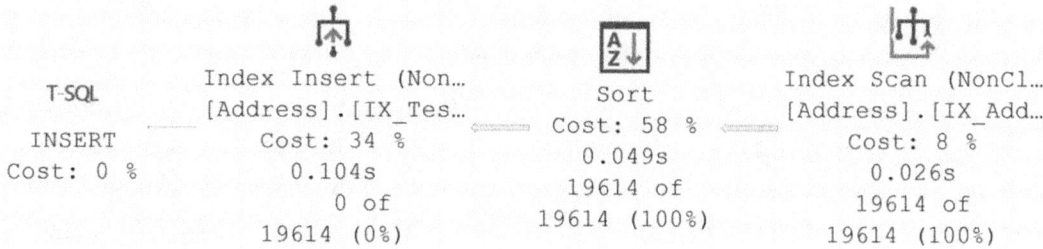

Figure 10-12. *The execution plan for a CREATE INDEX statement*

Instead of scanning the clustered index to arrive at the data set, the optimizer chose in this case to scan the nonclustered index, IX_Address_AddressLine1_AddressLine2_City_StateProvinceID_PostalCode. Both the clustered index and the nonclustered index used contain all the City values, but the nonclustered index is smaller, so fewer pages need to be read while creating the index.

Parallel Index Creation

Just as queries can run in parallel, SQL Server can create indexes using parallel execution, but only on the Enterprise edition. If you have a multiprocessor machine supporting your SQL Server instance, you can put those processors to work when creating an index. You control the number of processors used at the server level by setting the "Max Degree of Parallelism." You can also control it at the query level by using the MAXDOP query hint on your CREATE INDEX statement.

Online Index Creation

The default creation of an index is done as an offline operation. This means exclusive locks are placed on the table, restricting user access while the index is created. It is possible to create the indexes as an online operation. This allows users to continue to access the data while the index is being created. This comes at the cost of increasing the amount of time and resources it takes to create the index. Introduced in SQL Server 2012, indexes with varchar(MAX), nvarchar(MAX), and varbinary(MAX) can actually be rebuilt online. Online index operations are available only in SQL Server Enterprise editions. SQL Server 2025 introduces the ability to do an online rebuild for columnstore indexes; both clustered and nonclustered columnstore now support online rebuilds.

Considering the Database Engine Tuning Advisor

SQL Server has a tool called the Database Engine Tuning Advisor. In previous editions of the book, I dedicated a chapter to this. However, over the years I've lost more and more faith in the tool. Now, I never use it and won't advocate for its use. However, in some cases, people have found it to be helpful in deciding which indexes to apply to their systems. I will add that some of its suggestions are not helpful. Some of its suggestions may even be harmful. If you do choose to use the Tuning Advisor, please do extensive testing to validate its results.

OPTIMIZE_FOR_SEQUENTIAL_KEY

When you have an index on a value that is sequential, it's very common to see contention in the last page of the index, as multiple processes all attempt to insert values to the same page. Common values would be an IDENTITY column, a date or time column, or an ordered GUID. Starting with SQL Server 2019, and available in Azure SQL Database, you can enable OPTIMIZE_FOR_SEQUENTIAL_KEY. It will change the way the inserts occur in order to reduce the last page contention. You may also see this help other indexes that are experiencing similar contention.

Resumable Indexes and Constraints

Take advantage of the fact that index rebuilds can now be paused and restarted. This requires first that you create the index using the RESUMABLE option as shown in Listing 10-22.

Listing 10-22. Creating an index that can be paused

```
CREATE NONCLUSTERED INDEX IX_Resumable
ON Person.ADDRESS (
                City ASC,
                PostalCode DESC
            )
WITH (RESUMABLE = ON, ONLINE = ON);
```

The RESUMABLE option is part of the ONLINE index functionality, so you'll need to include both. Not only does this make it possible to pause the rebuild of an index while leaving the index in place, but you can restart failed index rebuilds. It's a handy function. You can also add MAX_DURATION to the command in order to have it pause automatically after a number of minutes.

If you have indexes in the middle of a rebuild, they've been paused; you check by querying sys.index_resumable_operations (Listing 10-23).

Listing 10-23. Getting information on paused index rebuilds

```
SELECT o.NAME AS ObjectName,
       i.NAME AS IndexName,
       iro.sql_text,
       iro.state_desc,
```

```
            iro.start_time,
            iro.last_pause_time,
            iro.total_execution_time,
            iro.percent_complete
FROM sys.index_resumable_operations AS iro
    JOIN sys.indexes AS i
        ON i.OBJECT_ID = iro.OBJECT_ID
            AND i.index_id = iro.index_id
    JOIN sys.objects AS o
        ON o.OBJECT_ID = i.OBJECT_ID;
```

In order to pause an index rebuild, you have to use a second connection. However, it's then fairly simple syntax as shown in Listing 10-24.

Listing 10-24. Pausing an index rebuild

```
ALTER INDEX IX_Resumable ON Person.ADDRESS PAUSE;
```

After pausing, you can either restart the process or get rid of it using the code in Listing 10-25.

Listing 10-25. Code to restart or abort an index rebuild

```
ALTER INDEX IX_Resumable ON Person.ADDRESS RESUME;
ALTER INDEX IX_Resumable ON Person.ADDRESS ABORT;
```

This does incur some disk storage overhead since the partially built index needs to be kept somewhere. Plan for at least as much storage as the index currently takes up. Using RESUMABLE means that you can't use SORT_IN_TEMPDB. Finally, you can't run a RESUMABLE index operation within an explicit transaction.

Special Index Types

As special data types and storage mechanisms are introduced to SQL Server by Microsoft, methods for indexing these special storage types are also developed. Explaining all the details possible for each of these special index types is outside the scope of the book. In the following sections, I introduce the basic concepts of each index type in order to facilitate the possibility of their use in tuning your queries.

Full-Text

You can store large amounts of text in SQL Server by using the MAX value in the VARCHAR, NVARCHAR, CHAR, and NCHAR fields. A normal clustered or nonclustered index against these large fields would be unsupportable because a single value can far exceed the page size within an index. So a different mechanism of indexing text is to use the full-text engine, which must be running to work with full-text indexes. You can also build a full-text index on VARBINARY data.

You need to have one column on the table that is unique. The best candidates for performance are integers: INT or BIGINT. This column is then used along with the word to identify which row within the table it belongs to, as well as its location within the field. SQL Server allows for incremental changes, either change tracking or time based, to the full-text indexes as well as complete rebuilds.

SQL Server 2012 introduced another method for working with text called Semantic Search. It uses phrases from documents to identify relationships between different sets of text stored within the database.

Spatial

Introduced in SQL Server 2008 is the ability to store spatial data. This data can be either a geometry type or the very complex geographical type, literally identifying a point on the earth. To say the least, indexing this type of data is complicated. SQL Server stores these indexes in a flat B-Tree, similar to regular indexes, except that it is also a hierarchy of four grids linked together. Each of the grids can be given a density of low, medium, or high, outlining how big each grid is. There are mechanisms to support indexing of the spatial data types so that different types of queries, such as finding when one object is within the boundaries of or near another object, can benefit from performance increases inherent in indexing.

A spatial index can be created only against a column of type geometry or geography. It has to be on a base table, it must have no indexed views, and the table must have a primary key. You can create up to 249 spatial indexes on any given column on a table. Different indexes are used to define different types of index behavior.

CHAPTER 10 INDEX BEHAVIORS

XML

Introduced as a data type in SQL Server 2005, XML can be stored not as text but as well-formed XML data within SQL Server. This data can be queried using the XQuery language as supported by SQL Server. To enhance the performance capabilities, a special set of indexes has been defined. An XML column can have one primary and several secondary indexes. The primary XML shreds the properties, attributes, and elements of the XML data and stores it as an internal table. There must be a primary key on the table, and that primary key must be clustered in order to create an XML index. After the XML index is created, the secondary indexes can be created. These indexes have types Path, Value, and Property, depending on how you query the XML.

Vector

Along with the Vector data type introduced in SQL Server 2025 and Vector functions, an index can be added to your Vector columns. Strictly speaking, it's not the same as many of the other indexes we've talked about in the last two chapters. Strictly speaking, this is a DiskANN index, which means Disk Approximate Nearest Neighbor. This means, unlike so many indexes that are focused on finding precise values faster, the Vector index is used to find approximate values within the Vector data type. There are a number of limitations on the new Vector index:

- Partitioning of a Vector index is unsupported.
- When a Vector index is created, the table becomes read-only.
- The table must have a single column, integer, and primary key that is also a clustered index.

When you create the index, you can control the mathematical constructs used to find the approximate nearest neighbor:

- Cosine
- Euclidean
- Dot

SQL Server 2025 supports a hybrid query mechanism. This means you can combine traditional T-SQL with your Vector functions. This also means that you can mix traditional indexes with the Vector index, as long as you meet the requirements for the primary key outlined earlier.

A full breakdown of how to use Vector data in order to take advantage of the Vector index is far beyond the scope of this book.

Summary

This chapter expanded on the capabilities, functions, and behaviors of the indexes that we introduced in the preceding chapter. Any, or all, of these can help improve performance on your systems, but be sure that you do test them, because they all come with some additional overhead.

In the next chapter, we'll explore lookups in detail and talk about possible ways to improve performance around them.

CHAPTER 11

Key Lookups and Solutions

Nonclustered indexes help query performance in all manner of ways. However, unlike clustered indexes, the data isn't stored with nonclustered indexes. Therefore, a common occurrence is the lookup, going back to the clustered index or the heap to retrieve the data not stored with the nonclustered index. In some cases, this is benign behavior. In other cases, this becomes a performance problem. Having ways to deal with this common issue can help your systems.

In this chapter, I cover the following topics:

- The purpose of lookups
- Performance issues caused by lookups
- Analysis of the cause of lookups
- Techniques to resolve lookups

Purpose of Lookups

As you know from previous chapters, you can store data in a heap or a clustered index. Then, you can create additional nonclustered indexes to aid queries that are searching for data, other than how the data is stored. The optimizer recognizes these indexes based on their utility to the query in question, usually around the WHERE, JOIN, and HAVING clauses. If the query refers to columns that are not a part of the nonclustered index, that data must be retrieved from the table. That process of finding the data from the source is what a lookup is.

If we look at Listing 11-1, we'll see a query where a nonclustered index can help us filter the data faster, but that index is not covering, and so a lookup is necessary.

G. Fritchey, *SQL Server 2025 Query Performance Tuning*, https://doi.org/10.1007/979-8-8688-1865-3_11

CHAPTER 11　KEY LOOKUPS AND SOLUTIONS

Listing 11-1. Retrieving sales data

```
SELECT p.NAME,
       AVG(sod.LineTotal)
FROM Sales.SalesOrderDetail AS sod
    JOIN Production.Product AS p
        ON sod.ProductID = p.ProductID
WHERE sod.ProductID = 776
GROUP BY sod.CarrierTrackingNumber,
         p.NAME
HAVING MAX(sod.OrderQty) > 1
ORDER BY MIN(sod.LineTotal);
```

The SalesOrderDetail table has a nonclustered index on the ProductID column. This is the index the optimizer can use to speed up data retrieval. The table has a clustered index defined on the SalesOrderID and SalesOrderDetailID columns, so they are a part of the nonclustered index as the row locator. However, since they're not referenced in the query, they don't do anything but act as the row locator. The other columns referenced in the query–LineTotal, CarrierTrackingNumber, and OrderQty–are not a part of the nonclustered index key or INCLUDE columns. This means the optimizer has to perform a lookup to retrieve the data as you see in Figure 11-1.

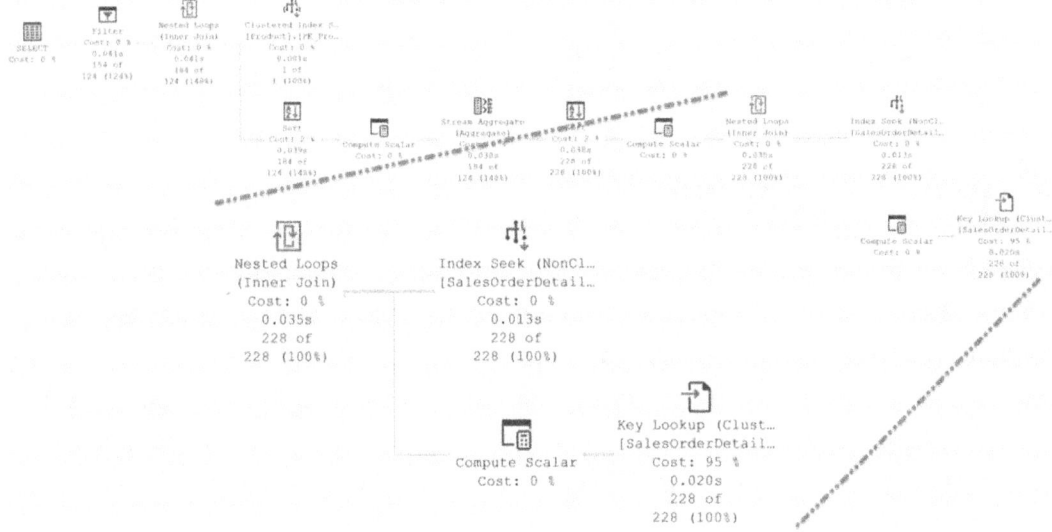

Figure 11-1. Execution plan for the query showing a key lookup

CHAPTER 11   KEY LOOKUPS AND SOLUTIONS

The lookup operation is blown up from the full execution plan in Figure 11-1. The Index Seek operation filters the rows returned down to 228. But then, an additional join operation, the Nested Loops, is added in order to work with the Key Lookup operation against the clustered index to return the additional columns needed. You can always check the properties of the Key Lookup operator to identify the output to see exactly which columns are retrieved in that way as illustrated in Figure 11-2.

Output List	[AdventureWorks].[Sales].[SalesOrderDetail].CarrierTrackingNumber, [
[1]	[AdventureWorks].[Sales].[SalesOrderDetail].CarrierTrackingNumber
[2]	[AdventureWorks].[Sales].[SalesOrderDetail].OrderQty
[3]	[AdventureWorks].[Sales].[SalesOrderDetail].UnitPrice
[4]	[AdventureWorks].[Sales].[SalesOrderDetail].UnitPriceDiscount

Figure 11-2. *The Output List property showing the columns in the lookup*

Performance Issues Caused by Lookups

A lookup necessitates retrieving pages from where the data is stored as well as the pages from the nonclustered index. Accessing more pages quite simply increases the number of logical reads for a given query. Additionally, if the pages are not available in memory, a lookup will probably require a random (nonsequential) I/O operation on the disk to go from the index page to the data page. On top of that, there is CPU processing necessary to marshal the data and perform the operations.

In addition to that cost, you also add the cost of the join operation necessary to put the two sets of data together.

These costs associated with lookups are why it's recommended to keep data retrieval from nonclustered indexes to small sets of data. As the data set size increases, the costs associated with lookups go up as well.

Let's look at an example to illustrate this point. Listing 11-2 shows a query that returns a relatively large data set and all columns through the SELECT * operation (used intentionally for illustration purposes).

Listing 11-2. *A larger data set from the SalesOrderDetail table*

```
SELECT *
FROM Sales.SalesOrderDetail AS sod
WHERE sod.ProductID = 793;
```

While a very simple query, it is returning more than 700 rows, as well as all the columns of the table. The optimizer chooses to perform a Clustered Index Scan as shown in Figure 11-3.

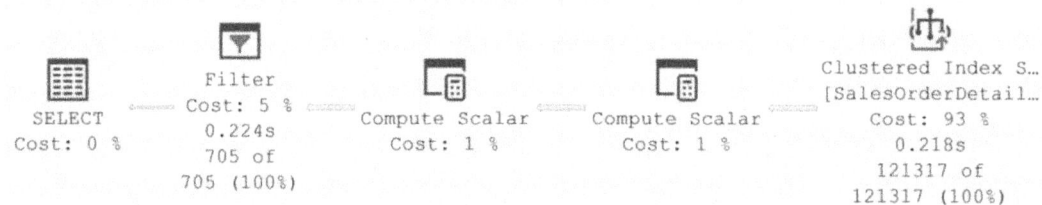

Figure 11-3. A scan in order to retrieve a larger data set

We can force the optimizer to use the nonclustered index on the ProductID column by using an index hint as shown in Listing 11-3.

Listing 11-3. Forcing an index to be used

```
SELECT *
FROM Sales.SalesOrderDetail AS sod WITH (INDEX(IX_SalesOrderDetail_ProductID))
WHERE sod.ProductID = 793;
```

This query will change the plan to one with an index seek and a key lookup, similar to what we saw earlier in Figure 11-1. However, the reads for the query in Listing 11-3 went to 2,278 from the value of 1,248 for Listing 11-2.

As you can see, while the lookup operation is a necessary one, it can be quite costly.

Analysis of the Causes of Lookups

Not all lookups have to be eliminated because some queries aren't called very frequently and they run fast enough as they are. However, when a query needs to run faster, and there's a lookup operation, depending on the number of columns that have to be dealt with, that lookup can be some low-hanging fruit to improve performance.

Listing 11-4 shows another query, retrieving information from the HumanResources. Employee table using an index on the NationalIDNumber column.

CHAPTER 11 KEY LOOKUPS AND SOLUTIONS

Listing 11-4. Retrieving basic information from the Employee table

```
SELECT NationalIDNumber,
       JobTitle,
       HireDate
FROM HumanResources.Employee AS E
WHERE E.NationalIDNumber = '693168613';
```

Running this query results in the execution plan you see in Figure 11-4.

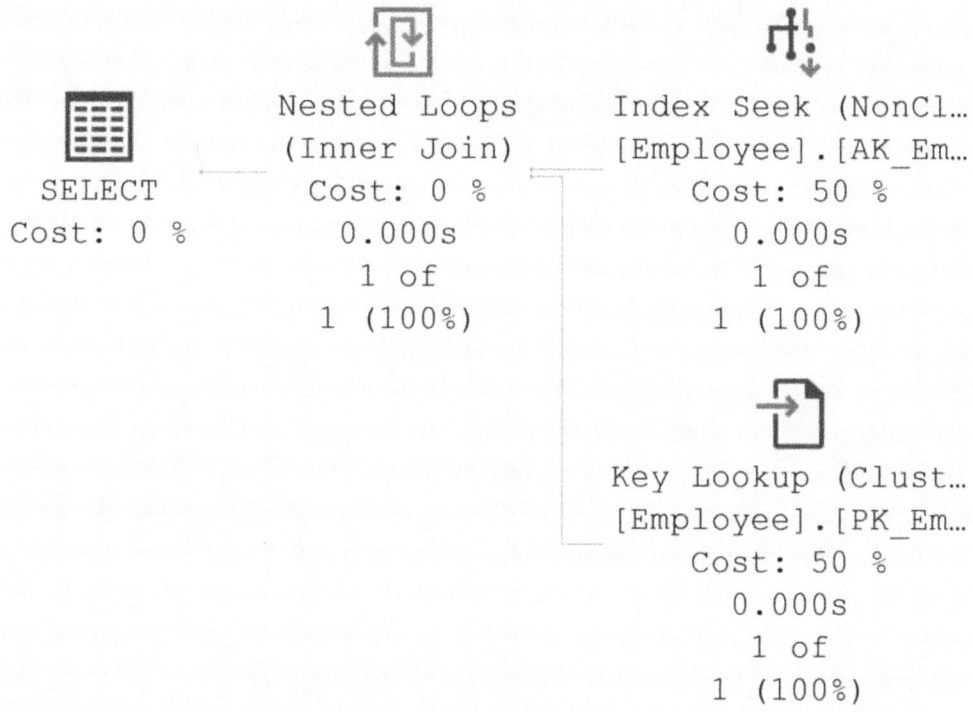

Figure 11-4. *A standard Key Lookup operation*

In the example in Listing 11-4, since we're only retrieving three columns from the table, and we know the index is on the NationalIDNumber column, it's pretty easy to infer that the lookup is for the other two columns. However, with large queries, columns in use in multiple clauses, it can be tricky to simply look at a query and understand which columns you need to deal with.

CHAPTER 11 KEY LOOKUPS AND SOLUTIONS

To know exactly which columns are taking part in the lookup operation, go to the lookup operator and open up the properties. The output columns will tell you what you need to know. Figure 11-5 shows the output for the Key Lookup operator.

Figure 11-5. *The two columns in the Output List of the Key Lookup operator*

You can see all the details available, the column, table, and schema, everything you need. On the right of the "Output List" property in SSMS, you'll see an ellipsis. Clicking that opens the columns up in a text window, making it easy to copy, as illustrated in Figure 11-6.

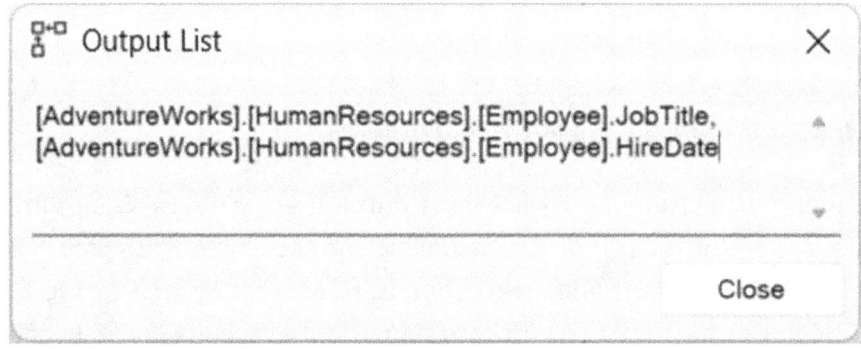

Figure 11-6. *Columns highlighted in a text window*

With this information, you can now decide how you plan to resolve the lookup operation.

Techniques to Resolve Lookups

I've said it already in this chapter, but it bears repeating, not every lookup operation requires immediate attention. Understanding how the query in question is working within the system can help you decide if you need to fix the lookup. However, you're usually unaware of lookups in queries that are running fast enough. You're looking at the execution plan of a query because it's running slowly.

To fix a lookup, you have three basic approaches:

- Create a clustered index.
- Use a covering index.
- Take advantage of index joins.

Let's explore all three of these in a little more detail.

Create a Clustered Index

Since the leaf pages of a clustered index contain all the columns for a table (with a few exceptions), when a clustered index is used to retrieve the rows, no lookup operations are needed. If the index used for Listing 11-4 earlier was recreated as the clustered index for the table, no lookup operation would occur.

In most cases, this just isn't an option. You've already designed the table around a good, clustered index. You can't–in fact, you shouldn't–simply swap those indexes around. At least, not without extensive testing. However, if you're working with a heap table, you have the opportunity to create a new clustered index, which would resolve any RID Lookup operations.

Use a Covering Index

In Chapter 10, I explained that a covering index is one that has all the columns needed to satisfy a given query. This means that the index would not need to go to where the data is stored in order to retrieve all the columns.

CHAPTER 11 KEY LOOKUPS AND SOLUTIONS

You have two mechanisms for making a nonclustered index into a covering index. The first of these is to change the key of the index to include all the columns needed for a given query. This choice has serious implications for the index. Let's take a look at the density graph of the existing index, AK_Employee_NationalIDNumber, using Listing 11-5.

Listing 11-5. Using DBCC SHOW_STATISTICS to see the density graph

```
DBCC SHOW_STATISTICS('HumanResources.Employee', 'AK_Employee_
NationalIDNumber') WITH DENSITY_VECTOR;
```

The results are visible in Figure 11-7.

	All density	Average Length	Columns
1	0.003448276	17.66207	NationalIDNumber
2	0.003448276	21.66207	NationalIDNumber, BusinessEntityID

Figure 11-7. *Density graph for the original index*

The average key length for the existing index, which includes the indexed column, NationalIDNumber, and the row identifier, in this case, the clustered index key, BusinessEntityID, is 21.66.

We can try to address the lookup by modifying the existing index using Listing 11-6.

Listing 11-6. Recreating the index with a new key

```
CREATE UNIQUE NONCLUSTERED INDEX AK_Employee_NationalIDNumber
ON [HumanResources].[Employee] (
                        NationalIDNumber ASC,
                        JobTitle,
                        HireDate
                )
WITH DROP_EXISTING;
```

If you were to rerun the original code in Listing 11-4, you'd see that the lookup operation is gone. The execution plan now looks like Figure 11-8.

CHAPTER 11 KEY LOOKUPS AND SOLUTIONS

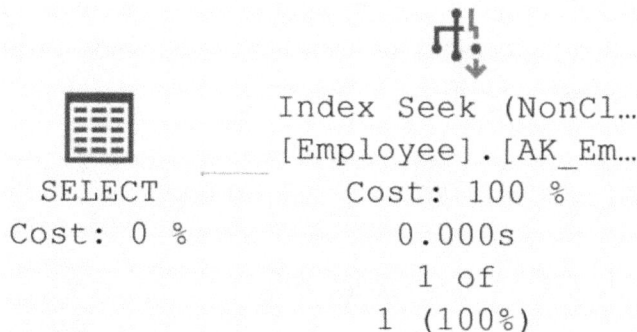

Figure 11-8. Lookup operation eliminated

However, when we now run Listing 11-5 to get the density graph, we see the results in Figure 11-9.

	All density	Average Length	Columns
1	0.003448276	17.66207	NationalIDNumber
2	0.003448276	67.48276	NationalIDNumber, JobTitle
3	0.003448276	70.48276	NationalIDNumber, JobTitle, HireDate
4	0.003448276	74.48276	NationalIDNumber, JobTitle, HireDate, BusinessE...

Figure 11-9. The density graph for the new index

The average length of the key has gone from 21.66 to 74.48, more than three times bigger. That means fewer rows per page, and so page reads will go up when accessing this new index. That doesn't even address the fact that the index behavior is now going to be different overall.

The other way to get a covering index is to leave the key alone and simply add the columns you want to the leaf level of the index, using the INCLUDE clause as shown in Listing 11-7.

Listing 11-7. Using the INCLUDE clause to recreate the index

```
CREATE UNIQUE NONCLUSTERED INDEX AK_Employee_NationalIDNumber
ON [HumanResources].[Employee] (NationalIDNumber ASC)
INCLUDE (
        JobTitle,
        HireDate
    )
WITH DROP_EXISTING;
```

CHAPTER 11 KEY LOOKUPS AND SOLUTIONS

This will end up with an execution plan basically identical to what you see in Figure 11-8. However, with this new index in place, the density graph looks a little different, as shown in Figure 11-10.

	All density	Average Length	Columns
1	0.003448276	17.66207	NationalIDNumber
2	0.003448276	21.66207	NationalIDNumber, BusinessEntityID

Figure 11-10. *Average key length is back down*

The average key length is back to what it was because while we've added data to the index, it's stored at the leaf, not on with the key. Overall, this should perform better in terms of reads, although for such a small key and data set, you're unlikely to see it here in this example.

Before we go, there is one other way to make an index into a covering index. I'm going to reset the index all the way back to the beginning using Listing 11-8.

Listing 11-8. Resetting the index

```
CREATE UNIQUE NONCLUSTERED INDEX AK_Employee_NationalIDNumber
ON [HumanResources].[Employee] (NationalIDNumber ASC)
INCLUDE (
        JobTitle,
        HireDate
    )
WITH DROP_EXISTING;
```

Now, if we actually modify the query, to change the columns retrieved, we can see a covering index again. Listing 11-9 shows the updated query.

Listing 11-9. A modified query

```
SELECT NationalIDNumber,
       E.BusinessEntityID
FROM HumanResources.Employee AS E
WHERE E.NationalIDNumber = '693168613';
```

Once more, this results in an execution plan that looks like Figure 11-8. It's a covering index because the clustered index key, BusinessEntityID, is included with the index as the row locator. So we can modify code to make an index covering. However, to be fair, we've changed the result set. If you need the columns in question, JobTitle and HireDate, this is a horrible solution.

Take Advantage of Index Joins

I introduced the concept of index joins in Chapter 10. As stated there, these are somewhat rare, so counting on them could be problematic as a tuning strategy. For example, the original code we've been testing with throughout the chapter, Listing 11-4, cannot be tuned with an index join. This is primarily because there is no filtering on the other columns, so indexes on those columns just won't help performance at all. To see this in action, we'll take a new example from Listing 11-10.

Listing 11-10. Query against the PurchaseOrderHeader table

```
SELECT poh.PurchaseOrderID,
       poh.VendorID,
       poh.OrderDate
FROM Purchasing.PurchaseOrderHeader AS poh
WHERE VendorID = 1636
      AND poh.OrderDate = '2014/6/24';
```

This query runs with the following performance metrics and the execution plan in Figure 11-11:

```
614mcs
10 reads
```

CHAPTER 11 KEY LOOKUPS AND SOLUTIONS

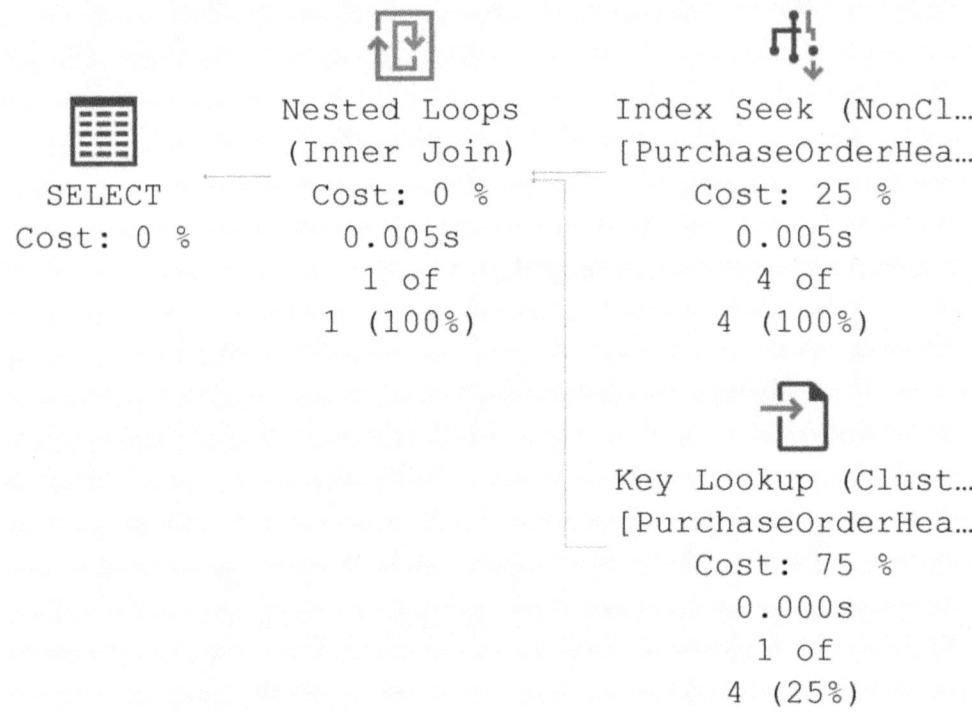

Figure 11-11. *Query resulted in a key lookup*

As with the other queries in this chapter, the columns in the query are not contained in any of the nonclustered indexes on the table. This means that even though the IX_PurchaseOrderHeader_VendorID index filters the data based on the WHERE criteria, the rest of the columns in the query have to be retrieved from the clustered index.

As we've shown earlier, you could modify the index and add columns to make it a covering index. However, that does change the index, either the key or just the overall size with columns at the leaf level. What if modifying the existing index negatively impacted other queries?

We can experiment to see if an index join is possible by adding the index in Listing 11-11.

Listing 11-11. Creating a new nonclustered index

```
CREATE NONCLUSTERED INDEX IX_TEST
ON Purchasing.PurchaseOrderHeader (OrderDate);
```

CHAPTER 11 ■ KEY LOOKUPS AND SOLUTIONS

Running Listing 11-10 for a second time, we get new performance metrics and a new execution plan in Figure 11-12:

```
4.66mcs
4 reads
```

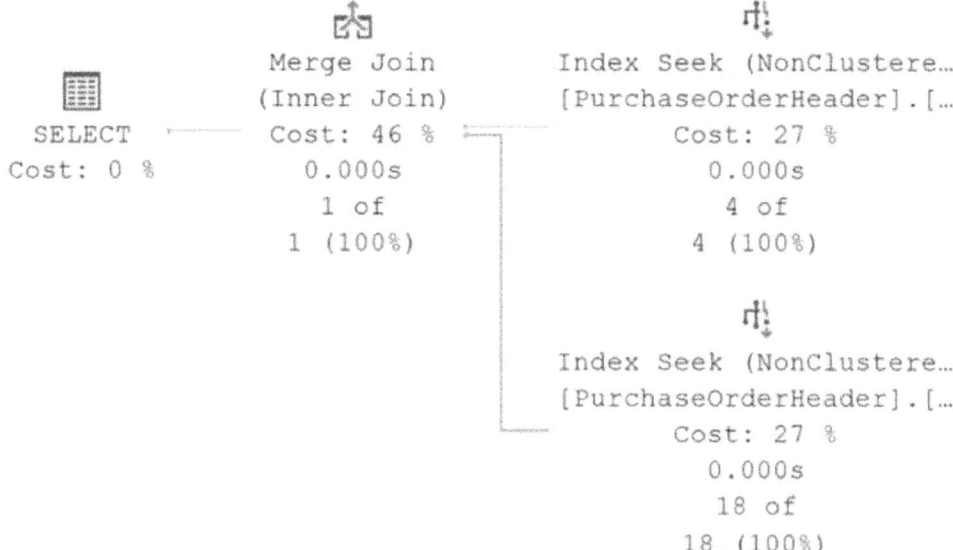

Figure 11-12. An index join works as a covering index

In the execution plan, both indexes are used to seek against. Because the data is ordered in both seek operations, a Merge Join is used to put together the one matching row. The reads went from 10 to 4, and you saw a similar improvement in performance.

Changing the index IX_PurchaseOrderHeader_VendorID to be covering would perform even better than this, since it eliminates the join operation as well as the reads against the second index. However, as we discussed, we're avoiding it in this case.

Summary

As you can see from the code and examples in this chapter, there are mechanisms for dealing with lookups, whether a heap or a clustered index. Lookup operations are not free, so they can be a good choice to help improve the performance of a given query.

Analyzing the lookup itself is easy since the lookup operation tells you what you need to know. Then it's just a question of picking one of the possible solutions to fix the issue.

In the next chapter, we're going to discuss a somewhat controversial topic: index fragmentation. We'll talk about whether or not fragmentation is a problem and, if it becomes a problem, how best to deal with it.

CHAPTER 12

Dealing with Index Fragmentation

As people work with the data in your databases, they make changes. They may be inserting new information, deleting information they no longer need, or modifying other information or all of the above. As the data changes, your indexes are directly affected, both rowstore and columnstore, albeit in different ways. For your rowstore indexes, the acts of modifying the data can lead to page splits, pages getting rearranged, and pages getting emptied, all summed up in a term called fragmentation. In your columnstore indexes, you're not dealing with the same kind of fragmentation, but you are dealing with the deltastore, marking data that has been deleted, or keeping updated and inserted data ready for when it gets pivoted and compressed. Fragmentation can, in some circumstances, lead to performance degradation. Unfortunately, fixing fragmentation can also lead to performance degradation.

In this chapter, I cover the following topics:

- The causes of rowstore index fragmentation
- The causes of columnstore index fragmentation
- An explanation of fragmentation's impact on performance
- How to analyze the amount of fragmentation on rowstore and columnstore indexes
- Techniques to resolve fragmentation
- The significance of fill factor in controlling fragmentation in rowstore indexes
- Automation techniques for fragmentation

Causes of Rowstore Fragmentation

Making changes to the data in a database can lead to index fragmentation. Adding or removing a row, through INSERT or DELETE operations, leads to changes in the clustered and nonclustered indexes on the table. UPDATES can also lead to fragmentation. We'll discuss the various mechanisms for rowstore fragmentation here and address columnstore fragmentation in the next section.

How Fragmentation Occurs in Rowstore Indexes

The key to understanding fragmentation goes right back to understanding how indexes store data. Everything goes on a page, fixed in size to 8KB. Removing data from a page leaves gaps. Adding data to a page that is full results in the need for a new page. Modifying data in a page that is full can also lead to the need for a new page. As new pages get added to the index, they're not necessarily next to the existing pages on the disk. Logically, the data will absolutely maintain the correct order as defined by the index key. However, the physical order and logical order may not be in any way related.

Let's take a simplified approach and talk about an index with nine key values. Let's also simplify our page structure and say, just for this explanation, instead of 8KB worth of information, we can only store four rows on a page. The pages in an index are in a doubly linked list, as explained in Chapter 9. Figure 12-1 shows the layout of our imaginary index.

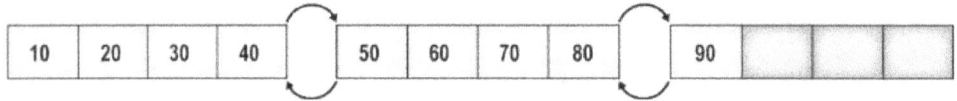

Figure 12-1. *Leaf pages in order*

If someone comes along and adds a piece of data with a value of 25, it has to go between 20 and 30 on the first page of the index. There is no room, so a new page must be allocated. This is a process referred to as a page split, since the contents of the page are split. Half will remain on the existing page, and half will move to a new page. Rather than going to the trouble of completely reordering all the pages on the index so that the logical and the physical order match, the new page is just added at the end so that now our index is laid out like Figure 12-2.

CHAPTER 12   DEALING WITH INDEX FRAGMENTATION

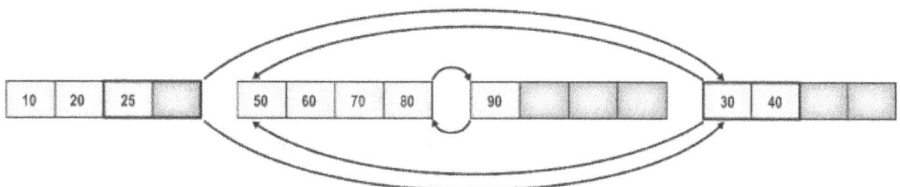

Figure 12-2. *Leaf pages out of order*

SQL Server actually groups the pages, eight at a time, into a storage unit called *an extent*. Instead of allocating single pages, in order to help with things just like this, an eight-page extent gets allocated. When an index first gets created, most of a given range in the index will be on a single extent. There will be little extent switching. However, as Figure 12-3 shows, when our new page was allocated, it was placed in a second extent.

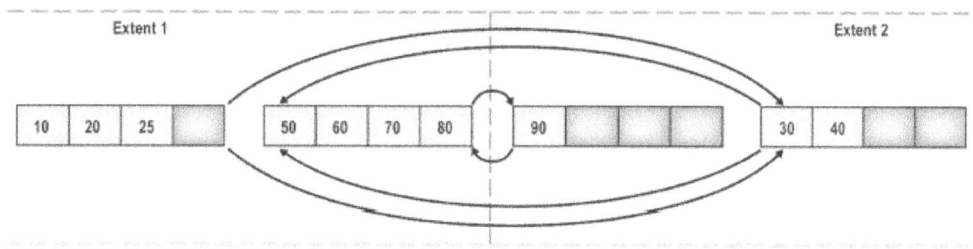

Figure 12-3. *Pages distributed across extents*

Fragmentation of the pages across extents as shown here is called external fragmentation. The fragmentation, free space, left by page splits or deletes, inside of a page, is called internal fragmentation. Both types of fragmentation can lead to poor performance.

To understand this, let's imagine a query that retrieves all the values between 25 and 90. There will be three extent switches as follows:

- The extent is switched to get the value 30 after the value 25.
- The extent switches back to get the value of 50 after the value of 40.
- Finally, another extent switch occurs to get the value of 90.

Interestingly enough, free space on the pages can help in a highly transactional system. In our example index, if the value of 26 is added, it can go right on the page next to 25.

All of this is exacerbated when we talk about tables that are stored as heaps. The fragmentation is exactly the same. However, when you decide to use the ALTER TABLE REBUILD command to eliminate fragmentation, you cause a major problem. Since any nonclustered indexes on the heap tables must point to the physical location of the data through the row identifier (RID), when the pages are rearranged to remove fragmentation, the nonclustered indexes must also be completely rebuilt in order to obtain the RID of the new location.

Enough theory. Let's explore page splits and fragmentation through physical examples.

Page Split from an UPDATE Statement

I'm going to build a table and add data to it in order to set things up for a page split. All the data from Listing 12-1 fits on a single page.

Listing 12-1. Creating a table in support of a page split

```
DROP TABLE IF EXISTS dbo.SplitTest;
GO
CREATE TABLE dbo.SplitTest
(
    C1 INT,
    C2 CHAR(999),
    C3 VARCHAR(10)
);
INSERT INTO dbo.SplitTest
(
    C1,
    C2,
    C3
)
VALUES
(100, 'C2', ''),
(200, 'C2', ''),
(300, 'C2', ''),
(400, 'C2', ''),
(500, 'C2', ''),
```

```
(600, 'C2', ''),
(700, 'C2', ''),
(800, 'C2', '');
CREATE CLUSTERED INDEX iClustered ON dbo.SplitTest (C1);
```

Since all the data is stored at the leaf level of a clustered index, the average size of a row (excluding internal overhead) is the combined average of the key columns and the data columns. If we wanted to express this mathematically for our table, SplitTest, it would look like this:

```
(Average size of [C1]) + (Average size of [C2]) + (Average size of [C3])
bytes = (Size of INT) + (Size of CHAR(999)) + (Average size of data in
[C3]) bytes
4 + 999 + 0 = 1,003 bytes
```

The maximum size of a row in SQL Server is 8,060 bytes. All eight rows will fit on that single page. We can even query the index to see how it is laid out using sys.dm_db_index_physical_stats as shown in Listing 12-2.

Listing 12-2. Querying the index to get its physical layout

```
SELECT ddips.avg_fragmentation_in_percent,
       ddips.fragment_count,
       ddips.page_count,
       ddips.avg_page_space_used_in_percent,
       ddips.record_count,
       ddips.avg_record_size_in_bytes
FROM sys.dm_db_index_physical_stats(DB_ID('AdventureWorks'), OBJECT_
ID(N'dbo.SplitTest'), NULL, NULL, 'Sampled') AS ddips;
```

The results of this query are here in Figure 12-4.

avg_fragmentation_in_percent	fragment_count	page_count	avg_page_space_used_in_percent	record_count	avg_record_size_in_bytes
0	1	1	100	8	1010

Figure 12-4. *Physical attributes of the index iClustered*

CHAPTER 12 DEALING WITH INDEX FRAGMENTATION

Our estimations have been born out. There is a single page in the page_count column. Our fragmentation is shown in avg_fragmentation_in_percent, and it's zero. We've used 100% of the space as shown in avg_page_space_used_in_percent. That last piece of information is the most interesting. Let's now run Listing 12-3.

Listing 12-3. Updating a column in one row

```
UPDATE dbo.SplitTest
SET C3 = 'Add data'
WHERE C1 = 200;
```

We're going to see changes in sys.dm_db_index_physical_stats, visible in Figure 12-5.

	avg_fragmentation_in_percent	fragment_count	page_count	avg_page_space_used_in_percent	record_count	avg_record_size_in_bytes
1	50	2	2	50.0741289844329	8	1011.75

Figure 12-5. *Fragmentation in the index iClustered*

We now have two pages. Each page has approximately half of the rows (if there were an odd number of rows, one would have slightly more). You can see that all the other values, except for the record_count, have been updated.

Page Split by an INSERT Statement

To see the page split from an INSERT in action, I'm going to recreate the SplitTest table from Listing 12-1. We know that the page that defines the table is completely full. Listing 12-4 adds a row to the middle of the page.

Listing 12-4. Adding a row to SplitTest

```
INSERT INTO dbo.SplitTest
VALUES
(110, 'C2', '');
```

Querying sys.dm_db_index_physical_stats again, we see the results of the split in Figure 12-6.

	avg_fragmentation_in_percent	fragment_count	page_count	avg_page_space_used_in_percent	record_count	avg_record_size_in_bytes
1	50	2	2	56.2391895231035	9	1010

Figure 12-6. *Fragmentation from an INSERT in iClustered*

CHAPTER 12 DEALING WITH INDEX FRAGMENTATION

Once more, approximately half of the rows were moved, and we get a new distribution of the data about the index. There is now space in the rows, and new inserts won't immediately cause a page split again. This is the advantage of free space in an index.

What would happen if you added a row to the trailing edge of the index, for example, with a value of 501? You will get a new page, but you won't get a page split. New data will be accommodated on a newly allocated page.

How Fragmentation Occurs in Columnstore Indexes

Columnstore indexes can be fragmented, after a manner, as well. If we assume that the columnstore index has at least 102,400 rows when it's first loaded, the data is stored in the compressed column segments that make up a columnstore index as we talked about in Chapter 9. If it's fewer than 102,400 rows, the data just gets stored in the deltastore, a standard B-Tree index. Once the data is stored in compressed column segments, it's not fragmented in any way. In order to avoid fragmentation, the changes to the data are stored in the deltastore. Changes to the data, whether updates or deletes, are stored as logical changes. By logical changes, I mean that a delete doesn't actually delete a given value, but instead the data is marked as deleted, but it is not removed. Updates are also marked as deleted, and the updated value from the deltastore is used in its place. All this means that a columnstore doesn't suffer from page splits and empty space but instead has to deal with all the logically modified data. These logical deletes represent the fragmentation of the columnstore indexes.

To see this fragmentation in action, I'm going to use the MakeBigAdventure scripts and tables that I used in Chapter 9. Using Listing 12-5, I'm going to modify one of the tables in order to make it into a clustered columnstore index. I'll also make sure I've cleaned up previous testing in Listing 12-5.

Listing 12-5. Creating a clustered columnstore index

```
ALTER TABLE dbo.bigTransactionHistory
DROP CONSTRAINT pk_bigTransactionHistory;

DROP INDEX IF EXISTS ix_csTest ON dbo.bigTransactionHistory;

CREATE CLUSTERED COLUMNSTORE INDEX cci_bigTransactionHistory
ON dbo.bigTransactionHistory;
```

CHAPTER 12 ■ DEALING WITH INDEX FRAGMENTATION

To see the fragmentation within columnstore, we're going to look at a system view, sys.column_store_row_groups, as shown in Listing 12-6.

Listing 12-6. Querying sys.column_store_row_groups

```
SELECT OBJECT_NAME(i.OBJECT_ID) AS TableName,
       i.NAME AS IndexName,
       csrg.row_group_id,
       csrg.state_description,
       csrg.total_rows,
       csrg.deleted_rows,
       100 * (total_rows - ISNULL(deleted_rows, 0)) / total_rows AS
       PercentFull
FROM sys.indexes AS i
    JOIN sys.column_store_row_groups AS csrg
        ON i.OBJECT_ID = csrg.OBJECT_ID
           AND i.index_id = csrg.index_id
WHERE NAME = 'cci_bigTransactionHistory'
ORDER BY OBJECT_NAME(i.OBJECT_ID),
         i.NAME,
         row_group_id;
```

Because we've just created the columnstore index and it contains more than 102,400 rows, we won't have any issues. The percentage full of all the groups, with the possible exception of the last one, will be 100%. So let's delete some rows (Listing 12-7).

Listing 12-7. Deleting rows in bigTransactionHistory

```
DELETE dbo.bigTransactionHistory
WHERE Quantity = 13;
```

Now when we run the query from Listing 12-6, you can see the logical fragmentation of a columnstore index in Figure 12-7.

	TableName	IndexName	row_group_id	state_description	total_rows	deleted_rows	PercentFull
1	bigTransactionHistory	cci_bigTransactionHistory	0	COMPRESSED	1048576	10491	98
2	bigTransactionHistory	cci_bigTransactionHistory	1	COMPRESSED	1048576	10579	98
3	bigTransactionHistory	cci_bigTransactionHistory	2	COMPRESSED	1048576	10550	98
4	bigTransactionHistory	cci_bigTransactionHistory	3	COMPRESSED	1048576	10268	99
5	bigTransactionHistory	cci_bigTransactionHistory	4	COMPRESSED	1048576	10437	99
6	bigTransactionHistory	cci_bigTransactionHistory	5	COMPRESSED	1048576	10428	99
7	bigTransactionHistory	cci_bigTransactionHistory	6	COMPRESSED	1048576	10597	98
8	bigTransactionHistory	cci_bigTransactionHistory	7	COMPRESSED	1048576	10637	98
9	bigTransactionHistory	cci_bigTransactionHistory	8	COMPRESSED	1048576	10506	98
10	bigTransactionHistory	cci_bigTransactionHistory	9	COMPRESSED	1048576	10802	98
11	bigTransactionHistory	cci_bigTransactionHistory	10	COMPRESSED	1048576	10453	99
12	bigTransactionHistory	cci_bigTransactionHistory	11	COMPRESSED	1048576	10578	98
13	bigTransactionHistory	cci_bigTransactionHistory	12	COMPRESSED	1048576	10642	98
14	bigTransactionHistory	cci_bigTransactionHistory	13	COMPRESSED	1048576	10351	99
15	bigTransactionHistory	cci_bigTransactionHistory	14	COMPRESSED	1048576	10508	98
16	bigTransactionHistory	cci_bigTransactionHistory	15	COMPRESSED	1048576	10539	98
17	bigTransactionHistory	cci_bigTransactionHistory	16	COMPRESSED	1048576	10579	98
18	bigTransactionHistory	cci_bigTransactionHistory	17	COMPRESSED	1048576	10638	98
19	bigTransactionHistory	cci_bigTransactionHistory	18	COMPRESSED	1048576	10458	99
20	bigTransactionHistory	cci_bigTransactionHistory	19	COMPRESSED	1048576	10640	98
21	bigTransactionHistory	cci_bigTransactionHistory	20	COMPRESSED	1048576	10560	98
22	bigTransactionHistory	cci_bigTransactionHistory	21	COMPRESSED	1048576	10499	98
23	bigTransactionHistory	cci_bigTransactionHistory	22	COMPRESSED	1048576	10499	98
24	bigTransactionHistory	cci_bigTransactionHistory	23	COMPRESSED	1048576	10387	99
25	bigTransactionHistory	cci_bigTransactionHistory	24	COMPRESSED	446032	4526	98

Figure 12-7. Fragmentation within a clustered columnstore index

The percentage full, the column PercentFull, is now less than 100 for every single group as that DELETE statement hit all of them. This is the kind of fragmentation you may see over time within a columnstore index.

Fragmentation Overhead

This is a somewhat tough discussion. Fragmentation does come with overhead for both rowstore and columnstore indexes. However, the fixes for fragmentation come with overhead as well. We'll discuss the fixes at length in the following section, resolving fragmentation. However, before we get there, we need to talk about whether or not you should worry about fragmentation at all.

While fragmentation does have some overhead, it also has some benefits. Once an index has been split, it can accommodate a number of new rows and expansion of existing rows before it splits again, enhancing performance of inserts and updates. Defragmentation hits you twice for performance. First, you pay a cost in resources, time, and potentially blocking while you run any of the fragmentation solutions. Second, you then begin to pay a cost in large amounts of page splits as your indexes take on new data or receive updates. A page split also causes blocking and additional resource use, especially I/O. Further, some of the more modern disk storage systems are so fast that the jumps between pages during a range scan are practically free.

Because of all this, the old, default stance that of course you're going to address fragmentation immediately has fallen into serious question. Instead, with monitoring and testing to validate the result, some are simply letting fragmentation occur and are seeing no major performance hit because of it. Others are carefully choosing their fill factor on the index, to keep a certain amount of free space on each page when the index is created–in short, sacrificing storage, and memory, to reduce the overhead caused by page splits and the defragmentation process.

Keep these opposing views in mind as we discuss the overhead of fragmentation. Also, plan on carefully measuring performance regardless of the path you choose.

Rowstore Overhead

Both internal and external fragmentation can adversely affect data retrieval performance.

External fragmentation means that index pages are no longer physically stored in order. While the logical order is maintained, the physical order could be all over the disk. This means a range scan on an index will have multiple context switches between extents, slowing down performance. Also, any range scans on the index will be unable to benefit from read-ahead operations.

You'll generally see superior performance when using sequential I/O, since this can read an entire extent (eight 8KB pages at once) in a single disk I/O operation. A noncontiguous layout of pages results in nonsequential I/O, which means only a single 8KB page can be read at a time.

However, single-row retrieval, or very limited range scans, can perform just fine, despite the fragmentation of an index. If a single page is all that is required to retrieve the necessary data, then the fragmentation doesn't hurt performance at all.

Internal fragmentation is when the rows are distributed sparsely within a page, increasing the number of pages that must be accessed in order to retrieve the necessary rows. However, internal fragmentation also has benefits since updates and inserts can take advantage of the free space on the index.

CHAPTER 12 DEALING WITH INDEX FRAGMENTATION

To see fragmentation in action, and the costs it has on a query, I'm going to create a clustered index and then induce fragmentation within it. Listing 12-8 shows how.

Listing 12-8. Fragmenting a clustered index

```
DROP TABLE IF EXISTS dbo.FragTest;
GO
CREATE TABLE dbo.FragTest
(
    C1 INT,
    C2 INT,
    C3 INT,
    c4 CHAR(2000)
);
CREATE CLUSTERED INDEX iClustered ON dbo.FragTest (C1);
WITH Nums
AS (SELECT TOP (10000)
           ROW_NUMBER() OVER (ORDER BY (SELECT 1)) AS n
    FROM MASTER.sys.all_columns AS ac1
        CROSS JOIN MASTER.sys.all_columns AS ac2)
INSERT INTO dbo.FragTest
(
    C1,
    C2,
    C3,
    c4
)
SELECT n,
       n,
       n,
       'a'
FROM Nums;
WITH Nums
AS (SELECT 1 AS n
    UNION ALL
    SELECT n + 1
```

CHAPTER 12 DEALING WITH INDEX FRAGMENTATION

```
    FROM Nums
    WHERE n < 10000)
INSERT INTO dbo.FragTest
(
    C1,
    C2,
    C3,
    c4
)
SELECT 10000 - n,
       n,
       n,
       'a'
FROM Nums
OPTION (MAXRECURSION 10000);
```

We're now going to run two queries. One will retrieve a larger result set and the other a smaller one (Listing 12-9).

Listing 12-9. Querying the FragTest table

```
--Reads 6 rows
SELECT ft.C1,
       ft.C2,
       ft.C3,
       ft.c4
FROM dbo.FragTest AS ft
WHERE C1
BETWEEN 21 AND 23;
--Reads all rows
SELECT ft.C1,
       ft.C2,
       ft.C3,
       ft.c4
FROM dbo.FragTest AS ft
WHERE C1
BETWEEN 1 AND 10000;
```

The performance is as follows:

```
6 rows
Reads: 8
Duration: 886mcs
All rows
Reads: 10,034
Duration: 461ms
```

I can eliminate the fragmentation using Listing 12-10.

Listing 12-10. Removing fragmentation in iClustered

```
ALTER INDEX iClustered ON dbo.FragTest REBUILD;
```

Now, since the index has been completely rebuilt from scratch, all fragmentation is removed. This results in the following performance metrics:

```
6 rows
Reads: 6
Duration: 401mcs
All rows
Reads: 6,695
Duration: 303ms
```

Both queries ran faster, but the obvious and real jump was in the second query that went from 461ms to 303ms, slightly more than 25% increase. This coincides with the reduction in reads from just over 10k to almost 7k.

So it really matters what kind of queries you're running predominantly. Smaller queries are unlikely to benefit from defragmenting indexes, while large scans will receive some benefit.

Columnstore Overhead

While what we call fragmentation within the columnstore index is not an artifact of page splits, it still has some negative impact on performance. Deleted and updated values are stored in a B-Tree index associated with the row group. Data retrieval has to go through an internal, additional, join against that index. This added join is not visible in an execution plan. It is visible in the performance metrics, though.

To see this in action, we'll be testing with the query in Listing 12-11.

Listing 12-11. Querying bigTransactionHistory

```
SELECT bth.Quantity,
       AVG(bth.ActualCost)
FROM dbo.bigTransactionHistory AS bth
WHERE bth.Quantity
BETWEEN 8 AND 15
GROUP BY bth.Quantity;
```

The performance metrics on this query are as follows:

Reads: 154,494
Duration: 104ms

I'm now going to remove information from the table using Listing 12-12.

Listing 12-12. Deleting data from bigTransactionHistory

```
DELETE dbo.bigTransactionHistory
WHERE Quantity
BETWEEN 9 AND 12;
```

Testing the query in Listing 12-11 again, we get the following metrics:

Reads: 154,238
Duration: 212ms

I was even surprised at that change in performance. The reads stayed nearly identical, but the duration doubled as it dealt with the fragmented data. As you can see, while the root cause of the fragmentation is different, the negative impact on performance is real.

Analyzing the Amount of Fragmentation

We've already introduced the mechanisms to look at the level of fragmentation inside the rowstore and columnstore indexes: sys.dm_db_index_physical_stats and sys.column_store_row_groups, respectively. While sys.dm_db_index_physical_stats is used for clustered and nonclustered indexes, it's also used for heap tables in the same way.

CHAPTER 12 DEALING WITH INDEX FRAGMENTATION

The output of sys.dm_db_index_physical_stats shows information on the pages and extents of an index (or a heap). A row is returned for each level of the B-Tree in the index. A single row for each allocation unit in a heap is returned.

SQL Server stores the data on 8KB pages. These pages are arranged into eight contiguous pages called an extent. Tables that contain less than the 64KB of data necessary to occupy an extent will share an extent with another table. This is referred to as mixed extents, and it helps SQL Server save space. You can't defragment mixed extents.

As a table or index grows and requests more than eight pages, SQL Server creates an extent dedicated to the table/index. This type of extent is called a uniform extent. Uniform extents help SQL Server lay out the pages of the table/index contiguously, enhancing performance. While information within an extent can still be fragmented, you're still going to see efficiencies from storing the pages of an extent together.

The dynamic management function `sys.dm_db_index_physical_stats` scans the pages of an index to return the data. You can control the level of the scan, which affects the speed and the accuracy of the scan. To quickly check the fragmentation of an index, use the Limited option. You can obtain increased accuracy with only a moderate decrease in speed by using the Sample option, as in the previous example, which scans 1% of the pages. For the most accuracy, use the Detailed scan, which hits all the pages in an index. Just understand that the Detailed scan can have a major performance impact depending on the size of the table and index in question. If the index has fewer than 10,000 pages and you select the Sample mode, then the Detailed mode is used instead. This means that despite the choice made in the earlier query, the Detailed scan mode was used. The default mode is Limited.

By defining the different parameters, you can get fragmentation information on different sets of data. By removing the `OBJECTID` function in the earlier query and supplying a `NULL` value, the query would return information on all indexes within the database. Don't get surprised by this and accidentally run a Detailed scan on all indexes. You can also specify the index you want information on or even the partition with a partitioned index.

The output from `sys.dm_db_index_physical_stats` includes 24 different columns. I selected the basic set of columns used to determine the fragmentation and size of an index. This output represents the following:

- `avg_fragmentation_in_percent`: This number represents the logical average fragmentation for indexes and heaps as a percentage. If the table is a heap and the mode is Sampled, then this value will be NULL. If average fragmentation is less than 10–20% and the table isn't massive, fragmentation is unlikely to be an issue. If the index is between 20% and 40%, fragmentation might be an issue, although it might not be. Remember, removing fragmentation removes free space. It's entirely possible that 20–40% free space is a nice operating margin. Large-scale fragmentation, usually greater than 40%, may require an index rebuild. Your system may have different requirements than these general numbers. They are meant as guidelines, not hard values.

- `fragment_count`: This number represents the number of fragments, or separated groups of pages, that make up the index. It's a useful number to understand how the index is distributed, especially when compared to the `page_count` value. `fragment_count` is NULL when the sampling mode is Sampled. A large fragment count is an additional indication of storage fragmentation.

- `page_count`: This number is a literal count of the number of index or data pages that make up the statistic. This number is a measure of size but can also help indicate fragmentation. If you know the size of the data or index, you can calculate how many rows can fit on a page. If you then correlate this to the number of rows in the table, you should get a number close to the `page_count` value. If the `page_count` value is considerably higher, you may be looking at a fragmentation issue. Refer to the `avg_fragmentation_in_percent` value for a precise measure.

- `avg_page_space_used_in_percent`: To get an idea of the amount of space allocated within the pages of the index, use this number. This value is NULL when the sampling mode is Limited.

- `record_count`: Simply put, this is the number of records represented by the statistics. For indexes, this is the number of records within the current level of the B-Tree as represented from the scanning mode.

(Detailed scans will show all levels of the B-Tree, not simply the leaf level.) For heaps, this number represents the records present, but this number may not correlate precisely to the number of rows in the table since a heap may have two records after an update and a page split.

- avg_record_size_in_bytes: This number simply represents a useful measure for the amount of data stored within the index or heap record.

Running sys.dm_db_index_physical_stats with a Detailed scan will return multiple rows for a given index. That is, multiple rows are displayed if that index spans more than one level. Multiple levels exist in an index when that index spans more than a single page. To see what this looks like and to observe some of the other columns of data present in the dynamic management function, run the query in Listing 12-13.

Listing 12-13. Retrieving the complete, detailed scan of the index

```
--Intentionally using SELECT *
SELECT ddips.*
FROM sys.dm_db_index_physical_stats(DB_ID('AdventureWorks'), OBJECT_ID(N'dbo.FragTest'), NULL, NULL, 'Detailed') AS ddips;
```

There are only three rows, but with 24 columns, I've had to break apart the columns into what you see in Figure 12-8.

database_id	object_id	index_id	partition_number	index_type_desc	alloc_unit_type_desc
5	404196490	1	1	CLUSTERED INDEX	IN_ROW_DATA
5	404196490	1	1	CLUSTERED INDEX	IN_ROW_DATA
5	404196490	1	1	CLUSTERED INDEX	IN_ROW_DATA

index_depth	index_level	avg_fragmentation_in_percent	fragment_count	avg_fragment_size_in_pages	page_count
3	0	0.28472950696838	305	21.8786885245902	6673
3	1	95	20	1	20
3	2	0	1	1	1

avg_page_space_used_in_percent	record_count	ghost_record_count	version_ghost_record_count	min_record_size_in_bytes	max_record_size_in_bytes
74.959649122807	20000	0	0	2019	2027
82.4017790956264	6673	0	0	14	22
3.9288361749444	20	0	0	14	14

avg_record_size_in_bytes	forwarded_record_count	compressed_page_count	hobt_id	columnstore_delete_buffer_state
2022.999	NULL	0	72057594071547904	0
17.995	NULL	0	72057594071547904	0
14	NULL	0	72057594071547904	0

columnstore_delete_buffer_state_desc	version_record_count	inrow_version_record_count	inrow_diff_version_record_count
NOT VALID	0	0	0
NOT VALID	0	0	0
NOT VALID	0	0	0

total_inrow_version_payload_size_in_bytes	offrow_regular_version_record_count	offrow_long_term_version_record_count
0	0	0
0	0	0
0	0	0

Figure 12-8. Complete results from sys.dm_db_index_physical_stats

We have three rows in Figure 12-8 because it represents the three levels of the current B-Tree index. There is a ton of extra data, including information on columnstore indexes. Yes, you can query here for columnstore as well. In fact, more detail for columnstore indexes is now provided in dm_db_index_physical_stats in SQL Server 2025. However, for older versions of SQL Server, and mostly for SQL Server 2025, you'll get more actionable information from the system view I provided earlier. Further, one new DMV is provided for columnstore index evaluation, dm_db_column_store_row_group_physical_stats. This shows more detailed compression and fragmentation across the columnstore row groups. Most of the rest of this information isn't necessary for your average look to see how fragmented an index is. Instead, a lot of this is used for additional, detailed, examination of the physical layout of the index.

Analyzing the Fragmentation of a Small Table

A small table or index with fewer than eight pages will be stored on mixed extents. That extent may have other indexes or tables within it. The output from sys.dm_db_index_physical_stats can be misleading. You're likely to see fragmentation in a small index or table, but since it is a small table, you don't need to worry about defragmenting it. In fact, while you can run an index rebuild on a small table, you may not see fragmentation get relieved in any way. For this reason, if you are dealing with a table or index below eight pages, don't even try to defragment it.

Fragmentation Resolutions

The key to resolving fragmentation is to rearrange the pages of the index so that their physical order and their logical order are the same. On the columnstore index, you're invoking the Tuple Mover, which will close the deltastore tables and put them into compressed segments. In addition, for a columnstore index, you may be forcing a reorganization of the data to get better compression. All this is achieved in one of four ways:

- Drop and recreate the index.
- Recreate the index with the DROP_EXISTING clause.
- Execute the ALTER INDEX REBUILD command.
- Execute the ALTER INDEX REORGANIZE command.

Drop and Recreate the Index

Dropping the index and creating it again guarantees that the index will be rebuilt with the logical and the physical order matching. This approach has major shortcomings:

- Blocking: Recreating the index puts a high amount of overhead on the system, and it will cause blocking. Dropping and recreating the index blocks all other requests on the table (or on any other index on the table). It can also be blocked by other requests against the table.

- Missing Index: With the index dropped, and possibly being blocked, waiting to be recreated, queries against the table will not have that index available for use. You'll also get a recompile of any query that was using the index.

- Nonclustered Index: If the index being dropped is a clustered index, then all the nonclustered indexes on the table will have to be rebuilt after the clustered index is dropped. They then have to be rebuilt again after the clustered index is recreated. This leads to further blocking and other problems such as statement recompiles.

- Unique Constraints: Indexes that are used to define a primary key or a unique constraint cannot be removed using the DROP INDEX statement. Also, both unique constraints and primary keys can be referred to by foreign key constraints. Prior to dropping the primary key, all foreign keys that reference the primary key would have to be removed first.

For all these reasons, dropping and recreating the index is a poor choice unless you can do it during scheduled down times.

Recreating the Index with the DROP_EXISTING Clause

You can avoid the overhead of recreating the nonclustered indexes while rebuilding a clustered index if you use the DROP_EXISTING clause. This recreates the clustered index in a single atomic step. Listing 12-14 shows the syntax in action.

Listing 12-14. Recreating the Person.EmailAddress primary key

```
CREATE UNIQUE CLUSTERED INDEX PK_EmailAddress_BusinessEntityID_
EmailAddressID
ON Person.EmailAddress (
                        BusinessEntityID,
                        EmailAddressID
                      )
WITH (DROP_EXISTING = ON);
```

You can use the DROP_EXISTING clause for both clustered and nonclustered indexes. You can even use it to convert a nonclustered index to a clustered index. You can't do the reverse though and change a clustered index into a nonclustered index through DROP_EXISTING.

The drawbacks to this approach of dealing with fragmentation are severe:

- Blocking: Most of the very same blocking problems discussed in the "Drop and Recreate the Index" section apply here.

- Index with Constraints: Unlike the first method, the CREATE INDEX statement with the DROP_EXISTING clause can be used to recreate indexes with constraints. If the constraint is a primary key or the unique constraint is associated with a foreign key, then failing to include the UNIQUE keyword in the CREATE statement will result in an error.

Execute the ALTER INDEX REBUILD Command

ALTER INDEX REBUILD rebuilds an index in one atomic step, just like CREATING INDEX with the DROP_EXISTING clause. Using the ALTER INDEX REBUILD command makes SQL Server allocate new pages and extents as it populates them with the data ordered logically and physically. However, unlike CREATE INDEX with the DROP_EXISTING clause, it allows the index to be rebuilt without forcing you to drop and recreate the constraints.

SQL Server 2025 changes the REBUILD command for columnstore indexes. Prior to 2025, a REBUILD command on a columnstore would take the index completely offline. It will invoke the Tuple Mover to remove the deltastore, and it will rearrange the data to ensure effective compression. Now, you can do the ONLINE REBUILD, which gets you a more effective rearrangement of the columnstore index without taking it offline.

With rowstore indexes, the preferred mechanism is ALTER INDEX REBUILD. For columnstore indexes, however, after testing to see if the new online index rebuild works for you, the preferred mechanism may be ALTER INDEX REORGANIZE, covered in the next section.

Rebuilding an index will also compact any large object (LOB) pages associated with the table. You can choose not to do this by setting LOB_COMPACTION = OFF. You'll need to experiment with this to determine if it's needed in your system.

When you use the PAD_INDEX setting while creating an index, it determines how much free space to leave on the index intermediate pages, which can help you deal with page splits. This is taken into account during an index rebuild. New pages will be set back to the original values you determined at the time of index creation.

If you don't specify otherwise, the default behavior is to defragment all indexes across all partitions. If you want to control the process, you just need to specify which partition you want to rebuild.

You can also use ALTER INDEX REBUILD to rebuild all indexes on a given table in a single command like Listing 12-15.

Listing 12-15. Rebuilding all indexes on a table

```
ALTER INDEX ALL ON dbo.FragTest REBUILD;
```

While this is the preferred mechanism to deal with fragmentation in rowstore indexes (and you can use it for columnstore indexes if you choose), it does come with some overhead:

- Blocking: Just like the other two techniques discussed, ALTER INDEX REBUILD introduces blocking to the system. It blocks all other queries trying to access the table (or any index on the table). It can also be blocked by other queries.

- Transaction Rollback: Since ALTER INDEX REBUILD is fully atomic in action, if it is stopped before completion, then all the defragmentation actions performed up to that point in time are lost.

You can run ALTER INDEX REBUILD using the ONLINE keyword, which will reduce the locking mechanisms but will increase the time involved in rebuilding the index.

Execute the ALTER INDEX REORGANIZE Command

For a rowstore index, ALTER INDEX REORGANIZE reduces the fragmentation of an index by rearranging the existing leaf pages to better match the logical order of the index. It compacts the rows within the pages, reducing internal fragmentation, and discards the resultant empty pages. When dealing with rowstore fragmentation, the REORGANIZE technique, while having the least overhead of all the techniques discussed, is also the most ineffectual. The amount of resources used to REORGANIZE an index is not as high as rebuilding it, but it is still a very expensive operation, especially when you consider the meager results. I do not recommend using this command on your rowstore indexes.

For a columnstore index, ALTER INDEX REORGANIZE will ensure that the deltastore within the columnstore index gets cleaned out and that all the logical deletes are taken care of as actual, physical, deletes. It performs these actions while keeping the index online and accessible. You can also choose to force compression of all the row groups. This function is very similar to running ALTER INDEX REBUILD, but it keeps the index online and accessible during the process. This is why I recommend using ALTER INDEX REORGANIZE for columnstore indexes. However, with the introduction of ONLINE REBUILD for columnstore indexes in 2025, I would test that on your systems to see which gives you the best results.

CHAPTER 12 DEALING WITH INDEX FRAGMENTATION

Another issue with rowstore indexes is that the REORGANIZE command uses a nonatomic method to clean up the index. As it processes the data, it requests a small number of locks for as short a period as possible. If it attempts to access a page that is locked, the process skips that page and never returns to it. While this makes REORGANIZE have a much lower overhead, it's also part of what makes it so ineffectual.

If I recreate the fragmented table from Listing 12-8, it has the level of fragmentation shown in Figure 12-9.

	avg_fragmentation_in_percent	fragment_count	page_count	avg_page_space_used_in_percent	record_count	avg_record_size_in_bytes
1	74.7574757475748	7568	9999	50.017358537188	20000	2022.999

Figure 12-9. *Fragmentation of the dbo.FragTest table*

I'm using Listing 12-16 to run the REORGANIZE command.

Listing 12-16. Using REORGANIZE on dbo.FragTest

```
ALTER INDEX iClustered ON dbo.FragTest REORGANIZE;
```

The results are shown in Figure 12-10.

	avg_fragmentation_in_percent	fragment_count	page_count	avg_page_space_used_in_percent	record_count	avg_record_size_in_bytes
1	0.239377618192699	101	6684	74.836236718557	20000	2022.999

Figure 12-10. *dbo.FragTest after running REORGANIZE*

The fragmentation was reduced quite a lot, but you'll notice that there is still some fragmentation. This would be worse if there were other queries running against the table at the same time.

If the index is highly fragmented, as this one was, ALTER INDEX REORGANIZE can take a lot longer than rebuilding the index. If an index spans multiple files, ALTER INDEX REORGANIZE doesn't migrate pages between the files.

To see REORGANIZE in action against a columnstore index, we'll need to remove some more data. This is because REORGANIZE will only clean up deleted data when more than 10% of the data in a rowgroup has been deleted. I'm going to run Listing 12-17 to take out more data from the table.

387

CHAPTER 12 DEALING WITH INDEX FRAGMENTATION

Listing 12-17. Deleting data in dbo.bigTransactionHistory

```
DELETE dbo.bigTransactionHistory
WHERE Quantity
BETWEEN 8 AND 17;
```

We can use the new DMV to query for fragmentation similar to how we used the system views before as shown in Listing 12-18.

Listing 12-18. Querying fragmentation from sys.dm_db_column_store_row_group_physical_stats

```
SELECT OBJECT_NAME(ddcsrgps.object_id) AS TableName,
       i.name IndexName,
       100 * (ddcsrgps.total_rows - ISNULL(ddcsrgps.deleted_rows, 0)) /
       total_rows AS PercentFull,
       ddcsrgps.row_group_id,
       ddcsrgps.state_desc
FROM sys.dm_db_column_store_row_group_physical_stats AS ddcsrgps
    JOIN sys.indexes AS i
        ON i.object_id = ddcsrgps.object_id
           AND i.index_id = ddcsrgps.index_id;
ORDER BY ddcsrgps.row_group_id ASC
```

The results are shown in Figure 12-11.

CHAPTER 12 DEALING WITH INDEX FRAGMENTATION

	TableName	IndexName	PercentFull	row_group_id	state_desc
1	bigTransactionHistory	cci_bigTransactionHistory	89	0	COMPRESSED
2	bigTransactionHistory	cci_bigTransactionHistory	89	1	COMPRESSED
3	bigTransactionHistory	cci_bigTransactionHistory	89	2	COMPRESSED
4	bigTransactionHistory	cci_bigTransactionHistory	90	3	COMPRESSED
5	bigTransactionHistory	cci_bigTransactionHistory	90	4	COMPRESSED
6	bigTransactionHistory	cci_bigTransactionHistory	90	5	COMPRESSED
7	bigTransactionHistory	cci_bigTransactionHistory	89	6	COMPRESSED
8	bigTransactionHistory	cci_bigTransactionHistory	89	7	COMPRESSED
9	bigTransactionHistory	cci_bigTransactionHistory	89	8	COMPRESSED
10	bigTransactionHistory	cci_bigTransactionHistory	89	9	COMPRESSED
11	bigTransactionHistory	cci_bigTransactionHistory	90	10	COMPRESSED
12	bigTransactionHistory	cci_bigTransactionHistory	89	11	COMPRESSED
13	bigTransactionHistory	cci_bigTransactionHistory	90	12	COMPRESSED
14	bigTransactionHistory	cci_bigTransactionHistory	90	13	COMPRESSED
15	bigTransactionHistory	cci_bigTransactionHistory	89	14	COMPRESSED
16	bigTransactionHistory	cci_bigTransactionHistory	89	15	COMPRESSED
17	bigTransactionHistory	cci_bigTransactionHistory	89	16	COMPRESSED
18	bigTransactionHistory	cci_bigTransactionHistory	89	17	COMPRESSED
19	bigTransactionHistory	cci_bigTransactionHistory	90	18	COMPRESSED
20	bigTransactionHistory	cci_bigTransactionHistory	90	19	COMPRESSED
21	bigTransactionHistory	cci_bigTransactionHistory	90	20	COMPRESSED
22	bigTransactionHistory	cci_bigTransactionHistory	90	21	COMPRESSED
23	bigTransactionHistory	cci_bigTransactionHistory	89	22	COMPRESSED
24	bigTransactionHistory	cci_bigTransactionHistory	90	23	COMPRESSED
25	bigTransactionHistory	cci_bigTransactionHistory	89	24	COMPRESSED
26	bigTransactionHistory	cci_bigTransactionHistory	89	38	COMPRESSED
27	bigTransactionHistory	cci_bigTransactionHistory	90	39	COMPRESSED
28	bigTransactionHistory	cci_bigTransactionHistory	90	40	COMPRESSED
29	bigTransactionHistory	cci_bigTransactionHistory	89	42	COMPRESSED
30	bigTransactionHistory	cci_bigTransactionHistory	89	44	COMPRESSED
31	bigTransactionHistory	cci_bigTransactionHistory	89	45	COMPRESSED
32	bigTransactionHistory	cci_bigTransactionHistory	90	48	COMPRESSED

Figure 12-11. Several rowgroups are missing 10%

Now we can run the REORGANIZE command in Listing 12-19.

Listing 12-19. Reorganizing the columnstore index dbo.bigTransactionHistory

```
ALTER INDEX cci_bigTransactionHistory ON dbo.bigTransactionHistory
REORGANIZE;
```

The results are shown in Figure 12-12.

CHAPTER 12 ■ DEALING WITH INDEX FRAGMENTATION

	TableName	IndexName	PercentFull	row_group_id	state_desc
1	bigTransactionHistory	cci_bigTransactionHistory	89	0	TOMBSTONE
2	bigTransactionHistory	cci_bigTransactionHistory	89	1	TOMBSTONE
3	bigTransactionHistory	cci_bigTransactionHistory	89	2	TOMBSTONE
4	bigTransactionHistory	cci_bigTransactionHistory	90	3	COMPRESSED
5	bigTransactionHistory	cci_bigTransactionHistory	90	4	COMPRESSED
6	bigTransactionHistory	cci_bigTransactionHistory	90	5	COMPRESSED
7	bigTransactionHistory	cci_bigTransactionHistory	89	6	TOMBSTONE
8	bigTransactionHistory	cci_bigTransactionHistory	89	7	TOMBSTONE
9	bigTransactionHistory	cci_bigTransactionHistory	89	8	TOMBSTONE
10	bigTransactionHistory	cci_bigTransactionHistory	89	9	TOMBSTONE
11	bigTransactionHistory	cci_bigTransactionHistory	90	10	COMPRESSED
12	bigTransactionHistory	cci_bigTransactionHistory	89	11	TOMBSTONE
13	bigTransactionHistory	cci_bigTransactionHistory	90	12	COMPRESSED
14	bigTransactionHistory	cci_bigTransactionHistory	90	13	COMPRESSED
15	bigTransactionHistory	cci_bigTransactionHistory	89	14	TOMBSTONE
16	bigTransactionHistory	cci_bigTransactionHistory	89	15	TOMBSTONE
17	bigTransactionHistory	cci_bigTransactionHistory	89	16	TOMBSTONE
18	bigTransactionHistory	cci_bigTransactionHistory	89	17	TOMBSTONE
19	bigTransactionHistory	cci_bigTransactionHistory	90	18	COMPRESSED
20	bigTransactionHistory	cci_bigTransactionHistory	90	19	COMPRESSED
21	bigTransactionHistory	cci_bigTransactionHistory	90	20	COMPRESSED
22	bigTransactionHistory	cci_bigTransactionHistory	90	21	COMPRESSED
23	bigTransactionHistory	cci_bigTransactionHistory	89	22	TOMBSTONE
24	bigTransactionHistory	cci_bigTransactionHistory	90	23	COMPRESSED
25	bigTransactionHistory	cci_bigTransactionHistory	89	24	TOMBSTONE
26	bigTransactionHistory	cci_bigTransactionHistory	89	38	TOMBSTONE
27	bigTransactionHistory	cci_bigTransactionHistory	90	39	TOMBSTONE
28	bigTransactionHistory	cci_bigTransactionHistory	90	40	COMPRESSED
29	bigTransactionHistory	cci_bigTransactionHistory	89	42	TOMBSTONE
30	bigTransactionHistory	cci_bigTransactionHistory	89	44	TOMBSTONE
31	bigTransactionHistory	cci_bigTransactionHistory	89	45	TOMBSTONE
32	bigTransactionHistory	cci_bigTransactionHistory	90	48	TOMBSTONE
33	bigTransactionHistory	cci_bigTransactionHistory	100	49	COMPRESSED
34	bigTransactionHistory	cci_bigTransactionHistory	100	50	COMPRESSED
35	bigTransactionHistory	cci_bigTransactionHistory	100	51	COMPRESSED
36	bigTransactionHistory	cci_bigTransactionHistory	100	52	COMPRESSED
37	bigTransactionHistory	cci_bigTransactionHistory	100	53	COMPRESSED
38	bigTransactionHistory	cci_bigTransactionHistory	100	54	COMPRESSED
39	bigTransactionHistory	cci_bigTransactionHistory	100	55	COMPRESSED
40	bigTransactionHistory	cci_bigTransactionHistory	100	56	COMPRESSED
41	bigTransactionHistory	cci_bigTransactionHistory	100	57	COMPRESSED
42	bigTransactionHistory	cci_bigTransactionHistory	100	58	COMPRESSED
43	bigTransactionHistory	cci_bigTransactionHistory	100	59	COMPRESSED
44	bigTransactionHistory	cci_bigTransactionHistory	100	60	COMPRESSED
45	bigTransactionHistory	cci_bigTransactionHistory	100	61	COMPRESSED
46	bigTransactionHistory	cci_bigTransactionHistory	100	62	COMPRESSED
47	bigTransactionHistory	cci_bigTransactionHistory	100	63	COMPRESSED
48	bigTransactionHistory	cci_bigTransactionHistory	100	64	COMPRESSED
49	bigTransactionHistory	cci_bigTransactionHistory	100	65	COMPRESSED
50	bigTransactionHistory	cci_bigTransactionHistory	100	66	COMPRESSED

Figure 12-12. *Results of REORGANIZE on dbo.bigTransactionHistory*

CHAPTER 12 DEALING WITH INDEX FRAGMENTATION

There are quite a few things to note here. First, you'll see that a bunch of rowgroups have switched from COMPRESSED to TOMBSTONE. That's the result of the REORGANIZE command. You'll see that some rowgroups are now COMPRESSED and at 100%, while a number of rowgroups that were at 89% deleted are now marked TOMBSTONE. That means that the data has been moved from them, and at some point in the future, those rowgroups will get removed from the index entirely.

Remember, this index is online and accessible during this operation, so the fact we didn't get all the defragmentation possible is OK. You can still use ALTER INDEX REBUILD with a columnstore index if you choose. The ONLINE option means it will radically reduce blocking while arriving at a more complete rebuilt index.

We can get more defragmentation if we add row compression in Listing 12-20.

Listing 12-20. REORGANIZE using row compression

```
ALTER INDEX cci_bigTransactionHistory
ON dbo.bigTransactionHistory
REORGANIZE
WITH (COMPRESS_ALL_ROW_GROUPS = ON);
```

The results are in Figure 12-13.

	TableName	IndexName	PercentFull	row_group_id	state_desc
1	bigTransactionHistory	cci_bigTransactionHistory	90	3	COMPRESSED
2	bigTransactionHistory	cci_bigTransactionHistory	90	4	COMPRESSED
3	bigTransactionHistory	cci_bigTransactionHistory	90	5	COMPRESSED
4	bigTransactionHistory	cci_bigTransactionHistory	90	10	COMPRESSED
5	bigTransactionHistory	cci_bigTransactionHistory	90	12	COMPRESSED
6	bigTransactionHistory	cci_bigTransactionHistory	90	13	COMPRESSED
7	bigTransactionHistory	cci_bigTransactionHistory	90	18	COMPRESSED
8	bigTransactionHistory	cci_bigTransactionHistory	90	19	COMPRESSED
9	bigTransactionHistory	cci_bigTransactionHistory	90	20	COMPRESSED
10	bigTransactionHistory	cci_bigTransactionHistory	90	21	COMPRESSED
11	bigTransactionHistory	cci_bigTransactionHistory	90	23	COMPRESSED
12	bigTransactionHistory	cci_bigTransactionHistory	90	40	COMPRESSED
13	bigTransactionHistory	cci_bigTransactionHistory	100	49	COMPRESSED
14	bigTransactionHistory	cci_bigTransactionHistory	100	50	COMPRESSED
15	bigTransactionHistory	cci_bigTransactionHistory	100	51	COMPRESSED
16	bigTransactionHistory	cci_bigTransactionHistory	100	52	COMPRESSED
17	bigTransactionHistory	cci_bigTransactionHistory	100	53	COMPRESSED
18	bigTransactionHistory	cci_bigTransactionHistory	100	54	COMPRESSED
19	bigTransactionHistory	cci_bigTransactionHistory	100	55	COMPRESSED
20	bigTransactionHistory	cci_bigTransactionHistory	100	56	COMPRESSED
21	bigTransactionHistory	cci_bigTransactionHistory	100	57	COMPRESSED
22	bigTransactionHistory	cci_bigTransactionHistory	100	58	COMPRESSED
23	bigTransactionHistory	cci_bigTransactionHistory	100	59	COMPRESSED
24	bigTransactionHistory	cci_bigTransactionHistory	100	60	COMPRESSED
25	bigTransactionHistory	cci_bigTransactionHistory	100	61	COMPRESSED
26	bigTransactionHistory	cci_bigTransactionHistory	100	62	COMPRESSED
27	bigTransactionHistory	cci_bigTransactionHistory	100	63	COMPRESSED
28	bigTransactionHistory	cci_bigTransactionHistory	100	64	COMPRESSED
29	bigTransactionHistory	cci_bigTransactionHistory	100	65	COMPRESSED
30	bigTransactionHistory	cci_bigTransactionHistory	100	66	COMPRESSED

Figure 12-13. *More defragmentation of the columnstore index*

You can see that the TOMBSTONE rowgroups are now gone. We did get just a little more defragmentation. One point worth noting, the row_group_id values are not reused, so it's common to see gaps like we have here. Finally, Table 12-1 lays out the various mechanisms for defragmenting indexes and details their pluses and minuses.

Table 12-1. *Characteristics of rowstore defragmentation techniques*

Characteristics/Issues	Drop and Create Index	Create Index with DROP_EXISTING	ALTER INDEX REBUILD	ALTER INDEX REORGANIZE
Rebuild nonclustered index on clustered index fragmentation	Twice	No	No	No
Missing indexes	Yes	No	No	No
Defragment index with constraints	Highly complex	Moderately complex	Easy	Easy
Defragment multiple indexes together	No	No	Yes	Yes
Concurrency with others	Low	Low	Medium, depending on concurrent user activity	High
Intermediate cancellation	Dangers with no transaction	Progress lost	Progress lost	Progress preserved
Degree of defragmentation	High	High	High	Moderate to low
Apply new fill factor	Yes	Yes	Yes	No
Statistics are updated	Yes	Yes	Yes	No

Defragmentation and Partitions

If you have massive databases, a standard mechanism to help effectively manage the data is to break it up into partitions. While partitioning can, in some very rare cases, help with performance, it is first and foremost a tool for managing data. You'll notice there is no chapter on partitioning for performance. That's because it's not an effective performance-enhancing tool. One of the issues in rebuilding an index is that it takes it offline during the process. However, if you had a partitioned index, you could use the ONLINE command to help deal with it like Listing 12-21.

Listing 12-21. Using ONLINE = ON

```
ALTER INDEX i1 ON dbo.Test1 REBUILD PARTITION = ALL WITH (ONLINE = ON);
```

This rebuilds all the partitions but keeps the index online. This will run longer than a normal rebuild and will use a lot of extra resources, especially in tempdb. You can also define individual partitions for rebuilding as a way to get around this as shown in Listing 12-22.

Listing 12-22. Setting the partition

```
ALTER INDEX i1 ON dbo.Test1 REBUILD PARTITION = 1 WITH (ONLINE = ON);
```

Now you're only rebuilding a single partition and using the ONLINE = ON to keep the index available.

Talking about the locking involved with index rebuild operations in partitions, you also have one other piece of functionality introduced in SQL Server 2014. You can modify the lock priority used during the rebuild operation by again adjusting the REBUILD command (Listing 12-23).

Listing 12-23. Changing the lock priority

```
ALTER INDEX i1
ON dbo.Test1
REBUILD PARTITION = 1
WITH (    ONLINE = ON
         (
             WAIT_AT_LOW_PRIORITY
             (
                 MAX_DURATION = 20,
                 ABORT_AFTER_WAIT = SELF
             )
         )
     );
```

What this does is set the duration that the rebuild operation is willing to wait, in minutes. Then, it allows you to determine which processes get aborted in order to clear the system for the index rebuild. You can have it stop itself or the blocking process. The most interesting thing is that the waiting process is set to low priority, so it's not using a lot of system resources, and any transactions that come in won't be blocked by this process.

Significance of the Fill Factor

On rowstore indexes, the best performance comes when more rows are stored on a given page. More rows on a page mean fewer pages have to be read from disk and put into memory. This is one of the prime reasons for defragmenting indexes. However, when pages are full, especially in a high-transaction OLTP system, you get more page splits, which hurts performance. Therefore, a balance between maximizing the number of rows on a page and avoiding page splits has to be maintained.

SQL Server allows you to control the amount of free space of an index by using the fill factor. If you know that there will be a lot of data manipulation and addition, you can pre-add free space to the pages of the index using the fill factor to help minimize the number of page splits. On the other hand, if the data is read-only, you can again use the fill factor to minimize the amount of free space.

The default fill factor is 0. When the fill factor is 0, the pages are packed to 100%. The fill factor for an index is applied only when the index is created. As keys are inserted and updated, the density of rows in the index eventually stabilizes within a narrow range. As you saw in the previous chapter's sections on page splits caused by UPDATE and INSERT, when a page split occurs, generally half of the original page is moved to a new page, which happens irrespective of the fill factor used during the index creation.

To understand the significance of the fill factor, let's use a small test table with 24 rows (Listing 12-24).

Listing 12-24. Creating a test table

```
DROP TABLE IF EXISTS dbo.Test1;
GO
CREATE TABLE dbo.Test1
(
    C1 INT,
    C2 CHAR(999)
);
WITH Nums
AS (SELECT 1 AS n
    UNION ALL
    SELECT n + 1
    FROM Nums
```

CHAPTER 12　DEALING WITH INDEX FRAGMENTATION

```
    WHERE n < 24)
INSERT INTO dbo.Test1
(
    C1,
    C2
)
SELECT n * 100,
       'a'
FROM Nums;
```

Increase the maximum number of rows in the leaf (or data) page by creating a clustered index with the default fill factor (Listing 12-25).

Listing 12-25. Adding a clustered index to the table

```
CREATE CLUSTERED INDEX FillIndex ON Test1(C1);
```

Since the average row size is 1,010 bytes, a clustered index leaf page (or table data page) can contain a maximum of eight rows. Therefore, at least three leaf pages are required for the 24 rows. You can confirm this in the sys.dm_db_index_physical_stats output shown in Figure 12-14.

	avg_fragmentation_in_percent	fragment_count	page_count	avg_page_space_used_in_percent	record_count	avg_record_size_in_bytes
1	33.3333333333333	2	3	100	24	1010

Figure 12-14. *Fill factor set to the default value of 0*

Note that avg_page_space_used_in_percent is 100%, since the default fill factor allows the maximum number of rows to be compressed in a page. Since a page cannot contain a part row to fill the page fully, avg_page_space_used_in_percent will be often a little less than 100%, even with the default fill factor.

To reduce the initial frequency of page splits caused by INSERT and UPDATE operations, create some free space within the leaf (or data) pages by recreating the clustered index with a fill factor (Listing 12-26).

Listing 12-26. Altering the index using a fill factor

```
ALTER INDEX FillIndex ON dbo.Test1 REBUILD
WITH (FILLFACTOR= 75);
```

CHAPTER 12 ■ DEALING WITH INDEX FRAGMENTATION

Because each page has a total space for eight rows, a fill factor of 75% will allow six rows per page. Thus, for 24 rows, the number of leaf pages should increase to four, as in the sys.dm_db_index_physical_stats output shown in Figure 12-15.

avg_fragmentation_in_percent	fragment_count	page_count	avg_page_space_used_in_percent	record_count	avg_record_size_in_bytes
25	2	4	74.9938225846306	24	1010

Figure 12-15. Fill factor set to 75

Note that avg_page_space_used_in_percent is about 75%, as set by the fill factor. This allows two more rows to be inserted in each page without causing a page split. You can confirm this by adding two rows to the first set of six rows (C1 = 100–600, contained in the first page) (Listing 12-27).

Listing 12-27. Adding two more rows

```
INSERT  INTO dbo.Test1
VALUES  (110, 'a'),   --25th row
        (120, 'a') ;  --26th row
```

Figure 12-16 shows the current fragmentation.

avg_fragmentation_in_percent	fragment_count	page_count	avg_page_space_used_in_percent	record_count	avg_record_size_in_bytes
25	2	4	81.2453669384729	26	1010

Figure 12-16. Fragmentation after new records

From the output, you can see that the addition of the two rows has not added any pages to the index. Accordingly, avg_page_space_used_in_percent increased from 74.99% to 81.25%. With the addition of two rows to the set of the first six rows, the first page should be completely full (eight rows). Any further addition of rows within the range of the first eight rows should cause a page split and thereby increase the number of index pages to five (Listing 12-28).

Listing 12-28. Adding one more row

```
INSERT  INTO dbo.Test1
VALUES  (130, 'a') ;  --27th row
```

Now sys.dm_db_index_physical_stats displays the difference in Figure 12-17.

avg_fragmentation_in_percent	fragment_count	page_count	avg_page_space_used_in_percent	record_count	avg_record_size_in_bytes
40	3	5	67.4919693600198	27	1010

Figure 12-17. *The number of pages goes up*

Note that even though the fill factor for the index is 75%, `Avg. Page Density (full)` has decreased to 67.49%, which can be computed as follows:

```
Avg. Page Density (full)
= Average rows per page / Maximum rows per page
= (27 / 5) / 8
= 67.5%
```

From the preceding example, you can see that the fill factor is applied when the index is created. But later, as the data is modified, it has no significance. Irrespective of the fill factor, whenever a page splits, the rows of the original page are distributed between two pages, and `avg_page_space_used_in_percent` settles accordingly. Therefore, if you use a nondefault fill factor, you should ensure that the fill factor is reapplied regularly to maintain its effect.

You can reapply a fill factor by recreating the index or by using `ALTER INDEX REORGANIZE` or `ALTER INDEX REBUILD`, as was shown. `ALTER INDEX REORGANIZE` takes the fill factor specified during the index creation into account. `ALTER INDEX REBUILD` also takes the original fill factor into account, but it allows a new fill factor to be specified, if required.

Without periodic maintenance of the fill factor, for both default and nondefault fill factor settings, `avg_page_space_used_in_percent` for an index (or a table) eventually settles within a narrow range.

One other option to consider is that you can create an index with PAD_INDEX. This will ensure that the intermediate pages are also using the fill factor. While the intermediate page splits are less costly overall than the rest, it's still an impact that you can help to mitigate.

An argument can be made that rather than attempting to defragment indexes over and over again, with all the overhead that implies, you could be better off settling on a fill factor that allows for a fairly standard set of distribution across the pages in your indexes. Some people do use this method, sacrificing some read performance and disk space to avoid page splits and the associated issues in which they result. Testing on your own systems to both find the right fill factor and determine if that method works will be necessary.

Automatic Maintenance

As I said at the start of the chapter, more and more people are largely leaving fragmented indexes alone. They are either adjusting their fill factors, as we just finished discussing, or they're carefully targeting exactly which indexes need to be defragmented and how frequently. Your system likely presents unique problems, and you'll have to figure out if you intend to automatically maintain your indexes through a defragmentation process or not.

For a fully functional script that includes a large degree of capability, I strongly recommend using Ola Hallengren's scripts at `http://bit.ly/JijaNI`.

In addition to those scripts, you can use the maintenance plans built into SQL Server. However, I don't recommend them because you surrender a lot of control for a little bit of ease of use. You'll be much happier with the results you get from one of the sets of scripts recommended previously.

Summary

As you learned in this chapter, in a highly transactional database, page splits caused by INSERT and UPDATE statements may fragment the tables and indexes, increasing the cost of data retrieval. You can avoid these page splits by maintaining free spaces within the pages using the fill factor. Since the fill factor is applied only during index creation, you should reapply it at regular intervals to maintain its effectiveness. Data manipulation of columnstore indexes also leads to fragmentation and performance degradation. You can determine the amount of fragmentation in an index (or a table) using sys.dm_db_index_physical_stats for a rowstore index or sys.column_store_row_groups for a columnstore index. Upon determining a high amount of fragmentation, you can use either ALTER INDEX REBUILD or ALTER INDEX REORGANIZE, depending on the required amount of defragmentation, database concurrency, and if you are dealing with a rowstore or columnstore index.

Defragmentation rearranges the data so that its physical order on the disk matches its logical order in the table/index, thus improving the performance of queries. However, unless the optimizer decides upon an effective execution plan for the query, query performance even after defragmentation can remain poor. Therefore, it is important to have the optimizer use efficient techniques to generate cost-effective execution plans.

In the next chapter, we're going to discuss a pernicious problem and several ways to address it: bad parameter sniffing.

CHAPTER 13

Parameter-Sensitive Queries: Causes and Solutions

Stored procedures and prepared statements can use parameters as placeholders for values. The optimizer can use the values in the parameter when the plans compile to get specific statistics, commonly known as parameter sniffing. Most of the time, this enhances performance. However, some queries suffer poor performance because they are very sensitive to exactly which values are used to create the plan. These are known as parameter-sensitive queries. Dealing with these queries can be a challenge.

In this chapter, I'll cover the following topics:

- How parameter sniffing works
- Identifying queries that are sensitive to parameter values
- Mechanisms for addressing parameter-sensitive queries

How Does Parameter Sniffing Work?

Parameter sniffing is a very simple concept. When you have a stored procedure, or a prepared statement with a parameter, the literal values passed to that parameter are available to the query optimizer when it compiles the query. That's it. The query optimizer can access those values and then use the exact value passed to the parameter to look up row estimates in the statistics of the table being referenced. Because of this, in many cases, you get execution plans that more accurately reflect the data because an actual value is used. If no actual value was used, an average would be used instead.

CHAPTER 13   PARAMETER-SENSITIVE QUERIES: CAUSES AND SOLUTIONS

The first thing to note is that while parameters and variables look similar within a given T-SQL statement where they are consumed, they are not the same. The definition of a parameter is part of the definition of the prepared statement. The definition of a variable is instead within the T-SQL of a batch or procedure. That difference matters. For example, the following code snippet shows the definition of a pair of parameters:

```
CREATE PROCEDURE dbo.AddressList
(
    @City VARCHAR(30),
    @PostalCode VARCHAR(15)
)
AS...
```

In contrast, the following snippet is the definition of a variable:

```
DECLARE @City VARCHAR(30);
```

Because a variable is defined within the code, it's not possible for the optimizer to know the value in the variable, so it's not sniffed automatically the way parameters are. However, in the event of a statement-level recompile, things change. During the recompile, any variables used in the statement being recompiled now have known values. The optimizer will take advantage of that in order to get more accurate row estimates.

To see parameter sniffing in action, we're going to use the stored procedure in Listing 13-1.

Listing 13-1. A stored procedure with a parameter

```
CREATE OR ALTER PROC dbo.ProductTransactionHistoryByReference
(@ReferenceOrderID INT)
AS
BEGIN
    SELECT p.NAME,
           p.ProductNumber,
           th.ReferenceOrderID
    FROM Production.Product AS p
```

CHAPTER 13 PARAMETER-SENSITIVE QUERIES: CAUSES AND SOLUTIONS

```
    JOIN Production.TransactionHistory AS th
        ON th.ProductID = p.ProductID
    WHERE th.ReferenceOrderID = @ReferenceOrderID;
END;
```

There's nothing special or unusual about the query inside the stored procedure in Listing 13-1. What's actually special is the distribution of data for the ReferenceOrderID column in the Production.TransactionHistory table. Some values return a larger number of rows and work best with one plan, while other values return very few rows and work better with a different plan.

To see how parameter sniffing works, I'll run the query in Listing 13-2.

Listing 13-2. Executing the ProductTransactionHistoryByReference query

```
EXEC dbo.ProductTransactionHistoryByReference @ReferenceOrderID = 53465;
```

The query has the following execution plan and runtime metrics:

```
2.2ms
245 reads
```

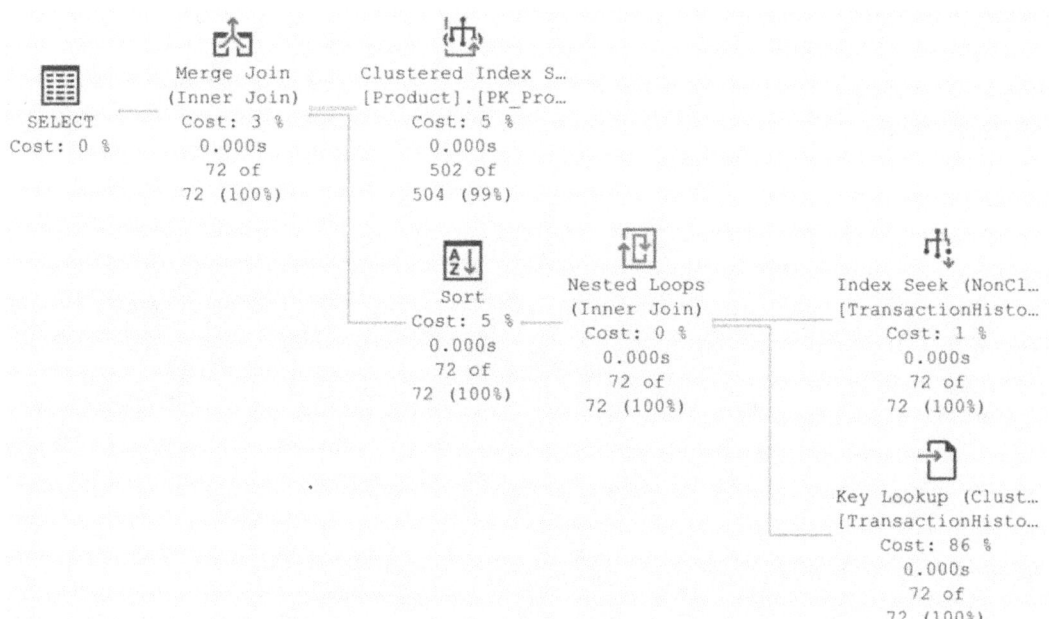

Figure 13-1. *Execution plan for a value returning more rows*

403

CHAPTER 13　PARAMETER-SENSITIVE QUERIES: CAUSES AND SOLUTIONS

There's nothing remarkable about the execution plan. Based on the value passed to the parameter, the optimizer chose to scan the Product table's clustered index, PK_Product_ProductID. Also, it decided that the most efficient join would be the Merge. While the Clustered Index Scan was ordered (which you can verify by looking at the properties of that operator), a Sort operator was necessary to order the output from the Nested Loops join. All this took just over two milliseconds and had 245 reads.

I'll remove the plan from cache using the query in Listing 13-3.

Listing 13-3. Removing a single plan from cache

```
DECLARE @planhandle VARBINARY(64);
SELECT @planhandle = deps.plan_handle FROM sys.dm_exec_procedure_
stats AS deps
WHERE deps.object_id = OBJECT_ID('dbo.
ProductTransactionHistoryByReference')
IF @planhandle IS NOT NULL
DBCC FREEPROCCACHE(@planhandle);
```

With that removed, I can execute the procedure with a different value, 816. This results in the plan in Figure 13-2.

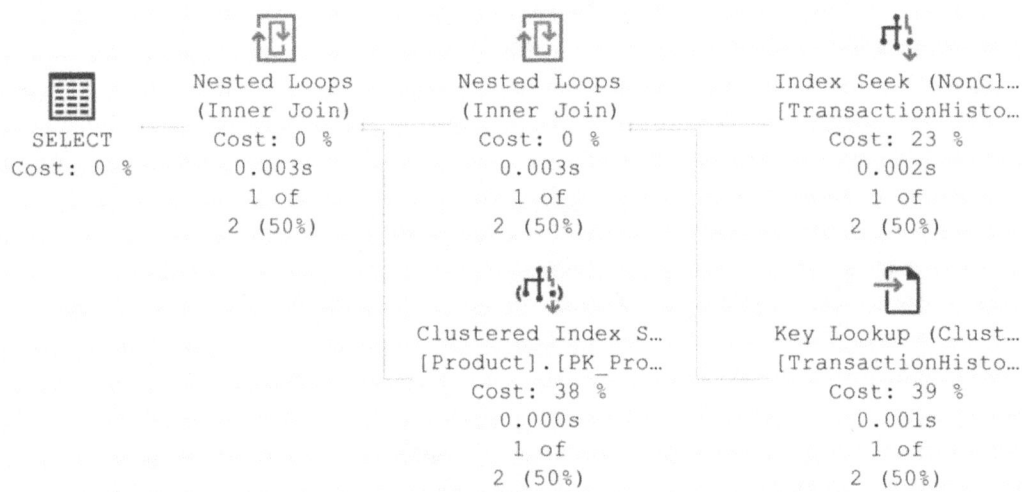

Figure 13-2. *A different execution plan for a different value*

CHAPTER 13　PARAMETER-SENSITIVE QUERIES: CAUSES AND SOLUTIONS

The plan has changed from the one shown in Figure 13-1. Because fewer rows are returned, a scan is not needed. The optimizer chose to use a Nested Loops join instead of a Merge, so no sort operations are needed either. This change in execution plans is the result of parameter sniffing. Specific values are used to look at the statistics, and then plans are chosen based on those values.

If I run the query outside the stored procedure, using a local variable, the code will look like Listing 13-4.

Listing 13-4. Executing the same query with a variable

```
DECLARE @ReferenceOrderID INT = 53465;
SELECT p.Name,
       p.ProductNumber,
       th.ReferenceOrderID
FROM Production.Product AS p
    JOIN Production.TransactionHistory AS th
        ON th.ProductID = p.ProductID
WHERE th.ReferenceOrderID = @ReferenceOrderID;
```

This results in the following execution plan in Figure 13-3 and these runtime metrics:

634mcs
362 reads

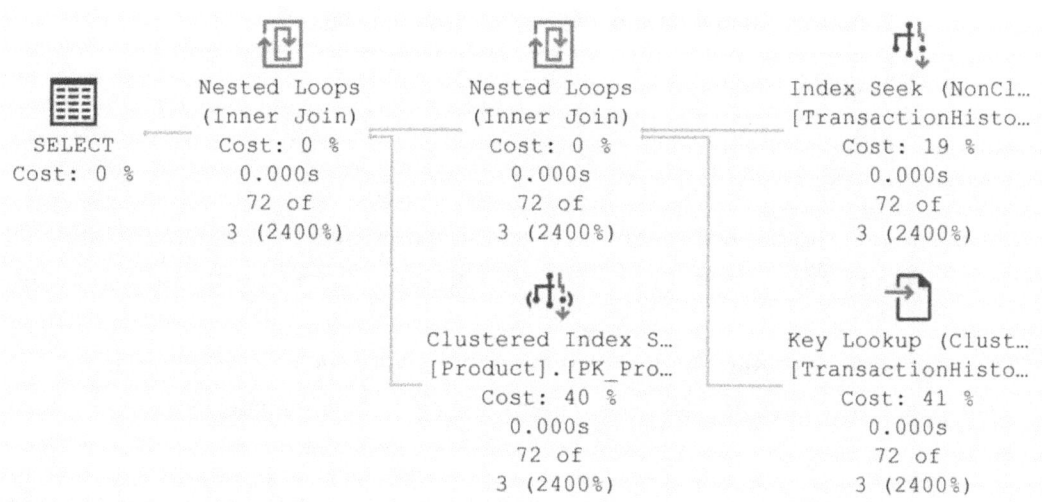

Figure 13-3. An average execution plan

The first thing we should address is that the query ran faster on average, by about 1.2ms on my machine. However, the reads went up from 245 to 362. That could be OK or a serious problem depending on the system and where any bottlenecks may be.

Next, note the actual rows, 72 for all the operators, vs. the estimated rows, 3. It's that difference in the estimated values that results in differences in the execution plans. For larger data sets, the plan shown in Figure 13-1 performs nominally better (at least for the reads). For the average number of rows across the entire data set, it matches the plan shown in Figure 13-2, which performs better for smaller data sets.

To see the estimations go the other way, I'm going to perform the following steps:

1. Run Listing 13-3 to remove the plan from cache.

2. Run Listing 13-2 with the larger data set in order to generate that plan.

3. Execute the procedure again with the value 816 and measure performance.

4. Run Listing 13-3 again to remove the plan from cache.

5. Execute the procedure a final time with the value of 816 and measure performance.

The results are shown in Table 13-1.

Table 13-1. Query performance metrics for two plans

Parameter Compile Value	Execution Time	Reads
53465 (72 rows)	529mcs	11
816 (2 rows)	271mcs	7

As you can see, both the reads and the execution time degrade when the smaller data set uses the plan created for the larger data set. This is the problem with bad parameter sniffing.

You have to decide which plan is better overall for your systems, and it's not always going to be obvious. Let's discuss how to identify the problematic queries.

Identifying Queries That Are Sensitive to Parameter Values

Encountering bad parameter sniffing can be a very frustrating experience. The problem is almost always an intermittent one. Performance will be fine for a long period of time, and then suddenly performance will degrade badly. Then, without any action from you, it may suddenly go back to performing just fine. This is occurring as plans age out of cache or are updated through other processes (discussed in Chapters 7 and 8) and new plans, possibly not the best for the majority of your queries, take their place.

Presumably you're going to be able to identify which query is causing this problem. Then, it's a question of getting the execution plans for the query. We need to see the execution plans in order to determine if the intermittent slow performance is caused by changes in the plan or has other causes. You have three choices in capturing plans.

One way to do this would be to capture the plan when behavior is good and again when behavior is bad, using the plan cache and sys.dm_exec_query_plan like in Listing 13-5.

Listing 13-5. Using sys.dm_exec_query_plan to retrieve execution plans

```
SELECT deps.EXECUTION_COUNT,
       deps.total_elapsed_time,
       deps.total_logical_reads,
       deps.total_logical_writes,
       deqp.query_plan
FROM sys.dm_exec_procedure_stats AS deps
   CROSS APPLY sys.dm_exec_query_plan(deps.plan_handle) AS deqp
WHERE deps.OBJECT_ID = OBJECT_ID('dbo.ProductTransactionHistoryByReference');
```

Just remember that this method is cache dependent, so you have to capture the plans while they are still in cache.

Another approach would be to use the Query Store, if that's enabled on the database in question. The nice thing about the Query Store is that it will automatically have all the plans associated with a given query. Listing 13-6 shows how I can aggregate the aggregations from the Query Store to get the execution plans.

Listing 13-6. Using the Query Store to retrieve execution plans

```
SELECT SUM(qsrs.count_executions) AS ExecutionCount,
       AVG(qsrs.avg_duration) AS AvgDuration,
       AVG(qsrs.avg_logical_io_reads) AS AvgReads,
       AVG(qsrs.avg_logical_io_writes) AS AvgWrites,
       CAST(qsp.query_plan AS XML) AS QueryPlan,
       qsp.query_id,
       qsp.plan_id
FROM sys.query_store_query AS qsq
    JOIN sys.query_store_plan AS qsp
        ON qsp.query_id = qsq.query_id
    JOIN sys.query_store_runtime_stats AS qsrs
        ON qsrs.plan_id = qsp.plan_id
WHERE qsq.OBJECT_ID = OBJECT_ID('dbo.ProductTransactionHistoryByReference')
GROUP BY qsp.query_plan,
         qsp.query_id,
         qsp.plan_id;
```

I've used the CAST to change the query_plan value to XML from the text that it's stored as. For very large execution plans, this might not work because of the nesting level limit of the XML data type. However, I do this because it makes it possible to click the column in SSMS and open the graphical plan.

Finally, you can use Extended Events to capture the execution plans. I'll show you how to do this, but I would suggest caution because this is an expensive Extended Events session and could put an undue load on your system. I'd suggest only running this for very short periods of time. Listing 13-7 shows the necessary session.

Listing 13-7. An Extended Events session to capture execution plans

```
CREATE EVENT SESSION [ExecutionPlans]
ON SERVER
    ADD EVENT sqlserver.query_post_execution_showplan
    (WHERE (
                [sqlserver].[equal_i_sql_unicode_string]([sqlserver].
                [database_name], N'AdventureWorks')
                AND [object_name] = N'ProductTransactionHistoryByReference'
```

```
            )
        ),
        ADD EVENT sqlserver.rpc_completed
        (WHERE (
                    [sqlserver].[equal_i_sql_unicode_string]([sqlserver].
                    [database_name], N'AdventureWorks')
                    AND [object_name] = N'ProductTransactionHistoryByReference'
                )
        )
        ADD TARGET package0.event_file
        (SET FILENAME = N'ExecutionPlans')
WITH
(
    TRACK_CAUSALITY = ON
);
```

Even with good filtering in place, this Event can be extremely expensive. If your system is already under stress, you may not want to use this approach. However, it really does make it easy to capture both the runtime metrics and the execution plan at the same time.

The goal, once again, is to have the two (or more) execution plans generated for the query. Since this is an intermittent problem, you may want to save one of the plans to disk until you get the second. Right-click inside any graphical plan and select "Save execution plan as..." from the context menu. As I said before, it's likely that the Query Store will just have both plans available.

The target in the plan is the compile-time and runtime values for the parameter, which is stored in the first operator of an execution plan. Right-click the operator and select Properties from the context menu. I usually just leave the Properties window open in SSMS when I'm tuning queries. Figure 13-4 shows the Parameter List properties for the plan in question.

CHAPTER 13   PARAMETER-SENSITIVE QUERIES: CAUSES AND SOLUTIONS

Parameter List	@ReferenceOrderID
Column	@ReferenceOrderID
Parameter Compiled Value	(816)
Parameter Data Type	int
Parameter Runtime Value	(53465)

Figure 13-4. *Parameter List values for the query*

Now I have actual data that I can use to understand what's happening with our query. The key to understanding why the optimizer is making these choices is in the statistics. You could run DBCC SHOW_STATISTICS and find the values using the RANGE_HI_KEY column and then determine if our value matches, where we'd use RANGE_ROWS, or was simply within a range, where we'd use AVG_RANGE_ROWS. Instead, I prefer to just query that information directly from sys.dm_db_stats_histogram as shown in Listing 13-8.

Listing 13-8. Identifying statistics information through a query

```
DECLARE @KeyValue INT = 53465;
WITH histolow
AS (SELECT ddsh.step_number,
           ddsh.range_high_key,
           ddsh.range_rows,
           ddsh.equal_rows,
           ddsh.average_range_rows
    FROM sys.dm_db_stats_histogram(OBJECT_ID('Production.
    TransactionHistory'), 3) AS ddsh ),
     histojoin
AS (SELECT h1.step_number,
           h1.range_high_key,
           h2.range_high_key AS range_high_key_step1,
           h1.range_rows,
           h1.equal_rows,
           h1.average_range_rows
    FROM histolow AS h1
        LEFT JOIN histolow AS h2
```

```
              ON h1.step_number = h2.step_number + 1)
SELECT hj.range_high_key,
       hj.equal_rows,
       hj.average_range_rows
FROM histojoin AS hj
WHERE hj.range_high_key >= @KeyValue
      AND
      (
          hj.range_high_key_step1 < @KeyValue
          OR hj.range_high_key_step1 IS NULL
      );
```

This will show us the equivalent rows and the average number of rows within the histogram inside the statistics. You have to supply the appropriate OBJECT_ID and the correct statistics ID, both available from the sys.stats system table. Then set each of the two values, compiled and runtime, to the @KeyValue variable. The results for both queries are shown in Figure 13-5.

	range_high_key	equal_rows	average_range_rows
1	53465	72	30

	range_high_key	equal_rows	average_range_rows
1	1255	24	2.266428

Figure 13-5. Histogram results for two different values

The information in Figure 13-5 tells us what we need to know. For our compiled value of 816, it's not equal to the range_high_key, so you have to look to the average_range_rows, which shows 2.266 rows average across that step in the histogram, whereas the runtime value, 53465, is equal to the range_high_key. That means it will return exactly 72 rows. The difference between 72 rows and 2.266 rows results in two different execution plans.

We now know where the different plans came from. We can also see how the plans affect performance for the different queries. The last step is deciding how to best address the, in this case, bad parameter sniffing.

CHAPTER 13 PARAMETER-SENSITIVE QUERIES: CAUSES AND SOLUTIONS

Mechanisms for Addressing Plan-Sensitive Queries

There are a number of different ways you can try to address bad parameter sniffing. Each of the methods requires you to make a determination as to what kind of solution you're going to apply. With the exception of Multiplan, the last mechanism we'll examine, each mechanism for dealing with bad parameter sniffing requires a trade-off. I'll discuss the trade-offs as I detail each mechanism. The options for dealing with bad parameter sniffing are as follows:

- Disable parameter sniffing entirely.
- Use a local variable in place of a parameter.
- Recompile the query every time it executes.
- Use the query hint OPTIMIZE FOR.
- Use the force plan functionality of the Query Store.
- If your query meets the thresholds, automatically get Multiplan.

With each of these approaches, you will need to return to the queries over time. As your data changes, what was a good solution could turn into a problem, so keep that in mind as you apply any of these fixes. Let's discuss these mechanisms and their trade-offs.

Disable Parameter Sniffing

While most of the time, parameter sniffing is either benign or beneficial, it really can be problematic. There are two mechanisms that would allow you to disable parameter sniffing entirely. The first is a server-level setting using a trace flag. Listing 13-9 shows how to do this.

Listing 13-9. Enabling a trace flag

```
DBCC TRACEON (4136,-1);
```

The problem with this approach is that it disables parameter sniffing for the entire server. While you may have a database that is suffering from bad parameter sniffing, seldom will all databases be in the same situation.

Alternatively, you can take advantage of Database Scoped Configuration (2016 and greater as well as Azure SQL Database) to disable parameter sniffing for a single database as shown in Listing 13-10.

Listing 13-10. Using Database Scoped Configuration

```
ALTER DATABASE SCOPED CONFIGURATION SET PARAMETER_SNIFFING = OFF;
```

Using this mechanism allows you a more targeted approach to disable parameter sniffing, but you do lose any advantages that parameter sniffing confers on your database.

One more option is to take advantage of the USE HINT query hint to disable parameter sniffing on a single query. Listing 13-11 shows how this works.

Listing 13-11. Disabling parameter sniffing for one query

```
CREATE OR ALTER PROC dbo.ProductTransactionHistoryByReference
(@ReferenceOrderID INT)
AS
BEGIN
    SELECT p.NAME,
           p.ProductNumber,
           th.ReferenceOrderID
    FROM Production.Product AS p
        JOIN Production.TransactionHistory AS th
            ON th.ProductID = p.ProductID
    WHERE th.ReferenceOrderID = @ReferenceOrderID
    OPTION (USE HINT ('DISABLE_PARAMETER_SNIFFING'));
END;
```

This gives you the ability to control parameter sniffing at an even more granular level than the entire server or the entire database (SQL Server 2016 and greater). You can combine this with Query Store hints (covered in Chapter 6) or plan guides (covered in Chapter 8), so you don't have to modify the code. However, I usually find one of the other methods serves me better than disabling parameter sniffing entirely, most of the time.

Local Variables

Way back in SQL Server 2000 and before, there were almost no ways to deal with bad parameter sniffing. Because of this, in some situations, you could use a local variable in place of a parameter. This means that you will get an average value from the histogram, instead of a specific value. Listing 13-12 shows how this would work inside a stored procedure.

Listing 13-12. Using a local variable to address parameter sniffing

```
CREATE OR ALTER PROC dbo.AddressByCity
(@City VARCHAR(30))
AS
BEGIN
    --To help deal with parameter sniffing issues
    DECLARE @LocalCity VARCHAR(30) = @City;
    SELECT A.AddressID,
           A.PostalCode,
           sp.NAME,
           A.City
    FROM Person.ADDRESS AS A
        JOIN Person.StateProvince AS sp
            ON sp.StateProvinceID = A.StateProvinceID
    WHERE A.City = @LocalCity;
END;
```

As you are no doubt thinking, that looks odd. However, you may come across this in older code. I put the comment in place so people won't be confused when they see this. Between more methods for dealing with bad parameter sniffing and the fact that this will be sampled in the same way during a recompile, it's unlikely you'll see this much. I don't recommend this approach at all.

Recompile

Since parameter sniffing occurs when you compile a plan, if you want to get a specific plan for each possible value, you can use a query hint to recompile the statement within your procedure. Listing 13-13 shows an example of how this would work.

Listing 13-13. Recompiling a statement at each execution

```
CREATE OR ALTER PROC dbo.ProductTransactionHistoryByReference
(@ReferenceOrderID INT)
AS
BEGIN
    SELECT p.NAME,
           p.ProductNumber,
           th.ReferenceOrderID
    FROM Production.Product AS p
        JOIN Production.TransactionHistory AS th
            ON th.ProductID = p.ProductID
    WHERE th.ReferenceOrderID = @ReferenceOrderID
        OPTION(RECOMPILE);
END;
```

Now every time this stored procedure gets executed, the statement within will be recompiled. This means that when the parameter values are sampled, the plan generated each time will be based on that sampled value. This does address the issues caused by bad parameter sniffing. However, you now have to pay the added overhead of compiling the plan on each execution. Further, any query with a RECOMPILE hint will not have its plan stored in cache. While this approach does solve the bad parameter sniffing issue, you are going to have to pay the overhead associated with recompiles and no plan reuse.

You can also use the WITH RECOMPILE hint when you define the stored procedure or even when you execute it. Just know that unlike the code in Listing 13-13, that will result in recompiling every statement in the procedure. I prefer the targeted approach in most scenarios.

OPTIMIZE FOR Query Hint

Another approach to dealing with bad parameter sniffing is to use the OPTIMIZE FOR query hint. This hint comes with two options. You can have the plan generated for specific values, or you can tell it to only, ever, use an average from the statistics.

CHAPTER 13 PARAMETER-SENSITIVE QUERIES: CAUSES AND SOLUTIONS

As I outlined in the previous section, you'll likely identify a plan that works better for most of your data. When you have that specific data and you want to see just that plan, you modify your query as shown in Listing 13-14.

Listing 13-14. Applying the OPTIMIZE FOR query hint

```
CREATE OR ALTER PROC dbo.ProductTransactionHistoryByReference
(@ReferenceOrderID INT)
AS
BEGIN
    SELECT p.NAME,
           p.ProductNumber,
           th.ReferenceOrderID
    FROM Production.Product AS p
        JOIN Production.TransactionHistory AS th
            ON th.ProductID = p.ProductID
    WHERE th.ReferenceOrderID = @ReferenceOrderID
    OPTION (OPTIMIZE FOR (@ReferenceOrderID = 53465));
END;
```

If I alter my procedure in this manner, when I execute the procedure, even if I pass a value that I know will generate another plan, I'll still get the plan for the value of 53465. Listing 13-15 shows the execution.

Listing 13-15. Executing the query to generate a plan

```
EXEC dbo.ProductTransactionHistoryByReference @ReferenceOrderID = 816;
```

The resulting execution plan with runtime metrics is shown in Figure 13-6.

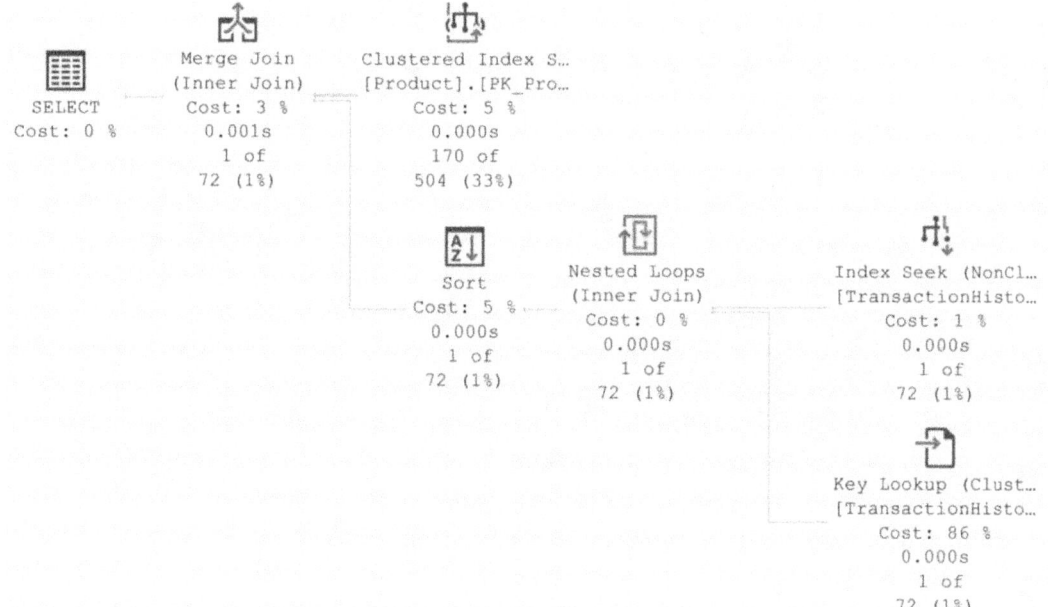

Figure 13-6. *Execution plan using a query hint*

Nothing in the plan itself will tell you that a query hint is in use. You have to look to the code. However, even though this query was recompiled because I altered the code, the plan generated used the value I gave it in the OPTIMIZE FOR hint. We can validate this by looking at the Parameter List in the properties of the first operator, visible in Figure 13-7.

Parameter List	@ReferenceOrderID
Column	@ReferenceOrderID
Parameter Compiled Value	(53465)
Parameter Data Type	int
Parameter Runtime Value	(816)

Figure 13-7. *Parameter runtime and compiled values*

While we executed the query with the value of 816, the value specified in the query hint was used. If you have more than one parameter value you want to reference in OPTIMIZE FOR, you can just comma separate them.

Another way to use OPTIMIZE FOR is not to specify an exact value, but instead, tell it that no value is known. Listing 13-16 shows how to modify the query.

Listing 13-16. Using the UNKNOWN option in OPTIMIZE FOR

```
CREATE OR ALTER PROC dbo.ProductTransactionHistoryByReference
(@ReferenceOrderID INT)
AS
BEGIN
    SELECT p.NAME,
           p.ProductNumber,
           th.ReferenceOrderID
    FROM Production.Product AS p
        JOIN Production.TransactionHistory AS th
            ON th.ProductID = p.ProductID
    WHERE th.ReferenceOrderID = @ReferenceOrderID
    OPTION (OPTIMIZE FOR (@ReferenceOrderID UNKNOWN));
END;
```

With no known value, the optimizer will use the average from the statistics as a row estimate. You also won't see compile values in the properties as you can see in Figure 13-8.

Parameter List	@ReferenceOrderID
Column	@ReferenceOrderID
Parameter Data Type	int
Parameter Runtime Value	(816)

Figure 13-8. No parameter compile-time value

The OPTIMIZE FOR hint gives you the ability to generate a plan based on a specific value, or a plan based on no value at all, as if it wasn't parameter sniffing. As with the other hints, you can modify code as in the examples or use plan guides or Query Store hints.

Force Plan

In Chapter 6, I covered how the Query Store can be used to force a plan. We're going to use our analysis of the query and plans to pick the one that works best across the most important queries. That may be the plan that is used the most. It may be the plan that

CHAPTER 13 PARAMETER-SENSITIVE QUERIES: CAUSES AND SOLUTIONS

runs the fastest for a given value. You'll have to make that call on a case-by-case basis. However, once decided, you simply force the plan as shown in Chapter 6. As with the other options, it's a good idea to revisit these plans as your data and structures change over time.

Multiplan

Introduced with SQL Server 2022 and available in Azure SQL Database, another mechanism available to deal with some instances of bad parameter sniffing is called Multiplan. Basically, SQL Server will create more than one plan for a given query if it identifies a wide variance in performance based on different execution plans.

There are two mechanisms at work within Multiplan. The first is Parameter-Sensitive Plan (PSP) Optimization. The nice thing about PSP is that it's entirely automatic. No code changes, query hints, or plan forcing required. Your database has to be set to compatibility mode 160 or higher, and you can't have disabled parameter sniffing at the server, database, or query level (discussed earlier in the "Disable Parameter Sniffing" section). You can get more than one plan cached in memory. The exact number of extra plans possible is limited to three in order to reduce plan cache bloat. These are plans for low, medium, and high cardinality.

Next is Optional Parameter Optimization (OPO). This is a somewhat specific scenario that involves parameters that are optional; they may have NULL values. Listing 13-17 shows the type of query that OPO is designed to help perform better.

Listing 13-17. A stored procedure with an optional parameter

```
CREATE OR ALTER PROCEDURE dbo.OptionalParameter @ReferenceOrderID
INT = NULL
AS
BEGIN
    SELECT p.ProductNumber
    FROM Production.Product AS p
        JOIN Production.TransactionHistory AS th
            ON th.ProductID = p.ProductID
    WHERE th.ReferenceOrderID = @ReferenceOrderID
        OR @ReferenceOrderID IS NULL;
END;
```

CHAPTER 13 PARAMETER-SENSITIVE QUERIES: CAUSES AND SOLUTIONS

If a value is passed to @ReferenceOrderID, it's possible that a SEEK operation could be performed if there's a good index on the th.ReferenceOrderID column. However, prior to SQL Server 2025 and OPO, you would be guaranteed a plan with a SCAN because of the OR to deal with the optional parameter value. Now, Multiplan will assist by making more than one plan for this query pattern.

Microsoft has not published specific information around the thresholds required for PSP to function. However, with some testing, as of this writing, I can say that approximately 100,000 rows and approximately one million rows are the dataset thresholds that a given query would have to meet in order to see PSP in action.

In order to test PSP, I modified data in the table dbo.bigTransactionHistory from the MakeBigAdventure script in order to have a value with over 100,000 rows. I also added a single row. I created a new index and a stored procedure as well, all in Listing 13-18.

Listing 13-18. Scripts to test Parameter-Sensitive Plan Optimization

```
--Modify data to get 100K rows
UPDATE dbo.bigTransactionHistory
SET ProductID = 1319
WHERE ProductID IN ( 28417, 28729, 11953, 35521, 11993, 29719, 20431,
29531, 29749, 7913, 29947, 10739, 26921, 20941,
27767, 27941, 47431, 31847, 32411, 39383, 39511, 35531, 28829, 35759,
29713, 29819, 16001, 29951, 10453, 34967, 16363, 41347, 39719, 39443,
39829, 38917, 41759, 16453, 16963, 17453, 16417, 17473, 17713, 10729,
21319, 21433, 21473, 29927, 21859, 16477
);
GO
--Add a single row to both tables
INSERT INTO dbo.bigProduct
(
    ProductID,
    Name,
    ProductNumber,
    SafetyStockLevel,
    ReorderPoint,
    DaysToManufacture,
    SellStartDate,
```

```
        MakeFlag,
        FinishedGoodsFlag,
        StandardCost,
        ListPrice
)
VALUES
(43, 'FarbleDing', 'CA-2222-1000', 0, 0, 0, GETDATE(), 1, 1, 42, 54);
INSERT INTO dbo.bigTransactionHistory
(
        TransactionID,
        ProductID,
        TransactionDate,
        Quantity,
        ActualCost
)
VALUES
(31263602, 42, GETDATE(), 42, 42);
GO
--Create an index for testing
CREATE INDEX ProductIDTransactionDate
ON dbo.bigTransactionHistory (
                                ProductID,
                                TransactionDate
                           );
GO
--Create a procedure
CREATE OR ALTER PROC dbo.TransactionInfo
(@ProductID INT)
AS
BEGIN
    SELECT bp.Name,
           bp.ProductNumber,
           bth.TransactionDate
    FROM dbo.bigTransactionHistory AS bth
```

CHAPTER 13   PARAMETER-SENSITIVE QUERIES: CAUSES AND SOLUTIONS

```
        JOIN dbo.bigProduct AS bp
            ON bp.ProductID = bth.ProductID
    WHERE bth.ProductID = @ProductID;
END;
```

You may have to adjust the first script depending on how your version of MakeBigAdventure runs.

With all that in place, I'm going to execute the procedure twice as shown in Listing 13-19.

Listing 13-19. Executing the TransactionInfo procedure

```
EXEC dbo.TransactionInfo @ProductID = 1319;
EXEC dbo.TransactionInfo @ProductID = 42;
```

I capture the execution plans for the two procedure calls, and you can see the results in Figure 13-9.

CHAPTER 13 PARAMETER-SENSITIVE QUERIES: CAUSES AND SOLUTIONS

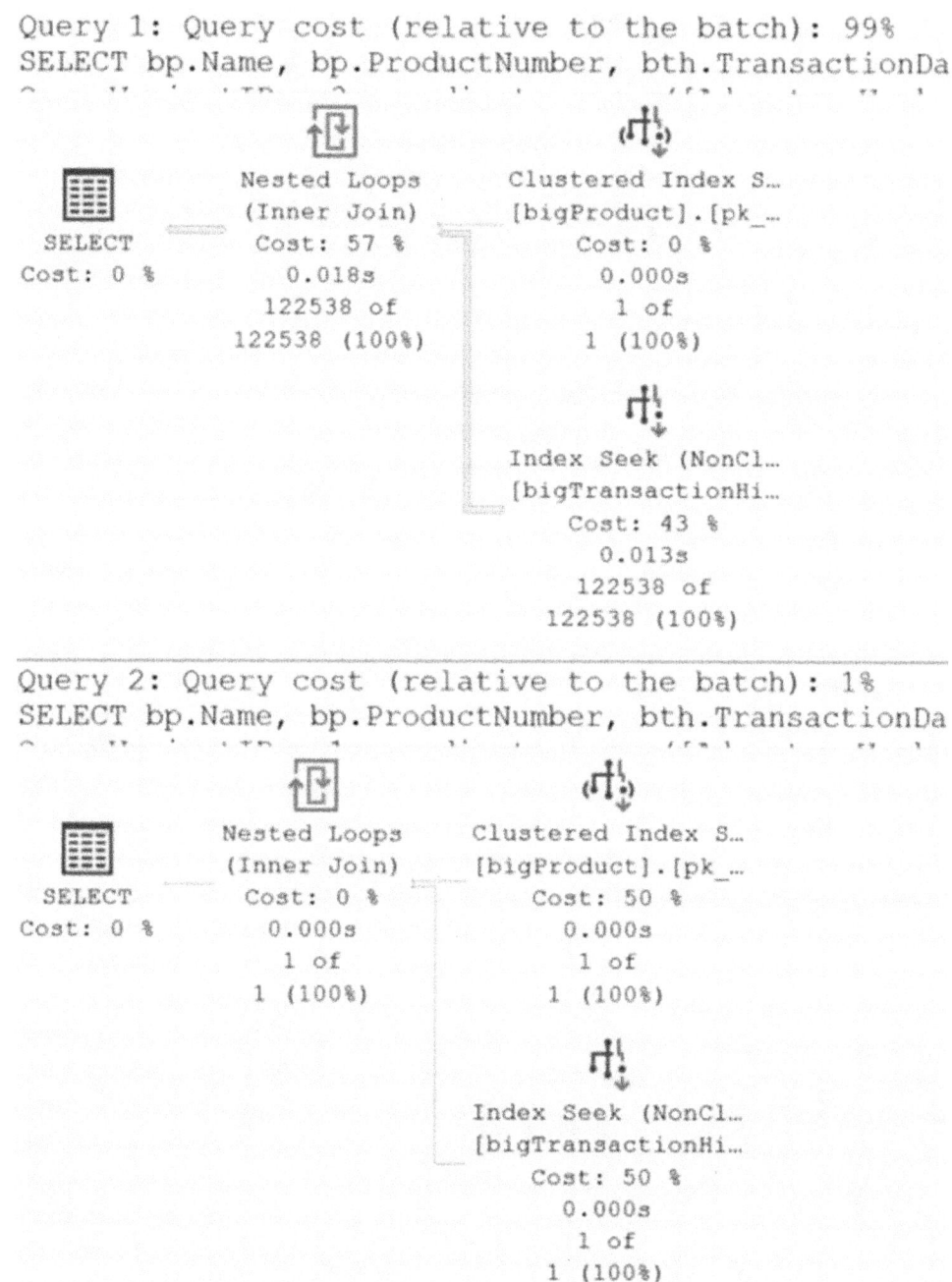

Figure 13-9. *Two different execution plans for the same query*

CHAPTER 13 PARAMETER-SENSITIVE QUERIES: CAUSES AND SOLUTIONS

While the overall plan shape for these two plans is the same, you can see that the top plan estimates 122,538 rows and returns that many. The bottom plan estimates and returns one row. These are two distinct execution plans. However, I didn't recompile the queries or procedures between executions. Instead, the optimization process is using Multiplan to implement PSP Optimization, so I have two different execution plans.

There are a number of other changes to the behavior of execution plans. In execution plans that also capture runtime metrics (a.k.a. actual plans), you get additional data in the properties as shown in Figure 13-10.

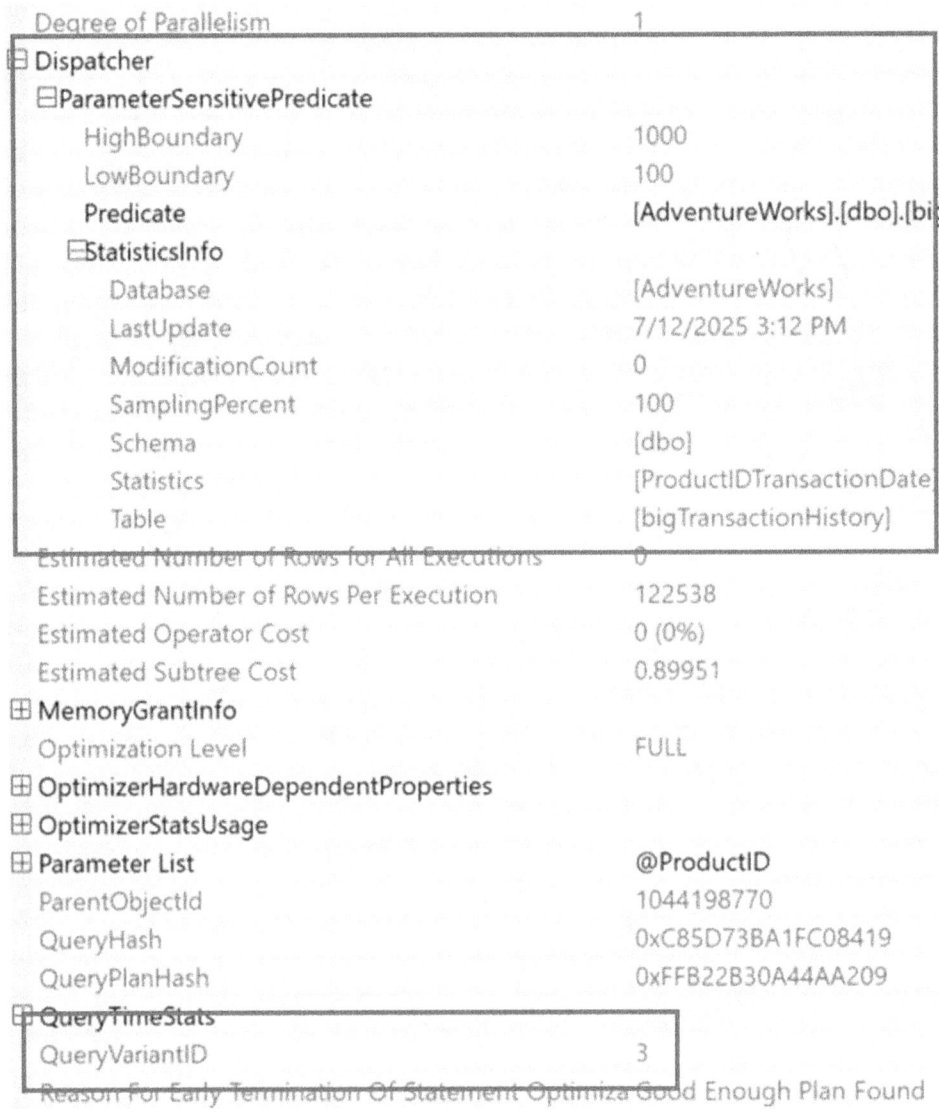

Figure 13-10. New properties in the execution plan

These new properties show information about how the optimizer is deciding which plan to run. At the top are Dispatcher settings, which show a boundary and the predicate in question, @ProductID. At the bottom is the marker for which variant of the query is in use. This is necessary because as a part of this process, changes are made to the query text. I used the query in Listing 13-20 to retrieve information from cache on our two plans.

Listing 13-20. Querying sys.dm_exec_query_stats for PSP information

```
SELECT deqs.query_hash,
       deqs.query_plan_hash,
       dest.text,
       deqp.query_plan
FROM sys.dm_exec_query_stats AS deqs
    CROSS APPLY sys.dm_exec_query_plan(deqs.plan_handle) AS deqp
    CROSS APPLY sys.dm_exec_sql_text(deqs.sql_handle) AS dest
WHERE dest.text LIKE '%SELECT bp.Name,
          bp.ProductNumber,
          bth.TransactionDate
    FROM dbo.bigTransactionHistory AS bth%';
```

The results of this query are shown in Figure 13-11.

	query_hash	query_plan_hash	text		query_plan
1	0xC85D73BA1FC08419	0xFFB22B30A44AA209	(@ProductID int)SELECT bp.Name,	bp.P...	<ShowPlanXML xmlns="http://schemas.microsoft.com...
2	0xC85D73BA1FC08419	0xFFB22B30A44AA209	(@ProductID int)SELECT bp.Name,	bp.P...	<ShowPlanXML xmlns="http://schemas.microsoft.com...

Figure 13-11. *Querying the plan cache for PSP information*

Notice that the query_hash values are the same, but the plan_handle values are different, one for each execution plan. The text for the query is shown here:

```
(@ProductID int)SELECT bp.Name,                    bp.
ProductNumber,                bth.TransactionDate      FROM dbo.
bigTransactionHistory AS bth            JOIN dbo.bigProduct AS
bp             ON bp.ProductID = bth.ProductID      WHERE bth.ProductID
= @ProductID option (PLAN PER VALUE(QueryVariantID = 3, predicate_
range([AdventureWorks].[dbo].[bigTransactionHistory].[ProductID] = @
ProductID, 100.0, 1000.0)))
```

CHAPTER 13   PARAMETER-SENSITIVE QUERIES: CAUSES AND SOLUTIONS

As you can see, the optimizer made a number of modifications to the query in order to take advantage of PSP.

You can disable PSP using DATABASE SCOPED CONFIGURATION as shown in Listing 13-21.

Listing 13-21. Disabling Parameter-Sensitive Plan Optimization

```
ALTER DATABASE SCOPED CONFIGURATION SET PARAMETER_SENSITIVE_PLAN_
OPTIMIZATION = OFF;
```

The Query Store captures information about PSP plans through a view, sys.query_store_query_variant. You can see the output in Figure 13-12.

	query_variant_query_id	parent_query_id	dispatcher_plan_id
1	926	907	86
2	927	907	86

Figure 13-12.   *Query Store information on PSP queries*

You can use the query_variant_query_id to find variations on the execution plan in the Query Store. The parent_query_id of course goes back to the original query within the Query Store. This makes it possible, when using the Query Store, to avoid queries like the one in Listing 13-20 where I used LIKE to track down the plans in cache. The dispatcher_plan_id refers to the plan that determines, based on cardinality, which of the different execution plans will be used.

Plans generated through PSP are subject to the same rules around aging out of cache, recompilation, and pretty much all other behaviors described throughout the book.

To see OPO we're going to execute the procedure from Listing 13-17. As with PSP Optimization, I'll execute the query twice as shown in Listing 13-22.

Listing 13-22.   Executing the OptionalParameter procedure

```
EXEC dbo.OptionalParameter @ReferenceOrderID = 1319;
EXEC dbo.OptionalParameter;
```

Figure 13-13 shows the execution plans for each query.

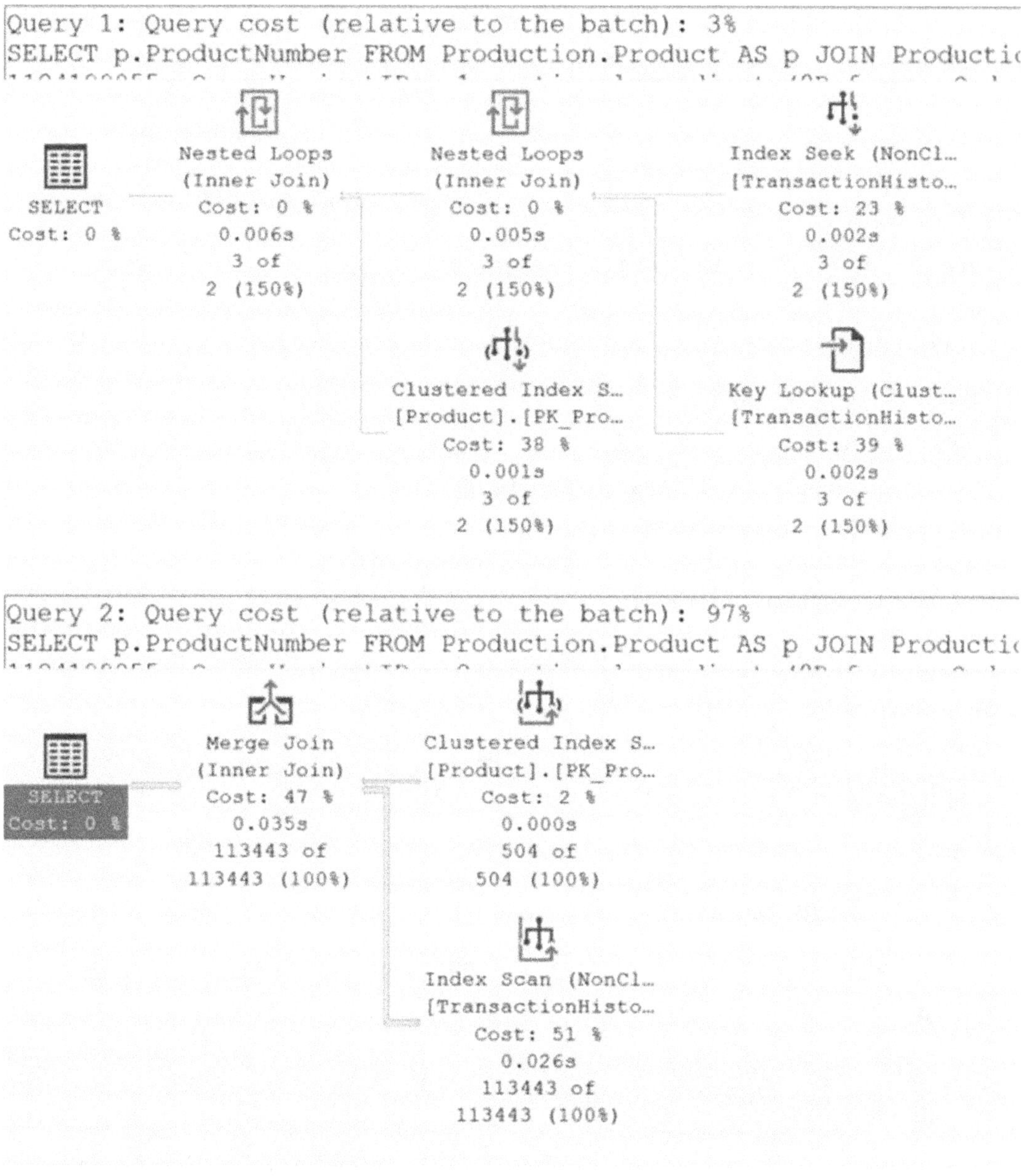

CHAPTER 13 ■ PARAMETER-SENSITIVE QUERIES: CAUSES AND SOLUTIONS

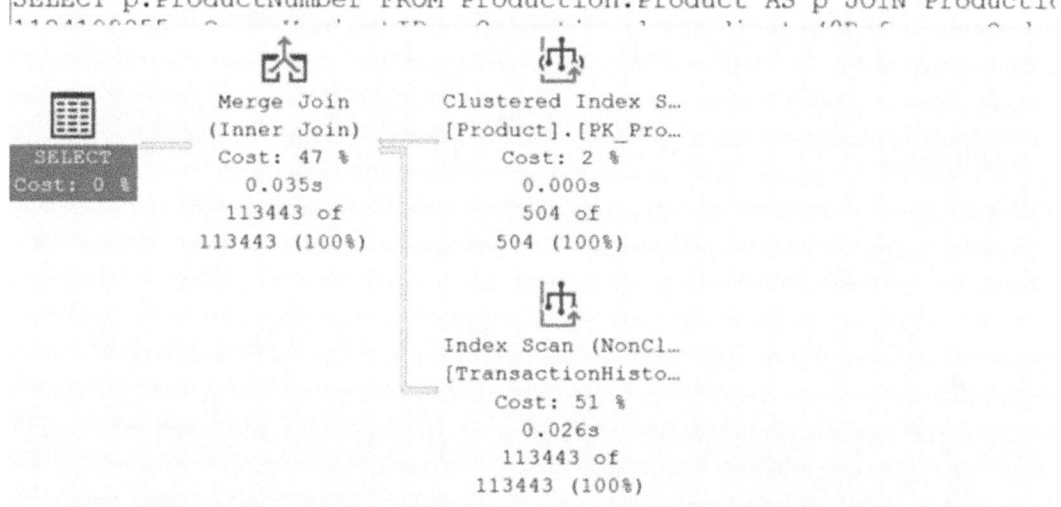

Figure 13-13. Two distinct execution plans

In this instance, the differences between the plans are quite stark. However, you can see that a plan for returning only a few rows was created as well as a plan for returning very large amounts of rows. As before, I haven't removed the plan from cache. There are two distinct plans depending on how the query is executed.

CHAPTER 13   PARAMETER-SENSITIVE QUERIES: CAUSES AND SOLUTIONS

As with PSP Optimization, OPO creates a dispatcher plan and any other plans. You can see the implementation in the properties of the execution plan in Figure 13-14.

```
Dispatcher
  OptionalParameterPredicate
    Predicate                                    [@ReferenceOrderID] IS NULL
```

Figure 13-14. *Dispatcher shows OPO predicate*

Multiplan also changes the code within the query as shown here:

```
SELECT p.ProductNumber
    FROM Production.Product AS p
        JOIN Production.TransactionHistory AS th
            ON th.ProductID = p.ProductID
    WHERE th.ReferenceOrderID = @ReferenceOrderID
        OR @ReferenceOrderID IS NULL option (PLAN PER VALUE(ObjectID
        = 1124199055, QueryVariantID = 2, optional_predicate(@
        ReferenceOrderID IS NULL)))
```

The OPO is enabled by default. Your database must be set to 170, SQL Server 2025, compatibility level. You can disable it using a DATABASE SCOPED CONFIGURATION setting as shown in Listing 13-23.

Listing 13-23. *Disabling OPO*

```
ALTER DATABASE SCOPED CONFIGURATION SET OPTIONAL_PARAMETER_
OPTIMIZATION = OFF;
```

As with the PSP Optimization, all other behaviors of OPO plans are the same as any other plan in the system.

Summary

While parameter sniffing can aid performance, sometimes, it can also hurt performance. However, the key is identifying which plans are going to work the best in your environment and then using one of the many mitigation methods to address the issue.

If you're working with SQL Server 2022 or in Azure SQL Database, you automatically get Parameter-Sensitive Plan Optimization, which, if you meet the thresholds, can address bad parameter sniffing with no action on your part.

In the next chapter, we'll cover common code smells and resolutions as we discuss query design analysis.

CHAPTER 14

Query Design Analysis

While a healthy amount of performance is determined by your hardware, your cloud service tier, server settings, indexes, and other data structures, the single most important aspect of SQL Server performance is your query. If your T-SQL is problematic, in many cases, none of the rest of functionality can save performance. There are a number of common coding issues, referred to as code smells, that can lead to bad performance. You may even have queries attempting to work on your data in a row-by-row fashion (quoting Jeff Moden, Row By Agonizing Row, abbreviated to RBAR). Focusing on fixing your T-SQL can be the single most important thing you can do to enhance the performance of your databases.

In this chapter, I cover the following topics:

- Common code smells in T-SQL
- Query designs to ensure effective index use
- Appropriate use of optimizer hints
- How database constraints affect performance

Query Design Recommendations

T-SQL is a very powerful language, and there is frequently more than one way to write a query and still get the exact same results. However, some queries are simply going to perform better than others. Certain query structures interfere with the optimizer finding the best execution plan. There are also query mechanisms that are more resource intensive than others. We'll cover that in the next chapter. In this chapter, I want to discuss the following recommendations:

- Keep your result sets as small as possible.
- Use indexes effectively.

- Use optimizer hints sparingly.
- Maintain and enforce referential integrity.

While all of my recommendations are tested, situationally they may not work for your queries or your environment. You should always make it a habit to test and validate code changes as you make them. Use the information put forward so far within the book, from capturing query metrics to reading execution plans, in order to understand how your own queries are performing.

Keep Your Result Sets Small

There's a classic saying, probably as old as computing:

Move only the data you need and only when you need to move it.

While this was originally stated back when networks could be easily overwhelmed by relatively benign data movement, the concept is still very applicable. By choosing to only select from columns that you need, you can easily reduce the overhead in your system. Further, limiting the rows being moved, you get to take advantage of indexes in assisting your performance. Follow these guidelines:

- Limit the columns in your SELECT list.
- Filter your data through a WHERE clause.

It's very common to hear someone say that the business requirement is to return 100,000 rows for a report. Yet if you drill down on this requirement, you may find that they simply need an aggregate or some other subset of the data. Humans simply do not process 100,000 rows on their own. Be sure you're only moving the data you need.

Limit the Columns in Your SELECT List

Strictly speaking, using SELECT * to retrieve every column is not a massive performance problem. However, retrieving all columns means that you won't be able to take advantage of covering indexes, indexes that provide all the columns needed for a given query. Listing 14-1 shows an example query.

Listing 14-1. Query with a limited column list

```
SELECT NAME,
       TerritoryID
FROM Sales.SalesTerritory AS st
WHERE st.Name = 'Australia';
```

The Sales.SalesTerritory table has a nonclustered index on the Name column. The clustered index on the table is on the TerritoryID column. Since the nonclustered index will use the clustered index key, you have a covering index for the query. Executing it, you get the metrics and execution plan shown in Figure 14-1:

Reads: 2
Duration: 127mcs

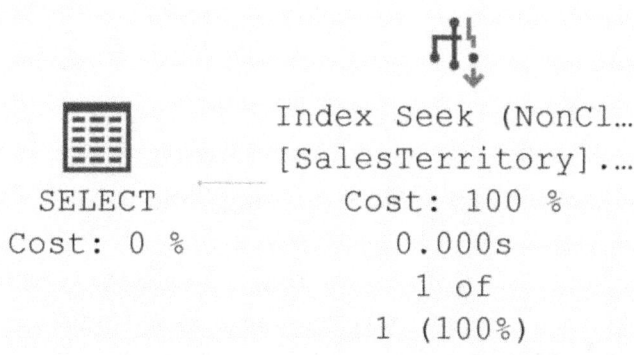

Figure 14-1. *An execution plan showing a covering index in action*

If I modify the query to return all columns on the table, we'll no longer see the nonclustered index used. Instead, we'll see the metrics and execution plan shown in Figure 14-2:

Reads: 4
Duration: 331mcs

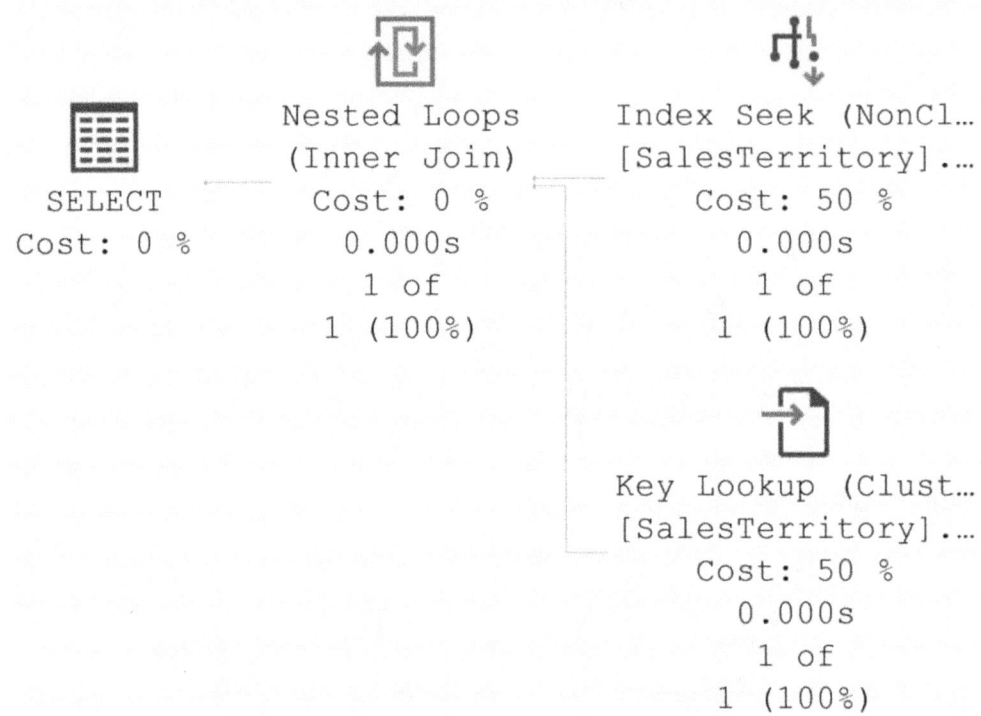

Figure 14-2. The query no longer has a covering index

I'm no longer getting the benefit of a covering index. The extra work required to both perform a Key Lookup to get the columns from the clustered index and then the Nested Loops to join the two result sets together ends up doubling the number of reads, from 2 to 4. The query duration on average doubled.

In short, only choose the columns you need at the moment.

Filter Your Data Through a WHERE Clause

In order to see benefits from an index on queries that involve looking up data, and this includes UPDATE and DELETE when they're finding the data being modified, INSERT when a referential integrity check occurs, and, of course, all SELECT statements, a WHERE clause must be used. Further, as explained in Chapter 8, the selectivity of the column, or columns, referenced in the WHERE, ON, and HAVING clauses determines how that index is used. As much as possible, your queries should be filtering data through these clauses. Where possible, you want to use the most selective column as well.

The majority of applications are going to be working off limited result sets. While you may need to perform data movement involving all, or a very large subset, of the data, generally speaking, you should be seeing mostly small data sets being retrieved. The exception of course is analytical queries, but you can better support queries of that type through columnstore indexes. In the event that you are in a situation where you regularly have to move extremely large result sets, you may need to look to external processes and hardware to improve performance.

Use Indexes Effectively

If a query is badly structured, it may not be able to take advantage of indexes. Since indexes are the most effective tool when it comes to performance tuning, it behooves you to ensure that your queries are structured such that they can use the indexes effectively. To improve the use of indexes, I'd suggest following these guidelines:

- Use effective search conditions.
- Avoid operations on columns in WHERE, ON, and HAVING clauses.
- Use care in creating custom scalar UDFs.

I'll break down these guidelines in the following sections.

Use Effective Search Conditions

Search conditions within a WHERE, ON, or HAVING clause can use a very large number of logical operations. Some of those operations are highly effective in allowing the query to work with indexes and statistics. Other operations are not as effective and can actively prevent the efficient use of indexes. Traditionally, we refer to the effective operations as being "Search ARGument ABLE" or sargable for short.

Note While the use of sargable conditions is in the HAVING, ON, and WHERE clauses, rather than saying all three every time, I'm going to simply reference the WHERE clause. Assume I mean all three when I reference just the one.

There are a few search conditions, introduced in more recent versions of SQL Server, for which these rules don't exactly apply. For example, SOME/ANY and ALL are dependent on the subquery that defines them. If you use a non-sargable condition in that subquery, then you'll have issues.

Table 14-1 shows both the sargable and non-sargable conditions within SQL Server. The sargable search conditions allow the optimizer to use an index on the column(s) in the WHERE clause. Generally, you're likely to see a seek to a row, or set of rows, in the index when using those conditions.

Table 14-1. Common sargable and non-sargable search conditions

Type	Search Conditions
Sargable	Inclusion conditions =, >, >=, <, <=, and BETWEEN and some LIKE conditions such as LIKE '<literal>%'
Non-sargable	Exclusion conditions <>, !=, !>, !<, NOT EXISTS, NOT IN, and NOT LIKE and some LIKE conditions such as '%<literal>' or '%<literal>%'

The non-sargable conditions listed will prevent good index use by the optimizer. Instead of a seek, you're much more likely to see scans when using these conditions. This is especially true to the logical NOT operators such as <>, !=, and NOT LIKE. Using these will always result in a scan of all rows to identify those that match.

Where you can, implement workarounds for these non-sargable search conditions to improve performance. In some cases, it may be possible to rewrite the logic of a query to use inclusion instead of exclusion operations. You will have to experiment with different mechanisms in order to determine which are going to work in a given situation. Also, don't forget that additional filtering could limit the scans necessary when multiple columns from one table are in a WHERE clause. Testing is your friend when you have to deal with these types of situations.

BETWEEN vs. IN/OR

Listing 14-2 is an example of a query using an IN condition.

Listing 14-2. A query using an IN condition

```
SELECT sod.CarrierTrackingNumber,
       sod.OrderQty
FROM Sales.SalesOrderDetail AS sod
WHERE sod.SalesOrderID IN ( 51825, 51826, 51827, 51828 );
```

Logically, this query could be written using an OR condition as shown in Listing 14-3.

Listing 14-3. A query using an OR condition

```
SELECT sod.CarrierTrackingNumber,
       sod.OrderQty
FROM Sales.SalesOrderDetail AS sod
WHERE sod.SalesOrderID = 51825
    OR sod.SalesOrderID = 51826
    OR sod.SalesOrderID = 51827
    OR sod.SalesOrderID = 51828;
```

Since the values we're searching for in this case are consecutive integers, another way to logically write this query is shown in Listing 14-4.

Listing 14-4. A query using a BETWEEN condition

```
SELECT sod.CarrierTrackingNumber,
       sod.OrderQty
FROM Sales.SalesOrderDetail AS sod
WHERE sod.SalesOrderID
BETWEEN 51825 AND 51828;
```

Logically, all three queries are the same. If you look at the result sets, they are all the same. If I capture all three execution plans and put them side by side, as shown in Figure 14-3, they are even visually identical.

CHAPTER 14   QUERY DESIGN ANALYSIS

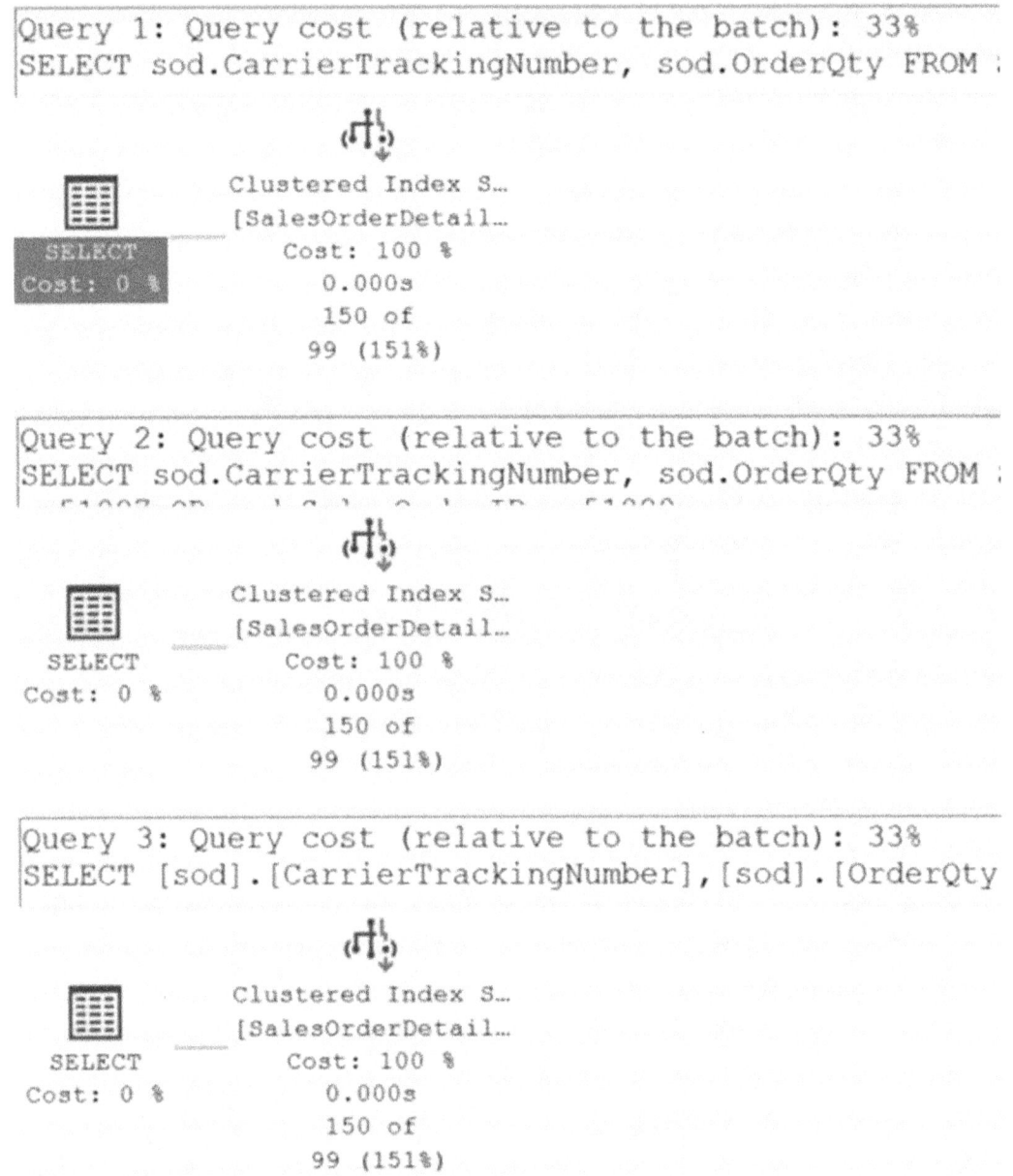

Figure 14-3. *Three visually identical execution plans*

Even though plans may be visually the same, if we look at the performance metrics, we can see differences. Here are the metrics for the three queries in order:

Using IN

CHAPTER 14 QUERY DESIGN ANALYSIS

Duration: 193mcs
Reads: 18

Using OR

Duration: 165mcs
Reads: 18

Using BETWEEN

Duration: 172mcs
Reads: 6

While the OR clause was slightly, 7 microseconds, faster than the BETWEEN, it used three times as many reads, 18 compared with 6. The key to understanding this is in how the optimizer chooses to deal with these queries. While they are logically the same, they are physically different, and the optimizer has choices. If we compare the IN execution plan with the BETWEEN plan using the plan comparison capabilities in SSMS (as explained in Chapter 4), we can quickly identify differences, especially this one in the Clustered Index Seek operator in Figure 14-4.

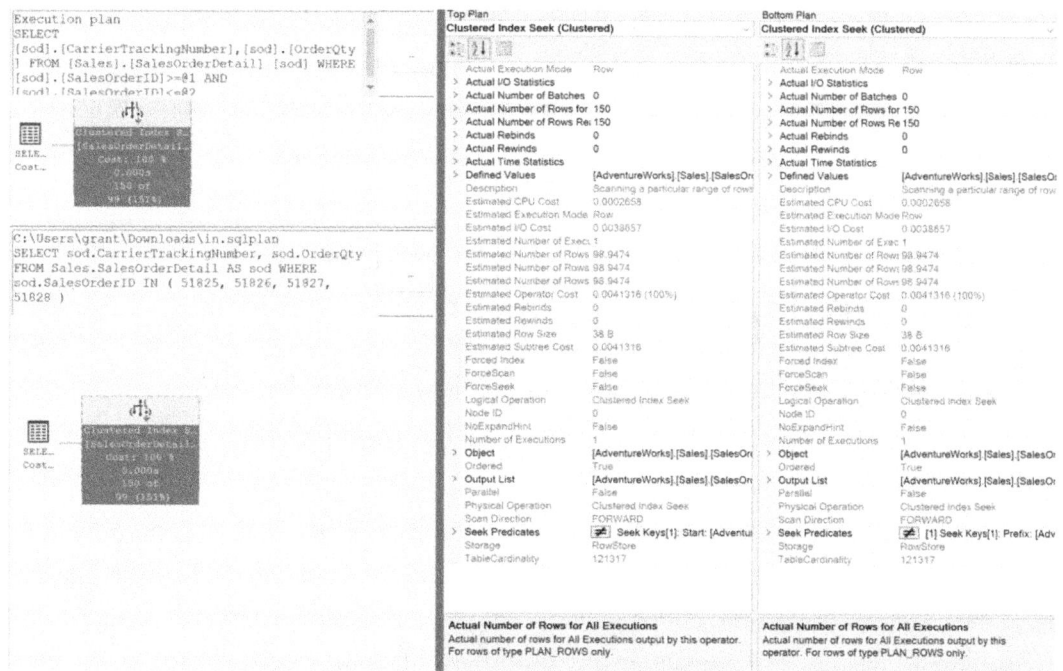

Figure 14-4. *Differences between two execution plans*

439

The only real difference is in the Seek Predicates values. Here is the predicate for both the IN and OR queries in Listings 14-2 and 14-3:

```
[1] Seek Keys[1]: Prefix: [AdventureWorks].[Sales].[SalesOrderDetail].
SalesOrderID = Scalar Operator((51825)), [2] Seek Keys[1]: Prefix:
[AdventureWorks].[Sales].[SalesOrderDetail].SalesOrderID = Scalar
Operator((51826)), [3] Seek Keys[1]: Prefix: [AdventureWorks].[Sales].
[SalesOrderDetail].SalesOrderID = Scalar Operator((51827)), [4] Seek
Keys[1]: Prefix: [AdventureWorks].[Sales].[SalesOrderDetail].SalesOrderID =
Scalar Operator((51828))
```

This is the predicate for the BETWEEN query in Listing 14-4:

```
Seek Keys[1]: Start: [AdventureWorks].[Sales].[SalesOrderDetail].
SalesOrderID >= Scalar Operator([@1]), End: [AdventureWorks].[Sales].
[SalesOrderDetail].SalesOrderID <= Scalar Operator([@2])
```

First, the optimizer has chosen to apply simple parameterization to this query as you can see in the @1 and @2 values within the second predicate. Also, instead of a BETWEEN operation, >= and <= have been substituted. In the end, this approach results in far fewer reads. On a production system under load, this will doubtless lead to superior performance.

If we also take a look at STATISTICS IO for the two queries, we get a better sense of what's happening:

For the OR query:

```
Table "SalesOrderDetail". Scan count 4, logical reads 18
```

For the BETWEEN query:

```
Table "SalesOrderDetail". Scan count 1, logical reads 6
```

As you can see, there are four scans to satisfy the OR condition, while a single scan satisfies the BETWEEN condition.

This is not to say that you will always see better performance under all circumstances when dealing with IN, OR, and BETWEEN. However, as you can tell, while three queries may share logical similarities, choosing different mechanisms can arrive at superior performance. Testing, and then using the tools to evaluate the queries, is the key. Different operators can, and will, use the indexes in different ways.

This is also an example where STATISTICS IO can give us additional information beyond what's available to us within Extended Events. You won't always need to use it, but keep that tool in mind when you need to drill down to better understand why you may be seeing differences in behavior between two queries.

LIKE Condition

Searches against text within the database are extremely common. Where possible, you should try to avoid using wild cards as part of the leading edge of that condition. Because it won't be able to use the histogram of the statistics to identify potential ranges of matching rows, it must scan the entire index to look for matching values. It's also a good idea to provide as many leading characters as you can in a LIKE condition in order to help the optimizer in identifying ranges. The optimizer also makes internal changes to queries when using the LIKE condition. Take Listing 14-5 as an example.

Listing 14-5. Using the LIKE condition

```
SELECT C.CurrencyCode
FROM Sales.Currency AS C
WHERE C.NAME LIKE 'Ice%';
```

The optimizer changes this predicate, and we can see it in the execution plan:

```
Seek Keys[1]: Start: [AdventureWork].[Sales].[Currency].Name >= Scalar
Operator(N'Ice'), End: [AdventureWork].[Sales].[Currency].Name <  Scalar
Operator(N'Ice')
```

The change is from a LIKE condition to >= and < conditions. You could rewrite the query to use those conditions yourself. If you did, the performance, including the reads, would be exactly the same. This simply means using leading characters in a LIKE condition means the optimizer can make good choices for the search using indexes on the table.

!< Condition vs. >= Condition

Even though both !< and >= are logically equivalent and you will see an identical result set in a query using them, the optimizer is going to implement execution plans differently using these two conditions. The key is in the equality operator for >=. That gives the optimizer a solid starting point for using an index. The other operation, !<, has no starting point, resulting in the entire index, or the entire table, having to be scanned.

CHAPTER 14   QUERY DESIGN ANALYSIS

However, as I've already shown you in multiple examples within the book, the optimizer is capable of some modifications to the T-SQL code you've submitted. Here, we have a pair of queries that are using the conditions just discussed (Listing 14-6).

Listing 14-6. Comparing !< and >= conditions

```
SELECT poh.TotalDue,
       poh.Freight
FROM Purchasing.PurchaseOrderHeader AS poh
WHERE poh.PurchaseOrderID >= 2975;
SELECT poh.TotalDue,
       poh.Freight
FROM Purchasing.PurchaseOrderHeader AS poh
WHERE poh.PurchaseOrderID !< 2975;
```

Capturing the execution plans for both queries, they look visually identical in Figure 14-5.

```
Query 1: Query cost (relative to the batch): 50%
SELECT [poh].[TotalDue],[poh].[Freight] FROM [Purchasing].[Purc
```

```
                                         Clustered Index S...
                                         [PurchaseOrderHea...
   SELECT       Compute Scalar            Cost: 99 %
   Cost: 0 %    Cost: 1 %                 0.006s
                                          1038 of
                                          1038 (100%)
```

```
Query 2: Query cost (relative to the batch): 50%
SELECT [poh].[TotalDue],[poh].[Freight] FROM [Purchasing].[Purc
```

```
                                         Clustered Index S...
                                         [PurchaseOrderHea...
   SELECT       Compute Scalar            Cost: 99 %
   Cost: 0 %    Cost: 1 %                 0.000s
                                          1038 of
                                          1038 (100%)
```

Figure 14-5. *Identical execution plans*

In fact, if you compare the plans, they are identical. It's the same execution plan, used for both queries. You can see what happened if you look at the T-SQL stored with the plan. First, the optimizer changed the !< to >=. Second, it used simple parameterization, which leads to plan reuse. This is an example of when code is logically equivalent, the optimizer can help the performance of your query.

Avoid Operations on Columns

Calculations such as mathematical operations or functions like DATEPART when used against columns prevent good statistics and index use. Listing 14-7 shows a calculation against a column in the WHERE clause.

Listing 14-7. Calculation on a column

```
SELECT poh.EmployeeID,
       poh.OrderDate
FROM Purchasing.PurchaseOrderHeader AS poh
WHERE poh.PurchaseOrderID * 2 = 3400;
```

The execution plan is shown in Figure 14-6.

CHAPTER 14   QUERY DESIGN ANALYSIS

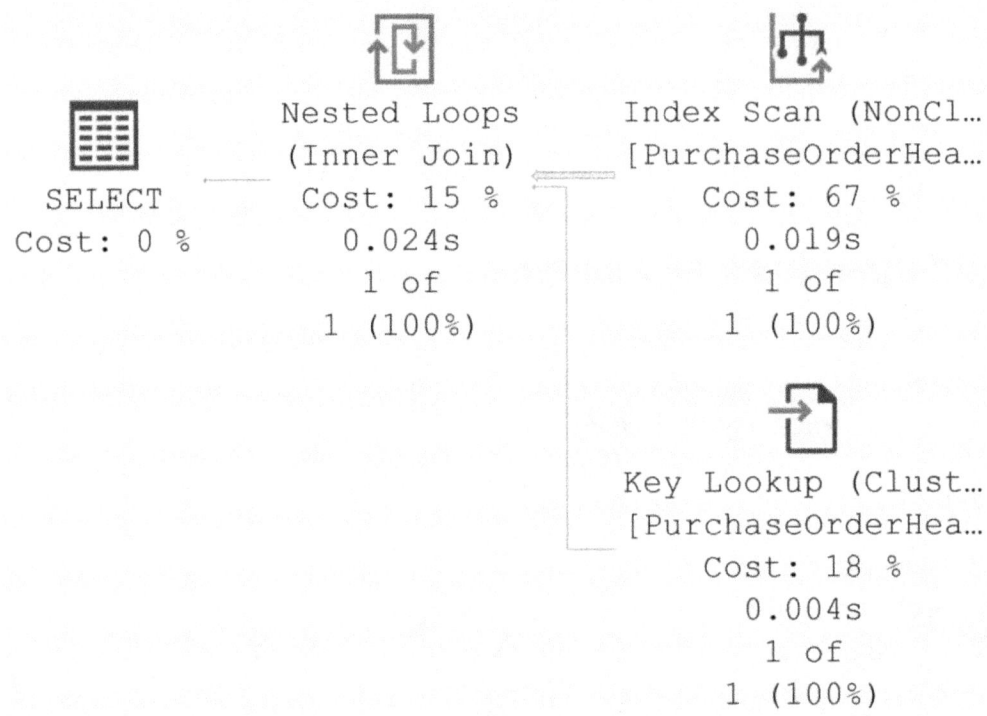

Figure 14-6. An index scan caused by a calculation

There is an index on the PurchaseOrderID column, so the optimizer scanned that instead of scanning the clustered index. This is because the nonclustered index is smaller. However, that scan results in the need to then pull the remaining columns from the clustered key through the Key Lookup operation and a join.

The query metrics are as follows:

Reads: 11
Duration: 2.15ms

In Listing 14-8, I move the calculation off the column to the hard-coded value.

Listing 14-8. Changing the query to not calculate on the column

```
SELECT poh.EmployeeID,
       poh.OrderDate
FROM Purchasing.PurchaseOrderHeader AS poh
WHERE poh.PurchaseOrderID = 3400 / 2;
```

Making this modification results in the runtime metrics and execution plan shown in Figure 14-7:

Reads: 2
Duration: 177mcs

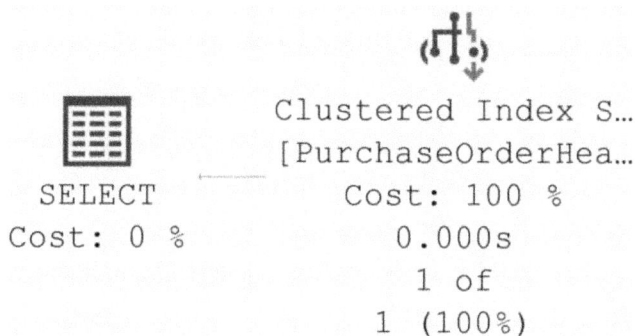

Figure 14-7. A seek with the calculation removed

There's not much to explain. Because of the calculation, the optimizer must scan the data. The optimizer tries to help you by scanning a smaller index and then looking up the remaining data, but as you can see, simply moving the calculation off the column makes all the difference. The problem with calculations on columns is so prevalent; even an AI can spot it in the code. Here's the suggestion from Perplexity (Figure 14-8).

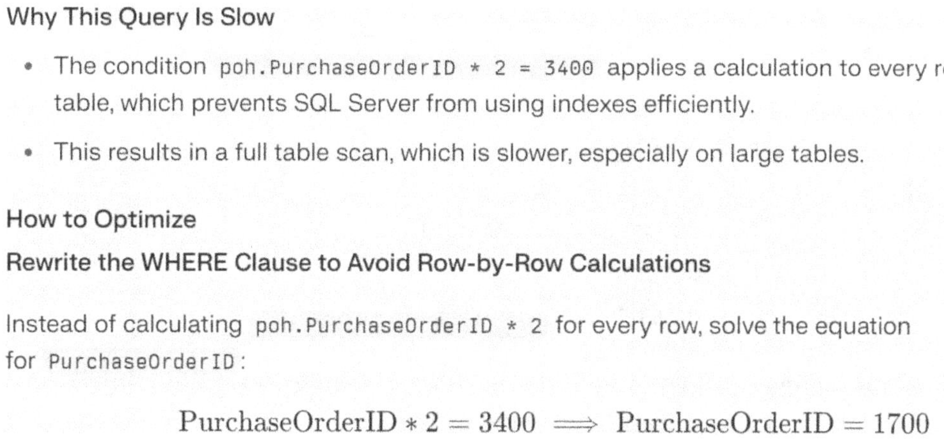

Why This Query Is Slow

- The condition `poh.PurchaseOrderID * 2 = 3400` applies a calculation to every row in the table, which prevents SQL Server from using indexes efficiently.
- This results in a full table scan, which is slower, especially on large tables.

How to Optimize

Rewrite the WHERE Clause to Avoid Row-by-Row Calculations

Instead of calculating `poh.PurchaseOrderID * 2` for every row, solve the equation for `PurchaseOrderID`:

$$\text{PurchaseOrderID} * 2 = 3400 \implies \text{PurchaseOrderID} = 1700$$

Figure 14-8. Perplexity AI explaining how to troubleshoot this query

This works for functions too. A classic problem arises when using DATETIME data types when you only need dates. An even worse issue is when people store date and time information as strings, in VARCHAR or CHAR columns, because you can store it formatted. To set up an example, I'm going to create an index on the Sales.SalesOrderHeader table as shown in Listing 14-9.

Listing 14-9. Creating an index on a DATETIME column

```
IF EXISTS
(
    SELECT *
    FROM sys.indexes
    WHERE OBJECT_ID = OBJECT_ID(N'[Sales].[SalesOrderHeader]')
        AND NAME = N'IndexTest'
)
    DROP INDEX IndexTest ON Sales.SalesOrderHeader;
GO
CREATE INDEX IndexTest ON Sales.SalesOrderHeader (OrderDate);
```

I'm going to query the data in the SalesOrderHeader table in order to retrieve sales that take place in the year 2008, in the month of April, as shown in Listing 14-10.

Listing 14-10. Querying for parts of dates

```
SELECT soh.SalesOrderID,
       soh.OrderDate
FROM Sales.SalesOrderHeader AS soh
    JOIN Sales.SalesOrderDetail AS sod
        ON soh.SalesOrderID = sod.SalesOrderID
WHERE DATEPART(yy, soh.OrderDate) = 2008
    AND DATEPART(mm, soh.OrderDate) = 4;
```

Because we're using DATEPART on the column, we're going to see poor index use in the execution plan in Figure 14-9 and the following metrics:

```
Reads: 73
Duration: 2.48ms
```

CHAPTER 14 QUERY DESIGN ANALYSIS

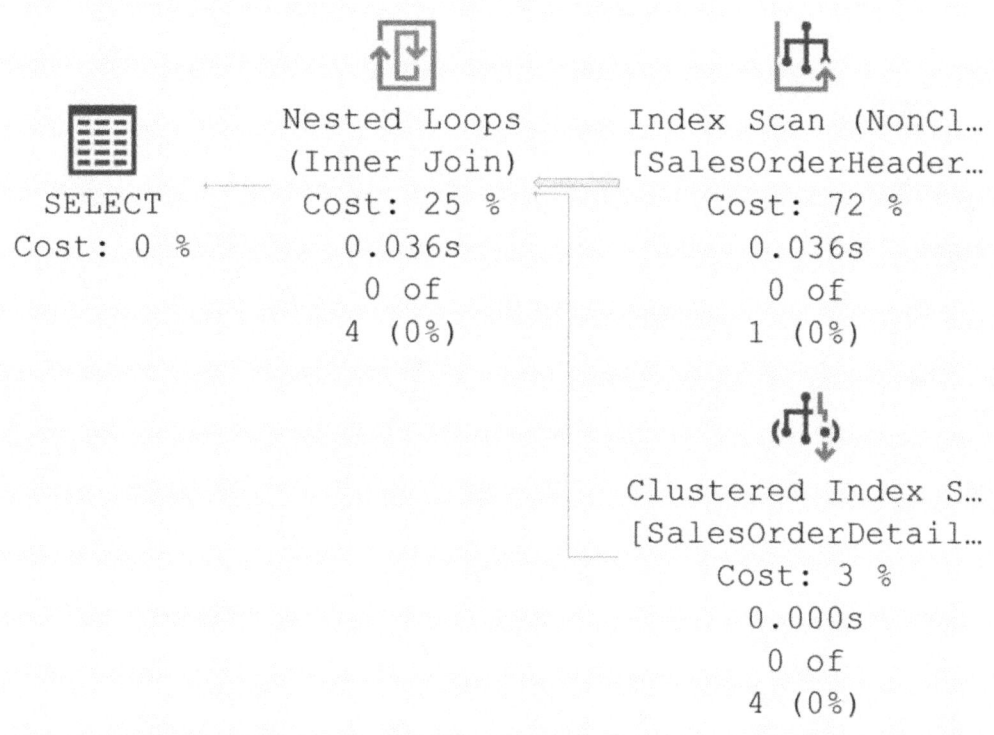

***Figure 14-9.** An index scan caused by the DATEPART function*

The thing is I can treat the dates as dates to arrive at the same result set by changing the logic of the query in Listing 14-11.

Listing 14-11. Modifying the date logic

```
SELECT soh.SalesOrderID,
       soh.OrderDate
FROM Sales.SalesOrderHeader AS soh
    JOIN Sales.SalesOrderDetail AS sod
        ON soh.SalesOrderID = sod.SalesOrderID
WHERE soh.OrderDate >= '2008-04-01'
    AND soh.OrderDate < '2008-05-01';
```

This version of the query has the following metrics and execution plan in Figure 14-10:

Reads: 2
Duration: 239mcs

CHAPTER 14 ■ QUERY DESIGN ANALYSIS

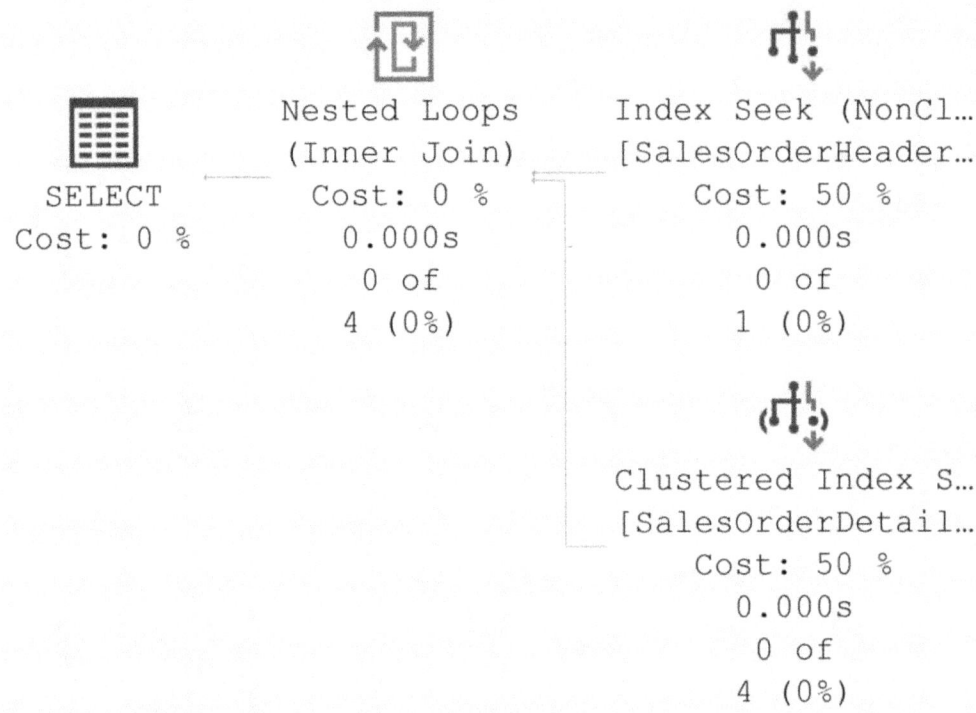

Figure 14-10. *A seek occurs when dates are treated appropriately*

It's not even close. In both examples, changing the logic to avoid running operations against columns results in radical performance enhancements.

Listing 14-12 removes the index I created.

Listing 14-12. Cleaning up after the test

```
DROP INDEX Sales.SalesOrderHeader.IndexTest;
```

Custom Scalar UDF

Scalar functions are an attractive means of code reuse, especially if you need only a single value. However, while you can use them for data retrieval, you can see poor performance because it's not an ideal use of scalar UDFs. In order to see this in action, Listing 14-13 creates a scalar function.

CHAPTER 14 QUERY DESIGN ANALYSIS

Listing 14-13. Scalar function to retrieve product costs

```
CREATE OR ALTER FUNCTION dbo.ProductStandardCost
(
    @ProductID INT
)
RETURNS MONEY
AS
BEGIN
    DECLARE @Cost MONEY;
    SELECT TOP 1
            @Cost = pch.StandardCost
    FROM Production.ProductCostHistory AS pch
    WHERE pch.ProductID = @ProductID
    ORDER BY pch.StartDate DESC;
    IF @Cost IS NULL
        SET @Cost = 0;
    RETURN @Cost;
END;
```

Listing 14-14 then uses the function in a simple query.

Listing 14-14. Consuming the scalar function

```
SELECT p.NAME,
       dbo.ProductStandardCost(p.ProductID)
FROM Production.Product AS p
WHERE p.ProductNumber LIKE 'HL%';
```

Running the query results in the runtime metrics and execution plan shown in Figure 14-11:

Reads: 14
Duration: 316mcs

CHAPTER 14   QUERY DESIGN ANALYSIS

Figure 14-11. *Execution plan with a scalar function*

This execution plan is a little difficult to see, so we'll break it down into its component parts. Older versions of SQL Server won't show this level of detail within the execution plan but instead will hide the scalar function within a single Compute Scalar operator. Capturing an estimated plan in older versions of SQL Server (prior to 2022) will show all the information you see here.

We'll start with the section that shows how the scalar function is performing its data retrieval. Figure 14-12 shows the detail of that part of the plan.

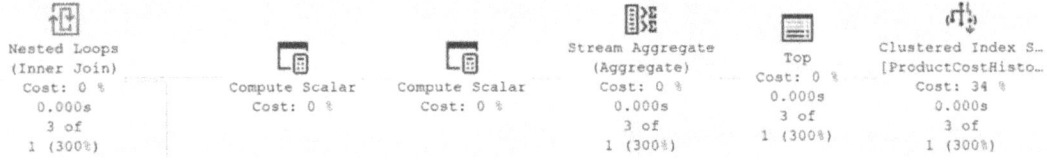

Figure 14-12. *Data retrieval inside the scalar function*

The function is able to use a Clustered Index Seek to retrieve the data. You can then see it performs the necessary functions to prep the information, using a Top operator to support the TOP 1 part of the query and a Stream Aggregate to define the values returned. The Compute Scalar operators simply ensure that the data types are correct.

450

CHAPTER 14 QUERY DESIGN ANALYSIS

The next section of the plan (Figure 14-13) at the bottom is how the optimizer deals with the IF clause in the query.

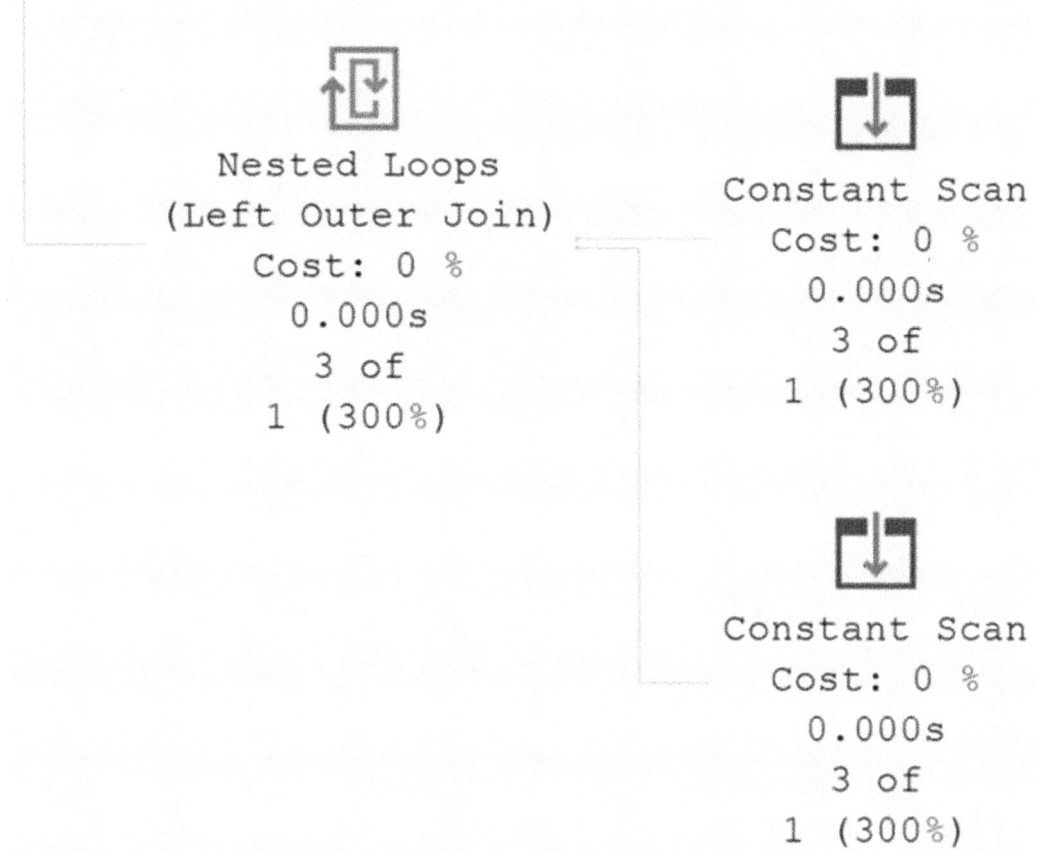

Figure 14-13. *IF statement within the execution plan*

The Constant Scan operators are used to evaluate whether or not the @Cost value is NULL. The join operation will ensure that a value, either the @Cost value or the value of 0, gets returned. This is then joined to the output of the data retrieval in the scalar operator.

At the top of the plan is the query from Listing 14-14, and it's part of the data retrieval in Figure 14-14.

CHAPTER 14 QUERY DESIGN ANALYSIS

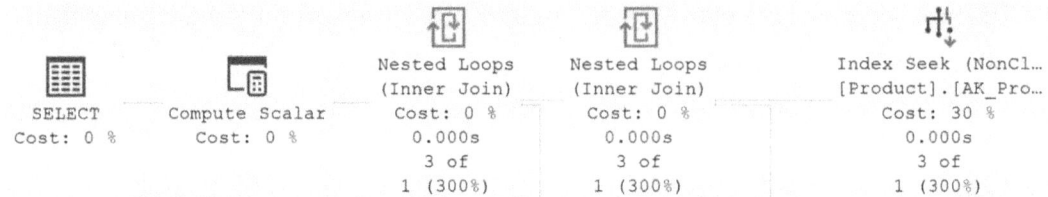

Figure 14-14. Satisfying the rest of the query

The Index Seek filters the data from the WHERE clause, and then the Name column is retrieved using the Key Lookup. This data is then joined and then joined again with the data from the scalar function.

The query is running fairly fast at 316 microseconds, but you can rewrite this query to avoid using the scalar function, seen here in Listing 14-15.

Listing 14-15. Replacing the scalar function

```
SELECT p.NAME,
       pc.StandardCost
FROM Production.Product AS p
    CROSS APPLY
(
    SELECT TOP 1
           pch.StandardCost
    FROM Production.ProductCostHistory AS pch
    WHERE pch.ProductID = p.ProductID
    ORDER BY pch.StartDate DESC
) AS pc
WHERE p.ProductNumber LIKE 'HL%';
```

This query runs in about 174 microseconds, a decent improvement over the scalar function. Figure 14-15 shows the execution plan for this query.

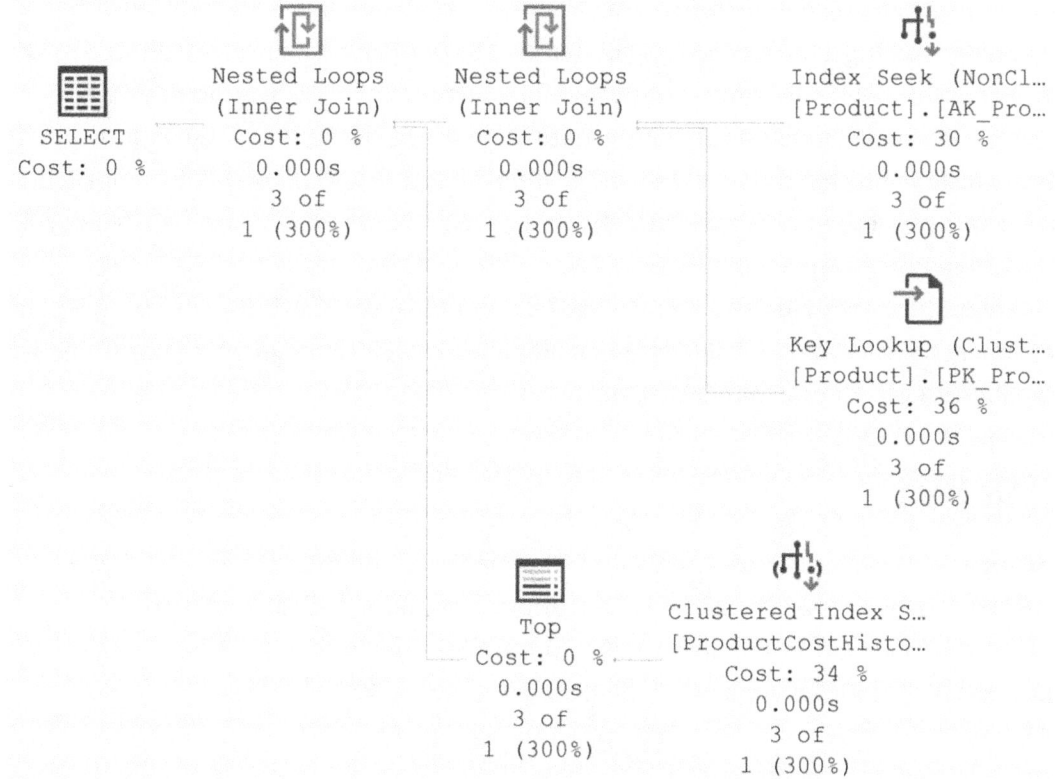

Figure 14-15. Simplified execution plan after eliminating the scalar function

If you compare this plan to the plan shown previously, you can see most of the same functionality in play. Yet because there are fewer overall operations, the speed is improved.

Minimize Optimizer Hints

The query optimizer within SQL Server is one of the most amazing pieces of software of which I'm aware. The way it uses your data structures, statistics, and its algorithms to make the queries you write run fast is incredible. However, the optimizer will not always get things perfectly correct, every time. Rarely, it may need some assistance, and you can take some aspects of control away from the optimizer in these cases through the use of what are called hints.

More often than not, the optimizer will give you a good enough plan for the query in question. However, like in the case of parameter sniffing (discussed in Chapter 13), the optimizer's choices can be less than optimal. As I showed, one way to deal with parameter sniffing gone bad is through the use of a query hint, such as OPTIMIZE FOR. It's extremely important to understand that a hint is not a suggestion nearly as much as it's a command for the optimizer to behave in a certain way. The majority of the time, I reserve hints to the very last option when attempting to improve the performance of a query. However, understanding what hints are and how they can be used when you need them is also important.

I don't have room in the book to cover all possible hints. I have already covered some in earlier chapters, and I'll cover more in later chapters. Here, I want to demonstrate two specific hints: JOIN hint and INDEX hint.

JOIN Hint

In Chapter 2, I explained how the optimizer dynamically determines a cost-effective JOIN strategy between two data sets. This strategy combines the data structures, constraints, and statistics to arrive at the appropriate type of join. Table 14-2 summarizes the types of JOIN operations within SQL Server.

Table 14-2. JOIN types supported by SQL Server

JOIN Types	Index on Joining Columns	Usual Size of Joining Tables	Sorted Data Requirement
Nested Loops	Inner table a must, outer table preferable	Small	Optional
Merge	Both tables a must	Large	Yes
Hash	Inner table **not** indexed	Any	No
Adaptive	Uses either Hash or Loops, so those requirements are needed	Generally, very large	Depends on the join type

There is no hint for the Adaptive Join since it's entirely determined by the optimizer when it will get used and then how it will get used based on the data, all covered in Chapter 8. Table 14-3 shows the possible JOIN hints.

CHAPTER 14 QUERY DESIGN ANALYSIS

Table 14-3. *JOIN hints*

JOIN Type	JOIN Hint
Nested Loops	LOOP
Merge	MERGE
Hash	HASH
	REMOTE

Note   There are four hints, but only three JOIN types because the REMOTE hint is used only when one of the tables in a JOIN is in a different database.

Listing 14-16 shows a query with a number of joins between different tables.

Listing 14-16. Joining multiple tables in a query

```
SELECT s.NAME AS StoreName,
       p.LastName + ', ' + p.FirstName
FROM Sales.Store AS s
    JOIN Sales.SalesPerson AS sp
        ON s.SalesPersonID = sp.BusinessEntityID
    JOIN HumanResources.Employee AS E
        ON sp.BusinessEntityID = E.BusinessEntityID
    JOIN Person.Person AS p
        ON E.BusinessEntityID = p.BusinessEntityID;
```

This query results in the following performance metrics and execution plan (Figure 14-16):

Reads: 2,364
Duration: 2.81ms

CHAPTER 14   QUERY DESIGN ANALYSIS

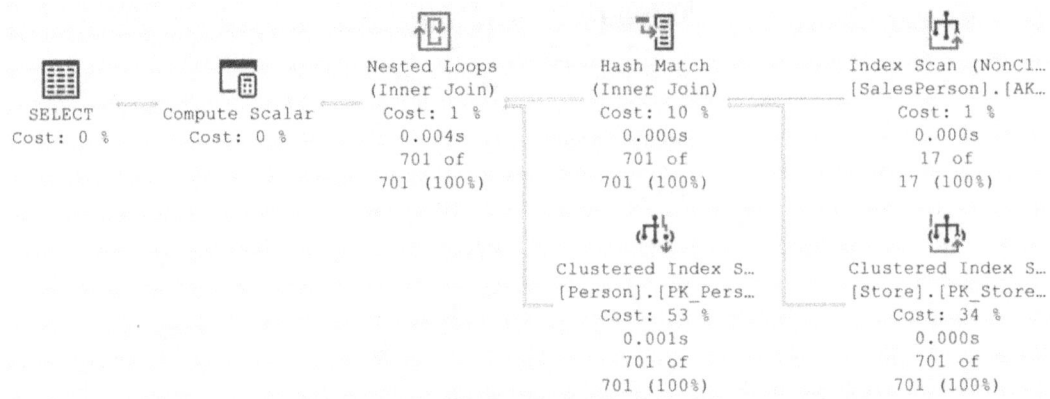

Figure 14-16. Execution for a query without any hints

The optimizer has made several choices based on the query and the objects. In this case, it's using a Hash Match for the first join and Nested Loops for the second. For simple queries of this type, with a small data set, a Nested Loops join makes sense. The optimizer saw no way for indexes to help with the other tables, so it ended up using a HASH to bring the data together. It's possible, since the number of rows coming from the Sales.SalesPerson table is relatively small, a loop join might be better. We can modify the code to test it out in Listing 14-17. Executing the query results in the plan you see in Figure 14-17.

Listing 14-17. Adding a JOIN hint

```
SELECT s.NAME AS StoreName,
       p.LastName + ', ' + p.FirstName
FROM Sales.Store AS s
    JOIN Sales.SalesPerson AS sp
        ON s.SalesPersonID = sp.BusinessEntityID
    JOIN HumanResources.Employee AS E
        ON sp.BusinessEntityID = E.BusinessEntityID
    JOIN Person.Person AS p
        ON E.BusinessEntityID = p.BusinessEntityID
OPTION (LOOP JOIN);
```

CHAPTER 14 QUERY DESIGN ANALYSIS

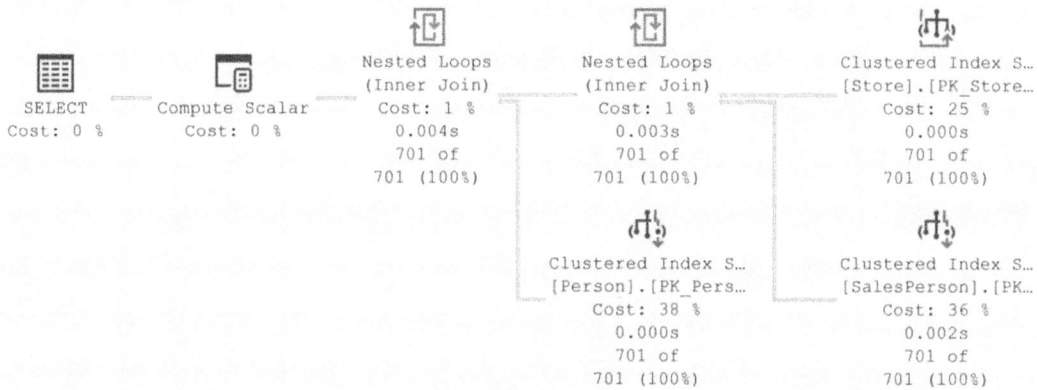

Figure 14-17. *Plan after forcing LOOPS joins*

The plan shape is roughly the same, but the Hash Match has been replaced by the Nested Loops, per the instruction. One point worth mentioning. In Figure 14-16, the Index Scan operation against the Sales.SalesPerson table estimated that 17 rows would be needed, and that's how many it returned. If you look at Figure 14-17, the Clustered Index Scan has hit all 701 rows in the table. This results in the following performance metrics:

Reads: 3,740
Writes: 3.6ms

That's almost 25% slower and close to 50% more reads. In short, we've received exactly what we asked for, all Nested Loops joins, but at the cost of worse performance. That's pretty bad, but it could be worse. In this case, we've told the optimizer to use Nested Loops for any joins it deems necessary. However, we could change things and only specify the join for the one table here in Listing 14-18.

Listing 14-18. Forcing just one join to behave a certain way

```
SELECT s.NAME AS StoreName,
       p.LastName + ', ' + p.FirstName
FROM Sales.Store AS s
    INNER LOOP JOIN Sales.SalesPerson AS sp
        ON s.SalesPersonID = sp.BusinessEntityID
```

```
JOIN HumanResources.Employee AS E
    ON sp.BusinessEntityID = E.BusinessEntityID
JOIN Person.Person AS p
    ON E.BusinessEntityID = p.BusinessEntityID;
```

This results in the execution plan visible in Figure 14-18.

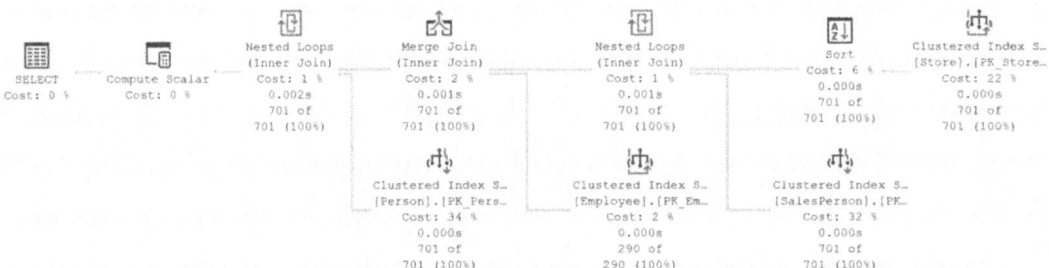

Figure 14-18. *Forcing a single join to change may have consequences*

The execution plans in Figures 14-16 and 14-17 showed three different references to pulling data from tables or indexes. Figure 14-18 now has four. In short, by forcing the join through the query hint as we did, we took away the optimizer's ability to put this query through the simplification process. Through the enforced referential constraints, the optimizer was able to eliminate a table from the execution plan, which it has now been forced to put back due to the query hint. The performance metrics reflect this change of course:

Reads: 3,749
Duration: 4ms

I haven't improved performance at all through these experiments. While there will absolutely be exceptions, in general, letting the optimizer choose how best to join together tables results in superior performance. The use of hints can

- Cause elimination of simplification
- Prevent auto-parameterization
- Prevent the optimizer from dynamically deciding the join order

While hints can sometimes improve performance, it's absolutely not a guarantee. Only use them after very thorough testing.

CHAPTER 14 QUERY DESIGN ANALYSIS

INDEX Hints

Because the optimizer is dependent on statistics, it is possible for an index that might help a query to get overlooked. However, the vast majority of the time, the optimizer is right. Still, people regularly try to outsmart the optimizer. Take our earlier example with the calculation against the column from Listing 14-7. There's an index on the table, PK_PurchaseOrderHeader_PurchaseOrderID, that, without the calculation, would surely have been used to retrieve the data. Listing 14-19 shows how to implement an index hint.

Listing 14-19. Forcing index choice through a query hint

```
SELECT poh.EmployeeID,
       poh.OrderDate
FROM Purchasing.PurchaseOrderHeader AS poh WITH (INDEX(PK_
PurchaseOrderHeader_PurchaseOrderID))
WHERE poh.PurchaseOrderID * 2 = 3400;
```

Figure 14-19 shows the resulting execution plan, and these are the runtime metrics:

Reads: 44
Duration: 682mcs

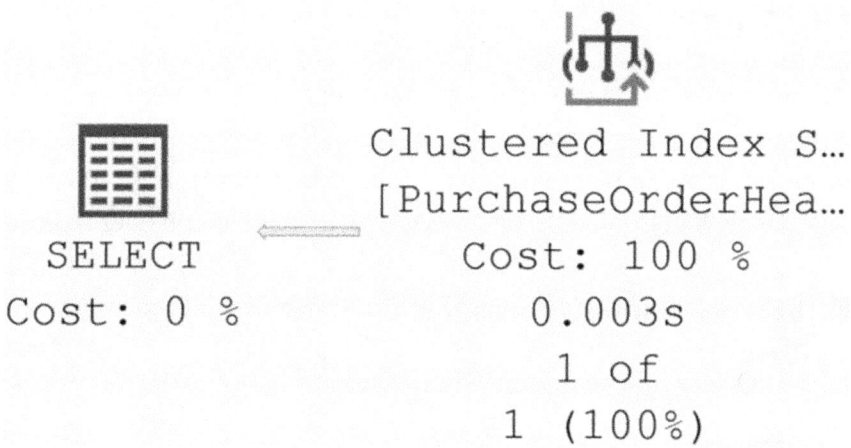

Figure 14-19. *A scan from an index hint*

This is a mixed result. The reads went from 11 to 44. However, the execution time went from 2.15ms to 434mcs, a very substantial reduction. It's still not as fast as simply removing the calculation from the column, which ran in 177mcs and only had 2 reads. Fixing the code is absolutely the superior choice by every measure. However, the INDEX hint did help the original query. This kind of experimentation can sometimes result in wins.

Using Domain and Referential Integrity

While the primary purpose of domain and referential integrity is to ensure good, clean data, the optimizer can also take advantage of these constraints. Knowing that a foreign key is enforced can change the row estimates and improve the choices made by the optimizer.

We'll explore three examples here:

- The NOT NULL constraint
- A check constraint
- Declarative referential integrity (DRI)

NOT NULL Constraint

The NOT NULL constraint ensures that a given column will never allow NULL values, helping ensure domain integrity of the data there. SQL Server will enforce this constraint in real time as data is manipulated within the table. The optimizer uses the information that there will be no NULL values to help improve the speed of the queries against the column.

Listing 14-20 contains two queries against similarly sized data sets and columns.

Listing 14-20. Querying the Person.Person table

```
SELECT p.FirstName
FROM Person.Person AS p
WHERE p.FirstName < 'B'
    OR p.FirstName >= 'C';
SELECT p.MiddleName
```

CHAPTER 14 QUERY DESIGN ANALYSIS

```
FROM Person.Person AS p
WHERE p.MiddleName < 'B'
      OR p.MiddleName >= 'C';
```

These two queries have visually identical execution plans as you see in Figure 14-20.

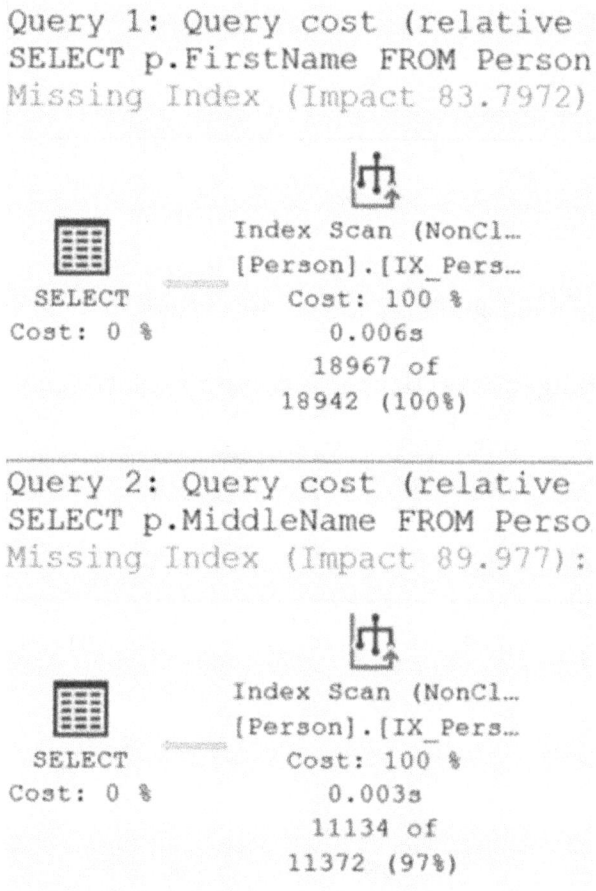

Figure 14-20. Two visually identical execution plans

The key difference is visible in the plan. The first query is returning 18,967 rows out of an estimated 18,942. The second is returning 11,134 out of 11,372. That's about the only real difference. Because neither the FirstName nor the MiddleName column has an index to support these queries, a scan of the IX_Person_LastName_FirstName_MiddleName index is used.

CHAPTER 14 QUERY DESIGN ANALYSIS

Further, because the second column, MiddleName, includes NULL values, which, by definition, do not equal the value of 'B', they need to be included. Listing 14-21 shows the adjusted query.

Listing 14-21. Fixing the logic of the second query

```
SELECT p.MiddleName
FROM Person.Person AS p
WHERE p.MiddleName < 'B'
    OR p.MiddleName >= 'C'
    OR p.MiddleName IS NULL;
```

In addition to fixing the logic of the query, I'm also going to take the Missing Index recommendations from the optimizer and create two indexes here in Listing 14-22.

Listing 14-22. Adding indexes to make the queries faster

```
CREATE INDEX TestIndex1 ON Person.Person (MiddleName);
CREATE INDEX TestIndex2 ON Person.Person (FirstName);
```

I'm now going to go back and rerun the queries, which results in the execution plans seen in Figure 14-21.

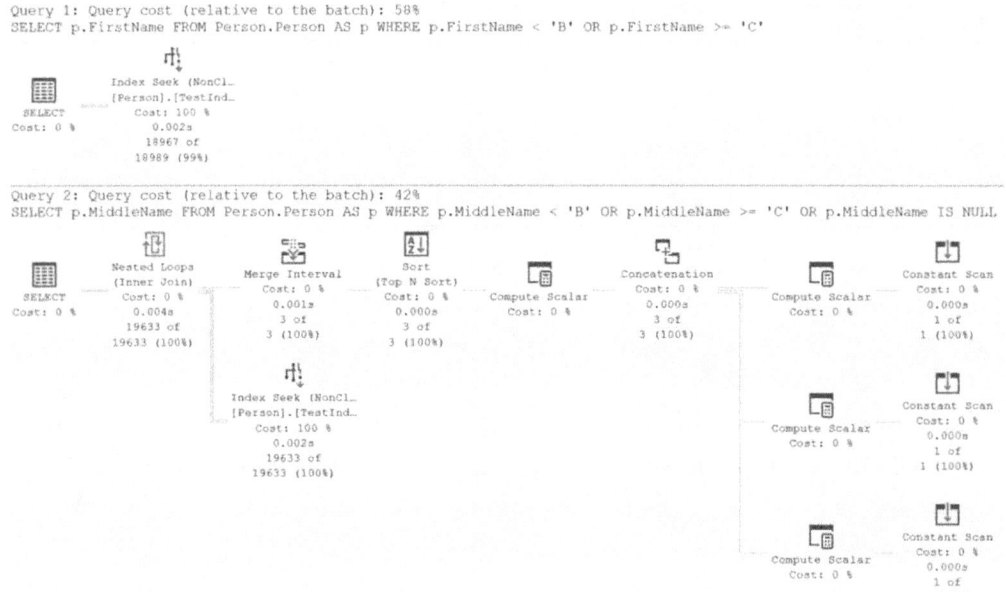

Figure 14-21. *Indexes and IS NULL changed the execution plans*

The first query against the FirstName column used the new index to simply retrieve the data. While the second query was able to use the new index, because of the IS NULL operation, you can see that the plan has greatly expanded in scope in order to satisfy that criterion. Three values are created using the three Constant Scan and Compute Scalar operators, one for each criterion in the WHERE clause. These are then sorted and merged and used in a join to arrive at the filtered data set.

An interesting point worth noting is that the first execution plan has a higher estimated cost. This is meaningless since the queries and data sets are different. However, there is some accuracy here as the first query runs in about 4.35ms, while the second runs in 3.05ms.

This is a place where experimenting with using a filtered index to deal with the NOT NULL may result in a performance enhancement. In this case, it actually doesn't. There are more reads and a slightly slower performance when making TestIndex1 a filtered index. One other point worth bringing up about NULL values is that you can use sparse columns. This helps reduce the overhead and space associated with storing NULL values. It's handy for analytical data when you have a lot of NULLs. However, it comes at a performance overhead, so generally it is not considered to be a way to enhance query behaviors.

Before going on, I'm dropping the test indexes I created (Listing 14-23).

Listing 14-23. Dropping the test indexes

```
DROP INDEX TestIndex1 ON Person.Person;
DROP INDEX TestIndex2 ON Person.Person;
```

User-Defined Constraints

Constraints are another way to help ensure that your data integrity is high. However, the optimizer can also use constraints to help you with performance. For example, Listing 14-24 shows a constraint from the AdventureWorks database.

Listing 14-24. Ensuring that the UnitPrice is greater than zero

```
ALTER TABLE Sales.SalesOrderDetail WITH CHECK
ADD CONSTRAINT CK_SalesOrderDetail_UnitPrice CHECK ((
                                        UnitPrice >= (0.00)
                                        ));
```

CHAPTER 14 ■ QUERY DESIGN ANALYSIS

If I run the query from Listing 14-25, we know it will return no rows.

Listing 14-25. No rows returned from this query

```
SELECT soh.OrderDate,
       soh.ShipDate,
       sod.OrderQty,
       sod.UnitPrice,
       p.Name AS ProductName
FROM Sales.SalesOrderHeader AS soh
    JOIN Sales.SalesOrderDetail AS sod
        ON sod.SalesOrderID = soh.SalesOrderID
    JOIN Production.Product AS p
        ON p.ProductID = sod.ProductID
WHERE p.Name = 'Water Bottle - 30 oz.'
      AND sod.UnitPrice < $0.0;
```

However, that's not the interesting part. The interesting part is how the optimizer chooses to satisfy this query here in Figure 14-22.

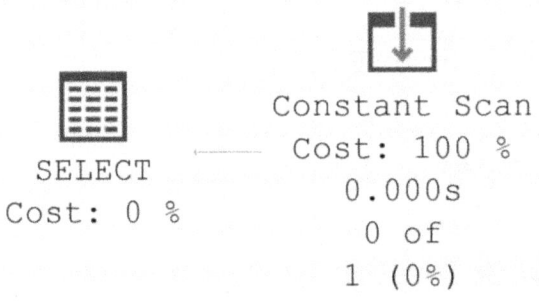

Figure 14-22. *An execution plan with no data access at all*

The Constant Scan operator is simply a placeholder that the optimizer will use in execution plans to build data sets against. However, in this case, there is only the Constant Scan operator. So what's happening?

The optimizer recognizes that this query cannot possibly return any rows at all. However, it still has to return a result set, even if it's just going to be empty. So it uses the Constant Scan to create the empty result set. You can see it in the Output List property in Figure 14-23.

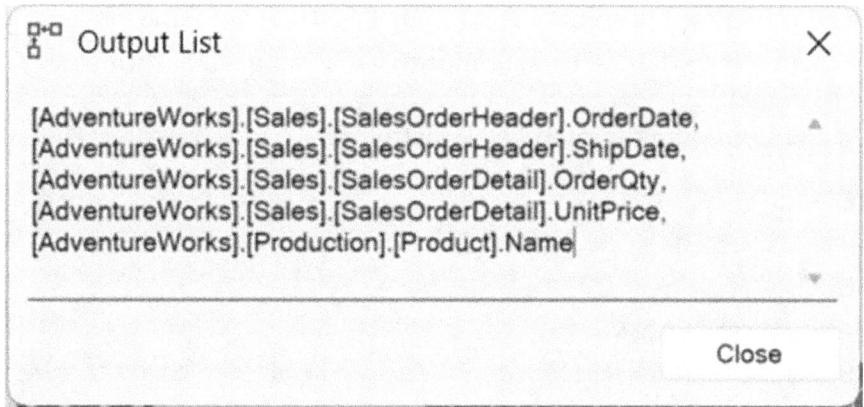

Figure 14-23. *The Output List to produce an empty result set*

If the optimizer didn't make this choice, since there is no index in support of the preceding query, you'd get a Clustered Index Scan, reading all the data in the table, but returning zero rows. The optimizer saved us from a nasty performance hit because it can read the constraints.

Note The optimizer can only use a check constraint if it was created using the WITH CHECK option. Otherwise, the constraint is untrusted because the data hasn't been validated.

Declarative Referential Integrity

Declarative referential integrity (DRI) is the most used mechanism within SQL Server to ensure data cleanliness between a parent and a child table. DRI ensures that rows in the child table only exist when the corresponding row exists in the parent table. The only exception here is when a child table has NULL values in the column, or columns, that refer back to the parent. In SQL Server, DRI is defined through the use of FOREIGN KEY constraint on the child that matches a PRIMARY KEY or UNIQUE INDEX on the parent.

When DRI is established between two tables and the foreign key columns of the child table are set to NOT NULL, the optimizer is assured that for every row in the child table, a corresponding row exists in the parent table. The optimizer can use this knowledge to improve performance because accessing the parent table isn't necessary to verify the existence of a row for the corresponding child row.

CHAPTER 14 QUERY DESIGN ANALYSIS

To see this in action, I'm going to run Listing 14-26 to remove the foreign key constraints between two tables: Person.Address and Person.StateProvince.

Listing 14-26. Removing foreign key constraints

```
IF EXISTS
(
    SELECT *
    FROM sys.foreign_keys
    WHERE OBJECT_ID = OBJECT_ID(N'[Person].[FK_Address_StateProvince_StateProvinceID]')
        AND parent_object_id = OBJECT_ID(N'[Person].[Address]')
)
    ALTER TABLE Person.ADDRESS
    DROP CONSTRAINT FK_Address_StateProvince_StateProvinceID;
```

With that out of the way, I have two queries in Listing 14-27.

Listing 14-27. Two nearly identical queries

```
SELECT A.AddressID,
       sp.StateProvinceID
FROM Person.ADDRESS AS A
    JOIN Person.StateProvince AS sp
        ON A.StateProvinceID = sp.StateProvinceID
WHERE A.AddressID = 27234;

--NOTE, Address.StateProvinceID
SELECT A.AddressID,
       A.StateProvinceID
FROM Person.ADDRESS AS A
    JOIN Person.StateProvince AS sp
        ON A.StateProvinceID = sp.StateProvinceID
WHERE A.AddressID = 27234;
```

The only difference between these two queries is that the second one, as noted, is using Address.StateProvinceID instead of StateProvince.StateProvinceID in the SELECT statement. With the foreign key constraint gone, these two queries generate the execution plans, shown in the Compare ShowPlan view, in Figure 14-24.

CHAPTER 14 ■ QUERY DESIGN ANALYSIS

Execution plan
SELECT A.AddressID, A.StateProvinceID F
sp.StateProvinceID WHERE A.AddressID =

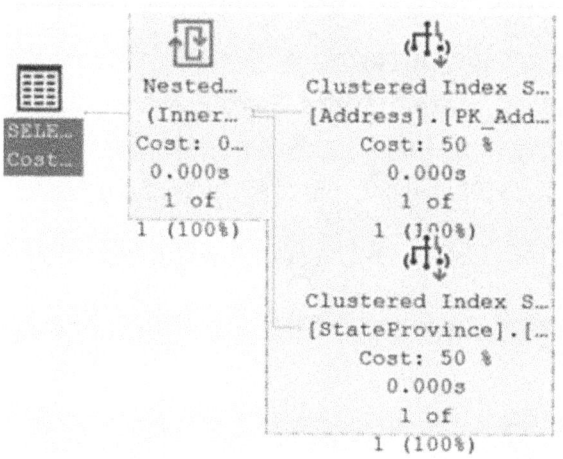

C:\Users\grant\Downloads\plan1.sqlplan
SELECT A.AddressID, sp.StateProvinceID
sp.StateProvinceID WHERE A.AddressID =

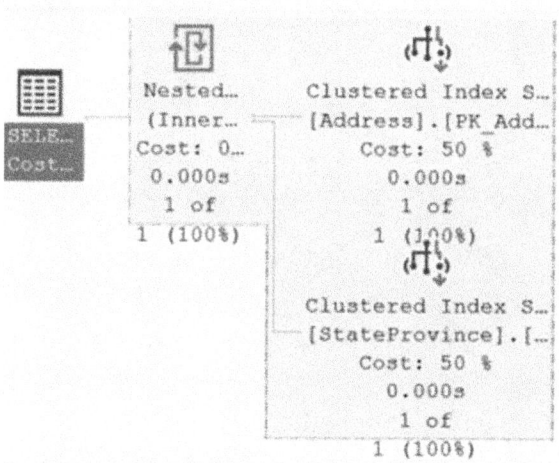

Figure 14-24. *Two identical execution plans*

467

CHAPTER 14 ■ QUERY DESIGN ANALYSIS

When using Compare ShowPlan, common parts of the structure are highlighted. As you can see, these are identical. I'm now going to use Listing 14-28 to replace the foreign key from earlier.

Listing 14-28. Creating a foreign key constraint on the Address table

```
ALTER TABLE Person.ADDRESS WITH CHECK
ADD CONSTRAINT FK_Address_StateProvince_StateProvinceID
    FOREIGN KEY (StateProvinceID)
    REFERENCES Person.StateProvince (StateProvinceID);
```

Running the queries from Listing 14-27 again, I get the execution plans shown in Figure 14-25.

CHAPTER 14 ■ QUERY DESIGN ANALYSIS

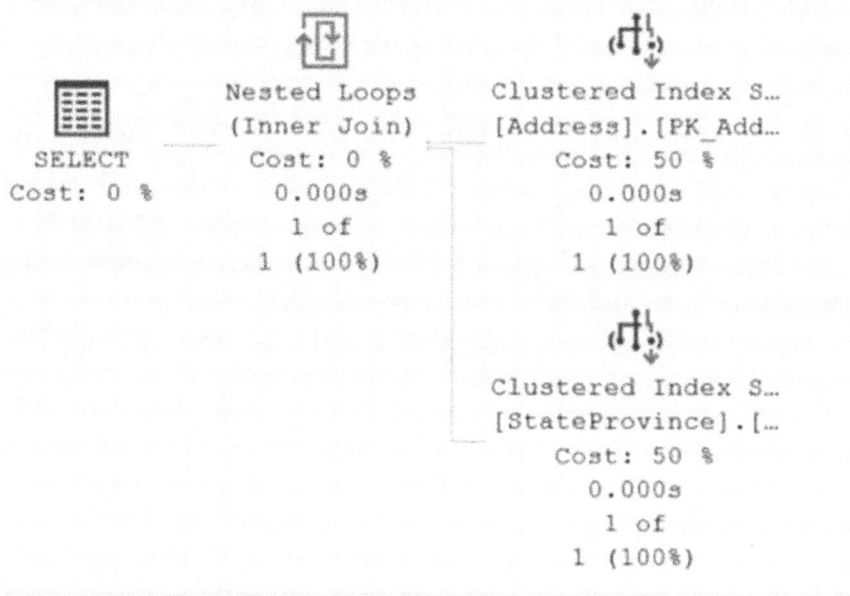

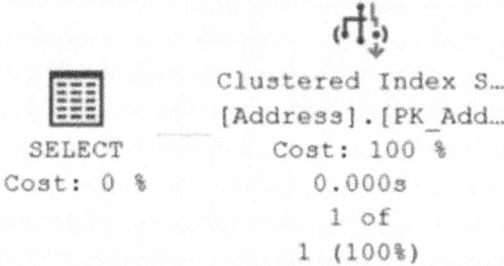

Figure 14-25. The execution plans are now different because of the foreign key

Clearly, the second query now has a new execution plan. When the foreign key wasn't present, the optimizer didn't know if rows in the parent and the child table, StateProvince and Address, matched. So it had to validate that by using a join operation, Nested Loops in this case. However, with the foreign key put back in place, specifically using the WITH CHECK option to validate the data, the optimizer could now simplify the execution plan and ignore the JOIN operation entirely, arriving at superior performance.

Summary

As important as your structures are, poor decisions with your T-SQL code can hurt performance just as much as if you had never taken the time to create appropriate indexes and maintain your statistics. The optimizer is extremely efficient at working out how best to retrieve your queries, but your queries need to be designed to work with the optimizer. While query hints are available and can be useful, thoroughly testing them before using them is a great practice. Finally, make sure you're taking advantage of constraints and referential integrity. It's not only important to make sure that queries are using your structure, but that they avoid excessive resource use.

The next chapter will be focused on reducing resource usage within queries.

CHAPTER 15

Reduce Query Resource Use

The previous chapter was focused on ensuring that your queries were able to take advantage of the indexes in your database. In this chapter, we'll be focusing on ensuring that we reduce the resource use of our queries. There are mechanisms with T-SQL that are more likely to use up memory, CPU, and I/O. Focusing on writing our queries in such a way as to reduce resource use not only helps individual queries but reduces the overall load on the system. We'll examine a number of different techniques focused on the following topics:

- Query designs that reduce resource use
- Mechanisms to enhance the use of the plan cache
- Reducing network overhead where possible
- Techniques to reduce the transaction cost of a query

Avoiding Resource-Intensive Queries

There are multiple ways to write almost any query. Many of those approaches will function just fine in terms of returning the appropriate data. However, some of those approaches are more likely to impact your system resources than others. Here are a number of mechanisms that will help reduce the resource use of your queries:

- Use the appropriate data types.
- Test EXISTS over COUNT(*) to verify data existence.
- Favor UNION ALL over UNION.

CHAPTER 15   REDUCE QUERY RESOURCE USE

- Ensure indexes are used in aggregation and sort operations.
- Be cautious with local variables in batch queries.
- Stored procedure names actually matter.

Use Appropriate Data Types

SQL Server supports a very large number of different data types. Also, SQL Server will automatically convert from one data type to another, depending of course on the data type. When this happens, it's called an *implicit conversion*. This is a situation where SQL Server helps and makes your life easier, but at the cost of performance issues. To maintain your performance, use parameters, variables, and constants that are the same data type as the column you're comparing.

To see the negative effects of an implicit conversion in action, let's take a look at Listing 15-1.

Listing 15-1. Creating a test table with data and running queries against it

```
DROP TABLE IF EXISTS dbo.Test1;
CREATE TABLE dbo.Test1
(
    Id INT IDENTITY(1, 1),
    MyKey VARCHAR(50),
    MyValue VARCHAR(50)
);
CREATE UNIQUE CLUSTERED INDEX Test1PrimaryKey ON dbo.Test1 (ID ASC);
CREATE UNIQUE NONCLUSTERED INDEX TestIndex ON dbo.Test1 (MyKey);

WITH Tally
AS (SELECT ROW_NUMBER() OVER (ORDER BY (SELECT NULL)) AS num
    FROM MASTER.dbo.syscolumns AS A
        CROSS JOIN MASTER.dbo.syscolumns AS B)
INSERT INTO dbo.Test1
(
    MyKey,
    MyValue
```

```
)
SELECT TOP 10000
        'UniqueKey' + CAST(Tally.num AS VARCHAR),
        'Description'
FROM Tally;

SELECT t.MyValue
FROM dbo.Test1 AS t
WHERE t.MyKey = 'UniqueKey333';
SELECT t.MyValue
FROM dbo.Test1 AS t
WHERE t.MyKey = N'UniqueKey333';
```

Listing 15-1 creates a table and two indexes and loads it all with data. Then, two queries are run, one of which will cause an implicit conversion. This is a fairly benign-looking conversion too. I'm simply taking a string from an NVARCHAR to a VARCHAR. You would think that wouldn't affect much. However, let's see the execution plans in Figure 15-1.

CHAPTER 15 REDUCE QUERY RESOURCE USE

```
Query 1: Query cost (relative to the batch): 12%
SELECT [t].[MyValue] FROM [dbo].[Test1] [t] WHERE [t].[MyKey]=@1
```

```
                   Nested Loops       Index Seek (NonCl...
                   (Inner Join)       [Test1].[TestInde...
    SELECT         Cost: 0 %          Cost: 50 %
    Cost: 0 %      0.000s             0.000s
                   1 of               1 of
                   1 (100%)           1 (100%)

                                      Key Lookup (Clust...
                                      [Test1].[Test1Pri...
                                      Cost: 50 %
                                      0.000s
                                      1 of
                                      1 (100%)
```

```
Query 2: Query cost (relative to the batch): 88%
SELECT [t].[MyValue] FROM [dbo].[Test1] [t] WHERE [t].[MyKey]=@1
```

```
                   Nested Loops       Index Scan (NonCl...
                   (Inner Join)       [Test1].[TestInde...
    SELECT         Cost: 12 %         Cost: 81 %
    Cost: 0 %      0.004s             0.004s
                   1 of               1 of
                   1 (100%)           1 (100%)

                                      Key Lookup (Clust...
                                      [Test1].[Test1Pri...
                                      Cost: 7 %
                                      0.000s
                                      1 of
                                      1 (100%)
```

Figure 15-1. *Two execution plans showing implicit conversion at work*

While the plan shapes are somewhat similar, two things should stand out. First, in the second plan, we can see a warning indicator on the first operator of the plan, the SELECT on the left. Next, again, in the second plan, we see that an Index Scan of the nonclustered index was done instead of the seek in the first plan. All of this was brought about by the need to convert the data type of the query from the NVARCHAR to VARCHAR because I set the hard-coded value through the use of "N" in front of the string definition at the end of Listing 15-1.

The warning indicator is telling us that there is something you should examine inside the execution plan. It may be nothing you need to worry about, or it could be vital to help improve performance. Just looking at the differences in estimates between these two plans, you can tell that this is likely a piece of vital information. Looking at the properties of the SELECT operator, we can see the warning itself:

```
Type conversion in expression (CONVERT_IMPLICIT(nvarchar(50),[t].
[MyKey],0)=[@1]) may affect "SeekPlan" in query plan choice, Type
conversion in expression (CONVERT_IMPLICIT(nvarchar(50),[t].
[MyKey],0)=N'UniqueKey333') may affect "SeekPlan" in query plan choice
```

Because of the conversion, even though the result sets are identical, performance went from 266mcs on average to 4,185mcs. The reads went from 4 to 38.

Conversions are always done to the comparison value, whether it's a variable, a parameter, or hard-coded, not to the column. The comparison process has to use the values stored with the table or index, so the conversion is done to the other value.

As you can see, while the implicit conversion process occurs simply and in the background, it can be extremely problematic for performance. The best solution is to always match your hard-coded values, variables, and parameters to the column data type.

Test EXISTS Over COUNT(*) to Verify Data Existence

A very common approach to validate that data exists in the table is to run a query similar to that in Listing 15-2.

Listing 15-2. Validating the existence of data through COUNT(*)

```
DECLARE @n INT;
SELECT @n = COUNT(*)
FROM Sales.SalesOrderDetail AS sod
WHERE sod.OrderQty = 1;
IF @n > 0
    PRINT 'Record Exists';
```

CHAPTER 15 ■ REDUCE QUERY RESOURCE USE

To satisfy the WHERE clause and the COUNT operation, a complete scan for all values matching the WHERE clause must be performed. However, in most circumstances, this kind of validation is more easily done through the EXISTS operation shown in Listing 15-3.

Listing 15-3. Validating data existence using EXISTS

```
IF EXISTS
(
    SELECT sod.OrderQty
    FROM Sales.SalesOrderDetail AS sod
    WHERE sod.OrderQty = 1
)
    PRINT 'Record Exists';
```

Figure 15-2 shows the execution plans for both listings as well as the performance metrics:

```
COUNT Reads: 1,248
Duration: 9.7ms
EXISTS Reads: 29
Duration: 1.66ms
```

CHAPTER 15 REDUCE QUERY RESOURCE USE

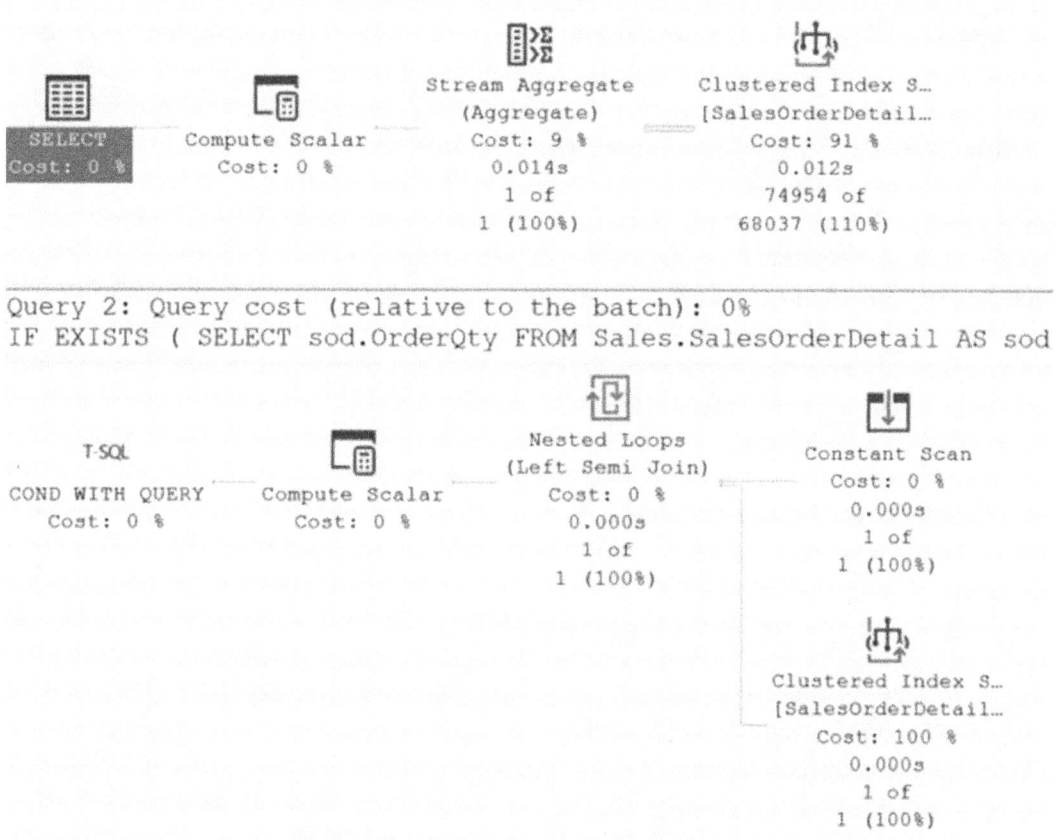

Figure 15-2. Different execution plans between COUNT and EXISTS

While this may look like an obvious win, negative results, where the entire data set has to be scanned, may run the same or even slower. This is why I say test this approach in your systems. Clearly going from 1,248 reads down to 29 is a win.

Worth noting, the optimizer is suggesting a different index for the first query from Listing 15-3. Following that suggestion could enhance performance a little, but not as much as using EXISTS in this case.

CHAPTER 15 REDUCE QUERY RESOURCE USE

Favor UNION ALL Over UNION

The UNION clause allows you to combine multiple result sets into a single result set. However, UNION is an aggregate operation. Listing 15-4 shows an example of combining results.

Listing 15-4. Combining result sets through UNION

```
SELECT sod.ProductID,
       sod.SalesOrderID
FROM Sales.SalesOrderDetail AS sod
WHERE sod.ProductID = 934
UNION
SELECT sod.ProductID,
       sod.SalesOrderID
FROM Sales.SalesOrderDetail AS sod
WHERE sod.ProductID = 932
UNION
SELECT sod.ProductID,
       sod.SalesOrderID
FROM Sales.SalesOrderDetail AS sod
WHERE sod.ProductID = 708;
```

This query results in the execution plan shown in Figure 15-3.

CHAPTER 15 REDUCE QUERY RESOURCE USE

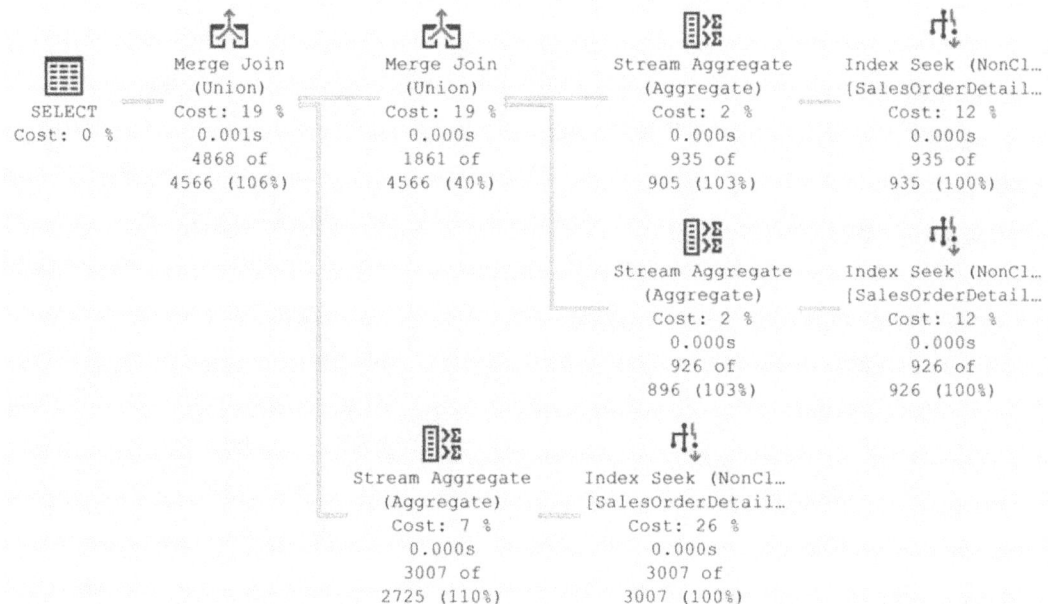

Figure 15-3. *Execution plan from a UNION query*

In this case, the optimizer has chosen to satisfy the query through the use of the Stream Aggregate operations. You'll note that each of the three data sets is retrieved through an Index Seek, but then they are aggregated, in order to eliminate duplicates, in the Stream Aggregate operations. The results of the aggregation are then combined through the two Merge Join operations.

However, in this case, each of our three queries is actually already unique. If you're in that situation or in a situation where the data doesn't have to be unique, then using the UNION ALL clause can dramatically improve performance. Figure 15-4 shows the results of changing Listing 15-4 to UNION ALL.

479

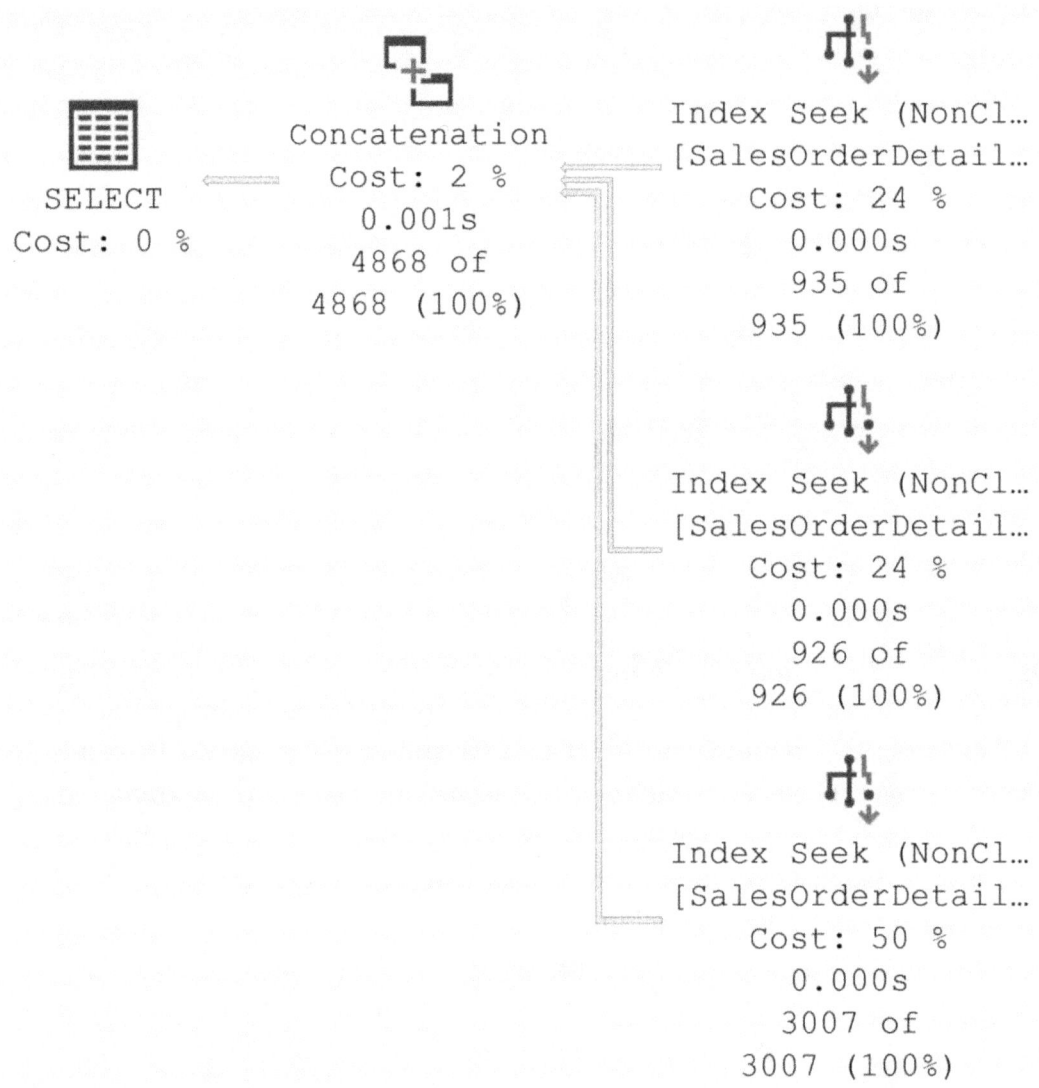

Figure 15-4. *An execution plan for UNION ALL*

The aggregation operations are gone as are the joins. Instead, we're left with just the data access through the Index Seek operations and then a combination of the data sets through the Concatenation operator. The plan is simpler, and the performance went from 2.4ms to 1.56ms. While it's not a huge gain in this case, it may be as data sets grow. Interestingly, the reads stayed the same at 20 for both queries. The additional work was primarily taken up through CPU.

Ensure Indexes Are Used for Aggregate and Sort Operations

The most optimal way to improve the performance of aggregate functions such as MIN or MAX is to take advantage of columnstore indexes. However, even traditional rowstore indexes can provide some performance improvements for aggregation queries. The lack of indexes supporting a query inevitably leads to table or index scans. For example, Listing 15-5 has a simple aggregate.

Listing 15-5. Looking for MIN UnitPrice

```
SELECT MIN(sod.UnitPrice)
FROM Sales.SalesOrderDetail AS sod;
```

Running this query results in the execution plan in Figure 15-5 and the following performance metrics:

```
Reads: 1,248
Duration: 15.2ms
```

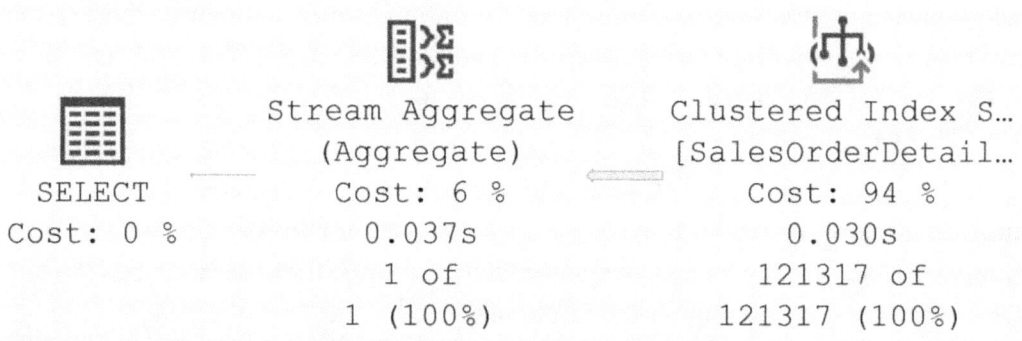

Figure 15-5. *No supporting index for the aggregate query*

To return a single value, the minimum UnitPrice, 1,248 reads were necessary as well as performing the aggregation operation through the Stream Aggregate operator. You can even see this visually as a thick arrow comes out of the Clustered Index Scan and only a very thin arrow from the Stream Aggregate. In order to attempt to improve performance, I'll add the index shown in Listing 15-6.

CHAPTER 15   REDUCE QUERY RESOURCE USE

Listing 15-6. Adding an index on the UnitPrice column

```
CREATE INDEX TestIndex ON Sales.SalesOrderDetail (UnitPrice ASC);
```

Rerunning the original query from Listing 15-5 results in the following performance metrics and the execution plan in Figure 15-6:

Reads: 3
Duration: 389mcs

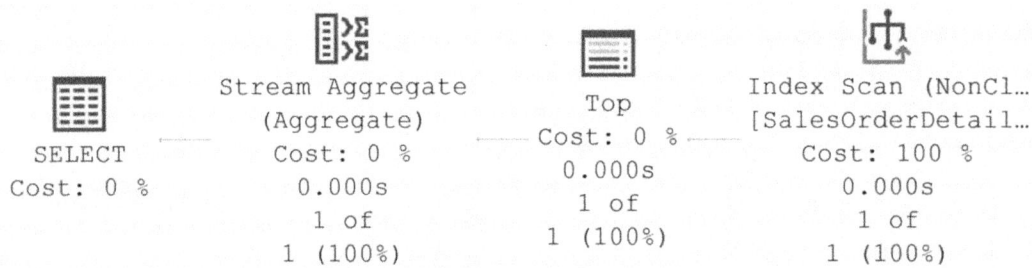

Figure 15-6. *An index supports the query*

While the plan is visually more complex since it has more operations, the performance metrics speak for themselves. The index is scanned, but it's a limited scan of a single row. The Top operator is to ensure that only one value is returned. The Stream Aggregate is merely a formality, validating the results.

You'll find similar behaviors in ORDER BY statements and indexes. It's all about having the data in a particular order to support the needs of the query. Overall, for analytical queries, you're still going to see superior performance enhancements from columnstore indexes, but you can see some from rowstore indexes as well. Before we proceed, Listing 15-7 will remove the test index.

Listing 15-7. Removing the test index

```
DROP INDEX IF EXISTS TestIndex ON dbo.Test1;
```

Be Cautious with Local Variables in a Batch Query

Running multiple statements through a batch process is extremely common. Just as common is to use local variables to pass values between the statements in the batch. However, local variables in filter criteria can, at times, lead to poor choices by the

CHAPTER 15 ■ REDUCE QUERY RESOURCE USE

optimizer. To keep things simple, instead of a large batch, we'll just look at the behavior of a single statement. The principles are the same in a larger set of queries. Listing 15-8 shows a query using a local variable.

Listing 15-8. Using a local variable to pass values

```
DECLARE @Id INT = 67260;
SELECT p.Name,
       p.ProductNumber,
       th.ReferenceOrderID
FROM Production.Product AS p
    JOIN Production.TransactionHistory AS th
        ON th.ProductID = p.ProductID
WHERE th.ReferenceOrderID = @Id;
```

Figure 15-7 is the resulting execution plan.

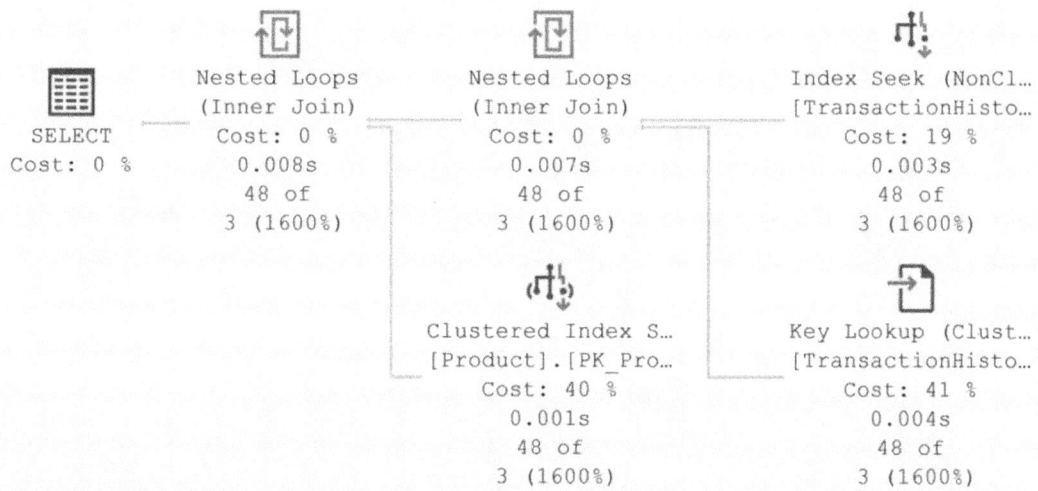

Figure 15-7. *Execution plan with a local variable*

We're filtering with the local variable on the ReferenceOrderID column of the TransactionHistory table. An Index Seek against a nonclustered index was used to satisfy the query. However, that means that additional values have to be pulled from the clustered index using the Key Lookup operation and a Nested Loops join. The rest of the data for the query comes from the Clustered Index Seek against the Product table and another Nested Loops join to pull them together.

483

CHAPTER 15   REDUCE QUERY RESOURCE USE

If we modify the code to use a hard-coded value, we'd see something like Listing 15-9.

Listing 15-9. Replacing the local variable

```
SELECT p.Name,
       p.ProductNumber,
       th.ReferenceOrderID
FROM Production.Product AS p
    JOIN Production.TransactionHistory AS th
        ON th.ProductID = p.ProductID
WHERE th.ReferenceOrderID = 67260;
```

With the query changed, we see a new execution plan in Figure 15-8.

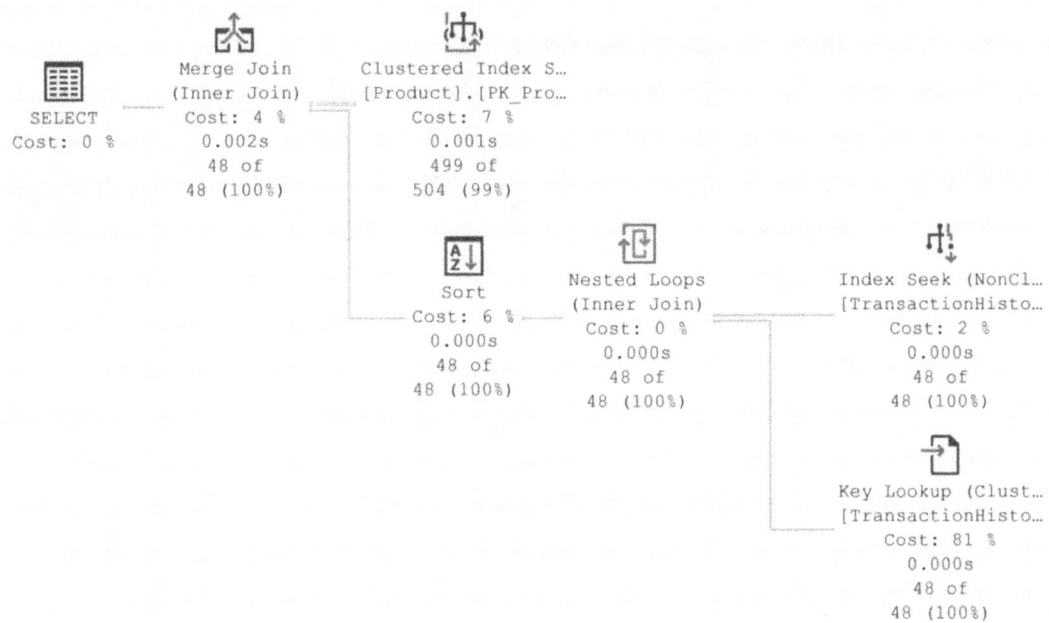

Figure 15-8. *The execution plan changes with a hard-coded value*

While we're retrieving the exact same data set, the optimizer has made new choices in how best to satisfy the query. Some of the plan shape is the same. The data access against the TransactionHistory table is still through the nonclustered Index Seek and the Key Lookup. However, the rest of the plan is different. A Merge Join is used, as well as an Index Scan against the Product table's clustered index. If you look at the properties of the Scan, you'll find it's an ordered scan, satisfying the need for the Merge Join to have ordered data. However, the other additional operator is the Sort, needed to get the data from the TransactionHistory table into order as well.

Things really get interesting when we look at the performance metrics. First, our original query from Listing 15-8:

Reads: 242
Duration: 333mcs

Now the metrics from Listing 15-9:

Reads: 170
Duration: 723mcs

Listing 15-8 is considerably faster. However, Listing 15-9 uses fewer resources in terms of reads, 170 vs. 242. The key difference here is in the row estimates. If you look at Figures 15-7 and 15-8, you'll notice that the number of rows estimated in Figure 15-7 is 3, while the number in Figure 15-8 is 48. You'll also notice that in both cases, the actual number of rows returned as 48.

The real value for the row estimate is in the properties of the execution plan from Figure 15-7, 3.05628, rounded to the value we see of 3. The reason such an inaccurate estimate was used is because the value of a variable is not known to the optimizer at compile time. Because of this, the optimizer uses the density graph from the statistics, 2.694111E-05, and the number of rows, 113,443, and multiplies the two together, arriving at a row estimate of 3.05628.

The difference with the hard-coded value is that the optimizer can use the histogram to decide how many rows will be returned by the value used, 67620. That value from the histogram is 48, the actual number returned. The optimizer decided that performing 48 Index Seek operations through the Nested Loops join would be more expensive than doing an ordered scan of the index and sorting the results of the initial data from the TransactionHistory table.

However, in this case, the optimizer arrived at a plan that used fewer resources (Figure 15-8) but actually ran slower. This is one of those points where we have to start making choices when attempting to tune queries. If all we care about is speed of execution, in this case, using the local variable is faster. However, if our system is under load and potentially suffering from I/O issues, there's a very good chance that the hard-coded value will perform better, since it performs fewer reads and will thus be in less conflict on the resources it uses.

I'm not advocating for hard-coded values, however. That leads to all sorts of code maintenance issues. Instead, you would want to explore the possibility of making the variable into a parameter so it can be sampled by the optimizer at compile time through parameter sniffing, although, again, that opens up issues as we explored in Chapter 13.

Sadly, there's not always going to be a single, right answer when it comes to query tuning. However, gaining the knowledge of how, and, more importantly, why, your queries are satisfied by the optimizer can help you make better choices.

Stored Procedure Names Actually Matter

Believe it or not, how you choose to name your stored procedures can have some impact on performance, albeit a very small one. A common approach to naming objects is to use an abbreviation, like "sp" for "stored procedure." Another common approach is to then separate this lead from the object name with an underscore, "sp_". This is so common as a naming standard; Microsoft was actually there first. This is how system stored procedures are designated. SQL Server then assumes that a stored procedure with that prefix is in the master database. In fact, the following are the search criteria:

- The master database
- The current database based on qualifiers (database name and/or owner)
- In the current database using "dbo" as the schema if none is provided

The performance hit from this is tiny, almost to the point of not being able to measure it. However, on very active systems, you're adding overhead that you simply don't need to add. Another issue comes when you create a procedure in your local database, with the same name as a system procedure. Attempting to execute the query, especially if it has a different set of parameters, will simply cause an error.

Reducing Network Overhead Where Possible

It's a rare process, report, analysis, or application that is running locally with the database. The network is always involved in moving the data around from SQL Server. While it's important to optimize your queries, you also have to think through how you work in batches of queries. A couple of approaches can help to reduce some network overhead:

- Execute multiple queries in sets.
- Use SET NOCOUNT.

To fully understand what I mean, we'll drill down on these approaches.

Execute Multiple Queries in Sets

Everything is subject to testing, but generally, it's a good approach to put sets of queries together in a batch or stored procedure. Rather than repeatedly connecting to the server, initiating a round trip across the network, call once and get the work done, returning what's needed. You may have to ensure that your code can deal with multiple result sets. You also may need to ensure that you can consume JSON or other mechanisms of moving sets of data around, not simply single-row inserts or updates.

Use SET NOCOUNT

After every query in a batch or stored procedure, SQL Server will, by default, report the number of rows affected:

(<Number> row(s) affected)

That information is transmitted across the network for every single statement. As you can imagine, while tiny, it accumulates to excessive network overhead. To change this behavior, use the T-SQL statement in Listing 15-10.

Listing 15-10. *Using the SET NOCOUNT command*

```
SET NOCOUNT ON;
```

You can also set the NOCOUNT to OFF if you choose. Using this statement at the start of a set of queries or in a batch will not cause recompiles. It simply stops the reporting of those row counts. It's a small thing, but it's a good coding practice.

CHAPTER 15 REDUCE QUERY RESOURCE USE

Techniques to Reduce Transaction Cost of a Query

Transactions are a fundamental part of how SQL Server protects the data in your system. Every action query–INSERT, UPDATE, DELETE, or MERGE–is performed as an atomic action in order to preserve the data in a consistent state, meaning data changes are successfully committed. This behavior cannot be disabled.

If the transition from one consistent state to another requires multiple database queries, then atomicity across the multiple queries should be maintained using explicitly defined database transactions. The old and new states of every atomic action are maintained in the transaction log (on the disk) to ensure durability, which guarantees that the outcome of an atomic action won't be lost once it completes successfully. An atomic action during its execution is isolated from other database actions using database locks.

Based on the characteristics of a transaction, here are two broad recommendations to reduce the cost of the transaction:

- Reduce logging overhead.
- Reduce lock overhead.

Reduce Logging Overhead

Your procedure or batch might consist of a series of action queries. If you attempt to maintain atomicity for each query separately, you get a lot more writes to the transaction log, possibly adding to contention there. To see this in action, let's consider Listing 15-11.

Listing 15-11. Inserting 10,000 rows of data

```
DROP TABLE IF EXISTS dbo.Test1;
CREATE TABLE dbo.Test1
(
    C1 TINYINT
);
GO
DBCC SQLPERF(LOGSPACE);
--Insert 10000 rows
DECLARE @Count INT = 1;
```

```
WHILE @Count <= 10000
BEGIN
    INSERT INTO dbo.Test1
    (
        C1
    )
    VALUES
    (@Count % 256);
    SET @Count = @Count + 1;
END;
DBCC SQLPERF(LOGSPACE);
```

The DBCC command, SQLPERF, is a really simple way to look at the amount of log space consumed. At the start of the operation, I have a small log in AdventureWorks, about 7.9MB in size and only 5% full. Running Listing 15-11 takes 39 seconds and blows the log up to about 72MB and it is 24% filled. For a very small system like this, that's a pretty massive impact.

One way to immediately change the behavior would be to wrap the code in a transaction like what you see here in Listing 15-12.

Listing 15-12. Adding a transaction

```
DECLARE @Count INT = 1;
DBCC SQLPERF(LOGSPACE);
BEGIN TRANSACTION;
WHILE @Count <= 10000
BEGIN
    INSERT INTO dbo.Test1
    (
        C1
    )
    VALUES
    (@Count % 256);
    SET @Count = @Count + 1;
END;
COMMIT;
DBCC SQLPERF(LOGSPACE);
```

Now, instead of 10,000 individual transactions, I have one. The size of the log remained the same. The percentage used dropped as the other transactions were aged out (I'm in Simple Recovery). The execution time went to 83ms. That alone is a massive win. However, we can improve this even more. The WHILE loop is a poor approach to set-based operations (and we'll be covering row-by-row processing in Chapter 18 in a lot more detail). Changing to a set-based operation like Listing 15-13 should have an even greater impact.

Listing 15-13. Eliminating the WHILE loop

```
DBCC SQLPERF(LOGSPACE);
BEGIN TRANSACTION;
WITH Tally
AS (SELECT ROW_NUMBER() OVER (ORDER BY (SELECT NULL)) AS num
    FROM master.dbo.syscolumns AS A
        CROSS JOIN master.dbo.syscolumns AS B)
INSERT INTO dbo.Test1
(
    C1
)
SELECT TOP 1000
       (Tally.num % 256)
FROM Tally;
COMMIT;
DBCC SQLPERF(LOGSPACE);
```

As with the simple addition of the transaction in Listing 15-12, we now have a single statement, so the size of the log didn't change. The percentage used of the log moved just a bit from 6.29% to 6.44%. The performance improved even more, dropping down to about 68.7ms. We've gone from being forced to grow the log and use a significant portion of the log to just almost nothing and 39 seconds to 68ms. It is possible to use fewer log resources.

However, a caution. Putting more work into a transaction can lead to a longer-running transaction overall in some circumstances. That can lead to resource contention and blocking (which we'll cover in Chapter 16). Also, longer transactions can add to the recovery time during a restore (although Accelerated Database Recovery certainly helps with this; for more, read the Microsoft documentation). As always, testing to validate how things work on your system is the best way to go.

Reduce Lock Overhead

By default, all T-SQL statements use some type of locking to isolate their work from that of other statements. Lock management adds performance overhead to a query. Another way to improve the performance of a query is to reduce the number of locks necessary to satisfy a given query. Further, reducing the locking of one query improves the performance of other queries because they are then waiting less for those resources.

This is a very large topic which we're going to drill down on in the next chapter. However, when talking about resource contention, I want to add a little detail on locking, here, in this chapter.

By default, SQL Server can use a row-level lock. However, if the query is working on a larger number of rows, row locks on each individual row add significant overhead to the lock management process. SQL Server will automatically attempt to manage the lock granularity by moving to a page-level or even a table-level lock. This process is dynamic and automatic and should generally be left to SQL Server to take care of. However, you can get directly involved by providing a lock hint as shown in Listing 15-14.

Listing 15-14. Pseudo-code to supply a lock hint

```
SELECT * FROM <TableName> WITH(PAGLOCK);  --Use page level lock
```

The example in Listing 15-14 would supply a page-level lock.

By default, SQL Server uses less intrusive locks for SELECT statements besides those for INSERT, UPDATE, and DELETE statements. This allows the SELECT statements to read data that isn't being modified. In some cases, the data may be quite static, and it doesn't go through much modification. In such cases, you can reduce the lock overhead of the SELECT statements in one of the following ways:

- Mark the database as READ_ONLY.
- Use snapshot isolation.
- Prevent SELECT statements from requesting a lock.

Mark the Database As READ_ONLY

This requires a situation where the database will not receive updates while it is set using the code from Listing 15-15.

Listing 15-15. Changing the database to be READ_ONLY

```
ALTER DATABASE <DatabaseName> SET READ_ONLY;
```

This allows users to retrieve data from the database, but it prevents them from modifying the data. The setting takes effect immediately. If occasional modifications to the database are required, then it may be temporarily converted to READ_WRITE mode in Listing 15-16.

Listing 15-16. Changing the database back to read/write

```
ALTER DATABASE <DatabaseName> SET READ_WRITE;
```

Use Snapshot Isolation

SQL Server provides a mechanism to put versions of data into tempdb as updates are occurring, radically reducing locking overhead and blocking for read operations. You can change the isolation level of the database by using an ALTER statement like Listing 15-17.

Listing 15-17. Changing the database isolation level

```
ALTER DATABASE AdventureWorks SET READ_COMMITTED_SNAPSHOT ON;
```

This will add overhead to the tempdb (again, except when using Accelerated Database Recovery). You can also set the isolation level in the connection string.

Prevent SELECT Statements from Requesting a Lock

I'm honestly hesitant to even mention the use of NOLOCK or READ UNCOMMITTED isolation levels. These are seen by many as the magic "run faster" switch in SQL Server. It is not. The use of NOLOCK prevents the SELECT statement from requesting any lock except the shared lock. NOLOCK is applicable to SELECT statements only. Although the NOLOCK hint can't be used directly on the tables referred to in the action queries (INSERT, UPDATE, and DELETE), it may be used on the data retrieval part of the action queries, as shown in Listing 15-18.

Listing 15-18. Using the NOLOCK with a DELETE statement

```
DELETE Sales.SalesOrderDetail
FROM Sales.SalesOrderDetail AS sod WITH (NOLOCK)
    JOIN Production.Product AS p WITH (NOLOCK)
        ON sod.ProductID = p.ProductID
           AND p.ProductID = 0;
```

You must know that the use of NOLOCK leads to dirty reads. Dirty reads can cause duplicate rows or missing rows. Therefore, NOLOCK should be considered only as a last resort to control locking. In fact, this is quite dangerous and will lead to improper results in queries. The best approach is to mark the database as read-only or use one of the snapshot isolation levels.

If you made any of the example changes to the database from this section, I recommend restoring from a backup.

Summary

Tuning queries is not simply about picking the right index and then ensuring that the code uses that index. As you can see, ensuring that you minimize the resources used by a query is also a big part of query tuning. Experimenting with different logical approaches to a given query can result in drastic performance enhancements or simply reduce the resource use of a bottlenecked resource. When resources are in use, you will begin to experience performance hits caused by blocking on those resources. In the next chapter, we'll examine how blocking affects SQL Server query performance.

CHAPTER 16

Blocking and Blocked Processes

SQL Server ensures that your data is protected even as the data is changed. It does this through a process called locking. However, even as SQL Server is locking within the I/O system in support of your data changes, this is causing what is called blocking, through contention for those resources. As the number of users on your systems increases, performance degrades as they contend for those resources. In order to understand how to deal with blocking, you need to understand how, and why, locking occurs.

In this chapter, I'll cover the following topics:

- The fundamentals of blocking in SQL Server
- The ACID properties of a transactional database
- Isolation levels within SQL Server
- Optimized Locking
- The effects of indexes on locking
- Information needed to analyze blocking
- Recommendations to minimize blocking

Blocking Fundamentals

Some degree of blocking is inevitable. There is simply no way for modern systems with large numbers of users and vast amounts of data to be set up or maintained in such a way that there will not be some amount of blocking. SQL Server takes control of managing the necessary locks through a process called the lock manager. It's the locks needed to ensure data integrity and consistency that lead to blocks.

© Grant Fritchey 2026
G. Fritchey, *SQL Server 2025 Query Performance Tuning*, https://doi.org/10.1007/979-8-8688-1865-3_16

CHAPTER 16   BLOCKING AND BLOCKED PROCESSES

A Short Discussion of Terminology

I'd like to take a moment to address an issue that comes up all the time. There are three terms in SQL Server that sound very similar and, in fact, are fairly tightly coupled. However, these three things are distinct and different processes within SQL Server. The three terms are as follows:

- Locking
- Blocking
- Deadlocking

Locking is an integral part of the process of SQL Server managing multiple sessions, all attempting to read or modify data. When a session needs access to a piece of data, the appropriate lock will be placed on it.

When one session holds a lock that another session needs, the second session can be said to be blocked. While blocked, the second session will wait until the first session, the blocking session, is complete. At which time the first session will release its lock, and then the blocking will end. These are two very distinct terms referring to two different, but clearly related, behaviors within SQL Server.

Finally, a situation can arise where two sessions each have a lock on two different pieces of data. Each session needs the piece of data locked by the other. These sessions are mutually blocking one another in what can be referred to as a deadly embrace. Neither can let go of the lock it has until it gets a lock on the other piece of data. Both will have to wait an infinite amount of time. This is what is referred to as a deadlock. We'll cover deadlocks in detail in Chapter 17.

The important information I want you to understand and remember is that while these three terms are absolutely interrelated, they are not the same. Locks can lead to blocks, and both blocks and locks play a part in deadlocks. However, they are three, completely distinct, processes within SQL Server. Keeping them separate in your head will absolutely assist in your understanding when you're faced with performance issues. Further, when you need assistance with locking, blocking, or deadlocks, using the right terminology will ensure that those attempting to help understand what the actual problem may be.

Introducing Blocking

A connection to a database that is used to run a query is called a session and comes with an identifier called the session ID. The sessions may be from one or more users in one or more applications. It's all the same inside SQL Server. When a session needs access to a piece of data, whether it's writing to that data through an INSERT, UPDATE, or DELETE or reading from that data in a SELECT, some kind of lock must be taken out on that piece of data, row, page, extent, or table.

When two sessions attempt to modify the same piece of data, well, one of them will get there first. That session takes out a lock. The second session is waiting for that lock to be released so that it can take out its own lock. This is the situation we refer to as blocking, one session waiting on another.

Now, when two sessions both wish to read a piece of data, they both read it. While there are still locks taken out for reads, they cooperate with other read locks on the data. Therefore, two sessions reading data won't block one another.

Blocking and locking are constantly taking place within SQL Server as queries are run. The majority of the time, this isn't noticeable. However, as the load increases on a server or there are bad or missing indexes or the code is written in an inefficient manner or transactions are poorly configured, for any or all of these reasons and more, locks are held longer. As locks are held longer, blocking occurs and extends. As you get more blocking, other sessions come along, looking to put locks on the same resources. These new sessions now must wait on other sessions, also blocked and waiting. Blocking gets worse and worse.

Because of all this, you need to minimize blocking on your servers in order to be able to support a large number of concurrent users.

Note Memory-optimized tables, also called in-memory tables, introduce some changes to how locking and blocking occur. I'll address them separately in Chapter 19.

CHAPTER 16 BLOCKING AND BLOCKED PROCESSES

Transactions and ACID Properties

Every query that runs within SQL Server is part of a transaction. It may be a part of an auto-commit transaction where you just connect up to SQL Server and run a query. It may be an explicit transaction where you use the BEGIN TRANSACTION statement and then have to either COMMIT the transaction to finish it or ROLLBACK the transaction to undo any work done. In order to make all this work across multiple transactions from multiple applications and people running queries, a set of rules have been established. These rules help to ensure that your data is stored properly and consistently on disk. We refer to these properties as the ACID properties:

- Atomicity
- Consistency
- Isolation
- Durability

Ensuring that these properties are met is a big part of why we get blocking in a database. Let's explore each of these properties in more detail.

Atomicity

The first property ensures that any given unit of work is completed, in its entirety, or everything gets undone, or rolled back. This is called an atomic operation and ensures the atomicity of a given transaction within SQL Server. The need for this is to ensure that all data write operations are successfully concluded. Listing 16-1 shows an example of an atomic operation (in fact, it shows several, but we'll concentrate on one).

Listing 16-1. Adding data in an atomic transaction

```
DROP TABLE IF EXISTS dbo.ProductTest;
GO
CREATE TABLE dbo.ProductTest
(
    ProductID INT
        CONSTRAINT ValueEqualsOne CHECK (ProductID = 1)
);
```

```
GO
--All ProductIDs are added into ProductTest as a logical unit of work
INSERT INTO dbo.ProductTest
SELECT p.ProductID
FROM Production.Product AS p;
GO
SELECT pt.ProductID
FROM dbo.ProductTest AS pt; --Returns 0 rows
```

The table defined in the CREATE TABLE statement includes a constraint that will only allow a value of 1 to be added to the table. Then, I attempt to INSERT rows to the table that don't have the value of 1. Of course, there's an error, so the SELECT statement will return zero rows.

The INSERT operation is atomic, meaning all the data goes or none of it does. There is one ProductID value in the Production.Product table that has the value of "1." That means I could add that row. However, since SQL Server insists on an atomic transaction, I don't get any rows. All must go, or none can go.

If we have multiple statements within a transaction, behavior is going to be a little different. Listing 16-2 shows an example.

Listing 16-2. More than one statement within a transaction

```
BEGIN TRAN;
--Start:  Logical unit of work
--First:
INSERT INTO dbo.ProductTest
SELECT p.ProductID
FROM Production.Product AS p;
--Second:
INSERT INTO dbo.ProductTest
VALUES
(1);
COMMIT; --End:   Logical unit of work
GO
```

Listing 16-2 explicitly defines a transaction. Now, if we run this query, we'll still see an error, just like in Listing 16-1. However, the second statement, where we only add a single value, which is within the definition of the constraint, succeeds.

While each of these statements is within a transaction, it's possible for some parts of a transaction to succeed while other parts fail and yet for it to still be an atomic operation.

Since the atomicity property requires that all the actions of a logical unit of work are completed or none of the changes are retained, SQL Server uses a process to isolate the work. Exclusive rights are granted to the affected resources while the atomic operation is being completed. These exclusive rights are what lead directly to blocking all other transactions from access to those resources. While atomicity is necessary to ensure data integrity, it automatically introduces the undesirable side effect of blocking.

There are two settings that directly affect how atomicity behaves within your connections:

- SET XACT_ABORT ON
- Explicit rollback

We should understand these before we move on.

SET XACT_ABORT ON

We can change the behavior of Listing 16-2 by using the "transaction abort" setting, SET XACT_ABORT ON, as shown in Listing 16-3.

Listing 16-3. Changing transaction behavior

```
SET XACT_ABORT ON;
GO
BEGIN TRAN;
--Start:  Logical unit of work
--First:
INSERT INTO dbo.ProductTest
SELECT p.ProductID
FROM Production.Product AS p;
--Second:
INSERT INTO dbo.ProductTest
```

CHAPTER 16 BLOCKING AND BLOCKED PROCESSES

```
VALUES
(1 );
COMMIT;
--End:   Logical unit of work GO
SET XACT_ABORT OFF;
GO
```

With the setting on, the entire transaction is rolled back with an error, making the whole transaction an atomic operation. The default setting for XACT_ABORT is off, so if you want this type of behavior, you will have to either modify code as shown in Listing 16-3 or change your connection strings.

Explicit Rollback

You can take a more active control in how atomicity is maintained by using the TRY/CATCH error trapping within your transactions. In this case, it can even act as a bit of a performance enhancement. Any statements within the TRY block of code that experience an error will cause the CATCH block of code to be initiated. Listing 16-4 shows an example.

Listing 16-4. Catching the error

```
BEGIN TRY
    BEGIN TRAN;
    --Start: Logical unit of work
    First:
    INSERT INTO dbo.ProductTest
    SELECT p.ProductID
    FROM Production.Product AS p;
    Second:
    INSERT INTO dbo.ProductTest
    (
        ProductID
    )
    VALUES
    (1 );
    COMMIT; --End: Logical unit of work
```

```
END TRY
BEGIN CATCH
    ROLLBACK;
    PRINT 'An error occurred';
    RETURN;
END CATCH;
```

When the error occurs, the first statement in the CATCH block is a ROLLBACK. This means that all work of the transaction is immediately undone. Further, no attempt at making the second INSERT is done, reducing the time this transaction is held open, possibly, slightly, improving performance. That's not to say that TRY/CATCH is a performance enhancement, but that it can be a side effect of their use.

Consistency

The next property that affects transactions, and therefore locking and blocking, is the need for your database to be consistent. This means that when a transaction is complete, the data is either written or rolled back. You will not be in an indeterminant state with your data.

SQL Server ensures this through a series of actions. First, when you're modifying a given data structure, all indexes, constraints, and other dependent objects that can be affected by the change in code are identified. Then, the optimization process assures that any data changes that must be done, such as adding or modifying a row in a nonclustered index after the clustered index is changed, are also taken into account.

The actual logical consistency of the data is maintained by SQL Server. However, it's your database design and the logical needs of the application being supported that drive that design. In order to ensure that all these constraints are maintained appropriately, exclusive rights must again be applied. This also leads to locks and blocking.

Isolation

It's expected in the multiuser environment of SQL Server for more than one transaction to be executing simultaneously. Isolation is the act of walling each of these transactions off from each other to ensure that one transaction's set of actions doesn't directly affect other transactions. Isolation is actually a setting within the database and can be controlled. We'll discuss it later in the chapter in the "Isolation Levels" section.

CHAPTER 16 BLOCKING AND BLOCKED PROCESSES

As data gets manipulated by a given transaction, SQL Server ensures that this transaction can conclude its operations before another transaction starts changing the data. The idea is two processes simply can't modify the exact same pieces of data at the same time.

Isolation is one of the factors that can most negatively impact performance. The necessary locks to allow data manipulation to occur, and complete, mean other transactions can't get to that data during the operation. This happens even if the second transaction is simply trying to read the data.

Durability

At the conclusion of a transaction, all data should be written to disk or, in short, be durable. If you turned a server off, an instant after the conclusion of a transaction, nothing should happen to that transaction. Transactions in flight, ones that are not completed, will of course have to be rolled back (this is a part of the recovery process and goes way beyond topic for a book on query tuning).

Durability in and of itself doesn't really contribute directly to blocking, unlike the other ACID properties. However, the requirements to maintain the transaction log, along with the data manipulation of the transaction itself, do add to the duration of a given transaction and, therefore, the time that locks are held.

However, you can use a setting called "delayed durability" to reduce the time of some transactions by letting the transaction conclude before it has been written to the transaction log.

Lock Types

To understand blocking, you first have to understand the root of blocking, locks. With the exception of certain data in flight and in-memory tables (which we'll discuss in Chapter 19), all the data within SQL Server is stored on disk. However, in order to ensure that what is stored on disk is there successfully, SQL Server uses the ACID properties of a transaction, as discussed in the last section.

In order to meet some of the ACID requirements, resources are given to transactions, either exclusively or through a shared process. Regardless, we need to understand exactly what it is that is being locked. SQL Server has a series of granular locking levels, from all the way down to a single row up to an entire database. The locks and the order of granularity are as follows (including the identifier you'll see in code later in the chapter within the parentheses):

- Row (RID)
- Key (KEY)
- Page (PAG)
- Extent (EXT)
- Heap or B-Tree (HoBT)
- Rowgroup()
- Table (TAB)
- File (FIL)
- Application (APP)
- Metadata (MDT)
- Allocation unit (AU)
- Transaction (XACT)
- Database (DB)

These locks are directly related to how the data is stored within SQL Server. I'm going to detail some of the behaviors on the most important of these lock types.

Row Locks

At the lowest level of storage is the row within a heap table. Consequently, this is as granular as you can get within SQL Server. For single-row data modifications, this is the most common lock. Listing 16-5 shows this in action.

Listing 16-5. Observing a row-level lock in action

```
DROP TABLE IF EXISTS dbo.LockTest;
CREATE TABLE dbo.LockTest
(
    C1 INT
```

CHAPTER 16 BLOCKING AND BLOCKED PROCESSES

```
);
INSERT INTO dbo.LockTest
VALUES
(1);
GO
BEGIN TRAN;
DELETE dbo.LockTest
WHERE C1 = 1;
SELECT dtl.request_session_id,
       dtl.resource_database_id,
       dtl.resource_associated_entity_id,
       dtl.resource_type,
       dtl.resource_description,
       dtl.request_mode,
       dtl.request_status
FROM sys.dm_tran_locks AS dtl
WHERE dtl.request_session_id = @@SPID;
ROLLBACK;
```

The code in Listing 16-5 first creates a table, dbo.LockTest. Then, it adds a single row to the table. With that in place, as part of a transaction, I delete the row and query sys.dm_tran_locks. The DMV sys.dm_tran_locks is a simple way to pull information about locking within a transaction. In this case, Figure 16-1 shows the results from the DMV.

	request_session_id	resource_database_id	resource_associated_entity_id	resource_type	resource_description	request_mode	request_status
1	64	5	0	DATABASE		S	GRANT
2	64	5	72057594073186304	PAGE	1:2480	IX	GRANT
3	64	5	72057594073186304	RID	1:2480:0	X	GRANT
4	64	5	1476200309	OBJECT		IX	GRANT

Figure 16-1. *A row-level lock for the DELETE statement*

There is a lot of detail on display here, but I want to focus rather tightly at the moment. I will explore all the information on display in more detail throughout this chapter. If you look at line 3, you'll see that the resource_type is "RID" for this session, indicating a row lock. Further, you'll see the request_mode is a value of "X," which means it is exclusive. The DELETE statement received an exclusive lock on the row in order to remove it.

Some of the additional information on display is the database identifier in the resource_database_id column. That lets you know where the action is occurring. You can also see the exact resource being locked in the resource_description column: "1:2480:0". This represents

>   FileID:PageID:Slot(row)

So we have the FileID value of 1, or the primary data file. The PageID value is 2480, which is a page on the dbo.LockTest table. Finally, the Slot, or row, represents placement, which is the very first, and only, row in the table. Finally, the resource_associated_entity_id column corresponds to the value in the resource_type table. So, for example, the object in question is shown in the row where the resource_type equals "OBJECT." Listing 16-6 shows how to find the name of the object.

Listing 16-6. Retrieving the object name from the object ID value

```
SELECT OBJECT_NAME(1476200309),
       DB_NAME(5);
```

No lock is superior to another in terms of performance. They all serve a different need. However, in this case, a single-row delete should see a row lock that will provide high concurrency.

Key Locks

A KEY lock occurs within an index, similar to a row lock on a table. As I outlined in Chapter 9, a clustered index defines data storage, keeping all the data at the leaf level of the index. When you then need to modify a single row, or a limited range of rows, with a clustered index, the key value of the index is used to find the row, or rows, and then a KEY lock is used while the data is being manipulated. Same concept applies to nonclustered indexes if you're modifying data stored at the leaf level with an INCLUDE operator or if you're modifying the key value for the nonclustered index.

We can use the LockTest table from Listing 16-5 and add a clustered index to the table as shown in Listing 16-7.

Listing 16-7. Adding a clustered index to the LockTest table

```
CREATE CLUSTERED INDEX TestIndex ON dbo.LockTest (C1);
```

CHAPTER 16 ■ BLOCKING AND BLOCKED PROCESSES

With that in place, I'll run the DELETE statement similar to Listing 16-5 here in Listing 16-8.

Listing 16-8. Deleting rows within a clustered index

```
BEGIN TRAN;
DELETE dbo.LockTest
WHERE C1 = 1;
SELECT dtl.request_session_id,
       dtl.resource_database_id,
       dtl.resource_associated_entity_id,
       dtl.resource_type,
       dtl.resource_description,
       dtl.request_mode,
       dtl.request_status
FROM sys.dm_tran_locks AS dtl
WHERE dtl.request_session_id = @@SPID;
ROLLBACK;
```

We can then observe how the locks were done as shown in Figure 16-2.

	request_session_id	resource_database_id	resource_associated_entity_id	resource_type	resource_description	request_mode	request_status
1	90	5	0	DATABASE		S	GRANT
2	90	5	1476200309	OBJECT		IX	GRANT
3	90	5	72057594073251840	PAGE	1:269816	IX	GRANT
4	90	5	72057594073251840	KEY	(de42f79bc795)	X	GRANT

Figure 16-2. *A KEY lock to DELETE data from a clustered index*

The X request_mode shows us that the intent is for an exclusive lock on the key, in order to delete the row requested in Listing 16-8.

Page Locks

When more than a few rows or key values are needed to be locked, it can be much more efficient for SQL Server to take out a single lock on a page, identified as a PAGE lock (or a PAG lock in older versions of SQL Server). The optimizer provides estimates for the number of rows that will be locked, and from that, the engine manages the locks, ensuring as few locks as possible since each one not only locks the resources in question but takes up memory and CPU. So as the lower-level locks increase, it's more efficient to take a higher-level lock, reducing resource use, even as the granularity of the lock decreases.

While you will see increased performance for a given query due to a broader lock, you will also see a decrease in concurrency since all rows on a given page will be locked.

Extent Locks

An extent is a group of eight contiguous data or index pages. An extent lock is then a lock of eight pages identified as an EXTENT lock. Just as excessive row or key locks lead to a page lock, a larger number of page locks can lead to an extent lock.

Heap or B-Tree Locks

A heap or B-Tree lock is used to describe when a lock to either type of object could be made. The target object could be an unordered heap table, a table without a clustered index, or a B-Tree object, usually referring to partitions. A setting within the ALTER TABLE function allows you to exercise a level of control over how locking escalation (covered in the "Lock Escalation" section) is affected with the partitions. Because partitions can be across multiple file groups, each one has to have its own data allocation definition. This is where the HoBT lock comes into play. It acts like a table-level lock but on a partition instead of on the table itself.

Rowgroup Locks

When dealing with columnstore indexes, you still have to take into account locking as data gets manipulated. However, instead of worrying about a row or a page, columnstore focuses on the rowgroup as a locking mechanism. As discussed in Chapter 9, the columnstore uses a rowgroup as its mechanism of storage. When data moves from the deltastore into the pivoted, compressed storage, you'll see rowgroup locks as that data moves.

Table Locks

It's possible to lock an entire table using a TAB lock. This reserves not just the table itself but all associated indexes.

As before, when there are too many lower-level locks, it can be much more efficient to take out a single lock on the entire table. You'll see a single value in the resource_description column for the OBJECT lock, the ID value for the table in question.

While this lock takes up as few resources as a single KEY lock, the concurrency is radically reduced.

Transaction Locks

Introduced with SQL Server 2025, XACT locks are a part of Optimized Locking and will be covered in detail in a section later in this chapter. With Optimized Locking enabled, transactions are taken out based on the transaction ID, or xactid, value. These locks are taken out instead of row- and page-level locks. Therefore, this type of locking, when enabled on a given database, can result in superior performance and reduced resource use, specifically memory. Taking out a lock on a transaction can also help prevent lock escalation (covered in another section later in the chapter).

When Accelerated Database Recovery (ADR) is enabled or when any of the row-versioning isolation levels are in use, every row in the database has a transaction ID value. Each transaction that modifies a given row supplies that row with its transaction ID (TID, or xactid). This is the value that is used for transaction locks.

Database Locks

Every connection that opens on your system sets a shared database lock on the database being used. This prevents the database from being dropped or overwritten through a restore operation while people are using it.

Lock Operations and Modes

Locks are not just a question of deciding what is being modified and then taking the lowest-level lock. Instead, a fairly complex set of decisions has to be completed within SQL Server. Not only does the appropriate lock have to be placed on the objects being modified, but the type of lock has to be determined and locking escalation has to be accounted for.

CHAPTER 16 BLOCKING AND BLOCKED PROCESSES

Lock Escalation

I've already discussed how the locks are arranged from extremely granular at the RID and KEY levels to not granular at all at the TABLE or DATABASE level. An initial estimate is made for the kind of locks needed within SQL Server. As the query executes, the lock manager monitors the number of locks requested by a given query. If that number grows beyond internal thresholds, lock escalation can occur, meaning a higher-level, less granular, lock is taken.

Key and page locks can be automatically escalated to a table lock as the internal thresholds are exceeded. At that point, the higher-level lock is taken out, and all the resources for the lower-level locks are released. While this decreases the concurrency on the table, it increases the resources available for other sessions running on the server. The dynamic nature of lock management helps queries to run faster.

You can exert some control over how locks are managed within SQL Server. Listing 16-9 shows how.

Listing 16-9. Preventing lock escalation on a table

```
ALTER TABLE schema.table
SET (LOCK_ESCALATION = DISABLE);
```

Running that code, supplying an appropriate schema and table name, will eliminate most lock escalations (but not every possible one).

Alternatively, you can set the LOCK_ESCALATION value to TABLE. In that case, every time escalation occurs, it goes straight to a TABLE-level lock.

Setting the value to AUTO re-enables the dynamic lock management within SQL Server for the table in question. This kind of control over locking should only be done after extensive testing to establish that you're not doing more harm than good on your system.

You also have the option to disable lock escalation on a wider basis by using trace flag 1224. This disables lock escalation based on the number of locks but leaves intact lock escalation based on memory pressure. You can also disable the memory pressure lock escalation as well as the number of locks by using trace flag 1211, but that's a dangerous choice and can lead to errors on your systems. I strongly suggest thorough testing before using either of these options.

Lock Modes

I've already mentioned locking modes in several places throughout the chapter. Not every lock taken is exclusive. In fact, there are a number of different ways that any of the locks can behave. For example, if a query is just reading data, it's not going to take out an exclusive lock, but rather a shared one, so more than one query can easily read the same piece of data. Further, while the data is being read, because of those shared locks, exclusive locks can't be taken. Here are the various lock modes that I'll cover in more detail in the rest of this section:

- Shared (S)
- Update (U)
- Exclusive (X)
- Intent
  - Intent Shared (IS)
  - Intent Exclusive (IX)
  - Shared with Intent Exclusive (SIX)
- Schema
  - Schema Modification (Sch-M)
  - Schema Stability (Sch-S)
- Bulk Update (BU)
- Key-Range

Shared (S) Mode

Shared mode is used for queries that are going to read data, like a SELECT statement. A shared lock doesn't prevent other queries that are only reading data from accessing the data simultaneously. This is because the integrity of the data is not affected in any way by concurrent reads. However, concurrent data modification queries are intentionally stopped in order to protect data integrity. The (S) lock is released immediately after the data is read.

Even if the SELECT query is part of a transaction, each of the necessary (S) locks is released as soon as the read on that row, or page, whatever, is completed. This is the default behavior under the read_committed isolation level (more on isolation levels later in the chapter). You can change the behavior of the shared (S) lock by using different isolation levels or a lock hint within the query.

Update (U) Mode

The Update (U) mode is actually indicating a read operation. However, the read is being done with the intention to then modify the data. Since the data is going to be modified, only one U lock on a single resource is possible in order to protect data integrity. The (U) lock is a common part of an UPDATE statement, which consists of two actions: reading the data to be modified and then modifying that data.

There are actually multiple lock modes that will take place during an UPDATE of data. As the data is being read in preparation for the possibility of being updated, a (U) lock is taken. If the data is then going to be modified, the (U) lock is converted to an exclusive lock for the actual data modification. If no data is being updated (e.g., it doesn't match the WHERE criteria), then the (U) lock is immediately released.

In order to see this action, I'm going to run a series of queries in multiple connections. Table 16-1 shows the code that I'm running in each T-SQL window (the easy way to get multiple connections within SSMS). It also shows the order in which the queries are run. The goal here is to have an observable blocked process.

Table 16-1. *Scripts running in multiple T-SQL windows to arrive at a blocked process*

Script Order	T-SQL Window 1(Connection 1)	T-SQL Window 2(Connection 2)	T-SQL Window 3(Connection 3)
1	BEGIN TRANSACTION LockTran2; --Retain an (S) lock on the resource SELECT * FROM Sales.Currency AS c WITH (REPEATABLEREAD) WHERE c.CurrencyCode = 'EUR'; --Allow DMVs to be executed before second step of -- UPDATE statement is executed by transaction LockTran1 WAITFOR DELAY '00:00:10'; COMMIT;		
2		BEGIN TRANSACTION LockTran1; UPDATE Sales.Currency SET Name = 'Euro' WHERE CurrencyCode = 'EUR'; -- NOTE: We're not committing yet	

(*continued*)

Table 16-1. (*continued*)

Script Order	T-SQL Window 1(Connection 1)	T-SQL Window 2(Connection 2)	T-SQL Window 3(Connection 3)
3			SELECT dtl.request_session_id, dtl.resource_database_id, dtl.resource_associated_entity_id, dtl.resource_type, dtl.resource_description, dtl.request_mode, dtl.request_status FROM sys.dm_tran_locks AS dtl ORDER BY dtl.request_session_id;

(*continued*)

CHAPTER 16 BLOCKING AND BLOCKED PROCESSES

Table 16-1. (*continued*)

Script Order	T-SQL Window 1 (Connection 1)	T-SQL Window 2 (Connection 2)	T-SQL Window 3 (Connection 3)
4			--wait 10 seconds
5			SELECT dtl.request_session_id, dtl.resource_database_id, dtl.resource_associated_entity_id, dtl.resource_type, dtl.resource_description, dtl.request_mode, dtl.request_status FROM sys.dm_tran_locks AS dtl ORDER BY dtl.request_session_id;
6		COMMIT;	

You may want to edit this code and put in a longer delay if you need more time to switch between windows to make this all work.

Step 1 modifies some data but waits on the commit. Step 2 modifies the same data, so it's blocked while the first step is waiting on the ten seconds. Step 3 allows you to use sys.dm_tran_locks to see the locks taken out by the two queries. In step 4, we wait out the ten seconds. In step 5, I query sys.dm_tran_locks a second time to see the locks used by the uncommitted code from step 2. Finally, in step 6, I commit the code.

One note, I'm using the REPEATABLEREAD locking hint in step 1, running in Connection 1, to ensure that the (S) lock is retained on the code through the transaction.

Figure 16-3 shows the locks held after the first two steps.

CHAPTER 16   BLOCKING AND BLOCKED PROCESSES

	request_session_id	resource_database_id	resource_associated_entity_id	resource_type	resource_description	request_mode	request_status
1	56	5	0	DATABASE		S	GRANT
2	56	5	72057594048675840	KEY	(0d881dadfc5c)	S	GRANT
3	56	5	1589580701	OBJECT		IS	GRANT
4	56	5	72057594048675840	PAGE	1:12304	IS	GRANT
5	58	5	0	DATABASE		S	GRANT
6	59	5	0	DATABASE		S	GRANT
7	72	5	72057594048675840	KEY	(0d881dadfc5c)	U	GRANT
8	72	5	72057594048675840	KEY	(0d881dadfc5c)	X	CONVERT
9	72	5	1589580701	OBJECT		IX	GRANT
10	72	5	72057594048675840	PAGE	1:12304	IX	GRANT
11	72	5	0	DATABASE		S	GRANT

Figure 16-3. Locks held by initial UPDATE statements

The focus here is on the *U* or *UPDATE* lock taken out by the `session_id` 72. It's against the key where the data is stored. However, the plan is, as you can see, to *CONVERT* to an exclusive, *X*, lock (visible on line 8, described in the `request_status` column).

After the ten-second wait, the transaction commits, and the next transaction (run from Connection 2 in the code sample from Table 16-1) can complete. This results in the locks visible in Figure 16-4.

	request_session_id	resource_database_id	resource_associated_entity_id	resource_type	resource_description	request_mode	request_status
1	56	5	0	DATABASE		S	GRANT
2	58	5	0	DATABASE		S	GRANT
3	59	5	0	DATABASE		S	GRANT
4	72	5	0	DATABASE		S	GRANT
5	72	5	72057594053918720	PAGE	1:9336	IX	GRANT
6	72	5	72057594053918720	KEY	(f62981d8cb14)	X	GRANT
7	72	5	72057594048675840	KEY	(0d881dadfc5c)	X	GRANT
8	72	5	1589580701	OBJECT		IX	GRANT
9	72	5	72057594048675840	PAGE	1:12304	IX	GRANT
10	72	5	72057594053918720	KEY	(3a34c4e89226)	X	GRANT

Figure 16-4. Locks held only by the second UPDATE statement

The reason a *U* lock is used is because other resources can continue to read the data until the changes are committed. That means until the exclusive lock is needed, other processes can continue to read data, increasing concurrency in the system. However, once an update lock is taken on a resource, only one of those is allowed. While other resources can read the data, nothing else can modify the data until the first transaction is complete.

Exclusive (X) Mode

I've already shown exclusive, X, mode in action in the examples shown previously. The purpose of the exclusive locking mode is to hold a resource within the database while data manipulation is completed. No concurrent transactions are allowed, ensuring ACID compliance. While you saw that UPDATE uses lock conversion as a way to ensure a higher degree of concurrency, INSERT and DELETE statements immediately take exclusive locks on the necessary resources.

The exclusive lock has two primary purposes:

- Other transactions can't access the resource while the change is being made, ensuring that they are reading either before or after the modification, with no ongoing modifications being read.

- Exclusive locks provide the mechanism to roll back transactions safely without modifying data since no other process has access to the data until the transaction is complete.

Intent Shared (IS), Intent Exclusive (IX), and Shared with Intent Exclusive (SIX) Modes

The intent modes indicate that the query will take out locks, corresponding to the appropriate type, at a lower-lock level. To see this in action, consider the code in Listing 16-10.

Listing 16-10. DELETE statement and a query for locks within a transaction

```
BEGIN TRAN;
DELETE Sales.Currency
WHERE CurrencyCode = 'ALL';
SELECT tl.request_session_id,
       tl.resource_database_id,
       tl.resource_associated_entity_id,
       tl.resource_type,
       tl.resource_description,
       tl.request_mode,
       tl.request_status
FROM sys.dm_tran_locks AS tl;
ROLLBACK TRAN;
```

The locks are shown in Figure 16-5.

	request_session_id	resource_database_id	resource_associated_entity_id	resource_type	resource_description	request_mode	request_status
1	59	5	0	DATABASE		S	GRANT
2	58	5	0	DATABASE		S	GRANT
3	56	5	0	DATABASE		S	GRANT
4	73	5	0	DATABASE		S	GRANT
5	78	5	0	DATABASE		S	GRANT
6	56	5	72057594053918720	KEY	(f9b93c451603)	X	GRANT
7	56	5	72057594053918720	PAGE	1:9336	IX	GRANT
8	56	5	1589580701	OBJECT		IX	GRANT
9	56	5	72057594048675840	KEY	(cadf591d32de)	X	GRANT
10	56	5	72057594048675840	PAGE	1:12304	IX	GRANT

Figure 16-5. *Locks taken out for a DELETE include Intent locks*

The Intent lock here is *IX*, Intent Exclusive, at the *PAGE* level. That means it will lock at the page, row, or key level. There's a second *IX* lock as well for a second object, a nonclustered index, on the table where the DELETE is occurring. Again, this means it will be using a page or key lock to deal with the DELETE operation.

The Intent locks are meant to ensure that while a lower-level lock is likely going to be used, no other resource can take out a higher-level lock that would cover the same resource. Without this type of lock, a process intending to take out a higher-level lock would need to scan all the locks in order to determine if it could take out its lock. The Intent lock ensures that high-level locking is optimized.

Only one Shared with Intent Exclusive, *SIX*, lock is allowed on a given resource. Other processes can place IS locks on a given resource at a lower level while the *SIX* lock is in place.

Schema Modification (Sch-M) and Schema Stability (Sch-S) Modes

Schema Modification and Schema Stability locks are acquired on a table by SQL statements that depend on the schema of the table. A DDL statement, working on the schema of a table, acquires an (Sch-M) lock on the table and prevents other transactions from accessing the table. An (Sch-S) lock is acquired for database activities that depend on the schema but do not modify the schema, such as a query compilation. It prevents an (Sch-M) lock on the table, but it allows other locks to be granted on the table.

Since, on a production database, schema modifications are infrequent, (Sch-M) locks don't usually become a blocking issue. And because (Sch-S) locks don't block other locks except (Sch-M) locks, concurrency is generally not affected by (Sch-S) locks either.

Bulk Update (BU) Mode

The Bulk Update lock mode is unique to bulk load operations. These operations are the older-style bcp (bulk copy), the BULK INSERT statement, and inserts from the OPENROWSET using the BULK option. As a mechanism for speeding up these processes, you can provide a TABLOCK hint or set the option on the table for it to lock on bulk load. The key to (BU) locking mode is that it will allow multiple bulk operations against the table being locked but prevent other operations while the bulk process is running.

Key-Range Mode

The Key-Range mode is applicable only while the isolation level is set to Serializable (you'll learn more about transaction isolation levels in the "Isolation Levels" section). The Key-Range locks are applied to a series, or range, of key values that will be used repeatedly while the transaction is open. Locking a range during a serializable transaction ensures that other rows are not inserted within the range, possibly changing result sets within the transaction. The range can be locked using the other lock modes, making this more like a combined locking mode rather than a distinctively separate locking mode. For the Key-Range lock mode to work, an index must be used to define the values within the range.

Lock Compatibility

SQL Server provides isolation to a transaction by preventing other transactions from accessing the same resource in an incompatible way. However, if a transaction attempts a compatible task on the same resource, then to increase concurrency, it won't be blocked by the first transaction. SQL Server ensures this kind of selective blocking by preventing a transaction from acquiring an incompatible lock on a resource held by another transaction. For example, an (S) lock acquired on a resource by a transaction allows other transactions to acquire an (S) lock on the same resource. However, an (Sch-M) lock on a resource by a transaction prevents other transactions from acquiring any lock on that resource.

CHAPTER 16 BLOCKING AND BLOCKED PROCESSES

Isolation Levels

The purpose of the locks and lock modes described in the previous section is very tightly coupled around the simple concept of ensuring data consistency through ACID compliance. However, the locks and modes are not the only driving factors for the behavior of data isolation within transactions. When you need to adjust how some of the locking processes are controlled, you use the isolation levels within SQL Server.

There are six isolation levels within SQL Server. The first four are standard:

- Read Uncommitted
- Read Committed
- Repeatable Read
- Serializable

The next two isolation levels are unique to SQL Server, providing mechanisms for row versions (although, to be clear, other relational databases have similar operations, e.g., PostgreSQL and the Multi-version Concurrency Control, just not these specific isolation levels). Basically, a copy of a row, or rows, is made while the data is being modified. This ensures that resources that only need to read the data have a mechanism to bypass the exclusive locks taken out on the resources. These are

- Snapshot
- Read Committed Snapshot (technically a subset of the Read Committed isolation level)

The first four isolation levels are in the order of the degree of isolation. The isolation levels can be set at the database, connection, or query level. You can use the SET TRANSACTION ISOLATION level or the locking hints to affect this behavior at the query level. Connection settings for the isolation level are maintained throughout the connection unless a SET statement is used to change them.

Read Uncommitted

Read Uncommitted is the least restrictive of the four standard isolation levels. Read Uncommitted allows SELECT queries to access data without taking out a shared, S, lock. Since there is no S lock taken, not only do the queries running SELECT statements not interfere with data manipulation queries taking out exclusive, X, locks, but the reads are not affected by those same X locks. In short, you can read data that is being actively manipulated. This is what is called a dirty read.

The common explanation of a dirty read goes as follows. The column stores the value "Cat," and it's actively being updated to the value "Dog." A dirty read could get the value "Cat" or the value "Dog." Because there are no locks taken for the reads, either could be returned.

However, that explanation for dirty reads does not go far enough. The data could be getting deleted, but you'll still retrieve a value. In the event of scans across indexes at the leaf level, it's possible to get duplicated values as page splits (explained earlier in Chapter 12) can cause rows to be moved before, or after, the point where a scan is occurring. Dirty reads could also miss rows, again, because of page splits moving their location.

Dirty reads can then lead to

- Incorrect data
- Duplicate data
- Missing data

While many people treat Read Uncommitted (primarily through the query hint NOLOCK) as a magic "run faster" switch in SQL Server, this is not true.

In order to apply Read Uncommitted (and by extension NOLOCK), you should be able to ensure that you're dealing with a system with a low need for accuracy in the data. For example, a banking or retail application would be a poor choice for using Read Uncommitted.

You can set the database default to be Read Uncommitted, or you can use the SET statement in Listing 16-11.

Listing 16-11. Setting Read Uncommitted for a connection

```
SET TRANSACTION ISOLATION LEVEL READ UNCOMMITTED;
```

It bears repeating, using Read Uncommitted (and the NOLOCK query hint) on systems that have a high level of transaction activity can result in radically undependable data. Read Uncommitted is meant for reporting systems that have little to no data changes occurring in real time. While you may see a performance improvement in OLTP systems using Read Uncommitted, few organizations realize that they're sacrificing data accuracy for that speed improvement.

Read Committed

Read Committed is the next most restrictive isolation level. With Read Committed, you will see shared, S, locks. It's in the name: it's only going to read from data where the transactions have been committed. No dirty reads. You control the isolation level in the same way as shown in Listing 16-12.

Listing 16-12. Setting Read Committed for a connection

```
SET TRANSACTION ISOLATION LEVEL READ COMMITTED;
```

Read Committed is the default isolation level within SQL Server, and it will serve well for most databases. Because of the S locks, you may see contention between reads and data manipulation queries.

An option you have for dealing with read contention is to use the Read Committed Snapshot isolation level. Turning this isolation level on means that data manipulation queries will use row versioning in the tempdb. Basically, a copy of the row is created that SELECT queries will use until the data manipulation is complete. This is further enhanced with Optimized Locking, discussed in a separate section in this chapter.

Using Read Committed Snapshot will place additional load on the tempdb, so you'll need to plan for that. However, you'll see an improvement in speed since you're eliminating contention between the reads and writes within the database. Also, unlike using NOLOCK or Read Uncommitted, you will not have an issue with page splits since there are no dirty reads taking place. Unlike SQL Server, the default isolation level in Azure SQL Database is Read Committed Snapshot.

To see this in action, I'll use Listing 16-13 to change the isolation level for my database.

Listing 16-13. Setting Read Committed Snapshot for a database

```
ALTER DATABASE AdventureWorks SET READ_COMMITTED_SNAPSHOT ON;
```

There can be no connections to the database in order to make this change. With that in place, I'm going to query data using the SELECT statement in Listing 16-14 in one query window, our first connection.

CHAPTER 16 ■ BLOCKING AND BLOCKED PROCESSES

Listing 16-14. Retrieving Color from the Production.Product table

```
BEGIN TRANSACTION;
SELECT p.Color
FROM Production.Product AS p
WHERE p.ProductID = 711;
```

Running this query against my version of AdventureWorks returns the value "Blue." Please note, I haven't committed the transaction.

Now, I want to change the data using the UPDATE statement in Listing 16-15, from a second query window, our second connection.

Listing 16-15. Changing the Color in the Production.Product table

```
BEGIN TRANSACTION;
UPDATE Production.Product
SET Color = 'Coyote'
WHERE ProductID = 711;
--test that change
SELECT p.Color
FROM Production.Product AS p
WHERE p.ProductID = 711;
```

You'll see, within this transaction, the value returned is "Coyote," not "Blue." If I go back to the first connection, where Listing 16-14 is located, I can run the SELECT statement again (but not the BEGIN TRAN again). It won't be blocked by the uncommitted transaction from Listing 16-15. The value returned will still be "Blue." If I then commit the transaction in Listing 16-15 and then rerun our original query, the results now come back as "Coyote" because the transaction has been committed.

Before we continue, I'm going to disable Read Committed Snapshot using Listing 16-16 (although I will have to re-enable it for the "Optimized Locking" section).

Listing 16-16. Disabling Read Committed Snapshot at the database

```
ALTER DATABASE AdventureWorks SET READ_COMMITTED_SNAPSHOT OFF;
```

One point you should know about tempdb and row versioning. If tempdb fills, you won't see issues with data manipulation queries. However, you may see errors on reads because the row versions will not be available.

523

CHAPTER 16 BLOCKING AND BLOCKED PROCESSES

Repeatable Read

The next most restrictive isolation level is Repeatable Read. In Read Committed, a shared lock, S, is taken as the data is read, but as soon as the read completes, that lock is dropped, regardless of the state of the transaction (we saw that in action with Read Committed Snapshot). Repeatable Read, on the other hand, maintains the S lock until the transaction is complete. In short, no data updates can be performed until the open transaction reading the data is committed or rolled back. This ensures that multiple queries within a given transaction will have identical results.

To see this action, let's use the following contrived example. I have two processes I intend to apply to my data:

- For a single product, I want to change the price if it's currently greater than ten.
- For all products in the table, I want to discount the prices by 40%.

First, I'm going to create a table with some data in Listing 16-17.

Listing 16-17. Creating a test table and data

```
DROP TABLE IF EXISTS dbo.MyProduct;
GO
CREATE TABLE dbo.MyProduct
(
    ProductID INT,
    Price MONEY
);
INSERT INTO dbo.MyProduct
VALUES
(1, 15.0),
(2, 22.0),
(3, 9.99);
```

Next, Listing 16-18 shows the two transactions that I'll run from two query windows as noted in the comments.

CHAPTER 16 BLOCKING AND BLOCKED PROCESSES

Listing 16-18. Applying discounts to prices in the MyProduct table

```
DECLARE @Price INT;
BEGIN TRAN NormailizePrice;
SELECT @Price = mp.Price
FROM dbo.MyProduct AS mp
WHERE mp.ProductID = 1;
/*Allow transaction 2 to execute*/
WAITFOR DELAY '00:00:10';
IF @Price > 10
    UPDATE dbo.MyProduct
    SET Price = Price - 10
    WHERE ProductID = 1;
COMMIT;
--Transaction 2 from Connection 2
BEGIN TRAN ApplyDiscount;
UPDATE dbo.MyProduct
SET Price = Price * 0.6 --Discount = 40%
WHERE Price > 10;
COMMIT;
```

Running each transaction in order from two different query windows results in the Price where ProductID = 1 being –1.0.

The issue here is that the second transaction is allowed to modify the data while the first is still running through its processes, reading the data. In order for Transaction 1 to not be affected in this way, a more stringent isolation level than Read Committed will be required.

This is where Repeatable Read comes into the picture. Rather than release a shared lock before the transaction is over, that lock is maintained throughout the transaction, meaning that any and all reads from within the transaction will be the same, or repeatable. Listing 16-19 shows how you could resolve this issue.

Listing 16-19. Changes to the first transaction

```
SET TRANSACTION ISOLATION LEVEL REPEATABLE READ;
GO
--Transaction 1 from Connection 1
```

```
DECLARE @Price INT;
BEGIN TRAN NormalizePrice;
SELECT @Price = Price
FROM dbo.MyProduct AS mp
WHERE mp.ProductID = 1;
/*Allow transaction 2 to execute*/
WAITFOR DELAY '00:00:10';
IF @Price > 10
    UPDATE dbo.MyProduct
    SET Price = Price - 10
    WHERE ProductID = 1;
COMMIT;
GO
SET TRANSACTION ISOLATION LEVEL READ COMMITTED; --Back to default
GO
```

Now if both transactions are run together, the second transaction cannot update the data until the first transaction completes. You could also add a lock hint to the query like this: `...FROM dbo.MyProduct AS mp WITH (REPEATABLEREAD)`.

Serializable

Serializable is the highest of the isolation levels and the most restrictive. Instead of acquiring a lock only on the row to be accessed, transactions under the Serializable isolation level will take a lock on the row in question and on the next row in the order of the data set. This does two things. First, transactions cannot insert rows into the data set being locked. Next, it prevents additional rows being discovered after the fact, also known as a phantom read.

To see this in action, I want to set up another data set in Listing 16-20.

Listing 16-20. Creating the MyEmployees table and data

```
DROP TABLE IF EXISTS dbo.MyEmployees;
GO
CREATE TABLE dbo.MyEmployees
(
    EmployeeID INT,
```

```
    GroupID INT,
    Salary MONEY
);
CREATE CLUSTERED INDEX i1 ON dbo.MyEmployees (GroupID);
INSERT INTO dbo.MyEmployees
VALUES
(1, 10, 1000),
(2, 10, 1000),
(3, 20, 1000),
(4, 9, 1000);
```

In this new data set, you'll note that two employees belong to GroupID = 10. The plan here is to distribute a bonus of $100 evenly to each employee in that group. However, we're also hiring a new employee at the same time. The code necessary to accomplish this is in Listing 16-21.

Listing 16-21. Applying the bonus and hiring a new employee

```
--Transaction 1 from Connection 1
DECLARE @Fund MONEY = 100,
        @Bonus MONEY,
        @NumberOfEmployees INT;
BEGIN TRAN PayBonus;
SELECT @NumberOfEmployees = COUNT(*)
FROM dbo.MyEmployees
WHERE GroupID = 10;
/*Allow transaction 2 to execute*/
WAITFOR DELAY '00:00:10';
IF @NumberOfEmployees > 0
BEGIN
    SET @Bonus = @Fund / @NumberOfEmployees;
    UPDATE dbo.MyEmployees
    SET Salary = Salary + @Bonus
    WHERE GroupID = 10;
    PRINT 'Fund balance =
' + CAST((@Fund - (@@ROWCOUNT * @Bonus)) AS VARCHAR(6)) + '   $';
END;
```

```
COMMIT;
--Transaction 2 from Connect 2
BEGIN TRAN NewEmployee;
INSERT INTO MyEmployees
VALUES
(5, 10, 1000);
COMMIT;
```

Running these two transactions, the result of the final @Fund is $-50. The addition of the new employee meant that the bonus fund was overdrawn. The solution here, like in the previous examples, is to change the locking mechanism to prevent this sort of thing from occurring, using Serializable isolation level.

There are several considerations when working with all these locking levels. On the one hand, reducing the locking as much as possible can help performance. However, it comes at the cost of data consistency and behavioral consistency. On the other hand, increasing locking can prevent these kinds of issues but increases contention, hurting performance. In short, this is all a balancing act.

Snapshot

Snapshot isolation is the second of the row-versioning isolation levels available in SQL Server since SQL Server 2005. Unlike Read Committed Snapshot isolation, Snapshot isolation requires an explicit call to SET TRANSACTION ISOLATION LEVEL at the start of the transaction. It also requires setting the isolation level on the database. Snapshot isolation is meant as a more stringent isolation level than the Read Committed Snapshot isolation. Snapshot isolation will attempt to put an exclusive lock on the data it intends to modify. If that data already has a lock on it, the snapshot transaction will fail. It provides transaction-level read consistency, which makes it more applicable to financial-type systems than Read Committed Snapshot.

Optimized Locking

Introduced with SQL Server 2025 and available in Azure SQL Database and SQL Database for Fabric, but not in Azure Managed Instance, Optimized Locking is new locking behavior that changes some of the fundamentals of locks within SQL Server.

Optimized Locking is enabled by default within Azure. Before you can enable it on your SQL Server 2025 database, you first have to enable Accelerated Database Recovery (ADR). ADR is a way to optimize recovery times on failovers, restores, and any other process that goes through the recovery process in a database. While this is a performance enhancement for certain actions in your database, it's not related to query performance tuning, so we won't be covering it beyond this explanation. I'll enable both as shown in Listing 16-22.

Listing 16-22. Enabling Optimized Locking

```
ALTER DATABASE AdventureWorks SET ACCELERATED_DATABASE_RECOVERY = ON;
ALTER DATABASE AdventureWorks SET OPTIMIZED_LOCKING = ON;
```

Optimized Locking has two fundamental behaviors that it adds to the way locks are managed during data manipulation queries such as an INSERT or a DELETE. These are TransactionID locking and Lock After Qualification. These two processes help to radically reduce the number of locks taken out as data is modified. This not only enhances query performance but helps with memory management as well. Let's look at both these processes.

TransactionID Locking

When you're using one of the snapshot isolation levels or when you have Accelerated Database Recovery enabled, every row in the database gets a transaction identifier. Optimized Locking can take advantage of this TransactionID. Instead of a set of locks across rows and pages, a single exclusive (X) lock is taken out on the TransactionID. Then, individual row or page locks are taken out and immediately released as the row modification completes. These locks are not held for the entire transaction as before. Only the lock on the TransactionID is maintained.

It's easy to see this in action. The DELETE query in Listing 16-23 deletes 121 rows from the ProductCostHistory table.

Listing 16-23. Deleting rows to see Optimized Locking in action

```
BEGIN TRAN;
DELETE Production.ProductCostHistory
WHERE StandardCost < 50;
```

CHAPTER 16 BLOCKING AND BLOCKED PROCESSES

```
SELECT dtl.request_session_id,
       dtl.resource_database_id,
       dtl.resource_associated_entity_id,
       dtl.resource_type,
       dtl.resource_description,
       dtl.request_mode,
       dtl.request_status
FROM sys.dm_tran_locks AS dtl
WHERE dtl.request_session_id = @@SPID;
ROLLBACK;
```

When this query is run and Optimized Locking is disabled, I get 126 locks, most of them KEY locks, to remove the necessary rows. Figure 16-6 shows the results with Optimized Locking enabled.

	request_session_id	resource_database_id	resource_associated_entity_id	resource_type	resource_description	request_mode	request_status
1	58	5	0	DATABASE		S	GRANT
2	58	5	770101784	OBJECT		IX	GRANT
3	58	5	0	XACT	XACT: 5:268081:0	X	GRANT

Figure 16-6. *XACT locks for Optimized Locking*

Instead of a large series of locks, we basically get one, the XACT lock on the TransactionID value. Not only does this reduce memory resource use and make for less contention between queries, but the performance changes too. I went from 1.9ms on average to only 1.7ms on average. That's not a huge win, but it's a win. The reads and writes did not change of course since the same rows must be found and modified, regardless of how the locks are taken out.

Microsoft's current guidance is to enable Read Committed Snapshot isolation (RCSI) if you are also going to enable Optimized Locking. This further reduces locking contention since readers won't take out a lock at all. Microsoft also suggests avoiding using locking hints on your queries. This is good advice generally, but with Optimized Locking enabled a locking hint changes behavior pretty radically since it's going to eliminate TransactionID locking entirely.

From a monitoring standpoint, you'll also see XACT wait types.

Lock After Qualification

In addition to TransactionID locking, another change to standard locking processes is introduced with Optimized Locking. Traditionally, before Optimized Locking, when a row was potentially going to modified by a query, an update (U) lock would be taken. After the U lock is in place, the predicate for the query validates whether or not the lock gets changed to exclusive (X). These locks are held until the transaction completes.

When both Optimized Locking and Read Committed Snapshot isolation are enabled, a new process takes over. Basically, the predicate check from the WHERE clause of the query is run first, without taking any locks since it's a read. If the predicate matches, then an X lock is taken out. However, that lock is only taken out long enough to complete the modification, and then the lock is released. That is what Lock After Qualification means. Locks are only taken out after it has been determined that this data matches the criteria of the predicate. This is going to radically reduce resource contention on busy systems.

To see this in action, I'm going to run the code in Listing 16-24. I'm first going to run it with both Optimized Locking and Read Committed Snapshot disabled.

Listing 16-24. Transactions to test Lock After Qualification

```
--Setup
DROP TABLE IF EXISTS dbo.LAQTest;
GO
CREATE TABLE dbo.LAQTest
(
    LAQID INT,
    LAQValue VARCHAR(25)
);
GO
INSERT INTO dbo.LAQTest
(
    LAQID,
    LAQValue
)
VALUES
(1, 'Value 1'),
(2, 'Value 2'),
```

```
(3, 'Value 3');

--Run from 1st connection
BEGIN TRAN
UPDATE dbo.LAQTest
SET LAQValue = 'Value 1a'
WHERE LAQID = 1;

--Run from 2nd connection
BEGIN TRAN
UPDATE dbo.LAQTest
SET LAQValue = 'Value 2a'
WHERE LAQID = 2;
```

Naturally, the first transaction is going to block the second transaction. Even though they are updating different values on different rows, the locks taken out will prevent the second transaction from starting until the first completes.

When Optimized Locking and Read Committed Snapshot are both enabled, well, there's nothing to show. The first UPDATE statement is no longer holding a U lock against any rows in the table; therefore, the second transaction just completes.

Lock After Qualification (LAQ) has a number of limits on when and where it can work. As I've already stated, you have to have Optimized Locking enabled, of course. In addition, Read Committed Snapshot must be enabled. The connection is set to Read Committed isolation level (the default). After that, here are the limitations:

- MERGE statements
- When there are conflicting locking hints
- If the modified table has a columnstore index
- When the query in question includes a variable assignment
- When the query has an OUTPUT clause
- If the execution plan has more than one seek or scan operator in order to read the necessary rows (think index joins as discussed in Chapter 14)

Any of these scenarios will prevent Lock After Qualification from being used. And there's one more.

LAQ uses an optimistic approach to the locks. However, it is possible internally for a query to be aborted and restarted, without LAQ being enabled. Obviously, restarting a query is going to add overhead and reduce performance. Because of this, SQL Server has an internal set of heuristics to monitor queries getting aborted before they can use LAQ. Internally, Microsoft measures the queries involved in LAQ in terms of the pages modified. If queries are aborted and restarted or even if they are considered for being aborted, their page count is recorded. Once an internal threshold is reached, Lock After Qualification is disabled until the number of pages is reduced below the threshold again. You can observe queries that are aborted using the Extended Event lock_after_qual_stmt_abort.

Before we go on, just to see consistent behavior in the rest of the code in this chapter, I'm going to disable both Optimized Locking and Read Committed Snapshot isolation, using the commands in Listing 16-25.

Listing 16-25. Disabling Optimized Locking

```
ALTER DATABASE AdventureWorks SET SINGLE_USER WITH ROLLBACK IMMEDIATE;
ALTER DATABASE AdventureWorks SET OPTIMIZED_LOCKING = OFF;
ALTER DATABASE AdventureWorks SET READ_COMMITTED_SNAPSHOT OFF;
ALTER DATABASE AdventureWorks SET MULTI_USER;
```

Effect of Indexes on Locking

If a table is a heap, meaning no clustered index defining data storage, then it can only have a very limited set of locks: row (RID), page (PAG), and table (TAB). Adding indexes to a table changes what resources can be, and must be, locked in support of the transactions. The effect of an index on locking varies with the index type and that index's ability to support WHERE, ON, and HAVING clauses that are part of the data manipulation queries. I'm going to explore some of the effects of an index on locking.

Effect of a Nonclustered Index

While a nonclustered index is stored separately from the data pages of the table, SQL Server still has to take locks on the nonclustered index to protect it from corruption. To see this in action, first, we'll create a new test table and an index using Listing 16-26.

Listing 16-26. Creating a nonclustered index on MyEmployees

```
DROP TABLE IF EXISTS dbo.LockTest;
GO
CREATE TABLE dbo.LockTest
(
    C1 INT,
    C2 DATETIME
);
INSERT INTO dbo.LockTest
VALUES
(1, GETDATE());
CREATE NONCLUSTERED INDEX iTest ON dbo.LockTest (C1);
```

I'm now going to run a query that will hold all the locks on the table using the REPEATABLEREAD query hint in Listing 16-27.

Listing 16-27. Running a named transaction, LockBehavior

```
BEGIN TRAN LockBehavior;
UPDATE dbo.LockTest WITH (REPEATABLEREAD) --Hold all acquired locks
SET C2 = GETDATE()
WHERE C1 = 1;
--Observe lock behavior from another connection
WAITFOR DELAY '00:00:10';
COMMIT;
```

If I run this query, the locks are shown in Figure 16-7.

	request_session_id	resource_database_id	resource_associated_entity_id	resource_type	resource_description	request_mode	request_status
1	53	5	0	DATABASE		S	GRANT
2	66	5	0	DATABASE		S	GRANT
3	53	5	72057594073972736	PAGE	1:398816	IU	GRANT
4	53	5	72057594073907200	RID	1:398800:0	X	GRANT
5	53	5	72057594073907200	PAGE	1:398800	IX	GRANT
6	53	5	72057594073972736	KEY	(cbdadd645ae0)	U	GRANT
7	53	5	816721962	OBJECT		IX	GRANT

Figure 16-7. *Locking in a nonclustered index*

CHAPTER 16 BLOCKING AND BLOCKED PROCESSES

The following locks (on request_session_id of 53) are acquired by the transaction:

- An (IU) lock on the page containing the nonclustered index row
- A (U) lock on the nonclustered index row within the index page
- An (IX) lock on the table
- An (IX) lock on the page containing the data row
- An (X) lock on the data row within the data page

You can then see that additional locking overhead is introduced. This can, possibly, negatively impact performance. Also, in some cases, you may see more contention. That's not to say we won't be using nonclustered indexes. Of course, we will.

Now, you can take control of the behavior of locking with a nonclustered index. We can use options when we create the index as shown in Listing 16-28.

Listing 16-28. Changing the locking behavior for an index

```
ALTER INDEX TestIndex
ON dbo.LockTest
SET (ALLOW_ROW_LOCKS = OFF, ALLOW_PAGE_LOCKS = OFF);
```

This approach is inherently dangerous. You're taking control away from SQL Server. Using this method, only a table lock will be taken out, radically increasing contention on the table. Only perform this sort of action as a last resort and try changing just one setting at a time.

Effects of a Clustered Index

Because the data is stored at the leaf level of the clustered index, it actually results in fewer locks than a nonclustered index will require. I'll use Listing 16-29 to create a clustered index on the LockTest table.

Listing 16-29. Replacing the nonclustered index with a clustered index

```
CREATE CLUSTERED INDEX iTest ON dbo.LockTest (C1) WITH DROP_EXISTING;
```

As before, I'll run the transaction from Listing 16-23 and capture the output of sys.dm_tran_locks from a second connection. The resulting locks are shown in Figure 16-8.

CHAPTER 16 BLOCKING AND BLOCKED PROCESSES

	request_session_id	resource_database_id	resource_associated_entity_id	resource_type	resource_description	request_mode	request_status
1	53	5	0	DATABASE		S	GRANT
2	66	5	0	DATABASE		S	GRANT
3	53	5	0	METADATA	$hash = 0x6a11181b:0x3e6005e0:0xb8	Sch-S	GRANT
4	53	5	72057594074038272	KEY	(de42f79bc795)	X	GRANT
5	53	5	816721962	OBJECT		IX	GRANT
6	53	5	72057594074038272	PAGE	1:397928	IX	GRANT

Figure 16-8. *Effects of a clustered index on locking behavior*

The following locks are acquired by the transaction:

- An (IX) lock on the table
- An (IX) lock on the page containing the clustered index row
- An (X) lock on the clustered index row within the table or clustered index

The locks on the clustered index row and the leaf page are actually the locks on the data row and data page, too, since the data pages and the leaf pages are the same. Thus, the clustered index reduced the locking overhead on the table compared with the nonclustered index.

Reduced locking overhead of a clustered index is another benefit of using a clustered index over a heap.

Capturing Blocking Information

With a good understanding of how locking occurs, the next step is to look at the blocking that occurs between processes caused by those locks. While the locks are entirely necessary to maintain ACID compliance and data consistency, excessive blocking from the locks is a performance concern. Understanding where blocking is occurring will help you improve concurrency and therefore performance.

You need a few important pieces of information in order to fully understand a blocking scenario:

- Connection information about both the blocking and blocked sessions
- The lock information about the blocking and blocked sessions
- The SQL statements being executed by the blocking and blocked sessions

CHAPTER 16 BLOCKING AND BLOCKED PROCESSES

There are several ways to gather this information. You can use the Activity Monitor within Management Studio. The Process page provides basic blocked processing information including the process identifier (SPID) for blocking processes, the blocked processes (called the block chain), and information about the queries. You can also query directly against the Dynamic Management Objects/Views (DMVs) to pull back detailed information. Finally, Extended Events come with a blocked process report event that supplies a lot of detail, along with all that you can do in Extended Events (detailed in Chapter 3).

Here, I'm going to cover the most flexible and most powerful methods: T-SQL and the DMVs and Extended Events.

Capturing Blocking Information Using T-SQL

The DMVs provide a lot of information about what's happened and what is currently happening within your SQL Server instances. Further, the DMVs are available everywhere, from Azure to AWS and Google Cloud Platform to SQL Server instances running in containers, VMs, and good old-fashioned hardware. Listing 16-30 shows one possible approach to gathering a detailed set of blocking information using the DMVs.

Listing 16-30. Querying the DMVs for blocking information

```
SELECT der.blocking_session_id AS BlockingSessionID,
       dtl.request_session_id AS WaitingSessionID,
       dowt.resource_description AS ResourceDesc,
       deib.event_info AS BlockingTsql,
       dest.text AS WaitingTsql,
       der.wait_type AS WaitType,
       dtl.request_type AS WaitingRequestType,
       dowt.wait_duration_ms AS WaitDuration,
       DB_NAME(dtl.resource_database_id) AS DatabaseName,
       dtl.resource_associated_entity_id AS WaitingAssociatedEntity,
       dtl.resource_type AS WaitingResourceType
FROM sys.dm_tran_locks AS dtl
    JOIN sys.dm_os_waiting_tasks AS dowt
        ON dtl.lock_owner_address = dowt.resource_address
    JOIN sys.dm_exec_requests AS der
        ON der.session_id = dtl.request_session_id
```

```
    CROSS APPLY sys.dm_exec_sql_text(der.sql_handle) AS dest
    CROSS APPLY sys.dm_exec_input_buffer(der.blocking_session_id, 0)
AS deib;
```

In order to see this in action, I'll need to create a blocking scenario. Listing 16-31 creates a table we can use for blocking.

Listing 16-31. Creating the BlockTest table

```
DROP TABLE IF EXISTS dbo.BlockTest;
GO
CREATE TABLE dbo.BlockTest
(
    C1 INT,
    C2 INT,
    C3 DATETIME
);
INSERT INTO dbo.BlockTest
VALUES
(11, 12, GETDATE()),
(21, 22, GETDATE());
```

With the table in place, I'm going to need three different query windows in order to have three connections. In one, I'll run my monitor script from Listing 16-30. In the other two, the scripts labeled in Listing 16-32 here will be executed.

Listing 16-32. Two scripts that will result in a blocked process

```
--First connection, executed first
BEGIN TRAN User1;
UPDATE dbo.BlockTest
SET C3 = GETDATE();
--Second connection, executed second
BEGIN TRAN User2;
SELECT C2
FROM dbo.BlockTest
WHERE C1 = 11;
COMMIT;
```

Since the transaction, User1, is started but not committed, it's going to hold the locks on the BlockTest table until we stop the script, roll it back, or cancel the execution.

Using the DMV script from Listing 16-30, we can get the core information outlined at the beginning of this section: session IDs, lock information, and queries. That information is on display for both the blocking and blocked processes. Figure 16-9 shows all the data collected.

	BlockingSessionID	WaitingSessionID	ResourceDesc			BlockingTsql
1	70	66	ridlock fileid=1 pageid=397920 dbid=5 id=lockd1c..			BEGIN TRAN User1; UPDATE dbo.BlockTest SET C3...
WaitingTsql				WaitType	WaitingRequestType	WaitDuration
(@1 tinyint)SELECT [C2] FROM [dbo].[BlockTest] W...				LCK_M_S	LOCK	8842
DatabaseName	WaitingAssociatedEntity		WaitingResourceType			
AdventureWorks	72057594074103808		RID			

Figure 16-9. *Information about the blocked and blocking processes*

You can easily spot the blocking session and the waiting session. You can also see the details about exactly which resource the contention is over. Both queries are available, and then you can see additional information about the objects, database, and more. The duration in this case is in milliseconds.

I included the database name because the DMVs are system wide, so you'll want to see which database is involved as a part of your investigation.

Before going forward, be sure to commit or roll back the transaction for User1.

Extended Events and the blocked_process_report Event

Built right into Extended Events is the blocked_process_report event. The event is driven by a system setting, the blocked process threshold. You can directly control that threshold using code in Listing 16-33.

Listing 16-33. Changing the blocked process threshold

```
EXEC sp_configure 'show advanced option', '1';
RECONFIGURE;
EXEC sp_configure 'blocked process threshold', 5;
RECONFIGURE;
```

The default value for the threshold is zero (0), meaning it will never actually fire the blocked process event. Using the script in Listing 16-33, I changed mine to 5. Determining this value is an important part of configuring your systems. There is no single correct answer. For some systems, a one-second blocked process may be too long, while others may not care until minutes have passed. However, setting this value controls the behavior of the blocked_process_report and any emails, Slack messages, tweets, or whatever you use from your alerting system. I would suggest setting a relatively low value to start and then adjusting from there.

Listing 16-34 shows how to create a session for the blocked_process_report event.

Listing 16-34. Extended Events session for blocked_process_report

```
CREATE EVENT SESSION BlockedProcess
ON SERVER
    ADD EVENT sqlserver.blocked_process_report;
```

Yeah, it really is that easy.

I'm going to use the blocking queries from Listing 16-32 again to create a blocked process. I will have to wait a full five seconds before the event will fire. Once it fires, Figure 16-10 shows the data returned.

Field	Value
blocked_process	<blocked-process-report monit...
database_id	5
database_name	AdventureWorks
duration	9908000
index_id	0
lock_mode	S
object_id	0
resource_owner_type	LOCK
transaction_id	468276

Event:blocked_process_report (2025-08-05 17:10:40.5061466)
Details

Figure 16-10. *Data from the blocked_process_report Extended Event*

The basic information shown gives you a little bit of an idea what's happening. There's a blocked process in the AdventureWorks database, and the duration, in microseconds, is 9908000, or just over ten seconds. By the way, every five seconds you'll get a new copy of the report, with an ever-increasing duration, so, again, as I say, experiment with the appropriate setting for your system.

CHAPTER 16 BLOCKING AND BLOCKED PROCESSES

The real details of the blocking and blocked processes are in the XML of the blocked_process field:

```
<blocked-process-report monitorLoop="10061">
 <blocked-process>
  <process id="processd15cc6478" taskpriority="0" logused="0"
waitresource="RID: 5:1:397920:0" waittime="9908" ownerId="468276"
transactionname="User2" lasttranstarted="2025-08-05T22:10:30.593"
XDES="0xd15d00450" lockMode="S" schedulerid="12" kpid="736"
status="suspended" spid="66" sbid="0" ecid="0" priority="0"
trancount="1" lastbatchstarted="2025-08-05T22:10:30.593" lastba
tchcompleted="2025-08-05T22:10:13.227" lastattention="1900-01-0
1T00:00:00.227" clientapp="Microsoft SQL Server Management Studio - Query"
hostname="NECESSARY" hostpid="30180" loginname="sa" isolationlevel="read
committed (2)" xactid="468276" currentdb="5" currentdbname="AdventureWorks"
lockTimeout="4294967295" clientoption1="671090784" clientoption2="390200">
    <executionStack>
     <frame line="2" stmtstart="24" stmtend="118" sqlhandle="0x02000000cc
     f3e6045e680885750c3f36d7cc549d8ff01368000000000000000000000000000
     0000000000" />
     <frame line="2" stmtstart="38" stmtend="124" sqlhandle="0x020000005b56
     8d2c021b28973c650340cb1ccc0dae9560860000000000000000000000000000
     0000000000" />
    </executionStack>
    <stackFrames>
       <frame id="00" address="0x78014301F" pdb="ntdll.pdb" age="1"
guid="AE37D054-B390-3562-6F0E-C5408377AABC" module="ntdll" rva="0x10301F"
/><frame id="01" address="0x781C1D78E" pdb="kernelbase.pdb" age="1"
guid="912DCD17-F367-183E-B940-91377218571F" module="kernelbase"
rva="0x3D78E" /><frame id="02" address="0x7893627D3" pdb="SqlDK.pdb"
age="2" guid="815A0963-09AE-4C9A-B67D-2523A2AA307C" module="SqlDK"
rva="0x27D3" /><frame id="03" address="0x789362DA5" pdb="SqlDK.pdb"
age="2" guid="815A0963-09AE-4C9A-B67D-2523A2AA307C" module="SqlDK"
rva="0x2DA5" /><frame id="04" address="0x789363CD2" pdb="SqlDK.pdb"
age="2" guid="815A0963-09AE-4C9A-B67D-2523A2AA307C" module="SqlDK"
rva="0x3CD2" /><frame id="05" address="0x7825BE11A" pdb="sqlmin.pdb"
```

age="2" guid="EE10BE3A-FA07-4A83-8081-3ACA652818C5" module="sqlmin"
rva="0x9E11A" /><frame id="06" address="0x7825BDE8A" pdb="sqlmin.pdb"
age="2" guid="EE10BE3A-FA07-4A83-8081-3ACA652818C5" module="sqlmin"
rva="0x9DE8A" /><frame id="07" address="0x782531512" pdb="sqlmin.pdb"
age="2" guid="EE10BE3A-FA07-4A83-8081-3ACA652818C5" module="sqlmin"
rva="0x11512" /><frame id="08" address="0x7828F85D3" pdb="sqlmin.pdb"
age="2" guid="EE10BE3A-FA07-4A83-8081-3ACA652818C5" module="sqlmin"
rva="0x3D85D3" /><frame id="09" address="0x78292CCEE" pdb="sqlmin.pdb"
age="2" guid="EE10BE3A-FA07-4A83-8081-3ACA652818C5" module="sqlmin"
rva="0x40CCEE" /><frame id="10" address="0x782552178" pdb="sqlmin.pdb"
age="2" guid="EE10BE3A-FA07-4A83-8081-3ACA652818C5" module="sqlmin"
rva="0x32178" /><frame id="11" address="0x7825542EE" pdb="sqlmin.pdb"
age="2" guid="EE10BE3A-FA07-4A83-8081-3ACA652818C5" module="sqlmin"
rva="0x342EE" /><frame id="12" address="0x782AB8849" pdb="sqlmin.pdb"
age="2" guid="EE10BE3A-FA07-4A83-8081-3ACA652818C5" module="sqlmin"
rva="0x598849" /><frame id="13" address="0x7827AA41C" pdb="sqlmin.pdb"
age="2" guid="EE10BE3A-FA07-4A83-8081-3ACA652818C5" module="sqlmin"
rva="0x28A41C" /><frame id="14" address="0x782551DF0" pdb="sqlmin.pdb"
age="2" guid="EE10BE3A-FA07-4A83-8081-3ACA652818C5" module="sqlmin"
rva="0x31DF0" /><frame id="15" address="0x78255F0DE" pdb="sqlmin.pdb"
age="2" guid="EE10BE3A-FA07-4A83-8081-3ACA652818C5" module="sqlmin"
rva="0x3F0DE" /><frame id="16" address="0x785B4BC80" pdb="sqllang.pdb"
age="2" guid="1B7CF56B-B861-4605-89C3-47BF07B8F68A" module="sqllang"
rva="0x1BC80" /><frame id="17" address="0x785B4BF62" pdb="sqllang.pdb"
age="2" guid="1B7CF56B-B861-4605-89C3-47BF07B8F68A" module="sqllang"
rva="0x1BF62" /><frame id="18" address="0x785E39AD3" pdb="sqllang.pdb"
age="2" guid="1B7CF56B-B861-4605-89C3-47BF07B8F68A" module="sqllang"
rva="0x309AD3" /><frame id="19" address="0x785E39170" pdb="sqllang.pdb"
age="2" guid="1B7CF56B-B861-4605-89C3-47BF07B8F68A" module="sqllang"
rva="0x309170" /><frame id="20" address="0x785B45B90" pdb="sqllang.pdb"
age="2" guid="1B7CF56B-B861-4605-89C3-47BF07B8F68A" module="sqllang"
rva="0x15B90" /><frame id="21" address="0x785E3ACD1" pdb="sqllang.pdb"
age="2" guid="1B7CF56B-B861-4605-89C3-47BF07B8F68A" module="sqllang"
rva="0x30ACD1" /><frame id="22" address="0x785B4627D" pdb="sqllang.pdb"
age="2" guid="1B7CF56B-B861-4605-89C3-47BF07B8F68A" module="sqllang"

CHAPTER 16 BLOCKING AND BLOCKED PROCESSES

```
rva="0x1627D" /><frame id="23" address="0x785B46B0E" pdb="sqllang.pdb"
age="2" guid="1B7CF56B-B861-4605-89C3-47BF07B8F68A" module="sqllang"
rva="0x16B0E" /><frame id="24" address="0x785B45B90" pdb="sqllang.pdb"
age="2" guid="1B7CF56B-B861-4605-89C3-47BF07B8F68A" module="sqllang"
rva="0x15B90" /><frame id="25" address="0x785B5078B" pdb="sqllang.pdb"
age="2" guid="1B7CF56B-B861-4605-89C3-47BF07B8F68A" module="sqllang"
rva="0x2078B" /><frame id="26" address="0x785B58436" pdb="sqllang.pdb"
age="2" guid="1B7CF56B-B861-4605-89C3-47BF07B8F68A" module="sqllang"
rva="0x28436" /><frame id="27" address="0x785B58612" pdb="sqllang.pdb"
age="2" guid="1B7CF56B-B861-4605-89C3-47BF07B8F68A" module="sqllang"
rva="0x28612" /><frame id="28" address="0x789367874" pdb="SqlDK.pdb"
age="2" guid="815A0963-09AE-4C9A-B67D-2523A2AA307C" module="SqlDK"
rva="0x7874" /><frame id="29" address="0x789367D4F" pdb="SqlDK.pdb"
age="2" guid="815A0963-09AE-4C9A-B67D-2523A2AA307C" module="SqlDK"
rva="0x7D4F" /><frame id="30" address="0x7893679B3" pdb="SqlDK.pdb"
age="2" guid="815A0963-09AE-4C9A-B67D-2523A2AA307C" module="SqlDK"
rva="0x79B3" /><frame id="31" address="0x789397EE5" pdb="SqlDK.pdb"
age="2" guid="815A0963-09AE-4C9A-B67D-2523A2AA307C" module="SqlDK"
rva="0x37EE5" /><frame id="32" address="0x789397DEC" pdb="SqlDK.pdb"
age="2" guid="815A0963-09AE-4C9A-B67D-2523A2AA307C" module="SqlDK"
rva="0x37DEC" /><frame id="33" address="0x789397B76" pdb="SqlDK.pdb"
age="2" guid="815A0963-09AE-4C9A-B67D-2523A2AA307C" module="SqlDK"
rva="0x37B76" /><frame id="34" address="0x789398BBB" pdb="SqlDK.pdb"
age="2" guid="815A0963-09AE-4C9A-B67D-2523A2AA307C" module="SqlDK"
rva="0x38BBB" /><frame id="35" address="0x781B34CD0" pdb="kernel32.pdb"
age="1" guid="0EE2AD2B-010C-8E9E-1218-E334FD46AF0F" module="kernel32"
rva="0x14CD0" />
    </stackFrames>
  <inputbuf>
BEGIN TRAN User2;
SELECT C2
FROM dbo.BlockTest
WHERE C1 = 11;
COMMIT;

  </inputbuf>
```

```
    </process>
  </blocked-process>
  <blocking-process>
    <process status="sleeping" spid="70" sbid="0" ecid="0" priority="0"
trancount="1" lastbatchstarted="2025-08-05T22:10:26.610" lastba
tchcompleted="2025-08-05T22:10:26.613" lastattention="1900-01-0
1T00:00:00.613" clientapp="Microsoft SQL Server Management Studio - Query"
hostname="NECESSARY" hostpid="30180" loginname="sa" isolationlevel="read
committed (2)" xactid="468241" currentdb="5" currentdbname="AdventureWorks"
lockTimeout="4294967295" clientoption1="671090784" clientoption2="390200">
      <executionStack />
      <inputbuf>
BEGIN TRAN User1;
UPDATE dbo.BlockTest
SET C3 = GETDATE();   </inputbuf>
    </process>
  </blocking-process>
</blocked-process-report>
```

Reading through XML is certainly not enjoyable. However, all the information we're looking for, and more, is available in the report. The session ID values are listed, as the "spid." You can see the query, lock mode, wait resource, and all the other information we pulled from the DMVs, but this time automatically gathered through Extended Events.

Recommendations to Reduce Blocking

It bears repeating, blocking is a normal part of the operation of SQL Server. It's only when it becomes excessive that you need to focus on it. There are a few things you can do to focus on reducing contention and therefore reducing blocking. The core concept is to keep your transactions as short as possible. The fewer resources you have to lock and the less amount of time you lock them are the primary means of reducing contention. The following is a list of tips to help with this:

- Keep transactions short.
- Perform the minimum steps/logic within a transaction.

- Do not perform costly external activity within a transaction, such as sending an acknowledgment email or performing activities driven by the end user.

- Optimize the queries involved.

- Create indexes as required to ensure optimal performance of the queries within the system.

- Avoid a clustered index on frequently updated columns. Updates to clustered index key columns require locks on the clustered index and all nonclustered indexes (since their row locator contains the clustered index key).

- Consider using a covering index to serve the blocked SELECT statements.

- Use query timeouts or a resource governor to control runaway queries. For more on the resource governor, consult Microsoft's documentation.

- Avoid losing control over the scope of the transactions because of poor error-handling routines or application logic.

- Use SET XACT_ABORT ON to avoid a transaction being left open on an error condition within the transaction.

- Execute the following SQL statement from a client error handler (TRY/CATCH) after executing a SQL batch or stored procedure containing a transaction: `IF @@TRANCOUNT > 0 ROLLBACK`.

- Use the lowest isolation level required.

- Consider using row versioning, one of the SNAPSHOT isolation levels, to help reduce contention.

- Test Optimize Locking on your system and enable it if it works well for you.

Summary

Blocking may be inevitable, but understanding the root causes through the ACID properties of the database, locks and locking, isolation levels, and all the rest of the information in this chapter can help you reduce it. The goal is having your servers scale as you add more and more users with more and more data. However, some blocking is inevitable. Therefore, learn to use the DMVs and Extended Events to capture blocking information. With that, you can help to alleviate contention and make your databases run faster and scale better.

Blocking not only hurts concurrency but can actually cause a major performance problem known as a deadlock. This is when processes mutually block one another, which we'll cover in the next chapter.

CHAPTER 17

Causes and Solutions for Deadlocks

A deadlock is a special form of blocking that occurs when two or more transactions each have locks that the other needs. Since neither transaction can release their locks until the transaction is complete, SQL Server is forced to roll back one of the transactions. An error is returned naming the rolled-back transaction as a deadlock victim. This is fundamentally a performance problem, but one that is exacerbated by the need to roll back the transaction and then resubmit the query for processing a second time. Dealing with deadlocks can be challenging.

In this chapter, I'll cover the following:

- Deadlock fundamentals
- Analyzing the causes of deadlocks
- Error handling for deadlocks
- Mechanisms to prevent deadlocks

Deadlock Fundamentals

Deadlocks are rooted in blocking. The core concept is relatively straightforward. Session 1 has a lock, probably exclusive, on a resource that Session 2 needs. This is a normal blocking situation. However, add in the idea that Session 2 has a different lock, probably exclusive, on a resource that Session 1 needs. Neither process can release its lock until it completes its transaction. Yet neither process can complete its transaction. Figure 17-1 illustrates the situation.

CHAPTER 17 CAUSES AND SOLUTIONS FOR DEADLOCKS

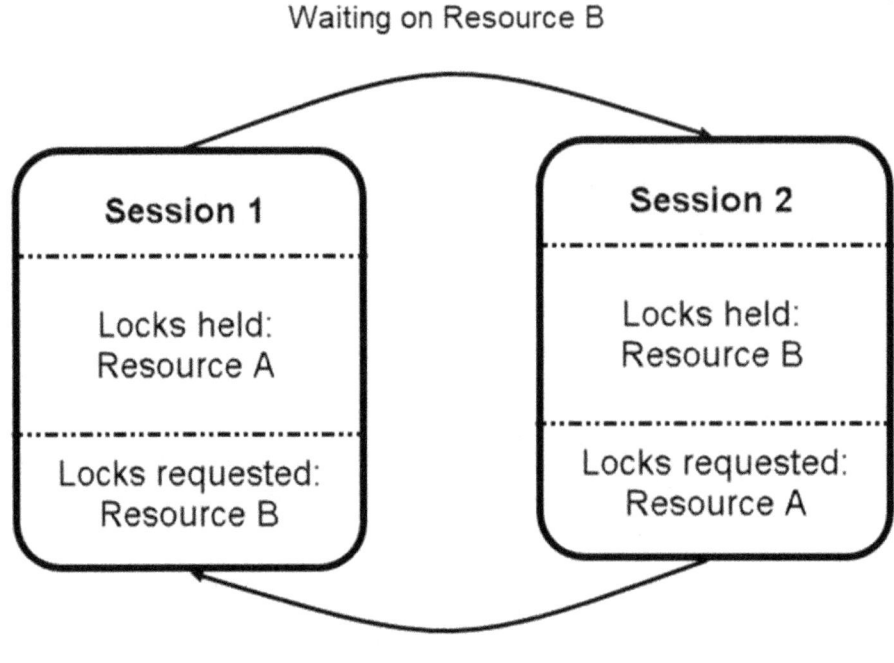

Figure 17-1. A graphical representation of a deadlock

Another way deadlocks occur is when processes attempt to escalate their locks on the same resource. The situation is usually started with each process having a shared lock on a resource, and then both sessions attempt to promote the lock from shared to exclusive. However, the same situation arises; neither can escalate while the other is holding the shared lock, yet neither can release the shared lock either. One of the two processes is then chosen as the deadlock victim.

One other possible way to get deadlocks is when a single session has gone parallel in its operations. It's possible for a thread to be holding a lock on Resource A while waiting on Resource B, held by another thread, while the second thread is waiting on Resource A. It's highly unlikely you'll see this type of deadlock because Microsoft has changed the code to address it in the more modern versions of SQL Server.

The core issue with deadlocks is that they would simply sit there, blocked and waiting forever. SQL Server has a secondary process to break the circular block. This process is called the *lock monitor*. The lock monitor watches for the presence of deadlocks. When a deadlock is detected, one of the sessions gets selected to be rolled back. Technically the rolled-back session is referred to as a victim, usually the process with the smallest estimated cost. In theory, the lowest estimated cost will have the easiest rollback process on its transaction.

Fundamentally, deadlocks are a performance issue. If your queries are running fast enough, taking out minimal locks, and releasing them as fast as possible, you will see very few, if any, deadlocks. This is why something like Optimized Locking (discussed in Chapter 16) can have such a beneficial impact. Adding to the performance problem, rollbacks use up resources, too, so that's additional overhead. Plus, in most circumstances, the person at the other end of the process chosen as a deadlock victim is just going to resubmit their query, again, using up resources for a second time in an attempt to complete their transaction. All this taken together is why it's important to minimize, or, where possible, eliminate, deadlocks within your system.

Choosing the Deadlock Victim

The basic choice of the deadlock victim is based on the estimated cost of the execution plan for the query. A lower cost implies that the rollback will be easier; therefore, the higher-cost query is allowed to proceed. You can influence these choices somewhat within the code by changing the priority level of a connection. Listing 17-1 shows how to set a connection to a lower deadlock priority.

Listing 17-1. Changing the deadlock priority

```
SET DEADLOCK_PRIORITY LOW;
```

With this set, the connection, and the queries, will be more likely to be chosen as the deadlock victim. There's no guarantee that it will always be that way. You can also change the priority to NORMAL or HIGH. When set to HIGH, it's more likely that the process will never be chosen as a victim.

You also have the option to use numeric values, running from -10 to 10, low to high priority. This gives you the option to get more granular in this level of control if you need to.

Normally, I would not mess with the deadlock priority. If I did, it would generally be on some high-value process that I want to try to prevent from being rolled back as a deadlock victim.

If there is a tie in priority, the process with the least cost will be rolled back. There are a few processes, marked in the deadlock graph (more about that later in the chapter), that can't be the deadlock victim. The only ones I've seen do this were processes being rolled back.

Analyzing the Causes of Deadlocks

The key to preventing deadlocks is understanding the underlying causes. In order to put this together, you have to have three pieces of information:

- The sessions involved in the deadlock
- The resources under contention, on both sides of the deadlock
- The queries executed by each session

Capturing Deadlock Information

There are four mechanisms for capturing deadlock information. Here, they are in the order of preference:

- Extended Events
- Trace flag 1222
- Trace Events
- Trace flag 1204

I list the methods in this order for several reasons. First, Extended Events are just a more efficient way to capture information within SQL Server. Further, on every machine since SQL Server 2008, unless you explicitly remove it, is an Extended Events session called system_health. Included in system_health is the basic deadlock graph information. You don't have to enable this; it's just there.

Next, trace flag 1222 is preferred over trace flag 1204 because it has more detailed information, even though they both work the same way. I also prefer trace flag 1222 over Trace Events because it has far less overhead than Trace Events. That overhead is why Trace Events are third. Trace flag 1204 is last because it has the least information.

CHAPTER 17 CAUSES AND SOLUTIONS FOR DEADLOCKS

I'll cover the information returned from both Extended Events and trace flag 1222 in the next section, "Analyzing the Deadlock Graph." Let's look at how to configure both data-capturing mechanisms first.

Trace Flag

The trace flags are very simple to enable. However, you do have to ensure that they are enabled on each server, or you won't have this information at all. Listing 17-2 shows how to turn on trace flag 1222.

Listing 17-2. Enabling the trace flag

```
DBCC TRACEON (1222, -1);
```

That will enable the trace flag on a server on which it is not currently enabled. However, if there's a failover or the server restarts, it will be lost. A common practice is to ensure that the trace flag is enabled at server startup. You can do this by setting the -T option on your server startup. Another approach is to use the SQL Server Configuration Manager. Here again, you're setting the -T option using the following steps:

1. Open the Properties dialog box of the instance of SQL Server.

2. Switch to the Startup Parameters tab of the dialog box, shown in Figure 17-2.

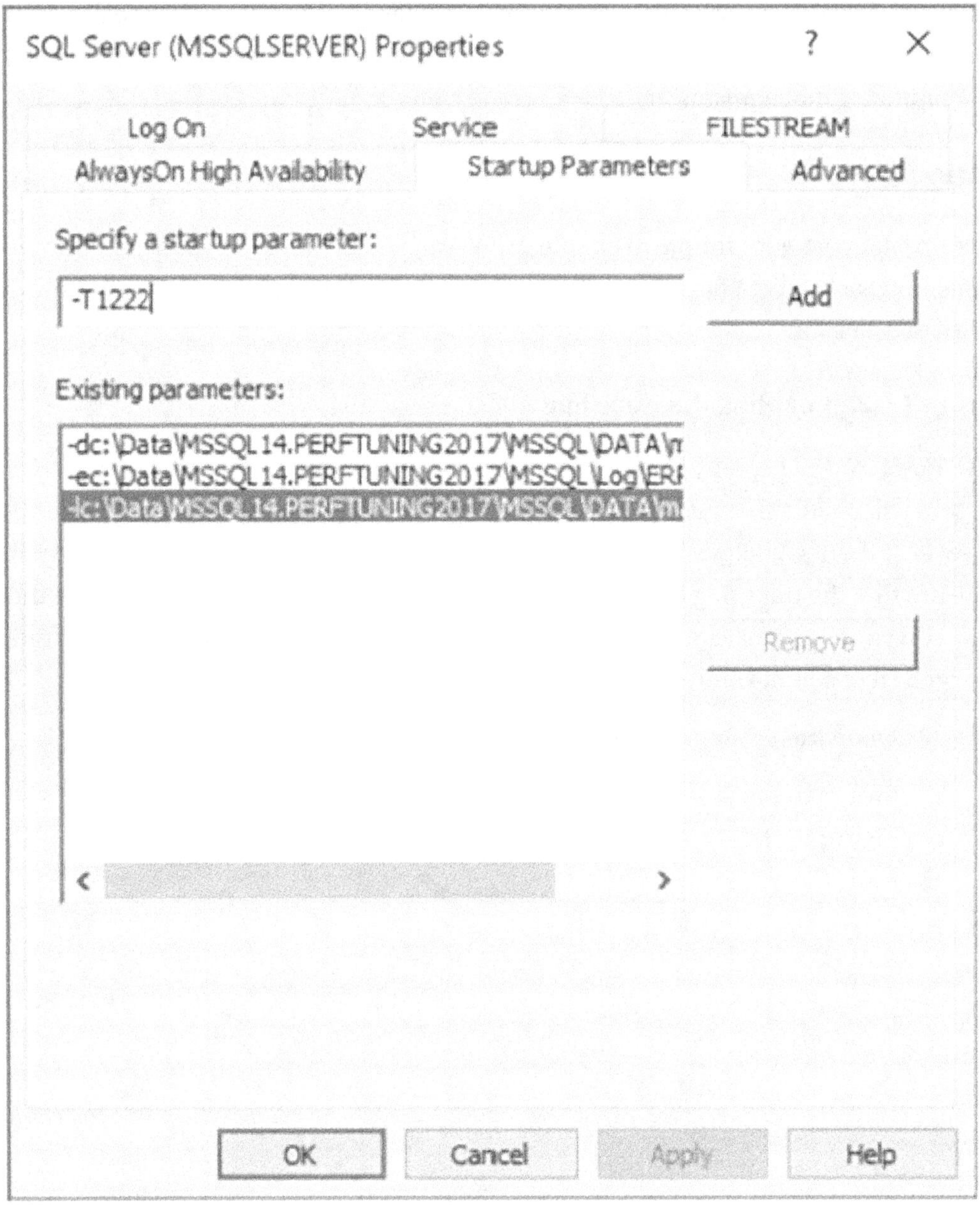

CHAPTER 17 CAUSES AND SOLUTIONS FOR DEADLOCKS

Figure 17-2. SQL Server Configuration Manager window

3. Type -T1222 in the "Specify a startup parameter" text box.

4. Click the Add button.

5. Click the OK button to close the dialog box.

When this instance restarts, the trace flag will be enabled by default. You also could use PowerShell to modify the Registry to enable this trace flag. Another option is the undocumented extended procedure, xp_instance_regaddvalue. That's not recommended, but it is available. Finally, it's possible to pass trace flags as part of the startup of SQL Server inside a container using MSSQL_OPTS and the -T1222 definition.

Output from the trace flag goes to the error log of SQL Server. You'll have to read it from there.

Extended Events

The easiest way to capture deadlock information is using the system_health Extended Events session. It's built in and turned on for all instances, by default. No extra work is needed, and you aren't adding any overhead to the system. You can query this information directly using the code in Listing 17-3.

Listing 17-3. Querying the system_health Extended Events session

```
DECLARE @path NVARCHAR(260);
--to retrieve the local path of system_health files
SELECT @path = dosdlc.path
FROM sys.dm_os_server_diagnostics_log_configurations AS dosdlc;

SELECT @path = @path + N'system_health_*';

WITH fxd
AS (SELECT CAST(fx.event_data AS XML) AS Event_Data
    FROM sys.fn_xe_file_target_read_file(@path, NULL, NULL, NULL) AS fx )
SELECT dl.deadlockgraph
FROM
(
    SELECT dl.query('.') AS deadlockgraph
    FROM fxd
        CROSS APPLY event_data.nodes('(/event/data/value/deadlock)')
AS d(dl)
) AS dl;
```

The output goes to XML in a format that you can click to open the deadlock graph, visible in Figure 17-3.

	deadlockgraph
1	<deadlock><victim-list><victimProcess id="proces...

Figure 17-3. Results from querying the system_health session

The system_health session has a fixed number of files, of fixed size. They roll over as they get filled. Depending on the load on your system, you may not see the particular deadlock you're looking for. Also, my query returned only a single deadlock graph because I'm working on a test system. A production system may return a very large number of deadlock graphs. So while the system_health session is probably the easiest, and functional enough for most, you may want to customize an Extended Events session to capture deadlock graphs.

There are a number of options for capturing deadlock information, but I'm going to focus on only two:

- xml_deadlock_report: The fundamental deadlock graph
- xml_deadlock_report_filtered: A deadlock graph with queries removed in order to protect sensitive data

The most common is going to be the first, xml_deadlock_report. The second, xml_deadlock_report_filtered, removes queries so that this information could be used with the General Data Protection Regulation (GDPR) or California Privacy Rights Act (CPRA) or any other privacy requirement. That does present a problem since the query is one of the three things we need to resolve deadlocks. However, situationally, it may be the appropriate event to use.

Analyzing the Deadlock Graph

To see a deadlock in action, I'm going to use the following scripts, run from two connections as commented within Listing 17-4.

Listing 17-4. Queries that will cause a deadlock

```
--Run from connection 1
BEGIN TRANSACTION PODSecond;
UPDATE Purchasing.PurchaseOrderHeader
SET Freight = Freight * 0.9 --9% discount on shipping
```

```
WHERE PurchaseOrderID = 1255;

--Run from connection 2
BEGIN TRANSACTION PODFirst;
UPDATE Purchasing.PurchaseOrderDetail
SET OrderQty = 2
WHERE ProductID = 448
      AND PurchaseOrderID = 1255;

--Run from connection 1
UPDATE Purchasing.PurchaseOrderDetail
SET OrderQty = 4
WHERE ProductID = 448
      AND PurchaseOrderID = 1255;
```

You can see we're creating two transactions: PODSecond and PODFirst. In the transactions, PODSecond is referencing the PurchaseOrderDetail after referencing the PurchaseOrderHeader table, while PODFirst is immediately attempting to update the PurchaseOrderDetail table. Locks will be taken out accordingly. Then, when the second query runs from the first connection, it will be chosen as a deadlock victim, resulting in the following error:

```
Msg 1205, Level 13, State 51, Line 7
Transaction (Process ID 56) was deadlocked on lock resources with another
process and has been chosen as the deadlock victim. Rerun the transaction.
```

I have set up an Extended Events session to capture deadlocks, and there I have the following information from the xml_deadlock_report, shown in Figure 17-4.

Figure 17-4. *Information captured by the xml_deadlock_report event*

CHAPTER 17 CAUSES AND SOLUTIONS FOR DEADLOCKS

That is the full XML deadlock graph. You can open that up in a window somewhere and start reading it. Or you can click the "Deadlock" tab you see in the figure. This will open the graphical deadlock graph, shown in Figure 17-5.

Figure 17-5. The graphical representation of the deadlock graph

We immediately see two of the three things we need to evaluate the causes of a deadlock. On the left and the right are the sessions involved in the deadlock. In this case, the victim is the one on the left with the large "x" through it.

Between these session details are the objects and locks involved in the deadlock. You get errors showing who owns which object and who is requesting which object. Inside the objects are the details needed to identify them, as shown in Figure 17-6.

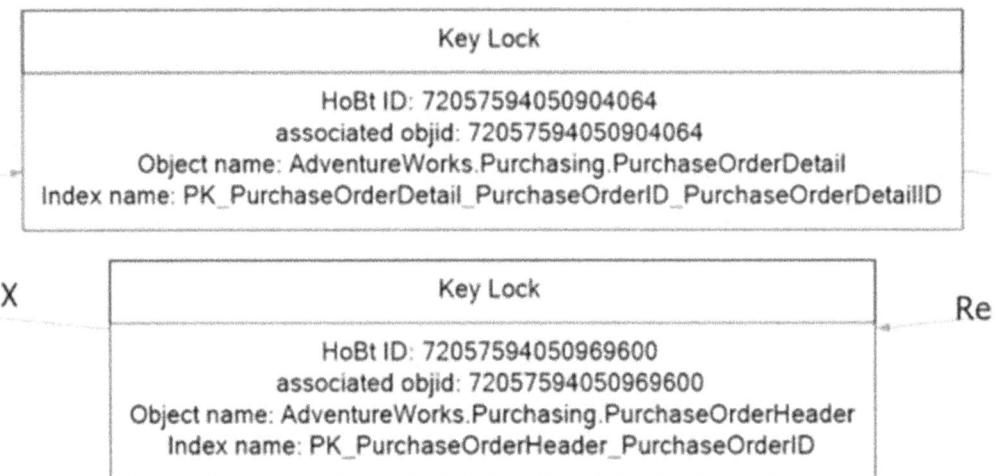

Figure 17-6. The locks and objects involved in the deadlock

The HoBt means "Heap or B-tree." The ID is referring to where the data is stored. You can already see the object and index names, but if you needed to, you could use the HoBt ID to identify them using the query in Listing 17-5.

CHAPTER 17 ■ CAUSES AND SOLUTIONS FOR DEADLOCKS

Listing 17-5. Getting the object_name from the HoBt ID

```
SELECT OBJECT_NAME(object_id)
FROM sys.partitions
WHERE hobt_id = 72057594050969600;
```

The only piece of data remaining is the query itself. In the deadlock graph, if you hover over either of the sessions, you'll see the query being called similar to Figure 17-7.

```
Server process Id: 64
Server batch Id: 0
Execution context Id: 0
Deadlock priority: 0
Statement:   BEGIN TRANSACTION PODFirst;  UPDATE Purchasing.PurchaseOrderDetail  SET OrderQty = 2  WHERE ProductID = 448      AND PurchaseOrderID = 1255;
Owner Id: 1004573
Transaction descriptor: 0x1018500450
```

Figure 17-7. *The query for the session involved in the deadlock*

Now you have everything you need to analyze the query. Sometimes, it might be easier to look directly at the XML for this information. Figure 17-8 shows a section of the XML from the current deadlock graph.

```xml
<deadlock>
  <victim-list>
    <victimProcess id="process100053f048" />
  </victim-list>
  <process-list>
    <process id="process100053f048" taskpriority="0" logused="440" waitresource="KEY: 5:72057
    <executionStack>
      <frame procname="adhoc" line="1" stmtstart="64" stmtend="278" sqlhandle="0x02000000d0c7
unknown    </frame>
      <frame procname="adhoc" line="1" stmtend="222" sqlhandle="0x02000000f4349d3899cff20344d
unknown    </frame>
    </executionStack>
    <stackFrames>
      <frame id="00" address="0xB8014301F" pdb="ntdll.pdb" age="1" guid="AE37D054-B390-3562
    </stackFrames>
    <inputbuf>
UPDATE Purchasing.PurchaseOrderDetail
SET OrderQty = 4
WHERE ProductID = 448
    AND PurchaseOrderID = 1255;    </inputbuf>
  </process>
  <process id="process1000aebc18" taskpriority="0" logused="11128" waitresource="KEY: 5:720
    <executionStack>
      <frame procname="AdventureWorks.Purchasing.uPurchaseOrderDetail" line="39" stmtstart="2
UPDATE [Purchasing].[PurchaseOrderHeader]
            SET [Purchasing].[PurchaseOrderHeader].[SubTotal] =
                (SELECT SUM([Purchasing].[PurchaseOrderDetail].[LineTotal])
                 FROM [Purchasing].[PurchaseOrderDetail]
                 WHERE [Purchasing].[PurchaseOrderHeader].[PurchaseOrderID]
                     = [Purchasing].[PurchaseOrderDetail].[PurchaseOrderID])
            WHERE [Purchasing].[PurchaseOrderHeader].[PurchaseOrderID]
                IN (SELECT inserted.[PurchaseOrderID] FROM inserted    </frame>
      <frame procname="adhoc" line="2" stmtstart="64" stmtend="278" sqlhandle="0x02000000d0c7
```

Figure 17-8. *A subset of the XML describing the deadlock*

Again, you can see the object IDs, key values, queries, and all the rest of the information you need to understand the root causes of this deadlock.

If you look through the details of the XML you'll find in this case, there's code that wasn't part of what I wrote. That's because there's a trigger on the PurchaseOrderDetail table that fired as part of this transaction.

You also have additional information that could prove useful. For example, the sqlhandle can be used, if the query is still in cache or the Query Store, to see the full batch that was involved in the deadlock. You'll have the execution plans for the queries because the plans get built and stored in cache, and the Query Store, prior to the transaction being chosen as a deadlock victim.

To fully understand everything involved, I'm going to break down the XML in detail in Table 17-1. If you were using trace flags, you'd get similar information, but it would be in the error log. Since that's a less effective way to collect this data, I'm just going to focus here on the XML.

Table 17-1. XML deadlock graph data

XML Info	Description
<deadlock> <victim-list>	The beginning of the deadlock information. It immediately starts with the victim processes.
<victimProcess id="process1300416ca8" />	Physical memory address of the process picked as the victim.
<process-list>	Processes that define the victim of the deadlock. There may be more than one involved. Not in this case.

(continued)

Table 17-1. (*continued*)

XML Info	Description
`<process id="process1300416ca8" taskpriority="0" logused="376" waitresource="KEY: 5:72057594050904064 (4ab5f0d47ad5)" waittime="572" ownerId="795760" transactionname="user_transaction" lasttranstarted="2022-06-30T19:52:08.177" XDES="0x13182fc040" lockMode="U" schedulerid="4" kpid="240" status="suspended" spid="56" sbid="0" ecid="0" priority="0" trancount="3" lastbatchstarted="2022-06-30T19:52:33.950" lastbatchcompleted="2022-06-30T19:52:16.613" lastattention="1900-01-01T00:00:00.613" clientapp="Microsoft SQL Server Management Studio - Query" hostname="DESKTOP-DEQGMOV" hostpid="12540" loginname="sa" isolationlevel="read committed (2)" xactid="795760" currentdb="5" currentdbname="AdventureWorks" lockTimeout="4294967295" clientoption1="671090784" clientoption2="390200">`   `<stackFrames>`   `<frame id="00" address="0x3FFFA0992717" pdb="sqlpal.pdb" age="1" guid="2148D596-D088-44AF-8A8E-E613596D33CF" module="sqlpal.dll" rva="0x392717" /><frame id="01" address="0xFFFFFFFFFFFFFFFF" /><frame id="02" address="0x10E149CB90" /><frame id="03" address="0xFFFFFFFDE943B9C7" /><frame id="04" address="0x132144C000" />`     `</stackFrames>`   `<executionStack>`     `<frame procname="adhoc" line="1" stmtstart="64" stmtend="278" sqlhandle="0x02000000d0c7f31a30fb1ad425c34357fe8ef6326793e7aa0000000000000000000000000000000000000000">` unknown   `</frame>`     `<frame procname="adhoc" line="1" stmtend="222" sqlhandle="0x02000000f4349d3899cff20344d9e8029adb969c032ee18a0000000000000000000000000000000000000000">` unknown   `</frame>`	All the information about the session picked as the deadlock victim.

(*continued*)

CHAPTER 17   CAUSES AND SOLUTIONS FOR DEADLOCKS

Table 17-1. (*continued*)

XML Info	Description
</executionStack> <inputbuf> UPDATE Purchasing.PurchaseOrderDetail SET OrderQty = 4 WHERE ProductID = 448 AND PurchaseOrderID = 1255; </inputbuf> </process>	

<process id="process1311b33468" taskpriority="0" logused="20400" waitresource="KEY: 5:72057594050969600 (4bc08edebc6b)" waittime="7127" ownerId="804479" transactionname="user_transaction" lasttranstarted="2022-06-30T19:52:21.280" XDES="0x13239f4040" lockMode="U" schedulerid="1" kpid="1020" status="suspended" spid="55" sbid="0" ecid="0" priority="0" trancount="3" lastbatchstarted="2022-06-30T19:52:27.303" lastbatchcompleted="2022-06-30T19:52:25.420" lastattention="1900-01-01T00:00:00.420" clientapp="Microsoft SQL Server Management Studio - Query" hostname="DESKTOP-DEQGMOV" hostpid="12540" loginname="sa" isolationlevel="read committed (2)" xactid="804479" currentdb="5" currentdbname="AdventureWorks" lockTimeout="4294967295" clientoption1="673319008" clientoption2="390200">
  <stackFrames>
    <frame id="00" address="0x3FFFA0992717" pdb="sqlpal.pdb" age="1" guid="2148D596-D088-44AF-8A8E-E613596D33CF" module="sqlpal.dll" rva="0x392717" /><frame id="01" address="0x5CD0FFFFFFFF" /><frame id="02" address="0x10E149CB90" /><frame id="03" address="0xFFFFFFFFFFF68A20" /><frame id="04" address="0x10821A2B99" pdb="sqlmin.pdb" age="2" guid="64A716B4-2836-4AEE-BE5A-D9CCB4066C0F" module="sqlmin.dll" rva="0x12B99" /><frame id="05" address="0x1088914C21" pdb="SqlDK.pdb" age="2" guid="B5987070-BA8C-4403-8529-567D529CF9F4" module="sqldk.dll" rva="0x4C21" /><frame id="06" address="0x600" />
	The second process involved in the deadlock. This one includes not just information about the query I submitted, near the bottom with the inputbuf, but also the trigger, in the call stack.

(*continued*)

Table 17-1. (*continued*)

XML Info	Description

</stackFrames>
<executionStack>
<frame procname="AdventureWorks.Purchasing.uPurchaseOrderDetail" line="39" stmtstart="2732" stmtend="3830" sqlhandle="0x0300050025999f1142d8ef0019a800000000000000000000000000000000000000000000000000000000000000">
UPDATE [Purchasing].[PurchaseOrderHeader]
    SET [Purchasing].[PurchaseOrderHeader].[SubTotal] =
      (SELECT SUM([Purchasing].[PurchaseOrderDetail].[LineTotal])
        FROM [Purchasing].[PurchaseOrderDetail]
        WHERE [Purchasing].[PurchaseOrderHeader].[PurchaseOrderID]
          = [Purchasing].[PurchaseOrderDetail].[PurchaseOrderID])
    WHERE [Purchasing].[PurchaseOrderHeader].[PurchaseOrderID]
      IN (SELECT inserted.[PurchaseOrderID] FROM inserted </frame>
<frame procname="adhoc" line="2" stmtstart="64" stmtend="278" sqlhandle="0x02000000d0c7f31a30fb1ad425c34357fe8ef6326793e7aa00000000000000000000000000000000000000000000">
unknown </frame>
<frame procname="adhoc" line="2" stmtstart="38" stmtend="260" sqlhandle="0x02000000dd281331f05b8769e24f99d2bd5ec6e2b696956d00000000000000000000000000000000000000000000">	

(*continued*)

Table 17-1. (*continued*)

XML Info	Description
unknown </frame> </executionStack> <inputbuf> BEGIN TRANSACTION UPDATE Purchasing.PurchaseOrderDetail SET OrderQty = 2 WHERE ProductID = 448 AND PurchaseOrderID = 1255; </inputbuf> </process> </process-list>	

(*continued*)

Table 17-1. (*continued*)

XML Info	Description

`<resource-list>`
  `<keylock hobtid="72057594050904064" dbid="5" objectname="AdventureWorks.Purchasing.PurchaseOrderDetail" indexname="PK_PurchaseOrderDetail_ PurchaseOrderID_PurchaseOrderDetailID" id="lock1307c3f600" mode="X" associatedObjectId="72057594050904064">`
    `<owner-list>`
    `<owner id="process1311b33468" mode="X" />`
    `</owner-list>`
    `<waiter-list>`
    `<waiter id="process1300416ca8" mode="U" requestType="wait" />`
    `</waiter-list>`
  `</keylock>`
  `<keylock hobtid="72057594050969600" dbid="5" objectname="AdventureWorks.Purchasing.PurchaseOrderHeader" indexname="PK_PurchaseOrderHeader_ PurchaseOrderID" id="lock131867c080" mode="X" associatedObjectId="72057594050969600">`
    `<owner-list>`
    `<owner id="process1300416ca8" mode="X" />`
    `</owner-list>`
    `<waiter-list>`
    `<waiter id="process1311b33468" mode="U" requestType="wait" />`
    `</waiter-list>`
  `</keylock>`
`</resource-list>`
`</deadlock>`
	Finally, the objects involved in the deadlock, the types of locks, the lock owners, pretty much everything to determine where the problem occurred.

So this example is a classic deadly embrace. It's not immediately apparent, but the deadlock is caused by the trigger. When the Quantity value gets updated on the PurchaseOrderDetail table, it attempts to update the PurchaseOrderHeader table. When the first two queries are run, it's just a blocking situation. The second query is waiting on the first to clear so that it can also update the PurchaseOrderHeader table. However, when the next query within the PODSecond transaction from Listing 17-4 gets run, we are now in a deadlock scenario. That means one of the transactions gets chosen as the victim and is then rolled back.

Error Handling for Deadlocks

When a deadlock occurs, SQL Server raises an error with the error number value of 1205. This means you can use the TRY/CATCH construct within T-SQL to handle the error. Because SQL Server has to protect the integrity of the data, it immediately rolls back a transaction chosen as a deadlock victim. What you can do is attempt to restart the transaction. However, in the interest of performance, I would only attempt it a few times before just letting go and returning the error to the calling application.

Listing 17-6 is just an example of how you could trap the deadlock.

Listing 17-6. Trapping a deadlock error

```
DECLARE @retry AS TINYINT = 1,
        @retrymax AS TINYINT = 2,
        @retrycount AS TINYINT = 0;
WHILE @retry = 1 AND @retrycount <= @retrymax
BEGIN
    SET @retry = 0;
    BEGIN TRY
        UPDATE HumanResources.Employee
        SET LoginID = '54321'
        WHERE BusinessEntityID = 100;
    END TRY
    BEGIN CATCH
        IF (ERROR_NUMBER() = 1205)
        BEGIN
            SET @retrycount = @retrycount + 1;
```

```
            SET @retry = 1;
        END;
    END CATCH;
END;
```

The idea is simple. You know the error number will be 1205. Check to see if that's what happened. If so, try again, but not too many times. I have two attempts shown here. I wouldn't go beyond three personally–the reason being each attempt takes time, resources, and more. Further, on each attempt, the person making the request is waiting. The longer the wait, the more likely they'll just kill the connection or relaunch the query themselves.

While this lets you easily, and automatically, retry a transaction, your best approach is to analyze the deadlock and resolve it, if possible.

Mechanisms to Prevent Deadlocks

It's not abnormal for there to be the occasional deadlock on a system. Sometimes, it just happens. However, most deadlocks can be prevented or, if you're experiencing them, resolved. These techniques are how you go about ensuring that you've minimized the number of deadlocks you must deal with:

- Access resources in the same order.
- Decrease the amount of resources accessed.
- Minimize lock contention.
- Tune your queries.

Access Resources in the Same Order

As I showed in the example deadlock in Listing 17-4, the easiest way to get a deadlock is to try to get locks on resources in the opposite order from two different transactions. If two transactions are attempting to access resources in exactly the same order, the very first exclusive lock taken by the first transaction will block the second. At no point will the second transaction have a way to take locks because it's still waiting on the first one. It's that simple.

One thing to watch for is generated code from tools like NHibernate or Entity Framework that can create transactions that do access tables and indexes in a very mixed order. You can work directly with the development teams to ensure that doesn't happen (changes in how the code is generated quickly fix the issue). While having your code in stored procedures or prepared statements means it's repeatable in its execution, you can still mess up the order within those procedures.

Decrease the Amount of Resources Accessed

A deadlock involves at least two resources. A transaction holds an exclusive lock on the first resource and then requests the second. The other transaction holds the second and requests the first. If you can prevent either, or both sessions from needing a given resource, you can prevent the deadlock. Generally, the best way to do this is to change the code. However, that's not always possible. Another couple of possibilities are as follows:

- Convert a nonclustered index to a clustered index.
- Use a covering index.

Convert a Nonclustered Index to a Clustered Index

Since the data isn't stored with a nonclustered index, you get at least two locks: one for the data (either a cluster or a heap) and one for the nonclustered index. Since a clustered index stores the data, you can see fewer locks. You may be in a situation where you need to convert your heap table to a clustered index (almost always the better choice), or you have your clustered index in the wrong place. It's possible converting your nonclustered index to a clustered index may help with the deadlocks. Testing and validation would be a requirement in this situation.

Use a Covering Index

A covering index decreases the number of resources needed for some queries. If a covering index is used, then locks don't have to be taken out on the heap or clustered index. That may help to alleviate deadlocks.

Minimize Lock Contention

Since deadlocks occur because of contention over locks, the more you can reduce the amount of locking with the system, the better off you'll be. Any time you modify a resource, you're going to be taking out exclusive locks, so there's little you can do to reduce contention there. However, reads, and the shared locks they require, can be reduced. Here are several mechanisms that will help:

- Implement row versioning.
- Decrease the isolation level.
- Enable Optimized Locking.
- Use locking hints (do this very judiciously).

Implement Row Versioning

Implementing one of the row-versioning mechanisms, SNAPSHOT, or, even better, READ_COMMITTED_SNAPSHOT, you can immediately reduce the contention caused by reads. Blocking reduction is the entire point of row versioning. Since they reduce locks, they help prevent deadlocks.

This is not a magic switch. You do have to take into account the added overhead on tempdb. Also, not all reads are helped by row versioning, just the ones taking part on data actively being modified. Still, reducing locking at any point will help with deadlocks.

Decrease the Isolation Level

At times, the shared lock required for a SELECT statement helps contribute to the formation of circular blocking. Reducing the isolation level of your databases can help reduce the amount of shared locks needed. As with anything else, there are trade-offs. You may require the more stringent isolation level for business or other purposes.

Enable Optimized Locking

We went over this in detail in Chapter 16. Optimized Locking reduces all types of resource contention related to locking. It won't eliminate the possibility of deadlocks. However, it reduces the likelihood of deadlocks. When fewer locks are taken out, for shorter periods of time, the possibility of deadlocks is naturally reduced.

Use Locking Hints

I am strongly against this approach. I think the dirty reads (missing or extra rows, incorrect data) are too high a cost to pay for a reduction in resource contention. However, another common method to reduce locking is to add one of the following hints:

- NOLOCK
- READUNCOMMITTED

Like the READ UNCOMMITTED isolation level, the NOLOCK and READUNCOMMITTED locking hints avoid shared locks entirely. That will help with deadlocks.

Using the locking hints can be a good idea since they only affect the objects referenced in a given query. Conversely, some organizations require the NOLOCK hint on every query, and you'd be better off using the READ UNCOMMITTED isolation level instead.

Once more, except in very targeted circumstances, this is a poor practice.

Tune the Queries

Since deadlocks are all about performance, making queries faster will mitigate the number of deadlocks. If all queries are completed before any resource contention even occurs, the chances of a deadlock are zero.

Summary

This chapter has shown you how to understand the "deadly embrace" that defines a deadlock. Remember that the focus of your attention should initially be on identifying the queries at the root cause. The best way to retrieve this information is through the system_health Extended Events session or by setting up your own session using the xml_deadlock_report event.

There are a number of ways to avoid deadlocks depending on the queries involved. You can address deadlocks by introducing or adjusting indexes. However, most of the time, the required fix is going to be adjusting code to run your queries differently.

Never forget, at the core of it all, deadlocks are about performance and contention. Anything you do to increase performance or reduce contention will also help you address deadlocks on your systems.

The next chapter talks about cursors and their impacts on performance.

CHAPTER 18

Row-by-Row Processing from Cursors and Other Causes

The best way to manipulate data within SQL Server is through the use of set-based operations. However, as humans, we tend to think about data in a more row-by-row way. It's true that Oracle uses a construct called a cursor to facilitate rapid data access. It's not the same in SQL Server. When accessing data using cursors within SQL Server, row by row can be one of the slowest ways to work with data. Jeff Moden has famously called this type of processing "ree-bar," abbreviated as RBAR, standing for "Row By Agonizing Row" to point out just how slow it can be. However, there is sometimes a valid purpose behind cursors, so it's best to try to use them the right way.

This chapter will cover

- Cursor fundamentals
- The cost analysis of different mechanisms within cursors
- The benefits and drawbacks of a default result set over cursors
- Recommendations to minimize the cost overhead of cursors

Cursor Fundamentals

A cursor within T-SQL is a mechanism to pull together a set of data in order to walk through it, one row at a time. The following steps are generally followed to create and use a cursor:

1. Declare the cursor and associate it with a SELECT statement as well as define cursor characteristics.

2. Open the cursor in order to gain access to the data set.

3. Retrieve a row from the cursor. Optionally, modify the row through the cursor.

4. Move through additional rows in the result set.

5. When processing is completed, close the cursor in order to release the resources consumed in creating and working with the cursor.

You can close a cursor before you walk through all the rows if you need to.

Cursors can be created through T-SQL or through data access mechanisms external to SQL Server. Cursors created through the data access layer are commonly called client cursors. Cursors written in T-SQL are called server cursors.

The key driver behind how much overhead a given cursor consumes comes from cursor characteristics. There are three broad categories of cursor characteristics:

- Cursor Location: Where was the cursor created from
- Cursor Concurrency: The degree of isolation and synchronization of a cursor with the underlying content
- Cursor Type: Specific characteristics of the different kinds of cursors

Cursor Location

Based on the location of its creation, a cursor is classified as either a client-side cursor or a server-side cursor. T-SQL cursors are always server-side cursors. Cursors created from the client can be either client or server side, depending on the code used.

Client-Side Cursors

Client-side cursors have the following characteristics:

- They are created externally to the server.
- The cursor metadata is maintained in the external code.

- They work on most of the common data access layers such as OLEDB or ODBC.
- Cursors can only be defined as forward-only or static (I'll define those terms in the "Cursor Types" section).

Server-Side Cursors

Server-side cursors are created on the SQL Server instance and have the following characteristics:

- They are created internally within the instance or database.
- The metadata for these cursors is maintained on the server.
- They can be created through either T-SQL or data access layers.
- Server-side cursors can be any cursor type.

All examples within the book will be server-side cursors.

Cursor Concurrency

Cursors can interact directly with the data within them, depending on how they are defined. This gives the cursor either isolation or synchronization with the underlying data. There are three concurrency models:

- Read-Only: A cursor that cannot be updated
- Optimistic: A cursor that can be updated and uses an optimistic concurrency model, meaning no locks are retained on the underlying rows until they are updated
- Scroll Locks: A cursor that can be updated and holds locks on the underlying data

Read-Only

A read-only cursor cannot be updated, and no locks are held on the base tables. While fetching a cursor row, whether a shared (S) lock will be acquired on the underlying row depends on the isolation level of the connection. In addition, any locking hints in the SELECT statement may affect locking. However, once the row is retrieved, by default, the locks are released. Listing 18-1 shows an example of creating a read-only cursor.

Listing 18-1. Declaring a cursor as READ_ONLY

```
DECLARE MyCursor CURSOR READ_ONLY FOR
SELECT adt.NAME
FROM Person.AddressType AS adt
WHERE adt.AddressTypeID = 1;
```

Because a read-only cursor has little to no locking, it's the fastest and safest cursor to use. Just remember, you are trading off the ability to modify data for speed.

Optimistic

Defining a cursor as optimistic means that you can update the data within that cursor. By default, while you're not modifying the data, the optimistic cursor will largely act as a read-only cursor. It will only take shared (S) locks as it reads data.

There are two mechanisms that an optimistic cursor can use to determine if the underlying data has changed prior to being updated. The first requires the data to have a ROWVERSION column in the table when the cursor is created. The second simply compares the value of the cursor with the values in the table. Of the two, the ROWVERSION mechanism is more efficient because of how the ROWVERSION data type works.

The ROWVERSION data type is a binary number that indicates the relative sequence of modifications on any given row. Each time a row with a ROWVERSION column gets modified, SQL Server updates the ROWVERSION column with the latest value of the global variable @@DBTS, and it increments the @@DBTS value.

Before applying a modification through the optimistic cursor, the engine determines if the ROWVERSION value in the cursor matches that in the underlying table. If they match, the data is updated. If they do not match, an error is raised. In the case of an error, you'll have to refresh the cursor data.

When there is no ROWVERSION column, then each piece of data gets matched to the underlying table before being updated. As you can guess, this is far less efficient. To get good performance with optimistic cursors, you should modify the tables to contain a ROWVERSION column.

Listing 18-2 shows an example of creating an optimistic cursor.

Listing 18-2. Declaring a cursor as OPTIMISTIC

```
DECLARE MyCursor CURSOR OPTIMISTIC FOR
SELECT adt.NAME
FROM Person.AddressType AS adt
WHERE adt.AddressTypeID = 1;
```

Scroll Locks

When a cursor is defined with scroll locks, you can update the data within the cursor. The cursor takes an update (U) lock on the underlying row until another cursor row is fetched or the cursor is closed. This prevents other users from modifying the underlying row. Listing 18-3 is an example of a cursor with scroll locks.

Listing 18-3. Declaring a cursor with SCROLL_LOCKS

```
DECLARE MyCursor CURSOR SCROLL_LOCKS FOR
SELECT adt.NAME
FROM Person.AddressType AS adt
WHERE adt.AddressTypeID = 1;
```

The idea here is that it's more important that you update the data through the cursor than you get good performance. You will get a reduction in database concurrency.

Cursor Types

Just like you can control the concurrency behavior of a cursor, you have additional behaviors you can control. These are set through the cursor types:

- Forward-only
- Static

- Keyset-driven
- Dynamic
- WHILE loop

Forward-Only Cursors

The core concept here is simple. You can't bounce around or reverse the order of the cursor. The following characteristics define the forward-only cursors:

- Cursors operate directly from base tables.
- Rows from the underlying tables are usually not retrieved until the cursor rows are called through the FETCH operation. However, the database API forward-only cursor type, with the following additional characteristics, retrieves all the rows from the underlying table in a single step:
    - Client-side cursor location
    - Server-side cursor location and read-only cursor concurrency
- They support forward scrolling only (FETCH NEXT).
- They allow all changes (INSERT, UPDATE, and DELETE) through the cursor. Also, these cursors reflect changes made to the underlying data.

There are differences in how forward-only cursors are implemented depending on their location. Client-side cursors are defined as different cursor types. T-SQL doesn't define different cursors so much as properties about the cursor. This means you can define any of the next three cursor types as being only able to scroll forward-only through the property.

T-SQL syntax also provides a specific cursor type that is also forward-only: FAST_FORWARD. The nickname for the FAST_FORWARD cursor is the fire hose because it is the single fastest way to move data through a cursor. Despite this, the "fire hose" still isn't as fast as set-based operations.

Listing 18-4 shows how to define a forward-only cursor.

Listing 18-4. Declaring a FAST_FORWARD cursor

```
DECLARE MyCursor CURSOR FAST_FORWARD FOR
SELECT adt.NAME
FROM Person.AddressType AS adt
WHERE adt.AddressTypeID = 1;
```

Static Cursors

A static cursor creates a snapshot of the underlying data and has the following characteristics:

- The snapshot cursor uses tempdb as a location to store the data defined by the cursor, separating it from the underlying data.
- Data is retrieved from the underlying tables when the cursor gets opened.
- Static cursors support all scrolling options: FETCH FIRST, FETCH NEXT, FETCH PRIOR, FETCH LAST, FETCH ABSOLUTE n, and FETCH RELATIVE n.
- The data in the static cursor is always read-only.
- Data in the underlying tables is not reflected in this cursor.

In some situations, you may find that the static cursor runs even faster than a forward-only cursor. Testing this in your situation can be a good idea. Listing 18-5 shows how to define a static cursor.

Listing 18-5. Declaring a STATIC cursor

```
DECLARE MyCursor CURSOR STATIC FOR
SELECT adt.NAME
FROM Person.AddressType AS adt
WHERE adt.AddressTypeID = 1;
```

Keyset-Driven Cursors

A keyset-driven cursor has a unique identifier, or key, that controls access with the following characteristics:

- The keyset is built from a column, or columns, that uniquely identifies each row in the cursor data set.

- The data generated for the keyset cursor is stored in tempdb.

- Somewhat similar to the static cursor, the keys, but not the data, are loaded into the keyset cursor when the cursor is opened.

- When fetching a row, the keyset rows are retrieved from tempdb, and then the data rows are retrieved from the underlying tables.

- All scrolling options are supported.

- Keyset cursors allow changes through the cursor.

If data is added to the underlying tables, it's not reflected in the cursor since the keyset is built and stored in tempdb. If you INSERT data through the cursor, all data added is appended to the end of the cursor. If data is deleted from the underlying tables, an error is generated if that key is used to attempt to retrieve data. Updates to the underlying tables will be retrieved using the appropriate key. Any UPDATE operations to the keyset are done as a DELETE and INSERT, with the new information appended as before. The keyset within the cursor is never reordered due to these data changes.

Listing 18-6 illustrates a keyset-driven cursor.

Listing 18-6. Declaring a KEYSET cursor

```
DECLARE MyCursor CURSOR KEYSET FOR
SELECT adt.NAME
FROM Person.AddressType AS adt
WHERE adt.AddressTypeID = 1;
```

Dynamic Cursors

Dynamic cursors operate directly with the underlying tables and have the following characteristics:

- There is no fixed membership in the cursor since the information comes from the underlying tables.

- Similar to forward-only cursors, rows from the tables are not retrieved until the row is called through a FETCH operation.

- Dynamic cursors support all but one of the scrolling options. FETCH ABSOLUTE n cannot work since the membership within the cursor is not fixed.

- These cursors allow all changes through the cursor. Also, all changes made to the underlying tables are reflected in the cursor.

Dynamic cursors don't support all properties and methods implemented by API cursors. Properties like AbsolutePosition, Bookmark, and RecordCount, as well as methods such as Clone and Resync, are not supported. If these are needed, you'll want to look at keyset-driven cursors.

Listing 18-7 provides an example of a dynamic cursor.

Listing 18-7. Declaring a DYNAMIC cursor

```
DECLARE MyCursor CURSOR DYNAMIC FOR
SELECT adt.NAME
FROM Person.AddressType AS adt
WHERE adt.AddressTypeID = 1;
```

The dynamic cursor is the slowest possible cursor in all situations. More locks are required, and they are held longer than any other cursor.

WHILE Loop

From a pure T-SQL standpoint, the WHILE loop is absolutely not a cursor. However, it is one additional way to walk through your data, one row at a time. The WHILE loop fully qualifies as an example of Jeff Moden's ree-bar, Row By Agonizing Row. However, situationally, a WHILE loop will perform better than a cursor.

A WHILE loop doesn't have characteristics like a cursor. Instead, you're performing a loop until a certain criterion is met.

The core issue for the WHILE loop is that you have to define some kind of count or limit that provides your steps. Then, you have to have a query that can retrieve one row at a time, usually based on those same steps.

Listing 18-8 covers an example of how a WHILE loop can work to retrieve one row at a time.

CHAPTER 18 ROW-BY-ROW PROCESSING FROM CURSORS AND OTHER CAUSES

Listing 18-8. Using a WHILE loop as a cursor substitute

```
--A table for identifying SalesOrderID values based on iteration
DECLARE @LoopTable TABLE
(
    LoopID INT IDENTITY(1, 1),
    SalesOrderDetailID INT
);
--defining our data set through a query
INSERT INTO @LoopTable
(
    SalesOrderDetailID
)
SELECT sod.SalesOrderDetailID
FROM Sales.SalesOrderDetail AS sod
WHERE sod.OrderQty > 23
ORDER BY sod.SalesOrderDetailID DESC;
DECLARE @MaxRow INT,
        @Count INT,
        @SalesOrderDetailID INT;
--retrieving the limit of the data set
SELECT @MaxRow = MAX(lt.LoopID),
       @Count = 1
FROM @LoopTable AS lt;
--looping through the results
WHILE @Count <= @MaxRow
BEGIN
    SELECT @SalesOrderDetailID = lt.SalesOrderDetailID
    FROM @LoopTable AS lt
    WHERE lt.LoopID = @Count;
    SELECT sod.OrderQty
    FROM Sales.SalesOrderDetail AS sod
    WHERE sod.SalesOrderDetailID = @SalesOrderDetailID;
    SET @Count += 1;
END;
```

There are discussions to be had here. A temporary table might provide superior performance to the table variable. An index on the table variable might enhance performance. However, overall, this is how a WHILE loop acts as a cursor. You have to define the limit, in this case, the @MaxRow value. Then you have to define a value that will be used to iterate through the set, @Count. I can then use the @Count value, which will correspond directly to the LoopID column value, to retrieve specific SalesOrderDetailID values. I have to do it that way because we can't guarantee that those values will not have gaps, messing up any possibility of iterating through the rows.

If this seems complex, it is. However, in some cases, it will perform faster than a cursor.

Cursor Cost Comparison

With a general understanding of the types of cursors available and how they behave, let's examine how those differences in behavior affect the resources used by the different cursor types. In situations where you've determined that you have to use a cursor, you should always strive for the most lightweight type and behavior.

Cost Comparison Based on Location

There are distinct behaviors between the client-side and server-side cursors that affect their overall cost.

Client-Side Cursors

Client-side cursors have the following benefits when compared with server-side cursors:

- Higher Scalability: With the management of the cursor being done outside the server, fewer resources within the server are being used, making it more scalable.

- Fewer Network Round Trips: The result set is sent to the client where the cursor is being maintained, so fewer network resources are in use.

- Faster Scrolling: With the client working the cursor, not the server, it's possible for quicker access to the rows.

- Highly Portable: With the cursor being worked on the client side, more databases are supported, not just SQL Server, but Oracle and PostgreSQL and others.

Those are the advantages, but there are also downsides to using client-side cursors:

- Higher Pressure on Client Resources: Nothing is ever free. Moving the work from the server alleviates resource use there but simply moves it to the client side. Within something like a web server where a lot of cursors would be if coded that way, you'd see a massive resource drain.

- Limited Cursor Type Support: Dynamic and keyset-driven cursors are not supported.

- Only One Active Cursor Statement on One Connection: While the cursor is being retrieved from the client, no other processing can occur.

Server-Side Cursors

Server-side cursors have the following benefits:

- Multiple Active Cursor Statements on One Connection: A single connection can fire multiple cursor processes.

- Row Processing Near the Data: Processing where the data is stored can mean less lag on network round trips. This is especially true if the cursor is doing data manipulation to other tables.

- Less Pressure on Client Resources: Just as moving a cursor to the client alleviates the server, a server-side cursor will alleviate the client's resource use.

- Support for All Cursor Types: There are no limits on the types of cursors available, unlike client-side cursors.

There are also costs associated with server-side cursors:

- Lower Scalability: The more resources being consumed by cursors mean less for other processing.

- More Network Round Trips: Where the client is involved with cursor processing from the server, you'll see a lot more network traffic.

- Less Portable: Cursors written in T-SQL will not work the same way in other database systems.

Cost Comparison Based on Concurrency

Cursors with a higher concurrency model create the least amount of blocking. Less blocking simply means a more scalable system. The following sections discuss the concurrency model's impact on cost.

Read-Only

The read-only concurrency model provides the following cost benefits:

- Lowest Locking Overhead: The read-only concurrency model introduces the least locking and synchronization overhead on the database. Since (S) locks are not held on the underlying row after a cursor row is fetched, other users are not blocked from accessing the row. Furthermore, the (S) lock acquired on the underlying row while fetching the cursor row can be avoided by using the NO_LOCK locking hint in the SELECT statement of the cursor, but only if you don't care about what kind of data you get back because of dirty reads.

- Highest Concurrency: Since additional locks are not held on the underlying rows, the read-only cursor doesn't block other users from accessing the underlying tables. The shared lock is still acquired.

The main drawback of the read-only cursor is as follows:

- Nonupdatable: The content of underlying tables cannot be modified through the cursor.

Optimistic

The optimistic concurrency model provides the following benefits:

- Low Locking Overhead: Similar to the read-only model, the optimistic concurrency model doesn't hold an (S) lock on the cursor row after the row is fetched. To further improve concurrency, the NOLOCK locking hint can also be used, as in the case of the read-only concurrency model. But please know that NOLOCK can absolutely lead to incorrect data or missing or extra rows, so its use requires careful planning. Modification through the cursor to an underlying row requires exclusive rights on the row as required by an action query.

- High Concurrency: Since only a shared lock is used on the underlying rows, the cursor doesn't block other users from accessing the underlying tables. But the modification through the cursor to an underlying row will block other users from accessing the row during the modification.

The following examples detail the cost overhead of the optimistic concurrency model:

- Row Versioning: Since the optimistic concurrency model allows the cursor to be updatable, an additional cost is incurred to ensure that the current underlying row is first compared (using either version-based or value-based concurrency control) with the original cursor row fetched before applying a modification through the cursor. This prevents the modification through the cursor from accidentally overwriting the modification made by another user after the cursor row is fetched.

- Concurrency Control Without a ROWVERSION Column: As explained previously, a ROWVERSION column in the underlying table allows the cursor to perform an efficient version-based concurrency control. In case the underlying table doesn't contain a ROWVERSION column, the cursor resorts to value-based concurrency control, which requires matching the current value of the row to the value when the row was read into the cursor. This increases the cost of the concurrency control. Both forms of concurrency control will cause additional overhead in tempdb.

Scroll Locks

The major benefit of the scroll locks concurrency model is as follows:

- Simple Concurrency Control: By locking the underlying row corresponding to the last fetched row from the cursor, the cursor assures that the underlying row can't be modified by another user. This eliminates the versioning overhead of optimistic locking. Also, since the row cannot be modified by another user, the application is relieved from checking for a row mismatch error.

The scroll locks concurrency model incurs the following cost overhead:

- Highest Locking Overhead: The scroll locks concurrency model introduces a pessimistic locking characteristic. A (U) lock is held on the last cursor row fetched, until another cursor row is fetched or the cursor is closed.

- Lowest Concurrency: Since a (U) lock is held on the underlying row, all other users requesting a (U) or an (X) lock on the underlying row will be blocked. This can significantly hurt concurrency. Therefore, please avoid using this cursor concurrency model unless absolutely necessary.

Cost Comparison Based on Cursor Type

Each of the basic four cursor types mentioned in the "Cursor Fundamentals" section earlier in the chapter incurs a different cost overhead on the server. Choosing an incorrect cursor type can hurt database performance. Besides the four basic cursor types, a fast-forward-only cursor (a variation of the forward-only cursor) is provided to enhance performance. The cost overhead of these cursor types is explained in the sections that follow.

Forward-Only Cursors

These are the cost benefits of forward-only cursors:

- Lower Cursor Open Cost Than Static and Keyset-Driven Cursors: Since the cursor rows are not retrieved from the underlying tables and are not copied into the tempdb database during cursor open, the forward-only T-SQL cursor opens quickly. Similarly, the forward-only, server-side API cursors with optimistic/scroll locks concurrency open quickly since they do not retrieve the rows during cursor open.

- Lower Scroll Overhead: Since only FETCH NEXT can be performed on this cursor type, it requires less overhead to support different scroll operations.

- Lower Impact on the tempdb Database Than Static and Keyset-Driven Cursors: Since the forward-only T-SQL cursor doesn't copy the rows from the underlying tables into the tempdb database, no additional pressure is created on the database.

The forward-only cursor type has the following drawbacks:

- Lower Concurrency: Every time a cursor row is fetched, the corresponding underlying row is accessed with a lock request depending on the cursor concurrency model (as noted earlier in the discussion about concurrency). It can block other users from accessing the resource.

- No Backward Scrolling: Applications requiring two-way scrolling can't use this cursor type. But if the applications are designed properly, then it isn't difficult to live without backward scrolling.

Fast-Forward-Only Cursor

The fast-forward-only cursor is the fastest and least expensive cursor type. This forward-only and read-only cursor is specially optimized for performance. Because of this, you should always prefer it to the other SQL Server cursor types.

Furthermore, the data access layer provides a fast-forward-only cursor on the client side. That type of cursor uses a so-called *default result set* to make cursor overhead almost disappear.

> **Note** The default result set is explained later in the chapter in the "Default Result Set" section.

Static Cursors

These are the cost benefits of static cursors:

- Lower Fetch Cost Than Other Cursor Types: Since a snapshot is created in the tempdb database from the underlying rows on opening the cursor, the cursor row fetch is targeted to the snapshot instead of the underlying rows. This avoids the lock overhead that would otherwise be required to fetch the cursor rows.

- No Blocking on Underlying Rows: Since the snapshot is created in the tempdb database, other users trying to access the underlying rows are not blocked.

On the downside, the static cursor has the following cost overhead:

- Higher Open Cost Than Other Cursor Types: The cursor open operation of the static cursor is slower than that of other cursor types since all the rows of the result set have to be retrieved from the underlying tables and the snapshot has to be created in the tempdb database during the cursor open.

- Higher Impact on tempdb Than Other Cursor Types: There can be significant impact on server resources for creating, populating, and cleaning up the snapshot in the tempdb database.

Keyset-Driven Cursors

These are the cost benefits of keyset-driven cursors:

- Lower Open Cost Than the Static Cursor: Since only the keyset, not the complete snapshot, is created in the tempdb database, the keyset-driven cursor opens faster than the static cursor. SQL Server populates the keyset of a large keyset-driven cursor asynchronously, which shortens the time between when the cursor is opened and when the first cursor row is fetched.

- Lower Impact on tempdb Than That with the Static Cursor: Because the keyset-driven cursor is smaller, it uses less space in tempdb.

The cost overhead of keyset-driven cursors is as follows:

- Higher Open Cost Than Forward-Only and Dynamic Cursors: Populating the keyset in the tempdb database makes the cursor open operation of the keyset-driven cursor costlier than that of forward-only (with the exceptions mentioned earlier) and dynamic cursors.

- Higher Fetch Cost Than Other Cursor Types: For every cursor row fetch, the key in the keyset has to be accessed first, and then the corresponding underlying row in the user database can be accessed. Accessing both the tempdb and the user database for every cursor row fetch makes the fetch operation costlier than that of other cursor types.

- Higher Impact on tempdb Than Forward-Only and Dynamic Cursors: Creating, populating, and cleaning up the keyset in tempdb impact server resources.

- Higher Lock Overhead and Blocking Than the Static Cursor: Since row fetch from the cursor retrieves rows from the underlying table, it acquires an (S) lock on the underlying row (unless the NOLOCK locking hint is used) during the row fetch operation.

Dynamic Cursor

The dynamic cursor has the following cost benefits:

- Lower Open Cost Than Static and Keyset-Driven Cursors: Since the cursor is opened directly on the underlying rows without copying anything to the tempdb database, the dynamic cursor opens faster than the static and keyset-driven cursors.

- Lower Impact on tempdb Than Static and Keyset-Driven Cursors: Since nothing is copied into tempdb, the dynamic cursor places far less strain on tempdb than the other cursor types.

The dynamic cursor has the following cost overhead:

- Higher Lock Overhead and Blocking Than the Static Cursor: Every cursor row fetch in a dynamic cursor requeries the underlying tables involved in the SELECT statement of the cursor. The dynamic fetches are generally expensive because the original select condition might have to be re-executed.

For a summary of the different cursors, their positives, and negatives, please refer to Table 18-1.

Table 18-1. Comparing cursors

Cursor Type	Positives	Negatives
Forward-only	Lower cost, lower scroll overhead, lower impact on tempdb	Lower concurrency, no backward scrolling
Fast-forward-only	Fastest cursor, lowest cost, lowest impact	No backward scrolling, no concurrency
Static	Lower fetch cost, no blocking, forward and backward scrolling	Higher open cost, higher impact on tempdb, no concurrency
Keyset-driven	Lower open cost, lower impact on tempdb, forward and backward scrolling, concurrency	Higher open cost, highest fetch cost, highest impact on tempdb, higher locking costs
Dynamic	Lower open cost, lower impact on tempdb, forward and backward scrolling, concurrency	Highest locking costs

Default Result Set

The default cursor type for the data access layers (ADO, OLEDB, and ODBC) is forward-only and read-only. The default cursor type created by the data access layers isn't a true cursor but a stream of data from the server to the client, generally referred to as the *default result set* or *fast-forward-only cursor* (created by the data access layer). In ADO.NET, the DataReader control has the forward-only and read-only properties, and it can be considered as the default result set in the ADO.NET environment. SQL Server uses this type of result set processing under the following conditions:

- The application, using the data access layers (ADO, OLEDB, and ODBC), leaves all the cursor characteristics at the default settings, which requests a forward-only and read-only cursor.

- The application executes a SELECT statement instead of executing a DECLARE CURSOR statement.

Note Because SQL Server is designed to work with sets of data, not to walk through records one by one, the default result set is always faster than any type of cursor.

The only request sent from the client to SQL Server is the SQL statement associated with the default cursor. SQL Server executes the query, organizes the rows of the result set in network packets (filling the packets as best it can), and then sends the packets to the client. These network packets are cached in the network buffers of the client. SQL Server sends as many rows of the result set to the client as the client-network buffers can cache. As the client application requests one row at a time, the data access layer on the client machine pulls the row from the client-network buffers and transfers it to the client application.

The following sections outline the benefits and drawbacks of the default result set.

Benefits

The default result set is generally the best and most efficient way of returning rows from SQL Server for the following reasons:

- Minimum Network Round Trips Between the Client and SQL Server: Since the result set returned by SQL Server is cached in the client network buffers, the client doesn't have to make a request across the network to get the individual rows. SQL Server puts most of the rows that it can in the network buffer and sends to the client as much as the client-network buffer can cache.

- Minimum Server Overhead: Since SQL Server doesn't have to store data on the server, this reduces server resource utilization.

Multiple Active Result Sets

SQL Server 2005 introduced the concept of multiple active result sets, wherein a single connection can have more than one batch running at any given moment. In prior versions, a single result set had to be processed or closed out prior to submitting the next request. MARS allows multiple requests to be submitted at the same time through the same connection. MARS is enabled on SQL Server all the time. It is not enabled by a connection unless that connection explicitly calls for it. Transactions must be handled at the client level and have to be explicitly declared and committed or rolled back. With MARS in action, if a transaction is not committed on a given statement and the connection is closed, all other transactions that were part of that single connection will be rolled back. MARS is enabled through application connection properties.

Drawbacks

While there are advantages to the default result set, there are drawbacks as well. Using the default result set requires some special conditions for maximum performance:

- It Doesn't Support All Properties and Methods: Properties such as AbsolutePosition, Bookmark, and RecordCount, as well as methods such as Clone, MoveLast, MovePrevious, and Resync, are not supported.

- Locks May Be Held on the Underlying Resource: SQL Server sends as many rows of the result set to the client as the client-network buffers can cache. If the size of the result set is large, then the client-network buffers may not be able to receive all the rows. SQL Server then holds a lock on the next page of the underlying tables, which has not been sent to the client.

To demonstrate these concepts, I'm going to create a test table and data in Listing 18-9.

Listing 18-9. A test table for a client-side cursor

```
DROP TABLE IF EXISTS dbo.Test1;
GO
CREATE TABLE dbo.Test1
```

```
(
    C1 INT,
    C2 CHAR(996)
);
CREATE CLUSTERED INDEX Test1Index ON dbo.Test1 (C1);
INSERT INTO dbo.Test1
VALUES
(1, '1'),
(2, '2');
```

To activate a client-side cursor, I'm going to use a PowerShell script shown in Listing 18-10. However, this one is using the ADODB.Recordset object, which is not how I would normally work with PowerShell and databases. However, it will let me illustrate how a client-side cursor behaves.

Listing 18-10. PowerShell to create a client-side cursor

```
$SqlConnection = New-Object System.Data.SqlClient.SqlConnection
$SqlConnection.ConnectionString = 'Server=localhost;Database=AdventureWorks
;trusted_connection=false;user=sa;password=*cthulhu1988'

$SqlCommand = New-Object System.Data.SqlClient.SqlCommand
$SqlCommand.CommandText = "SELECT * FROM dbo.Test1;"
$SqlCommand.Connection = $SqlConnection

$SqlConnection.Open()
$Reader = $SqlCommand.ExecuteReader()

while ($Reader.Read()) {
    $C1 = $Reader["C1"]
    $C2 = $Reader["C2"]
    Write-Output "C1 = $C1 and C2 = $C2"
}

$Reader.Close()
$SqlConnection.Close()
```

CHAPTER 18 ROW-BY-ROW PROCESSING FROM CURSORS AND OTHER CAUSES

The table as it's currently configured has two rows of data equal to 1,000 bytes (4 bytes for INT and 996 bytes for CHAR(996)), not counting internal overhead. The size of a result set from the current data in the table would then be 2,000 bytes for the two rows.

Since the size of the result set is small enough to be cached by the client-network buffer, all the cursor rows are cached on the client machine during the cursor open statement. Also, no locks will be held on the dbo.Test1 table. The only statement made to SQL Server is the SELECT statement of the cursor as shown in the Extended Events in Figure 18-1.

name	timestamp	batch_text	duration	logical_reads
rpc_completed	2025-08-09 1...	NULL	25	0
sql_batch_co...	2025-08-09 1...	SELECT * FROM dbo.Test1;	1951	20

Figure 18-1. *Query performance metrics for the cursor*

In order to see the results for a larger data set, we'll need to add additional data to the test table (Listing 18-11).

Listing 18-11. Creating more rows in the test table

```
SELECT TOP 100000
        IDENTITY(INT, 1, 1) AS n
INTO #Tally
FROM MASTER.dbo.syscolumns AS sc1,
     MASTER.dbo.syscolumns AS sc2;
INSERT INTO dbo.Test1
(
    C1,
    C2
)
SELECT n,
       n
FROM #Tally AS t;
```

With a larger data set, only part of the results can be cached. On execution of the Ado.Recordset.Open statement, the default result set on the client machine will only get a subset of the data. SQL Server will be waiting on the other end to return more information, holding locks on resources.

Figure 18-2 shows the locks on my machine.

	request_session_id	resource_database_id	resource_associated_entity_id	resource_type	resource_description	request_mode	request_status
1	60	5	0	DATABASE		S	GRANT
2	54	5	0	DATABASE		S	GRANT
3	64	5	0	DATABASE		S	GRANT
4	53	5	0	DATABASE		S	GRANT
5	53	5	72057594074234880	PAGE	1:400460	IS	GRANT
6	53	5	1440724185	OBJECT		IS	GRANT

Figure 18-2. *Locks held by the default result set*

The (IS) lock on the table will block other transactions attempting to acquire an exclusive lock. To minimize this, follow these recommendations:

- Process all rows in the default result set immediately.
- Keep the result set as small as you can in order to transfer all rows without locking.

Cursor Overhead

If you are implementing cursors in your code, you can use Extended Events to observe the behavior of cursors directly using the following events:

- cursor_open
- cursor_close
- cursor_execute
- cursor_prepare

There are other events as well, but most of them are only useful for troubleshooting specific problems. Otherwise, you'll use the standard metrics from batch completion and/or procedure completion.

Let's take an example to see the overhead associated with row-by-row processing. The business has defined some requirements:

- Identify all products in the Production.WorkOrder table that have been scrapped.

CHAPTER 18 ROW-BY-ROW PROCESSING FROM CURSORS AND OTHER CAUSES

- For each scrapped product, determine the money lost, where the money lost per product equals the units in stock multiplied by the unit price of the product.

- Calculate the total loss.

- Based on the total loss, determine the business status.

The phrase "for each" in the second point suggests that these requirements could be best met by using a cursor. Listing 18-12 shows the cursor in action.

Listing 18-12. Defining a stored procedure with a cursor

```
CREATE OR ALTER PROC dbo.TotalLossCursorBased
AS
DECLARE ScrappedProducts CURSOR FOR
SELECT p.ProductID,
       wo.ScrappedQty,
       p.ListPrice
FROM Production.WorkOrder AS wo
    JOIN Production.ScrapReason AS sr
        ON wo.ScrapReasonID = sr.ScrapReasonID
    JOIN Production.Product AS p
        ON wo.ProductID = p.ProductID;
--Open the cursor to process one product at a time
OPEN ScrappedProducts;
DECLARE @MoneyLostPerProduct MONEY = 0,
        @TotalLoss MONEY = 0;
--Calculate money lost per product by processing one product
--at a time
DECLARE @ProductId INT,
        @UnitsScrapped SMALLINT,
        @ListPrice MONEY;
FETCH NEXT FROM ScrappedProducts
INTO @ProductId,
    @UnitsScrapped,
    @ListPrice;
WHILE @@FETCH_STATUS = 0
```

```
BEGIN
    SET @MoneyLostPerProduct = @UnitsScrapped * @ListPrice; --Calculate
total loss
    SET @TotalLoss = @TotalLoss + @MoneyLostPerProduct;
    FETCH NEXT FROM ScrappedProducts
    INTO @ProductId,
        @UnitsScrapped,
        @ListPrice;
END;
--Determine status
IF (@TotalLoss > 5000)
    SELECT 'We are bankrupt!' AS STATUS;
ELSE
    SELECT 'We are safe!' AS STATUS;
--Close the cursor and release all resources assigned to the cursor
CLOSE ScrappedProducts;
DEALLOCATE ScrappedProducts;
GO
```

With the procedure in place, Listing 18-13 is how we'll execute it.

Listing 18-13. Executing the TotalLossCursorBased procedure

```
EXEC dbo.TotalLossCursorBased;
```

This results in the following runtime metrics:

```
Duration: 193ms
Reads: 8888
```

When you consider that the entire Production.Product table only has 6,196 pages and the Production.WorkOrder table has only 926 pages, 8,888 reads is a lot of activity.

Most of the time, you can avoid cursors by working on set-based mechanisms for accessing the data. For example, the business process defined previously could be satisfied by the stored procedure in Listing 18-14.

Listing 18-14. Creating the TotalLoss stored procedure

```
CREATE OR ALTER PROC dbo.TotalLoss
```

```
AS
SELECT CASE  --Determine status based on following computation
         WHEN SUM(MoneyLostPerProduct) > 5000 THEN
             'We are bankrupt!'
         ELSE
             'We are safe!'
     END AS STATUS
FROM
( --Calculate total money lost for all discarded products
    SELECT SUM(wo.ScrappedQty * p.ListPrice) AS MoneyLostPerProduct
    FROM Production.WorkOrder AS wo
        JOIN Production.ScrapReason AS sr
            ON wo.ScrapReasonID = sr.ScrapReasonID
        JOIN Production.Product AS p
            ON wo.ProductID = p.ProductID
    GROUP BY p.ProductID
) AS DiscardedProducts;
GO
```

Instead of walking through the rows, we use aggregation to put together the data as defined by the business. The results are identical, but the performance metrics look like this:

Duration: 50ms
Reads: 603

We've gone from 193ms to 50ms and 8,888 reads to 603. Clearly, a set-based approach is superior.

Cursor Recommendations

An ineffective use of cursors can degrade the application performance by introducing extra network round trips and load on server resources. To keep the cursor cost low, try to follow these recommendations:

- Use set-based SQL statements over T-SQL cursors since SQL Server is designed to work with sets of data.

- Use the least expensive cursor.
  - When using SQL Server cursors, use the FAST_FORWARD cursor type.
  - When using the API cursors implemented by ADO, OLEDB, or ODBC, use the default cursor type, which is generally referred to as the *default result set*.
  - When using ADO.NET, use the DataReader object.
- Minimize impact on server resources.
  - Use a client-side cursor for API cursors.
  - Do not perform actions on the underlying tables through the cursor.
  - Always deallocate the cursor as soon as possible. This helps free resources, especially in tempdb.
  - Redesign the cursor's SELECT statement (or the application) to return the minimum set of rows and columns.
  - Avoid T-SQL cursors entirely by rewriting the logic of the cursor as set-based statements, which are generally more efficient than cursors.
  - Use a ROWVERSION column for dynamic cursors to benefit from the efficient, version-based concurrency control instead of relying upon the value-based technique.
- Minimize impact on tempdb.
  - Minimize resource contention in tempdb by avoiding the static and keyset-driven cursor types.
  - Static and keyset-driven cursors put additional load on tempdb, so take that into account if you must use them, or avoid them if your tempdb is under stress.

- Minimize blocking.
  - Use the default result set, fast-forward-only cursor, or static cursor.
  - Process all cursor rows as quickly as possible.
  - Avoid scroll locks or pessimistic locking.
- Minimize network round trips while using API cursors.
  - Use the `CacheSize` property of ADO to fetch multiple rows in one round trip.
  - Use client-side cursors.
  - Use disconnected record sets.

Summary

As you learned in this chapter, a cursor is the natural extension to the result set returned by SQL Server, enabling the calling application to process one row of data at a time. Cursors add a cost overhead to application performance and impact the server resources.

You should always be looking for ways to avoid cursors. Set-based solutions work better in almost all cases. However, if a cursor operation is mandated, then choose the best combination of cursor location, concurrency, type, and cache size characteristics to minimize the cost overhead of the cursor.

In the next chapter, we explore the special functionality introduced with in-memory tables, natively compiled procedures, and the other aspects of memory-optimized objects.

CHAPTER 19

Memory-Optimized OLTP Tables and Procedures

One of the principal needs in Online Transaction Processing (OLTP) systems is to get as much speed as possible in order to support more transactions. Some systems simply cannot support the transaction loads necessary because of limitations on the speed of disks and disk controllers. Microsoft introduced the memory-optimized, also called in-memory, technology in SQL Server and Azure SQL Database to help deal with this situation. While the memory-optimized tools are extremely useful, they are also extremely specialized. As such, they should be approached with some caution. However, on systems with the right amount of memory, in-memory tables and native stored procedures produce lightning-fast speed.

In this chapter, I cover the following topics:

- The basics of how in-memory tables work

- Improving performance by natively compiling stored procedures

- The benefits and drawbacks of natively compiled procedures and in-memory tables

- Recommendations for when to use the in-memory technologies

In-Memory OLTP Fundamentals

Disks, disk controllers, and the whole architecture around permanent storage of the information that SQL Server manages have gone through radical changes over the last few years. As such, storage systems are blazingly fast. And yet, it is still possible to have systems that bottleneck on those storage systems.

CHAPTER 19   MEMORY-OPTIMIZED OLTP TABLES AND PROCEDURES

At the same time, memory operations have also improved equally radically. The amount of memory that can be put on systems has increased in enormous ways, making memory even faster than disks. However, never forget, memory is only, ever, temporary storage. If you want your data persisted, it has to have a way to get to the disk.

What if we could write everything to memory first and then, eventually, write it out to permanent storage? Wouldn't that speed things up? That's what memory-optimized OLTP tables are, although there's even more to it than that. You can define tables to be

- Durable: Meaning they get written to disk

- Delayed Durability: Meaning they get written to disk eventually but could suffer some data loss, the second fastest mechanism

- Nondurable: Meaning they're only ever written to memory with nothing ever written to disk, the fastest, but least safe, mechanism

Microsoft recognized that in order to make transactions faster, they would have to remove the pessimistic locks on data. The in-memory tables use an optimistic locking approach. They're using a data versioning scheme to allow multiple transactions to write data, with a "last one in wins" kind of approach. That eliminates all sorts of locking and blocking.

Additionally, instead of forcing all transactions to wait until they are written to the log to complete, an assumption is made that most transactions complete. Therefore, log writes occur asynchronously so that they don't slow down transactions for the in-memory tables.

Yet another step was to make memory management itself optimistic. In-memory tables work off an eventually consistent model. There is a conflict resolution process that could roll back a transaction but won't allow a transaction to block another. All operations within memory-optimized tables are then subsequently faster.

Additionally, internally, they've changed the way that the buffer pool works so that there are optimized scans for systems with extremely large memory pools. Without this, you would simply be moving where the slowdown occurs.

With SQL Server 2025, improvements were made to garbage collection, removing deleted or outdated rows. This further enhances the performance of memory-optimized tables, reducing latency on writes. The improved garbage collection also means that long-running transactions have less negative impact on memory-optimized table performance. This is because the improved garbage collection isn't blocked by the long-running transaction. Further, in 2025, they improved the file merging processes

CHAPTER 19 MEMORY-OPTIMIZED OLTP TABLES AND PROCEDURES

to make writing data to disk on durable tables more efficient. This combines with the improved garbage collection to reduce memory use and contention while increasing performance overall.

Finally, in addition to all the optimizations to data access, Microsoft added natively compiled stored procedures. This is T-SQL code that is turned into a DLL and run within the SQL Server OS. There is a lengthy, and expensive, compile process, but then, execution is radically enhanced, especially when working with the memory-optimized tables.

Best of all, largely, you can treat memory-optimized tables largely the same way you treat other tables, although you can't do just anything you want. There are a number of limitations on behaviors and some specific system requirements.

System Requirements

The system requirements are actually fairly simple. You have to have

- A modern 64-bit processor
- Twice the amount of free disk storage for the data you're putting into memory
- A lot of memory

You can, if you choose, run memory-optimized tables on a system with minimal memory. You must have enough memory to load the data, or you'll get an error. However, to do this well, you have to have a lot of memory. Remember, all the memory needed by SQL Server to support your system as is will likely still be needed. Then you're adding additional memory to load tables into for the performance enhancements.

Basic Setup

To begin to use in-memory tables, you have to modify your databases, adding a specific new file group that will store and manage your in-memory tables.

Warning Prior to SQL Server 2025, after you add a memory-optimized file group to your database, you can never remove it. Do not experiment with memory-optimized tables on a production system on older systems.

Usually, you want your in-memory tables to write to disk (at least I assume you do; most people usually like their data) in addition to the memory. Writing to disk is about persisting data; in the event of a power loss, failover, etc., your data is still there. You get a choice with in-memory tables. You can make them durable or nondurable. Durability is part of the ACID properties, explained in Chapter 16. The crux of the issue is with a nondurable table, you may lose data, even though it was written out to memory. If you're dealing with data such as session state, it might not matter if that data can be lost, so nondurable means just a little faster still, on top of all the rest, but with the potential for data loss.

Regardless, since disk storage is different from memory-optimized tables, a separate file group must be added to the database. Just remember, prior to 2025, this was not a reversable process. Listing 19-1 illustrates how I did it.

Listing 19-1. Adding a MEMORY_OPTIMIZED_DATA file group to a database

```
ALTER DATABASE AdventureWorks
ADD FILEGROUP InMemoryData
CONTAINS MEMORY_OPTIMIZED_DATA;
ALTER DATABASE AdventureWorks
ADD FILE
    (
        NAME = 'InMemoryFile',
        FILENAME = '/var/opt/mssql/data/inmemoryfile.ndf'
    )
TO FILEGROUP InMemoryData;
```

AdventureWorks will now support memory-optimized tables. If I did wish to remove the file and file group, I could. However, first, you must delete all memory-optimized tables and procedures from the database. Once they're clear, Listing 19-2 shows how to remove the file and file group.

Listing 19-2. Removing a MEMORY_OPTIMIZED_DATA file group from a database

```
ALTER DATABASE AdventureWorks REMOVE FILE InMemoryFile;

ALTER DATABASE AdventureWorks REMOVE FILEGROUP InMemoryData;
```

CHAPTER 19 MEMORY-OPTIMIZED OLTP TABLES AND PROCEDURES

There are a few limitations on what you can do with a database that has a memory-optimized file group:

- DBCC CHECKDB: Consistency checks run as normal, but they skip the memory-optimized tables. If you attempt CHECKTABLE on the memory-optimized table, you'll generate an error.

- AUTO_CLOSE: This is supported, but actively discouraged since it will cause massive performance hits.

- Database Snapshot: This is not supported.

- ATTACH_REBUILD_LOG: This is not supported.

- Database Mirroring: You cannot mirror a database with a MEMORY_OPTIMIZED_DATA file group. Availability Groups, however, work perfectly.

Creating Tables

Creating memory-optimized tables is largely the same process you're used to. There are a few wrinkles worth noting. Listing 19-3 is an attempt to replicate the Person.Address table from AdventureWorks.

Listing 19-3. Creating a memory-optimized version of the Address table

```
CREATE TABLE dbo.ADDRESS
(
    AddressID INT IDENTITY(1, 1) NOT NULL PRIMARY KEY NONCLUSTERED HASH
                                          WITH (BUCKET_COUNT = 50000),
    AddressLine1 NVARCHAR(60) NOT NULL,
    AddressLine2 NVARCHAR(60) NULL,
    City NVARCHAR(30) NOT NULL,
    StateProvinceID INT NOT NULL,
    PostalCode NVARCHAR(15) NOT NULL,
    --SpatialLocation geography NULL,
    --rowguid uniqueidentifier ROWGUIDCOL  NOT NULL CONSTRAINT DF_Address_
      rowguid  DEFAULT (newid()),
```

```
    ModifiedDate DATETIME NOT NULL
        CONSTRAINT DF_Address_ModifiedDate
            DEFAULT (GETDATE())
)
WITH (MEMORY_OPTIMIZED = ON, DURABILITY = SCHEMA_AND_DATA);
```

The primary magic is in the WITH statement. First, I'm identifying this table as being specifically MEMORY_OPTIMIZED. That will ensure that it goes to the correct file group. Additionally, I'm defining my durability, here a fully durable table supporting both schema and data.

The next thing worth noting is the index. This is not one of the indexes we've referenced throughout the book. This index, NOCLUSTERED HASH, is unique to memory-optimized tables. We'll drill down on indexing a little later in the chapter.

Finally, the only point worth noting here is that I've commented the SpatialLocation and rowguid columns. That's because their data types, geography and user defined, are not supported for in-memory tables. The complete list is here:

- GEOGRAPHY/GEOMETRY
- XML
- DATETIMEOFFSET
- ROWVERSION
- HIERARCHYID
- SQL_VARIANT
- User-defined data types

Otherwise, all the data types are supported. You can also use foreign keys, check constraints, and unique constraints ever since SQL Server 2016. Also, memory-optimized tables support off-row columns, meaning a single row can be greater than 8,060 bytes.

I'm going to run Listing 19-4 in order to put some data into my memory-optimized table, pulling directly from AdventureWorks.

Listing 19-4. Loading the dbo.Address table

```
INSERT dbo.ADDRESS
(
```

CHAPTER 19　MEMORY-OPTIMIZED OLTP TABLES AND PROCEDURES

```
    AddressLine1,
    AddressLine2,
    City,
    StateProvinceID,
    PostalCode
)
SELECT A.AddressLine1,
       A.AddressLine2,
       A.City,
       A.StateProvinceID,
       A.PostalCode
FROM Person.Address AS a;
```

Another limitation is that a memory-optimized table can't take part in a cross-database query or, more specifically, in a transaction. However, if you do need to use memory-optimized data in a cross-database query, you can use a memory-optimized table variable since it is not transactional. We'll explore the memory-optimized table variable more later in the chapter.

In order to have more to work with, I'll use Listing 19-5 to create and load several additional tables.

Listing 19-5. Setting up a more complete database of tables

```
CREATE TABLE dbo.StateProvince
(
StateProvinceID INT IDENTITY(1, 1) NOT NULL PRIMARY KEY NONCLUSTERED HASH
                                            WITH (BUCKET_COUNT = 10000),
    StateProvinceCode NCHAR(3) COLLATE Latin1_General_100_BIN2 NOT NULL,
    CountryRegionCode NVARCHAR(3) NOT NULL,
    NAME VARCHAR(50) NOT NULL,
    TerritoryID INT NOT NULL,
    ModifiedDate DATETIME NOT NULL
        CONSTRAINT DF_StateProvince_ModifiedDate
            DEFAULT (GETDATE())
)
```

CHAPTER 19 MEMORY-OPTIMIZED OLTP TABLES AND PROCEDURES

```sql
WITH (MEMORY_OPTIMIZED = ON);
CREATE TABLE dbo.CountryRegion
(
    CountryRegionCode NVARCHAR(3) NOT NULL,
    NAME VARCHAR(50) NOT NULL,
    ModifiedDate DATETIME NOT NULL
        CONSTRAINT DF_CountryRegion_ModifiedDate
            DEFAULT (GETDATE()),
    CONSTRAINT PK_CountryRegion_CountryRegionCode
        PRIMARY KEY CLUSTERED (CountryRegionCode ASC)
);
GO
INSERT dbo.StateProvince
(
    StateProvinceCode,
    CountryRegionCode,
    NAME,
    TerritoryID
)
SELECT StateProvinceCode,
       CountryRegionCode,
       NAME,
       TerritoryID
FROM Person.StateProvince AS sp
INSERT dbo.CountryRegion
(
    CountryRegionCode,
    NAME
)
SELECT cr.CountryRegionCode,
       cr.NAME
FROM Person.CountryRegion AS cr;
```

With additional tables, I can now write a complete query to see our memory-optimized table in action in Listing 19-6.

CHAPTER 19 ■ MEMORY-OPTIMIZED OLTP TABLES AND PROCEDURES

Listing 19-6. Querying memory-optimized tables

```
SELECT A.AddressLine1,
       A.City,
       A.PostalCode,
       sp.NAME AS StateProvinceName,
       cr.NAME AS CountryName
FROM dbo.ADDRESS AS A
   JOIN dbo.StateProvince AS sp
      ON sp.StateProvinceID = A.StateProvinceID
   JOIN dbo.CountryRegion AS cr
      ON cr.CountryRegionCode = sp.CountryRegionCode
WHERE A.AddressID = 42;
```

Notice, this is a mix of memory-optimized tables and a standard SQL Server table. Yet the query runs just fine. We can even capture an execution plan with runtime metrics in Figure 19-1.

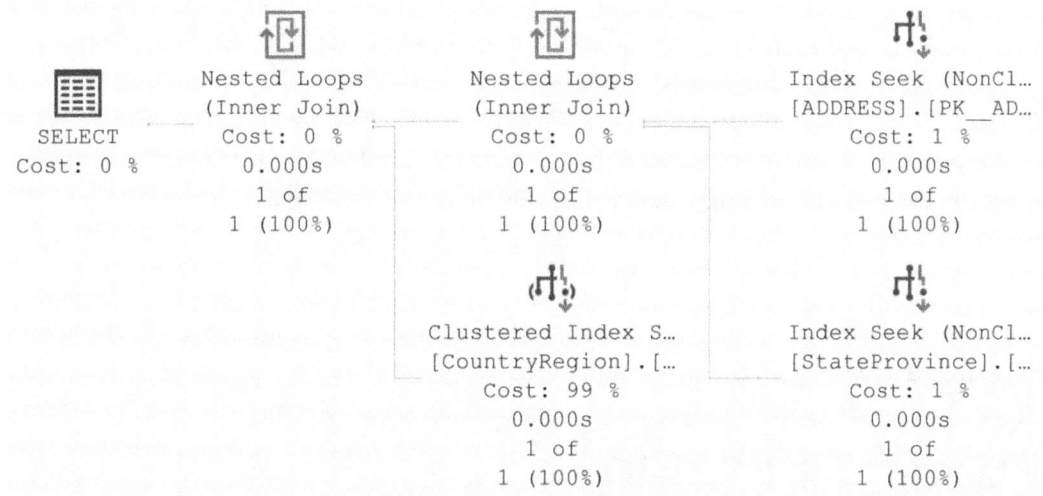

Figure 19-1. *Execution plan showing a mix of table types*

The best part is that the optimizer thinks that the single row, Clustered Index Seek, against the standard clustered index is 99% of the cost of the query.

However, the important point here is how mundane this is. It's just an execution plan. Yes, it has seeks against a nonclustered hash table instead of any of the indexes we've covered throughout the book, but if you've read straight through to this point, you know what an index seek represents. It's no different because it's in memory-optimized tables.

While much of the performance enhancements with memory-optimized tables are focused on enabling high-volume inserts and updates while simultaneously allowing for read queries, those same read queries are enhanced as well. If we compare the metrics of this query in the InMemoryTest database to a similar query against the AdventureWorks tables we pulled our data from, Table 19-1 shows the results.

Table 19-1. Comparing performance for a simple SELECT query

Database	Duration	Reads
InMemoryTest	148mcs	2
AdventureWorks	192mcs	6

This is a very small example returning a single row, but approximately 22% faster, and a 66% reduction in reads indicates the possibility of other performance enhancements as other queries get run.

One point I need to make here. The reads that we've been using throughout the book are not the same as reads with memory-optimized tables. No data is read off disk except during the recovery of the database during startup or failover. That means while we still have the value of reads, we can't do what I just did, a straight comparison on those reads. Fewer reads with memory-optimized tables are better, of course, but it's not the same values. Duration is your better comparison measurement, at least when comparing traditional behaviors with the in-memory ones.

In-Memory Table Variables

As I mentioned earlier in the chapter, you can create a memory-optimized, or in-memory, table variable. Earlier I stated that these could be used in cross-database queries, but that's just one example. Their real use would be to get better performance out of your use of table variables. Table variables are extremely ephemeral, temporary, storage. As such, putting them into in-memory storage is likely to perform much better than putting them into tempdb, as a standard table variable will be.

CHAPTER 19 MEMORY-OPTIMIZED OLTP TABLES AND PROCEDURES

In order to use in-memory table variables, you first have to create a TYPE that defines a memory-optimized table as shown in Listing 19-7.

Listing 19-7. Creating an in-memory table TYPE

```
CREATE TYPE dbo.PostalCodeType AS TABLE
(
    ID INT NOT NULL PRIMARY KEY NONCLUSTERED,
    City NVARCHAR(30) NOT NULL,
    PostalCode NVARCHAR(15) NOT NULL,
    INDEX CityIndex HASH (City) WITH (BUCKET_COUNT = 100)
)
WITH (MEMORY_OPTIMIZED = ON);
```

The requirements for the TYPE are reflected in the code. You have to have an index, either hash or nonclustered. In this example I have both. You also have to use MEMORY_OPTIMIZED = ON in order to make this an in-memory table variable.

We can then use the TYPE very much in traditional ways. Listing 19-8 shows the code to load the table variable.

Listing 19-8. Loading an in-memory table variable

```
DECLARE @PostalCode AS dbo.PostalCodeType;

INSERT INTO @PostalCode
(
    City,
    PostalCode
)
SELECT DISTINCT
      a.City,
      a.PostalCode
FROM Person.Address AS a;
```

As you can see, once it's declared, the in-memory table variable is addressed within T-SQL the same way as a traditional table variable would be. The difference is in performance. Listing 19-9 shows the same code for a standard table variable.

Listing 19-9. Loading a traditional table variable

```
DECLARE @OldPostalCode AS TABLE
(
    id INT IDENTITY NOT NULL PRIMARY KEY NONCLUSTERED,
    City NVARCHAR(30) NOT NULL,
    PostalCode NVARCHAR(15) NOT NULL,
    INDEX CityIndex NONCLUSTERED (City)
);

INSERT INTO @OldPostalCode
(
    City,
    PostalCode
)
SELECT DISTINCT
       a.City,
       a.PostalCode
FROM Person.Address AS a;
```

The performance difference is stark. The in-memory temp table gets loaded in 15.1ms, while the traditional table variable takes 25.8ms.

We can see differences in queries as well. Listing 19-10 shows how we could query the table variable.

Listing 19-10. Querying a table variable

```
DECLARE @PostalCode AS dbo.PostalCodeType;

INSERT INTO @PostalCode
(
    City,
    PostalCode
)
SELECT DISTINCT
      a.City,
      a.PostalCode
```

```
FROM Person.Address AS a;

SELECT * FROM @PostalCode AS pc
WHERE pc.City = 'London';
```

Once more, comparing this with the traditional table variable, we see a stark performance difference with the single SELECT statement running in 118mcs on the memory-optimized table variable and about three times slower at 339mcs on the traditional table variable.

To sum up, memory-optimized table variables offer a major performance enhancement over traditional table variables.

In-Memory Indexes

Every memory-optimized table must have one index. Since the row is stored as a unit within the in-memory table, an index has to be there in order to make a table. The data is not stored on a page, which is why reads are not the same. Because of this, there is no worry about index fragmentation. An UPDATE consists of a logical DELETE and an INSERT. A process comes along later to clean things up.

Prior to SQL Server 2017, you were limited to eight indexes per table. Now, the limit is 999 (but remember, it's a limit, not a goal).

The indexes on a memory-optimized table live in memory in the same way that the table does. Their durability matches that of the table they're created on.

Let's explore these indexes in more detail.

Hash Index

The hash index is different from the other index types within SQL Server. A hash index uses a calculation to create a hash value of the key. The hash values are stored in buckets, or a table of values. The hash calculation is a constant, so for any given value, the same hash value will always be calculated.

Hash tables are very efficient. A hash value is a good way to retrieve a single row. However, when you start to have a lot of rows with the same hash value, that efficiency begins to drop.

The key to making the hash index efficient is getting the correct distribution across your hash buckets. When you create the index, you supply a bucket count. In the example in Listing 19-3, I supplied a value of 50,000 for the bucket count. When you consider there are currently about 19,000 rows in the table, I've made the bucket count more than big enough to hold the existing data, and I left room for growth over time.

The bucket count has to be big enough without being too big. If the bucket count is small, a lot of values are inside a single bucket, making the index less efficient. If you have a lot of empty buckets, when a scan occurs, they are all read, even though they are empty, slowing down the scan.

Figure 19-2 illustrates how hash buckets work.

Figure 19-2. *Hash values in buckets with a shallow and deep distribution*

The first set of buckets is what is defined as a shallow distribution, that is to say, a few hash values distributed across a lot of buckets. The second set of buckets at the bottom of Figure 19-2 represents a deep distribution—in that case, fewer buckets with more values in them.

With a shallow distribution, point lookups, individual rows, are going to be extremely efficient, but scans will suffer. However, in the deep distribution, point lookups won't be as fast, but scans will be faster. However, if you are in a situation where your queries are doing a lot of scans of a memory-optimized table, you may want to switch back to a regular table again.

CHAPTER 19 ■ MEMORY-OPTIMIZED OLTP TABLES AND PROCEDURES

The recommendation for bucket counts completely depends on your data and your data growth. If you don't expect any data growth at all, set the number of buckets equal to your row count. If your data is going to grow over time, set it somewhere between one and two times the row count. Don't worry too much about this. Even with too many, or too few, buckets, performance is likely to be great. Just remember, the more buckets you allocate, the more memory you're using.

You also have to be concerned with how many values can be returned by the hash value. Unique indexes and primary keys are excellent choices for a hash index because their values will be unique. The general recommendation is a ratio of total rows to unique values being less than 10.

The hash value is simply a pointer to the bucket. If there are multiple rows, they are chained together, each row pointing to the next row. When a bucket is found, you've found the first value in the chain. You then scan through the chain to find the actual row you're interested in. This means a point lookup turns into a bit of a scan, hence keeping the number of duplicates in the hash to a minimum.

You can see the distribution of your data within the hash index using the query in Listing 19-11.

Listing 19-11. Querying sys.dm_db_xtp_hash_index_stats

```
SELECT i.NAME AS [index name],
       hs.total_bucket_count,
       hs.empty_bucket_count,
       hs.avg_chain_length,
       hs.max_chain_length
FROM sys.dm_db_xtp_hash_index_stats AS hs
    JOIN sys.indexes AS i
        ON hs.OBJECT_ID = i.OBJECT_ID
           AND hs.index_id = i.index_id
WHERE OBJECT_NAME(hs.OBJECT_ID) = 'Address';
```

The results are in Figure 19-3.

	index name	total_bucket_count	empty_bucket_count	avg_chain_length	max_chain_length
1	PK__ADDRESS__091C2A1A5CD944A3	65536	48652	1	5

Figure 19-3. *Results from sys.dm_db_xtp_hash_index_stats*

CHAPTER 19 MEMORY-OPTIMIZED OLTP TABLES AND PROCEDURES

There are several important pieces of information here. First, you should note the total_bucket_count value of 65,536. I called for 50,000 buckets, but SQL Server rounded it up to the next power of 2 value. I have about 48,652 empty buckets, which is a little high, but maybe I'm anticipating growth. The average chain length is 1, which is very good. The maximum chain length is 5, which is good enough being below 10.

If there were even more empty buckets, the average chain length was above 5, and the max chain length was greater than 10, it might be time to consider a nonclustered index for the memory-optimized table.

Nonclustered Indexes

A nonclustered index on a memory-optimized table is no different than a nonclustered index on a regular table, other than where the data is stored. Durability again will be dictated by the durability of the table.

Consider the query in Listing 19-12.

Listing 19-12. A query in need of an index

```
SELECT A.AddressLine1,
       A.City,
       A.PostalCode,
       sp.NAME AS StateProvinceName,
       cr.NAME AS CountryName
FROM dbo.ADDRESS AS A
    JOIN dbo.StateProvince AS sp
        ON sp.StateProvinceID = A.StateProvinceID
    JOIN dbo.CountryRegion AS cr
        ON cr.CountryRegionCode = sp.CountryRegionCode
WHERE A.City = 'Walla Walla';
```

Running this query results in the execution plan in Figure 19-4.

CHAPTER 19 MEMORY-OPTIMIZED OLTP TABLES AND PROCEDURES

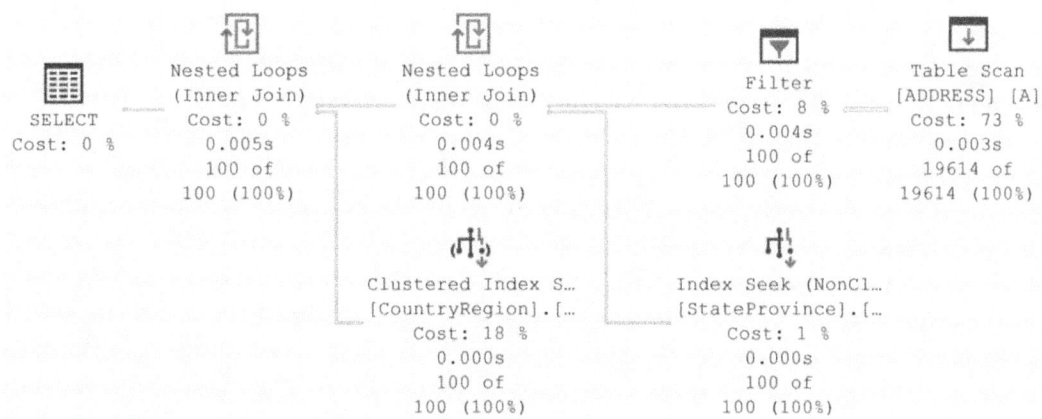

Figure 19-4. *A scan of an in-memory table*

Because the WHERE clause is unsupported by any index, we're getting a scan of the dbo.Address table. While a scan of an in-memory table will be faster than one stored on disk, it's still a performance issue in the same way it would be on another query.

You can't simply run CREATE INDEX on a memory-optimized table. Instead, you have to either recreate the table or use ALTER TABLE as a way to add an index. Listing 19-13 shows how.

Listing 19-13. ALTER a memory-optimized table to add an index

```
ALTER TABLE dbo.ADDRESS ADD INDEX nci (City);
```

Running the query from Listing 19-12 again results in a different execution plan (Figure 19-5).

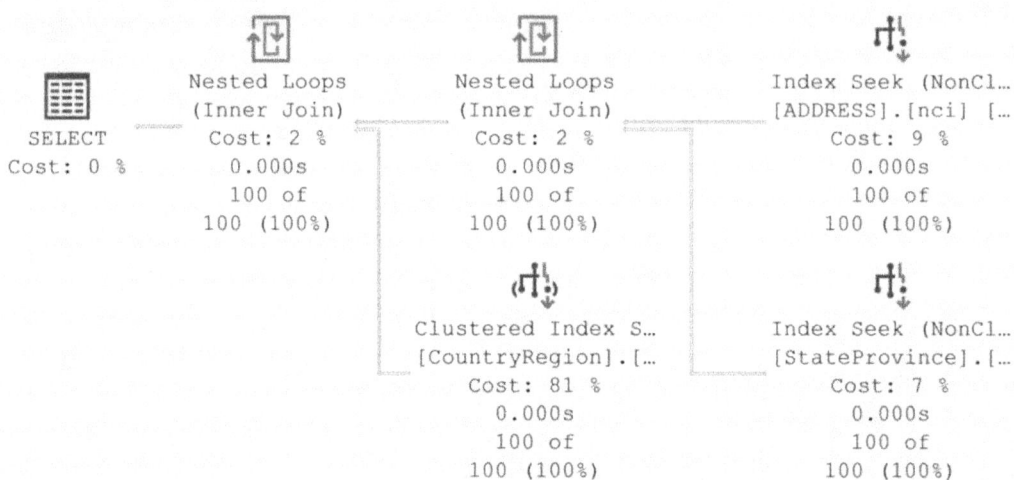

Figure 19-5. Scan replaced with a seek

The nonclustered index replaces the scan. Because of how the data is stored in a memory-optimized table, no Key Lookup operation is needed. Performance went from 3.8ms to 947mcs, a considerable gain.

Columnstore Index

There are no major distinctions between a memory-optimized table and a regular table when it comes to a columnstore index. You are limited to only a clustered columnstore. You have to have the memory to support the data stored in the index. Otherwise, it's just a columnstore index.

Statistics Maintenance

Memory-optimized tables still have statistics, and those statistics must be maintained. Information about the statistics can be gathered using standard means. Listing 19-14 shows the properties of the statistics on the Address table.

Listing 19-14. Querying sys.dm_db_stats_properties

```
SELECT s.NAME,
       s.stats_id,
       ddsp.last_updated,
```

CHAPTER 19 MEMORY-OPTIMIZED OLTP TABLES AND PROCEDURES

```
       ddsp.ROWS,
       ddsp.rows_sampled,
       ddsp.unfiltered_rows,
       ddsp.persisted_sample_percent,
       ddsp.steps
FROM sys.STATS AS s
    CROSS APPLY sys.dm_db_stats_properties(s.OBJECT_ID, s.stats_id) AS ddsp
    WHERE s.OBJECT_ID = OBJECT_ID('Address');
```

The results from my table are in Figure 19-6.

	NAME	stats_id	last_updated	ROWS	rows_sampled	unfiltered_rows	persisted_sample_percent	steps
1	PK__ADDRESS__091C2A1A5CD944A3	2	2025-08-10 15:14:52.9200000	19614	19614	19614	0	3
2	_WA_Sys_00000005_59B045BD	3	2025-08-10 13:52:51.1733333	19614	19614	19614	0	71
3	_WA_Sys_00000004_59B045BD	4	2025-08-10 15:09:58.7433333	19614	19614	19614	0	200
4	nci	5	2025-08-10 15:14:52.9300000	19614	19614	19614	0	200

Figure 19-6. *Statistics on the memory-optimized table*

As you can see, statistics are created for the indexes on the table, but also system-generated statistics are created. You can use standard mechanisms to look at the data within the statistics, including hash indexes. Listing 19-15 shows a query for retrieving a histogram from the hash index.

Listing 19-15. Querying sys.dm_db_stats_histogram

```
SELECT ddsh.step_number,
       ddsh.range_high_key,
       ddsh.range_rows,
       ddsh.equal_rows,
       ddsh.distinct_range_rows,
       ddsh.average_range_rows
FROM sys.dm_db_stats_histogram(OBJECT_ID('Address'), 2) AS ddsh;
```

This returns the values shown in Figure 19-7.

	step_number	range_high_key	range_rows	equal_rows	distinct_range_rows	average_range_rows
1	1	1	0	1	0	1
2	2	19613	19611	1	19611	1
3	3	19614	0	1	0	1

Figure 19-7. *Histogram of the hash index*

Statistics are automatically maintained in SQL Server 2016 and greater as long as the database compatibility level is set to at least 130. Prior to that, or with the compatibility level set lower, you will have to maintain statistics manually.

You can use sp_updates or UPDATE STATISTICS. However, in SQL Server 2014, you will have to use FULLSCAN or RESAMPLE along with RECOMPUTE as shown in Listing 19-16.

Listing 19-16. Updating statistics in 2014

```
UPDATE STATISTICS dbo.ADDRESS
WITH FULLSCAN,
    NORECOMPUTE;
```

Otherwise, you will generate an error.

Apart from that exception, statistics are largely the same as described in Chapter 5.

Natively Compiled Stored Procedures

If the performance of your memory-optimized tables isn't enough, you can also look to compiling stored procedures as DLLs so that they run within the SQL Server operating system itself. There are limitations on the T-SQL allowed within them documented on the Microsoft website. SQL Server 2025 radically reduced the amount of unsupported T-SQL functionality. All the tables must be memory-optimized for use within the compiled procedure. Listing 19-17 rebuilds the CountryRegion table.

Listing 19-17. Recreating the CountryRegion table as memory-optimized

```
DROP TABLE IF EXISTS dbo.CountryRegion;
GO
CREATE TABLE dbo.CountryRegion
(
    CountryRegionCode NVARCHAR(3) NOT NULL,
    NAME VARCHAR(50) NOT NULL,
    ModifiedDate DATETIME NOT NULL
        CONSTRAINT DF_CountryRegion_ModifiedDate
            DEFAULT (GETDATE()),
    CONSTRAINT PK_CountryRegion_CountryRegionCode
```

```
        PRIMARY KEY NONCLUSTERED (CountryRegionCode ASC)
)
WITH (MEMORY_OPTIMIZED = ON);
GO
INSERT dbo.CountryRegion
(
    CountryRegionCode,
    NAME
)
SELECT cr.CountryRegionCode,
       cr.Name
FROM Person.CountryRegion AS cr;
```

With that, Listing 19-18 shows how to create the procedure.

Listing 19-18. Creating a natively compiled stored procedure

```
CREATE PROC dbo.AddressDetails @City NVARCHAR(30)
WITH NATIVE_COMPILATION, SCHEMABINDING, EXECUTE AS OWNER AS
BEGIN ATOMIC WITH (TRANSACTION ISOLATION LEVEL = SNAPSHOT, LANGUAGE = N'us_
english')
    SELECT A.AddressLine1,
           A.City,
           A.PostalCode,
           sp.NAME AS StateProvinceName,
           cr.NAME AS CountryName
    FROM dbo.ADDRESS AS A
        JOIN dbo.StateProvince AS sp
            ON sp.StateProvinceID = A.StateProvinceID
        JOIN dbo.CountryRegion
        AS
        cr
            ON cr.CountryRegionCode = sp.CountryRegionCode
    WHERE A.City = @City;
END;
```

Executing the natively compiled procedure for the value of 'Walla Walla' in the same way as Listing 19-12 results in a query running in 893mcs compared with the 947mcs from before.

There are other restrictions and requirements visible in the code in Listing 19-18. First, parameters cannot accept NULL values. You have to enforce schema binding to the underlying tables. Finally, the procedure must exist within an ATOMIC BLOCK. Atomic blocks require that all statements within the transaction succeed or all statements within the transaction get rolled back.

Starting in SQL Server 2019, you can capture execution plans with runtime metrics, also called actual plans. You can also see estimated plans. Figure 19-8 shows the plan from this procedure.

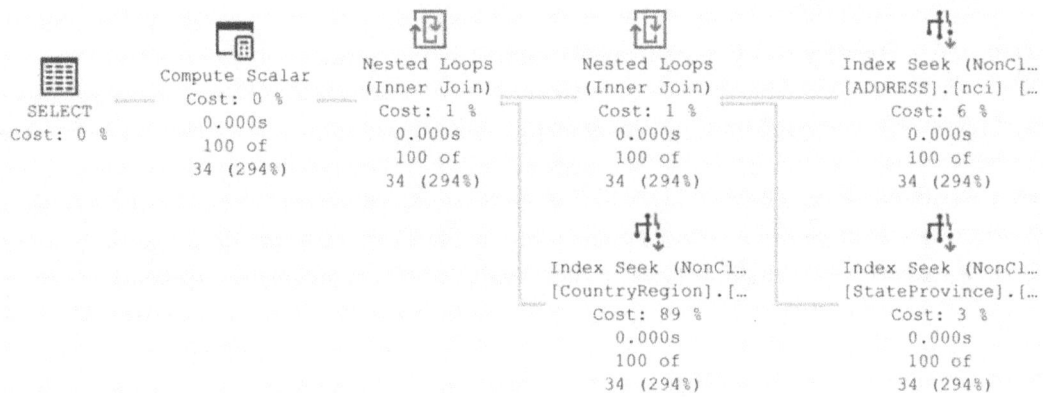

Figure 19-8. Execution plan for a natively compiled procedure

The plans for natively compiled procedures are created when you create the procedure. These plans look the same, but there are some differences in the properties. Figure 19-9 shows the SELECT operator properties from the plan.

Misc	
Estimated Number of Rows for All Execu	0
Estimated Operator Cost	0 (0%)
Estimated Subtree Cost	0.0176351
NonParallelPlanReason	NoParallelForNativelyCompiledModule
Statement	SELECT A.AddressLine1, A.City,

Figure 19-9. SELECT operator properties

Because this procedure executes within the OS, most of the properties we're used to seeing aren't applicable.

You should use execution plans the same way as you would with a regular query. You'll see where there may be optimization opportunities looking for scans and so on. One note, all join operations within a natively compiled procedure will be Nested Loops. No other join operations are supported.

Recommendations

While the performance enhancements of memory-optimized tables and natively compiled procedures are simply huge, you should not simply, blindly, start migrating your databases and objects to in-memory. There are serious hardware requirements that you must meet. Here are a number of considerations you should work through prior to implementing this technology.

Baselines

The very first thing you should have in hand is a good understanding of the existing performance and behavior of your system. This means implementing Extended Events and all the other tools to gather performance metrics. With that information in hand, you'll know if you're in a situation where locking and latches are leading to performance bottlenecks that memory-optimized tables could solve.

Correct Workload

The name of the technology is in-memory OLTP. That's because it is oriented and designed to better support Online Transaction Processing, not analytics or reporting. If your system is primarily read focused, has only intermittent data loads, or simply has a very low level of transaction processing, this technology is not right for you. You may see only marginal improvements in performance for a substantial amount of work. Microsoft outlines a series of possible workloads in more detail in their documentation.

CHAPTER 19 MEMORY-OPTIMIZED OLTP TABLES AND PROCEDURES

Memory Optimization Advisor

As a way to help, Microsoft has supplied functionality within SSMS that will test individual tables for supporting a move to in-memory. Right-clicking a table and selecting "Memory Optimization Advisor" from the context menu is all that is required. Figure 19-10 shows the information from the Person.Address table in the AdventureWorks database.

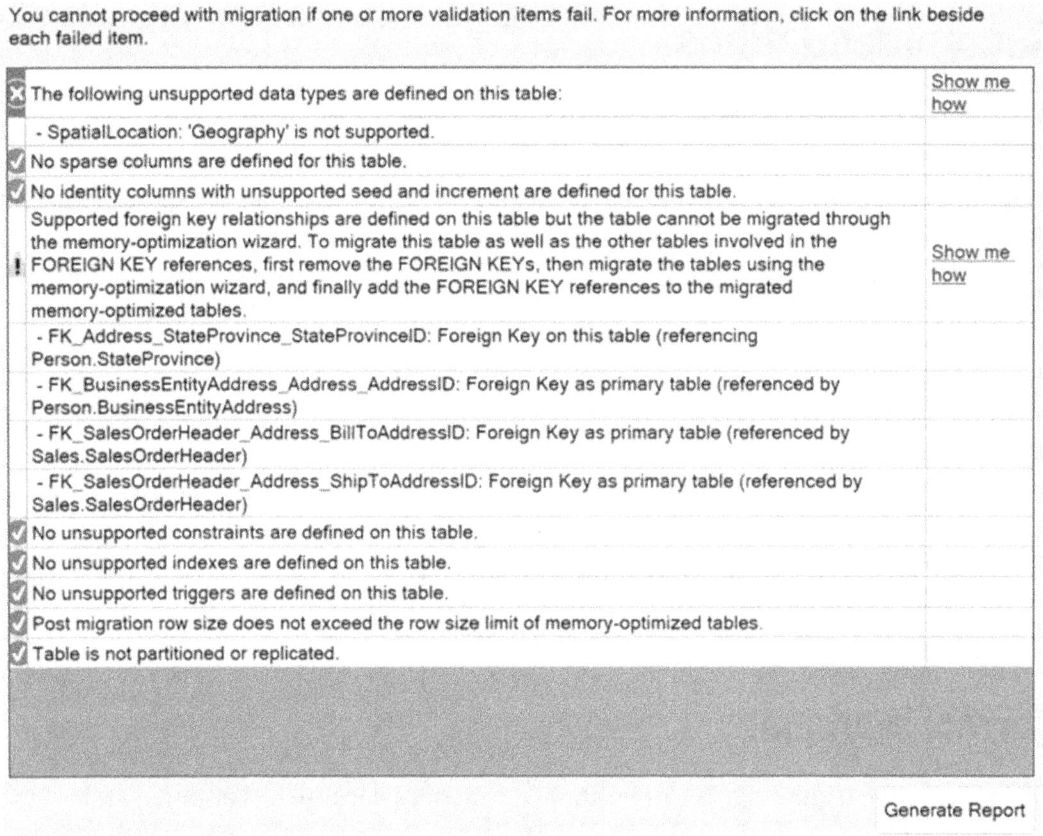

Figure 19-10. Results of the Memory Optimization Advisor

Because the geography data type isn't allowed in memory-optimized tables, this fails the initial test. You can see that it passed several other tests and received a warning that for a migration scenario, other tables would have to be processed without foreign keys.

In order to see the next steps, I'll use Listing 19-19 to create a test table in the InMemory database.

CHAPTER 19 ■ MEMORY-OPTIMIZED OLTP TABLES AND PROCEDURES

Listing 19-19. Setting up a table for migration to memory-optimized

```
CREATE TABLE dbo.AddressMigrate
(
    AddressID INT NOT NULL IDENTITY(1, 1) PRIMARY KEY,
    AddressLine1 NVARCHAR(60) NOT NULL,
    AddressLine2 NVARCHAR(60) NULL,
    City NVARCHAR(30) NOT NULL,
    StateProvinceID INT NOT NULL,
    PostalCode NVARCHAR(15) NOT NULL
);
```

The table shown in Figure 19-11 passed the initial checks.

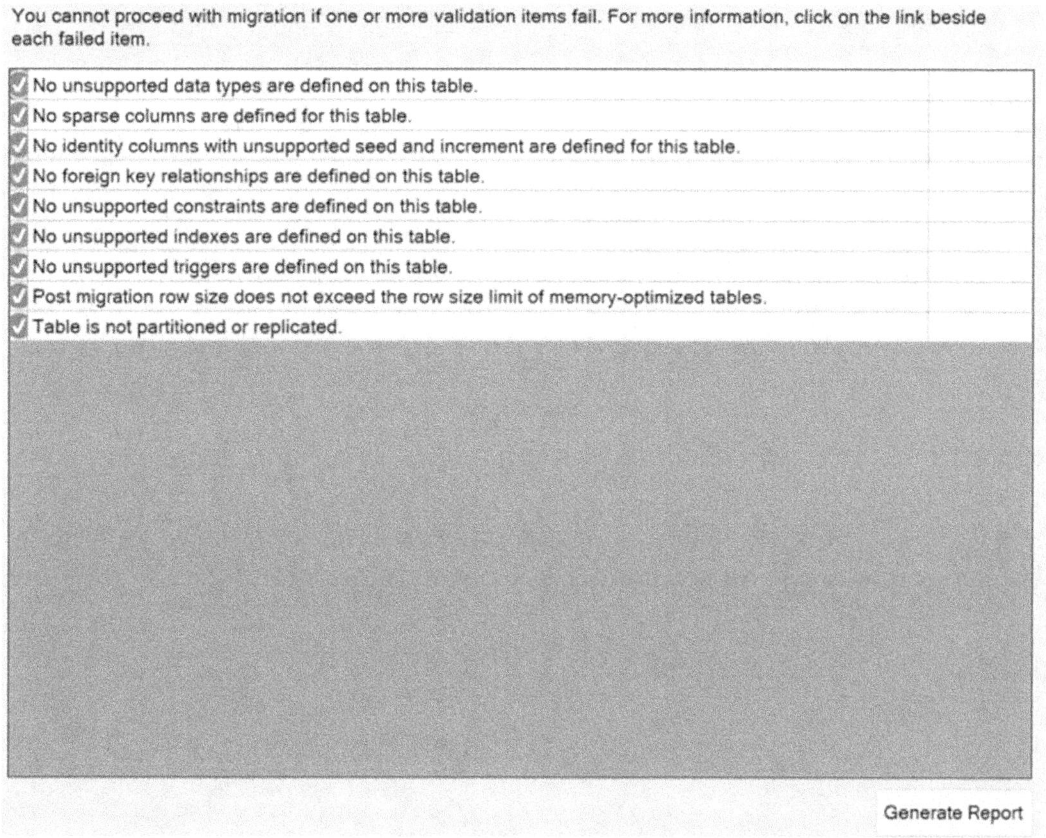

Figure 19-11. *All checks are passed*

CHAPTER 19 MEMORY-OPTIMIZED OLTP TABLES AND PROCEDURES

Next, Microsoft supplies a series of warnings for the migration to memory-optimized (Figure 19-12).

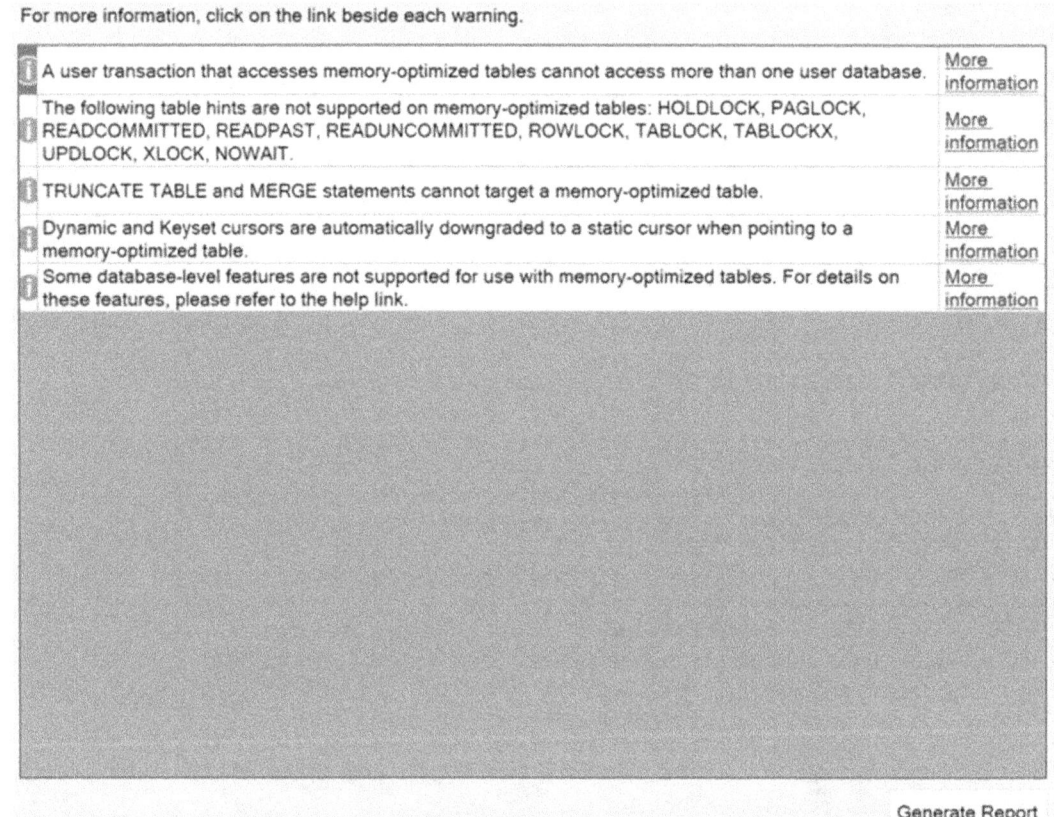

Figure 19-12. Warnings about migrating a table to in-memory storage

It doesn't simply perform the checks and warnings; it will actually migrate the table. Next, you get the options for naming and data migration (Figure 19-13).

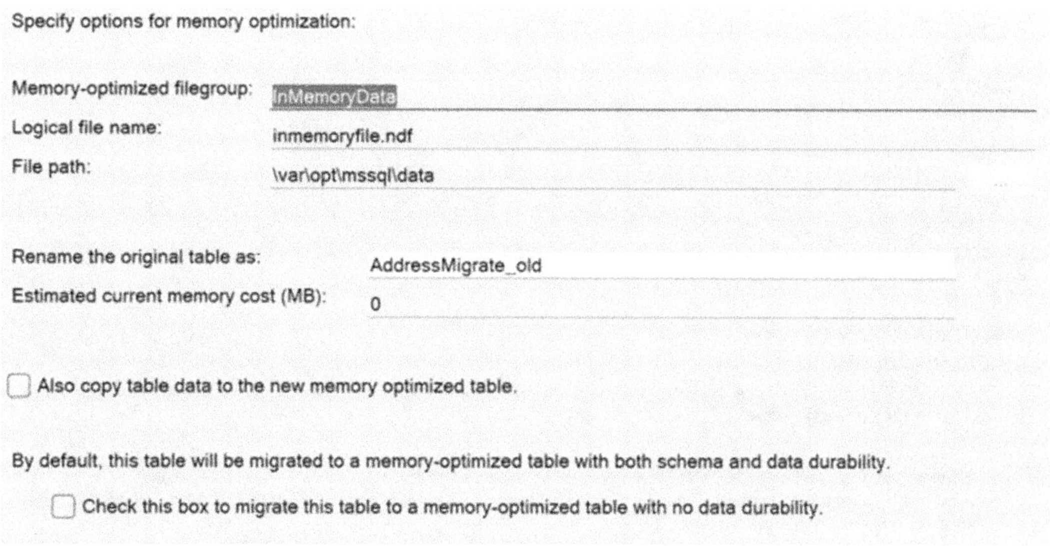

CHAPTER 19 MEMORY-OPTIMIZED OLTP TABLES AND PROCEDURES

Specify options for memory optimization:

Memory-optimized filegroup: InMemoryData
Logical file name: inmemoryfile.ndf
File path: \var\opt\mssql\data

Rename the original table as: AddressMigrate_old
Estimated current memory cost (MB): 0

☐ Also copy table data to the new memory optimized table.

By default, this table will be migrated to a memory-optimized table with both schema and data durability.

☐ Check this box to migrate this table to a memory-optimized table with no data durability.

Figure 19-13. *Naming the table and migrating data*

After that, since every memory-optimized table must have an index, you choose which type of index you want for your table (Figure 19-14).

CHAPTER 19　MEMORY-OPTIMIZED OLTP TABLES AND PROCEDURES

Please choose the appropriate conversion for this primary key:

Column	Type
AddressID	int

Select a new name for this primary key:　AddressMigrate_primaryKey

Select the type of this primary key:

◉ Use NONCLUSTERED HASH index

A NONCLUSTERED HASH index provides the most benefit for point lookups. It provides no discernible benefit if a query is running a Range scan.

Bucket Count:

The Bucket Count of a NONCLUSTERED HASH index is the number of buckets in the hash table. It is recommended to set the fill factor to 50 to 60% if the table requires a lot of space for growth. Bucket Count will be rounded up to the nearest power of two.

○ Use NONCLUSTERED index

A NONCLUSTERED index provides the most benefit for range predicates and ORDER BY clauses. NONCLUSTERED indexes are unidirectional. It provides no benefit for ORDER BY clauses with orders different from the index.

Sort column and order:

Column	Sort Order

Figure 19-14. Selecting an index for the in-memory table

You will need to supply a bucket count if you're using the hash index. At this point, you can generate a report, or a script that does all the work, or you can click the Migrate button and see it all go. Figure 19-15 shows the results of clicking that button.

Action	Result
✓ Renaming the original table. 　New name:AddressMigrate_old	Passed
✓ Creating the memory-optimized table in the database. 　Adding index:AddressMigrate_primaryKey	Passed

Figure 19-15. After migrating the table to in-memory storage

That table has been moved to in-memory storage. While the advisor will help you move a table to in-memory, it doesn't help you determine which tables should be moved. You're still on your own for that evaluation.

Native Compilation Advisor

Just as you can evaluate a table for migration to memory-optimized storage, you also have an advisor for stored procedures. Listing 19-20 shows two procedures: one that will fail the migration and one that will pass.

Listing 19-20. Procedures for testing the Native Compilation Advisor

```
CREATE OR ALTER PROCEDURE dbo.FailWizard
(@City NVARCHAR(30))
AS
SELECT A.AddressLine1,
       A.City,
       A.PostalCode,
       sp.NAME AS StateProvinceName,
       cr.NAME AS CountryName
FROM dbo.ADDRESS AS A
    JOIN dbo.StateProvince AS sp
        ON sp.StateProvinceID = A.StateProvinceID
    JOIN dbo.CountryRegion AS cr WITH (NOLOCK)
        ON cr.CountryRegionCode = sp.CountryRegionCode
WHERE A.City = @City;
GO
CREATE OR ALTER PROCEDURE dbo.PassWizard
(@City NVARCHAR(30))
AS
SELECT A.AddressLine1,
       A.City,
       A.PostalCode,
       sp.NAME AS StateProvinceName,
       cr.NAME AS CountryName
FROM dbo.ADDRESS AS A
    JOIN dbo.StateProvince AS sp
```

CHAPTER 19 MEMORY-OPTIMIZED OLTP TABLES AND PROCEDURES

```
            ON sp.StateProvinceID = A.StateProvinceID
    JOIN dbo.CountryRegion AS cr
            ON cr.CountryRegionCode = sp.CountryRegionCode
WHERE A.City = @City;
GO
```

The first procedure has a NOLOCK hint that isn't allowed in the natively compiled procedures. Right-clicking that procedure and selecting the "Native Compilation Advisor" from the context menu results in Figure 19-16.

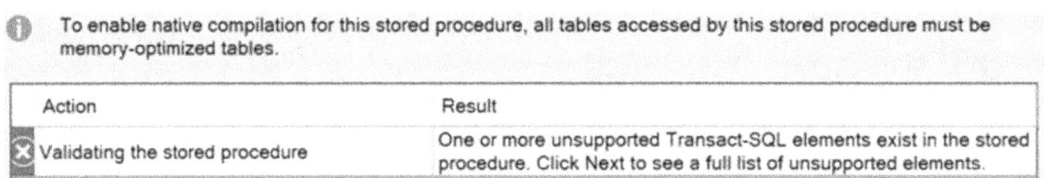

Figure 19-16. *Native Compilation Advisor failed this procedure*

You can click ahead in the Advisor to get more details (Figure 19-17).

Transact-SQL Element	Occurrences in the Stored Procedure	Start Line
NOLOCK	NOLOCK	9

Figure 19-17. *Explanation for the failure from the Native Compiled Advisor*

Running the Advisor against the good procedure just reports that it doesn't have any issues that you need to address. Unlike the Table Advisor, there is no actual migration wizard. Instead, you'd have to write the code yourself.

630

CHAPTER 19 MEMORY-OPTIMIZED OLTP TABLES AND PROCEDURES

Summary

You've been introduced to the concepts behind memory-optimized tables and natively compiled procedures as a part of the in-memory OLTP suite of tools. This is a specialized set of functionality that will absolutely help some workloads. Just remember that there are a lot of limitations on which tables can be migrated and what kind of code can be run against them. You also must have the hardware to support this functionality. However, with all that in place, the performance benefits of memory-optimized tables and natively compiled procedures are difficult to overemphasize.

In the next chapter, I'll introduce graph tables and the performance issues you may encounter there.

CHAPTER 20

Graph Databases

Introduced in SQL Server 2017, the graph database stores nodes and edges within SQL Server, allowing you to use T-SQL to query graph data. Graph data is specifically oriented around many-to-many relationships. Graph data doesn't lend itself to traditional relational structures but instead is focused on hierarchies and relationships past those more traditional structures. Graph data is separated from either traditional analytical data, better served by columnstore indexes, or OLTP systems, better served by rowstore indexes. However, when you have a data set that consists of complex hierarchical data, focused on the relationships between that data, the graph database comes into play.

In this chapter, I'll cover the following:

- Introduction to graph databases
- Querying graph data
- Performance considerations of graph data

Introduction to Graph Databases

You're allowed to create one graph per database. A graph consists of node and edge tables. Node tables describe an object. Edge tables describe the relationships between the values in the node tables. For this chapter, I'm going to create this simple graph data set in Figure 20-1.

CHAPTER 20   GRAPH DATABASES

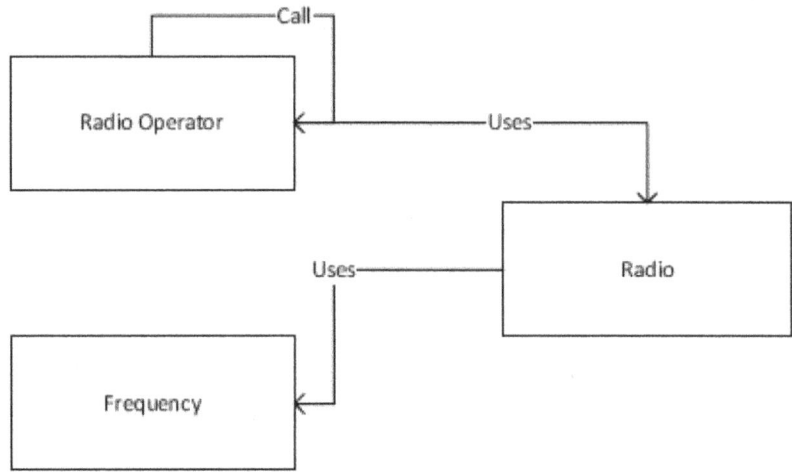

Figure 20-1. *A graph relationship with nodes and edges*

In the example, I'll have three nodes, or objects:

- Radio operators
- Frequencies
- Radios

This will be with two edges, or relationships:

- Call
- Uses

In short, many radio operators will use many frequencies using radios to call out to make many contacts with each other.

While the definition is that we're going to create a database, in fact, we're mainly just working with node and edge tables, more or less like regular tables. We could easily build out a structure using traditional relational mechanisms to store the data for functionality outlined previously. However, graph queries give us a much more efficient way to query that data.

You can easily see deeper relationships in the data, determining the number of different steps between radio operators who haven't contacted each other but have contacted others for example.

To work on this, I'm going to create a database along with a set of node and edge tables. Listing 20-1 is the start.

CHAPTER 20 GRAPH DATABASES

Listing 20-1. Creating a database for graph data

```
CREATE DATABASE RadioGraph;
GO
USE RadioGraph;
GO
--Create schema to hold different structures
CREATE SCHEMA grph;
GO
CREATE SCHEMA rel;
GO
```

Notice that there's nothing special about the database. All the work will be done with tables and T-SQL. I've created two schemas in the database:

- grph: Will hold the graph structures
- rel: Will hold a relational equivalent so that we can compare some query performance

Listing 20-2 shows the three node tables.

Listing 20-2. Creating node tables

```
CREATE TABLE grph.RadioOperator
(
    RadioOperatorID int IDENTITY(1, 1) NOT NULL,
    OperatorName varchar(50) NOT NULL,
    CallSign varchar(9) NOT NULL
) AS NODE;
CREATE TABLE grph.Frequency
(
    FrequencyID int IDENTITY(1, 1) NOT NULL,
    FrequencyValue decimal(6, 3) NOT NULL,
    Band varchar(12) NOT NULL,
    FrequencyUnit varchar(3) NOT NULL
) AS NODE;
CREATE TABLE grph.Radio
(
```

```
    RadioID int IDENTITY(1, 1),
    RadioName varchar(50) NOT NULL
) AS NODE;
```

As you can see, the only thing special I do while creating the tables is use the AS NODE command. Other than that definition, there's nothing unique that you have to do. Creating the edge tables is quite a lot different (Listing 20-3).

Listing 20-3. Creating edge tables

```
CREATE TABLE grph.Calls AS EDGE;
CREATE TABLE grph.Uses AS EDGE;
```

In this case, I don't define columns of any kind. They are created for me. Additionally, the node tables also get new columns. Figure 20-2 shows the new folder, graph tables, and the associated tables with columns.

CHAPTER 20 GRAPH DATABASES

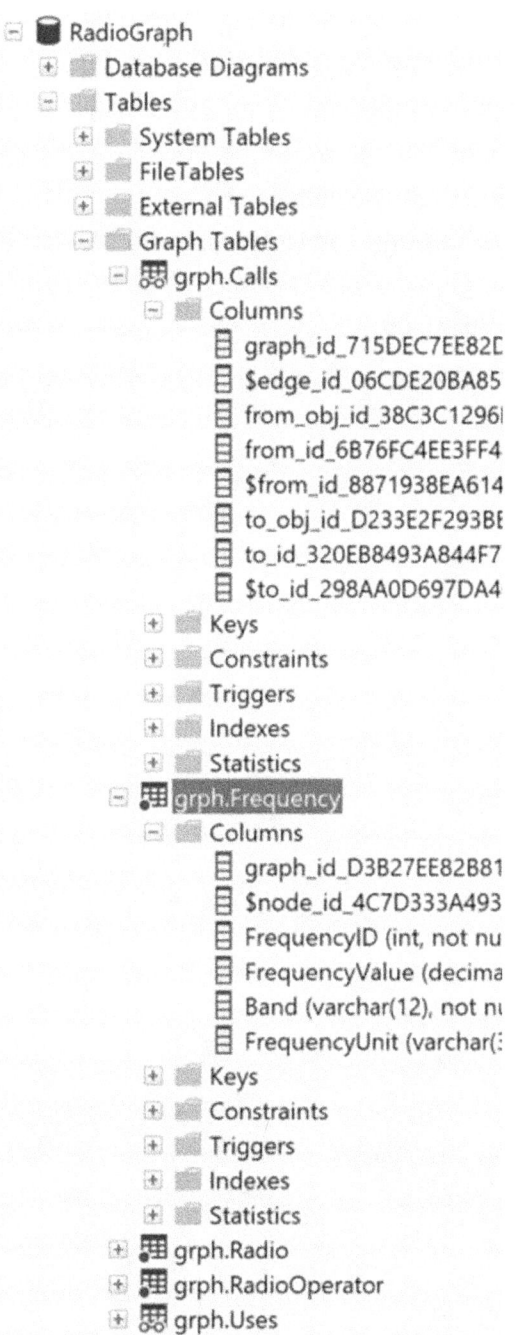

Figure 20-2. *Tables inside of a graph database*

CHAPTER 20 GRAPH DATABASES

For the node table, grph.Frequency highlighted in Figure 20-2, you can see that a $graph_id and a $node_id column have been added. We'll be using the node_id quite a bit. The edge table, in this case, grph.Calls, has a bunch of columns created, despite our CREATE TABLE statement not including any. Before I explain the $node_id, $from_id, and $to_id columns, let's load some data.

First, I'm going to load the node tables using Listing 20-4.

Listing 20-4. Adding data to node tables

```
INSERT INTO grph.RadioOperator
(
    OperatorName,
    CallSign
)
VALUES
('Grant Fritchey', 'KC1KCE'),
('Bob McCall', 'QQ5QQQ'),
('Abigail Serrano', 'VQ5ZZZ'),
('Josephine Wykovic', 'YQ9LLL');
INSERT INTO grph.Frequency
(
    FrequencyValue,
    Band,
    FrequencyUnit
)
VALUES
(14.250, '20 Meters', 'MHz'),
(145.520, '2 Meters', 'MHz'),
(478, '630 Meters', 'kHz'),
(14.225, '20 Meters', 'MHz'),
(14.3, '20 Meters', 'MHz'),
(7.18, '40 Meters', 'MHz');
INSERT INTO grph.Radio
(
    RadioName
)
```

CHAPTER 20 GRAPH DATABASES

```
VALUES
('Yaesu FT-3'),
('Baofeng UV5'),
('Icom 7300'),
('Raddiodity GD-88'),
('Xiegu G90');
```

The only really important point to understand here is that I'm not populating the $node_id column. It's taken care of similar to an IDENTITY column by internal processes.

> **Note** Just as an aside, my call sign is real. The other three call signs are fake along with the names of the people.

I am going to use the $node_id column when I go to load the edge table as shown in Listing 20-5.

Listing 20-5. Adding data to an edge table

```
INSERT INTO grph.Uses
(
    $from_id,
    $to_id
)
VALUES
(
    (
        SELECT $node_id FROM grph.RadioOperator AS ro WHERE
        ro.RadioOperatorID = 1
    ),
    (
        SELECT $node_id FROM grph.Radio AS r WHERE r.RadioID = 1
));
```

CHAPTER 20 GRAPH DATABASES

Here's where graph databases get a little tricky. I'm going to define the $from_id and $to_id however I want, but I have to do it consistently. In my case, I'm saying that a RadioOperator uses a radio. So the $from_id is the $node_id from the RadioOperator table—in this case, for RadioOperatorID = 1.

We can load all sorts of relationships within the Uses table. In the next code listing, I also make the association between radios and frequencies to understand which radio uses which frequency. However, you must be consistent. If you accidentally reverse the $from_id and $to_id, you're creating a new type of relationship, not simply a new relationship within the table.

Listing 20-6 loads some more data into the grph edge tables.

Listing 20-6. Loading the remaining data into the edge tables

```
INSERT INTO grph.Uses
(
    $from_id,
    $to_id
)
VALUES
(
    (
        SELECT $node_id FROM grph.RadioOperator AS ro WHERE
        ro.RadioOperatorID = 1
    ),
    (
        SELECT $node_id FROM grph.Radio AS r WHERE r.RadioID = 2
    )),
(
    (
        SELECT $node_id FROM grph.RadioOperator AS ro WHERE
        ro.RadioOperatorID = 1
    ),
    (
        SELECT $node_id FROM grph.Radio AS r WHERE r.RadioID = 3
    )),
(
```

CHAPTER 20   GRAPH DATABASES

```
    (
        SELECT $node_id FROM grph.RadioOperator AS ro WHERE
        ro.RadioOperatorID = 2
    ),
    (
        SELECT $node_id FROM grph.Radio AS r WHERE r.RadioID = 2
    )),
(
    (
        SELECT $node_id FROM grph.RadioOperator AS ro WHERE
        ro.RadioOperatorID = 3
    ),
    (
        SELECT $node_id FROM grph.Radio AS r WHERE r.RadioID = 4
    )),
(
    (
        SELECT $node_id FROM grph.RadioOperator AS ro WHERE
        ro.RadioOperatorID = 1
    ),
    (
        SELECT $node_id FROM grph.Radio AS r WHERE r.RadioID = 5
    )),
(
    (
        SELECT $node_id FROM grph.RadioOperator AS ro WHERE
        ro.RadioOperatorID = 3
    ),
    (
        SELECT $node_id FROM grph.Radio AS r WHERE r.RadioID = 1
    )),
(
    (
        SELECT ro.$node_id FROM grph.RadioOperator AS ro WHERE
        ro.RadioOperatorID = 4
```

CHAPTER 20 GRAPH DATABASES

```
    ),
    (
        SELECT r.$node_id FROM grph.Radio AS r WHERE r.RadioID = 1
    ));
--edges for radio uses frequency
INSERT INTO grph.Uses
(
    $from_id,
    $to_id
)
VALUES
(
    (
        SELECT $node_id FROM grph.Radio AS r WHERE r.RadioID = 1
    ),
    (
        SELECT $node_id FROM grph.Frequency AS F WHERE F.FrequencyID = 2
    )),
(
    (
        SELECT $node_id FROM grph.Radio AS r WHERE r.RadioID = 2
    ),
    (
        SELECT $node_id FROM grph.Frequency AS F WHERE F.FrequencyID = 2
    )),
(
    (
        SELECT $node_id FROM grph.Radio AS r WHERE r.RadioID = 1
    ),
    (
        SELECT $node_id FROM grph.Radio AS r WHERE r.RadioID = 2
    ));
--edges for calls
INSERT INTO grph.Calls
(
```

```
        $from_id,
        $to_id
)
VALUES
(
    (
        SELECT $node_id FROM grph.RadioOperator AS ro WHERE
        ro.RadioOperatorID = 1
    ),
    (
        SELECT $node_id FROM grph.RadioOperator AS ro WHERE
        ro.RadioOperatorID = 4
    )),
(
    (
        SELECT $node_id FROM grph.RadioOperator AS ro WHERE
        ro.RadioOperatorID = 1
    ),
    (
        SELECT $node_id FROM grph.RadioOperator AS ro WHERE
        ro.RadioOperatorID = 3
    )),
(
    (
        SELECT $node_id FROM grph.RadioOperator AS ro WHERE
        ro.RadioOperatorID = 2
    ),
    (
        SELECT $node_id FROM grph.RadioOperator AS ro WHERE
        ro.RadioOperatorID = 3
    )),
(
    (
        SELECT $node_id FROM grph.RadioOperator AS ro WHERE
        ro.RadioOperatorID = 3
    ),
```

CHAPTER 20 GRAPH DATABASES

```
        (
            SELECT $node_id FROM grph.RadioOperator AS ro WHERE
            ro.RadioOperatorID = 4
        )),
    (
        (
            SELECT $node_id FROM grph.RadioOperator AS ro WHERE
            ro.RadioOperatorID = 3
        ),
        (
            SELECT $node_id FROM grph.RadioOperator AS ro WHERE
            ro.RadioOperatorID = 1
        )),
    (
        (
            SELECT $node_id FROM grph.RadioOperator AS ro WHERE
            ro.RadioOperatorID = 3
        ),
        (
            SELECT $node_id FROM grph.RadioOperator AS ro WHERE
            ro.RadioOperatorID = 2
        ));
```

It's not a large data set, but it does take up quite a bit of space here.

With the data defined, we can query the information. This query shows which of our operators has called out to other operators (Listing 20-7).

Listing 20-7. Querying graph tables

```
SELECT Calling.OperatorName,
       Calling.CallSign,
       Called.OperatorName,
       Called.CallSign
FROM grph.RadioOperator AS Calling,
     grph.Calls AS C,
     grph.RadioOperator AS Called
WHERE MATCH(Calling-(C)->Called);
```

This is a new way of querying data, so we should break things down a bit. First up, your FROM clause simply lists the tables. We're not defining JOIN operations using an ON clause. Instead, we have a new command, MATCH. In that, we're looking for where the first table RadioOperator, aliased as Calling, through the edge table of grph.Calls, aliased as C, matches values in RadioOperator again, but this time, aliased as Called. The results look like Figure 20-3.

	OperatorName	CallSign	OperatorName	CallSign
1	Grant Fritchey	KC1KCE	Josephine Wykovic	YQ9LLL
2	Grant Fritchey	KC1KCE	Abigail Serrano	VQ5ZZZ
3	Bob McCall	QQ5QQQ	Abigail Serrano	VQ5ZZZ
4	Abigail Serrano	VQ5ZZZ	Josephine Wykovic	YQ9LLL
5	Abigail Serrano	VQ5ZZZ	Grant Fritchey	KC1KCE
6	Abigail Serrano	VQ5ZZZ	Bob McCall	QQ5QQQ

Figure 20-3. *Which radio operators have called out to which other operators*

This is just one example of how a graph database works. However, it's not an exciting example. If we take Listing 20-8 and create and load traditional tables, I can show the same behavior.

Listing 20-8. Building a relational table to do the same thing

```
CREATE TABLE rel.RadioOperator
(
    RadioOperatorID int IDENTITY(1, 1) NOT NULL,
    OperatorName varchar(50) NOT NULL,
    CallSign varchar(9) NOT NULL
);
CREATE TABLE rel.RadioOperatorCall
(
    CallingOperatorID INT NOT NULL,
    CalledOperatorID INT NOT NULL
);
INSERT INTO rel.RadioOperator
(
    OperatorName,
    CallSign
```

CHAPTER 20 GRAPH DATABASES

```
)
VALUES
('Grant Fritchey', 'KC1KCE'),
('Bob McCall', 'QQ5QQQ'),
('Abigail Serrano', 'VQ5ZZZ');
INSERT INTO rel.RadioOperatorCall
(
    CallingOperatorID,
    CalledOperatorID
)
VALUES
(1, 2),
(1, 3),
(2, 3),
(3, 1),
(3, 2),
(3, 4);
```

With the same data loaded into a many-to-many relationship, we can then write a query like Listing 20-9.

Listing 20-9. Querying the relational table

```
SELECT Calling.OperatorName,
       calling.CallSign,
       CALLED.OperatorName,
       CALLED.CallSign
FROM rel.RadioOperator AS Calling
    JOIN rel.RadioOperatorCall AS roc
        ON Calling.RadioOperatorID = roc.CallingOperatorID
    JOIN rel.RadioOperator AS CALLED
        ON roc.CalledOperatorID = CALLED.RadioOperatorID;
```

The results from Listings 20-7 and 20-9 are the same. However, the performance is quite different with the graph query running in 247mcs and the relational query returning in over 1.1ms, five times slower.

Querying Graph Data

We've already seen one example of a query for graph data in Listing 20-7, but getting relationships like that is just the start of what can be done with graph data. The syntax is relatively straightforward. As was already demonstrated in Listing 20-7, there are no substantive changes to the SELECT and FROM clauses. The only real change there is that you won't use an ON clause to put the relationships together. Instead, within the WHERE clause, you'll use the new MATCH function along with ASCII-art to define the relationship. Here is the WHERE clause again:

```
WHERE MATCH(Calling-(C)->Called);
```

I'm defining a node, Calling, to node, Called, relationship through the edge table, C. The direction consists of a dash on either side of the edge table and a dash and arrow showing the direction of the relationship on the other side of the graph table. I could rewrite it this way:

```
WHERE MATCH(Called<-(C)-Calling);
```

The use of the arrow is what is meant by ASCII-art. You can even extend the relationships and add filtering. For example, Listing 20-10 shows how a query shows all the people I called and who they called.

Listing 20-10. Multiple relationships

```
SELECT Calling.OperatorName,
       Calling.CallSign,
       CALLED.OperatorName,
       CALLED.CallSign,
       TheyCalled.OperatorName,
       TheyCalled.CallSign
FROM grph.RadioOperator AS Calling,
    grph.Calls AS C,
    grph.RadioOperator AS CALLED,
    grph.Calls AS C2,
    grph.RadioOperator AS TheyCalled
WHERE MATCH(Calling-(C)->CALLED-(C2)->TheyCalled)
          AND Calling.RadioOperatorID = 1;
```

CHAPTER 20 GRAPH DATABASES

I can add traditional filtering to limit the data returned. It all functions as you would expect. The results are in Figure 20-4.

	OperatorName	CallSign	OperatorName	CallSign	OperatorName	CallSign
1	Grant Fritchey	KC1KCE	Abigail Serrano	VQ5ZZZ	Josephine Wykovic	YQ9LLL
2	Grant Fritchey	KC1KCE	Abigail Serrano	VQ5ZZZ	Grant Fritchey	KC1KCE
3	Grant Fritchey	KC1KCE	Abigail Serrano	VQ5ZZZ	Bob McCall	QQ5QQQ

Figure 20-4. *The people called by the people I called*

You can also write a query to find everyone who called the same person as shown in Listing 20-11.

Listing 20-11. Relationships can occur in multiple directions

```
SELECT AllCalled.CallSign AS WasCalledBy,
       WeCalled.CallSign AS CALLED,
       TheyCalled.CallSign AS AlsoCalled
FROM grph.RadioOperator AS AllCalled,
     grph.RadioOperator AS WeCalled,
     grph.RadioOperator AS TheyCalled,
     grph.Calls AS C,
     grph.Calls AS C2
WHERE MATCH(Wecalled-(C)->Allcalled<-(C2)-TheyCalled)
ORDER BY WasCalledBy ASC;
```

So each set of relation is expressed to a common person in the same way, from a node table, through an edge table to a node table. The results are shown in Figure 20-5.

CHAPTER 20 GRAPH DATABASES

	WasCalledBy	CALLED	AlsoCalled
1	KC1KCE	VQ5ZZZ	VQ5ZZZ
2	QQ5QQQ	VQ5ZZZ	VQ5ZZZ
3	VQ5ZZZ	KC1KCE	KC1KCE
4	VQ5ZZZ	KC1KCE	QQ5QQQ
5	VQ5ZZZ	QQ5QQQ	KC1KCE
6	VQ5ZZZ	QQ5QQQ	QQ5QQQ
7	YQ9LLL	VQ5ZZZ	KC1KCE
8	YQ9LLL	VQ5ZZZ	VQ5ZZZ
9	YQ9LLL	KC1KCE	KC1KCE
10	YQ9LLL	KC1KCE	VQ5ZZZ

Figure 20-5. *Relationships can be expressed in multiple ways*

There is one additional piece of functionality within the graph data that we should explore: the ability to track a path through relationships.

Shortest Path

The shortest path function, SHORTEST_PATH, allows you to find several different things:

- The single shortest path between two nodes
- The shortest path between multiple nodes
- A single source path

Basically, this action is performed by aggregating and ordering a set of relationships as a PATH. Once that data is defined, using functions and syntax within the MATCHING clause, you can then apply aggregate functions such as STRING_AGG to aggregate on a string, COUNT to see a path count, and LAST_VALUE to see the end of the path.

All this requires some changes to the standard syntax. Listing 20-12 illustrates the changes.

Listing 20-12. Implementing SHORTEST_PATH in a graph query

```
SELECT op1.OperatorName,
       STRING_AGG(op2.OperatorName, '->')WITHIN GROUP(GRAPH PATH) AS
    Friends, LAST_VALUE(op2.OperatorName)WITHIN GROUP(GRAPH PATH) AS
    LastNode, COUNT(op2.OperatorName)WITHIN GROUP(GRAPH PATH) AS levels
```

CHAPTER 20 GRAPH DATABASES

```
FROM grph.RadioOperator AS op1,
     grph.Calls FOR PATH AS C,
     grph.RadioOperator FOR PATH AS op2
WHERE MATCH(SHORTEST_PATH(op1(-(C)->op2)+));
```

I'll start at the FROM clause. You'll notice that we've now added the syntax FOR PATH to two of the tables: grph.Calls and grph.RadioOperator. That informs the engine that these tables are involved in a path operation.

Next, the MATCH command has added the function SHORTEST_PATH. Further, the definition of the path has also changed. We're starting with op1 the same as any of the other examples. However, we're placing the path definition within parentheses so that it is separated from just normal relationships. We've also added a plus (+) sign to indicate that the pattern can be repeated as many times as necessary to find the path. You can limit that using an integer value.

Finally, back in the SELECT operation, I've used three aggregate values to show the STRING_AGG, LAST_VALUE, and COUNT. That lets us see the basic layout of the paths as shown in Figure 20-6.

	OperatorName	Friends	LastNode	levels
1	Grant Fritchey	Abigail Serrano	Abigail Serrano	1
2	Grant Fritchey	Josephine Wykovic	Josephine Wykovic	1
3	Bob McCall	Abigail Serrano	Abigail Serrano	1
4	Abigail Serrano	Grant Fritchey	Grant Fritchey	1
5	Abigail Serrano	Bob McCall	Bob McCall	1
6	Abigail Serrano	Josephine Wykovic	Josephine Wykovic	1
7	Grant Fritchey	Abigail Serrano->Grant Fritchey	Grant Fritchey	2
8	Grant Fritchey	Abigail Serrano->Bob McCall	Bob McCall	2
9	Bob McCall	Abigail Serrano->Grant Fritchey	Grant Fritchey	2
10	Bob McCall	Abigail Serrano->Bob McCall	Bob McCall	2
11	Bob McCall	Abigail Serrano->Josephine Wykovic	Josephine Wykovic	2
12	Abigail Serrano	Grant Fritchey->Abigail Serrano	Abigail Serrano	2

Figure 20-6. *The paths and levels showing which operators have called who*

We can also take advantage of a function called LAST_NODE that lets us use the final node in a path with other paths such as this one showing only radio operators using a radio called "Xiegu G90" in Listing 20-13.

650

Listing 20-13. Adding additional relationships to a path

```
SELECT op1.OperatorName,
       STRING_AGG(op2.OperatorName, '->')WITHIN GROUP(GRAPH PATH) AS
Friends,
       LAST_VALUE(op2.OperatorName)WITHIN GROUP(GRAPH PATH) AS LastNode,
       COUNT(op2.OperatorName)WITHIN GROUP(GRAPH PATH) AS levels
FROM grph.RadioOperator AS op1,
     grph.Calls FOR PATH AS C,
     grph.RadioOperator FOR PATH AS op2,
        grph.Uses AS u,
        grph.Radio AS r
WHERE MATCH(SHORTEST_PATH(op1(-(C)->op2)+) AND LAST_NODE(op2)-(u)->r)
AND r.RadioName = 'Xiegu G90';
```

The LAST_NODE knows that it's going to be using values from the defined node, in this case, op2, to match to another path, through our grph.Uses and grph.Radio edge and node. Note that neither is defined as FOR PATH since they're used in a normal graph set.

There is more that can be done with querying graph data, but from these examples, you get the understanding. This is a point where AI could also be put to work. For example, I can actually pass my data structure to an AI—for this example I'm using Perplexity—and then ask it to generate a graph query for me. It came back with a functional query and an explanation for how it works as shown in Figure 20-7.

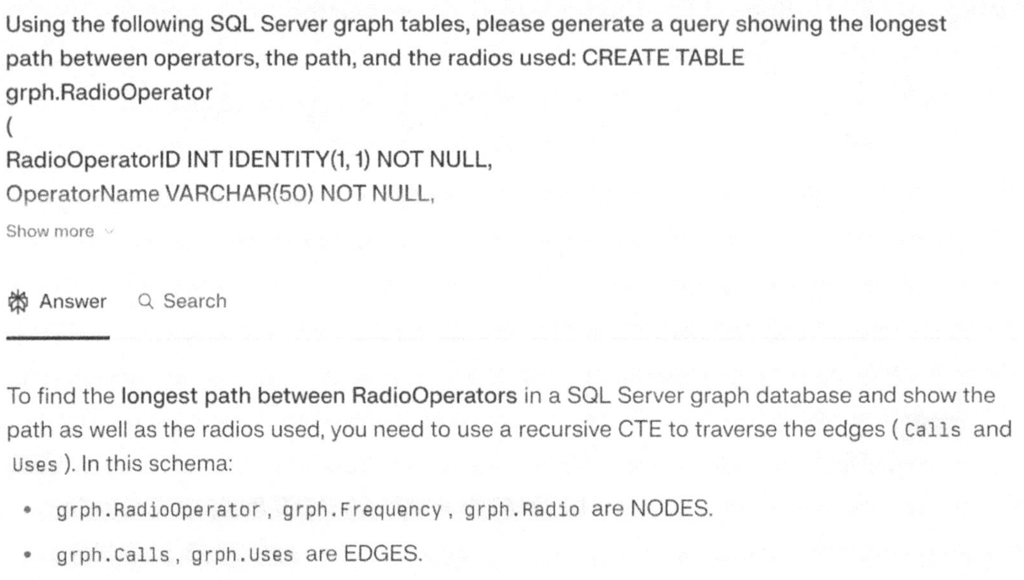

CHAPTER 20   GRAPH DATABASES

Using the following SQL Server graph tables, please generate a query showing the longest path between operators, the path, and the radios used: CREATE TABLE grph.RadioOperator
(
RadioOperatorID INT IDENTITY(1, 1) NOT NULL,
OperatorName VARCHAR(50) NOT NULL,

Show more

✦ Answer   Q Search

To find the **longest path between RadioOperators** in a SQL Server graph database and show the path as well as the radios used, you need to use a recursive CTE to traverse the edges (`Calls` and `Uses`). In this schema:

- `grph.RadioOperator`, `grph.Frequency`, `grph.Radio` are NODES.
- `grph.Calls`, `grph.Uses` are EDGES.

Figure 20-7. *The beginning of the results of an AI search*

Now, let's examine the performance implications of graph data.

Performance Considerations of Graph Data

As you've already seen, for a simple comparison between traditional many-to-many relational structures and graph structures, the performance comparison between Listings 20-7 and 20-9 is stark. For this small data set, we saw a five times improvement in speed. However, more can be attained. Let's take a look at the execution plan from Figure 20-8.

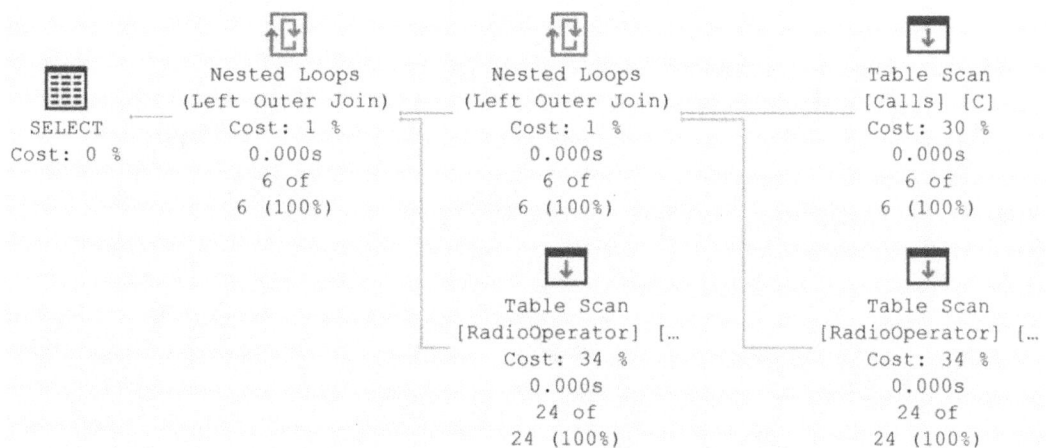

Figure 20-8. A fairly normal execution plan from a graph query

As you can see, this is a relatively standard execution plan with few surprises. Indexes are created on the graph tables as you create the tables, a unique, nonclustered index acting as a primary key. However, you can add your own indexes. In fact, Microsoft recommends that you define an index on the $NodeID columns of node tables as you define them. You should also add an index to edge tables on the $from_id and $to_id columns. In Listing 20-14, I do just that, putting a clustered index in place.

Listing 20-14. Creating an index on an edge table

```
CREATE UNIQUE CLUSTERED INDEX CallsToFrom ON grph.Calls ($from_id, $to_id);
```

With that index in place, let's take a look at the execution plan now (Figure 20-9).

CHAPTER 20 GRAPH DATABASES

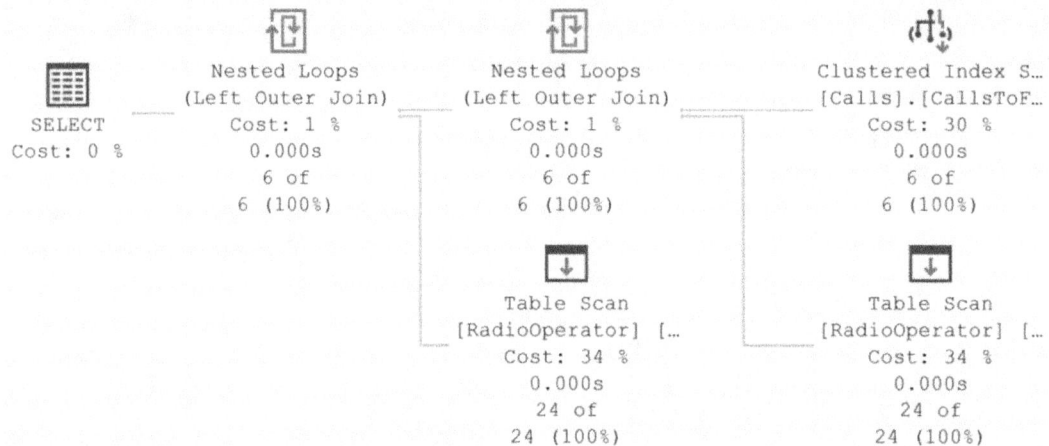

Figure 20-9. Table scan has been replaced

The Calls table is no longer being scanned. Instead, we have a Clustered Index Seek. With this tiny data set, performance only improved marginally, from 247mcs to 210mcs. Reads went from 39 to 38. With a larger data set, and additional indexes on other tables, those improvements will be much higher.

Obviously, you can keep going from there. Graph tables support clustered and nonclustered indexes, both rowstore and columnstore. You can use INCLUDE columns and more. In short, they act similarly to relational tables.

Graph queries will suffer from the same problems as other queries, so putting functions on columns in the WHERE clause and other bad practices will hurt performance here in the same way.

Summary

This chapter introduced the concept of a graph database within SQL Server consisting of node and edge tables. The most important thing to focus on when working with graph tables is the type of queries you intend to run. If they are many to many, or hierarchical, the graph data type will absolutely improve performance. Get in the habit of creating indexes on the $node_id columns when you create your tables. Also, make sure you add an index to the $from_id and $to_id columns. These can improve performance. Lastly, write your queries with the same thoughts in mind as with relational data avoiding bad code smells.

The next chapter deals with all the mechanisms that Microsoft has introduced to dynamically enhance query performance on the fly: Intelligent Query Processing.

CHAPTER 21

Intelligent Query Processing

As you have seen throughout the book, query tuning isn't easy. Microsoft has recognized this and has introduced a large number of automatic performance enhancements into SQL Server over the last four versions. These are all mechanisms to attempt to deal with common query performance issues without forcing people to rewrite their code or restructure their databases. There are many ways that Microsoft can use the internals of the engine to deal with what would have been in the past problematic code. In this chapter, I'll be covering

- Adaptive query processing
- Approximate query processing
- Table variable deferred compilation
- Scalar UDF inlining

I've already covered other aspects of some of the Intelligent Query Processing including optimized plan forcing and Parameter-Sensitive Plan Optimization in other chapters. I also covered adaptive joins in Chapter 9 while discussing columnstore indexes.

As wonderful as this new technology is, it won't fix bad code choices or poor structures. Even with all these new, better, methodologies for query execution, standard tuning will still have to take place. However, even a well-tuned system will see benefits from various aspects of Intelligent Query Processing.

CHAPTER 21 INTELLIGENT QUERY PROCESSING

Adaptive Query Processing

Adaptive query processing is Microsoft's attempt to deal with what has in the past been best handled by changes to code and structure. Some options within SQL Server aren't always the best for query performance such as multi-statement table-valued functions. Adaptive query processing attempts to deal with these through several processes:

- Adaptive joins (which were already covered)
- Interleaved execution
- Query processing feedback
- Optimized plan forcing (covered in Chapter 6)

Interleaved Execution

I have a standing recommendation to avoid using multi-statement table-valued functions, and nothing I'm about to share with you changes that recommendation. However, there are still going to be situations where you have these functions in place and your performance could suffer.

Starting in SQL Server 2017, however, Microsoft has changed the way that multi-statement functions behave. The optimizer can identify that this type of function is being executed. SQL Server can allow those functions to execute and then, based on the rows being processed, can adjust the row counts on the fly in order to get a better execution plan.

To see this in action, I'm going to create three different functions as shown in Listing 21-1.

Listing 21-1. Multi-statement user-defined table-valued functions

```
CREATE OR ALTER FUNCTION dbo.SalesInfo
()
RETURNS @return_variable TABLE
(
    SalesOrderID INT,
    OrderDate DATETIME,
    SalesPersonID INT,
```

CHAPTER 21 INTELLIGENT QUERY PROCESSING

```sql
        PurchaseOrderNumber dbo.OrderNumber,
        AccountNumber dbo.AccountNumber,
        ShippingCity NVARCHAR(30)
)
AS
BEGIN;
    INSERT INTO @return_variable
    (
        SalesOrderID,
        OrderDate,
        SalesPersonID,
        PurchaseOrderNumber,
        AccountNumber,
        ShippingCity
    )
    SELECT soh.SalesOrderID,
           soh.OrderDate,
           soh.SalesPersonID,
           soh.PurchaseOrderNumber,
           soh.AccountNumber,
           A.City
    FROM Sales.SalesOrderHeader AS soh
        JOIN Person.ADDRESS AS A
            ON soh.ShipToAddressID = A.AddressID;
    RETURN;
END;
GO
CREATE OR ALTER FUNCTION dbo.SalesDetails
()
RETURNS @return_variable TABLE
(
    SalesOrderID INT,
    SalesOrderDetailID INT,
    OrderQty SMALLINT,
    UnitPrice MONEY
)
```

```
AS
BEGIN;
    INSERT INTO @return_variable
    (
        SalesOrderID,
        SalesOrderDetailID,
        OrderQty,
        UnitPrice
    )
    SELECT sod.SalesOrderID,
           sod.SalesOrderDetailID,
           sod.OrderQty,
           sod.UnitPrice
    FROM Sales.SalesOrderDetail AS sod;
    RETURN;
END;
GO
CREATE OR ALTER FUNCTION dbo.CombinedSalesInfo
()
RETURNS @return_variable TABLE
(
    SalesPersonID INT,
    ShippingCity NVARCHAR(30),
    OrderDate DATETIME,
    PurchaseOrderNumber dbo.OrderNumber,
    AccountNumber dbo.AccountNumber,
    OrderQty SMALLINT,
    UnitPrice MONEY
)
AS
BEGIN;
    INSERT INTO @return_variable
    (
        SalesPersonID,
        ShippingCity,
```

```
        OrderDate,
        PurchaseOrderNumber,
        AccountNumber,
        OrderQty,
        UnitPrice
    )
    SELECT si.SalesPersonID,
           si.ShippingCity,
           si.OrderDate,
           si.PurchaseOrderNumber,
           si.AccountNumber,
           sd.OrderQty,
           sd.UnitPrice
    FROM dbo.SalesInfo() AS si
        JOIN dbo.SalesDetails() AS sd
            ON si.SalesOrderID = sd.SalesOrderID;
    RETURN;
END;
GO
```

This example is a very common antipattern (code smell) that can be found all over. It's basically an attempt to make SQL Server into more of an object-oriented programming environment. Define one function to retrieve a set of data, a second to retrieve another, then a third that calls the other functions as if they were tables. I've seen this as deep as 75 levels. To say the least, performance was abysmal.

In older versions of SQL Server, prior to 2014, the optimizer assumed these tables returned a single row, regardless of how much data is actually returned. The newer cardinality estimation engine, introduced in SQL Server 2014, assumes 100 rows, if the compatibility level is set to 140 or greater.

In order to see the new interleaved execution in action, first, I'm going to use Listing 21-2 to capture the query metrics after disabling interleaved execution.

Listing 21-2. Executing the functions both ways

```
ALTER DATABASE SCOPED CONFIGURATION SET INTERLEAVED_EXECUTION_TVF = OFF;
GO
SELECT csi.OrderDate,
```

```
            csi.PurchaseOrderNumber,
            csi.AccountNumber,
            csi.OrderQty,
            csi.UnitPrice,
            sp.SalesQuota
FROM dbo.CombinedSalesInfo() AS csi
    JOIN Sales.SalesPerson AS sp
        ON csi.SalesPersonID = sp.BusinessEntityID
WHERE csi.SalesPersonID = 277
      AND csi.ShippingCity = 'Odessa';
GO
ALTER DATABASE SCOPED CONFIGURATION SET INTERLEAVED_EXECUTION_TVF = ON;
ALTER DATABASE SCOPED CONFIGURATION CLEAR PROCEDURE_CACHE;
GO
SELECT csi.OrderDate,
       csi.PurchaseOrderNumber,
       csi.AccountNumber,
       csi.OrderQty,
       csi.UnitPrice,
       sp.SalesQuota
FROM dbo.CombinedSalesInfo() AS csi
    JOIN Sales.SalesPerson AS sp
        ON csi.SalesPersonID = sp.BusinessEntityID
WHERE csi.SalesPersonID = 277
      AND csi.ShippingCity = 'Odessa';
GO
```

Figure 21-1 shows the two execution plans for both queries in Listing 21-2.

CHAPTER 21 INTELLIGENT QUERY PROCESSING

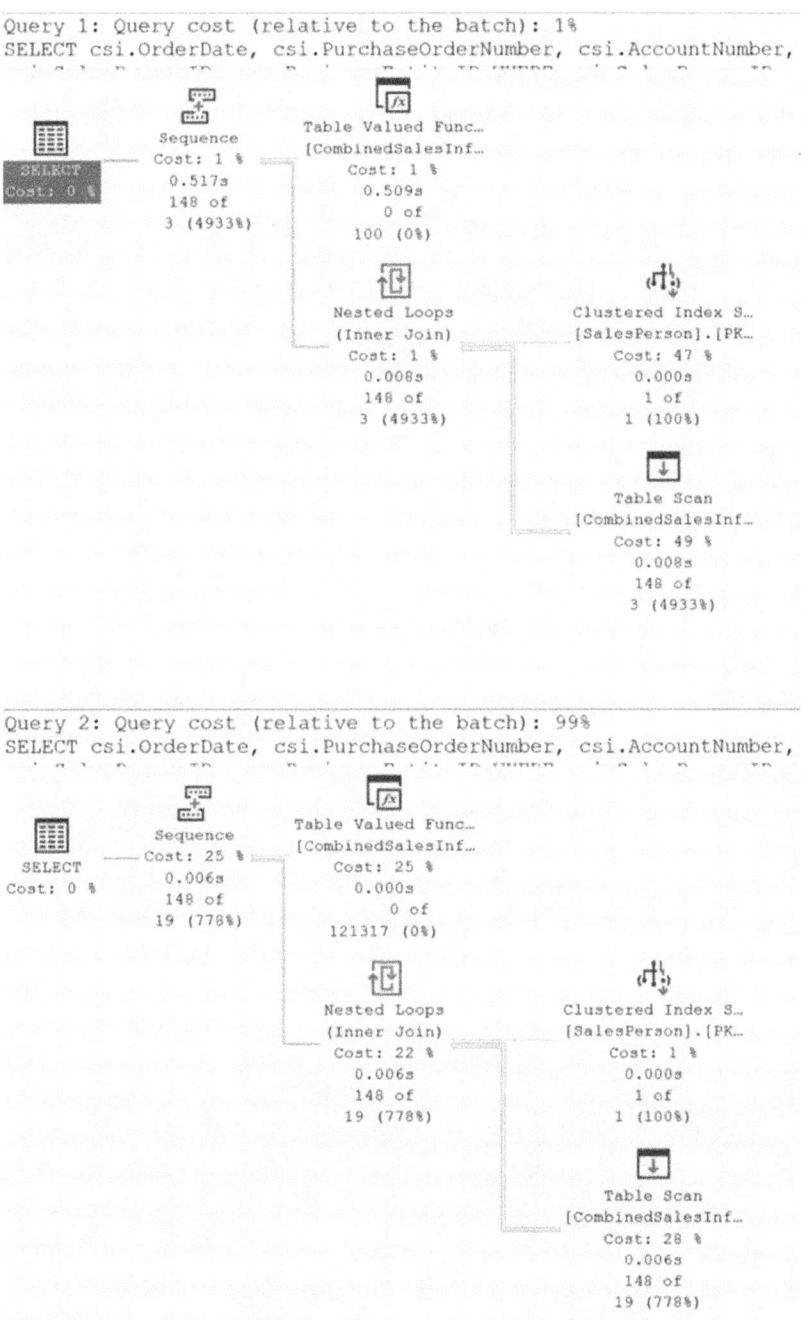

Figure 21-1. *Execution plan for a non-interleaved execution and an interleaved execution*

The overall shape of the execution plans is the same. However, there are very distinct differences. For example, since these queries were run as part of a single batch, each plan is measured against the other. The top plan is estimated at only 1% of the cost of the execution, while the second plan is 99%. Why is that?

In both plans, the Sequence operator runs the subtrees attached to it in order, top to bottom. That means the first thing executed is the table-valued function, CombinedSalesInfo. That function is used to supply data to the Table Scan operation lower in the plan. That Scan operation shows us data movement and, for our purposes, the estimated number of rows. Figure 21-2 shows the properties of that operator from the first plan.

Actual Execution Mode	Row
⊞ Actual I/O Statistics	
⊞ Actual Number of Batches	0
⊞ Actual Number of Rows for All Executions	148
⊞ Actual Number of Rows Read	121317
⊞ Actual Rebinds	0
⊞ Actual Rewinds	0
⊞ Actual Time Statistics	
⊞ Defined Values	[AdventureWorks].[dbo].
Description	Scan rows from a table.
Estimated CPU Cost	0.000267
Estimated Execution Mode	Row
Estimated I/O Cost	0.003125
Estimated Number of Executions	1
Estimated Number of Rows for All Executions	3.16228
Estimated Number of Rows Per Execution	3.16228
Estimated Number of Rows to be Read	100
Estimated Operator Cost	0.003392 (49%)

Figure 21-2. *Properties from scan on the non-interleaved plan*

At the top, you can see the actual number of rows as 148. At the bottom, you can see that the estimates were for 100 rows total and 3.16228 for all executions. It's that disparity in the estimated number of rows, 3.16228 vs. 148, that frequently causes performance headaches when using table-valued functions.

CHAPTER 21 INTELLIGENT QUERY PROCESSING

Figure 21-3 shows the same properties from the second plan, which executed in an interleaved fashion.

Actual Execution Mode	Row
⊞ Actual I/O Statistics	
⊞ Actual Number of Batches	0
⊞ Actual Number of Rows for All Executions	148
⊞ Actual Number of Rows Read	121317
⊞ Actual Rebinds	0
⊞ Actual Rewinds	0
⊞ Actual Time Statistics	
⊞ Defined Values	[AdventureWorks].[dbo].|
Description	Scan rows from a table.
Estimated CPU Cost	0.133606
Estimated Execution Mode	Row
Estimated I/O Cost	0.003125
Estimated Number of Executions	1
Estimated Number of Rows for All Executions	18.663
Estimated Number of Rows Per Execution	18.663
Estimated Number of Rows to be Read	121317
Estimated Operator Cost	0.136731 (28%)

Figure 21-3. *Properties from an interleaved execution*

Of course, the same number of rows was returned since I haven't changed the query or parameters. The interesting parts are at the bottom. Instead of 100 rows, it's clear that we're dealing with larger data sets at 121,317. Also, instead of an estimated 3.16228 rows, we're seeing 18.663. While this isn't perfect as an estimate, it's better, and that's the point.

The differences in execution times between these are trivial. The non-interleaved execution was approximately 542ms with 372,637 reads on average. The interleaved execution was 512ms with 368,636 average reads. The improvement is small, but it is there.

We can improve this considerably if we restructure the code. I'll still use a multi-statement function, but I'll eliminate the internal functions as shown in Listing 21-3.

CHAPTER 21 INTELLIGENT QUERY PROCESSING

Listing 21-3. An improved multi-statement function

```
CREATE OR ALTER FUNCTION dbo.AllSalesInfo
(
    @SalesPersonID INT,
    @ShippingCity VARCHAR(50)
)
RETURNS @return_variable TABLE
(
    SalesPersonID INT,
    ShippingCity NVARCHAR(30),
    OrderDate DATETIME,
    PurchaseOrderNumber dbo.OrderNumber,
    AccountNumber dbo.AccountNumber,
    OrderQty SMALLINT,
    UnitPrice MONEY
)
AS
BEGIN;
    INSERT INTO @return_variable
    (
        SalesPersonID,
        ShippingCity,
        OrderDate,
        PurchaseOrderNumber,
        AccountNumber,
        OrderQty,
        UnitPrice
    )
    SELECT soh.SalesPersonID,
           A.City,
           soh.OrderDate,
           soh.PurchaseOrderNumber,
           soh.AccountNumber,
           sod.OrderQty,
           sod.UnitPrice
```

```
    FROM Sales.SalesOrderHeader AS soh
        JOIN Person.ADDRESS AS A
            ON A.AddressID = soh.ShipToAddressID
        JOIN Sales.SalesOrderDetail AS sod
            ON sod.SalesOrderID = soh.SalesOrderID
    WHERE soh.SalesPersonID = @SalesPersonID
        AND A.City = @ShippingCity;
    RETURN;
END;
GO
```

We can now rewrite our query to execute this function as shown in Listing 21-4.

Listing 21-4. Using parameters instead of a WHERE clause

```
SELECT asi.OrderDate,
       asi.PurchaseOrderNumber,
       asi.AccountNumber,
       asi.OrderQty,
       asi.UnitPrice,
       sp.SalesQuota
FROM dbo.AllSalesInfo(277, 'Odessa') AS asi
    JOIN Sales.SalesPerson AS sp
        ON asi.SalesPersonID = sp.BusinessEntityID;
```

By changing the code so that we're pushing the parameters into the function instead of using a WHERE clause, the interleaved execution can actually get even more accurate estimates. We can see it in the execution plan in Figure 21-4.

CHAPTER 21   INTELLIGENT QUERY PROCESSING

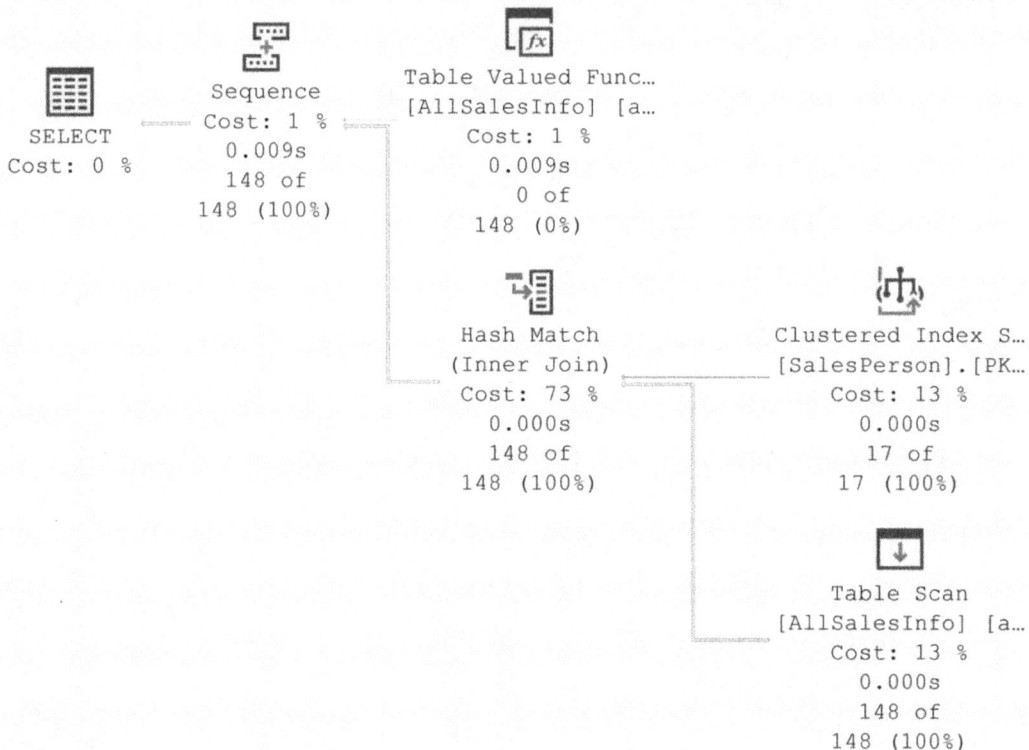

Figure 21-4. A new execution plan with better estimates

The estimated number of rows and the actual number of rows perfectly match. Further, the plan has changed from using a Loops Join to a Hash Match since that will be more effective for the amount of data involved.

Performance went down to 6ms with 1,120 reads, an enormous improvement. However, it's worth noting that the non-interleaved performance improved as well. It was 8.1ms with 1,414 reads. So we're still only talking about 2ms improvement here. As before, faster is faster, and no code changes are required to get the improved performance since interleaved execution is just a part of the engine now.

One more thing to keep in mind when talking about interleaved execution, especially using parameters like this. The plan created is based on the parameters supplied and the data they'll return. That plan is stored in cache. To a degree, this can act like parameter sniffing if you have a wildly varying data set. This is why you have the ability to turn off interleaved execution if you need to. You can also turn it off through a query hint.

Query Processing Feedback

The optimizer makes a number of decisions based on calculations against the statistics and cardinality of the data in the objects involved in a query. Depending on the accuracy of those calculations, performance can be good or bad. Starting with memory grants in SQL Server 2017, the optimizer and the query engine can now use feedback mechanisms to adjust a number of behaviors as queries execute in order to get better performance. The following mechanisms use feedback to change query behavior dynamically:

- Memory grants
- Cardinality estimates
- Degree of Parallelism
- Feedback persistence

Memory Grants

When introduced, memory grant feedback worked only for batch-mode processing. In SQL Server 2019, row-mode memory grant feedback was also introduced. SQL Server 2025 enhanced the feedback algorithms. Part of the calculations from the optimizer is the amount of memory that will need to be allocated to execute a query. If not enough memory gets allocated, then the excess data gets written out to disk through tempdb in a process called a spill. If too much memory is allocated, the query is simply using more than it should. Either way, both these scenarios lead to performance issues.

SQL Server can now adjust the memory allocation after analyzing how memory was used during the execution of the query. Adjustments can be made, up or down, to ensure better performance and better memory management.

To observe this in action, we'll first set up an Extended Events session that lets us capture the memory grant feedback process (Listing 21-5).

Listing 21-5. Creating an Extended Events session for memory grant feedback

```
CREATE EVENT SESSION MemoryGrant
ON SERVER
    ADD EVENT sqlserver.memory_grant_feedback_loop_disabled
    (WHERE (sqlserver.database_name = N'AdventureWorks')),
    ADD EVENT sqlserver.memory_grant_updated_by_feedback
```

```
        (WHERE (sqlserver.database_name = N'AdventureWorks')),
        ADD EVENT sqlserver.sql_batch_completed
        (WHERE (sqlserver.database_name = N'AdventureWorks'))
WITH
(
    TRACK_CAUSALITY = ON
);
GO
ALTER EVENT SESSION MemoryGrant ON SERVER STATE = START;
```

For this session, in the event a query is suffering from parameter sensitivity, also known as parameter sniffing, memory grant feedback could be all over the map. The engine can recognize this, and the memory_grant_feedback_loop_disabled event will fire for that query. When a query experiences changes in its memory allocation due to feedback, the next event, memory_grant_updated_by_feedback, will return information about the feedback process. Finally, I have the sql_batch_completed event so I can see the query associated with the other events, and I have it all tied together through Causality Tracking (explained in Chapter 3).

To see this in action, I'm going to run a query against the MakeBigAdventure tables we created earlier in the book (available here: http://dataeducation.com/thinking-big-adventure/) as shown in Listing 21-6.

Listing 21-6. Creating the CostCheck procedure

```
CREATE OR ALTER PROCEDURE dbo.CostCheck
(@Cost MONEY)
AS
SELECT p.NAME,
       AVG(th.Quantity),
       AVG(th.ActualCost)
FROM dbo.bigTransactionHistory AS th
    JOIN dbo.bigProduct AS p
        ON p.ProductID = th.ProductID
WHERE th.ActualCost = @Cost
GROUP BY p.NAME;
```

CHAPTER 21 INTELLIGENT QUERY PROCESSING

Executing this procedure with a value to @Cost = 0 results in events in Extended Events, as shown in Figure 21-5.

name	timestamp	attach_activity_i...	attach_activity_i...	batch_text
memory_grant_updated_by_feedback	2025-08-16 0...	34C52EBB-D584...	1	NULL
sql_batch_completed	2025-08-16 0...	34C52EBB-D584...	2	EXEC dbo.CostC...

Event:memory_grant_updated_by_feedback (2025-08-16 09:45:07.6071388)
Details

Field	Value
adjustment_count	0
attach_activity_id.guid	34C52EBB-D584-4EF6-9EA5-9E10A0AEE611
attach_activity_id.seq	1
attach_activity_id_xfer.guid	43B2D38A-C482-417B-83F4-029BBBECAA3F
attach_activity_id_xfer.seq	0
current_execution_count	1
failed_concurrent_update_count	0
history_current_execution_count	0
history_update_count	0
ideal_additional_memory_after_kb	3072
ideal_additional_memory_before_kb	16192
is_persisted_feedback_used	False
memory_summary_by_operator_kb	[{"Node":4,"Granted":18880,"Used":1440},{"Node":6,"Granted":30240,"Used":7040},{"Node":9,"Granted":26880,"Used":688...

Figure 21-5. *Results of memory grant feedback*

A few points are illustrated here. First, by looking at the sequence from Causality Tracking, we can tell that the memory grant feedback occurs before the query finishes executing. We can see, right at the bottom, the amount of memory granted for Node 4 was 18,880, but the memory used was 1,440, a large overallocation. Anything where the allocated memory is more than twice the used memory is considered an overallocation.

However, if you execute the procedure a second time with the same value, you'll find that no memory_grant_updated_by_feedback event occurs. This is because the memory grant has been adjusted and is now stored in cache with the plan.

If you execute the procedure with a different value, say 325.7354 on my system returns only one row (as opposed to over 9,000), the memory grant is not readjusted. This is because the difference is small enough it doesn't require a readjustment.

We can also see this in the execution plan properties of the first operator, within the MemoryGrantInfo property set, as shown in Figure 21-6.

CHAPTER 21   INTELLIGENT QUERY PROCESSING

```
MemoryGrantInfo
    DesiredMemory                          74408
    GrantedMemory                          74408
    GrantWaitTime                          0
    IsMemoryGrantFeedbackAdjusted          YesAdjusting
    LastRequestedMemory                    87528
    MaxQueryMemory                         977264
    MaxUsedMemory                          20488
    RequestedMemory                        74408
    RequiredMemory                         71208
    SerialDesiredMemory                    5632
    SerialRequiredMemory                   2560
```

Figure 21-6. *Evidence of memory grant feedback within an execution plan*

You can see that the optimizer has adjusted the memory allocation based on feedback, and based on the executions, it has adjusted the memory allocation, but it may make more adjustments. Other values can be as follows:

- YesStable: Memory grant feedback has been applied, and it is now stable.

- NoFirstExecution: Memory grant feedback is not generally applied during the first compile and execution.

- NoAccurateGrant: There has been no spill, and more than half the allocated memory is in use.

- NoFeedbackDisabled: There has been thrash; memory adjusts up and down multiple times, probably from parameter sniffing or statistics issues; and memory feedback is disabled.

For this behavior to be automatic, you have to set the compatibility mode to 150 or greater. You can disable, or enable, memory grant feedback using Listing 21-7.

Listing 21-7. Disabling memory grant feedback

```
ALTER DATABASE SCOPED CONFIGURATION SET ROW_MODE_MEMORY_GRANT_FEEDBACK =
OFF; --or ON
```

Memory grant feedback is completely cache dependent. If a plan with feedback is removed from cache, when it is recompiled, it will have to go through the feedback process again. However, it is possible to store this information in the Query Store. I'll discuss that in a separate section on feedback persistence later in the chapter.

This example was a batch-mode execution, but the row-mode processing is exactly the same in both behavior and how to monitor it using Extended Events.

Finally, prior to SQL Server 2022, memory grant feedback was subject to some thrash, meaning if a query needed more memory, it was granted. Then, if the next execution required less, it was cut back again. This can lead to poor performance. So in SQL Server 2022, the memory grant is adjusted as a percentile over time, not as a raw number. That then arrives at a better place for performance. This behavior is on by default, and there's nothing you have to do to enable it. If you choose to disable it, you can alter Database Scoped Configuration using the MEMORY_GRANT_FEEDBACK_PERCENTILE = OFF command.

Cardinality Estimates

Starting with SQL Server 2022, the cardinality estimates can benefit from a feedback process. The compatibility mode for the database has to be 160 or greater, and the Query Store must be enabled. The reason for this is the feedback mechanism uses Query Store hints (described in Chapter 6) to adjust how cardinality is estimated.

We can observe the cardinality estimation (CE) feedback in action through this Extended Events session (Listing 21-8).

Listing 21-8. Observing CE feedback

```
CREATE EVENT SESSION [CardinalityFeedback]
ON SERVER
    ADD EVENT sqlserver.query_ce_feedback_telemetry(),
    ADD EVENT sqlserver.query_feedback_analysis(),
    ADD EVENT sqlserver.query_feedback_validation(),
    ADD EVENT sqlserver.sql_batch_completed();
GO
ALTER EVENT SESSION CardinalityFeedback ON SERVER STATE = START;
```

CHAPTER 21   INTELLIGENT QUERY PROCESSING

There are a limited number of scenarios that are likely to lead to a situation where (CE) feedback can help. The first of these is in dealing with data correlation. In the old cardinality estimation engine (compatibility 70), prior to SQL Server 2014, the assumption was that there is no correlation between columns within a table. The modern cardinality estimation engine (compatibility 120 or greater) assumes a partial correlation between columns. There are of course situations where there is direct correlation between the data in columns as well. CE feedback will look at if the data is underestimated or overestimated compared with the actual rows. It will then apply hints through the Query Store to get better row estimates for the plan.

This simple query from Microsoft's documentation can illustrate the point (Listing 21-9).

Listing 21-9. Filtering on two columns in the table

```
SELECT AddressID,
       AddressLine1,
       AddressLine2
FROM Person.ADDRESS
WHERE StateProvinceID = 79
      AND City = N'Redmond';
```

I've seen the CE feedback fire on the first execution of the query, but usually by the 17th. If you are attempting this on your own, you may have to execute it more than once. The idea is if a query is only called a single time, no need to try to adjust its behavior. However, ultimately, you'll see CE feedback events within the Extended Events session, as shown in Figure 21-7.

name	timestamp
query_ce_feedback_telemetry	2025-08-16 1...
query_feedback_analysis	2025-08-16 1...
sql_batch_completed	2025-08-16 1...
query_feedback_validation	2025-08-16 1...

Figure 21-7. *CE feedback events caused by a query*

The first event to fire is query_ce_feedback_telemetry, and the data it returns looks like the one shown in Figure 21-8.

Field	Value
analysis_count	0
corrective_action	2
filter_strategy	2
guess_type	0
join_strategy	2
max_overestimation	0
max_rowgoalmisestimate	0
max_underestimation	2.72778654285278
new_filter_strategy	1
new_join_strategy	2
new_rowgoal_strategy	2
overestimation_nodes	0
prev_feedback	0
query_id	4
rowgoalmisestimation_nodes	1
total_nodes	0
underestimation_nodes	1

Figure 21-8. *query_ce_feedback_telemetry*

This shows you the data that is being used as a part of the CE feedback process. The columns cover all three scenarios, not just the first one. I've included this for informational purposes. There's not a lot here that you can use for evaluating your own queries or system behaviors. However, you can use it to have the data that Microsoft is using internally.

The next event is query_feedback_analysis, shown in Figure 21-9.

Field	Value
check_queue_size	0
feedback_hint	OPTION(USE HINT('ASSUME_MIN_SELECTIVITY_FOR_FILTER_ESTIMATES'))
max_check_queue_size	12189713
max_validation_queue_size	14627656
plan_id	1
query_id	4
validation_queue_size	0

Figure 21-9. *query_feedback_analysis*

Here, you get the hint that will be used to address the functionality. You also get the plan_id and query_id so you can pull the information straight from the Query Store.

Looking back at Figure 21-7, you'll next see that the query was executed again. After that, you get query_feedback_validation in Figure 21-10.

Field	Value
feedback_validation_cpu_time	1448
feedback_validation_plan_hash	1315970081
original_cpu_time	0
original_plan_hash	1315970081
plan_id	1
query_id	4
stdev_cpu_time	0

Figure 21-10. *query_feedback_validation*

The important information here is the two hash values. In this case, they're the same, showing that while this query was evaluated for CE feedback, no hint was applied at this time.

We can also use the catalog view sys.query_store_plan_feedback to see what's going on with any queries that have been evaluated. Listing 21-10 shows an example query.

Listing 21-10. Retrieving data from sys.query_store_plan_feedback

```
SELECT qsqt.query_sql_text,
       CAST(qsp.query_plan AS XML) AS queryplan,
       qspf.feature_id,
       qspf.feature_desc,
       qspf.feedback_data,
       qspf.STATE,
       qspf.state_desc
FROM sys.query_store_plan_feedback AS qspf
    JOIN sys.query_store_plan AS qsp
        ON qsp.plan_id = qspf.plan_id
    JOIN sys.query_store_query AS qsq
        ON qsq.query_id = qsp.query_id
    JOIN sys.query_store_query_text AS qsqt
        ON qsqt.query_text_id = qsq.query_text_id;
```

The results of the query are here in Figure 21-11.

CHAPTER 21 INTELLIGENT QUERY PROCESSING

query_sql_text	queryplan	feature_id	feature_desc	feedback_data	STATE	state_desc
1 SELECT AddressID, AddressLine1,	<ShowPlanXML xmlns="http://schemas.microsoft.com...	1	CE Feedback	{"Feedback hints" ""}	4	VERIFICATION_REGRESSED

Figure 21-11. *Status of CE feedback on a query*

The most important information here is the state_desc that lets us know that after evaluation, the plan was regressed back to its original.

The next condition applies to row goals. When a query specifies that a specific number of rows are going to be returned, such as when using the TOP operator, then the optimizer will limit all estimates to be below the goal count. However, in the case where data is not uniformly distributed, the row goal may become inefficient. In that case, the CE feedback can disable the row goal scan.

Listing 21-11 shows a query that will cause the evaluation of the CE feedback.

Listing 21-11. Querying the bigProduct table with a TOP operation

```
SELECT TOP (1500)
       bp.Name,
       bp.ProductNumber,
       bth.Quantity,
       bth.ActualCost
FROM dbo.bigProduct AS bp
    JOIN dbo.bigTransactionHistory AS bth
        ON bth.ProductID = bp.ProductID
WHERE bth.Quantity = 10
    AND bth.ActualCost > 357
        ORDER BY bp.Name;
```

Executing this 17 times does get me a query_ce_feedback_telemetry event. I also get an entry in sys.query_store_plan_feedback. However, the result is NO_RECOMMENDATION. The evaluator for the CE decided that even attempting a hint wouldn't be worth it on this query.

The final scenario is related to join predicates. Depending on the CE engine, either 70 or 120 and greater, different assumptions are made regarding the correlation of join predicates. The old behavior was similar to compound keys, full correlation is assumed, and the filter selectivity is calculated and then the join selectivity. This is referred to as simple containment. The modern CE assumes no correlation, base containment, where the join selectivity is calculated first and then the WHERE and HAVING clauses get added.

Listing 21-12 shows this type of CE feedback.

Listing 21-12. Querying the bigProduct and bigTransactionHistory tables

```
--intentionally using SELECT *
SELECT *
FROM dbo.bigTransactionHistory AS bth
    JOIN dbo.bigProduct AS bp
        ON bp.ProductID = bth.ProductID
WHERE bth.Quantity = 10
    AND bth.ActualCost > 357;
```

Figure 21-12 shows the output for the query_feedback_analysis event.

Field	Value
check_queue_size	0
feedback_hint	OPTION(USE HINT('ASSUME_FULL_INDEPENDENCE_FOR_FILTER_ESTIMATES'))
max_check_queue_size	12189713
max_validation_queue_size	14627656
plan_id	7
query_id	46
validation_queue_size	0

Figure 21-12. *New feedback hint being evaluated*

So there is the new hint, *ASSUME_FULL_INDEPENDENCE_FOR_FILTER_ ESTIMATES*; in short, it tested whether simple containment would work better for this query.

You can disable CE feedback using ALTER DATABASE SCOPED CONFIGURATION SET CE_FEEDBACK = OFF. You can turn it back on the same way. You can also pass a query hint, DISABLE_CE_FEEDBACK.

If you have a hint in the query, you're using Query Store hints, or you're forcing a plan, CE feedback won't occur. You can, however, override the hints using Database Scoped Configuration again, this time setting FORCE_CE_FEEDBACK = ON.

Degree of Parallelism (DOP) Feedback

Parallel execution of queries can be extremely beneficial for some queries. However, there are other queries that suffer badly when they go parallel. As I discussed in Chapter 2, the best way to deal with getting the right plans to go, or not go, parallel is to use the Cost Threshold for Parallelism. Even then, some queries that exceed that threshold may still suffer from poor performance due to parallelism.

To see DOP feedback in action, the Query Store must be enabled, and you must be at compatibility level 160 or higher. In SQL Server 2025, the DOP feedback mechanism is on by default. With older versions of SQL Server, you have to alter the database as shown in Listing 21-13.

Listing 21-13. Turning on DOP feedback

```
ALTER DATABASE SCOPED CONFIGURATION SET DOP_FEEDBACK = ON;
```

In order to see how the DOP feedback occurs, we can use Extended Events to set up a session as shown in Listing 21-14.

Listing 21-14. Extended Events session for monitoring DOP feedback

```
CREATE EVENT SESSION [DOPFeedback]
ON SERVER
    ADD EVENT sqlserver.dop_feedback_eligible_query(),
    ADD EVENT sqlserver.dop_feedback_provided(),
    ADD EVENT sqlserver.dop_feedback_reverted(),
    ADD EVENT sqlserver.dop_feedback_validation(),
    ADD EVENT sqlserver.sql_batch_completed();
```

Setting up a demo for DOP feedback is complicated. It requires even more data than we've loaded into AdventureWorks so far. Instead of listing all the required code here, making the book artificially larger, I'm going to suggest you reference this example by Bob Ward: https://github.com/microsoft/bobsql/blob/master/demos/sqlserver2022/IQP/readme.md (github.com).

Running these examples takes a long time depending on the machine you're using. However, eventually, you'll get the example query to run a few times. At which point, our first Extended Event will fire, dop_feedback_eligible_query, with the output shown in Figure 21-13.

Details

Field	Value
adjusted_elapsed_time_ms	64974
cpu_time_ms	449746
disable_dop_feedback_hint	False
internal_query	False
is_eligible	True
plan_id	37
query_dop	20
query_hash	18160936266318353147
query_hash_signed	-285807807391198469
query_id	37
query_plan_hash	4128150668158729174
query_plan_hash_signed	4128150668158729174
recompile_hint	False
sql_text	EXEC Warehouse.GetStocklte...
statement_key_hash	752307041
total_elapsed_time_ms	68112

Figure 21-13. *A query that may benefit from DOP feedback*

This won't immediately cause changes in behavior. Instead, through the use of the query_hash and plan_hash values, the engine is now tracking the behavior of this query. After a larger number of executions, the next event fires, dop_feedback_provided. The details are shown in Figure 21-14.

Details

Field	Value
avg_adjusted_elapsed_time_ms	57458
avg_cpu_time_ms	226982
avg_parallelism_wait_time_ms	933914
baseline_avg_adjusted_elapsed_time_ms	57458
baseline_avg_cpu_time_ms	226982
baseline_avg_parallelism_wait_time_ms	933914
baseline_std_dev_adjusted_elapsed_time_ms	8626
baseline_std_dev_cpu_time_ms	45129
baseline_std_dev_parallelism_wait_time_ms	151557
feedback_dop	16
plan_id	37
query_dop	20
query_hash	18160936266318353147
query_hash_signed	-285807807391198469
query_id	37
query_plan_hash	4128150668158729174
query_plan_hash_signed	4128150668158729174
sql_text	EXEC Warehouse.GetStockIte..
statement_key_hash	752307041
std_dev_adjusted_elapsed_time_ms	8626
std_dev_cpu_time_ms	45129
std_dev_parallelism_wait_time_ms	151557

Figure 21-14. *A suggested change to the DOP for this query*

There is useful information here to help you track which query, which statement, the plan, etc. However, the interesting piece is the fact that the query DOP has been 20 and is now suggested to be better at 16.

Figure 21-15 shows the beginning of the testing process with dop_feedback_validation.

Details

Field	Value
avg_adjusted_elapsed_time_ms	57458
avg_cpu_time_ms	226982
avg_parallelism_wait_time_ms	933914
baseline_avg_adjusted_elapsed_time_ms	57458
baseline_avg_cpu_time_ms	226982
baseline_avg_parallelism_wait_time_ms	933914
baseline_std_dev_adjusted_elapsed_time_ms	8626
baseline_std_dev_cpu_time_ms	45129
baseline_std_dev_parallelism_wait_time_ms	151557
feedback_dop	16
plan_id	37
query_dop	20
query_hash	18160936266318353147
query_hash_signed	-285807807391198469
query_id	37
query_plan_hash	4128150668158729174
query_plan_hash_signed	4128150668158729174
sql_text	EXEC Warehouse.GetStockIte..
statement_key_hash	752307041
std_dev_adjusted_elapsed_time_ms	8626
std_dev_cpu_time_ms	45129
std_dev_parallelism_wait_time_ms	151557

Figure 21-15. Validating that the suggested DOP change is working

You get the information showing you the behaviors that are being measured and their standard deviation from the baseline. On my machine, a second feedback was provided, taking the Degree of Parallelism from 16 to 12. Then more validations are run against the new feedback. Ultimately, you'll either see a validation run feedback_state value is "Stable," meaning it has found the DOP adjustments to have worked, or you'll see it revert to the previous DOP.

The engine will try this more than once. After it achieves an actual improvement, it will lock it into place. The lowest it will go is a DOP value of 2.

Feedback Persistence

The ability to get feedback on memory, statistics, and Degree of Parallelism and then adjust query behavior based on the feedback is actually pretty wonderful. However, prior to SQL Server 2022, that feedback did not persist, meaning when a query went out of cache, any history of it having benefited from feedback was lost. Now, with the Query Store, by default, the feedback is persisted to the Query Store. This means when a query is removed from cache, for whatever reason, when it gets recompiled, the existing feedback applied to the query is used again when compiling the new plan. This is a massive win in regard to performance with all the feedback processes.

Only feedback that has been validated is written out permanently. Otherwise, it's in evaluation and won't be persisted until it passes.

Prior to SQL Server 2022, there was a possibility of seeing the memory grant feedback oscillate between a min and a max on the memory allocation. After SQL Server 2022, multiple data points, multiple executions of the query, were used to arrive at a percentile allocation of memory over time. This makes for a more steady state allocation and less of a tendency toward memory spills (writing memory out to disk).

You can disable this behavior using Database Scoped Configuration settings through MEMORY_GRANT_FEEDBACK_PERSISTENCE = OFF. When you set this to OFF, it's off for all the feedback mechanisms. They're all driven through this one setting.

Approximate Query Processing

Getting precise counts in aggregations is vital for some queries. Even though this accuracy may be costly, you'll have to use it for some queries. However, other queries may not need a perfectly accurate accounting. There are three approximate functions you can use to get faster, if less accurate, data:

- APPROX_COUNT_DISTINCT
- APPROX_PERCENTILE_CONT
- APPROX_PERCENTILE_DISC

Unlike a lot of the other aspects of Intelligent Query Processing, the approximate functions require a change to code.

APPROX_COUNT_DISTINCT

This first function, APPROX_COUNT_DISTINCT, is the easiest to explain and understand. It's simply taking an approximation of data instead of a precise count. We can best explore this with two example queries, both in Listing 21-15.

Listing 21-15. Comparing COUNT and APPROX_COUNT_DISTINCT

```
SELECT COUNT(DISTINCT bth.TransactionID)
FROM dbo.bigTransactionHistory AS bth
GROUP BY bth.TransactionDate,
        bth.ActualCost;
GO
SELECT APPROX_COUNT_DISTINCT(bth.TransactionID)
FROM dbo.bigTransactionHistory AS bth
GROUP BY bth.TransactionDate,
        bth.ActualCost;
GO
```

The performance here is slightly better, from 103 seconds to 93 seconds, for the APPROX_COUNT_DISTINCT. The goal for this function is to deal with large data sets, in the millions of rows, and to avoid spills that are common with a COUNT(DISTINCT...) query.

Documentation says that a 2% error rate is likely with a 97% probability. In short, it's going to be close in places where close works well enough.

APPROX_PERCENTILE_CONT and APPROX_PERCENTILE_DISC

PERCENTILE_CONT is used to calculate a percentile over a continuous distribution. Therefore, APPROX_PERCENTILE_CONT is a way to get the same percentile, but by doing it this way, it will result in less overall accuracy. PERCENTILE_DISC is used to return a specific value across a distribution based on the input. APPROX_PERCENTILE_DISC is once more an approximation to help with performance. Listing 21-16 shows two examples that look for the median value across a data set.

Listing 21-16. Comparing the functions and the approximate functions

```
SELECT DISTINCT
       bp.NAME,
       PERCENTILE_CONT(0.5)WITHIN GROUP(ORDER BY bth.ActualCost) OVER
       (PARTITION BY bp.NAME) AS MedianCont,
       PERCENTILE_DISC(0.5)WITHIN GROUP(ORDER BY bth.ActualCost) OVER
       (PARTITION BY bp.NAME) AS MedianDisc
FROM dbo.bigTransactionHistory AS bth
    JOIN dbo.bigProduct AS bp
        ON bp.ProductID = bth.ProductID
WHERE bth.Quantity > 75
ORDER BY bp.Name;
GO
SELECT bp.NAME,
       APPROX_PERCENTILE_CONT(0.5)WITHIN GROUP(ORDER BY bth.ActualCost) AS
       MedianCont,
       APPROX_PERCENTILE_DISC(0.5)WITHIN GROUP(ORDER BY bth.ActualCost) AS
       MedianDisc
FROM dbo.bigTransactionHistory AS bth
    JOIN dbo.bigProduct AS bp
        ON bp.ProductID = bth.ProductID
WHERE bth.Quantity > 75
GROUP BY bp.NAME
ORDER BY bp.Name;
GO
```

The most important aspect of the APPROX* functions is that you are not guaranteed the same result set from one execution to another. They both use a random sampling process that means they won't be working from the same data set every time.

Execution times here are pretty severe. The first query runs about 48 seconds. The second runs in 6.1. Reads for the first query are 244,367. The second query has a varying number of reads as it randomly samples the data. However, generally it was about 140,000 reads.

Interestingly, looking at the data, the approximate functions were fairly close as you can see in Figure 21-16.

	NAME	MedianCont	MedianDisc
52	All-Purpose Bike Stand10000	11300.6197	11300.6197
53	All-Purpose Bike Stand11000	14107.1428	14107.1428
54	All-Purpose Bike Stand12000	12522.6171	12522.6171
55	All-Purpose Bike Stand13000	14209.0272	14209.0272
56	All-Purpose Bike Stand14000	13376.9882	13376.9882

	NAME	MedianCont	MedianDisc
52	All-Purpose Bike Stand10000	11300.6197	11300.6197
53	All-Purpose Bike Stand11000	14107.1428	13964.7788
54	All-Purpose Bike Stand12000	12396.9581	12801.4515
55	All-Purpose Bike Stand13000	14058.890…	14345.1724
56	All-Purpose Bike Stand14000	13286.047…	13393.1183

Figure 21-16. *Accuracy from the approximate functions*

This is consistent with Microsoft's claim that this function will be 1.33% accurate. At least based on the values in the figure, it's doing well.

Table Variable Deferred Compilation

The strength of table variables is the fact that they do not have statistics. This makes them a great choice in scenarios where statistics are not needed and would be painful due to maintenance overhead and recompiles. However, the one weakness of table variables is that they don't have statistics, so the optimizer just makes assumptions about how many rows will be returned: one (1) row. With deferred compilation, the plan involving a table variable isn't completed until actual row counts are available to provide better choices to the optimizer, similar to how temporary tables work, but without the added overhead of recompiles. SQL Server 2025 tuned the plan choices when dealing with table variables in order to better enhance performance.

To be able to take advantage of deferred compilation, the compatibility level has to be 150 or greater. Also, you can use Database Scoped Configuration to disable deferred recompile, DEFERRED_COMPILATION_TV = OFF. That must be enabled.

To see this in action, I'm going to run the same query twice in Listing 21-17.

Listing 21-17. Executing without and with deferred compilation

```
--Disable deferred compilation to see the old behavior
```

```sql
ALTER DATABASE SCOPED CONFIGURATION SET DEFERRED_COMPILATION_TV = OFF;
GO
DECLARE @HeaderInfo TABLE
(
    SalesOrderID INT,
    SalesOrderNumber NVARCHAR(25)
);
INSERT @HeaderInfo
(
    SalesOrderID,
    SalesOrderNumber
)
SELECT soh.SalesOrderID,
       soh.SalesOrderNumber
FROM Sales.SalesOrderHeader AS soh
WHERE soh.DueDate > '6/1/2014';
SELECT hi.SalesOrderNumber,
       sod.LineTotal
FROM @HeaderInfo AS hi
    JOIN Sales.SalesOrderDetail AS sod
        ON sod.SalesOrderID = hi.SalesOrderID;
GO
--Enabled deferred compilation
ALTER DATABASE SCOPED CONFIGURATION SET DEFERRED_COMPILATION_TV = ON;
GO
DECLARE @HeaderInfo TABLE
(
    SalesOrderID INT,
    SalesOrderNumber NVARCHAR(25)
);
INSERT @HeaderInfo
(
    SalesOrderID,
    SalesOrderNumber
)
```

CHAPTER 21 INTELLIGENT QUERY PROCESSING

```
SELECT soh.SalesOrderID,
       soh.SalesOrderNumber
FROM Sales.SalesOrderHeader AS soh
WHERE soh.DueDate > '6/1/2014';
SELECT hi.SalesOrderNumber,
       sod.LineTotal
FROM @HeaderInfo AS hi
    JOIN Sales.SalesOrderDetail AS sod
        ON sod.SalesOrderID = hi.SalesOrderID;
```

The SELECT statement from the first query results in the execution plan in Figure 21-17.

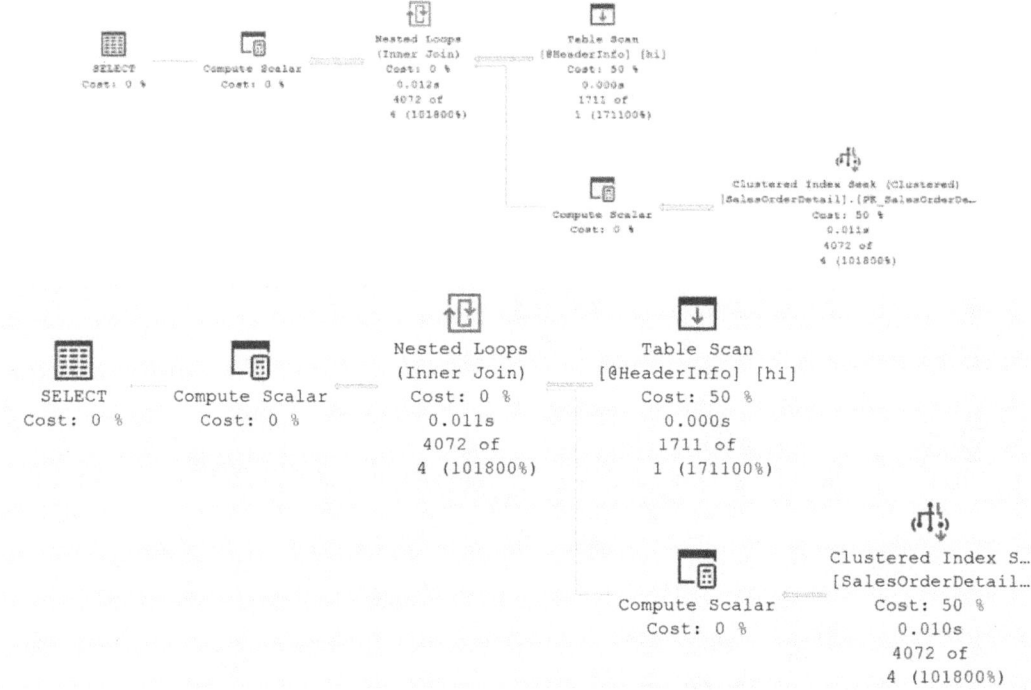

Figure 21-17. *Row counts reflecting the estimate of one row*

If you look at the Table Scan, you can see how there were 1,711 rows returned after an estimate of one. Figure 21-18 shows the plan from the second query.

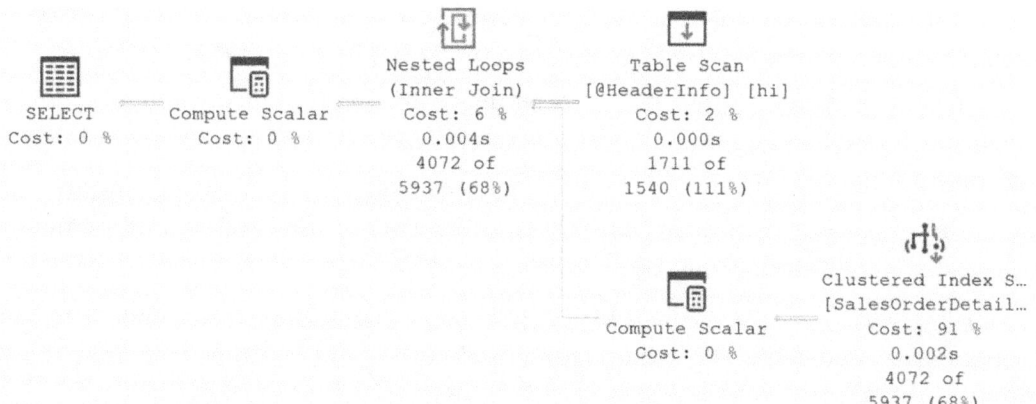

Figure 21-18. *Deferred compilation results in more accurate row counts*

While the basic plan shape in this example didn't change, you can see that the plan is now based on accurate row counts. The Table Scan now shows an estimated value of 1,711 as well as the actual identical count.

Deferred compilation doesn't increase recompile frequency. You may not always see improvements in performance. In fact, if you have a wildly varying row count for your table variables, you may see no benefit from deferred compilation at all.

Scalar User-Defined Function Inlining

User-defined functions can often be a source of problems. I talked earlier about multi-statement, table-valued functions, user-defined functions (UDFs), and their inherent problems (partially addressed through interleaved execution). While inline table-valued functions can perform just fine, they can also be abused. Scalar UDFs are also something that can be a fine tool or can be abused.

The issue with scalar functions is that by their nature, they have to be applied to each row in the query. Some scalar functions, such as simple arithmetic, formatting, and something similar, will perform perfectly fine. Other scalar UDFs, such as ones that independently access data, can perform quite poorly.

The poor performance comes from multiple sources. As already mentioned, each row will get an execution of the function in an iterative fashion. Since scalar functions aren't relational, they are not properly costed by the optimizer, which can lead to poor

CHAPTER 21 INTELLIGENT QUERY PROCESSING

choices. Also, each UDF statement is compiled independently of the rest of the query, potentially missing out on optimizations. Finally, UDFs under the old system are executed serially, with no parallelism, further degrading performance potential.

Starting in SQL Server 2019 (which means a compatibility level of 150 or greater), scalar UDFs are automatically transformed into scalar subqueries. Because they are subqueries, they can be optimized with the rest of the query. This means most of the standard issues with scalar functions are eliminated.

Not all scalar functions can be transformed to inline. In fact, there is a lengthy set of exceptions outlined in the Microsoft documentation here: https://docs.microsoft.com/en-us/sql/relational-databases/user-defined-functions/scalar-udf-inlining?view=sql-server-ver17.

Let's take an example from AdventureWorks shown in Listing 21-18.

Listing 21-18. Scalar UDF dbo.ufnGetProductStandardCost

```
CREATE OR ALTER FUNCTION dbo.ufnGetProductStandardCost
(
    @ProductID int,
    @OrderDate datetime
)
RETURNS money
AS
-- Returns the standard cost for the product on a specific date.
BEGIN
    DECLARE @StandardCost money;
    SELECT @StandardCost = pch.StandardCost
    FROM Production.Product p
        INNER JOIN Production.ProductCostHistory pch
            ON p.ProductID = pch.ProductID
            AND p.ProductID = @ProductID
            AND @OrderDate
            BETWEEN pch.StartDate AND COALESCE(pch.EndDate,
CONVERT(datetime, '99991231', 112)); -- Make sure we get all the prices!
    RETURN @StandardCost;
END;
```

CHAPTER 21   INTELLIGENT QUERY PROCESSING

Since this is already created as a part of the AdventureWorks database, we can validate whether or not the function can be executed inline by running this query in Listing 21-19.

Listing 21-19. Validating whether a query can be executed inline

```
SELECT sm.is_inlineable
FROM sys.sql_modules AS sm
    JOIN sys.objects AS o
        ON o.OBJECT_ID = sm.OBJECT_ID
WHERE o.NAME = 'ufnGetProductStandardCost';
```

When a value of 1 is returned from sys.sql_modules, it means the scalar function can be executed inline.

To see it in action, we'll run the same query twice as shown in Listing 21-20.

Listing 21-20. Executing the scalar UDF within a query

```
--Disable scalar inline
ALTER DATABASE SCOPED CONFIGURATION SET TSQL_SCALAR_UDF_INLINING = OFF;
GO
--not inline
SELECT sod.LineTotal,
       dbo.ufnGetProductStandardCost(sod.ProductID, soh.OrderDate)
FROM Sales.SalesOrderDetail AS sod
    JOIN Production.Product AS p
        ON p.ProductID = sod.ProductID
    JOIN Sales.SalesOrderHeader AS soh
        ON soh.SalesOrderID = sod.SalesOrderID
WHERE sod.LineTotal > 1000;
GO
--Enable scalar inline
ALTER DATABASE SCOPED CONFIGURATION SET TSQL_SCALAR_UDF_INLINING = ON;
GO
--inline
SELECT sod.LineTotal,
```

CHAPTER 21 INTELLIGENT QUERY PROCESSING

```
        dbo.ufnGetProductStandardCost(sod.ProductID, soh.OrderDate)
FROM Sales.SalesOrderDetail AS sod
    JOIN Production.Product AS p
        ON p.ProductID = sod.ProductID
    JOIN Sales.SalesOrderHeader AS soh
        ON soh.SalesOrderID = sod.SalesOrderID
WHERE sod.LineTotal > 1000;
GO
```

Capturing the performance metrics results in the following:

```
Not inline
Duration: 579ms
Reads: 130821
Inline
Duration: 182ms
Reads: 130943
```

While there are slightly more reads with the inline scalar function, you can clearly see that performance was radically improved. It's easy to see why when we take a look at the execution plans (Figure 21-19).

CHAPTER 21 INTELLIGENT QUERY PROCESSING

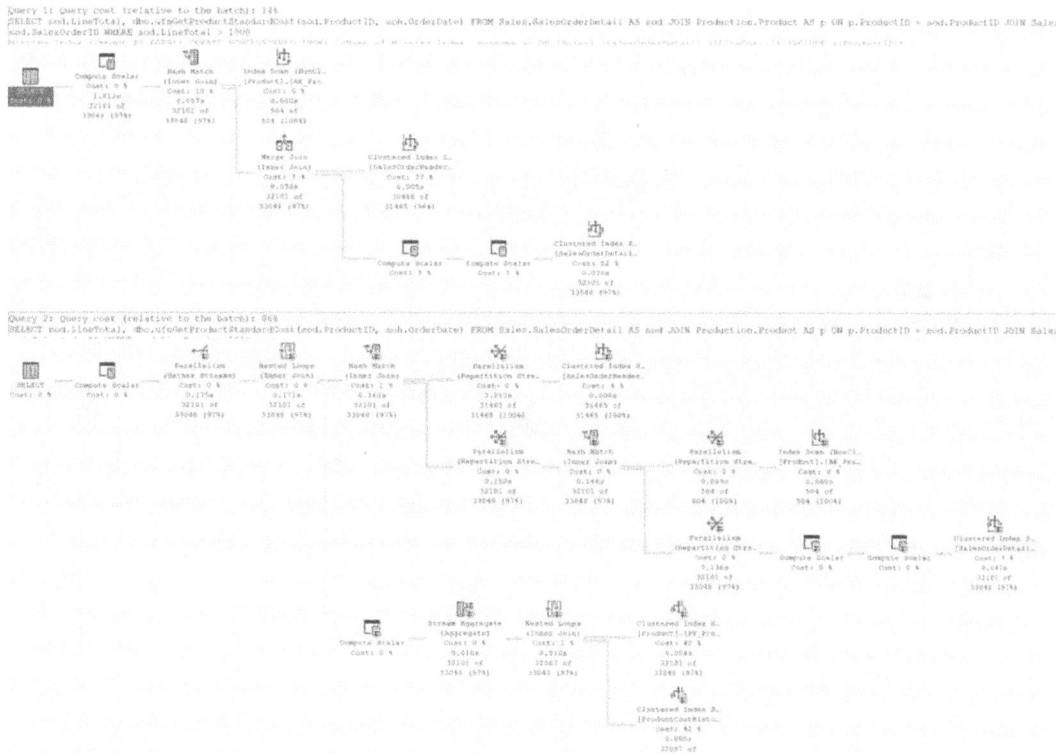

Figure 21-19. *Inline scalar function vs. not inline*

Don't worry about trying to read the details of the plan here in the book. There are a few simple facts that are immediately apparent. First, the plan for the UDF executed without being inline has a Missing Index suggestion, which is absent from the other plan. This implies that the second plan's optimization is probably better since all the indexes it needed were available to it.

Next, you can see that the second execution went parallel. This also helped to enhance performance.

Finally, and you'd have to break down the plan into detail to see it, the location of the production of the data from the UDF queries has moved. In the original plan, the queries necessary to satisfy the UDF are done at the very end of execution, whereas they're done sooner throughout the second plan. Also, there is no Compute Scalar operator for the UDF in the second plan.

Obviously, since the plan has changed, things like hints, the query and plan hash, and dynamic data masking may all work differently. You may also see warnings that were previously masked inside the plan for the scalar function (by the way, that plan can be seen by looking at the estimated plan for a query using a scalar function).

While some queries may not benefit from this functionality, clearly, others will.

Summary

Intelligent Query Processing covers a lot of ground, from automated feedback to changes in the query itself and to code changes that can better support performance. Don't forget that as excellent as this functionality is, and it is excellent, it won't fix bad code or incorrect structures. Standard query tuning is still going to be a part of the process. However, where you have common issues, there may be some solutions that simply occur automatically, thanks to Intelligent Query Processing.

Speaking of automated fixes, the next chapter will cover automated tuning in SQL Server and Azure SQL Database.

CHAPTER 22

Automated Tuning in Azure and SQL Server

Certain aspects of query tuning, especially around simple index creation and recognizing a superior execution plan, are mechanical in nature. A simple evaluation (this makes things faster, or it doesn't) is all that's needed in some situations. With this in mind, Microsoft has automated some aspects of index creation in Azure SQL Database. Also, certain plan choices can be automated within SQL Server and Azure SQL Database. While these mechanisms will absolutely help, especially in the situation where you manage thousands, or more, of databases, you'll still have to develop query tuning skills as well.

This chapter will cover the following:

- Automatic plan correction
- Azure SQL Database automatic index management

Automatic Plan Correction

The simple ability that the Query Store offers (detailed in Chapter 6) is a way to track query and plan behavior over time. With that ability, Microsoft simply wrote functionality into SQL Server that takes advantage of that information. When you can tell that, for a given query, performance degraded after a recompile, getting the last good plan just makes sense.

So when you're in situations such as parameter-sensitive queries (discussed in detail in Chapter 13), Cumulative Updates changing behavior, or just changing data, plans change. Automating tracking when these changes cause regression, worse performance, is straightforward. Basically, Microsoft is following the same process you would:

CHAPTER 22   AUTOMATED TUNING IN AZURE AND SQL SERVER

1. Monitor query performance, using the Query Store, and note when a query's performance degrades.
2. Determine if that regression is from a change in plan.
3. If the plan changed, force the last plan.
4. Measure performance again to determine if that helped.
5. If performance degrades or doesn't improve, undo the change.

While there is doubtless a lot more to this process internally, externally, that's what's happening.

Within SQL Server, this behavior is not on by default. Within Azure SQL Database, it is.

Tuning Recommendations

First, you have to be running SQL Server 2017 or greater or be in Azure SQL Database. Then, the Query Store must be enabled. From this point, SQL Server is already capturing the data needed to identify regressed plans.

To see this in action, we're going to use the tables from MakeBigAdventure again (as a reminder, the script can be downloaded from here: http://dataeducation.com/thinking-big-adventure/). You may need to recreate the tables depending on which experiments you have in place from throughout the book. Listing 22-1 shows the setup needed.

Listing 22-1. Creating indexes and procedures and preparing the Query Store

```
CREATE INDEX ix_ActualCost ON dbo.bigTransactionHistory (ActualCost);
GO
--a simple query for the experiment
CREATE OR ALTER PROCEDURE dbo.ProductByCost
(@ActualCost MONEY)
AS
SELECT bth.ActualCost
FROM dbo.bigTransactionHistory AS bth
    JOIN dbo.bigProduct AS p
        ON p.ProductID = bth.ProductID
```

```
WHERE bth.ActualCost = @ActualCost;
GO
--ensuring that Query Store is on and has a clean data set
ALTER DATABASE AdventureWorks SET QUERY_STORE = ON;
ALTER DATABASE AdventureWorks SET QUERY_STORE CLEAR;
ALTER DATABASE SCOPED CONFIGURATION SET PARAMETER_SENSITIVE_PLAN_
OPTIMIZATION = OFF;
GO
```

The following code can be affected by the Parameter-Sensitive Plan Optimization, so for these tests, I'm going to disable it. With everything set up, we're going to execute the query, using one parameter value to establish a pattern of behavior. With that in place, I'll remove the plan from cache and then establish a new pattern of behavior, all as shown in Listing 22-2.

Listing 22-2. Establishing two different query performance histories

```
--establish a history of query performance
EXEC dbo.ProductByCost @ActualCost = 54.838;
GO 30
--remove the plan from cache
DECLARE @PlanHandle VARBINARY(64);
SELECT  @PlanHandle = deps.plan_handle
FROM    sys.dm_exec_procedure_stats AS deps
WHERE   deps.object_id = OBJECT_ID('dbo.ProductByCost');
IF @PlanHandle IS NOT NULL
    BEGIN
        DBCC FREEPROCCACHE(@PlanHandle);
    END
GO
--execute a query that will result in a different plan
EXEC dbo.ProductByCost @ActualCost = 0.0;
GO
--establish a new history of poor performance
EXEC dbo.ProductByCost @ActualCost = 54.838;
GO 15
```

I have very intentionally executed the query both 30 times in the first instance and 15 in the second. That's because these minimums must be met. The first establishes a baseline of behavior. The second validates that performance has really degraded. After executing these, we can take a look to see if Microsoft has a recommendation. We just have to query sys.dm_db_tuning_recommendations as shown in Listing 22-3.

Listing 22-3. Retrieving tuning recommendations

```
SELECT ddtr.TYPE,
       ddtr.reason,
       ddtr.STATE,
       ddtr.score,
       ddtr.details
FROM sys.dm_db_tuning_recommendations AS ddtr;
```

The results of this query are shown in Figure 22-1.

Figure 22-1. *Tuning recommendations from sys.dm_db_tuning_recommendations*

The type lets us know what kind of tuning opportunity this is (there will be more over time)—in this case, FORCE_LAST_GOOD_PLAN. We'll explore why that is in just a minute. The reason given is that performance went from 1.03ms to 4,607ms, a distinct degradation of performance. The state value lets us know that this is purely advisory since we haven't yet enabled the behavior. There's a score; higher is definitely something to pay attention to. Finally, we get the details as shown here:

{"planForceDetails":{"queryId":31,"queryHash":"0x5F791E9D3FE1F510", "regressedPlanId":3,"regressedPlanHash":"0x04CB9DE3C20315A3","regressedPlan ExecutionCount":15,"regressedPlanErrorCount":0,"regressedPlanCpuTime Average":7.046529466666667e+006,"regressedPlanCpuTimeStddev":5.768587089464084 e+006,"recommendedPlanId":2,"recommendedPlanHash":"0x6F1B019D25F6B1A2", "recommendedPlanExecutionCount":47,"recommendedPlanErrorCount":0,"recommended PlanCpuTimeAverage":1.519361702127659e+002,"recommendedPlanCpuTimeStddev": 2.886145853980385e+002},"implementationDetails":{"method":"TSql","script": "exec sp_query_store_force_plan @query_id = 31, @plan_id = 2"}}

CHAPTER 22 AUTOMATED TUNING IN AZURE AND SQL SERVER

Let's unpack that information so you know what's there in Table 22-1.

Table 22-1. *Details from sys.dm_db_tuning_recommendations*

planForceDetails		
	queryID	31
	queryHash	0x5F791E9D3FE1F510
	regressedPlanId	3
	regressedPlanHash	0x04CB9DE3C20315A3
	regressedPlanExecutionCount	15
	regressedPlanErrorCount	0
	regressedPlanCpuTimeAverage	7.046529466666667e+006
	regressedPlanCpuTimeStddev	5.768587089464084e+006
	recommendedPlanId	2
	recommendedPlanHash	0x6F1B019D25F6B1A2
	recommendedPlanExecutionCount	47
	recommendedPlanErrorCount	0
	recommendedPlanCpuTimeAverage	1.519361702127659e+002
	recommendedPlanCpuTimeStddev	2.886145853980385e+002
implementationDetails		
	method	TSql
	Script	exec sp_query_store_force_plan @query_id = 31, @plan_id = 2

We have yet to enable automated tuning, yet we could put this to work in our own systems. Not only has it identified a query that is clearly regressed based on the execution plan change, but it has provided us with the precise T-SQL to fix the situation.

The question is, how did this happen? Figure 22-2 shows the original execution plan for the first execution of the stored procedure in Listing 22-2.

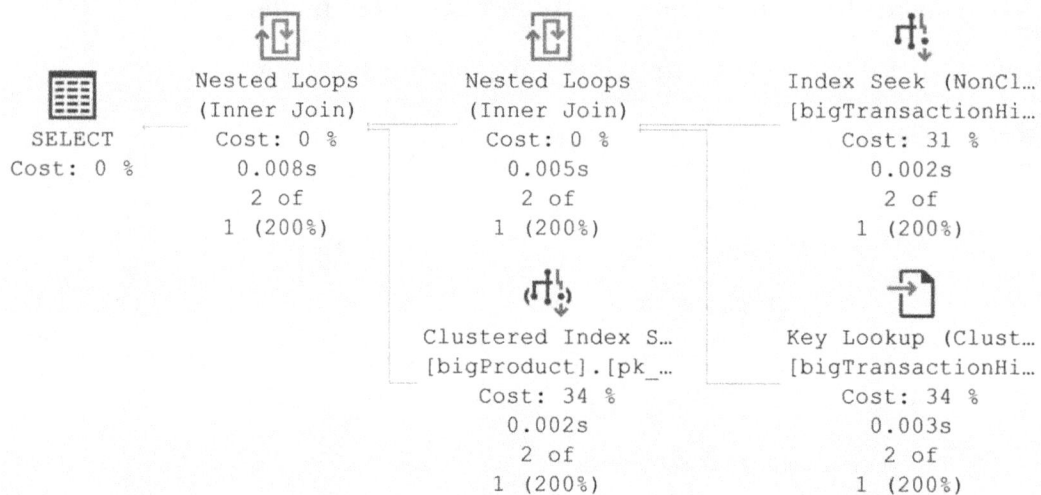

Figure 22-2. First execution of dbo.ProductByCost

Since the query returns only a single row for the value of 54.838, this plan makes sense. By executing it 30 times, I establish a basis of behavior for the query. Please note that 30 seems to work, but that's not a guaranteed value. Microsoft may move that up or down as they see fit.

After the plan is removed from cache, I re-execute the query, but this time with a value of 0.0, which results in the execution plan in Figure 22-3.

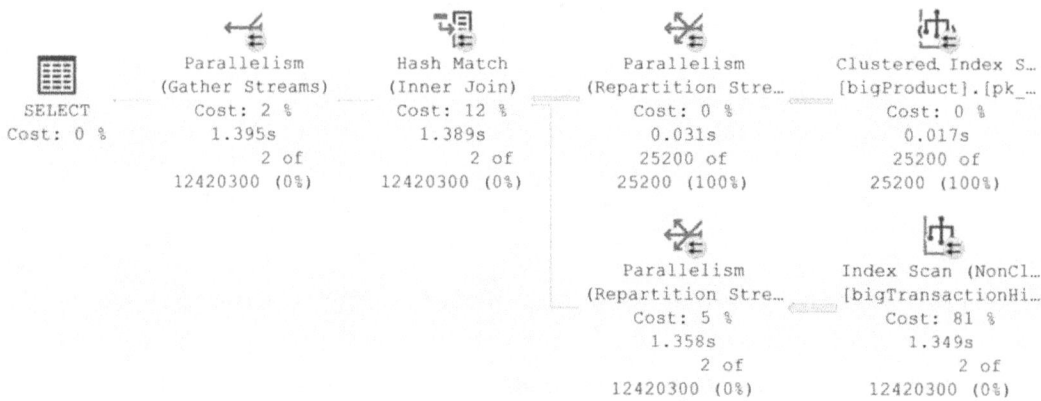

Figure 22-3. Second execution of dbo.ProductByCost after recompile

CHAPTER 22 AUTOMATED TUNING IN AZURE AND SQL SERVER

Since 12 million of the 30-million-row table is returned by this query, this execution plan also makes a lot of sense. However, you can clearly see that one of these plans is optimized for a very large data set, while the other plan is optimized for a very small data set. That difference alone is why performance went from just over 1ms to 42 seconds.

We can get even more sophisticated in querying the tuning recommendations. It's possible to pull the information from within the JSON and combine it with retrieving the execution plans as shown in Listing 22-4.

Listing 22-4. Combining multiple result sets to get detailed recommendations

```
WITH DbTuneRec
AS (SELECT ddtr.reason,
           ddtr.score,
           pfd.query_id,
           pfd.regressedPlanId,
           pfd.recommendedPlanId,
           JSON_VALUE(ddtr.STATE, '$.currentValue') AS CurrentState,
           JSON_VALUE(ddtr.STATE, '$.reason') AS CurrentStateReason,
           JSON_VALUE(ddtr.details, '$.implementationDetails.script') AS
           ImplementationScript
    FROM sys.dm_db_tuning_recommendations AS ddtr
        CROSS APPLY
        OPENJSON(ddtr.details, '$.planForceDetails')
        WITH
        (
            query_id INT '$.queryId',
            regressedPlanId INT '$.regressedPlanId',
            recommendedPlanId INT '$.recommendedPlanId'
        ) AS pfd)
SELECT qsq.query_id,
       dtr.reason,
       dtr.score,
       dtr.CurrentState,
       dtr.CurrentStateReason,
       qsqt.query_sql_text,
       CAST(rp.query_plan AS XML) AS RegressedPlan,
```

```
        CAST(sp.query_plan AS XML) AS SuggestedPlan,
        dtr.ImplementationScript
FROM DbTuneRec AS dtr
    JOIN sys.query_store_plan AS rp
        ON rp.query_id = dtr.query_id
            AND rp.plan_id = dtr.regressedPlanId
    JOIN sys.query_store_plan AS sp
        ON sp.query_id = dtr.query_id
            AND sp.plan_id = dtr.recommendedPlanId
    JOIN sys.query_store_query AS qsq
        ON qsq.query_id = rp.query_id
    JOIN sys.query_store_query_text AS qsqt
        ON qsqt.query_text_id = qsq.query_text_id;
```

With this information in hand, you have everything you need to make your own choice as to whether or not to use plan forcing to fix the problem. You may even decide other solutions are needed. However, these mechanisms give you a fast way to identify problematic queries that may need tuning.

The information in sys.dm_db_tuning_recommendations doesn't survive a restart or failover of the instance. If the database goes offline, this data is also lost. You'll need your own mechanisms to protect this data if you want it to survive a reboot.

Enabling Automatic Tuning

There are two different ways to enable automatic tuning. One is for Azure, and the other is for a SQL Server instance. You must also be running the Query Store on the database in question, which is likely since the Query Store is now on by default in SQL Server since 2022 and Azure SQL Database. Azure supports two mechanisms: the portal and T-SQL. SQL Server requires that everything be done through T-SQL. I'll show you the Azure portal, and then I'll use T-SQL on SQL Server. It will work the same within Azure when using T-SQL.

> **Note** The Azure portal is frequently updated. Screen captures in this book may be out of date at the time you read it. You may see some difference in the graphics and layout.

CHAPTER 22 AUTOMATED TUNING IN AZURE AND SQL SERVER

Azure Portal

Connect to your Azure account and then open an Azure SQL Database to get started. The settings will be on the left side of the screen by default, with details on the right side, something like Figure 22-4.

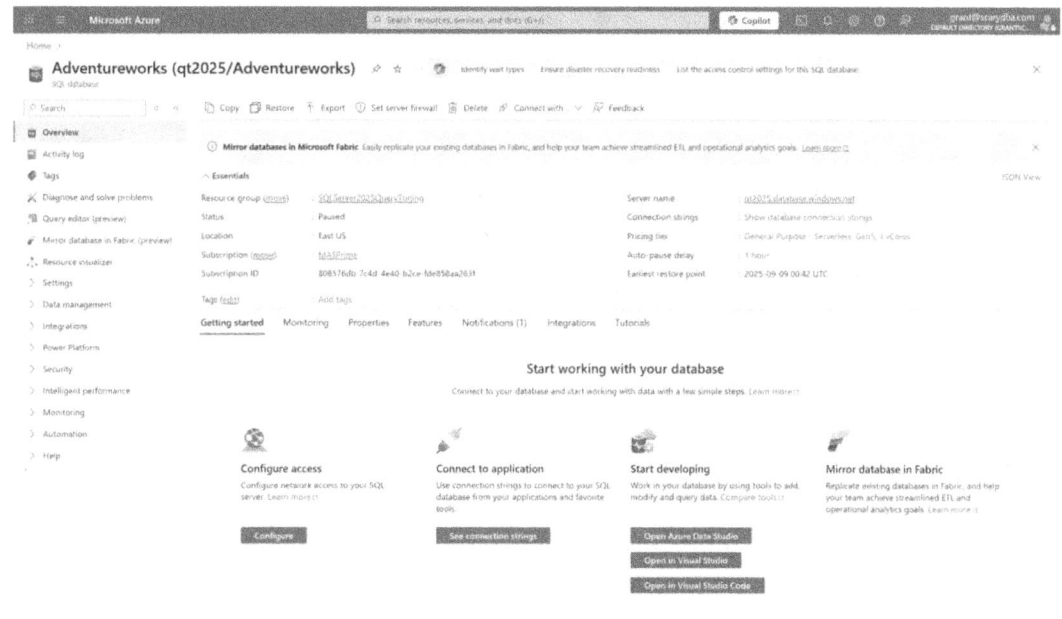

Figure 22-4. *The Azure SQL Database portal*

You can scroll down the left side of the screen until you see Intelligent performance. Expanding that menu choice will look something like Figure 22-5.

701

CHAPTER 22   AUTOMATED TUNING IN AZURE AND SQL SERVER

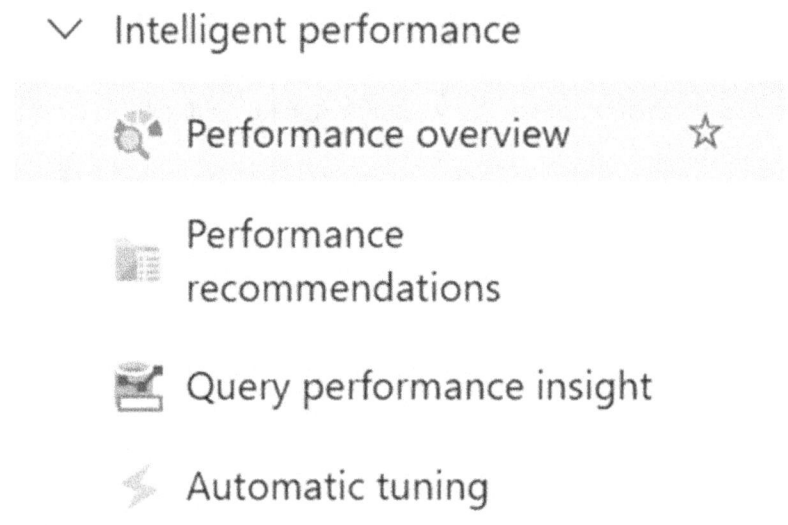

Figure 22-5. Intelligent performance selection in the Azure portal

Selecting "Automatic tuning" from there, or choosing the button that exists on the bottom of the page, will open the details for automatic tuning within your Azure SQL Database as shown in Figure 22-6.

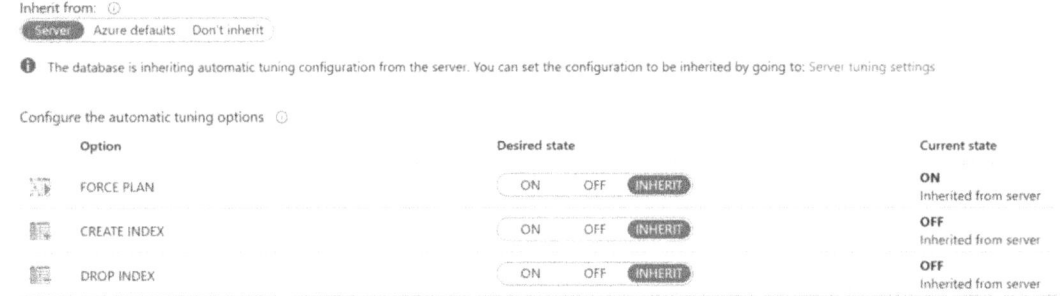

Figure 22-6. Automatic tuning features of the Azure SQL Database

By default, the settings are inherited from the server. The defaults on the server are as you see here:

- FORCE PLAN: ON
- CREATE INDEX: OFF
- DROP INDEX: OFF

CHAPTER 22 AUTOMATED TUNING IN AZURE AND SQL SERVER

We're starting in this section with the FORCE PLAN settings. We'll be covering the other two options later in this chapter in the "Azure SQL Database Automatic Index Management" section.

From this point forward, any tuning recommendations will be automatically applied. You can see the recommendations and any actions on the *performance recommendations* page visible in Figure 22-7.

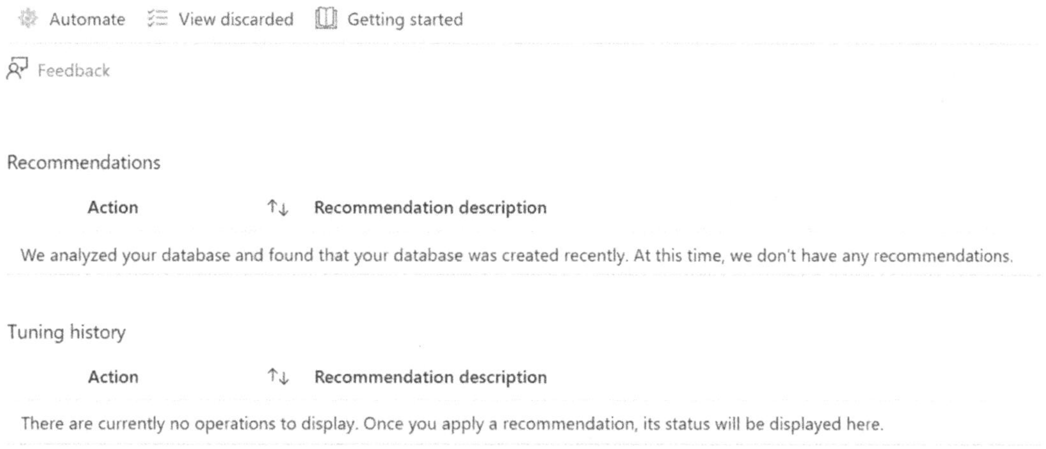

Figure 22-7. Performance recommendations on the portal

This part of the behaviors within Azure is basically the same as on an instance of SQL Server. You can manually apply recommendations if you have the automation turned off. This information can also be lost since it's stored in the same DMVs as a SQL Server instance.

SQL Server

SQL Server Management Studio doesn't have anything like the Azure portal when it comes to automatic tuning. Instead, we'll simply use the T-SQL syntax supplied in Listing 22-5.

Listing 22-5. Enabling automatic tuning using T-SQL

```
ALTER DATABASE CURRENT SET AUTOMATIC_TUNING(FORCE_LAST_GOOD_PLAN = ON);
```

To disable it, you simply run the same command to OFF. You can substitute a database name for the word CURRENT I used in the example.

Automatic Tuning in Action

With automatic tuning in place, we can simply rerun Listing 22-2 to see the plan handled automatically. However, if you're not sure what the status of your automatic tuning is, you can query the settings using Listing 22-6.

Listing 22-6. Validating the status of automatic tuning

```
SELECT NAME,
       desired_state,
       desired_state_desc,
       actual_state,
       actual_state_desc,
       reason,
       reason_desc
FROM sys.database_automatic_tuning_options;
```

Before rerunning Listing 22-2, you might want to clear both the Query Store and the cache. That ensures that you're starting from a clean slate. I only recommend that for testing and development systems. On a production system, you can pull the information for a single query from the Query Store and the same with the cache.

After running Listing 22-2, I can query sys.dm_db_tuning_recommendations using the query in Listing 22-3. Figure 22-8 shows the results.

Figure 22-8. *Results in place with automatic tuning in action*

The CurrentState value is now Verifying, and the reason is "LastGoodPlanForced." This means that SQL Server will continue measuring performance to validate that choosing the last plan was a good decision. If performance doesn't improve or gets worse, then the forced plan will be removed by SQL Server, completely automatically. If there are errors or timeouts, you'll also see the plan forcing removed. That will also mark the plan as error_prone in the sys.dm_db_tuning_recommendations.

If the server were to restart, all the information in sys.dm_db_tuning_ recommendations would be removed, as I've stated several times already. However, any plans that are forced, such as the one for dbo.ProductByCost, will remain forced. However, the verification process, if it wasn't complete, won't be completed.

If you look at the plan through the Query Store DMVs or reports, or even look for the Use Plan property in the execution plan, they'll all be there as if it were a normally forced execution plan. To all respects, it is a normal forced plan.

Azure SQL Database Automatic Index Management

Azure SQL Database is defined as a Platform as a Service (PaaS). In this case, the platform on offer is a SQL Server database. This means that patching, backups, high availability, corruption, and more are all managed by Microsoft through the Azure platform. Adding in the concept of automatic index creation and index drops is perfectly in line with the idea of a PaaS offering of a database.

Since Microsoft has full control over the hardware running within their data centers in Azure, they can also put to work all the information they have with machine learning, analysis, and AI. These are incorporated into their management of Azure SQL Database in general and the automatic index management in particular.

Please note that Microsoft doesn't gather private information from your queries, data, or any of the information stored there. It simply uses the query metrics to measure behavior. You need to know this because there is still misinformation regarding this topic being passed around.

I'm using the AdventureWorksLT database in Azure. There, I'm creating several stored procedures shown in Listing 22-7.

Listing 22-7. Creating stored procedures on the AdventureWorksLT database

```
CREATE OR ALTER PROCEDURE dbo.CustomerInfo
(@Firstname NVARCHAR(50))
AS
SELECT C.FirstName,
       C.LastName,
       C.Title,
       A.City
FROM SalesLT.Customer AS C
    JOIN SalesLT.CustomerAddress AS ca
        ON ca.CustomerID = C.CustomerID
    JOIN SalesLT.ADDRESS AS A
        ON A.AddressID = ca.AddressID
```

```sql
WHERE C.FirstName = @Firstname;
GO
CREATE OR ALTER PROCEDURE dbo.EmailInfo
(@EmailAddress nvarchar(50))
AS
SELECT C.EmailAddress,
       C.Title,
       soh.OrderDate
FROM SalesLT.Customer AS C
    JOIN SalesLT.SalesOrderHeader AS soh
        ON soh.CustomerID = C.CustomerID
WHERE C.EmailAddress = @EmailAddress;
GO
CREATE OR ALTER PROCEDURE dbo.SalesInfo
(@firstName NVARCHAR(50))
AS
SELECT C.FirstName,
       C.LastName,
       C.Title,
       soh.OrderDate
FROM SalesLT.Customer AS C
    JOIN SalesLT.SalesOrderHeader AS soh
        ON soh.CustomerID = C.CustomerID
WHERE C.FirstName = @firstName;
GO
CREATE OR ALTER PROCEDURE dbo.OddName
(@FirstName NVARCHAR(50))
AS
SELECT C.FirstName
FROM SalesLT.Customer AS C
WHERE C.FirstName
BETWEEN 'Brian' AND @FirstName;
GO
```

CHAPTER 22   AUTOMATED TUNING IN AZURE AND SQL SERVER

Before we continue with executing the queries, we have to finish preparing the Azure SQL Database. If you look at Figure 22-9, you can see that I've enabled both index creation and index dropping on my instance.

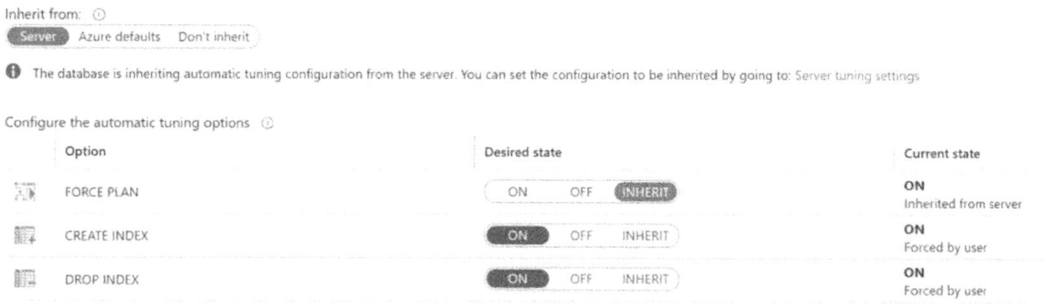

Figure 22-9. Enabling all possible automatic query performance tuning in Azure

To get the queries to run, you could use Microsoft's ostress.exe tool. Or you could write your own PowerShell, maybe using DBATools. I have a simple script here that will run the procedures. You just have to run the queries for approximately 24 hours in order for Azure to recognize that you have a load in place. Listing 22-8 shows that script.

Listing 22-8. PowerShell to execute the procedures in a loop

```
$SqlConnection = New-Object System.Data.SqlClient.SqlConnection
$SqlConnection.ConnectionString = 'Server=qpf.database.windows.net;Database
=QueryPerformanceTuning;trusted_connection=false;user=UserName;password=You
rPassword'
## load customer names
$DatCmd = New-Object System.Data.SqlClient.SqlCommand
$DatCmd.CommandText = "SELECT c.FirstName, c.EmailAddress
FROM SalesLT.Customer AS c;"
$DatCmd.Connection = $SqlConnection
$DatDataSet = New-Object System.Data.DataSet
$SqlAdapter = New-Object System.Data.SqlClient.SqlDataAdapter
$SqlAdapter.SelectCommand = $DatCmd
$SqlAdapter.Fill($DatDataSet)
$Proccmd = New-Object System.Data.SqlClient.SqlCommand
$Proccmd.CommandType = [System.Data.CommandType]'StoredProcedure'
$Proccmd.CommandText = "dbo.CustomerInfo"
```

CHAPTER 22 AUTOMATED TUNING IN AZURE AND SQL SERVER

```
$Proccmd.Parameters.Add("@FirstName",[System.Data.SqlDbType]"nvarchar")
$Proccmd.Connection = $SqlConnection
$EmailCmd = New-Object System.Data.SqlClient.SqlCommand
$EmailCmd.CommandType = [System.Data.CommandType]'StoredProcedure'
$EmailCmd.CommandText = "dbo.EmailInfo"
$EmailCmd.Parameters.Add("@EmailAddress",[System.Data.SqlDbType]"nvarchar")
$EmailCmd.Connection = $SqlConnection
$SalesCmd = New-Object System.Data.SqlClient.SqlCommand
$SalesCmd.CommandType = [System.Data.CommandType]'StoredProcedure'
$SalesCmd.CommandText = "dbo.SalesInfo"
$SalesCmd.Parameters.Add("@FirstName",[System.Data.SqlDbType]"nvarchar")
$SalesCmd.Connection = $SqlConnection
$OddCmd = New-Object System.Data.SqlClient.SqlCommand
$OddCmd.CommandType = [System.Data.CommandType]'StoredProcedure'
$OddCmd.CommandText = "dbo.OddName"
$OddCmd.Parameters.Add("@FirstName",[System.Data.SqlDbType]"nvarchar")
$OddCmd.Connection = $SqlConnection
while(1 -ne 0)
{
    foreach($row in $DatDataSet.Tables[0])
        {
        $name = $row[0]
        $email = $row[1]
        $SqlConnection.Open()
        $Proccmd.Parameters["@FirstName"].Value = $name
        $Proccmd.ExecuteNonQuery() | Out-Null
        $EmailCmd.Parameters["@EmailAddress"].Value = $email
        $EmailCmd.ExecuteNonQuery() | Out-Null
        $SalesCmd.Parameters["@FirstName"].Value = $name
        $SalesCmd.ExecuteNonQuery() | Out-Null
        $OddCmd.Parameters["@FirstName"].Value = $name
        $OddCmd.ExecuteNonQuery() | Out-Null
        $SqlConnection.Close()
 }
 }
```

You also have to ensure that you have the Query Store turned on. It's on by default in Azure SQL Database, so unless you've explicitly turned it off, it's available. If you've turned the Query Store off, turn it back on.

With all this enabled, I'll start running the code to generate a load and leave it in place for at least 24 hours. While you're waiting, if you look at the recommendations, it'll just say the following:

> *We analyzed your database and found that your database was created recently. At this time, we don't have any recommendations.*

The process does require quite a bit of information before it functions. Eventually though, you'll see Figure 22-10.

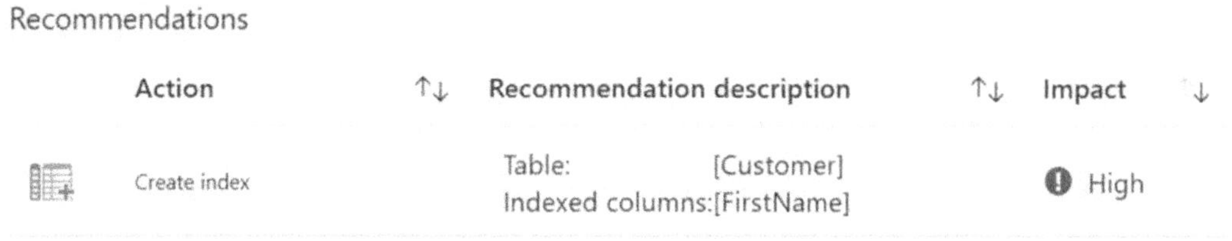

Action	Recommendation description	Impact
Create index	Table: [Customer] Indexed columns:[FirstName]	High

Recommendations

Figure 22-10. *An index tuning recommendation has been made*

If you look at the queries from Listing 22-7, each one has a Missing Index recommendation. They were intentionally written to query data not covered by a good index in order to get scans and Key Lookup operations. These are the precise types of queries that are covered by that somewhat mechanical performance tuning process.

We can see the details in the Azure portal as shown in Figure 22-11.

CHAPTER 22　AUTOMATED TUNING IN AZURE AND SQL SERVER

Create index
[SalesLT].[Customer]

╋ Apply　⊘ Discard　</> View script

Recommended action	Status	Last update	Initiated by
Create index Learn more	Active	9/13/2025 5:47:52 AM	N/A

Estimated impact

Impact	High
Disk space needed	0.29 MB

Details

Index name	nci_msft_1_Customer_578ACD92335C36DF8D59CE26BA4F0DBB
Index type	NONCLUSTERED
Schema	[SalesLT]
Table	[Customer]
Index key columns	[FirstName]
Included columns	

Figure 22-11. Automated tuning recommendation

In this case, the index has not yet been created, but it soon will be. After the index is created, it goes into a process that validates that it worked. Because Microsoft can capture metrics over time, it can use that information to determine if the index worked. In this case, it will work extremely well, radically improving performance.

You can immediately apply the recommendation by clicking the "Apply" button shown in the figure. If the index was already automatically created, you would have a "Revert" button that would drop the index. You can also review the script ahead of applying it or, if it were applied, see what script had been run.

The accuracy of the process is quite high. Since it can only create nonclustered indexes, not clustered ones, this process can't solve all indexing issues in queries. Also, it can't create columnstore indexes when the query pattern is better suited to that style of index.

The process can also drop indexes that you already have in place. However, it won't drop a clustered index, ever. Also, it won't drop unique indexes. There are many reasons for this, but one of the principal ones is that it can be quite hard to determine exactly which queries benefit from a unique index. Since the optimizer can simply use the fact that there exists a unique index as part of determining estimated row counts, it doesn't even have to actually use the index in the plan to get a performance benefit. In short, the process errs on the side of being conservative and cautious.

Summary

As more and more people are managing larger data estates, the ability to be on top of every possible query shrinks. This is why having the ability to automatically get the last good plan can help performance. This type of problem increases on the cloud as people manage large numbers of databases. Getting the simpler aspects of query tuning automated, such as index creation, means that you can spend time on the more complex aspects. Still, as with so many other things, it's always best to test these mechanisms thoroughly in order to understand their benefits and costs in your own system.

The next and final chapter of the book will be an exhaustive checklist of tuning recommendations: a query tuning methodology.

CHAPTER 23

A Query Tuning Methodology

As I stated at the start of the book, query tuning can be challenging. The goal of the book is to, of course, reduce the size of that challenge. With that in mind, this final chapter is intended to act as a kind of guide around applying all the information from the rest of the book. Following the methodology laid out here will enable you to improve the performance of your SQL Server systems.

In this chapter, I'll cover the following topics:

- Database design
- Configuration settings
- Database administration
- Query design

A lot of new information will be introduced throughout this chapter. I'll also be referring back to earlier chapters for a lot of detail on some of the topics we'll cover here.

Database Design

While more and more databases seem to be created from tools like Entity Framework, relational database design remains a vital part of building databases within SQL Server. I'm not going to attempt to do a treatise on relational storage here. However, a number of topics within the basics of database design directly impact performance. As such, I am going to cover a few aspects of that design:

- Use entity-integrity constraints.
- Maintain domain and referential integrity constraints.

- Adopt index-design best practices.
- Avoid the use of sp_ prefix when naming stored procedures.
- Minimize the use of triggers.
- Put tables into in-memory storage.
- Use columnstore indexes.
- Take advantage of graph storage where appropriate.

Use Entity-Integrity Constraints

The phrase "garbage in, garbage out" must have had data in mind. Data integrity, data cleanliness, is probably the single most important aspect of modern data management and one that is frequently ignored. Simple entity integrity, being able to identify a row as a unique entity within a table, is the foundation of data integrity. The column or columns that uniquely identify rows within a table are the starting point for all database design.

A table can have multiple columns, or sets of columns, that could uniquely identify a given row. For example, the Employee table could have an EmployeeID column, a SEQUENCE or IDENTITY data type, and a SocialSecurityNumber column that identify the row. You may designate the EmployeeID as the primary key, while the SocialSecurityNumber is an alternate key. Those alternate keys can be defined as unique constraints, basically unique indexes.

There remains an ongoing debate about the use of artificial primary keys like the EmployeeID above. Some will argue, with plenty of evidence in their corner, that a better approach is to only use the natural keys, something like SocialSecurityNumber, as the primary key of a database. I've seen both types of designs succeed, but allow me to make a few points in each direction.

IDENTITY columns are frequently made from an INT or BIGINT data type, great choices for an index. Separating the value of the primary key from business knowledge, especially from General Data Protection Regulation (GDPR) personally identifying information (and other legal data management requirements), is an excellent design choice. Another choice is the use of GUIDs as primary keys. They are hard to read and share, making troubleshooting a little more challenging, but overall, they are still a good option, although they make for wider keys, possibly negatively impacting performance. Finally, when using artificial keys, you will still need to have a unique constraint on the natural keys of a table, increasing storage and I/O overhead.

CHAPTER 23　A QUERY TUNING METHODOLOGY

Natural keys, on the other hand, make for simple, clear, human-readable identifiers for a row. They do tend to be wider columns, making for bigger, therefore less performant, indexes. Data tends to change, and changing primary key values has knock-on effects to data storage, foreign keys, and more. Natural keys also are more problematic when it comes to GDPR compliance.

Either approach can work well. Each provides plenty of tuning opportunities. Both approaches will ensure the core entity integrity of your data.

The unique indexes that define data integrity are vital to query performance. The optimizer knows that when a unique index exists, for any given value of the key of the index, only a single row will ever get returned. Columns used in sort operations (also GROUP BY or DISTINCT) benefit from unique constraints. Unique constraints also assist the optimizer in making cardinality estimations, sometimes without even referencing the index itself in the query plan. In fact, you won't see counts increase in sys.dm_db_index_usage_stats from these types of operations.

If we were to remove the UNIQUE constraint from an index, as in Listing 23-1, performance would degrade.

Listing 23-1. Removing a UNIQUE constraint

```
CREATE NONCLUSTERED INDEX AK_Product_Name
ON Production.Product (NAME ASC)
WITH (DROP_EXISTING = ON);
```

The Name column still has unique values, but without the constraint, the optimizer can't know that. If we take a simple query like Listing 23-2, the optimizer has fewer choices to aggregate the data.

Listing 23-2. Using a DISTINCT operation in a query

```
SELECT DISTINCT
       (p.NAME)
FROM Production.Product AS p;
```

This query results in the execution plan shown in Figure 23-1.

715

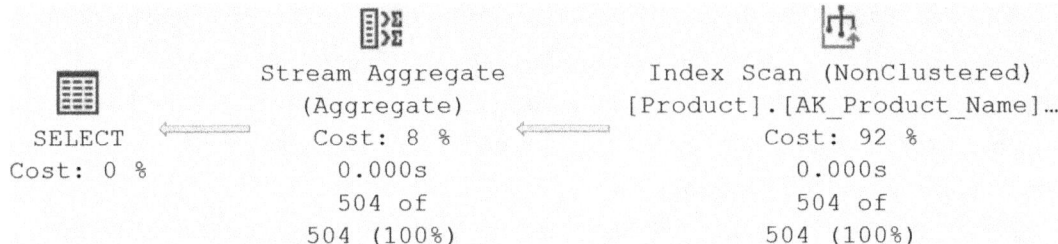

Figure 23-1. An aggregation operation with an execution plan

The index on the Name column is still useful to the optimizer since it's used to retrieve the data. However, because the optimizer doesn't know that data is unique, it uses the Stream Aggregate operator to create a unique data set. If the optimizer knows the data is unique, it makes different choices. Listing 23-3 recreates the original index.

Listing 23-3. Adding UNIQUE back to the index

```
CREATE UNIQUE NONCLUSTERED INDEX AK_Product_Name
ON Production.Product (NAME ASC)
WITH (DROP_EXISTING = ON);
```

Now, rerunning Listing 23-2, a different execution plan is generated (Figure 23-2).

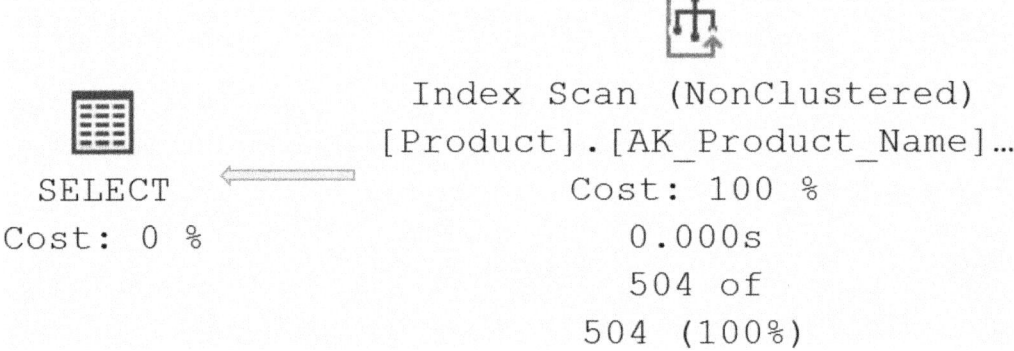

Figure 23-2. A UNIQUE constraint removes the need for aggregation

Entity integrity, unique constraints, provides the optimizer with choices that can result in better performance.

Maintain Domain and Referential Integrity Constraints

Domain and referential integrity may not sound like areas to focus on for performance, but they actually are. Domain integrity for a column is enforced by restricting the data type of the column, defining the format of the data, and limiting the range of acceptable values for the column. Referential integrity is enforced through the use of foreign key constraints between tables.

SQL Server provides the following features to implement the domain and referential integrity:

- Data types
- FOREIGN KEY constraints
- CHECK constraints
- DEFAULT definitions
- NOT NULL definitions

A given business definition of data can be maintained in the application code, in the database code and structures, or through both means. Implementing these types of rules within the database can help the optimizer generate more efficient execution plans.

For example, I'm going to build tables using Listing 23-4.

Listing 23-4. Defining the test tables

```
DROP TABLE IF EXISTS dbo.Test1;
GO
CREATE TABLE dbo.Test1
(
    C1 INT,
    C2 INT CHECK (C2
                BETWEEN 10 AND 20
                )
);
INSERT INTO dbo.Test1
VALUES
(11, 12);
GO
```

```
DROP TABLE IF EXISTS dbo.Test2;
GO
CREATE TABLE dbo.Test2
(
    C1 INT,
    C2 INT
);
INSERT INTO dbo.Test2
VALUES
(101, 102);
```

With these tables defined, I'm going to run two queries from Listing 23-5.

Listing 23-5. Two SELECT statements against a table with a constraint

```
SELECT T1.C1,
       T1.C2,
       T2.C2
FROM dbo.Test1 AS T1
    JOIN dbo.Test2 AS T2
        ON T1.C1 = T2.C2
           AND T1.C2 = 20;
GO
SELECT T1.C1,
       T1.C2,
       T2.C2
FROM dbo.Test1 AS T1
    JOIN dbo.Test2 AS T2
        ON T1.C1 = T2.C2
           AND T1.C2 = 30;
```

These two queries vary only by the hard-coded values in the WHERE clause. The CHECK constraint on the table ensures that there can't possibly be a value of 30. This directly affects the execution plan generated as you see in Figure 23-3.

CHAPTER 23   A QUERY TUNING METHODOLOGY

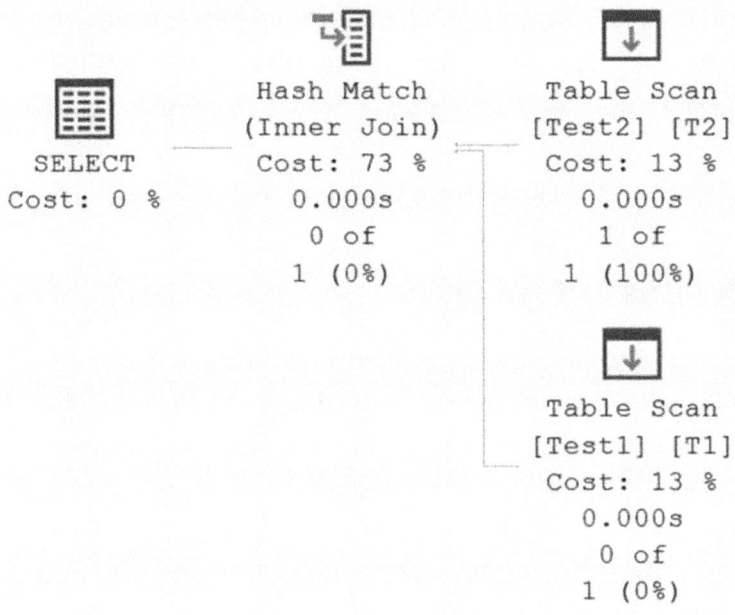

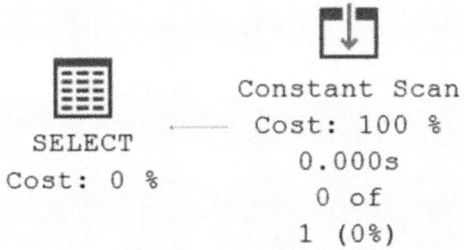

Figure 23-3. *Plans where the predicate is within and outside a CHECK constraint*

The first query, where the data will be within the CHECK constraint, generated a relatively unsurprising execution plan. The second query, where the data is absolutely outside the boundaries of the CHECK constraint, generated what appears to be a somewhat odd plan. The Constant Scan operator in this query is simply supplying the empty columns for the empty result set. The optimizer could tell that no data could possibly be returned from the table for the value in question. So it made sure that there would be an empty result set but otherwise didn't bother reading from the tables.

You should use domain and referential constraints, not simply to implement data integrity, but to facilitate the good choices the optimizer can make. Be sure that you use the WITH CHECK option when creating and maintaining the constraints; otherwise, the optimizer will ignore them. I covered all of this in more detail in Chapter 14.

Adopt Index-Design Best Practices

The single most common approach to enhance performance is to create a new index. Indexes are vital to query performance. While a table can be designed based simply on the knowledge of what's needed for storage, indexes are different. You have to know how you're querying the data in order to build appropriate indexes.

Except in common and obvious cases, such as primary keys and unique indexes supporting alternate keys, a poor design choice is to start building indexes before you know how the data is going to be queried. Even in the case of primary and alternate keys, some thought and planning has to be made around how the data will be queried.

I covered various aspects of indexes and index design in detail in Chapters 9–12 as well as in various other points throughout the book. I'm going to create a simple checklist here for how best to design, build, and apply indexes within your databases:

- Where possible, make the index key columns as narrow as you can.

- Ensure that the selectivity of the data in the column you are indexing is high (i.e., the column has a low number of values returned for a given query).

- Prefer columns with the integer data type (and variants of the integer) and avoid, where possible, indexing on string data types like VARCHAR.

- It's generally best to list columns having higher selectivity first in a multicolumn index.

- Use the INCLUDE list in an index as a way to create covering indexes.

- When choosing how to index for a given query, focus first on the WHERE, JOIN, and HAVING clauses. These filtering processes generally benefit the most from appropriate indexes.

- When choosing the type of index (rowstore or columnstore, clustered or nonclustered), keep in mind the advantages and disadvantages of query types, analytical or point lookups.

Because a clustered index defines data storage, and you only get one per table, there are additional considerations for picking the clustered index:

- Keep the clustered index key as narrow as possible since it will also be in every single nonclustered index.

- Create the clustered index first, and then create nonclustered indexes.

- If required, rebuild a clustered index in a single step using the DROP_EXISTING = ON command in the CREATE INDEX command. You don't want to rebuild all nonclustered indexes twice: once when the clustered index is dropped and again when it gets recreated.

- Avoid creating a clustered index on a frequently updated column. This leads to additional writes on all nonclustered indexes.

You can use sys.dm_db_index_usage_stats to get a pretty good idea which of your indexes are being actively used and which ones may be unnecessary. Indexes that are not used in support of queries are just overhead on your system. However, remember that the data in sys.dm_db_index_usage_stats does get refreshed and may not show all index use, so testing after you remove indexes is a good call.

While the optimizer will give you index suggestions through the Missing Index hints in execution plans and the sys.dm_db_missing_index_* DMVs, remember, these are just suggestions. You should test these indexes, not simply apply them blindly. Also worth noting, the information in the DMVs cannot be correlated with a query, so that information is not very useful.

Avoid the Use of the "sp_" Prefix for Stored Procedure Names

This is a very minor point, but every little bit helps. Procedures that have "sp_" at the front are assumed by the optimizer to be system procedures stored in the master database. So when one of these queries gets called, the optimizer looks first in the master database. If it doesn't find it there, it then looks in the database you're querying. While this is a tiny performance hit, it's easily avoided, so why not simply avoid it?

Minimize the Use of Triggers

Triggers provide an attractive method for automating behavior within the database. Since they fire as data is manipulated by other processes (regardless of the processes), triggers can be used to ensure certain functions are run as the data changes. That same functionality makes them dangerous since they are not immediately visible to the developer or DBA working on a system. They must be taken into account when designing queries and when troubleshooting performance problems. Because they carry a somewhat hidden cost, triggers should be considered carefully. Before using a trigger, make sure that the only way to solve the problem presented is with a trigger. If you do use a trigger, document that fact in as many places as you can to ensure that the existence of the trigger is taken into account by other developers and DBAs.

Put Tables into In-Memory Storage

While there are a large number of limitations on in-memory storage mechanisms, the performance benefits are high. If you have a high-volume OLTP system and you're seeing a lot of contention on I/O, especially around latches, the in-memory storage is a viable option. You may also want to explore using in-memory storage for table variables to help enhance their performance. If you have data that doesn't have to persist, you can even create the table in-memory using the SCHEMA_ONLY durability option. The general approach is to use the in-memory objects to help with high-throughput OLTP where you may have concurrency issues, as opposed to greater degrees of scans, and so on, experienced in a data warehouse situation. All these methods lead to significant performance benefits. But remember, you must have the memory available to support these options. There's nothing magic here. You're enhancing performance by throwing significant amounts of memory, and therefore money, at the problem. The good news is that SQL Server 2025 will allow you to drop the in-memory storage if all objects within it have been removed from the database, allowing for more experimentation and testing.

Use Columnstore Indexes

If the query load on your system is more analytic or data warehouse style, columnstore indexes may be a huge performance enhancer. You can also take advantage of nonclustered columnstore indexes on your OLTP system if there are reporting queries that you need to run there. The thing to remember here is that you can orient your index storage, by picking the right clustered index, so that you support either analytical or OLTP queries.

Take Advantage of Graph Storage

When you have a lot of many-to-many relationships or hierarchy data, you may see performance enhancements by moving data into graph storage. It really does depend on the type of data you have, and it won't help regular queries much at all. If you are storing your data in graph storage, don't forget about using functions like shortest path to gain additional behaviors.

Use Appropriate Data Types

Store your data in the data types that are appropriate to that data. Don't store dates as strings, for example. Sure, you can ensure formatting by storing it that way, but you surrender functionality such as date math in this example. Further, if you then have to convert your data types, or rely on implicit conversions, you negatively impact statistic and index use.

Configuration Settings

The vast majority of all your work is going to be adjusting structures and/or code in order to improve performance. However, there are a few system settings that can help you in your system's performance:

- Memory configuration options

- Cost Threshold for Parallelism

- Max Degree of Parallelism

- Optimize for Ad Hoc Workloads

- Blocked process threshold

- Database compression

Memory Configuration Options

Your SQL Server instances should have the max server memory set on them in order to avoid contention with the operating system or other applications. You can also allocate memory for index creation if that's something you're doing frequently on your system.

Cost Threshold for Parallelism

Queries can absolutely benefit from parallel execution. However, the management of parallel execution (splitting the data into threads, running through the processes, gathering the threads back together) has a lot of overhead. Therefore, simple queries that go parallel frequently don't see a performance benefit. In fact, they may run substantially slower.

A common, very mistaken, way to "fix" this is to set the Max Degree of Parallelism to 1 (I'll cover the Max Degree of Parallelism in more detail in the next section). That takes away the benefit for the more complex queries that would run better.

The right way to adjust which queries go parallel is to change the value of the Cost Threshold for Parallelism. The default value of 5 is far too low for most systems. I always increase that value.

There are two ways you can set a better value for this setting. First would be to query either the cache or Query Store to get your query costs. Listing 23-6 shows an example query that will retrieve the costs from the Query Store.

Listing 23-6. Gathering cost values from the Query Store

```
WITH XMLNAMESPACES
(
    DEFAULT N'http://schemas.microsoft.com/sqlserver/2004/07/showplan'
```

```
)
, QueryStore
AS (SELECT CAST(qsp.query_plan AS XML) AS QueryPlan
    FROM sys.query_store_plan AS qsp),
  QueryPlans
AS (SELECT RelOp.pln.value(N'@EstimatedTotalSubtreeCost', N'float') AS
EstimatedCost, RelOp.pln.value(N'@NodeId', N'integer') AS NodeId,
        qs.QueryPlan
    FROM QueryStore AS qs
        CROSS APPLY qs.queryplan.nodes(N'//RelOp') RelOp(pln) )
SELECT qp.EstimatedCost
FROM QueryPlans AS qp
WHERE qp.NodeId = 0;
```

It would be easy enough to get the same thing from cache. With the values in hand, calculate the average and the standard deviation. Then set your Cost Threshold for Parallelism two, or more, standard deviations above the average.

Another way is to just pick an arbitrary number, start there, and then monitor the system. This is a far less scientific way to approach the problem, but people sometimes find it easier. I'd start with a value of 35. Just make sure you are monitoring to validate if that works well or not.

Max Degree of Parallelism

When a system has multiple processors available, by default, SQL Server will use all of them during parallel executions. To better control the load on the machine, you may find it useful to limit the number of processors used by each parallel execution. Further, you may need to set the affinity so that certain processors are reserved for the operating system and other services running alongside SQL Server. OLTP systems may receive a benefit from disabling parallelism entirely, although that's usually a questionable choice. First, try increasing the Cost Threshold for Parallelism because even in OLTP systems, there are queries that will benefit from parallel execution, especially maintenance jobs. You may also explore the possibility of using the resource governor to control some workloads.

Optimize for Ad Hoc Workloads

Many systems can consist of primarily dynamic or ad hoc T-SQL, not stored procedures or prepared statements. In these cases, enabling the Optimize for Ad Hoc Workloads setting can help reduce memory use. Plan stubs are created and stored instead of whole plans. This was covered in more detail in Chapter 8.

Blocked Process Threshold

The blocked process threshold setting defines in seconds when a blocked process report is fired. When a query runs and exceeds the threshold, the report is fired. An alert, which can be used to send an email or a text message, is also fired. Testing an individual system determines what value to set this to. You can monitor for this using events within Extended Events.

Database Compression

SQL Server has supplied data compression since 2008 with the Enterprise and Developer editions of the product. This can provide a great benefit in space used and in performance as more data gets stored on a page. These benefits come at the cost of added overhead in the CPU and memory of the system; however, the benefits usually far outweigh the costs. Take this into account as you implement compression.

Database Administration

A lot of database administration is focused on high availability and disaster recovery. There are a few administrative activities that directly relate to enhancing performance:

- Keep the statistics up to date.
- Maintain a minimum amount of fragmentation.
- Avoid automatic database functions like AUTOCLOSE or AUTOSHRINK.

Keep Statistics Up to Date

I discussed statistics in detail in Chapter 5. I also reference them throughout the book. This is because statistics are one of the most important tools you have in assisting the optimizer. The more accurate your statistics are, the more accurate your query plans will be. Here are a few things to keep in mind:

- Allow SQL Server to automatically maintain the statistics on your system using the default settings for both AUTO_CREATE_STATISTICS and AUTO_UPDATE_STATISTICS.

- You can programmatically update the statistics on a scheduled basis. Monitor your systems to determine how frequent that should be.

- You can update statistics asynchronously. For some systems, that may be a benefit. For others, it won't be. Measure and test in order to be sure.

- If you schedule both index maintenance and statistics maintenance, be sure to put the statistics first since rebuilding an index automatically rebuilds the statistics. You wouldn't want to then run a statistics update, taking away accuracy.

Maintain a Minimum Amount of Index Fragmentation

My advice here has shifted over the years. I'm much more inclined to suggest working on getting the right fill factor for your indexes is a better use of your time than rebuilding indexes to remove fragmentation. If you are going to defragment your indexes, follow these guidelines:

- Run the defragment process during off hours to avoid blocking and resource contention.

- Determine the level of fragmentation on your indexes and deal with that using the scripts and queries from Chapter 12.

- Remember that very small tables can't be defragmented.

- Index rebuilds in Azure lead to a lot of I/O, which could lead to your system getting throttled.

Avoid Database Functions Such As AUTO_CLOSE or AUTO_SHRINK

AUTO_CLOSE cleanly shuts down a database and frees all its resources when the last user connection is closed. This means all data and queries in the cache are automatically flushed. When the next connection comes in, not only does the database have to restart but all the data has to be reloaded into the cache. Also, stored procedures and the other queries have to be recompiled. That's an extremely expensive operation for most database systems. Leave AUTO_CLOSE set to the default of OFF.

AUTO_SHRINK periodically shrinks the size of the database. It can shrink the data files and, when in Simple Recovery mode, the log files. While doing this, it can block other processes, seriously slowing down your system. More often than not, file growth is also set to occur automatically on systems with AUTO_SHRINK enabled, so your system will be slowed down yet again when the data or log files have to grow. Further, you're going to see the physical file storage get fragmented at the operating system level, seriously impacting performance. Set your database sizes to an appropriate size and monitor them for growth needs. If you must grow them automatically, do so by specific increments, not by percentages.

Query Design

The following are some of the best practices discussed throughout the book in various chapters. Please consider all of these as you write and tune your queries:

- Use the command SET NOCOUNT ON.
- Explicitly define the owner of an object.
- Avoid non-sargable search conditions.
- Avoid large IN clauses.
- Avoid a large number of OR clauses.
- Avoid arithmetic operators and functions on filtered columns.
- Avoid optimizer hints.
- Stay away from nesting views.

CHAPTER 23   A QUERY TUNING METHODOLOGY

- Ensure there are no implicit data type conversions.
- Adopt best practices for reusing execution plans.
- Adopt best practices for database transactions.
- Eliminate or reduce the overhead of database cursors.
- Use natively compiled stored procedures.
- Take advantage of columnstore indexes for analytical queries.
- Enable the Query Store.

Use the Command SET NOCOUNT ON

Always use the command SET NOCOUNT ON as the first statement in stored procedures, triggers, and other batch queries. With NOCOUNT set to ON, you avoid the network overhead caused by the return of a rows-affected count after each SQL statement executes. I covered this in more detail in Chapter 15.

Explicitly Define the Owner of an Object

As a performance best practice, always qualify a database object with its owner to avoid the runtime cost required to verify the owner of the object. The performance benefit of explicitly qualifying the owner of a database object is explained in detail in Chapter 7.

Avoid Non-sargable Search Conditions

One of the most common problems I see in queries is bad search conditions in the WHERE, ON, and HAVING clauses. If the search condition prevents the optimizer from getting good row estimates, then performance will suffer, even if good indexes are in place.

You also have to be very cautious when it comes to designing your search methodologies in your system. A common practice that leads to issues is to write code like you see in Listing 23-7.

CHAPTER 23 A QUERY TUNING METHODOLOGY

Listing 23-7. Querying using LIKE and a wild card

```
SELECT p.ProductID,
       p.Name,
       p.ProductNumber,
       p.SafetyStockLevel,
       p.ReorderPoint,
       p.StandardCost,
       p.ListPrice,
       p.Size,
       p.DaysToManufacture,
       p.ProductLine
FROM Production.Product AS p
WHERE p.NAME LIKE '%Caps';
```

In this case, someone wants to find everything that ends with "Caps." This results in the execution plan you see in Figure 23-4.

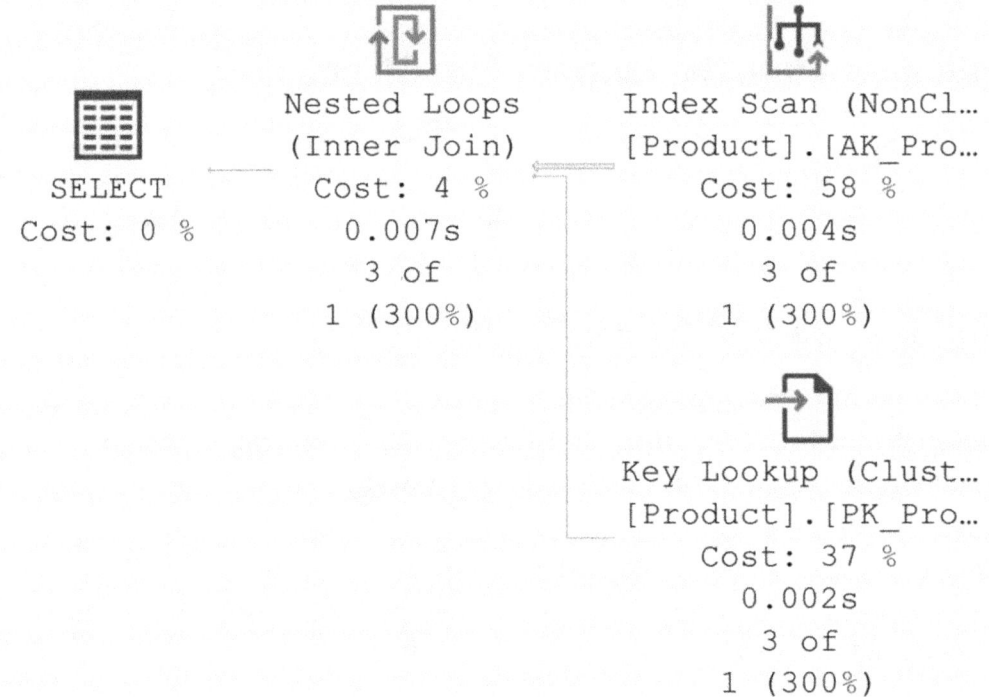

Figure 23-4. *Execution plan with poor performance*

The data is being retrieved based on an index scan. There is no way around it either. You could try using an index hint to improve performance, but chances are that would actually degrade it further.

Avoid Large IN Clauses

There isn't a hard and fast value for the number of values within an IN clause that will absolutely lead to problems. However, as you pass 100 values and certainly when you pass 1,000 or more values, you're very likely to see performance issues. This is a case where restructuring the query becomes extremely important. You're most likely to see very large numbers of IN clause values when working with Object Relational Mapping (ORM) tools. Using temporary tables or table variables can be a viable alternative.

SQL Server 2022 introduced a new Extended Event called query_antipattern. It uses heuristics internally to identify when an overly large set of IN clause values is in a query. It can also identify a large number of OR clauses, MAX values on columns without indexes, and implicit data conversions that could affect index use.

Avoid a Large Number of OR Clauses

Just as with the IN clause, there is no hard number for what defines too many OR clauses. However, generally speaking, we're talking about a dozen or so before you can see degradation in performance, depending on the query of course. Once more if you have more than a dozen OR clauses, restructuring the query to use alternative logic will be necessary. Using the query_antipattern Extended Event can help you identify these queries.

Avoid Arithmetic Expressions on Filter Clauses

Try to avoid using arithmetic operators and functions on columns in the WHERE, ON, and HAVING clauses. Using operators and functions on columns prevents the use of indexes. I covered this in detail in Chapter 14.

To take a quick look at how this works, take a look at Listing 23-8.

CHAPTER 23 ■ A QUERY TUNING METHODOLOGY

Listing 23-8. Two queries returning the same data

```
SELECT soh.SalesOrderNumber
FROM Sales.SalesOrderHeader AS soh
WHERE 'SO5' = LEFT(SalesOrderNumber, 3);
SELECT soh.SalesOrderNumber
FROM Sales.SalesOrderHeader AS soh
WHERE SalesOrderNumber LIKE 'SO5%';
```

Both queries have the same logic, but different approaches. The first query uses the LEFT function on the SalesOrderNumber column. These queries result in the execution plans you see in Figure 23-5.

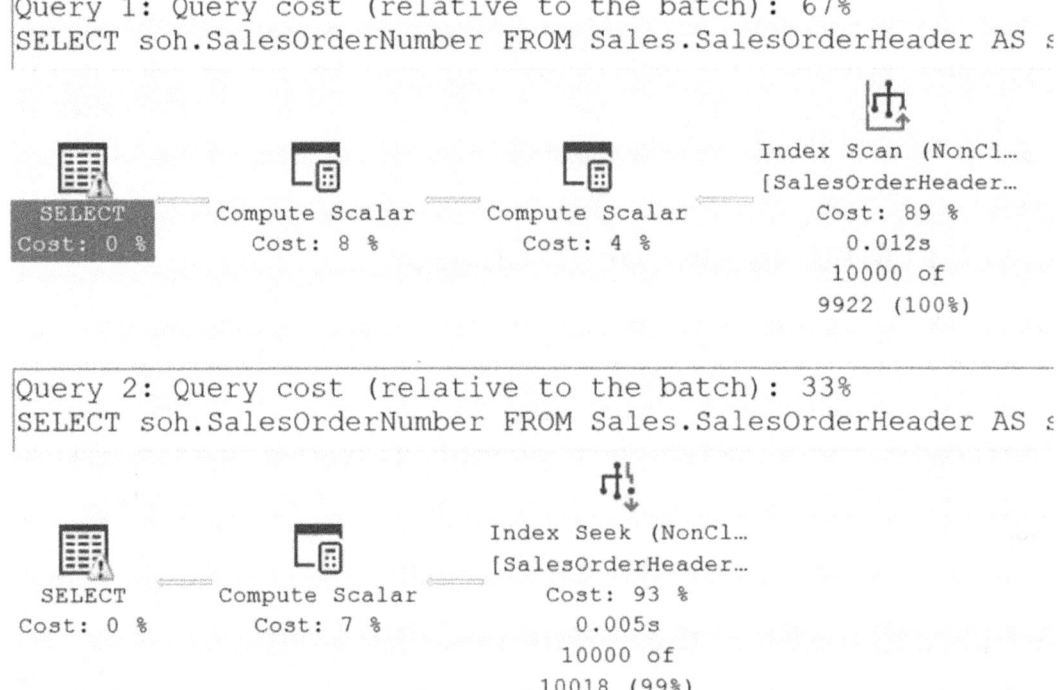

Figure 23-5. *One query not using an index*

The first query goes through an index scan, whereas the second is able to use a seek, which will perform faster.

The warning you see in the plans is caused by an implicit conversion in the calculated column in the SalesOrderHeader table. In this example, that's a false positive since the calculated column isn't used in any filtering criteria.

Avoid Optimizer Hints

There are perfectly valid reasons to apply hints to queries. For example, OPTIMIZE FOR UNKNOWN is one method for addressing parameter sniffing in parameter-sensitive queries. However, frequently, the hints being applied are just taking choices away from the optimizer and therefore hurting performance.

Stay Away from Nesting Views

When you create a view that calls or joins to other views, this is called nesting. This leads to a serious problem. The optimizer doesn't treat views as tables. It treats them as queries, which they are. As a query, the optimizer will be attempting to arrive at a good plan, but across a far more complex query since every query in every view being referenced has to all be put together. The biggest issue is caused when the simplification process of optimization, where objects that aren't needed get eliminated, can take up most of the query tuning process, resulting in timeouts and poor plans. The same rule applies to nesting user-defined functions.

Ensure No Implicit Data Type Conversions

Every variable and parameter should match the data types of the columns. SQL Server can convert, for example, a VARCHAR to a DATE. It's called an implicit conversion. However, it acts just like running an operator or function against the column, preventing index use.

You have to be just as careful in situations like table joins so that the primary key data type of one table matches the foreign key of the table being joined. You may occasionally see a warning in the execution plan to help you with this, but you can't count on this.

Minimize Logging Overhead

SQL Server maintains the old and new states of every atomic action (or transaction) in the transaction log to ensure database consistency and durability. This can place tremendous pressure on the log disk, often making the log disk a point of contention. Therefore, to improve database performance, you must try to optimize the transaction log overhead. In addition to the hardware solutions discussed later in the chapter, you should adopt the following query design best practices:

- Choose table variables over temporary tables for small result sets, less than 20–50 rows, where possible. Remember, if the result set is not small, you can encounter serious issues. The performance benefit of table variables is explained in detail in the "Use Table Variables" section in Chapter 8.

- Batch a number of action queries in a single transaction. You must be careful when using this option because if too many rows are affected within a single transaction, the corresponding database objects will be locked for a long time, blocking all other users trying to access the objects.

- Reduce the amount of logging of certain operations by using the Bulk Logged recovery model. This rule applies primarily when dealing with large-scale data manipulation. You also will use minimal logging when Bulk Logged is enabled, and you will use the WRITE clause of the UPDATE statement or drop or create indexes.

Adopt Best Practices for Reusing Execution Plans

You can help influence how the engine reuses your execution plans. Reuse of plans means that they don't have to be compiled, or recompiled, reducing CPU use quite a lot. There are two general mechanisms you should approach:

- Caching execution plans effectively
- Minimizing recompilation of execution plans

Caching Execution Plans Effectively

The key to reusing plans is storing them in cache in order to later retrieve them for use. There are a number of practices you can follow that will help this process along:

- Avoid executing queries as nonparameterized, ad hoc queries. Instead, parameterize the variable parts of a query and submit the parameterized query either as a stored procedure or as a prepared statement.

- If you must use ad hoc queries, enable the Optimize for Ad Hoc Workloads setting, which will create a plan stuff instead of a full plan the first time a query is called. This increases CPU use somewhat since the plan has to be compiled a second time. However, it helps memory and cache management a lot.

- Use the same environment settings (such as ANSI NULLS) in every connection that executes the same parameterized queries. This is important because the environment settings being different can result in additional execution plans.

- Explicitly qualify the owner of objects in your queries.

Minimize Recompilation of Execution Plans

In support of plan reuse, you want to ensure as few recompiles of those plans as possible. The following practices will absolutely help reduce the amount of recompiles you have:

- Do not interleave DDL and DML statements in your queries. You should put all the DDL statements at the beginning of the code.

- In a stored procedure, avoid using temporary tables created outside that stored procedure.

- Prefer table variables over temporary tables for small data sets.

- Do not change the ANSI SET options within a query.

Adopt Best Practices for Database Transactions

The more effectively you design your queries for concurrency, the faster the queries will be able to complete without blocking one another. Consider the following recommendations while designing the transactions in your queries:

- Keep the scope of the transactions as short as possible. In a transaction, include only the statements that must be committed together for data consistency.

- Prevent the possibility of transactions being left open because of poor error-handling routines or application logic. Do so using the following techniques.

- Use SET XACT_ABORT ON to ensure that a transaction is aborted or rolled back on an error condition within the transaction.

- After executing a stored procedure or a batch of queries containing a transaction from a client code, always check for an open transaction and then roll back any open transactions using the following SQL statement:

    IF @@TRANC0UNT > 0 ROLLBACK

- Use the lowest level of transaction isolation required to maintain data consistency as determined by your application requirements. The amount of isolation provided by the Read Committed isolation level, the default isolation level, is sufficient most of the time. If excessive locking is occurring, consider using the Read Committed Snapshot isolation level.

Eliminate or Reduce the Overhead of Database Cursors

Since SQL Server is designed to work with sets of data, processing multiple rows using DML statements is generally much faster than processing the rows one by one using database cursors. If you find yourself using a lot of cursors, re-examine the logic to see whether there are ways you can eliminate the cursors. If you must use a database cursor, then use the database cursor with the least overhead: the FAST_FORWARD cursor type (generally referred to as the fast-forward-only cursor). You can also use the equivalent DataReader object in ADO.NET.

Use Natively Compiled Stored Procedures

In situations where you're accessing only in-memory tables, you have one additional performance enhancement open to you, which is to compile your stored procedures into a DLL that runs within the SQL Server executable. As was shown in Chapter 24, this has fairly radical performance implications. Just be sure that you call the procedures in the correct fashion passing parameters by ordinal position rather than by parameter name. Although this feels like you're breaking a best practice, it leads to better performance of the compiled procedure.

Take Advantage of Columnstore for Analytical Queries

Most applications using relational databases to store their information have some degree of analytical queries. Either you have an OLTP system with a few analytical queries or you have a data warehouse or reporting system with a lot of analytical queries. Take advantage of columnstore indexes in support of the queries that do a lot of aggregation and analysis. A clustered columnstore is best when the majority of the queries are analytical but doesn't work as well for OLTP point lookup style of query. The nonclustered columnstore index adds analysis when the majority of queries are OLTP focused, but some of them need to do analysis. In this case, it's all about picking the right tool for the job.

Enable the Query Store

Enabling the Query Store on your databases doesn't just give you the ability to capture execution plans and query metrics. The Query Store is used by most of the Intelligent Query Processing mechanisms covered in Chapter 21. The Query Store is also used by the automatic tuning we discussed in Chapter 22. You can put the Query Store to work on your own as well, forcing plans as needed.

CHAPTER 23 A QUERY TUNING METHODOLOGY

Summary

Performance optimization never finishes. You're going to find that you always have more that you can do. This chapter was meant to provide something close to a checklist that you can apply, along with the knowledge in the rest of the book, to make your queries run faster.

Please, have a little fun along the way. Experimentation can be the key to successfully tuning queries. Try stuff out. You never know. Remember, if it's stupid and it works, it's not stupid.

Good luck!

Index

A

Accelerated Database Recovery (ADR), 509, 529
ACID, *see* Atomicity, consistency, isolation and durability (ACID)
ACID/TRANSACTION properties
    atomic operation
        connections, 500
        data adding, 498
        INSERT operation, 499
        ROLLBACK, 502
        SET XACT_ABORT ON, 500, 501
        TRY/CATCH error, 501, 502
    consistency, 502
    durability, 503
    isolation levels, 502
    properties, 498
    ROLLBACK, 498
Actions, 56, 57, 60
Actual Execution Plan, 42
Adaptive Join operator, 315, 316
Adaptive query processing
    feedback mechanisms, 667
        cardinality estimates, 671–676
        degree for parallelism, 677–681
        Extended Events session, 667
        memory grant, 667–671
        persistence, 681
    interleaved execution
        execution, 659, 660
        execution plan, 665, 666
        internal functions, 663, 665
        multi-statement functions, 656–659
        non-interleaved execution, 661–663
        properties, 662, 663
        WHERE clause, 665
    query performance, 656
Adaptive Threshold Rows property, 316
Addressing plan-sensitive queries
    approaches, 412
    disable parameter sniffing
        advantage, 413
        database scoped configuration, 413
        trace flag, 412
    force plan, 418
    local variables, 414
    multiplan (*see* Multiplan)
    OPTIMIZE FOR query hint, 415–418
    parameter sniffing, 412
    recompiling statement, 415, 416
Ad hoc queries, 236, 267
Ad hoc workload
    changing, 212
    compiled plan, 214
    defined, 210
    execution results, 211
    existence, 212
    forced parameterization, 219–221
    hard-coded values, 211
    optimization, 213, 215
    retrieving information, 210, 211
    simple parameterization, 215–219
    WHERE clause, 210

INDEX

ADR, *see* Accelerated Database Recovery (ADR)
ADS, *see* Azure Data Studio (ADS)
AdventureWorks, 3, 26, 59, 272
Aging, 37, 38
AI, *see* Artificial intelligence (AI)
Algebrizer, 24, 25
ALTER DATABASE command, 165
Analytical queries, 296
Arithmetic operations, 292
Artificial intelligence (AI), 1, 8, 126, 296
Asynchronous process, 183, 191
Asynchronous statistics, 130
Atomicity, consistency, isolation and durability (ACID), 17
Automatic tuning
   index management
      AdventureWorksLT database, 705, 706
      definition, 705
      index creation/dropping, 707
      PowerShell, 707, 708
      recommendation, 709
   plan correction, 693–705
   recommendation, 710
Availability Groups, 182
Azure Data Studio (ADS), 41

B

Batch-mode processing, 313, 314
Binding, 24–26
Blocking/blocked processes
   ACID (*see* ACID/TRANSACTION properties)
   blocked_process_report event, 539
   BlockTest table, 538
   definition, 495
   dynamic management objects/views, 537–539
   Extended Events, 539–544
   fundamentals, 495
   isolation levels
      committed snapshot, 522, 523
      factors, 520
      MyProduct table, 525
      Production.Product table, 523
      read uncommitted, 520, 521
      repeatable read, 524–526
      row versions, 520
      serializable, 526–528
      SET statement, 521
      snapshot, 528
      standards, 520
   locking (*see* Locking process)
   memory-optimized tables, 497
   process page, 537
   reducing contention, 544, 545
   scenario, 536
   sessions, 497
   terminology, 496
B-Tree, 275, 276, 281, 299

C

Cardinality, 137, 150–154
Cardinality estimation (CE), 150–152, 159–162
Causality tracking, 67, 68, 244
CE, *see* Cardinality estimation (CE)
CE feedback
   bigProduct table, 675
   bigTransactionHistory tables, 676
   correlation, 672
   Extended Events session, 671, 672
   query_ce_feedback_telemetry, 672, 673

INDEX

query_feedback_analysis, 673, 676
query_feedback_validation, 674
status, 675
sys.query_store_plan_feedback, 674
Cloud service provider, 5
Clustered index, 148, 273, 274, 279, 357
    accessing data, 303, 304
    creation, 300
    data retrieve, 284
    data storage, 296
    design practices
        updated columns, 306, 307
        wide keys, 307
    heap tables, 297
    narrow, 300, 301, 303
    retrieving pre-sorted data, 304, 306
    single step, 303
    uniquifier, 303
Columnstore index
    Adaptive Join, 314–316
    aggregate query, 310
    aggregations and counts, 280
    batch-mode processing, 313
    benefits, 281
    defined, 280
    execution plan, 312
    execution time, 311, 312
    filtering criteria, 310
    locally aggregated rows, 314
    operator, 313
    performance benefits, 280
    properties, 316
    recommendations, 317
    restrictions, 281
    scan, 313
    storage, 281, 282
    types, 280
Columnstore indexes

bigTransactionHistory, 377, 378
clustered index, 371
rowstore, 371–373
Compile storm, 229
Compute Scalar operators, 108, 109
Cost comparison (Cursor), 581
    comparison, 589
    concurrency model, 583
        optimistic model, 583
        read-only, 583
        scroll locks, 585
    cursor types, 585
    default result, 586
    dynamic model, 588
    fast-forward-only, 586
    forward-only, 586
    keyset-driven, 587
    location
        client-side, 581
        server-side, 582
    static model, 587
Cost threshold for parallelism, 34, 35
Covering index, 308, 310, 357–361
    defined, 321
    execution plan, 322, 323
    IX_Address_StateProvinceID
        index, 322
    pseudoclustered, 324
    recommendations, 324
    reverting, 323
    structure, 321
Cursors
    API cursors, 599
    blocking, 599
    characteristics, 572
    client-side, 572
    concurrency models, 573
        optimistic cursor, 574

Cursors (*cont.*)
    read-only, 574
    ROWVERSION data type, 574
    scroll locks, 575
  cost comparison, 581–589
  data access, 571
  default result set
    benefits, 590
    client-side, 591
    conditions, 589
    data access layers, 589
    disadvantages, 591
    locks, 594
    multiple active, 591
    PowerShell script, 592
    query performance metrics, 593
    test table, 593
  dynamic cursors, 578, 579
  Extended Events, 594
  forward-only, 576
  keyset-driven, 577, 578
  location, 572
  recommendations, 597
  requirements, 594
  server resources, 598
  server-side, 573
  static cursor, 577
  steps, 571, 572
  stored procedure, 595
  tempdb, 598
  TotalLossCursorBased procedure, 596
  types, 575
  WHILE loop, 579–581

D

Database design
  aspects, 713
  columnstore indexes, 723
  data types, 723
  domain and referential
    integrity, 717–720
    CHECK constraint, 718, 719
    features, 717
    SELECT statements, 718
    test tables, 717
  entity-integrity
    aggregation operation, 716
    cleanliness, 714
    DISTINCT operation, 715
    IDENTITY columns, 714
    natural keys, 715
    UNIQUE constraint, 715, 716
  graph storage, 723
  indexes and index design, 720, 721
  in-memory storage, 722
  stored procedures, 722
  triggers, 722
Database Engine Tuning Advisor, 344
DATABASEPROPERTYEX function, 139
Database scoped configuration, 160, 161
Data definition language (DDL), 26
Data distributions, 137, 140
Data manipulation, 277, 280
Data manipulation language (DML), 26
Data normalization, 7
Data storage, 62
DBATools, 70
Deadlocks, 17, 271, 547
  access resources, 565
  capturing information
    Extended Events session, 553, 554
    mechanisms, 550
    SQL server configuration manager
      window, 552
    system_health session, 554

INDEX

trace flags, 551–553
connections, 554, 555
covering index, 566
error handling, 564, 565
graphical representation, 547, 548, 556
Heap/B-tree, 556
lock contention
   hints, 568
   isolation level, 567
   mechanisms, 567
   NOLOCK and READUNCOMMITTED, 568
   optimized locking, 567
   queries, 568
   row-versioning mechanisms, 567
lock monitor, 548
locks/objects, 556
nonclustered/clustered index, 566
possibilities, 566
priority level, 549
rollback process, 549
xml_deadlock_report event, 555
XML graph data, 558–565
Deadly embrace, 17
Debug events, 81
Declarative referential integrity (DRI), 465–469
  address table, 468
  definition, 465
  execution plans, 467–469
  foreign key constraints, 466
  identical queries, 466
Deferred compilation, 251
Deferred object resolution
  DML statement, 248
  statement-level recompile, 250
  table recompilation, 248, 249
  temporary tables, 249, 250

Defragmentation techniques
  automatic maintenance, 399
  characteristics, 393, 394
  fill factor, 395–398
  INSERT/UPDATE operations, 396
  lock priority, 394
  maintenance plans, 399
  partitions, 393
  sys.dm_db_index_physical_stats, 397
  test table, 395
Degree of Parallelism (DOP) feedback
  benefits, 677, 678
  Extended Events session, 677
  parallel execution, 677
  query executions, 678, 679
  testing process, 679
  validation, 680
Deltastore, 281
Density, 148, 149
DMVs, *see* Dynamic management views (DMVs)
DOP, *see* Degree of Parallelism (DOP) feedback
Doubly linked list, 276
DRI, *see* Declarative referential integrity (DRI)
DROP STATISTICS command, 144
Dynamic management views (DMVs), 27, 32, 88, 90, 208, 230, 537
  actively executing queries, 44, 45
  categories, 43
  defined, 43
  previously executed queries, 45, 46
  reasons, 44

E

Early termination of optimization, 29

743

INDEX

Estimated *vs.* actual execution plans, 110–112
    capturing, 85
    DMVs, 88, 90
    Extended Events, 91–93
    highlighted query, 86
    information, 84
    Query Store, 90, 91
    runtime metrics, 84, 87
    sources, 84
    SQL Editor toolbar, 86, 87
    SSMS, 85–87
ETW, *see* Event Tracing for Windows (ETW)
Event Tracing for Windows (ETW), 62
Execution plans, 16, 19
    aging, 37, 38
    caching, 37, 38
    caching and reuse (*see* Plan cache)
    complex query, 31
    costly operations, 107
    estimated *vs.* actual, 84–93, 110–112
    extra operators, 108–110
    fat pipes, 108
    first operator, 103, 104
    identical, 264, 333
    nested loops operator, 100–102
    number of warnings, 144
    parallel, 33–37
    properties, 31
    runtime metrics, 42, 145
    scans, 110
    shortcuts, 102
    signposts, 113
    table scan, 134
    tools, 113–126
    warning indicator, 26
    warnings, 104–107

Extended events, 27, 91–93, 242, 277, 322
    adding and configuring, 51–56
    adding global fields, 56, 57
    causality tracking, 67, 68
    clicking, 54
    configuration window, 56
    creating session, 48–51
    defined, 47
    filtered, 53
    Live Data Explorer window, 70–80
    new session window, 50
    object explorer window, 66
    optional fields, 60, 61
    output, statistics updates, 133
    performance time, 337
    predicates, 57–60
    programmatic constructs, 47
    querying, 69
    recommendations, 80, 81
    scripting, 68–70
    selected list, 55
    session selection, 52
    targets, 62–66
    upgrades, 47
    working with sessions, 66
Extensible Markup Language (XML)
    deadlocks, 558–565
External fragmentation, 374
Extra operator, 108–110

F

Filtered indexes, 157–159, 330–334
Filtering criteria, 283–286
Forced parameterization, 219–221, 231
Fragmentation
    benefits, 373

columnstore (*see* Columnstore indexes)
definition, 365
defragmentation (*see* Defragmentation techniques)
dynamic management function, 379
page splits, 374
resolutions, 383
    ALTER INDEX REBUILD command, 385, 386
    blocking, 383
    dbo.bigTransactionHistory, 389, 390
    DROP_EXISTING clause, 384
    drop/recreation, 383, 384
    large object (LOB) pages, 385
    missing index, 383
    nonclustered index, 383
    REORGANIZE command, 386–393
    row compression, 391
    unique constraints, 384
row (*see* Rowstore fragmentation)
small table/index, 382
sys.dm_db_index_physical_stats, 379–382

G

GDPR, *see* General Data Protection Regulation (GDPR)
General Data Protection Regulation (GDPR), 714
Graph databases, 633
    database creation, 635
    edges/relationships
        data adding, 639
        loading, 640–644
        tables, 636
        types, 634

graph relationship, 633, 634
many-to-many relationship, 646
nodes/objects
    data adding, 638
    tables, 635
    types, 634
performance comparison, 652–654
querying data, 644
    AI search, 652
    multiple directions, 648
    multiple relationships, 647
    paths and levels, 650
    relationships, 649
    shortest path, 649–652
    traditional filtering data, 648
    WHERE clause, 647
radio operators, 645
relational table, 645
tables, 637, 638
table scan, 654

H

HashMatch, 316
Hash values, 230, 231, 233
Heap, 275
Heap table, 297
Hint forcing, 269
Histogram, 149, 150
Histogram Target, 65, 66

I

Inaccurate_cardinality_estimate, 174
Index characteristics
    column sort order, 342
    computed columns, 343
    creating index statement, 343, 344
    Database Engine Tuning Advisor, 344

Index characteristics (*cont.*)
   online index creation, 344
   OPTIMIZE_FOR_SEQUENTIAL_
      KEY, 345
   parallel index creation, 344
   resumable indexes and constraints,
      345, 346
Index compression, 340–342
Index-design
   AI, 296
   column order, 292–295
   data selectivity, 289–291
   data storage, 296
   data type, 292
   filtering criteria, 283–286
   forcing index seek, 290
   narrow indexes, 286–288
   options, 282
   query processing, 283
   WHERE clause, 283–285
Indexed view
   benefits, 334
   defined, 334
   overhead, 335
   removing, 339
   restrictions, 335, 336
   scenarios, 336–339
   usage, 339–342
Indexes
   mathematical operations/functions
      calculations, 443
      date logic modification, 447
      DATEPART function, 447
      DATETIME data types, 446
      execution plan, 443, 446
      index scan, 444
      metrics and execution plan, 445, 447
      query metrics, 444
   scalar functions, 448–453
      data retrieval, 450
      execution plan, 449
      IF statement, 451
      replacing option, 452
      retrieve product costs, 449
      satisfaction, 452
      simplified execution plan, 453
   search conditions
      BETWEEN, 437–442
      execution plans, 439
      identical execution plans, 438
      IN/OR condition, 436–441
      LIKE condition, 441
      logical operations, 435
      !< and >=, 441–443
      sargable and non-sargable
         conditions, 436
Index intersection, 324–328
Index joins, 328–330, 361–363
In-memory technologies
   ALTER TABLE, 617
   columnstore index, 618
   durable/nondurable, 604
   fundamentals, 601
   garbage collection, 602
   hash index, 613–616
   indexes, 613
   limitations, 605
   MEMORY_OPTIMIZED_DATA file, 604
   nonclustered index, 616–618
   shallow and deep distribution, 614
   storage systems, 601
   sys.dm_db_xtp_hash_index_stats, 615
   system requirements, 603
   table definition, 602
   table variables
      loading option, 611

queries, 612
traditional table variable, 611
TYPE, 610, 611
transactions, 602
Intelligent query processing, 203
adaptive (*see* Adaptive query processing)
approximate functions, 681
accuracy, 684
APPROX_COUNT_DISTINCT, 682
PERCENTILE_CONT, 682–684
PERCENTILE_DISC, 682, 683
deferred compilation, 684, 687
table variables, 684–687
user-defined functions, 687–692
Interior nodes, 276
Internet of Things (IoT), 7
IoT, *see* Internet of Things (IoT)
Iterators, 93, 101

J, K

JOIN operators, 101

L

LAQ, *see* Lock After Qualification (LAQ)
Large language model (LLM), 1, 126
Leading edge of index, 292
Lightweight profiling, 122
Live Data Explorer window
adding fields, 71, 72
aggregation, 77–80
choosing columns window, 73
columns selected on display, 73
filtering, 75–77
grouped by column, 78
grouping window, 77
initial view, 70, 71
search function, 74
toolbar, 72, 74
Live Data window, 48
LLM, *see* Large language model (LLM)
Lock After Qualification (LAQ), 532
Locking process
clustered index, 506
compatibility, 519
DELETE statement, 505
escalation, 510
extent, 508
granularity, 504
heap/B-Tree, 508
indexes
clustered index, 533, 535, 536
nonclustered index, 533–535
REPEATABLEREAD query, 534
transaction, 535
KEY lock, 506, 507
modes
blocked process, 513
bulk update (BU), 519
exclusive (IE), 518
exclusive (X), 517
intent shared (IS), 517
key-range, 519
modification (Sch-M), 518
sections, 511
shared(S) mode, 511
SIX lock, 518
stability (Sch-S), 518
T-SQL window, 512–516
UPDATE statements, 516–520
object ID value, 506
operations/modes, 509
optimization
fundamentals, 529

747

INDEX

Locking process (*cont.*)
    limitations, 532
    lock after qualification, 533
    qualification, 531–533
    recovery process, 529
    TransactionID, 529, 530
    transactions, 531
  PAGE lock, 507
  rowgroup, 508
  row-level, 504–506
  shared database, 509
  shared process, 503
  table, 509
  table-level, 508
  transactions, 509
Lookups
  causes, 354–357
  execution plan, 352
  operation, 355
  output list, 356
  Output List property, 353
  performance issues, 353, 354
  purpose, 351–353
  resolve techniques
    approaches, 357
    average key length, 360
    covering index, 357–361
    creating clustered index, 357
    density graph, 358, 359
    INCLUDE clause, 359
    modified query, 360
    operation eliminated, 359
    resetting, 360
  text window, 356

M

Mapping index, 308

Materialization, 334
Materialized views, 334, 336
Max degree of parallelism, 34, 35
Memory grant feedback
  compatibility mode, 670
  CostCheck procedure, 668
  execution plan, 669, 670
  Extended Events session, 667
  memory allocation, 670
  parameter sniffing, 668
  performance issues, 667
  results of, 669
  row-mode processing, 671
Memory-optimization
  advisor
    AdventureWorks database, 624
    checklists, 625
    index selection, 628
    InMemory database, 624
    naming and data migration, 626, 627
    native compilation, 629, 630
    results, 624, 628
    warnings, 626
  in-memory (*see* In-memory technologies)
  performance metrics, 623
  stored procedures
    CountryRegion table, 620
    creation, 621
    execution plan, 622
    SELECT operator properties, 622
  tables
    address table, 605
    database, 607, 608
    data types, 606
    dbo.Address table, 606
    execution plan, 609

INDEX

performance enhancements, 610
queries, 608
SELECT query, 610
statistics, 618–620
variables, 610–620
workloads, 623
Merge join, 329
Missing indexes, 317–320
Multicolumn density graph, 157
Multicolumn index, 154–157
Multiplan
   Database Scoped Configuration, 426, 428
   definition, 419
   dispatcher plan, 428
   execution plans, 422, 423, 426, 427
   optional parameter, 419
   OptionalParameter procedure, 426
   plan cache, 425
   properties, 424
   PSP optimization, 419, 420, 422
   query store information, 426
   SEEK operation, 420
   sys.dm_exec_query_stats, 425
   TransactionInfo procedure, 422
Multiple filter criteria, 60
Multi-statement selection, 121

N

Naming convention, 142
Nested Loops operator, 298
   and action, 93, 94
   data flow, 95, 96
   estimated cost, 94
   example, 93
   execution plan, 100–102
   properties, 98, 99
   runtime metrics, 94, 95
   tooltip, 96, 97
   warning description, 106
No_Event_Loss, 81
Nonclustered indexes, 128, 147, 242, 274
   benefits, 275
   concept, 307
   lookup operation, 308
   loop join, 309
   maintenance, 308
   mechanisms, 358
   relationships, 297–300
   requirements, 309
   RID, 275
   UPDATE operation, 309
Nonindexed columns
   ad hoc T-SQL queries, 137
   auto_stats events, 141
   benefits, 137–143
   cardinality and data distribution, 137
   data returned changes, 143
   performance comparison, 144, 145
   two tables without indexes, 140
Normalization, 18

O

Object relational mapping (ORM), 7, 229
OLTP, *see* Online transaction processing (OLTP)
Online transaction processing (OLTP), 29, 283, 296
   memory-optimization (*see* Memory-optimization)
Operators, 87
OPO, *see* Optional parameter optimization (OPO)
Optimization process, 27, 28

INDEX

OPTIMIZE FOR hint, 262
Optimizer behaviors, 31, 32
Optional parameter optimization (OPO), 246, 419
ORM, *see* Object relational mapping (ORM)
Out-of-date statistics, 175

P

PaaS, *see* Platform as a Service (PaaS)
Page-level compression, 340
Parallel execution, 33–37
Parameter-sensitive plans (PSPs), 246, 419, 420
   advantage, 426
   disable option, 426
   dispatcher plan, 428
   plan cache, 425
   properties, 424
   scripts, 420, 421
   sys.dm_exec_query_stats, 425
Parameter-sensitive queries, 401
   identification
      Extended Events, 408
      histogram results, 411
      parameter list properties, 409
      performances, 407
      query store, 408
      statistics information, 410
      sys.dm_exec_query_plan, 407
   mechanism (*see* Addressing plan-sensitive queries)
   sniffing process
      average execution plan, 405
      concepts, 401
      definition, 402
      execution plan, 404

      query performance metrics, 406
      runtime metrics, 405
      steps, 406
      stored procedure, 402, 403, 405
      value returning, 403
Parameter sniffing, 16, 225
Parse tree, 24
Parsing, 23, 24
Performance tuning
   core process, 9
   issues, 4–7
   needs, 9
Plan cache, 19, 37, 38
   ad hoc workload, 210–221
   categories, 209
   defined, 207
   memory space, 239
   methods, 209
   prepared workload
      defined, 221
      prepare/execute model, 229, 230
      sp_executesql, 226–229
      stored procedures, 222–226
      techniques, 221
   querying, 207, 208
   recommendations
      ad hoc queries, 236
      explicitly parameterize values, 235
      management, 234
      prepare/execute model, 236
      sp_executesql, 235
      stored procedures, 235
Plan correction (automation)
   advantages, 693
   automatic tuning, 704, 705
   enable automatic tuning, 700
      Azure account, 701–703
      features, 702

FORCE PLAN settings, 703
intelligent performance
   selection, 702
performance
   recommendations, 703
SQL Database portal, 701
T-SQL Server, 703
parameter-sensitive queries, 693
tuning process
   dbo.ProductByCost, 698
   indexes and procedures, 694
   query performance histories, 695
   result sets, 699, 700
   results of, 696
   stored procedure, 697
   sys.dm_db_tuning_
      recommendations, 696, 697
Plan forcing, 181, 262
   defined, 200
   hints, 202, 203
   implementation, 200
   optimization, 203, 204
   queries, 201
   upgrades, 204, 205
PlanGuideName property, 266
Plan guides, 265–269
Plan reuse, 209–230
Platform as a Service (PaaS), 705
Pseudoclustered index, 324
PSPs, *see* Parameter-sensitive
   plans (PSPs)

Q

Query degradation, 9
Query design analysis
   advantage, 432
   covering index, 434
   domain and referential
      integrity, 460–469
   indexes (*see* Indexes)
   index hints
      execution plan, 459
      forcing index, 459
   JOIN hints
      loops, 456, 457
      metrics/execution plan, 455, 456
      performance metrics, 457, 458
      single join, 458
      tables, 455
      types, 454
   metrics and execution plan, 433
   optimizer hints
      definition, 453
      index, 459, 460
      JOIN operations, 454–458
      parameter sniffing, 453
   recommendations, 431, 432
   SELECT list, 432–434
   WHERE clause, 434, 435
Query execution, 183
Query hash, 230–234
QueryHash, 104
Query hints, 202, 203, 262–265
Query optimization, 11, 183
   aggregated information, 33
   cost-based analysis, 21
   execution plan caching, 37, 38
   mathematical models, 22
   parallel execution plans, 33–37
   phases, 28–33
   resources, 21
   simplification, 28
   statistics (*see* Statistics)
   steps, 22–28
   Trivial Plans, 28

INDEX

Query performance metrics
    connection properties, 41
    DMVs (*see* Dynamic management views (DMVs))
    Include Client Statistics, 40
    measurement methods, 40
    mechanisms, 39
    SET STATISTICS TIME/IO, 41, 42
    timestats, 42
    Trace Events and profiler, 42, 43
Query performance tuning, 7
    comparison, 12
    methodology, 2
    problems, 14
        deadlocks, 17
        excessive blocking, 17
        execution plans, 16
        inaccurate/missing statistics, 15
        incorrect database design, 18
        insufficient/poor indexes, 15
        non-set-based operations, 18
        poor execution plan reuse, 19
        recompilation, 19
        T-SQL, 16
    repetitive process, 7-10
    root causes, 13
    survey, 13
    See also Performance tuning
Query plan hash, 230-234
QueryPlanHash, 104
Query processor tree, 24, 26
Query Store, 47, 90, 91, 240
    controlling
        capture mode, 192-194
        current settings, 191
        maximum storage size, 191
        memory disk, 191
        plan identifier, 191
        removing information, 190
    data collection, 183
    function and design, 182-184
    information collection, 184-188
    plan forcing, 200-204
    properties, 198
    reporting, 194-200
    runtime data, 188-190
Query tuning methodology
    analytical queries, 737
    arithmetic operators, 731, 732
    caching execution, 735
    configuration settings, 723
        Ad Hoc workloads, 726
        blocked process, 726
        cost threshold, 724
        data compression, 726
        memory options, 723
        parallel execution, 724, 725
    database administration
        activities, 726
        AUTO_CLOSE, 728
        AUTO_SHRINK, 728
        index fragmentation, 727
        statistics, 727
    database design (*see* Database design)
    data type conversions, 733
    eliminate/reduce cursors, 736
    execution plans, 734
    explicitly qualification, 729
    IN clause, 731
    logging process, 734
    nesting view, 733
    non-sargable search conditions, 729-731
    OPTIMIZE FOR UNKNOWN, 733
    OR clauses, 731
    queries, 728

INDEX

Query Store, 737
recompilation, 735
SET NOCOUNT ON, 729
stored procedures, 737
transactions, 736
Query tuning process, 4, 6, 10
    time testing, 11

R

RCSI, *see* Read Committed Snapshot isolation (RCSI)
Read Committed Snapshot isolation (RCSI), 530
Recompilation
    attach_activity_id_guid, 245
    benefits and drawbacks, 239–243
    causes, 245, 246
    changing SET options, 260, 261
    DDL and DML statements, 251–253
    deferred object resolution, 248–250
    identifying statements, 244, 245
    mechanisms
        hint forcing, 269
        plan forcing, 262
        plan guides, 265–269
        query hints, 262–265
    multiple events, 249
    practices, 251
    procedure, 240
    reasons, 247
    statistics changes
        disabling automatic statistics maintenance, 256, 257
        KEEPFIXED PLAN hint, 254–256
        options, 253
    table variables, 257–259
    temporary tables, 259, 260

useless statement, 243
Referential integrity/domain
    advantage, 460
    DRI, 465–469
    NOT NULL constraint
        execution plans, 461–463
        key difference, 461
        Person.Person table, 460
        test indexes, 463
    user-defined constraints, 463–465
Report configuration window, 199
Resource consumers report, 196
Resource-intensive queries
    aggregation operations, 480
    approaches, 471
    batch process, 482–486
    data types, 472–475
    different techniques, 471
    EXISTS operation, 476–478
    hard-coded values, 484, 486
    implicit conversion, 472
    local variables, 483–487
    lock management process
        ALTER statement, 492
        DELETE statement, 493
        NOLOCK, 493
        pseudo-code, 491
        READ_ONLY, 492
        row-level lock, 491
        SELECT statements, 491, 492
        snapshot isolation, 492
    network process
        approaches, 486
        query execution, 487
        SET NOCOUNT command, 487
    sort operations, 482
    stored procedures, 486
    table/indexes scans, 481, 482

INDEX

Resource-intensive queries (*cont.*)
    test exists COUNT(*), 475–477
    transaction cost
        action query, 488
        atomic action, 488
        characteristics, 488
        lock management process, 491
        logging process, 488–490
        WHILE loop, 490
    UNION clause, 478–480
Ring buffers, 62
Root node, 276
Row-by-row processing
    cursor (*see* Cursors)
Row identifier (RID), 274, 297, 298
Row-level compression, 340
Row locator, 297
Rowstore fragmentation
    clustered index, 373, 375
    clustered/nonclustered indexes, 366
    columnstore indexes, 371–373
    extents, 367
    external model, 367
    FragTest table, 376
    INSERT statement, 370, 371
    internal/external data, 374
    leaf pages, 366, 367
    noncontiguous layout, 374
    performance metrics, 377
    physical layout, 369
    row identifier (RID), 368
    simplified approach, 366
    UPDATE statement, 368–370
Rowstore index
    benefits, 275–277
    clustered indexes, 296–307
    data ordered and numbered, 272
    data reordered, 273
    defined, 271
    nonclustered index, 307–310
    overhead, 277–280
    random order, 275
    retrieving products ordered by
        name, 272
    sorted order, 276
    StandardCost column, 273, 274
    types, 274
Rowstore indexed columns
    auto_stats event, 134
    calculations, 129
    default automatic statistics
        maintenance, 129
    defined, 128
    methods, 129
    old statistics maintenance thresholds,
        129, 130
    outdated statistics, 135–137
    updated statistics, 130–135

S

Scan, 275
Showplan analysis, 121
SHOW_STATISTICS command, 147
Simple parameterization, 19, 25,
    215–219, 231
Simplification, 28
Sorted index, 293
Spatial indexes, 347
Special index types
    full-text, 347
    spatial data, 347
    vector, 348, 349
    XML, 348
sp_executesql, 226–229, 235
SQL Database

automatic tuning (*see*
    Automatic tuning)
SQL plan guide, 267
SQL Server Management Studio (SSMS),
    3, 6, 40, 48, 84–87, 191, 332
  Activity Monitor window, 124
  compare plans, 118–121
  description, 114
  dragging screen, 114
  estimated rows, 122
  find node, 115–118
  Live Query Statistics, 122–125
  third party
    AI, 126
    paste the plan, 126
    solarwinds plan explorer, 125
    supratimas, 125
SSMS, *see* SQL Server Management
    Studio (SSMS)
Statistics
  automatic creation, 139, 141
  cardinality, 150–154
  controlling cardinality
      estimator, 159–162
  creation, 167, 168
  data sets, 146
  definition, 127
  density, 148, 149
  execution plan, 169
  filtered indexes, 157–159
  filtering mechanisms, 128
  FirstIndex, 147
  header, 147
  histogram, 149, 150
  importance, 127
  maintenance, 128
    auto create, 163
    auto update, 163
    auto update asynchronously, 163
    configurations, 162
    manual maintenance, 164
    settings, 165, 166
  multicolumn index, 154–157
  nonindexed columns, 137–145
  performance measurements, 136
  Product table, 156
  recommendations
    amount of sampling, 178
    auto create, 177
    auto update, 177
    auto update asynchronously, 178
    backward compatibility, 177
  recompilation, 253–257
  resolving missing issue, 169–173
  resolving outdated issue, 174–176
  rowstore indexed columns, 128–137
  StatsCollectionId matching, 154
  testing table, 146
  unfiltered index, 158
Stored procedures, 235
  adding cache, 223
  behaviors, 224
  compilation, 224, 225
  DBATools, 223
  defined, 222
  events, 222
  nonperformance benefits, 226
  performance benefits, 225
Stream aggregate operations, 310
Supratimas, 125
Syntax-based optimization, 25, 26

T

Table Scan operator, 171
Table variables, 257–259

INDEX

Targets
    defined, 62
    event_file, 63–65
    histogram, 65, 66
    options, 62, 63
    page, 62
Templates, 50
Temporary tables, 257, 259, 260
Text plan, 85
Timeout, 29
Trace Events, 42, 43
Transacct-SQL (T-SQL)
    query design, 431
Trivial Plans, 28
T-SQL, 14, 16, 18, 41, 48, 211, 228
Type conversion, 26

U

Unfiltered index, 158
Uniquifier, 303
Unsorted table, 293
User-defined functions (UDFs)
    execution plan, 689
    execution plans, 690
    inherent problems, 687
    inline scalar function vs. not inline, 691
    performance metrics, 690
    scalar functions, 687
    ufnGetProductStandardCost, 688
    validation, 689

V

Vector index, 348
Views, 334
Virtual machines (VMs), 1, 5, 6
VMs, *see* Virtual machines (VMs)

W

Wide World Importers, 3

X, Y, Z

XEvent Profiler, 48
XML, *see* Extensible Markup Language (XML)
XQuery language, 348

GPSR Compliance

The European Union's (EU) General Product Safety Regulation (GPSR) is a set of rules that requires consumer products to be safe and our obligations to ensure this.

If you have any concerns about our products, you can contact us on

ProductSafety@springernature.com

In case Publisher is established outside the EU, the EU authorized representative is:

Springer Nature Customer Service Center GmbH
Europaplatz 3
69115 Heidelberg, Germany